European Competition Law and Economics:
A Comparative Perspective

AUSTRALIA
LBC Information Services
Sydney

CANADA and **USA**
The Carswell Company
Toronto

NEW ZEALAND
Brooker's
Auckland

SINGAPORE and **MALAYSIA**
Sweet & Maxwell Asia
Singapore and Kuala Lumpur

European Competition Law and Economics: A Comparative Perspective

2nd Edition

Roger Van den Bergh

Professor of Law, Erasmus University Rotterdam,
Rotterdam Institute of Law and Economcs

and

Peter Camesasca

Partner, Howrey LLP, Advocaat, Member of Brussels Bar and
Assistant Professor, Erasmus University Rotterdam

LONDON
SWEET & MAXWELL
2006

Published in 2006 by
Sweet & Maxwell
100 Avenue Road
London NW3 3PF
(*http://www.smlawpub.co.uk*)

Typeset by YHT Ltd, London
Printed in Great Britain by Athenaeum Press Ltd., Gateshead, Tyne & Wear

No natural forests were destroyed to make this product; only farmed timber was used
and replanted.

A CIP record for this book is available from the British Library

ISBN 0421965800
ISBN 9780421965805

PREFACE

The second edition of this book is substantially different from the first, published in 2001. Over the past five years, European competition law has undergone dramatic changes, largely inspired by the European Commission's move towards a more economics based approach. When the first edition came out, economic analysis had been introduced through the Market Definition Notice and the General Regulation on Vertical Restraints. Today, however, economic analysis permeates almost the entire field of European competition law. Modernisation has not only reorganised the enforcement of Articles 81 EC and 82 EC, it has also shifted the balance of power between the European Commission and the competition authorities (and judges) of the Member States and imposed an economic framework for assessing Article 81 EC. Clearly, the role of economic analysis is most advanced in the area of merger control. A number of high-profile rulings by the Court of First Instance urged the European Commission to refocus its merger review process, resulting in a new Merger Regulation and accompanying policy documents. At the time of writing, the last legalistic bulwark of European competition law, the assessment of abuse of dominance, is also being included in the discussion on the desirability of an economics based approach.

These changes necessitated a substantial revision of the first edition of this book. The chapters on merger control and allocation of regulatory powers in Europe (centralisation versus decentralisation) have been significantly expanded. In addition, the authors considered it appropriate to add separate chapters on the goals of competition law, and enforcement. Furthermore, the most important recent case law has been included and comparisons with US antitrust law extended. Boxes have been introduced to provide additional information, detailed case examples and further illustrations to the main text.

As with the first edition, the authors' aim is to provide students familiar with the basic notions of antitrust with a guide to the economic analysis of European competition law. Our hope is that its depth of content also makes it a useful text for newly qualified solicitors, regulators as well as those wishing to refresh their knowledge.

The authors wish to thank Luit Bakker and Roberto Pardolesi for useful comments, and Anne-Lise Domen and Erica Screen for valuable editorial assistance.

Roger Van den Bergh
Peter Camesasca
Sambuca Pistoiese, November 2005

CONTENTS

NUMBERICAL TABLE OF EUROPEAN CASES

ALPHABETICAL TABLE OF EUROPEAN CASES

Table of US Cases

Chapter 1

....

INTRODUCTION

_____

Throughout this book the position is taken that economic considerations deserve priority in applying competition rules to real-world cases. For a long time, European competition law was permeated by legal formalism. The permissibility of certain business practices was decided upon the basis of technical legal distinctions rather than their economic effects. This state of things has changed dramatically in the late 1990s and, even more decisively, at the beginning of the 21st century. The European Commission's increasing focus on economic analysis has been complemented by reinforcing the economic capabilities and resources of its administration. The apogee of this evolution has been the appointment of a Chief Economist at the Directorate General for Competition. The creation of this post is a significant step towards ensuring that European Commission decisions will be supported by rigorous economic analysis.

In current European competition law, economic arguments are regularly employed to justify conduct in terms of competition. For a long time economic arguments seem to have had a greater impact in American antitrust law than in European competition law. European competition lawyers were less familiar with economic arguments than their American colleagues. In particular, there was resistance to the view that economic considerations must be recognised as valid defences to lawsuits which challenge restrictions on competition. In the early days of European competition law, the European Commission often tried to divorce itself from decisions based on economic thinking. However, as early as 1969 the European Court of Justice stated that a lack of precise economic analysis may undermine the foundations of competition law.[1] The Court further paved the way for economic analysis by

_____

[1] Case 14/68 *Walt Wilhelm v Bundeskartellamt* [1969] E.C.R. 1, para.14.

requiring that all agreements must be evaluated by their factual, *legal and economic* context (our emphasis).[2]

It is clear from a number of aspects of the European Commission's work in recent years that increasingly greater emphasis is placed on economic issues. When Mario Monti took office as Commissioner for Competition, he advanced the development of an economic interpretation of EC competition rules as one of his main objectives.[3] A first step towards appreciating the relevance of economic arguments in competition cases was the publication of the Commission's Notice on the definition of the relevant market,[4] which tried to introduce new techniques of market definition based on economic analysis. In spite of all its shortcomings,[5] this was an important milestone in the European Commission's practice. A second milestone was the overhaul of the policy in relation to vertical restraints.[6] It must also be emphasized here that a number of rules (in particular the black-listed clauses) will still raise economists' eyebrows, but compared to the old legal formalistic regime important progress was certainly made. The role of economics in competition law further increased with the publication of the Guidelines on horizontal cooperation.[7] In the field of mergers, a number of decisions were taken that equally showed a greater receptiveness to more refined economic analysis.[8] Indeed, in the area of merger control, the role of economic analysis is probably most advanced.

- Economic analysis is required by the European Courts. Although confirming that "the substantive rules of the [Merger] Regulation, in particular Article 2, confer on the European Commission a certain discretion, especially with respect to assessments of an economic nature", the Court of First Instance now requires the European Commission to conduct "a particularly close examination of the circumstances which are relevant for an assessment of the [competitive] effects" supported by "convincing evidence" of an economic and empirical nature. In addition, given the necessarily prospective nature of the assessment of dominance in the merger context, the Court of First Instance points out that if the anticipated dominant position would only emerge after a certain lapse of time, then the European Commission's analysis of the merging

---

[2] Case 56/65 *Société Technique Minière v Maschinenbau Ulm GmbH* [1966] E.C.R. 235, para.8; Case 23/67 *Brasserie de Haecht v Wilkin* [1967] E.C.R. 407; Case C–234/89 *Delimitis v Henninger Bräu* [1991] E.C.R. I–935.

[3] M. Monti, "EU Competition Policy", Speech, Fordham Annual Conference on International Antitrust Law and Policy, New York, October 31, 2002.

[4] Commission Notice on the definition of the relevant market for the purposes of Community competition law [1997] O.J. C 372/1.

[5] Economic approaches were injected into an orthodox legal straitjacket. See P.D. Camesasca and R.J. Van den Bergh, "Achilles Uncovered: Revisiting the European Commission's 1997 Market Definition Notice" (2002) 44 Antitrust Bull. 143 and, for further discussion, Ch.4, s.4.2.2.

[6] Commission Regulation (EC) No 2790/1999 of December 22, 1999 on the application of Art.81(3) of the Treaty to categories of vertical agreements and concerted practices [1999] O.J. L 336/21. The preceding documents consisted of a Green Paper on vertical restraints in Community competition policy, COM(96)721 final; and a Communication from the Commission on the application of the Community competition rules to vertical restraints as a follow-up to the Green Paper on vertical restraints [1998] O.J. C 365/3.

[7] Commission Notice—Guidelines on the applicability of Article 81 of the EC Treaty to horizontal cooperation agreements [2001] O.J. C 3/2.

[8] See, e.g. Case COMP/M.1313 *Danish Crown/Vestjyske Slagterier* [2000] O.J. L 20/1; Case IV/M.623 *Kimberly-Clark/Scott Paper* [1996] O.J. L 183/1.

companies' future position must be "particularly plausible". Failure thereof will result in a "manifest error of assessment" (and consequently lead to the annulment of the European Commission's decision).[9]

Economic analysis is the cornerstone of the substantive analysis under the Merger Regulation and the EC Horizontal Merger Guidelines. The second revision of the Merger Regulation (after coming into force in 1990 and a first review in 1997) is to a large extent coloured by the grievous losses the European Commission had suffered at the hands of the Court of First Instance in *Airtours*,[10] *Schneider/Legrand*[11] and *Tetra Laval/Sidel*. The annulment of these three high-profile decisions—because of unsound substantive analysis—not only prompted an institutional shake-up of DG Comp's once-invincible Merger Task Force;[12] it also resulted in a much-welcomed focus on the competitive effects of concentrations in economics and the issuance of the EC Horizontal Merger Guidelines (the latter containing a detailed description of DG Comp's assessment standards, consistent with the principles of economic analysis).

The European Court of Justice has also moved towards requiring ever more advanced economic analysis.[13] The European Commission's new policy documents on merger control[14] reflect the criticisms of the Court that emphasised the proper application of economic theory standards. In addition to revising the Merger Regulation and issuing the EC Horizontal Merger Guidelines, the European Commission has also commissioned a number of expert reports dealing with economic theory and measurement of (a) unilateral effects,[15] (b) tacit collusion,[16] (c) differentiated product mergers,[17] and (d) the impact of vertical and conglomerate mergers.[18] Finally, the new ("modernisation") Regulation on enforcement[19] has removed the procedural obstacle to applying modern economic analysis in the assessment of Article 81 EC in its entirety. Both the European Commission and the network of national competition authorities (European Competition Network, ECN) and judges can now simultaneously assess the anti-competitive effects and the conditions for exemption, in particular the achievement of efficiencies. The last remaining bulwark of "economics light"—Article 82 EC—is currently under serious

---

[9] See Case T–5/02 *Tetra Laval v Commission* [2002] E.C.R. II–4381, paras 119, 155, 162, 308, 336–337; as confirmed in Case C–12/03P *Commission v Tetra Laval* [2005] E.C.R. I–987.

[10] Case T–342/99 *Airtours v Commission* [2002] E.C.R. II–2585.

[11] Case T–310/01 *Schneider v Commission* [2002] E.C.R. II–4071.

[12] Including a number of internal best practice guidelines aiming at checks and balances for its decision-making practice, see Best Practice Guidelines as available on the DG Comp website at: *http://europa.eu.int/comm/competition/mergers/legislation/index_new.html*.

[13] Joined Cases C–68/94 and C–30/95 *French Republic and Société Commerciale des Potasses et de l'Azote (SCPA) and Entreprise Minière et Chimique (EMC) v Commission* [1998] E.C.R. I–1375.

[14] Available on DG Comp's website at: *http://europa.eu.int/comm/competition/mergers/legislation/index_new.html*.

[15] M. Ivaldi, B. Jullien, P. Rey, P. Seabright and J. Tirole, *Economics of Unilateral Effects* (Final Report Prepared for DG Comp, 2003).

[16] *ibid.*

[17] R.J. Epstein and D.L. Rubinfeld, *Effects of Mergers Involving Differentiated Products* (Final Report Prepared for DG Comp, 2004).

[18] J. Church, *The Impact of Vertical and Conglomerate Mergers* (Final Report Prepared for DG Comp, 2004).

[19] Council Regulation (EC) No 1/2003 of December 16, 2002 on the implementation of the rules on competition laid down in Arts 81 and 82 of the Treaty [2003] O.J. L 1/1.

review with the European Commission intending to move to a more effects based approach.[20] In sum, European competition law has moved from a legalistic tradition to a framework of economic assessment of business practices affecting competition.

It would be premature, however, to describe the current state of affairs as an unqualified victory for economic efficiency. The scope of economic analysis must still be substantially extended to eliminate the use of legalistic arguments and to avoid decisions being taken on goals that conflict with efficiency concerns. Also, the quality of economic analysis must be further improved in order to avoid the use of outdated theories and to guarantee that poor economic arguments are identified. In particular, the use of quantitative techniques in proving violations of European competition law is still in its infancy.

Even though the harmony between economic insights and legal rules is not complete, in many fields of competition law legal formalism has been replaced by an economically oriented approach. In the Introduction to this book, ways in which competition lawyers may benefit from economic analysis are explored. To this end, the first section provides a brief overview of the strengths and remaining challenges of an economically oriented approach to competition. The second section explains the structure of the book and the third clarifies the scope of the analysis presented by formulating a number of qualifications.

1.1 The economic approach to competition law: its achievements and remaining challenges

The added value of an economically oriented approach to competition law manifests itself in three respects. First, economic analysis sheds light on the relevant normative standards for the purpose of competition policy and law. Second, economic criteria are extremely useful to clarify the meaning of the many vague concepts used in competition law. Third, economics (in particular econometrics) provides quantitative techniques that may be helpful in solving problems of evidence in real-world cases. In spite of these benefits, traditional competition lawyers may object to an increased use of economic analysis from a perspective of legal certainty. Also, economic models may not (yet) allow conclusions that are sufficiently general to be used in policy making. The first section of this Introduction closes with a consideration of these objections.

---

[20] See DG Competition Discussion Paper on the application of Art.82 of the Treaty to exclusionary abuses, at *http://europa.eu.int/comm/competition/antitrust/others/article_82_review.html*. See also J. Gual, M. Hellwig, A. Perot, M. Polo, P. Rey, K. Schmidt and R. Stenbacka (EAGCP), "An Economic Approach to Article 82, July 2005", to be downloaded from the same website address.

1.1.1 The goals of competition policy and law

A coherent discussion on the purpose of competition policy and law is not really taking place in Europe. Reading the statements of the European Commission (in particular, the Reports on Competition Policy published annually by the Commission since 1972), one encounters a multitude of goals attributed to competition policy, shifting in emphasis over time.[21] In the early years, European competition law was seen predominantly as a means to achieve market integration. The prohibition of cartel agreements (Article 81 EC) and the ban on abuses of dominant position (Article 82 EC) were regarded as necessary complements to the provisions of the EC Treaty on free movement of goods, persons, services and capital. Whereas the latter rules have been instrumental in undoing governmental regulations that keep national borders intact, the former rules have been used to avoid firms being able to achieve segregation of the internal market through private agreements and practices. In later reports, the European Commission advanced the protection of consumer welfare (by guaranteeing low prices) as the major goal, but at the same time emphasising the importance of efficiency savings (by stressing the cost reducing potential of mergers). However, efficiency savings and low consumer prices are goals that cannot easily be achieved simultaneously. In contrast with a consumer welfare view, which stresses that consumers should benefit from business practices, a total welfare view accepts that efficiency savings are advanced to compensate consumer losses. Hence, policy makers may not be able to escape from difficult trade-offs.[22] In 1998, Neven, Papandropoulos and Seabright, who conducted a survey of the Reports on Competition Policy, concluded that "the choice has clearly been made to favour income redistribution from producers with market power to consumers".[23] Aside from market integration, consumer welfare and efficiency considerations, competition policy and law may be inspired by other objectives, such as the protection of individual economic freedom and goals of social equity.

Today, the dominant view of the European Commission is that the goal of competition law is to protect competition in the market as a means of ensuring an efficient allocation of resources and enhancing consumer welfare.[24] However, current European competition law still exhibits a number of rules that can be explained only from different perspectives. Examples include the group exemption for car distribution agreements, which contains several rules to protect the "weak" car dealer from opportunistic behaviour by its "strong" counterparty, the car manufacturer.[25] Apart from the protection of business

---

[21] See Box 2.1. at p.33.

[22] For an elaboration of this point, see Ch.2, s.2.3.

[23] D. Neven, P. Papandropoulos and P. Seabright, *Trawling for Minnows: European Competition Policy and Agreements Between Firms* (1998), p.12 concluding on a survey of the Reports for the purpose of dealing with general competition law. Similarly inclined, see A. Schaub, "Competition Policy Objectives", in *The Objectives of Competition Policy* (C.D. Ehlermann and L.L. Laudati ed., 1998), p.119.

[24] Guidelines on the application of Art.81(3) of the Treaty [2004] O.J. C 101/97, para.13.

[25] See, for further elaboration, Ch.6, Box 6.4.

freedom, concerns about the achievement of social goals are equally over-riding efficiency concerns. Proof thereto is found in the case law of the European Court of Justice which has excluded collective labour agreements from the scope of the cartel prohibition.[26]

The first chapter of this book will present the different economic criteria that seem appropriate for the discussion of the goals of competition law, and it will also indicate the normative consequences of choosing a particular yardstick. Microeconomic theory provides valuable insights into the economic effects of different market forms (perfect competition, monopoly, oligopoly) and types of conduct (forms of strategic interaction limiting competition). Welfare economics offers criteria to judge the desirability of these outcomes (Pareto efficiency, Kaldor–Hicks efficiency). Economic analysis also illuminates the relation between the different goals of competition policy and reveals that policy makers will not be able to escape from trade-offs in cases of conflicting goals. As indicated earlier, the efficiency goal and the consumer welfare goal are not perfectly consistent with each other. Another source of potential inconsistencies is the objective of market integration. The emphasis on the market integration goal of European competition law may lead to rules which are different from their American counterparts. In Europe, efficiency may be sacrificed on the altar of the internal market. However, European competition law will continue to come more in line with US antitrust law—and thus more hospitable to pure economic arguments—as European economic integration reaches its stage of completion. It may be expected, though, that practices that are thought of as liable to undo the effects of market integration will continue to be subjected to strict prohibitions.

1.1.2 Interpretation of legal concepts

The goals of competition law are but one example of a debated area where economic analysis can bring important clarifications and contribute to greater overall consistency. In addition to the lack of transparency concerning the goal(s) to be achieved, the great number of vague notions contained in rules of competition law is equally amazing. Most of competition law's core principles are contained in overtly vague norms that need clarification throughout their application. Surely the most obvious is the concept of competition, a notion nowhere sufficiently clarified, neither in the Treaty, nor in rulings by the European Court of Justice, nor in the European Commission's decision making apparatus. On this point economic analysis offers tools of interpretation that are compatible with the normative standards.

The objective of competition policy at Community level is to ensure "that competition is not distorted" in order to promote, *inter alia*, a harmonious development of economic activities, sustainable growth and a "high degree of

---

[26] R.J. Van den Bergh and P.D. Camesasca, "Irreconcilable Principles? The Court of Justice Exempts Collective Labour Agreements from the Wrath of Antitrust", (2002) 25 E.L. Rev. 492–5.

competitiveness" (Article 2 *juncto* 3 EC). This aim was considerably strengthened by the Single Market project and reconfirmed by the Maastricht Treaty on the European Union, making the economic policy of the Community explicitly subject to the principle of an "open market economy with free competition" (Article 4 EC). The Treaty, however, nowhere defines what constitutes "competition". Matters are not made easier as the usage and meaning of terms, such as dominance and efficiency, shift depending on whether they are applied by lawyers or economists. Problems of interpretation thus abound.

Only if competition law consisted of unambiguously formulated *per se* rules could practitioners do without tools of economic analysis. This concept has its origin in American antitrust law, which distinguishes between types of conduct that are *per se* unlawful and other types of conduct that may pass the test of reasonableness. A *per se* rule prohibits certain acts without regard to the particular effects of the acts; it does not consider mitigating circumstances nor offsetting benefits of anti-competitive practices. A *per se* prohibition is justified for types of conduct that have manifestly anti-competitive implications and a very limited potential for pro-competitive benefits.[27] Conversely, a "rule of reason" requires an investigation of the effects of the challenged conduct, taking into account the particular facts of the case. According to the rule of reason the courts must decide whether the questioned practice imposes an unreasonable restraint on competition, taking into account a variety of factors, including specific information about the relevant business, its condition before and after the restraint was imposed, and the restraint's history, nature and effect.[28]

Not only lawyers stressing the need for legal certainty, but also some economists, notably those adopting the concept of freedom of competition (*Konzept der Wettbewerbsfreiheit*) as their principle guiding postulate,[29] have a preference for *per se* rules. However, few, if any, practices are so outrageously anti-competitive that an unequivocal prohibition could be formulated; rather, in most cases both pro-competitive and anti-competitive effects require a balancing act. This is also true with respect to "legal dogmas" of competition policy, in particular the ban on fixing minimum retail prices. The current *per se* prohibition under European law does not seem to be justified economically, as resale price maintenance may not only impede competition, but also cope with free riding problems and thus generate important efficiency savings.[30]

Consequently, one will rarely escape broadly formulated prohibition clauses that will have to be interpreted by competition authorities and courts. Under US antitrust law, the "rule of reason" approach allows for a weighing of the pernicious and beneficial repercussions on competition of the practices under investigation. The scope of the rule of reason can vary considerably with changes in competition law's underlying goals. For example, the expansion of capacity might be considered an exclusionary practice if the aim of antitrust is

---

[27] See, e.g. *Northern Pacific Railroad Co v United States*, 356 U.S. 1 (1958), at 5.
[28] *Board of Trade of Chicago v United States*, 246 U.S. 231 (1918), at 238.
[29] See Ch.3, s.3.7.3.
[30] See, for further elaboration, Ch.6, s.6.6.2.

to protect small businesses, but may conversely be judged legal if the goal is the maximisation of consumer welfare, since increased output results in lower prices.[31] Under European law the broad prohibition as formulated in Article 81(1) EC is softened by providing for the possibility of individual or group exemptions under Article 81(3) EC. Thereto four cumulative conditions must be satisfied. The extent to which exemptions resemble a rule of reason approach is being debated.[32] This matter will be pursued in more detail in later chapters of this book, but it already appears evident that even under the system of exemptions a continued interpretation of their terms and conditions remains a discretionary activity.

Throughout this book the reader will encounter numerous examples of how economic analysis may assist in illuminating the law's general norms. It suffices to mention at this point:

- the concept of restriction of competition in Article 81(1) EC;

- the interpretation of the four cumulative conditions of Article 81(3) EC: contribution to an improvement of production and distribution or promotion of technical or economic progress, fair share of the resulting benefits for consumers, indispensability of the restrictions to attaining the preceding objectives, and no elimination of competition in relation to a substantial part of the products in question;

- the concept of dominance, as contained in Article 82 EC and defined by the European Court of Justice;[33]

- the formulation of Article 82 EC types of abuse, such as "directly or indirectly imposing unfair purchase or selling prices or unfair trading conditions" (at a), as well as "applying dissimilar conditions to equivalent transactions with other trading parties, thereby placing them at a competitive disadvantage" (at c);

- the Merger Regulation's new substantive requirement of "significant impediment to effective competition" compared to the former criterion of dominance and the US concept of "substantially lessening competition";

- the Merger Regulation's criteria of appraisal as contained in Article 2(1) of the Merger Regulation, consisting of, *inter alia*, the need to maintain and develop effective competition, the taking into account of potential competition, barriers to entry, and the interests of the intermediate and ultimate consumers.

The interpretation of these concepts may be influenced by one's preference for a particular economic school of thought. As it will be made clear in Chapter 3

---

[31] Compare H. Hovenkamp, *Federal Antitrust Policy: The Law of Competition and its Practice* (1994), s.6.4.a.
[32] Compare D.G. Goyder, *EC Competition Law* (4th ed., 2003), pp.91–92; C.W. Bellamy and G. Child, *Common Market Law of Competition* (5th ed., 2001), para.2–063; A. Jones and B. Sufrin, *EC Competition Law: Text, Cases and Materials* (2nd ed., 2004), pp.201–204.
[33] Case 85/76 *Hoffmann-La Roche v Commission (Vitamins)* [1979] E.C.R. 461.

of this book, there is no single economic approach to competition but various principles and ideas underlying different economic interpretations of vague legal concepts. The alternative views will be contrasted in the following chapters.

1.1.3 Problems of evidence

Central questions of competition law are ultimately empirical issues. The Harvard–Chicago debate on the effects of mergers,[34] for example, is a clear illustration of how shaky theory may be provided without facts supported by empirical analysis. The questions whether cartel agreements raise prices above competitive levels (and, if yes, to what extent) and mergers may cause price increases could be answered by applying qualitative arguments. However, only quantitative (econometric) tests may provide hard evidence.[35] Quantitative techniques should be geared to the main concerns of antitrust in improving total welfare or consumer welfare. This is the case for:

- Market structure issues: how should one measure market concentration, market shares based on the delineation of relevant markets, entry barriers, and exit conditions? How responsive are potential entrants to increased prices?

- Pricing issues: are movements in market prices consistent with competition, with monopoly, or with collusion? Can firms increase post-merger prices unilaterally in markets characterised by product differentiation? Are price–costs relationships consistent with, or indicative of, predatory pricing?

- Vertical issues: to what extent do vertical restraints by leading firms, such as exclusive distribution and franchising, reduce competition and/or yield efficiencies?

- Exclusionary behaviour: to what extent do leading firms' non-price strategies, for example, on matters such as tying, refusals to deal, discrimination, advertising, or patent licensing, lessen competition or improve industry performance? Where both effects exist, can profit variations be explained by costs efficiency?

- Merger issues: how much might the merger under scrutiny change pricing and other market behaviour post-merger, either by lessening competition or by promoting efficiency?

The extent to which quantitative techniques are used to provide evidence in antitrust cases differs according to which side of the Atlantic ocean one

---

[34] See Ch.3, s.3.6.1.3.
[35] For further details, see Office of Fair Trading, *Quantitative Techniques in Competition Analysis* (1999).

resides. American antitrust has long moved beyond the stage of mere economic signalling. This is partly due to the more litigious nature of US antitrust law, which is very demanding in terms of supporting economic and factual evidence. Contrary to the investigative procedure in Europe, expert testimony is more often required in the US where the adversarial process invites each party to expose the weakness of the other party's arguments and evidence. Hereto the Supreme Court's *Daubert* rule[36] has stirred, but in principle reconfirmed, that it is "virtually impossible to proceed with an antitrust case without an economist".[37] Indeed, economic expertise dealing with statistics and multiple regression is a well-established regular,[38] prominently featured in the Court's evidence manual.[39] Despite, or because of, this high-profile setting, the US antitrust enforcement's adaptation of new developments is still prone to cyclical bouts of quandary.[40] Still, even if—the availability of econometric techniques notwithstanding—quantitative estimates are impossible or imprecise it seems to be established that knowledge of empirical measurement is crucial to weigh correctly the qualitative information that is available. In Europe, there is still less willingness to decide competition cases on the basis of quantitative evidence, as the current practice of market definition clearly shows.[41] At this point, one may take up the Commission staff's wording in that "while the Commission will use quantitative evidence whenever it is available and sufficiently sound, the assessment ... is still, in the large majority of cases, a qualitative analysis based on a mix of quantitative and qualitative evidence."[42]

Within the scope of this book an extensive overview of the range of empirical tools available cannot be provided, whereto the reader is invited to consult the specialised literature on the field.[43] However, in subsequent chapters, some illustrations are given on how quantitative techniques may

---

[36] *Daubert v Merrill Dow Pharmaceuticals, Inc*, 509 U.S. 579 (1993).

[37] Compare the articles contained in *Antitrust*'s Summer 1996 issue and A.I. Gavil, "After Daubert: Discerning the Increasingly Fine Line between the Admissibility and Sufficiency of Expert Testimony in Antitrust Litigation" (1997) 65 Antitrust L.J. 663 at pp.666–667. See, in general, E.L. Rubin, "The New Legal Process, the Synthesis of Discourse, and the Microanalysis of Institutions" (1996) 109 Harv. L. Rev. 1393 at p.1405.

[38] M. Tyson, "Presumed Guilty until Proven Innocent: Using Results of Statistical or Econometric Studies as Evidence" (1998) 10 St. Thomas L. Rev. 387.

[39] Compare D.H. Kaye and D.A. Friedman, "Reference Guide on Statistics" in *Reference Manual on Scientific Evidence* (1995), p.331; and D.L. Rubinfeld, "Reference Guide on Multiple Regression" in *Reference Manual on Scientific Evidence* (1995), p.415. For an early account, see D.L. Rubinfeld and P.O. Steiner, "Quantitative Methods in Antitrust Litigation" (1983) 46 Law and Contemp. Prob. 69.

[40] Compare, among many, the evidence noted in W.E. Kovacic, "Downsizing Antitrust: Is it Time to End Dual Federal Enforcement?" (1996) 41 Antitrust Bull. 505, at p.538; W.J. Liebeler, "Bureau of Competition: Antitrust Enforcement Activities", in *The Federal Trade Commission since 1870: Economic Regulation and Bureaucratic Behaviour*, (K.W. Clarkson and T.J. Muris ed., 1981) pp.65, 97.

[41] See Ch.4, s.4.2.2.2.

[42] P. Christensen, P. Owen and D. Sjöblom, "Mergers", in *The EC Law of Competition* (J. Faull and A. Nikpay ed., 1999) para.4.146.

[43] J.B. Baker and D.L. Rubinfeld, "Empirical Methods Used in Antitrust Litigation: Review and a Critique" (1999) 1 Amer. Law Econ. Rev. 386; Office of Fair Trading, *Quantitative Techniques in Competition Analysis* (1999); S. Bishop and M. Walker, *Economics of EC Competition Law: Concepts, Application and Measurement* (2nd ed., 2002); D.H. Kaye and D.A. Friedman, "Reference Guide on Statistics", in *Reference Manual on Scientific Evidence* (1995), p.331.

assist in answering the above questions typically arising during antitrust proceedings.

1.1.4 Objections and remaining challenges

The qualification of efficiency as the main goal of competition law is not necessarily the view of the politicians who wrote the laws, while having in their minds above all considerations of distributive justice, such as fairness, consumer welfare or the protection of small business. Also, there may be objections within the legal community to the efficiency goal, if its attainment implies different treatments of what (to most non-economists) appear to be identical cases. Gauging consumers' reactions and the overall profitability of projected price increases is by no means straightforward, and its complexity was augmented for a long time as the adaptation of economically enhanced rules had been fended off in Europe as leading to an undesirable measure of uncertainty in legal interpretation.[44] Courts may be very hesitant to accept arguments based on probability statements, conceptions of frequency, and on hypotheticals such as potential entry. Such considerations stem mainly from concerns of legal certainty. In sum, concepts of justice and the desire to avoid inequality, as well as legal uncertainty, have inhibited a full application of economic analysis.

However, these possible objections to a widespread use of economic arguments in solving real-world competition cases should be scaled down to their proper proportions. To some extent non-economic goals are consistent with efficiency considerations. Monopoly may be denounced both for efficiency and distributional motives. Not only does monopoly cause resource misallocation (the so-called deadweight loss[45]); it also increases the profits of the producer to the detriment of consumers, which may be seen as a less desirable distribution of income. Similarly, a prohibition of a large-scale merger that yields inappreciable efficiency benefits serves both the efficiency objective and the non-economic goal of dispersal of power. Even more importantly, if non-economic goals must give way to efficiency goals in the area of competition law, this does not at all imply that society cannot pursue the former objectives by different means. It is not asserted here that fairness is not an appropriate goal for public policy. However, distributional issues, such as the protection of small firms by giving them fair and equal chances to compete with larger rivals, are best addressed through means other than competition policy. Tax benefits seem to be superior in this respect. The difficulty in gaining sufficient political support for tax discrimination may explain why inefficient

---

[44] Summarising these fears: P. Erlinghagen, "Zur Verwendbarkeit wirtschaftswissenschaftlicher Theorien als Beweismittel in Kartellverfahren", in *Wettbewerbsordnung im Spannungsfeld von Wirtschafts- und Rechtswissenschaft, Festschrift für Günther Hartmann* (Forschungsinstitut für Wirtschaftsverfassung und Wettbewerb ed., 1976), p.95.
[45] For an explanation of this concept, see Ch.2, s.2.2.2.

competition rules are enacted, which allegedly serve to guarantee fair and equal opportunities for small traders.[46]

On the notion of legal certainty, the following observations seem appropriate. A lack of precise economic analysis threatens to undermine competition law's foundations. This is an important insight to which the European Court of Justice has cleared the way in requesting a more positive economically inspired reasoning in *Walt Wilhelm*.[47] Within the existing framework of European competition law, the general quality of reasoning may be improved substantially by referring to economic insights. In addition, the reliability of an economic approach for judging individual cases has increased due to the development of more advanced measurement techniques. Indeed, economic science has in the meantime cultivated a range of sophisticated empirical tools, enabling a more direct estimation of most competitive parameters' consequences. Although often complex in their application, these quantitative techniques do serve well the wider goal of assessing firms' behaviour and predicting its outcome. On the one hand, economic theory supported by reliable quantitative measurement techniques necessitates a case-by-case approach, which may reduce the predictability of decisions and increase legal uncertainty in individual antitrust cases. On the other hand, these costs may be outweighed by reducing the inconsistencies which European competition law still harbours.

1.2 Structure of this book

The structure of this book is as follows. The next chapter discusses the different goals that may underlie competition policy and law. It emphasises the negative welfare consequences of monopoly power which clearly justify the need for competition rules. At the same time, it stresses that economic efficiency (total welfare) is not the only possible goal of competition policy. Rules of competition law may be inspired by other considerations, such as consumer welfare, protection of business freedom or concepts of equity. The third chapter provides an overview of the evolution of economic thinking towards competition policy. In this way, different economic approaches to competition policy and law are identified. Competition rules may be adapted as the underlying economic theory changes. A chronological overview is particularly helpful to explain how the outcomes of competition cases may be affected by changes in economic theory. The fourth chapter then addresses the economic analysis of market power and shows how economic insights may be helpful in interpreting the legal concept of dominance. The largest part of this chapter is

[46] Compare R.J. Van den Bergh, "Belgian Public Policy towards the Retailing Trade", in *Law and Economics and the Economics of Legal Regulation* (M. Graf von der Schulenburg and G. Skogh ed., 1986), pp.185–205.
[47] Case 14/68 *Walt Wilhelm v Bundeskartellamt* [1969] E.C.R. 1, para.14. Compare R. Wesseling, "Subsidiarity in Community Antitrust Law: Setting the Right Agenda" (1997) 22 E.L. Rev. 35 at p.45.

devoted to a critical analysis of the concept of the relevant market, which forms the basis of an indirect assessment of market power based on market shares. The inherent limitations of market share analysis are illuminated and comparisons are made with alternative approaches, which try to assess market power directly. The fourth chapter concludes with an analysis of barriers to entry. In the absence of entry barriers, there is no possibility to exercise market power for a lasting period.

Chapters 5, 6 and 7 contain an economic analysis of the substantive rules of competition law contained in Articles 81 EC and 82 EC: the prohibition of (horizontal) cartel agreements, the regulation of vertical restraints, and the prohibition of abuses of dominant position (for example, tying and predatory pricing). Chapter 5 summarises the most important insights of economic theory relating to horizontal restrictions of competition. Thereafter it discusses the substantive rules prohibiting restrictive agreements and the four cumulative conditions for an exemption (Article 81 EC). This chapter also provides an economic assessment of the current law on competitor cooperation and horizontal restraints. Chapter 6 addresses vertical restraints of competition, which emanate from agreements between firms that are active at different stages of production (agreements between manufacturers and dealers). Also in this chapter, the major insights from economic theory are summarised and an economic assessment of current European competition law is provided. The topic of Chapter 7 is the prohibition of abuse of a dominant position (Article 82 EC). Different types of potential abuses are discussed: price discrimination, tying, and predatory pricing. Chapter 8 discusses how the cartel prohibition and the rules on abuse of dominant position are enforced. Three dimensions of law enforcement are analysed: the choice of sanctions (fines on companies only or also fines on individuals and eventually imprisonment), the role of private and public enforcement mechanisms, and the timing of the enforcement (*ex ante* control versus *ex post* monitoring). Chapter 9 contains an analysis of the Merger Regulation. The chapter will focus on the role of market share analysis, concentration ratios, competitive effects and efficiencies of horizontal concentrations. It will highlight the substantive issues raised by coordinated and non-coordinated effects, and provide examples to illustrate these complex concepts and their application in recent practice. Finally, Chapter 10 discusses the need for European competition law as a complementary instrument to national competition laws. Advantages and disadvantages of diverging competition laws are presented; from this perspective, the scope for European competition law is critically examined.

Throughout this book frequent comparisons with US antitrust law and competition laws of EC Member States (in particular German competition law) are included. Since competition laws are phrased in deliberately general terms, they get their precise meaning when competition authorities and courts interpret them. For this reason leading cases are also discussed, in order to find out whether their outcomes are consistent with economic principles. It is thus made clear how economic analysis may influence the practical results of competition law.

1.3 Caveats

Before closing this general introduction, a number of important caveats must be made. First, the limited scope of this book does not allow for a comprehensive review of the economic literature on the subject of competition. The major textbooks on industrial economics have several hundred pages.[48] The same is true for books on competition law.[49] The latter seldom contain an overview of the relevant economic theory, and the analysis of competition law in the former also remains limited. Although industrial economists and competition lawyers study the same subject matter, their approaches have unfortunately grown apart. The purpose of this book is to lay the foundations for a closer cooperation between industrial economists and competition lawyers. It is neither a substitute for textbooks on industrial organisation nor an introduction to competition law. The central aim is to stimulate an integrated approach, rather than assessing competition problems either by purely economic or strictly legal criteria. This reflects the key concern that decisions on competition issues should not be made solely on the basis of formalistic line drawing, using only technical legal categories. In order to develop a consistent and efficiency enhancing competition policy, the economic effects of legal rules and decisions in competition cases should always be borne in mind. Although in this book the application of economic principles will be far from exhaustive, it is hoped that the reader will develop some feeling for the relevance of an economic approach in relation to competition law.

Second, economic theory does not always provide clear-cut answers to judge the efficiency of certain types of conduct. For example, behaviour that is irrational in the Chicago sense of the word may be "rationalised" using recent game theoretic approaches. This may have an impact on the normative issues with which lawyers have to cope. In the field of the most controversial competition policy issues, such as the assessment of barriers to entry and predatory pricing, it does seem to be the case that there is only one consensus among economists as among lawyers, namely, that "competition is important". Hence, this book will disappoint those who seek an exact and authoritative guide to all kinds of competition policy issues, for it contains nothing of the kind.

Third, because the primary target group of this book consists of (competition) law students, familiarity with basic rules of competition law is assumed. This may make the text harder to understand for economics students who would like to contribute to bridging the gap between both disciplines. To inform industrial economists about the complexities of competition law is, of

---

[48] D.W. Carlton and J.M. Perloff, *Modern Industrial Organization* (4th ed., 2005); F.M. Scherer and D. Ross, *Industrial Market Structure and Economic Performance* (3rd ed., 1990); J. Tirole, *The Theory of Industrial Organization* (1988).

[49] L. Ritter, W.D. Braun and F. Rawlinson, *European Competition Law: A Practitioner's Guide* (2nd ed., 2000); J. Faull and A. Nikpay, *The EC Law of Competition* (1999); D.G. Goyder, *EC Competition Law* (4th ed., 2003); C.W. Bellamy and G. Child, *Common Market Law of Competition* (5th ed., 2001); A. Jones and B. Sufrin, *EC Competition Law: Text, Cases and Materials* (2nd ed., 2004).

course, a similarly important undertaking to stimulate interdisciplinary research. It may prevent an industrial organisation theory from living a life of its own and the development of pure theories, which do not pay sufficient attention to real-world problems in applying competition law. A further elaboration of this point, however, must find its place in a different introduction to a different book.

Chapter 2

....

THE GOALS OF COMPETITION LAW

2.1 Introduction

There has been an intense debate over the goals of competition law—or antitrust, as it is commonly called in the USA. Scholars working in the Chicago School tradition have rejected the propriety of any goals other than productive and allocative efficiency for competition policy. The promotion of total welfare (maximisation of producer surplus and consumer surplus in all sectors of the economy) was most clearly voiced by Robert Bork.[1] The Chicago School had a profound impact on American antitrust law in the 1970s and the 1980s.

---

[1] R.H. Bork, *The Antitrust Paradox: A Policy at War with Itself* (2nd ed., 1993). In this book consumer welfare is used as a synonym for total welfare, whereas—as will be explained below—these are different concepts.

However, recent policy statements by the American enforcement agencies stress consumer welfare, rather than total welfare, as the main goal of antitrust law.[2] If making consumers better off is seen as the major goal, allocative efficiency may remain the focal point of antitrust analysis but it will need to be supplemented by an investigation of distributive effects.

Even though most commentators may agree that European competition policy is concerned with the economic consequences of market power, they will not all subscribe to the view that allocative efficiency (eventually under the condition that it generates benefits for consumers) is the sole aim of European competition law. European competition policy embraces a multitude of political goals.[3] A traditional objective of European competition law is the achievement of market integration, which eventually may come at the expense of inefficiencies in the organisation of production and distribution.[4] European competition law is further distinct from American antitrust law in its embrace of small and medium-sized firms as a positive competitive force[5] and the related emphasis on fairness (equity) rather than efficiency. Also, the so-called ordoliberal view,[6] according to which any limitation of business freedom should be held as a virtual restriction of competition, has had an impact on the formulation of prohibitions in European competition law. On top of these different views, the EC Treaty mandates interaction between competition policy objectives and other goals, such as social policy, environmental protection and consumer protection.[7] The problems created by the multi-valued tradition of European competition law become even more aggravated when covert considerations of industrial policy seep into the competitive appraisal.

In spite of the lack of consensus on the goals to be achieved, an extensive body of European competition law has developed. Obviously, different goals may be inconsistent with each other and necessitate difficult trade-offs. Economic analysis forces policy makers and practitioners alike to be explicit about the law's underlying aims and thus guarantees a more consistent approach. This chapter discusses the different economic welfare standards that seem appropriate for competition law and indicates the normative consequences of choosing a particular yardstick. To revamp the discussion on the goals of competition policy, and profiting from the debate in the United States, one may contrast the following three options: first, efficiency as a measure of total

[2] See US Department of Justice, "Antitrust Enforcement and the Consumer", at *www.usdoj.gov/ atr/public/div_stats/1638.htm*; and Federal Trade Commission, "Promoting Competition, Protecting Consumers", at *www.ftc.gov/bc/compguide/index.htm*.

[3] See for an overview of its development: D.J. Gerber, *Law and Competition in Twentieth Century Europe* (1998).

[4] Compare in general: J. Pelkmans, *European Integration: Methods and Economic Analysis* (2nd ed., 2001), pp.223–245; R.J. Van den Bergh, "Modern Industrial Organisation and Old-fashioned European Competition Law" (1996) 17 E.C.L.R. 75.

[5] It may be added that in the USA antitrust law also embodies social and moral goals. The competitive process is believed to be a kind of disciplinary machinery for the development of character and the competitiveness of people is seen as the fundamental stimulus to national morale which needs protection. Compare R. Hofstadter, "What Happened to the Antitrust Movement?", in *The Paranoid Style in American Politics and Other Essays* (1965), p.200, reprinted in T.E. Sullivan, *The Political Economy of the Sherman Act: The First One Hundred Years* (1991).

[6] This view has its roots in Germany; see Ch.3, s.3.4.

[7] See the statement of former Commissioner for Competition Van Miert, quoted in Box 2.2.

societal welfare, second, consumer welfare, and third, other policy goals, such as market integration and protection of individual economic freedom. The authors of this book adhere to the view that only efficiency and consumer welfare are appropriate normative goals of competition law. Other objectives, such as market integration and protection of individual economic (business) freedom may be fully legitimate but should be pursued by other legal instruments.

To fully understand the different notions of efficiency and their relevance for competition policy, it is necessary to introduce some basic notions of micro-economics (consumer surplus, producer surplus, perfect competition, monopoly) and welfare economics (Pareto efficiency, Kaldor–Hicks efficiency). Economic theory offers tools that may help to interpret a great number of vague notions in competition law in accordance with the welfare standard opted for. The main purpose of this chapter is to make the reader familiar with the different concepts of efficiency (productive efficiency, allocative efficiency, dynamic efficiency) and consumer welfare, as well as with their relation to other possible goals of competition policy. In this chapter, the goals of European competition law are contrasted with the notions of welfare economics and some examples are given to illustrate the conflicts between different policy goals.

This chapter is structured as follows. In the next section, the notions of consumer surplus and producer surplus are explained and it is shown that total surplus is maximised under the conditions of perfect competition. The central insight from welfare economics is that perfectly competitive markets are Pareto efficient. Pareto improvements are no longer possible in a market which is allocatively efficient. Allocative efficiency implies that firms produce what buyers want and are willing to pay for. Whereas allocative efficiency is reached in a perfectly competitive market, monopoly causes welfare losses. In the second section of this chapter, the economic models of perfect competition and monopoly are contrasted with each other. The concept of allocative efficiency is explained and it is made clear that the model of perfect competition provides a strong theoretical basis for the desirability of competition law.

In the third section, the different concepts of efficiency are introduced. In some cases, allocative efficiency may conflict with other efficiency goals: productive efficiency and dynamic efficiency.[8] To enable policy decisions when the different efficiency goals are not consistent with each other, welfare economics offers the alternative criterion of Kaldor–Hicks efficiency. This alternative welfare notion—also called potential Pareto improvements— allows changes that increase total welfare, irrespective of the distribution of the gains that result from these modifications. In the last part of the third section, the total welfare view is contrasted with the consumer welfare goal requiring that consumers also profit from productive and dynamic efficiencies.

In the fourth section, how the current rules of European competition law

---

[8] W. Nicholson, *Microeconomic Theory: Basic Principles and Extensions* (7th ed., 1998), pp.611–620; European Commission, *The Single Market review: Impact on Competition and Scale Effects: Competition Issues* (1997), p.33; J.F. Brodley, "The Economic Goals of Antitrust: Efficiency, Consumer Welfare, and Technological Progress" (1987) 62 N.Y.U.L. Rev. 1020 at p.1025.

relate to the efficiency concepts and the consumer welfare standard introduced in the two previous sections is investigated. An answer will be sought to the question of whether the policy goals of European competition law can be supported by criteria of welfare economics. Particular attention will be devoted to welfare losses that may be caused by pursuing goals other than efficiency and consumer welfare. This section introduces the typical policy conflicts of the multi-valued tradition of European competition policy. Some first examples will be given to illustrate the unavoidable conflicts and trade-offs. The tensions between different policy goals are a recurrent topic of this book and will be further elaborated upon in the next chapters.

2.2 Allocative efficiency

To understand the relevance of the notion of allocative efficiency for the design and implementation of competition policy and law, some familiarity with notions of micro-economics is necessary. The scope of this book does not allow a complete introduction into micro-economic consumer and producer theory and an analysis of different market forms (perfect competition, monopoly, oligopoly, monopolistic competition) in a rigorous way.[9] However, a comparison of the market results under perfect competition and monopoly will suffice to show why the latter market form is suboptimal and antitrust provisions against monopoly power are warranted. The results of this simple analysis do not become invalid, if the economic reasoning becomes more elaborate or technical.

2.2.1 The model of perfect competition

Adam Smith's notion of an invisible hand as the guiding mechanism of an economy is essential to the economist's idea of a competitive market. Adam Smith gave a positive reply to the basic question concerning the desirability of a free market system which has served as a policy guideline for more than two centuries now.[10] However, the justification of Smith's answer is unsatisfactory according to the methodological standards of scientific neo-classical micro-economics. To highlight the beneficial welfare consequences of competition, the formal model of a perfectly competitive market has been constructed.

When economists speak of a perfectly competitive market they have in mind a market with the following characteristics:

- on the supply side of the market there is a large number of producers acting as price takers who decide independently, without collusion, on

---

[9] Interested readers are referred to R.S. Pindyck and D.L. Rubinfeld, *Microeconomics* (6th ed., 2005).
[10] See, for a more elaborate discussion, Ch.3, s.3.2.2.

Graph 2.1: Market equilibrium under perfect competition

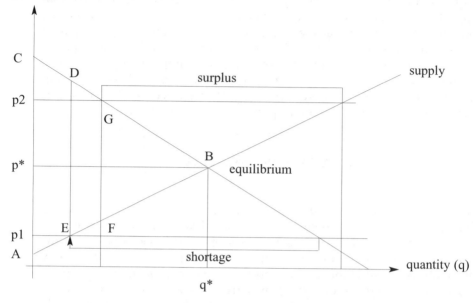

their actions. No single firm has a sufficiently large degree of market power to influence the market outcome or the actions of others;

- the demand side is similarly structured. The producers face a large number of buyers who are acting independently and have no power to control the market price through their behaviour;

- it is further assumed that entry and exit may occur instantaneously without prohibitively high costs for new firms. Producers must be able to start up or shut down operations if they find it in their interest to do so. There is thus free and easy entry and exit;

- the products traded on the market are homogeneous. This means that consumers perceive no quality differences between the goods and decide on the basis of prices alone from which producer they will buy;

- the transaction costs of a perfectly competitive market equal zero. The goods can be exchanged without costs and flow freely to their most valued use. Transaction costs are expenses that occur by the exchange of the produced good and cannot be considered as production costs;

- the (final) assumption of perfect information covers a wide range of sub-assumptions which will not be listed in full. Here, it suffices to reduce the assumptions to the following. The suppliers of the market know their production and cost function as well as the market price of the goods. Relying on this information they are able to make decisions on the optimal output and on whether to enter or exit the market. The consumers know the utility they derive from the consumption of the goods and determine the purchased quantity by taking into account their utility, income and price.

It can be shown that the equilibrium of a perfectly competitive market is allocatively efficient. An economist calls a resource allocation efficient if it is impossible to conceive a better outcome for society at large. In a perfectly competitive market it is not possible to effectuate a Pareto improvement, which is a change making at least one individual better off without making another individual worse off. When no further Pareto improvements are possible, the market reaches an equilibrium that is Pareto efficient.

The market equilibrium of a perfectly competitive market is the point where the demand curve and the supply curve intersect. The slope of demand and supply curves is explained below. The demand curve and the supply curve can be combined to model the market mechanism leading to the market equilibrium. The allocative efficiency of perfectly competitive markets is illustrated in the following graph.

The market demand curve shows the quantity that consumers will purchase at different prices. It indicates the relation between the price the consumer has to pay for each unit and the purchased quantity of goods. If the price of goods increases, the demand will fall; if the price decreases, the exchanged quantity will rise. The increase of the quantity can be explained in two ways. If the price is lowered, consumers who have already bought the product may buy additional units and those who were not yet buyers because of high prices will no longer refrain from purchasing. The demand curve will thus slope downward if the independent variable, the price, is placed on the vertical axis and the dependent variable, the quantity, is put on the horizontal axis. The demand curve in Graph 2.1 is the aggregate demand of the market. The aggregate demand is the relation between the total demand of all consumers in the market and the price of the goods. The individual demand curve describing the behaviour of an individual consumer and the aggregate demand curve have the same property: quantity increases in the case of a price decrease. The aggregate curve of the entire market is obtained by adding up the quantities demanded at each price as derived from the individual consumers' demand curves.

The market supply curve shows the quantities that producers will supply at different prices. It indicates the relation between the prices and the supplied quantities of goods. On the supply side, the response to price changes is the opposite of demand behaviour. If prices increase, supply will equally increase; if prices fall, quantities supplied will decrease accordingly. The supply curve will slope upward if the dependent variable, the quantity, is put on the horizontal axis and the independent variable, the price, is placed on the vertical axis. The curve slopes upward because with higher prices firms are willing to increase their output in the short run as prices cover the higher production costs per unit. In the long run new firms which could not cover production costs at low market prices will enter the market. The result of both adaptation processes is the explained joint increase of price and supplied quantity. The graph shows the aggregate supply curve of a market. The individual supply curve of a firm has similar, but not identical, properties as its aggregate counterpart. The short run aggregate supply curve is a straightforward summation of quantities expressed by individual supply curves. The derivation of the long run aggregate supply curve is more complicated and will not be covered in this book.[11]

The demand curve and the supply curve can be combined to model a market and the mechanism which leads to an equilibrium between demand and supply. The point where the demand and supply curves intersect is the market equilibrium. At this point the equilibrium price and quantity are determined. In Graph 2.1 this is at point B. If the price deviated from its equilibrium level, the market result would be either a surplus of production or a shortage of demand. If the market is not in equilibrium, the production surplus or the shortage of demand will disappear in the following way. In the case of a surplus, with the actual price being higher than the equilibrium value, the excess production will be reduced by a price decrease. This decline in the price level will lower production in two ways. The firms which are still able to cover their production costs will produce less; firms facing higher costs will incur losses and will thus be forced to leave the market and cease production. At the end of the adaptation processes only the most efficient firms remain in the market and the resulting market price will just cover the costs. In the case of a shortage the price of the product is lower than the equilibrium value and consumers are willing to pay more to satisfy their demand. The possibility of selling at higher prices encourages existing firms to expand their production and incites new firms to enter the market. Both factors will have a stimulating effect on the output level and the shortage will be continuously removed. The described adaptation processes, the removal of surplus (or shortage) through the reduction (or expansion) of production with the associated fall (or rise) of the market price are the spelled out version of the invisible hand of Adam Smith. This market mechanism guides all involved firms and consumers to the market equilibrium.

To describe the welfare consequences of perfect competition two additional notions must be introduced: consumer surplus and producer surplus. Market demand merely sums up the demands of individual consumers. Since some consumers are willing to pay higher amounts for the product than the market price, they earn a surplus. In Graph 2.1 the consumer surplus is the area between the demand curve and the horizontal line at the height of the equilibrium price. The area below the demand curve down to the horizontal axis measures the willingness to pay. The area between the market price line and the horizontal axis depicts the actual expenses. The difference is the triangle of consumer surplus. The producer surplus is the area between the market price

---

[11] The problem with the construction of the long run supply curve is that entry and exit of firms occur in the market. To construct the long run supply curve, one has to know how many firms are active in the market, how the prices for inputs and the produced goods change, and, maybe, even how production technology further develops. This requires additional assumptions which describe this process. The long run supply curve of an industry slopes upward too, if the costs of production rise with higher aggregate output.

line and the supply curve. This area is a measure for the difference between the revenue and production costs of firms. The revenue is defined as the price times the quantity sold and thus covers the area below the market price line. The area under the supply curve measures the variable costs of producing a certain number of goods. The difference between the revenue and the variable costs of production is defined as the producer surplus.

The yardstick for measuring the efficiency of the market outcome is simply the sum of consumer and producer surplus. This joint surplus makes it possible to compare the social welfare consequences of the competitive equilibrium and a market in disequilibrium. Referring to Graph 2.1, the welfare properties of a perfectly competitive market can be explained. The price and quantity combination A is the optimal equilibrium. In the market equilibrium, the consumer surplus is given by the triangle p*CB and the producer surplus by the triangle p*AB. The aggregate surplus is the area ABC. In the case of a shortage the consumer surplus is given by the area p1EDC and the producer surplus by the triangle AEp1. The triangle EBD measures the welfare loss of a shortage. In the case of a surplus the consumer surplus is measured by the triangle p2GC and the producer surplus is given by the area AFGp2. The aggregate loss is the triangle FBG. Total surplus, which is the sum of consumer and producer surplus, is maximised in the competitive equilibrium and the disequilibrium situation results in surplus losses. Total welfare will be maximised if the conditions of perfect competition prevail in all sectors of the economy.

Perfect competition is a situation in which it is impossible to introduce a change to make at least one person better off without making another person worse off. This situation is also known as Pareto efficient. Pareto optimality is realised when it is no longer possible to enhance the welfare of one or more economic subjects by a change in the transaction or production conditions without diminishing the welfare of some other subject. The market equilibrium achieved under conditions of perfect competition is, therefore, optimal from a perspective of economic welfare.

It should be emphasised that this equilibrium is a spontaneous order, attained by decentralised individual decisions which take into account personal benefits but not collective welfare. The coincidence of individual and collective interest may be considered the most important result of the analysis of the market mechanism. It was shown earlier that the market equilibrium is a social optimal state which cannot be improved upon. Spontaneous coordination and the welfare properties are the reasons for the attractiveness of the market equilibrium, achieved under conditions of perfect competition, as a policy guideline and its status as a reference point.

2.2.2 Monopoly

Monopoly is to be distinguished from perfect competition in two important respects. Instead of a large number of sellers there is only one firm supplying the entire market. In addition, it is assumed that the monopoly position is not challenged by new entrants. The monopolist thus faces neither actual nor potential competition. In other aspects, the monopoly model does not differ from the assumptions made for the competitive case: the goods sold are homogeneous, there is perfect information, transaction costs equal zero, and there is a large number of buyers. In contrast to a market characterised by perfect competition where firms act as price takers, the monopolist can influence the market outcome, the equilibrium price, and quantity, by his production decisions. Here, it is assumed that the monopolist is not able to discriminate between his customers according to their willingness to pay or, in other words, that he has no knowledge about their individual demand functions. This eliminates the possibility of price discrimination, where different prices are charged for different quantities and/or consumers. Price discriminating behaviour is a possible extension of the model which will not be covered here.[12]

The key difference between monopoly and perfect competition are the properties of the demand function which the firms face. In perfect competition the individual firm perceives the market demand as a horizontal line, as shown in Graph 2.2. The competitive firm takes the market price as given and adjusts its output until its marginal cost equals price.

Graph 2.2: Profit maximisation under perfect competition

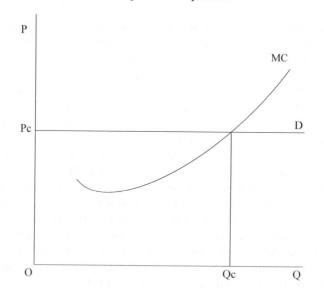

In contrast with a perfectly competitive firm, a monopolist faces a downward sloping market demand curve. When the monopolist produces and sells an extra unit of output, it must move down the market demand curve. To sell additional units the monopolist must reduce the price and will suffer a loss in

[12] See Ch.7, s.7.2.

rev-
enue
on
units
that

Graph 2.3: Profit maximisation and welfare losses under monopoly

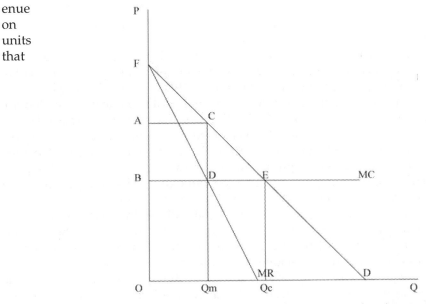

might have been sold at higher prices. Marginal revenue is the change in total revenue per unit change in the quantity demanded. The monopolist can gain a monopoly rent by selling at a higher price a smaller quantity compared to the perfectly competitive outcome. This leads to welfare losses measured by reference to the sum of producer and consumer surplus. How the profit maximising calculus of the monopolist differs from the competitive situation is the next step to develop.

For reasons of simplicity, it is assumed that average and marginal costs are equal and that marginal costs are constant. Hence, the marginal cost curve may be depicted as a horizontal line indicating the height of the constant unit costs of production. The monopolist knows the market demand function, which is a relation between the price charged and the quantity demanded by the consumers. Here, the price of the goods is not fixed, but depends on the quantity sold. The marginal revenue is the additional revenue of selling an additional unit of the monopolist's goods. Under perfect competition the marginal revenue is just the market price, which is the sum of money the firm earns by selling one unit of its product. A monopolist knows that the price will vary with the offered quantity and consequently the marginal revenue is not constant. The marginal revenue is derived from the revenue function by calculating its slope. The slope of a function is the value of variation of the dependent variable (the revenue), if the independent variable (the quantity) is incrementally changed. It can be shown that the marginal revenue function of a monopolist is the market demand function with the double slope.[13] The marginal revenue is the key variable to determine the profit maximising

---

[13] For an elaboration of this point, see J.R. Church and R. Ware, *Industrial Organization: A Strategic Approach* (1999), pp.32–36.

production quantity. In the case of perfect competition, the condition of profit maximisation is the equivalence of marginal revenue (the market price) and marginal cost. The same holds for the monopolist. His production quantity is determined in the same way; the difference is that the marginal revenue is not the constant market price, but a downward sloping curve. The intersection between the marginal cost and marginal revenue curve thus marks the point of the optimal output decision of a monopolist. This is shown in Graph 2.3.

D is the market demand curve, MR is the marginal revenue curve with twice the slope of the demand curve. MC is the marginal cost curve, which is constant in our example and equal to average costs. The marginal revenue curve and the marginal cost curve intersect at D which, when projected on the quantity axis, indicates the optimal output for the monopolist (Qm). The price the monopolist can charge is given by the value of the demand function with this quantity and denoted by A. This price is derived by projecting the optimal output on the demand curve (C), which then allows the fixing of the profit maximising price on the vertical axis at point A. The point C on the demand function is called the Cournot Point, in honour of the French economist Augustin Cournot who developed the model in 1838.[14]

It is now possible to compare the outcome of the monopoly market with the equilibrium of perfect competition. The latter equilibrium is characterised by the equality of the market price with marginal cost. This is point E in Graph 2.3, which, when projected on the horizontal axis, indicates the output of a competitive market (Qc). As can be seen, the quantity produced by the monopolist (Qm) is lower and the price charged higher (A = Pm) than the competitive outcome (Qc, B = Pc). The monopolist charges a price significantly higher than his marginal cost of production. Market prices higher than marginal costs always result in economic rents which exceed normal returns on investment. The notions of consumer and producer surplus can be used to evaluate the losses of a monopoly.

It can be seen from Graph 2.3 that monopolists are able to capture a part of the consumer surplus and that, apart from this surplus redistribution, monopoly causes a deadweight loss to society. The consumer surplus is, as usual, given by the area between the demand curve and the horizontal market price line. The producer surplus is the area between the marginal cost curve and the market price line. The consumer surplus in the monopoly situation is equal to the triangle FAC and the producer surplus to the area ABCD. The consumer surplus would be FBE in the case of perfect competition where (Qc, A = Pc) are realised. The loss of consumer surplus can be divided into two parts. The area ABCD represents a transfer of income from the consumers to the monopolist. This reduction in consumer surplus makes consumers worse off, but producers are better off to the extent that they earn a monopoly profit. With the assumption of constant marginal costs the producer surplus would be zero.[15] The triangle CDE represents the remaining loss of consumer surplus

---

[14] A.A. Cournot, *Researches into Mathematical Principles of the Theory of Wealth* (1971). (Original French title: *Recherches sur les Principes Mathématiques de la Théorie des Richesses.*)
[15] This does not mean that the firm would exit the market; rather, it is indifferent to produce or not.

that is not transferred to the monopolist. This net loss is the deadweight loss resulting from monopoly.

The welfare consequences of monopoly can be summarised as follows:

- a part of the consumer surplus is redistributed to the monopolist as producer surplus or monopoly rent. This is the so-called price effect of monopoly: consumers pay too much. This price effect in itself is not a loss in welfare, but it may be considered as a situation with a less preferable income distribution. In a political judgment this transfer of income may be considered as socially unacceptable;

- there is a deadweight loss which lowers the welfare of the concerned economy. This is the so-called allocation effect of monopoly: consumers purchase less of the product in question.

2.2.3 Competition law as an instrument to correct the undesirable effects of monopoly

The preceding analysis provides a strong theoretical basis for the design and implementation of a welfare-improving competition law. A great deal of the specialist literature on the economic effects of market power is dedicated to the magnitude of the deadweight loss triangle of an individual monopolist and the total deadweight loss caused by monopoly in the economy. The first attempt to measure the welfare costs of market power was made by Harberger. He estimated the deadweight loss due to market power for 73 US manufacturing industries. Harberger's empirical results for the period 1924–1928 showed that the welfare loss due to monopoly was a negligible part (0.1 per cent) of US national income.[16] Later studies investigated the losses for the American economy in the "golden sixties" and estimated the deadweight loss at between 0.2 and 0.7 per cent of national income.[17] These low estimates can best be seen as a lower limit. In his study Harberger assumed a price elasticity of demand equal to one; he estimated the normal rate of return on capital by the average rate of return on capital and used industry rather than firm data. By assuming higher price elasticities of demand and using a stock market measure of the normal rate of return and firm data, much higher estimates of welfare losses may be reached.[18] Cowling and Mueller estimated the welfare losses due to market power for 734 US firms for the period 1963–1966 and suggested that monopoly power costs the US economy no less than 13 per cent of national income per year. For the United Kingdom in the period 1968–1969,

---

[16] A.C. Harberger, "Monopoly and Resource Allocation" (1954) 44 Amer. Econ. Rev. 77.

[17] D.A. Worcester, "New Estimates of the Welfare Loss to Monopoly in the United States 1956–1969" (1973) 40 Southern Econ. J. 234.

[18] See for an overview of the literature: S. Martin, *Industrial Economics: Economic Analysis and Public Policy* (1994), pp.31–36.

Cowling and Mueller calculated losses between 4 and 7 per cent of national income.[19] For France in the period 1967–1970 Jenny and Weber estimated losses amounting to no less than 9 per cent of national income in the worst scenario.[20] In a classic survey written in 1990, after having corrected for a variety of errors and inconsistencies in Harberger's original methodology, Scherer and Ross suggested that "the deadweight welfare loss attributable to monopolistic resource misallocation in the United States lies somewhere between 0.5 and 2 percent of gross national product".[21]

It must be added that the high estimates of monopoly losses, which can best be seen as an upper limit, not only include profits earned by firms enjoying market power but also the costs of monopolisation ("rent seeking"). Economists believed for a long time that the deadweight loss depicted by the triangle CDE was the only social cost of a monopoly. However, when one measures the effects of market power, the costs incurred in acquiring and preserving a monopoly must also be included. Tullock has argued convincingly that all the resources which are applied to achieving monopoly profits (ABCD) should likewise be included in the social costs.[22] Tullock's argument is obviously relevant: the analysis of the welfare losses caused by a monopoly cannot be complete if the sums expended on achieving the transfer from consumers to the monopolist are excluded. Firms may compete for market power not only by incurring expenditure to influence regulatory agencies, but also by building excess capacity, excessive advertising or sales efforts coaxed from dealers through vertical restraints. To the extent that these practices contribute to the creation and/or preservation of monopoly power, they should be added to the social costs of monopoly. Moreover, it should not be forgotten that one of the major benefits of a monopoly is a "quiet life". Once the competitive pressures have disappeared, a firm may become slower to reorganise production when that needs to be done because there are no competitors nipping at its heels. Earlier technical efficiencies will then be replaced by waste in the form of X-inefficiencies. With a lazy monopolist, innovative activity may also slow down. Finally, market power may also have harmful effects on factors other than price that are valued by consumers, such as product quality and variety. When these additional costs of monopoly are taken into account the welfare losses may be quite substantial. The magnitude of these losses seems to justify the costs of enforcing competition law prohibitions.

By combating monopolies (and cartels that achieve monopoly power) competition authorities reduce the negative consequences of monopolies and improve upon allocative efficiency. An intervention by the competition authority will bring an end to the allocation effect of monopoly, which causes a reduction in the production factors that are deployed. The increase in

---

[19] K. Cowling and D. Mueller, "The Social Costs of Monopoly" (1978) 88 Econ. J. 724. The higher figure was obtained when the cost of rent seeking was also included.

[20] F. Jenny and A. Weber, "Aggregate Welfare Losses due to Monopoly Power in the French Economy: Some Tentative Estimates" (1983) 32 J. Ind. Econ. 113.

[21] F.M. Scherer and D. Ross, *Industrial Market Structure and Economic Performance* (3rd ed., 1990), p.667.

[22] G. Tullock, "The Welfare Costs of Tariffs, Monopolies and Theft" (1967) 5 Western Econ. J. 224.

activities results in additional demand and the extra sales serve partially as an input into business processes throughout the economy. As explained earlier, monopoly not only causes negative allocation effects but also price effects that may be regarded as undesirable. The price effect is determined by multiplying the price increase as a result of monopoly power by the quantity of products sold. The estimated effects of antitrust supervision, measured by the dead-weight loss (allocation effect) and the redistribution damage to consumers (price effect) can amount to several hundred million euro.[23]

2.3 Conflicting concepts of efficiency and consumer welfare

2.3.1 Allocative versus productive and dynamic efficiency

In the second section of this chapter, the economic models of perfect compe-tition and monopoly were contrasted with each other and it was made clear that the model of perfect competition provides a strong theoretical basis for the desirability of competition law. The central insight from welfare economics is that perfectly competitive markets are Pareto efficient, since it is no longer possible to enhance the welfare of a single individual without diminishing the welfare of another. When products are sold at prices covering the marginal costs of production, no consumer (producer) can be made better off without making a producer (consumer) worse off. Put differently, Pareto improve-ments are no longer possible in a market which is allocatively efficient. Allo-cative efficiency implies that firms produce what buyers want and are willing to pay for. Whereas allocative efficiency is reached in a perfectly competitive market, monopoly causes welfare losses: prices are persistently held above marginal costs and output is reduced. In sum, allocative efficiency can be convincingly presented as a major policy goal for competition law.

This section introduces a number of complications that may limit the attractiveness of allocative efficiency as the universal yardstick for competition policy and law. In some cases, allocative efficiency may conflict with other efficiency goals: productive efficiency and dynamic efficiency.[24] Productive or technical efficiency implies that output is maximised by using the most effective combination of inputs; hence internal slack (also called X-inefficiency) is absent. The goal of productive efficiency implies that more efficient firms, which produce at lower costs, should not be prevented from taking business away from less efficient ones. Obviously, the achievement of productive

---

[23] The Dutch competition authority estimates the effects of enforcement of the Dutch competition law as high as €900 million for the period 2002 to 2004. See: "Measuring the harm caused by cartels and assessing the benefits of competition enforcement—Analysing economic damage at the Netherlands Competition Authority" (NMa)-OECD Document DAF/COMP/WP3/RD(2005), 5.
[24] W. Nicholson, *Microeconomic Theory: Basic Principles and Extensions* (7th ed., 1998), pp.611–620; European Commission, *The Single Market Review: Impact on Competition and Scale Effects: Competition Issues* (1997), p.33; J.F. Brodley, "The Economic Goals of Antitrust: Efficiency, Consumer Welfare, and Technological Progress" (1987) 62 N.Y.U.L. Rev. 1020 at p.1025.

efficiency is not a Pareto improvement since the less efficient firms are made worse off. Dynamic efficiency is achieved through the invention, development and diffusion of new products and production processes that increase social welfare. Whereas productive efficiency and allocative efficiency are static notions, progressiveness or dynamic efficiency refers to the rate of techno-logical progress. Again, there will be losers in the dynamic competitive struggle, so that Pareto improvements cannot be reached. To enable policy decisions when the different efficiency goals are not consistent with each other, welfare economics offers the alternative criterion of Kaldor–Hicks efficiency.

A Kaldor–Hicks improvement allows changes in which there are both winners and losers, but requires that the gainers gain more than the losers lose. This condition being satisfied, the winners could compensate the losers[25] and still have a surplus left for themselves.[26] A Kaldor–Hicks improvement is also referred to as a potential Pareto improvement, since actual compensation would again satisfy the Pareto criterion. The central value judgment under-lying Kaldor–Hicks efficiency is that an exchange of money has a neutral impact on aggregate well-being, which may not be the case when the incomes of gainers and losers differ. By using the Kaldor–Hicks criterion total welfare is maximised. This welfare notion may allow clearing mergers that enable the merging firms to achieve important scale economies and thus improve pro-ductive efficiency, but at the same time enable previously independent firms to collude and raise prices above competitive levels. In terms of total welfare, it is irrelevant that producers rather than consumers capture the surplus pro-duced by achieving efficiencies, as the monopoly overcharge paid by pur-chasers to stockholders is treated as a transfer from one member of society to another and so is ignored in the balance.

There is also a possible trade-off between market power and technological progress. So far the analysis was limited to issues of allocative efficiency and possible trade-offs with productive efficiency. In a static analysis, Pareto improvements occur when firms realise costs efficiencies and pass on (a part of) these benefits to consumers. Aside from costs efficiencies, there are effi-ciencies in the form of new or improved products. Dynamic efficiency (in a broad sense: including both productivity increases and product innovation) raises additional issues. The relationship between market power and inno-vation is highly debated. The dispute initiated with the seminal contribution of Schumpeter, who argued that monopolists and large firms are better equipped to generate innovation since they can more easily finance costly research and, thanks to their size, can fully exploit the innovation achieved.[27] This idea was contested by Arrow, who showed that, theoretically, a monopolist has less incentive to innovate than a new entrant or a firm in a competitive industry.[28]

---

[25] The relevant criterion is potential compensation, since actual compensation would again satisfy the Pareto criterion.

[26] Compare N. Kaldor, "Welfare Propositions in Economics" (1939) 49 Econ. J. 549; and J.R. Hicks, "The Rehabilitation of Consumer's Surplus" (1941) 9 Rev. Econ. Studies 108.

[27] J. Schumpeter, *Capitalism, socialism and democracy* (1943).

[28] K.J. Arrow, "Economic Welfare and the Allocation of Resources for Invention", in *The Rate and Direction of Inventive Activity* (R. Nelson ed., 1962), p.609.

In the absence of unambiguous theoretical conclusions, the relationship between market power and innovation is ultimately an empirical matter. Empirical evidence, however, still fails to demonstrate any definitive relationship between firm size, market concentration and the pace of innovation. The individual circumstances of the industry under scrutiny weigh heavily on the final outcome.[29]

As was the case with productive efficiency, an improvement in terms of dynamic efficiency does not satisfy the Pareto criterion, since this will harm less innovative firms which will lose customers to their technically superior competitors. However, such improvements may satisfy the Kaldor–Hicks criterion since benefits both to pioneering firms and consumers may outweigh losses to non-innovative firms.

With respect to consumers' interests, it can be added that there are differences in applying the efficiency criteria of welfare economics in real-life cases. When the improvements concern allocative efficiency, it must be shown that there are costs efficiencies and that these efficiencies are sufficiently large to be passed on to consumers. In the case of dynamic efficiency, it must be shown that new and improved products create sufficient value for consumers. Whereas in the former case, it could still be possible to measure the amount of the efficiencies, it seems very difficult to assign values to dynamic efficiencies. The next section of this chapter will show how antitrust authorities cope with these differences.

2.3.2 An example of conflicting efficiency goals: the welfare trade-off in merger control

The tensions between the different efficiency goals are illustrated by using the example of merger control. Mergers may enable the merging firms to achieve important scale economies and thus improve productive efficiency, but at the same time enable previously independent firms to collude and raise prices above competitive levels,[30] thus causing allocative inefficiency. There is also a debate among economists concerning the possible trade-off between market power and technological progress. Costs may fall as a result of competition in technological innovation but, at the same time, market concentration may increase. On the one hand, this may lead to supra-competitive prices but, on the other hand, prices above marginal costs may be necessary to allow firms a suitable reward for their research investments.[31]

[29] For a survey of numerous studies, see F.M. Scherer, "Schumpeter and Plausible Capitalism" (1992) 30 J. Econ. Lit. 1416. Recent empirical work arguing a positive correlation between competition and innovation includes P. Geroski, *Innovation, Technical Opportunity and Market Structure*, Oxford Economic Papers 586 (1990), p.42. Other authors found that large firms tend to innovate more, but industry concentration has a counteracting effect (R. Blundell, R. Griffith and J. Van Reenen, "Dynamic Count Data Models of Technological Innovation" (1995) 105 Econ. J. 333).
[30] Prices may also increase without collusion if the merger eliminates competitive restraints from substitute rival products. For a discussion of these "unilateral effects", see Ch.9, s.9.2.2.
[31] See C.C. von Weizsäcker, "A Welfare Analysis of Barriers to Entry" (1980) 11 Bell J. Econ. 399.

It is well known that competition authorities are reluctant to accept an efficiency defence in merger control cases. This reluctance can be better understood by making the objections against a total welfare approach explicit. An efficiency defence (based on productive or dynamic efficiencies) fits a total welfare approach nicely, but it is at odds with the goal to avoid allocative inefficiencies and price increases for consumers. To put it in the terms of welfare economics: whereas an efficiency defence may fulfil the requirements of a Kaldor–Hicks improvement, it will not satisfy the Pareto criterion.

A useful starting point for an efficiency analysis of the effects of a horizontal merger is what has become known as the Williamsonian trade-off. In 1968 Oliver Williamson published a seminal article, in which he contrasted the anti-competitive and beneficial effects of a merger.[32] This trade-off may be best illustrated by Graph 2.4.

Graph 2.4: The Williamsonian welfare trade-off

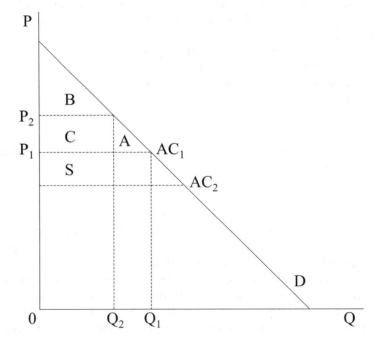

This Graph depicts a common merger scenario, namely of an amalgamation that yields economies of scale but, at the same time, increases market power. AC_1 represents the level of average costs of the two or more firms before combination, while AC_2 shows the level of average costs after the merger. The price before the merger is given by P_1 and is equal to AC_1 as an index of pre-merger market power. The price after the merger is given by P_2 and is assumed to exceed P_1. If this was not the case, the merger would be strictly

[32] O.E. Williamson, "Economies as an Antitrust Defense: The Welfare Trade-offs" (1968) 58 Amer. Econ. Rev. 18, 1372; (1969) 59 Amer. Econ. Rev. 954.

positive. The welfare effects of the merger are given by the different areas in the figure. The area designated A is the deadweight loss that results if price is increased from P_1 to P_2, assuming that costs remain constant. But, since average costs are actually reduced by the merger, the area designated S, which represents costs savings, must also be taken into account. In the Graph, area S is larger than area A, so that the effect of the merger on total welfare is positive. Williamson concluded that, for the net allocative effects to be negative, a merger which yields non-trivial economies must produce substantial market power and result in relatively large price increases.

Apart from well known theoretical and practical dilemmas in the application of this approach to merger policy (see Box 2.1), a major problem arises from the neglect of income distribution consequences. As a consequence of the merger, consumer surplus given by area ABC is reduced to area B. Area C indicates a wealth transfer from consumers to producers. From a competition policy perspective, it may be unacceptable to clear a merger that benefits shareholders but harms consumers. If consumers must also gain, a Kaldor–Hicks improvement as contained in the Williamsonian trade-off will be insufficient to give a green light to the merger.

Box 2.1: Practical value of the Williamsonian welfare trade-off

There are a number of well known theoretical and practical dilemmas in the application of this approach to merger policy.[33] In short, these include: (a) issues of second best, (b) the complications of appraising alternative methods of obtaining the scale gains associated with mergers, (c) the problems of external economies and diseconomies, and (d) the problems that arise from the neglect of income distribution consequences and the political considerations surrounding competition law enforcement. In addition, this model contains some more fundamental difficulties of which the main points can be summarised as follows.

The ability to conduct the Williamsonian welfare trade-off depends largely on knowledge of the elasticity of demand. This should be difficult enough to determine in its own right, but the model presupposes a lot more information as known which is internal to the merging firms, making it a cumbersome tool under real-life antitrust constraints. Indeed, assessing the external effects on consumers and rival firms requires much less information than assessing the overall welfare effect.[34] On the contrary, the determination of the insiders' profits depends on knowing the internal costs savings which are "easy to promise, yet may be difficult to deliver".[35] The

---

[33] Most of these were already recognised by Williamson; they are further developed in a number of other contributions: P. Ross, "Economies as An Antitrust Defense: Comment" (1968) 58 Amer. Econ. Rev. 1371; M.E. DePrano and J.B. Nugent, "Economies as An Antitrust Defense: Comment" (1969) 59 Amer. Econ. Rev. 947.

[34] J. Farrell and C. Shapiro, "Horizontal Mergers: An Equilibrium Analysis" (1990) 80 Amer. Econ. Rev. 107 at p.109.

[35] *ibid.*

exact location of any of the triangles and rectangles used in the original Williamsonian diagram remains vague, making it impossible to calculate their areas mathematically. Under antitrust constraints, we can rarely determine either the actual demand curve or the location of the initial cost curve, the distance this cost curve will shift, or the amount the output will change.

Because competition is a dynamic process, the concern in practice lies with the future development of the market and market power enduring over a period of time. The Williamsonian analysis depicts the effect of market power only as a static "snapshot" of the market in equilibrium[36] without taking into account the temporal effects of an increase in market power which may be more negative than positive.[37] The applicability of the model and its results therefore becomes questionable in real-world situations characterised by disequilibria.

Finally, the Williamsonian welfare trade-off assumes an increase in prices as a prerequisite for opposing a concentration as part of its basic framework. This, however, is not entirely consistent with the standard economic concern interpreting an increase in monopoly power as an increase in the Lerner index.[38] Although it is possible to establish a link between concentration ratios and methods of market power measurement such as the Lerner index, the concentration indices do not tell the whole story.

Despite these apparent weaknesses, this model still represents a useful tool in understanding the attitude of merger control systems towards potential trade-offs developed in the economic analysis of concentrations, as illustrated in the following Box 2.2. The biggest legal appeal of the Williamsonian welfare trade-off probably lies in its compelling terminology, which seemingly offers an additional line of defence in an otherwise lost case.

In recent economic literature authors have investigated how large cost savings of mergers would need to be in order to prevent price increases for consumers, so that the Pareto criterion would be satisfied. Froeb and Werden developed a test for welfare enhancing mergers among sellers of homogeneous products under Cournot competition.[39] The starting point of their analysis is that the reduction of marginal costs may offset the anti-competitive effects of the merger on prices. The size of the compensating marginal cost reduction for a Cournot model will depend on the firms' market share and the price elasticity of market demand. Modest marginal cost reductions may prevent price

---

[36] Quoting R.A. Kassamali, "Competition Law Survey: From Fiction to Fallacy: Reviewing the E.C. Merger Regulation's Community Dimension Thresholds in the Light of Economics and Experience in Merger Control" (1996) 21 E.L. Rev. 89 at p.93. See, for an overview of the discussion, Secretary of State for Prices and Consumer Protection, *A Review of Monopolies and Mergers Policy* (1978), paras 3.35 *et seq.*

[37] A.A. Fisher and R.H. Lande, "Efficiency Considerations in Merger Enforcement" (1983) 71 Calif. L. Rev. 1580 at pp.1634–1638.

[38] See later at Ch.4, s.4.2.1.1.

[39] The Cournot model assumes that firms produce a homogeneous product and that each firm chooses the quantity of output that maximises its profits, taking competitors' output as given.

increases following mergers of modest size. However, the cost reductions will need to be large to prevent large mergers from raising price. By way of example, if the merging firms' market shares are 20 per cent each, a 0.5 elasticity of demand would require a 66.67 per cent compensating marginal cost reduction, while a higher elasticity, say 1, would require a 25 per cent reduction in marginal costs.[40] In another paper, Werden investigated the case of differentiated good markets under Bertrand price competition.[41] The compensating marginal cost reduction required to offset the anti-competitive effects induced by mergers will depend on pre-merger product prices, diversion ratios[42] among products, and profit margins. By estimating the compensating marginal cost reduction for different levels of pre-merger profit margins and diversion ratios, Werden reached the conclusion that "if the products are highly differentiated and the merging firms compete intensively, large typically implausible cost reductions are necessary to restore pre-merger prices". For example, for a 25 per cent diversion ratio and 0.7 per cent profit margin, the compensating marginal cost reduction is 77.78 per cent.[43] In sum, the conclusion from these papers seems to be that, under a Pareto efficiency standard, the scope for an efficiency defence is negligible. Chapter 9, which deals with mergers, will come back to these insights and apply them to the practice of merger control.

It is immediately clear from these theoretical contributions that, in practice, an efficiency defence makes sense only if merger control would be based on the normative criterion of Kaldor–Hicks efficiency (total welfare). However, policy makers may object to this criterion because of the undesirable effects on the distribution of income. However, if an actual Pareto improvement is required (benefits to firms without any harm to consumers) the efficiency defence will fail in the vast majority of cases.

2.3.3 Efficiency and consumer welfare

In policy statements of competition authorities, the goal to improve allocative efficiency is quoted alongside the objective of furthering consumer welfare. For example, in the Guidelines on the application of Article 81(3) EC, the European Commission states that "the objective of Article 81 EC is to protect . competition on the market as a means of enhancing consumer welfare and of

---

[40] L.M. Froeb and G.J. Werden, "A Robust Test for Consumer Welfare Enhancing Mergers among Sellers of a Homogeneous Product" (1998) 58 Economics Letters 367.

[41] The Bertrand model describes the competitive scenario in markets where firms produce non-homogeneous (differentiated) products and, therefore, compete in prices rather than quantities. In this model, firms fix the price for their products in order to maximise profits. In equilibrium, each firm cannot, by changing its price, increase its profits, given the prices of competitors.

[42] The higher the demand substitutability among products, the smaller will be the anti-competitive effect.

[43] G.J. Werden, "A Robust Test for Consumer Welfare Enhancing Mergers among Sellers of Differentiated Products" (1996) 44 J. Ind. Econ. 409.

ensuring an efficient allocation of resources".[44] In the context of European competition policy, the question thus arises as to how consumer welfare relates to the concepts of efficiency explained in the previous paragraphs of this chapter. Since the notion of consumer welfare is vague, it needs to be defined explicitly before this question can be answered. Consumer welfare may be understood in different ways. Hereafter, two possible interpretations are presented.

The first interpretation requires that changes improving the individual welfare of producers also improve the welfare of individual consumers or at least do not make any individual consumer worse off. This is nothing else but an alternative formulation of the Pareto criterion. In this interpretation, there will be no conflict between allocative efficiency and consumer welfare. Under the conditions of perfect competition, both allocative efficiency and consumer welfare are optimally served. Producer surplus and consumer surplus are simultaneously maximised. The Pareto criterion is the basis for the assessment of perfectly competitive markets as allocatively efficient. Also, evaluations of why monopoly is bad rest upon the application of the Pareto criterion. The deadweight loss caused by monopoly precisely indicates the remaining scope for Pareto improvements.

Since it is not possible to achieve perfect competition in all sectors of the economy, the Pareto criterion puts heavy limitations on the desirability of policy changes. Policy decisions that make producers better off without making any consumer worse off may be rare. Examples include mergers increasing the profits of the merging firms and at the same time leading to lower prices for consumers[45] or mergers allowing cost savings without any negative impact on consumer prices.

The second interpretation defines consumer welfare as the maximisation of consumer surplus. This definition implies that a pre-eminent objective of competition law should be to prevent increases in consumer prices due to the exercise of market power by dominant firms.[46] The change in consumer surplus measures the consumer savings of antitrust intervention in markets that are not perfectly competitive. In Graph 2.3, this will be the trapezium ACEB. This second interpretation satisfies neither the Pareto criterion nor the Kaldor–Hicks criterion. Pareto improvements are excluded since interventions leading to reduced prices (or preventing price increases) will be invariably at the expense of the profits of the firms concerned. Kaldor–Hicks improvements are also excluded. The goal to maximise consumer surplus requires that consumers are made better off without accepting gains that accrue to producers only, even if these gains are sufficiently large to potentially compensate the losses to consumers.

---

[44] Guidelines on the application of Art. 81(3) EC, para.13.
[45] A.A. Fisher, R.H. Lande and W. Vandaele, "Could a Merger Lead to both Monopoly and Lower Price?" (1983) 71 Calif. L. Rev. 1697.
[46] See on the background, A.A. Fisher, F.I. Johnson and R.H. Lande, "Price Effects of Horizontal Mergers" (1989) 77 Calif. L. Rev. 777; A.A. Fisher, R.H. Lande and W. Vandaele, *ibid.*; and A.A. Fisher and R.H. Lande, "Efficiency Considerations in Merger Enforcement" (1983) 71 Calif. L. Rev. 1580 at p.1592.

The second definition has no basis in welfare economics and can be justified on equity grounds only. First, improvements in terms of allocation may be opposed if they increase producer surplus only. An example is price discrimination which increases output but enables the dominant firm to capture a larger part of the consumer surplus.[47] Second, efficiency savings may be regarded unfavourably if they do not lead to price decreases benefiting consumers. These negative policy judgments will be overcome if the size of the total surplus (Kaldor–Hicks efficiency) rather than consumer surplus is used as a benchmark for policy decisions. The important insight is that allocative efficiency (assessed in terms of total welfare, that is total surplus in the entire economy) and consumer welfare (defined as maximisation of consumer surplus) are conflicting concepts and that policy makers cannot escape from trade-offs if these goals are to be pursued simultaneously.

The main argument against a consumer welfare standard is that it discriminates between individuals in different interest groups (shareholders and consumers). The Kaldor–Hicks criterion precisely avoids this type of discrimination. The promotion of aggregate economic welfare has most clearly been voiced by the Chicago School.[48] The consequences of this view for competition law are far-reaching. The Kaldor–Hicks criterion accepts restraints of competition if they lead to an increase in the welfare of producers that is greater than the ensuing loss suffered by consumers. Hence, the total welfare model of antitrust rejects the view that enforcement agencies should require firms to pass on efficiency benefits to consumers, as this is unnecessary because total welfare is already increased by the very act of achieving efficiencies within the firm.[49] Unlike the total welfare approach, the consumer-welfare model views redistribution in the form of wealth transfers from consumers to producers as harmful rather than neutral.[50] A requirement that the achieved savings are passed on to consumers—partly or entirely, immediately or within a set time frame—does not flow from the efficiency analysis but is a value judgment based on equity.

The above analysis is subject to an important caveat, however. There may be circumstances when increasing producer surplus may also be in the interest of consumers. This will become clear when the static Chicago analysis is complemented by a dynamic approach. If profits are the necessary return on previous innovation or provide the funding for future innovation, consumers will be harmed if antitrust intervention focuses on low consumer prices only. To guarantee innovation (dynamic efficiency), the size of producer surplus should matter inasmuch as it generates future increases of consumer surplus.

---

[47] See Ch.7, s.7.2.
[48] R.H. Bork, *The Antitrust Paradox* (2nd ed., 1993), pp.90–91.
[49] H. Hovenkamp, *Federal Antitrust Policy: The Law of Competition and its Practice* (1994), para.2.3.c. For a summary of the critique, see R.H. Lande, "Chicago's False Foundation: Wealth Transfers (not just Efficiency) Should Guide Antitrust" (1989) 58 Antitrust L.J. 631 at pp.638–639; E.M. Fox, "The Battle for the Soul of Antitrust" (1987) 75 Calif. L. Rev. 917 at pp.918 *et seq*.
[50] R.H. Lande, "Wealth Transfers as the Original and Primary Concern of Antitrust: The Efficiency Interpretation Challenged" (1982) 34 Hastings L. J. 65; G.L. Roberts and S.C. Salop, "Dynamic Analysis of Efficiency Benefits" (1995/1996) 19. W.Comp.5.

In sum, conflicts between efficiency (total welfare) and consumer welfare (defined in terms of consumer surplus) cannot be excluded. This will be the case when distributional considerations prevail, so that improvements in terms of total welfare will be opposed because consumers are not made better off. The origins of producer surplus are inevitably mixed: sometimes market power, sometimes reward for efficiency or innovation. Distributional considerations prevent consumer losses (increased prices) being accepted since they lead to higher gains for producers (increased profits), even though consumers may also profit in their capacity as shareholders. Costs efficiencies, which are welfare enhancing for firms, may be opposed because they are achieved by a merger causing price increases to consumers (rejection of a Williamsonian welfare trade-off). The scope for conflicts between efficiency goals and consumer welfare seem to be smaller if dynamic efficiencies are realised, since consumers will also benefit from product innovation.

Box 2.2: The goals of European competition law

"[Competition policy's] aim is to ensure that business operates along competitive lines, while protecting the consumer by making goods and services available on the most favourable terms possible. It therefore endeavours to cut monopoly profits", quoted from: European Commission, *Sixth Report on Competition Policy* (1977), p.9.

"Effective competition preserves the freedom and right of initiative of the individual economic operators and it fosters the spirit of enterprise", quoted from European Commission, *Fifteenth Annual Report on Competition Policy* (1986).

"[Competition policy] is not an end in itself to be pursued dogmatically; it is an instrument, albeit an important one, for achieving agreed Community objectives", statement by Karel van Miert, Commissioner in charge of EC competition policy until 1999, quoted by A. Haid, "European Merger Control, Political Discretion, and Efficient Market Structures" in *Competition, Efficiency, and Welfare: Essays in Honor of Manfred Neumann* (D.C. Mueller, A. Haid and J. Weigand ed., 1999), p.167.

"The objective of Article 81 is to protect competition on the market as a means of enhancing consumer welfare and of ensuring an efficient allocation of resources. Competition and market integration serve these ends since the creation and preservation of an open single market promotes an efficient allocation of resources throughout the Community for the benefit of the consumer", quoted from Guidelines on the application of Article 81(3) of the Treaty [2004] O.J. C 101/98, para.13.

"Our aim is simple: to protect competition in the market as a means of enhancing consumer welfare and ensuring an efficient allocation of resources. An effects-based approach, grounded in solid economics, ensures that citizens enjoy the benefits of a competitive, dynamic market economy", Neelie Kroes, "European Competition Policy—Delivering Better Markets and Better Choices", Speech, London, September 15, 2005.

2.4 Goals of welfare economics and the policy objectives of European competition law

Clearly, textbook criteria of welfare economics have not been the driving force of European competition policy and law. The rules of European competition law reflect the concerns of European societies in the 20th century for freedom of business decisions, in particular for consumer welfare and social equity and freedom from exploitation. Moreover, competition law has been instrumental as a motor of European integration.[51] Hence, the European approach is different from US antitrust law and is set in a divergent economic culture, characterised by "dirigiste" instead of Anglo-Saxon progressive liberalisation of markets brought about by capitalist development.[52] In comparative analyses, there is not always sufficient awareness of the specificity of the European dimension, and this obscures the role competition law has played in the creation of contemporary Europe.

The policy consequences of the multivalued tradition of European competition law are highlighted below. It will be shown that rules of European competition law cannot be easily economically "rationalised" by referring to the notions of Pareto efficiency and Kaldor–Hicks efficiency (total welfare). Instead, a pragmatic concern for consumer welfare dominates current European competition policy and law. Aside from protecting the interests of consumers, the market integration goal, the wish to safeguard freedom of business decisions and concerns of social equity continue to exert an influence on the formulation of the substantive rules and the decisions of real-world cases. The multivalued tradition of European competition law, in particular the shifts in emphasis on different goals of competition law over time, is nicely illustrated by the statements in Box 2.2. The emphasis on market integration and individual economic freedom has gradually been replaced by focusing on misallocation of resources and consumer welfare. The history of American antitrust law equally witnesses changes in policy making. In the United States, the objective to protect small businesses has been discredited and replaced by concerns of efficiency and consumer welfare. Box 2.3 illustrates these changes. Looking at the statements over time on both sides of the Atlantic, there now seems to be convergence with respect to the consumer welfare goal.[53] In the remainder of this chapter, the policy goals of European competition law will be identified and contrasted with the notions of welfare economics that were developed in the third section.

---

[51] D.J. Gerber, *Law and Competition in Twentieth Century Europe* (1998).

[52] D.S. Landes, *The Unbound Prometheus: Technological Change and Industrial Development in Western Europe from 1750 to the Present* (1969), p.164.

[53] Whereas the consumer welfare standard seems to be the benchmark in US antitrust law and EC competition law, others countries (such as Canada, Australia and New Zealand) also take producer surplus into account (W. Kerber and U. Schwalbe, "Ökonomische Grundlagen des Wettbewerbsrechts" in *Münchener Kommentar zum Europäischen und Deutschen Wettbewerbsrecht*, Vol. I, nr. 101 (2006, forthcoming).

Box 2.3: The goals of US antitrust law
Senator Sherman defended his bill partly on the following ground: "If we will not endure a king as a political power we should not endure a king over the production, transportation, and sale of any of the necessities of life. If we would not submit to an emperor we should not submit to an autocrat of trade, with power to prevent competition and fix the price of any commodity", quoted by S. Martin, *Industrial Economics: Economic Analysis and Public Policy* (2nd ed., 1994), p.49.

"Of course, some of the results of large integrated or chain operations are beneficial to consumers. . . . But we cannot fail to recognize Congress' desire to promote competition through the protection of viable, small, locally owned business. Congress appreciated that occasional higher costs and prices might result from the maintenance of fragmented industries and markets. It resolved these competing considerations in favour of decentralization", quoted from *Brown Shoe Co v United States*, 370 US 294 (1962).

The Department of Justice states that the antitrust laws "prohibit business practices that unreasonably deprive consumers of the benefits of competition, resulting in higher prices for inferior products and services". As such, the government will "act promptly" to protect the "interest of American consumers" when competing firms engage in "anti-competitive arrangements that provide no benefits to consumers", see US Department of Justice, "Antitrust enforcement and the consumer", at *www.usdoj.gov/atr/public/div_stats/1638.htm*.

The revised American Merger Guidelines require that efficiencies are of a character and magnitude sufficient to reverse the merger's potential to harm consumers, see Section 4 of the 1997 Merger Guidelines. The Merger Guidelines will be discussed in more detail in Chapter 10.

"United States' primary commitment in enforcement of its antitrust laws is to serve the goal of the welfare of consumers", former FTC chairman Robert Pitofsky, "The Effect of Global Trade on United States Competition Law and Enforcement Policies", Speech, New York, October 15, 1999.

"Sound antitrust policy does not believe that big is bad or that success must be punished. Quite the contrary—where success is the result of skill, foresight and industry, consumer welfare is enhanced", former Assistant Attorney General, Antitrust Division, DOJ, Joel I. Klein, "Rethinking Antitrust Policies for the New Economy", Speech, Berkeley, May 9, 2000.

2.4.1 European competition law and the criterion of Pareto efficiency

The concept of Pareto efficiency puts a heavy burden on policy makers. In the field of competition law, interventions in markets should not be considered if at least one individual (producer or consumer) will be made worse off. In practice, the implementation of such a strict requirement would leave almost no scope for prohibiting anti-competitive practices and mergers (since producers would be made worse off) or granting exemptions and clearing mergers (since individual consumers may be harmed by such decisions). Consequently, it is not surprising that policy statements by competition authorities do not endorse the Pareto criterion. The view of the European Commission that Pareto efficiency is not the normative criterion for making policy decisions has always got the support from the European Court of Justice. In the landmark *Metro/Saba* judgment, the Court has stated that perfect competition (where Pareto efficiency is realised) is not the goal of European competition law. Instead, the Court advanced the criterion of "workable competition",[54] which allows that some market imperfections are kept in place. In the Guidelines on Article 81(3) EC the Commission states, in accordance with Community case law, that the decisive factor is the overall impact on consumers of the products within the relevant market and not the impact on individual members of this group of consumers.[55] This leaves the option open to clear anti-competitive agreements if not all consumers benefit or if some consumers are harmed by the restrictions of competition.

2.4.2 European competition law and the criterion of Kaldor–Hicks efficiency (total welfare)

Careful reading of the EC Treaty's formulations casts serious doubts as to whether total welfare can be the benchmarking standard for the purpose of European competition law. Article 81(3) EC provides for agreements being exempt from the ban on cartels, if they contribute:

> "… to improving the production or distribution of goods or to promoting technical or economic progress, while allowing consumers a fair share of the resulting benefit, and which does not: (a) impose on the undertakings concerned restrictions which are not indispensable to the attainment of these objectives; (b) afford such undertakings the possibility of eliminating competition in respect of a substantial part of the products in question".[56]

The explicit requirement that consumers must receive a fair share of the resulting benefits seems to exclude gains incurred by producers offering an alternative profit justifying consumer losses.

The formulation of Article 81(3) EC thus suggests that European competition law does not serve the goal of maximising the sum of consumer and producer surplus.[57] In this interpretation, even if total welfare increases, there may still be an unlawful restriction of competition if the agreement reduces consumer surplus. European competition law does not allow balancing efficiency savings and negative distributional effects on consumers. To the European legislator one euro of consumer surplus is not equivalent to one euro of

---

[54] Compare the discussion in Ch.3, s.3.5.1.2.
[55] Guidelines on the application of Art. 81(3) EC, para.87.
[56] Compare also the Merger Regulation's similar wording in Art. 2(1)(b) Merger Regulation.
[57] See also Art. 2(1)(b) Merger Regulation which contains a similar wording and does not, therefore, allow a trade-off between productive efficiency and allocative efficiency.

producer surplus (rejection of the constant euro assumption). This view does not match with the economist's definition of Kaldor–Hicks efficiency. Nevertheless, an economic interpretation of the European competition rules remains possible; it is only necessary to broaden the traditional theorems of welfare economics with a full consideration of the consequences of efficiency savings for consumers. This obviously adds an additional layer of complexity to the analysis.

Also, the formulation of the Merger Regulation, which mentions the development of technical and economic progress among the criteria to assess mergers, does not seem to allow clearing mergers as Kaldor–Hicks improvements. Under a total welfare approach, cost savings could offset price increases, but such an approach is at odds with the requirement that efficiencies should be taken into account only if they are "to consumers' advantage and [do] not form an obstacle to competition".[58]

Recent policy documents of the European Commission confirm that Kaldor–Hicks efficiency is not the benchmarking yardstick for European competition policy and law. As far as the formulations of the EC Treaty and the Merger Regulation left any scope for a total welfare approach, the Commission's documents have certainly excluded such an interpretation. Several statements in the Article 81(3) EC Notice make it clear that European competition law does not aim at maximising total welfare. Three passages of this policy document are highly illustrative for the rejection of the total welfare approach: the Commission's unwillingness to take account of costs savings that arise from the mere exercise of market power, the requirement of a direct link between restrictive agreements and efficiencies and the focus on the relevant market under investigation bypassing the effects of the agreements in the entire economy. First, according to the European Commission, cost reductions that are the consequence of a reduction in output and value do not produce any pro-competitive effects on the market and are therefore irrelevant for the granting of an exemption.[59] Consequently, high profits cannot compensate consumer losses (rejection of the constant euro assumption). Second, the requirement that the causal link between the agreement and the claimed efficiencies must be direct excludes from the scope of Article 81(3) EC a restrictive agreement that allows the undertakings concerned to increase their profits, enabling them to invest more in research and development to the ultimate benefit of the consumer.[60] This requirement may exclude reasonably close effects in the form of efficiencies that are considerable. Finally, the Commission states that: "Negative effects on consumers in one geographic market or product market cannot normally be balanced against and compensated by positive effects for consumers in another unrelated geographic market or product market".[61] From a welfare economics point of view, the criterion should be the overall welfare effect for consumers; if this is positive, the agreement should qualify for an exemption. In sum, in each of these three

[58] Art. 2(1)(b) Merger Regulation.
[59] Guidelines on the application of Art. 81(3) EC, para.49.
[60] ibid., para.54.
[61] ibid., para.43.

cases total welfare may be maximised if the gains are sufficiently large to compensate for the losses. In all three cases European competition policy, however, does not endorse the Kaldor–Hicks criterion.

With respect to the control of horizontal mergers, the Commission has declared that "The relevant benchmark in assessing efficiency claims is that consumers will not be worse off as a result of the merger".[62] This is again a clear rejection of the total welfare standard and Kaldor–Hicks improvements. A later passage of the Guidelines on the assessment of horizontal mergers re-affirms this conclusion by pointing out that "Cost reductions, which merely result from anti-competitive reductions in output, cannot be considered as efficiencies benefiting consumers".[63]

2.4.3 European competition policy: a pragmatic consumer welfare standard

The conclusion of the previous paragraphs that European competition law does not match the Pareto or Kaldor–Hicks criteria obviously raises the question of whether there is another welfare standard that underlies the current substantive rules. Is the goal of European competition law the pro-motion of consumer welfare? Here, a balanced answer seems necessary. In its Guidelines on the application of Article 81(3) EC, the European Commission does not require that any individual consumer receives a share of each and every efficiency gain. This would amount to a Pareto criterion, which is extremely difficult to implement in practice. Instead the European Commis-sion suggests a more pragmatic solution:

> "The concept of 'fair share' implies that the pass-on of benefits must at least com-pensate consumers for any actual or likely negative impact caused to them by the restriction of competition. ... The net effect must at least be neutral from the point of view of those consumers directly or likely affected by the agreement. If such con-sumers are worse off following the agreement, the second condition of Article 81(3) EC is not fulfilled".[64]

The latter approach can also be found in the Guidelines on the assessment of horizontal mergers, where the Commission states: "The relevant benchmark in assessing efficiency claims is that consumers will not be worse off as a result of the merger".[65]

An analysis of merger control, in particular the recent Guidelines, may further document the consumer welfare notion that underlies European policy and law. A total welfare approach, based on the Kaldor–Hicks criterion, necessarily implies that efficiencies are accepted as a reason to clear a merger which creates a dominant position. In the past, the Commission accepted

---

[62] Guidelines on the assessment of horizontal mergers, para.79.
[63] *ibid.*, para.80.
[64] Guidelines on the application of Art. 81(3) EC, para.85.
[65] Guidelines on the assessment of horizontal mergers, para.79.

efficiencies as an argument when no dominant position would be created by the merger.[66] Consequently, the efficiency defence was accepted in cases when there was no need for it. Taking efficiencies into account only as an argument to prevent the conclusion that a dominant position is created is not in conformity with a total welfare approach. Blocking the merger—in spite of its efficiencies—because of the fear that prices for consumers may increase, does not fit a total welfare approach either. Preventing price increases is in conformity only with a consumer welfare standard.

The limited practical relevance of an efficiency defence is again confirmed in recent policy documents of the European Commission. The European Commission requires that efficiencies brought about by a merger are verifiable and substantial: "Where reasonably possible, efficiencies and the resulting benefit to the consumers should therefore be quantified".[67] Outside the field of merger control, the approach seems to be even stricter. In the case of claimed costs efficiencies (including synergies from an integration of assets, economies of scale and economies of scope, and better planning of production) under Article 81(3) EC, the undertakings "must as accurately as reasonably possible calculate the (monetary) value of the efficiencies and describe in detail how the amount has been calculated". This seems possible only in a minority of cases, where the price reducing impact of efficiencies on marginal costs and changes in price–cost margins can be calculated.[68] The requirement that a fair share of the benefits must be passed on to consumers further limits the scope of efficiencies claims. In the European Commission's view, the second condition of Article 81(3) EC incorporates a sliding scale: "The greater the restriction of competition found under Article 81(1) EC the greater must be the efficiencies and the pass-on to consumers".[69] Remarkably, the European Commission's attitude towards dynamic efficiencies in the form of new and improved products seems less severe. Even though the objective of the assessment remains the same, the Commission acknowledges that it is difficult to assign precise values to dynamic efficiencies. Future practice will show whether the Commission will indeed more easily accept claims of dynamic efficiencies and apply a higher standard of proof concerning cost efficiencies, also in markets where the net price effect cannot be easily calculated. In this respect it should be remembered that costs efficiencies must be very substantial to guarantee that they are passed on to consumers. If quantification of dynamic efficiencies is not required, it may be easier to accept that they will create sufficient value for consumers to compensate for the anti-competitive effects of agreements or mergers. As argued earlier, a more tolerant view towards dynamic efficiencies is also in line with the insight that producers' gains may be necessary to finance research and development expenditures.

In sum, reading together its policy documents, it seems that the European Commission has found a pragmatic way to avoid interpretations of consumer

---

[66] P.D. Camesasca, *European Merger Control: Getting the Efficiencies Right* (2000).
[67] Guidelines on the assessment of horizontal mergers [2004] O.J. C 31/5, para.86.
[68] RBB Economics, "Art or Science? Assessing Efficiencies under the Commission's Article 81(3) Notice", RBB Brief 15 (2004).
[69] Guidelines on the application of Art. 81(3) EC, para.90.

welfare that are either impracticable (Pareto efficiency) or ill-suited (consumers must benefit) for policy making. With respect to the latter, it is remarkable that policy statements of the 1970s, urging price decreases for the benefit of consumers, have been replaced by the less demanding criterion that consumers should not be made worse off. However, other passages of the recent policy documents still describe consumer benefits in terms of lower prices. It would bring important benefits in terms of clarity and consistency if the European Commission would clearly formulate its consumer welfare standard and openly endorse it, rather than obscuring policy choices by paying lip service to efficiency arguments.

2.4.4 European competition policy and the goal of market integration

European competition law must be understood in the context of the need to break down the national boundaries between the Member States of the Community. Ever since the European Court of Justice's *Grundig*[70] case, the coherence between the ultimate Community task of creating an internal (common) market in accordance with the principle of an open market economy with free competition (as contained in Article 2 *juncto* 4 EC) and the policy means thereto of market integration (as contained in Article 3(1)(c) EC), has been clearly established. The goal of market integration can be defined as the elimination of economic frontiers between two or more economies. Neither Member States nor private enterprises may thus engage in practices that are in conflict with or undermine the unification of the common market. The former should not maintain or issue regulations that hinder the free movement of goods, services, persons or capital. The latter should not agree to restrictive business practices that could equally form effective barriers against competition originating in other Member States. In the European Commission's view, efforts aimed at removing national regulatory barriers to the full deployment of the four freedoms should not be jeopardised by business behaviours aimed at partitioning national markets. For example, national regulation on the composition of goods hindering free interstate trade[71] should not be replaced by agreements between producers limiting their commercial activities to particular Member States. The removal of public barriers may not be made ineffective by the creation of private barriers. Competition policy should ensure that such substitution cannot arise.

The view that competition law is an instrument to inhibit private initiatives (either agreements or unilateral practices) against the process of market integration has left European competition law with a heavy legacy. To reduce price differences across Member States, European competition law promotes

---

[70] Joined Cases 56/64 and 58/64 *Consten Sarl and Grundig-Verkaufs GmbH v Commission* [1966] ECR 299. See the discussion in Ch.6, Box 6.1.
[71] A classic example is the German purity law reserving the denomination ''beer'' to beer brewed from specific approved ingredients; see Case 178/84 *Commission v Germany* [1987] ECR 1227 (''Reinheitsgebot'').

intra-brand competition and stimulates parallel trade. Two examples may suffice to illustrate the potential conflicts between the objective of market integration, on the one hand, and the efficiency goals and the goal of consumer welfare, on the other hand. The first example is the persistent (almost *per se*) ban on absolute territorial protection: in spite of possible efficiency benefits in the organisation of distribution the practice is outlawed as an obvious instrument to segregate markets along national borders. The efficiency savings that are regularly attributed to intra-brand restrictions, such as coping with "free riding" and providing incentives for dealers to increase sales' efforts, are sacrificed on the altar of the internal market. The discussion in Chapter 6 on vertical restraints will show that the European Commission is willing to be more tolerant with regard to territorial restraints if they are objectively necessary in order for a distributor to penetrate a new market, but that the harmony with economic insights is still far from complete.[72]

The second example is the persisting uneasy attitude towards price discrimination across different Member States. As will be shown in Chapter 7 of this book, price discrimination may have beneficial consequences for consumers if it increases overall output. Consumer welfare will increase if a uniform price allows only consumers having an inelastic demand to buy the good concerned, whereas price discrimination would also allow sales to consumers with a more elastic demand, leaving the price to the former group unchanged.[73] However, different prices in different geographical areas seem to fly in the face of the market integration goal. Price convergence within the Member States may thus come at the expense of losses in terms of consumer welfare.

Often the question has been asked how the European system, devised for the primary purpose of market integration, will operate once that goal is achieved. A clear sign that market integration is losing importance as a goal to be achieved can be found in the *Adalat* case of the Court of Justice. The Court of First Instance censured an attempt by the European Commission to achieve price convergence by supporting parallel trade in the pharmaceutical industry. To this end, the Commission had extended the applicability of Article 81 EC (which requires the proof of an agreement) to a case where no concurrence of wills between economic operators could be shown. By annulling the Commission's decision, the Court made clear that Article 81 EC cannot be used to eliminate in an absolutely generic way the obstacles to interstate trade.[74] Remarkably, in the recent Guidelines on the application of Article 81(3) EC, the European Commission no longer mentions market integration as an objective of Article 81 EC. However, market integration is presented as an instrument which serves exactly the same goal as the protection of competition. In the words of the European Commission: "The creation and preservation of an open single market promotes an efficient allocation of resources throughout

---

[72] See Ch.6, s.6.4.3.
[73] J. Church and R. Ware, *Industrial Organization—A Strategic Approach* (2000), p.165.
[74] Case T–41/96 *Bayer AG v Commission* [2000] ECR II–3383; confirmed by Court of Justice in Joined Cases C–2/01P and C–3/01P *Commission v Bayer* [2004] ECR I–23.

the Community for the benefit of consumers".[75] It may be deplored that the European Commission has not taken the opportunity to fully discuss the multiple tensions between the goal of market integration and competition. Some of the most perverse consequences of the prohibition of territorial protection have been mitigated, but no indication is given as to the line beyond which community competition law will prohibit price discrimination because of the threat this practice poses to the single market. Such guidance might be found in the future Guidelines on the application of Article 82 EC, which are currently being prepared by the European Commission.

The authors of this book adhere to the view that only efficiency and consumer welfare are appropriate normative goals of competition law. The objectives of market integration may be fully legitimate but should be pursued by other legal instruments. It is highly questionable whether competition law is an appropriate instrument to further market integration.[76] This goal is largely impeded by factors, such as fiscal disparities and different regulatory interventions by the Member States, which are external to concerns of competition policy. Illustrative examples are the car industry, where price differences are caused by differences in tax levels, and the pharmaceutical industry, where price differences are the consequence of differences in the health policies of the Member States (varying between the two extremes of a single buyer and a competitive health insurance market). Prohibiting companies active in the European Union to adapt their sales policies to heterogeneous local conditions is nothing else but combating effects without reaching the causes of the existing disparities. Using rules of competition law to bring about price convergence by means of the arbitrage of parallel trade comes down to imposing the costs of non-Europe on companies, whereas the primary responsibility of persisting price differences lies with the governments of the Member States.

2.4.5 European competition policy and the protection of individual economic freedom

In analysing Articles 81 and 82 EC, one should always keep in mind that the wording of these provisions has been inspired by German ordoliberal thinking. According to the views of the Freiburg School,[77] any limitation of business freedom should be considered as a virtual restriction of competition and thus subject to prohibition unless exempted. If the emphasis is put on freedom of action, rather than the achievement of allocative efficiency, the scope for an economic analysis of the kind described in the previous sections of this chapter obviously diminishes. In liberalist thinking as conceived in the German tradition of law and economic freedom, competition is described as a beneficial process because it is the embodiment of liberty. Hoppmann's concept of

---

[75] Guidelines on the application of Art. 81(3), para.13.
[76] See R. Pardolesi, "Ritorno dall'isola che non c'è. Ovvero: l'intesa malintesa e l'integrazione del mercato come obiettivo dell'antitrust communitario" (2001) *Mercato Concorrenza Regole* 561.
[77] See Ch.3, s.3.4.

freedom of competition (*Konzept der Wettbewerbsfreiheit*) also grew out of this ordoliberal tradition.[78] Here it suffices to mention that, according to the German concept of *Wettbewerbsfreiheit*, restrictions on competition can occur both in relations with competitors and in relations with firms that are active as suppliers or buyers.

In European competition law, freedom of individual competitors is seen as an important benefit in preserving competition. The European Commission has held that "effective competition preserves the freedom and right of initiative of the individual economic operators and it fosters the spirit of enterprise".[79] The Article 81(3) EC Notice states that "a general principle underlying Article 81(1) EC, which is expressed in the case law of the Community Courts is that each economic operator must determine independently the policy which he intends to adopt on the market".[80] The emphasis on freedom of action may explain why the Commission often objects to contracts limiting the freedom of parties to take independent decisions (e.g. vertical restraints in distribution agreements[81]).

The influence of the Freiburg School can also clearly be felt in the Article 82 EC case law. According to the Court of Justice, the European dominant firm is endowed with a special responsibility *vis-à-vis* its customers: *Quod licet bovi non licet Iovi*. A dominant firm cannot engage in types of conduct (such as refusal to supply) that are perfectly lawful and feasible for its non-dominant competitors. The ordoliberal philosophy of Article 82 EC becomes immediately clear when it is contrasted with its American counterpart. Section 2 of the Sherman Act assumes the existence of a causal link between the contested conduct and some form of monopoly power. In contrast, European competition law ignores the process that led to the achievement of a dominant position and bans abuses by firms which achieved dominance. Consequently, the European approach is more formalistic and inhospitable to an analysis of economic effects.

As already indicated, the authors of this book adhere to the view that only economic efficiency and consumer welfare are appropriate goals for competition policy. Several reasons may be advanced why competition law should not be used to protect individual economic freedom. It is believed that guaranteeing a minimum protection to economically dependent contract parties (such as car dealers) will enable the latter to compete more intensively. Hence, protecting individual economic freedom of weak market parties would bring important benefits to consumers. However, competition law is ill-suited to protect weak contract parties. This task should be left to contract law, which is able to provide such protection in a more effective way than the indirect approach of competition law. If there are good reasons why Member States'

---

[78] See Ch.3, s.3.7.3.
[79] European Commission, *Fifteenth Annual Report on Competition Policy 1985* (1986).
[80] Guidelines on the application of Art. 81(3), para.14.
[81] See Ch.6, s.6.3.2 and Box 6.4.

contract laws remain ineffective, the European Community may consider issuing an appropriate Directive.[82] In this way, the absence of protective rules will be tackled directly instead of the indirect sanction of competition law that only withholds the benefit of an exemption. Protection of weak contract parties in the latter way may also cause counterproductive effects. Requiring stable relations between manufacturers and dealers is apt to freeze distribution networks and impede the market access of potentially more efficient dealers, as well as the development of innovative distribution channels. In sum, rules of contract law may be appropriate to protect freedom of business decisions. By contrast, achieving the latter goals through rules of competition law will cause inconsistencies and may create welfare losses.

2.4.6 European competition policy, industrial policy and goals of social equity

According to former Commissioner for Competition Van Miert,[83] competition policy does not take place in a vacuum; its effects in other policy areas, such as industrial, regional, social and environmental policy always have to be taken into account. The anchoring of competition values in the EC Treaty, as a result of the various amendments introduced by the Treaty of Amsterdam, actually increased pressure on the European Commission to consider these factors in making competition policy decisions,[84] and this inevitably required the European Commission to include political considerations.[85] Also the European Court of Justice seemed willing to limit the scope of competition law out of fears grounded in the non-attainability of social goals as contained in collective bargaining agreements when forced into a competition law regime.[86] As a result, the economic foundations of competition policy have been seriously shaken.

In recent policy documents, the European Commission no longer seems to share the view that competition law enforcement in the European Community serves a plurality of goals. The Guidelines on the interpretation of Article 81(3)

---

[82] This was done, for instance, to protect the rights of commercial agents (Council Directive 86/653/EEC of December 18, 1986 on the coordination of the laws of the Member States relating to self-employed commercial agents [1986] O.J. L 382/17).

[83] K. Van Miert, "Die Wettbewerbspolitik der neuen Kommission" (1995) 45 WuW 553, 554: "Die Wettbewerbspolitik der Kommission findet nicht in einem Vakuum statt. Sie hat stets auch ihre Auswirkungen in andere Politikbereichen der Kommission mit in Betracht zu ziehen, wie etwa Industrie-, Regional-, Sozial- und Umweltpolitik".

[84] A. Schmidt, "Die europäische Wettbewerbspolitik nach dem Vertrag von Amsterdam" (1999) 49 WuW 133, at pp.133–135.

[85] This is well-recognised: see "European Commission, Industrial Policy in an Open and Competitive Environment, COM(90)556" in *Bulletin of the European Communities* (1991), Supplement 3/91.

[86] Case C–67/96 *Albany International v Stichting Bedrijfspensioenfonds Textielindustrie* [1999] ECR I–5751; Joined Cases C–115/97, C–116/97 and C–117/97 *Brentjens' Handelsonderneming BV v Stichting Bedrijfspensioenfonds voor de Handel in Bouwmaterialen* [1999] ECR I–6025; Case C–219/97 *Maatschappij Drijvende Bokken BV v Stichting Pensioenfonds voor de Vervoer- en Havenbedrijven* [1999] ECR I–6121.

EC state that "goals pursued by other provisions of the Treaty can be taken into account to the extent that they can be subsumed under the four conditions of Article 81(3) EC". This statement leaves only a secondary, if not marginal role for considerations of social policy, environmental protection and protection of small and medium-sized enterprises. However, in current European competition law, several rules remain that can only be explained from a social or industrial policy perspective. Examples include the case law of the European Court of Justice, which exempted collective labour agreements from the scope of Article 81(1) EC[87] and the Regulation on distribution of cars.[88]

Industrial policy proposes an intervention in the free workings of the market, as opposed to competition policy's focus on the static and dynamic allocation of resources. The potential for policy conflicts is consequently quite large and this is aggravated because policies inherently have multiple objectives. Most explicitly, competition policy might work against industrial policy in R&D-intensive industries, if it is the case that large (and potentially dominant) firms are likely to invest more in R&D than small competitive firms. Both policies then reflect fundamentally different views of policy makers of the impact of government intervention on economic performance. At the same time, however, competition policy and industrial policy will be complementary if competition among firms is perceived as a major force behind industrial competitiveness.

Similarly, protecting small businesses leads to policy conflicts. Protection of small firms is seen as a component of a healthy competitive environment. The raging economic crisis launched a concern for small and medium-sized firms to become part of Community law.[89] The European Court of Justice referred to the "independence of small and medium sized firms" in *United Brands*[90] to counter the alleged ability of large firms to extract unfair prices and conditions from smaller enterprises.[91] The protection of small firms is often justified by referring to a particular concept of fairness: the preservation of "equal opportunities". This concept finds its roots in philosophical thought and has no direct link with allocative efficiency.[92] In spite of its shaky foundations, the view that the powers of large firms should be curtailed for reasons of economic democracy is not alien to European competition policy. Apart from efficiency goals, current competition policy embodies rules that aim to decentralise power, protect the freedom of decision of independent firms and maintain equal opportunities of competition for small businesses. In past decades examples of a "small is beautiful" approach could also be found on the other side of the Atlantic. In contrast with current US antitrust law, the

---

[87] For a critical comment, see R. J. Van den Bergh and P.D. Camesasca, "Irreconcilable Principles? The Court of Justice Exempts Collective Labour Agreements from the Wrath of Antitrust" (2000) 25 E.L.Rev. 492.

[88] See Ch.6, Box 6.4.

[89] R. Klotz and P. Zurkinden, "Die Anwendung des Kartellrechts auf kleine und mittlere Unternehmen" (1999) 49 WuW 120, at pp.121–128.

[90] Case 27/76 *United Brands v Commission* [1978] ECR 207.

[91] Compare A. Väth, *Die Wettbewerbskonzeption des Europäischen Gerichtshofs* (1987), pp.199–208.

[92] D. Neven, R. Nuttall and P. Seabright, *Merger in Daylight: The Economics and Politics of European Merger Control* (1993), p.12.

early Robinson–Patman Act,[93] as well as older American case law under the Sherman Act, expressed a wish to restrict the power of big firms in favour of smaller firms.[94] This power-sharing objective was pursued in spite of the noticeable inefficiencies that could ensue.[95] In current US antitrust law promotion of small business has been discredited as a policy goal[96] (see Box 2.3). European competition law and regulations of competitive processes in a number of Member States, however, continue to be influenced by considerations of fairness. Cartel agreements between small and medium-sized enterprises, which can often only compete effectively with larger enterprises by means of this sort of cooperation, is shielded from the ban on cartels.[97] Additionally, in some Member States, laws on "unfair" competition contain rules which are not consistent with an efficiency oriented competition policy.[98]

2.5 Conclusions

The goal of a competition policy that is primarily intended to increase economic welfare can be defined in terms of consumer surplus, producer surplus and total welfare. Consumer surplus is a concept used to describe the difference between what a consumer is willing to pay for a good and what the consumer actually pays when buying it. Producer surplus refers to the variance between the price in the market that producers collectively receive for their products and the sum of those producers' respective marginal costs at each level of output. Total surplus then is the sum of producer surplus and consumer surplus. Total welfare is a notion designed to take into account the

---

[93] For a critical analysis, partly from an economic perspective, see P. Elman, "The Robinson–Patman Act and Antitrust Policy: A Time for Reappraisal" (1969) 1 J. Reprints Antitrust L. and Econ. 561.

[94] Indeed, social and moral considerations also influenced the US case law, as the following quotation shows: "It is possible, because of its indirect social or moral effect, to prefer a system of small producers, each dependent for his success upon his own skill and character, to one in which the great mass of those engaged must accept the direction of a few", quoted from *United States v Aluminium Company of America*, 148 F. 2d 416 (1945).

[95] It should be added that the Federal Trade Commission no longer actively enforces the Robinson–Patman Act, even though private suits continue to be filed.

[96] Only a minority of authors favours protection of small firms as a goal for competition policy. See, e.g. E.M. Fox and L.A. Sullivan, "Antitrust-Retrospective and Prospective: Where are we Coming from and Where are we Going?" (1987) 62 N.Y.U.L. Rev. 936; they express concern for "the underdog".

[97] Commission Notice on agreements of minor importance which do not fall under Art. 81(1) of the Treaty establishing the European Community (*de minimis* Notice) [1997] O.J. C 372/13; Commission Notice concerning agreements, decisions, and concerted practices in the field of co-operation between enterprises, [1968] O.J. C 75/3.

[98] An example is the Belgian law on unfair trade practices (*Wet betreffende de handelspraktijken en de voorlichting en bescherming van de consument*) which prohibits sales at loss prices or with an exceptionally reduced profit margin, irrespective of the existence of a dominant market position. For a comment, see E. Dirix, Y.Montangie and H. Vanhees, *Handels-en Economisch Recht in Hoofdlijnen* (2005) at pp.373–377. Another example is price discrimination which is equally held illegal on the basis of laws banning unfair trade practices (in Belgium: Art. 93 of the above mentioned law; in Germany: Section 1 UWG). These rules are clearly over-inclusive since they also outlaw competitive uses of price discrimination.

welfare effects on the entire economy, bypassing the markets directly involved in the analysis of a particular industry. The total welfare view asserts that the chief objective of antitrust is increasing total welfare by allocating resources through the price system to those users who value these most.

Economic theory shows that consumer surplus and producer surplus are maximised in a market characterised by the conditions of perfect competition. Allocative efficiency implies that firms produce what buyers want and are willing to pay for. A perfectly competitive market is also qualified as Pareto efficient, since it is no longer possible to increase the welfare of one individual without harming another individual. In contrast to an allocatively efficient, perfectly competitive market, monopoly causes welfare losses. Aside from undesirable distributional consequences (the price effect of monopoly), the size of these losses (deadweight loss and "rent seeking") seems to justify the costs of formulating and enforcing the prohibitions of competition law. Hence, allocative efficiency can be advanced as a major policy goal of competition law.

However, allocative efficiency may conflict with other efficiency goals: productive efficiency and dynamic efficiency. Productive efficiency relates to the maximisation of output at a given input, so that internal slack (also called X-inefficiency) is absent. Dynamic efficiency is achieved through the invention, development and diffusion of new products and production processes that increase social welfare. To enable policy decisions when the different efficiency goals are not consistent with each other (and Pareto improvements are thus not possible), welfare economics offers the alternative criterion of Kaldor–Hicks efficiency. By using the Kaldor–Hicks criterion, total welfare will be maximised. In this way, competition authorities may clear mergers that enable the merging firms to achieve important scale economies and thus improve productive efficiency, but at the same time enable previously independent firms to collude and raise prices above competitive levels. In terms of total welfare, it is irrelevant that producers rather than consumers capture the surplus produced by achieving efficiencies, as the monopoly overcharge paid by purchasers to stockholders is treated as a transfer from one member of society to another and so is ignored in the balance. The total welfare standard accepts that producers capture the surplus as long as their gains are higher than the losses of consumer surplus.

This chapter has shown that total welfare (Kaldor–Hicks efficiency) is not the normative standard underlying current European competition law. It has brought forward the important insight that competition policy may be more inspired by equity considerations concerning the distribution of resources than by efficiency criteria. In the view of the European Commission, cost reductions which result from reductions in output cannot be considered as efficiencies benefiting consumers. Even if total welfare increases, there is still an unlawful restriction of competition if the agreement (or the merger) reduces consumer surplus. The European Commission seems to have endorsed a pragmatic consumer welfare standard, by requiring that the net effect of agreements (or a merger) must at least be neutral from the point of view of consumers affected by the agreement. Even though this benchmark is much less demanding than insisting on price decreases, it is not perfectly in line with an economic approach. The requirement that consumers in the relevant market are not made worse off excludes increases in total welfare. The latter may result either from gains of producers (shareholders) exceeding consumers' losses or from balancing negative effects in one relevant market against positive effects for consumers in different geographic or product markets. In sum, the use of consumer welfare criteria in competition law requires efficiency–equity trade-offs. The rejection of the Kaldor–Hicks criterion implies that more weight is given to competitive prices for consumers than to costs savings for efficient firms or profits for shareholders. Thus wealth transfers not efficiency considerations seem to be the driving force for formulating general rules and deciding hard cases. Competition authorities should be fully aware of these underlying value judgments and policy choices. Making these trade-offs explicit, rather than paying lip service to efficiency arguments, can improve the quality of the decision making.

Aside from distributional concerns about consumer welfare, European competition law has been inspired by other policy goals. These include market integration, protection of freedom of business decisions, and goals of fairness and social equity. The goal of market integration has left a heavy legacy on European competition law; up until today it has kept prohibitions into place (such as the ban on absolute territorial protection) which may cause substantial inefficiencies in the organisation of production or distribution. European competition law is also still permeated by rules aiming at the protection of the individual economic freedom of market players. A clear example can be found in the Regulation on distribution of cars, which lays down several requirements to protect the commercial freedom of the "weak" car dealer against supposedly abusive behaviour by the "strong" car manufacturer. In the view of the authors of this book, market integration and protection of business freedom are not appropriate goals of competition law; they should be pursued by other means, in particular rules of public law and contract law. Also, the wish to achieve social goals (such as protection of the labour force) and covert concerns about industrial policy will cause inconsistencies that will endanger the overall quality of competition law and cause economic welfare losses.

Chapter 3

....

ECONOMIC APPROACHES TO COMPETITION LAW

3.1 Introduction

Competition theory, competition policy and competition law are inextricably linked. Ever since competition law came into existence the economic theory of competition has exercised its influence upon it. The US Sherman Act, which is the oldest competition law, dating from 1890, is now more than 100 years old.[1] Competition theory has naturally changed since then, and this has had an impact on competition policy and competition law. This branch of the law has been characterised by a cyclical movement. The rules alter as and when the underlying economic theory changes, thus reflecting the fluctuating importance of economic theory in the decision-making process. When mathematics began to penetrate economic science, in price theory the microeconomic models of perfect competition and monopoly replaced the classical economic approach to competition. The criticisms of the strong underlying unrealistic assumptions of these models led to the development of oligopoly models, which are closer to the reality of actual markets. The early theories of imperfect competition and monopolistic competition did not, however, have an immediately clear influence on competition policy.

The influence of competition theory on competition policy and competition law increased dramatically once the so-called Harvard School had articulated the basic perceptions of industrial organisation theory[2] in the well-known "structure–conduct–performance" paradigm and claimed to be able to explain the relationships among these three variables (structuralist approach). This, together with the emergence of the new competitive ideal of "workable competition",[3] had a clear influence upon competition policy. In the light of the relationship between market structure, market conduct and market performance, competition law became an instrument for generating optimal outcomes by, *inter alia*, directly influencing market structure (merger control). When the Harvard School acquired a dominant influence in the 1960s, competition lawyers also began to refer to it. They did so in order to examine whether or not certain business activities that influenced market structure should be countered by competition law, depending on the effect those activities had upon efficiency. Insights derived from the Harvard doctrine of industrial organisation were also employed to evaluate concentration in markets for which, because economies of scale were present, the perfect competition model was not altogether appropriate.

The many shifts in American competition policy in the 1970s and 1980s can, without doubt, be attributed to the economic insights of the Chicago School. Chicago economists regard the Harvard approach as primarily descriptive and make a renewed use of concepts of price theory to explain firm behaviour and market structure. In the following chapters of this book, extensive

[1] On the history of American antitrust law, see R. Peritz, *Competition Policy in America: 1888–1992* (2nd ed., 2001).
[2] Industrial organisation (also termed industrial economics in European countries) has developed into an influential branch of learning. This discipline is devoted to the application of explanations and predictions concerning economic results in real-life markets. The Harvard School applies the traditional structure–conduct–performance paradigm in order to determine whether the competition in various branches of industry is "workable". This approach is thus labelled because it was developed in the late 1930s and early 1940s at the University of Harvard. The term "Harvard School" is less used in the USA, though. American authors do not have a common way of referring to the pre-Chicago era. The case law is often grouped under the heading "Warren Court" era, after the then-President of the Supreme Court.
[3] J.M. Clark, "Towards a Concept of Workable Competition" (1940) 30 Amer. Econ. Rev. 241; E. Kantzenbach, *Die Funktionsfähigkeit des Wettbewerbs* (1966).

consideration will be given to how the insights of the Chicago School have led to a sharply altered evaluation of particular competition issues. In recent years, three new theoretical approaches have won substantial support in industrial economics: the theory of contestable markets, transaction cost analysis, and game theory. The influence of these recent theories on competition policy and law is steadily increasing. Later chapters will attempt to show how the new insights afforded by these recent theoretical developments may be used to analyse some of the current hot issues in competition law (such as collusion in oligopolistic markets and predatory pricing).

In Europe, until the mid-1990s, economic theories had less influence upon competition policy and law than in the USA. The rules of European competition law and their application in practice were largely driven by the goal of achieving market integration. Integration of national markets in the European Union was a political necessity rather than an economic decision.[4] It resulted in an interventionist competition law, which strictly forbade any form of market division.[5] Moreover, rules of competition law were interpreted using technical legal distinctions only and focus on the economic effects of diverging interpretations was largely absent. If one looks for the economic foundations of European competition policy, one will discover that the drafting of the European competition rules was largely based on German ordoliberal ideas. Ordoliberalism covers the policy views of the Freiburg School, which greatly affected the development of German competition and economic policy. When the European (Economic) Community was founded, the leading German representatives managed to introduce ordoliberal views into the economic and competition policies of the EC. The influence of ordoliberal thoughts in European competition law has already been documented in the previous chapter.[6] For a proper understanding of the underlying principles and ideas of European competition law, the American Chicago–Harvard debate and the post-Chicago developments in the USA[7] are not sufficient. Up until the 1990s, European competition policy and law could be best understood as a manifestation of ordoliberalism complemented by the insights of the analytical model of the Harvard School. Influences by the ideas of the Chicago School were clearly absent. From the mid-1990s on, European competition law has been substantially revised and many ideas of modern industrial organisation theory have been integrated into the current legal framework.

As this chapter will illustrate, there is no such thing as *the* economic approach to competition law that offers exact and authoritative answers to all kinds of competition policy problems. This book will disappoint those who seek such guidance, for it contains nothing of the kind. Conversely, this chapter shows that there are different economic approaches to competition

---

[4] As will be illustrated in later chapters of this book, market integration may harm rather than improve productive and allocative efficiency. See Ch.6 on vertical restraints and Ch.10 on competition between competition laws and harmonisation.

[5] D.G. Goyder, *EC Competition Law* (4th ed., 2003), pp.45–47.

[6] See Ch.2, s.2.4.5.

[7] See the collection of articles in: A. Cucinotta, R. Pardolesi and R. Van Den Bergh, *Post-Chicago Developments in Antitrust Law* (2002).

policy and law. Even though most current industrial organisation research is grounded in the same formal economic theory, differences of opinion among economists on substantive points cannot be excluded when it comes to policy issues. The overview of economic approaches to competition policy and law, which is offered below, indicates both common opinions and the lines along which economists may disagree. The latter discord should by no means detract from the important added value to be derived from an economic analysis. It must be acknowledged that different opinions are often based upon differing underlying value judgments that rarely surface. Economics hereto offers a set of welfare criteria that may be used to guide antitrust. Total welfare, consisting of the sum of consumer and producer surplus as the measure for allocative efficiency, must be distinguished from consumer welfare,[8] which is often the more important political goal. If politics, rather than economics, is the decisive factor in shaping competition laws, other policy goals, such as protection of small firms and considerations of social policy, which are lacking objective benchmarks, may even supersede the economic criteria of efficiency.

In this chapter, a simple chronological subdivision is used for revealing various Schools of thought[9] in the field of competition policy. A sketch of the evolution in economic thinking and the impact of changes in the dominant economic thinking of the time on competition law is the easiest way to explain how economic theory may have a concrete impact on legal issues. For example, the change of direction in decisions from the US Supreme Court during the Reagan and Bush eras was clearly a response to the emergence of the Chicago School. Similarly, the recent evolution of European competition law can be best understood as a transition process from ordoliberalism to a modern economic framework. The presentation of different schools of thought is mainly done for didactical reasons. It should not give the false impression that there is complete disagreement among economists, so that a systematic economic approach to competition law would only increase legal uncertainty and therefore be of little use. The qualification "School" is a typical response to a paradigmatic change in a scholarly field, since new ideas are often threatening to established scholars. Today, in the USA, Chicago economics has established itself as central to the entire discipline and the term Chicago School does not necessarily have a negative connotation. The Harvard paradigm (structure–conduct–performance) and the Chicago paradigm (price theory) are not incompatible as organising principles and may therefore be used as complementary rather than as mutually exclusive.

The structure of this chapter is as follows. In the next section, the origins of the concept of competition are traced back in classical economics, where it

---

[8] Under the latter welfare standard producer gains cannot justify losses in consumer surplus, as is the case in a total welfare approach. See Ch.2, s.2.3.3.

[9] In Mackaay's definition, a School of thought is "a group of thinkers who adopt a common approach, including shared theoretical premises, on how and what to research in a particular field". Mackaay states that such a School can be distinguished when a group of scholars project their own axioms and defend their views, which must have a certain complexity and logical coherence, against other views. See E. Mackaay, "History of Law and Economics", in *Encyclopedia of Law and Economics* (B. Bouckaert and G. de Geest ed., 2000), Vol.I, pp.402–403.

figured prominently as the invisible hand guiding business decisions towards economic welfare. In the early days of economics, competition was seen as a dynamic process until it was replaced by the static notion of perfect competition devised in price theory. The third section of this chapter questions the relevance of the model of perfect competition as a yardstick for competition policy and law. Perfect competition, as monopoly's antithesis, allows for clear-cut predictions about the way firms will behave and the consequences of that behaviour on economic welfare. Most real-world markets, however, cannot be characterised by either perfect competition or monopoly. This insight has led to the development of more refined oligopoly models in the economic profession; at the same time, the evolution was not without cost, though, as consensus among economists disappeared. As a result, so-called Schools emerged, each projecting its own axioms. In the fourth section, the ideas of the Freiburg School (also known as ordoliberalism) are presented. Ordoliberals advanced the concept of a social market economy supported by a legal framework, in which competition law had to guarantee individual economic freedom. These ideas had a clear impact on the formulation of the prohibition of cartels and abuses of a dominant position in European competition law. Even though the views of the Freiburg School are outdated and at odds with modern economic insights, ordoliberal influences remain visible in European competition law up until today. In the fifth section, the Harvard approach to problems of competition policy will be presented. This School is also labelled the structuralist approach, since it produced numerous industry studies linking performance with structural characteristics of markets, often devoid of any but the vaguest theories. This provoked sharp criticism from scholars belonging to what has subsequently established itself as the Chicago School. Also, the structuralist point of convergence was rejected among European authors favouring a dynamic view of competition. In the sixth section of this chapter, the Harvard–Chicago controversy is commented on in some detail, given its continuing relevance for understanding current economic issues. The seventh section provides an overview of the most prominent dynamic approaches to competition: the work of Schumpeter, Austrian economics (von Hayek, von Mises) and the German concept of freedom of competition (*Konzept der Wettbewerbsfreiheit*, Hoppmann). The final three sections of this chapter are devoted to the most recent developments in industrial organisation. The theories of contestable markets, transaction cost analysis and game theory have emerged as important extensions of the Chicago approach. The eighth section discusses the theoretical concept of contestable markets and its relevance for competition policy. In the ninth section, it is shown how transaction costs analysis may supplement both the structuralist approach and the relevant insights from price theory (Chicago School). The policy conclusions flowing from taking transaction costs into account will also be presented. Finally, the tenth section introduces modern industrial organisation theory. The most recent literature builds upon the best insights from the Harvard–Chicago debate (without its extremes) and adds views from the theory of contestable markets, transaction cost economics and game theory. The implications of the modern theoretical and empirical literature for current competition law will be discussed in the following chapters.

3.2 The concept of competition in classical economics

The roots of the classical concept of competition go back at least to Adam Smith's famous book *The Wealth of Nations*.[10] Even before Smith's time, competition was a familiar concept in economic writing.[11] Smith systematised earlier thinking on the subject and elevated competition to the level of a general organising principle of economic society. Although much of Adam Smith's analysis is now obsolete, his arguments concerning the efficiency of free competition are as valid as ever. Since the days of Adam Smith, economists have naturally updated their views of competition and have developed various more refined competition models. These formal models not infrequently sacrifice their explanatory power in favour of mathematical refinement. Through the use of overtly simple assumptions, important insights of the classical theory have been lost in more recent developments of competition theory. A renewed acquaintance with the classical literature can, therefore, put us back on track to the origins of competition theory.

3.2.1 A dynamic view of competition

In classical economics, competition was a behavioural concept, the essence of which was the effort of the individual seller to undersell, or the individual buyer to outbid, his rivals in the marketplace. Competition was seen as a power which forced prices to a level just covering costs.[12] Smith incorporated this concept into his *Wealth of Nations* and gave it a significance it never had before by presenting competition as a force which would lead self-seeking individuals unconsciously to serve the general welfare. The reference to the "invisible hand" is the most frequently quoted passage of the book:

> "[Each individual] generally, indeed, neither intends to promote the public interest, nor knows how much he is promoting it. . . . [He] intends only his own gain, and he is in this, as in many other cases, led by an invisible hand to promote an end which was no part of his intention."[13]

Smith's invisible hand is the market prices which emerge in reaction to competitive forces. These forces oblige producers to take account of consumers' demands. If they ignore these demands, they will be excluded from

---

[10] A. Smith, *An Enquiry into the Nature and Causes of the Wealth of Nations* (1776).

[11] See P. McNulty, "A Note on the History of Perfect Competition" (1967) 75 J. Polit. Economy 395, with references to the 17th-century mercantilist Johann Joachim Becher, writings by Turgot and Hume (1766) and to Sir James Steuart (1767), who provided the most complete pre-Smithian analysis of competition.

[12] P. McNulty, "Economic Theory and the Meaning of Competition" (1968) 82 Quart. J. Econ. 639 at p.647.

[13] A. Smith, *An Enquiry into the Nature and Causes of the Wealth of Nations* (1776), p.423.

the market. Smith's suspicion of cartels and monopolies is well summarised in another well-known passage in the *Wealth of Nations*:

> "People of the same trade seldom meet together, even for merriment and diversion, but the conversation ends in a conspiracy against the public or in some contrivance to raise prices."[14]

The conception of competition as an ordering force dominated classical economics. When Adam Smith wrote of competition, he did not contrast competition and monopoly as market models, but rather the level of prices resulting from the presence or absence of competition as a regulatory force.[15] In classical economics, competition was seen as a process of rivalry between competing firms possessing reasonable knowledge of the market opportunities. Freedom of trade was stressed as a necessary condition for competition to work. Competition was seen as a process which achieves its results only in the long run. During the classical period market theory was: "to open the door of opportunity wide and to trust the results".[16] Most importantly, competition was viewed as a price-determining force and not as a market structure, although it was acknowledged that competition was more effective with a larger rather than smaller number of competitors. The idea of competition itself as a market structure was the distinguishing contribution of neo-classical economics. In neo-classical economics, a more precise and elegant model of perfect competition was developed. This model, however, focuses exclusively on the effects of competition. It therefore, in spite of its elegance, loses sight of the behavioural processes leading to these results.

Nobel prize-winner George Stigler[17] neatly summarised the Smithian conditions of competition as follows:

- the rivals must act independently, not collusively;

- the number of rivals, potential as well as present, must be sufficient to eliminate extraordinary gains;

- the economic units must possess tolerable knowledge of the market opportunities;

- there must be freedom (from social restraints) to act on this knowledge;

- sufficient time must elapse for resources to flow in the directions and quantities desired by their owners.

---

[14] A. Smith, *An Enquiry into the Nature and Causes of the Wealth of Nations* (1776), pp.127–128.
[15] P. McNulty, "Economic Theory and the Meaning of Competition" (1968) 82 Quart. J. Econ. 639 at p.643.
[16] H.C. Adams, *Description of Industry* (1918), p.27.
[17] G. Stigler, "Perfect Competition, Historically Contemplated" (1997) 65 J. Polit. Economy 2.

3.2.2 Policy conclusions

What were the lessons of classical economics for competition policy? It is a widespread fallacy that classical economics blindly placed its trust in the *laissez faire* principle. Many classical economists were against government interference in the market. They were of the opinion that the competitive process would lead to efficient results. Some of them nevertheless advocated limited regulation of competition. Although competition was hailed as a process, they considered some sort of government interference to be necessary in order to ensure that markets could operate freely, so that competitors could enter and leave the market without hindrance. Adam Smith, in particular, was well aware of the need for a legal framework to guarantee freedom of competition by preventing collusion between firms and abuses by dominant firms, consisting in the erection of barriers to entry to combat the erosion of their market power.[18]

In classical economics, competition signified both reciprocal rivalry and the absence of government restrictions, such as the exclusive privileges which characterised the mercantilist period. The common law in relation to restraints of trade reflected the classical view of competition. Modes of conduct limiting individual freedom were condemned as restraints on competition. The emphasis on freedom in the classical view of competition explains why the use of duress in entering into agreements and collective refusals to contract were regarded as unlawful, while at the same time agreements freely entered into were subsequently enforced. It also explains why, in the classical approach, no distinction was made between horizontal and vertical agreements.[19] In present-day competition law this distinction is accorded great significance; a critical analysis of the legal approach in relation to vertical restraints is to be found in Chapter 6.

3.3 The concept of perfect competition in price theory

3.3.1 A static view of competition

Adam Smith gave a positive reply on the desirability of a free market system which has served as a policy guideline for more than two centuries now. But the justification of his answer is not satisfying according to the methodological standards of scientific neo-classical micro-economics. With the mathematical economists (Cournot, Jevon, Edgeworth, Marshall), the concept of competition took a fundamentally different form. The emergence of price theory in the 19th

---

[18] H. Cox and H. Hübener, "Einführung in die Wettbewerbstheorie und -politik", in *Handbuch des Wettbewerbs* (H. Cox, U. Jens and K. Markert ed., 1981), pp.10–11.
[19] See in general H.J. Hovenkamp, "The Sherman Act and the Classical Theory of Competition" (1989) 74 Iowa L. Rev. 1019.

century led to the development of a structural and static notion of competition: the abstraction of perfect competition. This concept is still indispensable in modern economic theory today. In contrast with classical economics, which analysed competition as a dynamic process, price theory focuses on the properties of market equilibrium. An equilibrium may be defined as a final state in which all possibilities for mutually beneficial exchanges between market parties have been exhausted. Price theory does not consider how this equilibrium is attained dynamically. Perfect competition is a static notion; if the conditions of the model are satisfied no competitor can gain a lead on any of the others, and this results in a slowing-down of the competitive process. In German, this phenomenon is concisely described as *Schlafmützenkonkurrenz* (night-cap competition).[20] The equilibrium as a final state is a much simpler structure, but loses much of the richness of the classical model. However, the structural concept of perfect competition is very useful to analyse the welfare properties of a market system. According to Smith, an invisible hand guided the economic actors through the incentives of the price system to an optimal resource allocation. To restate this proposition in a modern fashion, the behaviour of consumers and producers must be analysed more precisely and a yardstick must be introduced for measuring economic efficiency or social welfare. Neither aspect was convincingly developed in the original invisible hand theorem. The price to be paid for progress in these questions is the unrealistic assumptions of the model of perfect competition.

A technical description of the basic models of perfect competition and monopoly was already provided in the previous chapter. As was shown, a market characterised by perfect competition must satisfy many (unrealistic) assumptions: the number of sellers and buyers must be large, products sold must be homogeneous, there must be no barriers to entry, and information concerning present and future market conditions must be perfect. It was also shown that the equilibrium of a perfectly competitive market is Pareto efficient.[21] Resource allocation is economically efficient if one cannot conceive a better outcome for the economic world and the individuals who populate it. It is thus the achievable social optimum for society. By contrast, in a situation of monopoly, in which there is only one producer in the market and there are significant barriers to entry, social welfare is not optimised. While the competitive market price is equal to marginal costs, the monopolist's price exceeds marginal costs.[22] This leads to an inefficient allocation of resources because the consumers' wishes are not fully satisfied. Under perfect competition, with prices equal to marginal costs, it is impossible to reallocate resources to achieve a higher output. By contrast, output is not maximised under a monopoly. This difference lies at the heart of economists' pleas in favour of perfect competition and against monopoly. In addition, a share of the consumer surplus is redistributed to the monopoly as producer surplus or monopoly rent. This is not in itself a loss in welfare, but it might lead to a

---

[20] F.A. Lutz, "Bemerkungen zum Monopolproblem" (1956) 8 ORDO 32.
[21] See Ch.2, s.2.1.
[22] R.S. Pindyck and D.L. Rubinfeld, *Microeconomics* (4th ed., 1998), pp.333–374.

situation with a less preferable income distribution. In addition, monopoly causes a deadweight loss, which lowers the economy's overall welfare.

3.3.2 Policy conclusions

The attractiveness of the model of perfect competition as a blueprint for competition policy is limited for a number of reasons. First, the concept of perfect competition is totally devoid of behavioural content. In contrast with Adam Smith's view, competition is no longer the force which drives prices down to costs, but a description of a particular idealised situation. Perfect competition is a market situation which, although it is the result of the free entry of formerly competing firms, has evolved to the point where no further competition within the industry is possible. Competition is by definition also excluded under monopoly since the monopolist is identified as the entire industry. Neither the monopolist nor the perfectly competitive firm is able to compete in the Smithian sense. As McNulty put it, the two concepts of competition are not only different, but also fundamentally incompatible. Whereas classical economics provided very close insights into real-life business experience, the equilibrium achieved under perfect competition is far away from reality. Perfect competition is a state of affairs quite incompatible with the idea of all-encompassing competition. Apart from its unrealistic and abstract character, the concept of perfect competition also reveals one of the great paradoxes of economic science: both perfect competition and monopoly are situations in which the possibility of competitive behaviour is ruled out by definition. Every act of competition in the classical sense of the word is valuable as evidence of welfare enhancing conduct, while in neo-classical economic theory it would be proof of some degree of monopoly power.[23] For Smith, competition was a process (disequilibrium) through which a predicted result, the equation of price and costs, was achieved. With Cournot it becomes the realised result itself (equilibrium).[24] Hence, those who favour a dynamic view of competition will refuse to base any policy recommendations on the model of perfect competition.

Second, the model of perfect competition may cause a serious bias in policy making. The magnitude of the welfare losses under monopoly (allocative inefficiencies, "rent seeking"[25] and technical inefficiencies) certainly seems to justify the costs of an antitrust law.[26] Even though the analysis of monopoly seems to demonstrate unambiguously that a monopoly is a bad thing, price theory, however, does not allow us easy conclusions as to the contents of

---

[23] P. McNulty, "Economic Theory and the Meaning of Competition" (1968) 82 Quart. J. Econ. 639 at 641. See also D.T. Armentano, *Antitrust and Monopoly: Anatomy of a Policy Failure* (1982).
[24] P. McNulty, "A Note on the History of Perfect Competition" (1967) 75 J. Polit. Economy 395 at p.398.
[25] A rent is the difference between the revenue from producing a good and the cost of production. Competition eliminates rents. By contrast, firms protected by regulation may retain rents. The process by which firms try to convince regulators to limit competition is thus called rent seeking.
[26] R.S. Pindyck and D.L. Rubinfeld, *Microeconomics* (4th ed., 1998), p.334.

competition policy in real life. In reality, markets differ sharply from the model of perfect competition and from the strict assumptions upon which that model is founded. A major problem in using the model of perfect competition is that it may lead policy makers to label every deviation from the perfectly competitive model caused by a less than perfectly elastic demand as a market imperfection. Suppliers selling differentiated products face downward sloping demand curves. Deviations of real-world conditions from the assumptions of the perfectly competitive model are pervasive throughout the economy. However, all these deviations are not imperfections in the antitrust policy sense. Taking advantage of uniqueness in pricing one's product is not anti-competitive, but actually encourages the investments in product features and firm reputations that consumers value. Product differentiation might pose antitrust concerns only if it is used strategically to limit market entry.

Third, if a general competitive equilibrium is to be achieved, the conditions of perfect competition must be satisfied in all sectors of the economy. The impossibility of achieving a general competitive equilibrium, rather than a partial equilibrium in some sectors of the economy, gives rise to the problem of "second best". Apart from the hypothetical case in which all market imperfections are either absent or simultaneously corrected, the analysis set out above throws no light on the question of whether perfect competition is better than monopoly. Political pressure can hinder the removal of market imperfections, just as the presence of economies of scale (production costs falling as output increases) can make their removal undesirable. Although the achievement of perfect competition in all sectors of the economy (the "first best" solution) necessarily brings about an increase in welfare, this is by no means certain once one less than optimal situation is transformed by com-petition policy into another less than optimal situation. Given the imperfec-tions in some markets, information about the most efficient market form in other markets (perfect competition, oligopoly or even monopoly) is not easily available. To generate a second-best solution a lot of research has to be done and to be repeated if the situation in only one market changes. Scherer and Ross conclude that: "The theory of second best is a counsel of despair". According to these authors, aiming at a "third best" solution is the best strategy for competition policy.[27] An approach such as this involves choosing from the various forms of general policy those which, on average, result in the most desirable allocation of resources. Seen in this light, a policy which sti-mulates competition appears to be superior. Such a policy aims to achieve that amount of competition which is compatible with economies of scale and with the desired degree of product differentiation. Because there is no reliable information concerning the second-best solutions, an improvement in welfare must be achievable by eliminating monopoly power where it is present, rather than by encouraging fresh obstacles to monopoly in markets where these obstacles did not previously exist.

---

[27] F.M. Scherer and D. Ross, *Industrial Market Structure and Economic Performance* (3rd ed., 1990), pp.37–38.

3.4 Ordoliberalism: the ideas of the Freiburg School

The Freiburg School was a neo-liberal School of thought that emerged in the 1930s and which played a significant role after the Second World War in the development of economic policy and competition law in Germany and in Europe. Its most prominent representatives were the economist Walter Eucken and the lawyer Franz Böhm. Thus, contrary to what is often believed, inter-disciplinary research in Competition Law and Economics did not start at the University of Chicago in the 1950s.[28] It was preceded by the German ordo-liberals, who endorsed a clear instrumentalist view of the legal system by viewing legal rules, such as cartel prohibition, as tools to attain economic goals. As stated by Franz Böhm, the language of economics must be translated into the language of legal sciences to create the conditions for an effectively functioning competitive market.[29]

The ordoliberal view of society was distinguished by a search for a third way between capitalism (market economy) and socialism (command economy). After the First World War, Europe experienced a renaissance of theoretical liberalism, which tried to avoid the disadvantages of the old liberal *laissez-faire* system without moving to extreme state interventionism and centrally planned economic systems (as came into existence in Russia after the October Revolution of 1917). After the Second World War, the question of the socialisation of production reached the top of the German political agenda. The close cooperation between German heavy industry and the Hitler regime, which led to a cartel stimulating policy (*Zwangskartelle*) had to be dismantled. Both socialists and liberals agreed on the need for anti-monopoly measures (*Dekartellierungsgesetze*). The liberals, however, took the position that individual freedom is a primary social goal, which can be guaranteed only if economic freedom and private property are protected. The third way between capitalism and socialism became known as the "social market economy", which is an open market with social justice and individual freedom. The ordoliberals of the Freiburg School accepted the main idea of classical liberalism, viewing economic freedom as the corollary of political freedom and competition as the main instrument to realise a free society. However, in the ordoliberal view, a legal framework is necessary to protect individual economic freedom not only against governmental interference, but also against private economic power. The role of the legislature is to define the basic rules governing economic activities in an economic constitution and then step back. Economic processes should remain free but need a framework to achieve their

---

[28] In the same period (but, again, later than in Europe) at Harvard University lawyers and economists also worked together in the field of competition policy. See the well-known book by C. Kaysen and D.F. Turner, *Antitrust Policy: An Economic and Legal Analysis* (1959), discussed in s.3.5.2.2.

[29] F. Böhm, cited in D.J. Gerber, *Law and Competition in Twentieth Century Europe* (1998), p.46.

beneficial results. As formulated by Eucken: "Staatliche Planung der Formen—ja; Staatliche Planung und Lenkung des Wirtschaftsprozesses—nein".[30] Consequently, competition law should also consist of general, broad rules and not be interventionist.

The Freiburg School assigned competition law a central role in the whole economic order. The ordoliberals believed that the economy operates better under fierce competition. In Eucken's view, the goal to be achieved is *vollständiger Wettbewerb* (complete competition). This notion is close to the notion of perfect competition. As explained in the first chapter, numerous unrealistic criteria must be satisfied to achieve perfect competition. But, according to Eucken, it should suffice to ensure that firms which are active in the market are price-takers. In this vein, Eucken also emphasised the importance of free access to the market, which excludes scope for coercion by incumbent firms. In a market of *vollständiger Wettbewerb*, no firm has the power to forcibly influence the conduct of other firms.[31] Accordingly, for ordoliberals, the ideal market form is a polyopoly.[32] According to the authors of the Freiburg School, the state should create the legal framework to make "complete competition" (*vollständiger Wettbewerb*) possible and must, where this ideal cannot be attained, enact regulations to simulate the outcome of "complete competition" (firms acting as price-takers). To achieve a competitive system, the ordoliberals proposed seven constitutive and three regulating principles. The former principles embraced the price system of "complete competition", the creation of a stable currency, private property, contractual freedom, liability of market participants (risk of bankruptcy), free access to markets and a continuous economic policy. The regulating principles were an active anti-monopoly policy, an income policy correcting the weaknesses of the market system and a social policy.

The main contribution of the Freiburg School is the emphasis put on the need to transfer responsibility for achieving competition from *laissez faire* to a strong state. With respect to the concrete contents of a competition law, different opinions existed among the members of the Freiburg School. They, however, all subscribed to the following common principles. The primary task of competition law is to protect the competitive process from private economic power. According to Böhm, competition rules should protect the freedom of individuals, which is an indispensable condition for attaining effective competition.[33] The mere existence of monopolies is completely inconsistent with the idea of *vollständiger Wettbewerb*, which excludes the possession of coercive power. According to the ordoliberal views, a strict and general prohibition of horizontal cartels and a preventive merger control should prevent the creation

---

[30] "State planning of structures—yes; state planning and direction of economic processes—no" (authors' translation), see W. Eucken, "Die Wettbewerbsordnung und ihre Verwirklichung" (1949) ORDO, Band 2, 93.

[31] W. Eucken, *Die Grundlagen der Nationalökonomie* (8th ed., 1965). On German ordoliberalism, see also W. Möschel, "Competition Policy from an Ordo Point of View", in *German Neo-Liberals and the Social Market Economy* (A. Peacock and H. Willgerodt ed., 1989), pp.142–159.

[32] H. Bartling, "Schlußfolgerungen aus Entwicklungstendenzen der Wettbewerbstheorie für die Wettbewerbspolitik" (1993) 43 WuW 28.

[33] F. Böhm, *Das Problem der privaten Macht* (1928), cited in D. Gerber, *op.cit.*, p.251.

of monopolies in markets where the conditions of complete competition are still satisfied. In other markets, state intervention requiring dissolution of cartels, divestitures and control of remaining monopolies should realise or simulate the outcomes under complete competition. Firms possessing economic power should be forced to behave "as if" *vollständiger Wettbewerb* existed, in particular with respect to their pricing decisions. The enforcement of the competition rules should be entrusted to an independent competition authority, which is free from pressure by interest groups. Many features of German competition law clearly reflect ordoliberal views. Examples are the concept of *Als-Ob-Preis*, which was used to assess excessive prices in the framework of the control of firms enjoying a dominant position[34] and the enforcement of the cartel prohibition by the relatively autonomous *Bundeskartellamt*. The German enforcement system thus clearly differs from its US counterpart. In the USA, there are two national competition agencies (Antitrust Division of the Department of Justice and the Federal Trade Commission) and private suits are equally possible. Ordoliberal ideas also affected European competition law. At this point, the reader may be referred to the discussion in the previous chapter, where it was shown that the formulation of the cartel prohibition (Article 81 EC) and the ban on abuses of a dominant position (Article 82 EC) have a clear ordoliberal touch.[35]

3.5 The Harvard approach to problems of competition policy

3.5.1 The structuralist conception of industrial organisation

In what follows the term Harvard School will be employed to indicate the extensive literature on competition policy that constituted the dominant approach until the 1970s. The Harvard School rejected the application of price theory. Researchers tried to find causal relationships to predict possible results in real-life markets (characterised by a limited number of large firms next to a fringe of small competitors). Under the Harvard approach, the performance of specific industries was seen as dependent on the conduct of firms, which in turn is dependent on the market structure of the industry under investigation. This has become widely known as the "structure–conduct–performance" paradigm which emphasises the direction of causality from structure to conduct to performance. Since the first industrial economists accorded an influential or even determinant role to market structure, their view became known as the structuralist conception of industrial organisation. On the normative level, Harvard scholars discarded perfect competition as the ideal to be aimed at. The concept of workable competition was suggested instead as a blueprint

---

[34] A landmark case is BGH, February 12, 1980, WRP, 1980, 259 (*Valium II*). For a comment, see V. Emmerich, *Kartellrecht* (1994), para.17.14.
[35] See Ch.2, s.2.4.5.

for competition policy. In order to determine whether a specific industry satisfies the criteria of workable competition, structural components, modes of conduct and performance criteria must be examined.

3.5.1.1 The structure–conduct–performance paradigm

The structure–conduct–performance paradigm was developed by Edward Mason at Harvard University in the late 1930s and early 1940s.[36] Some authors suggest that Chamberlin,[37] who, simultaneously with Robinson,[38] developed the model of monopolistic competition, laid the theoretical basis for the work on structure, conduct and performance.[39] In those works the theoretical relationship between industry structures, on the one hand, and prices and profits, on the other, was examined, and it was precisely this type of relationship that Harvard scholars started to test empirically in the 1950s. The original empirical applications of the new theory were made by Mason's colleagues and students, the most famous of whom being Joe Bain.

The Harvard paradigm implies that market performance (the success of an industry in producing benefits for consumers) in certain industries is dependent on the conduct of sellers and buyers (as regards, for example, prices, advertising, research and development). Conduct, in turn, is determined by the structure of the relevant market (number of buyers and sellers, barriers to entry of new firms, and degree of product differentiation). The structure of an industry depends on basic conditions on both the supply side (such as raw materials, technology, and unionisation of the labour force) and the demand side (such as price elasticity, rate of growth, and purchase method). Government policy, through antitrust laws, regulation and taxes, may affect the basic conditions, the structure of an industry, the conduct of the economic players, and the ultimate performance of an industry.[40] In the initial years of classical industrial organisation the reciprocal relationship between market structure and performance was the principal topic of investigation.[41] Chamberlin proceeded upon the reasonable assumption that firms are profit maximisers and showed that, under monopolistic competition, long-run equilibrium would be achieved where price was equal to average cost. In this vein, Bain stated that the conduct component did not add much information, since information about market structure was sufficient for predictions about performance. Later publications by scholars working in the Harvard tradition also included behavioural criteria as explanatory variables insofar as the relevant

---

[36] E.S. Mason, "Price and Production Policies of Large Scale Enterprises" (1939) 29 Amer. Econ. Rev. 61; E.S. Mason, "The Current State of the Monopoly Problem in the United States" (1949) 62 Harv. L. Rev. 1265.

[37] E.H. Chamberlin, *The Theory of Monopolistic Competition: A Re-orientation of the Theory of Value* (8th ed., 1969).

[38] J. Robinson, *The Economics of Imperfect Competition* (2nd ed., 1969).

[39] D.A. Hay and D.J. Morris, *Industrial Economics and Organization: Theory and Evidence* (1991).

[40] Scherer and Ross introduced Public Policy as a fifth block, next to Basic Conditions, Market Structure, Market Conduct and Market Performance; compare F.M. Scherer and D. Ross, *Industrial Market Structure and Economic Performance* (3rd ed., 1990), p.5.

[41] J.S. Bain, *Industrial Organisation* (2nd ed., 1968).

information was available. By the addition of conduct a much richer model arises and predictions can be made with more precision and confidence.[42]

The relationship among basic conditions, structure, conduct, performance and government policy is complex. The Bain paradigm analysed industries in terms of a causative chain from structure to conduct to performance. However, there are also feedback effects from conduct to market structure and basic conditions, and from market structure to basic conditions. For example, sellers' pricing policies (conduct) may either encourage entry or drive firms out of the market, thereby affecting the number of competitors (market structure), and advertising (conduct) may be used to make the demand for products offered less elastic (basic conditions). Together with the criticisms by the Chicago School relating to the weaknesses of the empirical work conducted by Harvard scholars, these feedback effects seem to diminish the predictive power of the structure–conduct–performance paradigm. Modern industrial organisation theory emphasises the effects of conduct (strategic interaction) on industry structure.[43]

There are hundreds of studies that attempt to relate market structure to market performance. In these studies three major measures of market performance are used: (1) the rate of return, which is based upon profits earned per dollar of investment; (2) the price–costs margin, which should be based upon the difference between price and marginal costs, although in practice some form of average costs is used instead; and (3) Tobin's q,[44] which is the ratio of the market value of a firm to its value based upon the replacement costs of its assets.[45] To examine how performance varies with structure additional measures of market structure are needed. Industry concentration is typically measured as a function of the market shares of some or all of the firms in a market. Examples include the eight-firm concentration ratio (CR8) which is the sum of the market shares of the eight largest firms and the four-firm concentration ratio (CR4) that focuses attention on the top four firms in measuring concentration. Alternatively, market structure may be measured by using a function of all the individual firms' market shares. The Herfindahl–Hirschman Index (HHI) is the sum of the squares of the market share of every firm in the relevant market.[46]

In 1951 Bain had already investigated 42 industries and separated them into two groups, depending upon whether the CR8 was higher than 70 per cent. He found evidence that the rate of return was higher for the more concentrated industries (11.8 per cent) than for the less concentrated industries (7.5 per cent).[47] In 1956 Bain published his seminal book *Barriers to New Competition*, in

[42] The most important textbook of the structuralist conception is: F.M. Scherer and D. Ross, *Industrial Market Structure and Economic Performance* (3rd ed., 1990), pp.37–38.
[43] See s.3.10.
[44] J. Tobin, "A General Equilibrium Approach to Monetary Theory" (1969) 1 J. Money Cred. Bank. 15.
[45] See for more details: D.W. Carlton and J.M. Perloff, *Modern Industrial Organization* (4th ed., 2005), pp.246–254.
[46] Further discussed in Ch.9, s.9.2.1.3.
[47] J. Bain, "Relation of Profit Rate to Industry Concentration: American Manufacturing 1936–1940" (1951) 65 Quart. J. Econ. 293.

which he argued that profit rates are higher in industries with high concentration and high barriers to entry. Bain's sample included 20 manufacturing industries with relatively high concentration levels. The CR4 was used as a
measure of market concentration. Even though Bain recognised the theoretical
superiority of the price–marginal cost margin, he used the accounting rate of
return on stockholder's equity as a measure of profitability for informational
reasons. Bain's 1956 study also included a detailed (but subjective[48]) analysis
of entry conditions, based on publicly available material and information from
a survey. The relationship between concentration and profitability appeared to
be consistent with his earlier work, especially when entry barriers were substantial. In addition, Bain discovered that large firms in industries with very
high barriers to entry (e.g. automobiles, cigarettes) generally earned higher
rates of return (23.9 per cent in the automobile industry and 18.6 per cent in
the liquor industry) than large firms in industries with lower entry barriers
(e.g. 10.1 per cent in the flour industry and 5.1 per cent in the meat packing
industry). In the Bain sample higher barriers to entry were associated with
greater profitability for large firms. Bain concluded that concentration allows
collusion (tacit or otherwise) and that collusion generates excess profit if entry
into the industry is difficult. These effects were observed mainly for large
firms.[49] Other authors replicated Bain's work for later time periods. The results
were generally consistent with Bain's findings.[50] An early econometric study
by Collins and Preston equally confirmed the relationship between profitability, used as a measure of market power, and various industry structural
characteristics.[51]

3.5.1.2 The concept of workable competition

The concept of workable competition came about as a result of the publication,
in 1940, of Clark's classic article "Toward a Concept of Workable Competition".[52] This publication ultimately brought about a radical change in thinking
concerning competition policy. In the 1930s Robinson and Chamberlin had
developed models of imperfect competition (oligopoly, monopolistic competition), but their viewpoints contained no radically altered perspective as far as
policy recommendations were concerned. Economic analysis of competition
problems was reoriented towards real-life market situations, but the model of

---

[48] In contrast to Bain's subjective judgments, later empirical work uses objective standards to
measure entry barriers: minimum efficient scale as a fraction of industry output (to assess scale
economies) and the advertising sales ratio (to assess product differentiation).
[49] J. Bain, *Barriers to New Competition* (1956).
[50] See, e.g. H.M. Mann, "Seller Concentration, Barriers to Entry and Rates of Return in Thirty
Industries, 1950–1960" (1966) 48 Rev. Econ. Statist. 296.
[51] N.R. Collins and L.E. Preston, "Price–Cost Margins and Industry Structure" (1969) 51 Rev. Econ.
Statist. 271. This study did not explicitly control for differences in entry conditions across industries. Later empirical work showed the importance of product differentiation in determining price–
costs margins (A.D. Strickland and L.W. Weiss, "Advertising, Concentration, and Price–Cost
Margins" (1976) 84 J. Pol. Econ. 1109. See for more recent research results, *inter alia*, I. Domowitz,
G.R. Hubbard and B.C. Petersen, "Business Cycles and the Relationship between Concentration
and Price–Cost Margins" (1986) 17 RAND J. Econ. 1.
[52] J.M. Clark, "Toward a Concept of Workable Competition" (1940) 30 Amer. Econ. Rev. 241.

perfect competition was still applied as a policy guideline. Market imperfections had to be corrected whenever and wherever possible in order to achieve, or at least approximate, perfect competition. Clark had an aversion to mathematic static equilibrium models and he followed Mason's approach to case studies. Initially, Clark also tried to maintain perfect competition as a norm. In his later work, which was influenced by Schumpeter, Clark emphasised the dynamics of competition once he had realised that perfect competition did not exist, could not exist, and had probably never existed. Accordingly, the theoretical model of perfect competition does not provide a reliable standard by which to evaluate real market conditions. Furthermore, Clark emphasised that, in the long run, market imperfections were not bound to be injurious *per se*. Not all market imperfections should be eliminated by competition policy, for market imperfections can neutralise each other—this became known as the "antidote theory". For example, informational uncertainty may be desirable to prevent collusion in markets with few suppliers. Persistent market imperfections are therefore no obstacle to workable competition. Competition policy should not seek to achieve the ideal of perfect competition, but should, instead, formulate criteria for judging to what extent an industry is workably competitive.

The views of Mason and Clark initiated a great number of case studies, starting with the structure–conduct–performance paradigm, in order to assess the existence of workable competition in different sectors of the economy. Sosnick published an admirable overview of the almost unmanageable bulk of the US literature on the subject.[53] Taking their cue from Sosnick's scheme, Scherer and Ross have established criteria for judging whether or not an industry is workably competitive.[54] The relevant criteria can be grouped into three categories, as summarised in Box 3.1.

Box 3.1: The structure–conduct–performance paradigm: criteria

STRUCTURAL CRITERIA:

- The number of firms must be at least as great as economies of scale will permit.

- There must be no artificial restraints on entry or mobility.

- The products on offer must have moderate and price-sensitive differences in quality.

---

[53] S. Sosnick, "A Critique of Concepts of Workable Competition" (1958) 72 Quart. J. Econ. 380.
[54] F.M. Scherer and D. Ross, *Industrial Market Structure and Economic Performance* (3rd ed., 1990), p.5.

CONDUCT CRITERIA:

- Competitors must be subject to a degree of uncertainty as to the extent to which price initiatives will be followed.

- Firms must pursue their objectives independently without reciprocal agreements.

- No unfair trade practices or exclusion measures must be used.

- Inefficient suppliers and customers must not be constantly protected.

- Advertising must be informative and not misleading.

- There must be no harmful, persistent price discrimination.

PERFORMANCE CRITERIA:

- Firms' production and distribution processes must be efficient and must not waste resources.

- Production levels and product quality (differentiation, product-life, safety, reliability) must accord with customers' wishes.

- Profits must reach just the right level to ensure investment, efficiency and innovation.

- Price levels must encourage rational choice, steer markets towards equilibrium and prevent the reinforcement of cyclical instability.

- Opportunities to introduce superior technical products and processes must be exploited.

- Advertising expenditure must not be excessive.

- Success must go to the sellers who respond best to consumers' wishes.

Box 3.1 shows, among other things, that there are a number of criteria whose fulfillment will be very difficult to measure. More important still is the fact that it is not clear how the presence of workable competition is to be established if some, but not all, of the criteria are satisfied. If the performance criteria are satisfied, but the structural ones are not, the main criterion in Harvard writings seems to be the acceptability of performance. Such difficulties will increase if some, but not all, performance dimensions are fulfilled. When the workability test is applied, the resulting second-best problems can thus be particularly serious. In addition, it must be stressed that the performance criteria may not be completely consistent with one another. Good performance is multi-dimensional. It embodies productive efficiency, allocative efficiency and dynamic efficiency (progress). If workable competition is to be used as the normative criterion, what decision must be taken when a proposed merger might allow firms to earn supernormal profits (allocative inefficiency) but at the same time produces substantial cost savings (increased productive efficiency)?[55] How does one solve Clark's well-known dilemma according to which economic progress requires acceptance of restrictions on competition (for example, patents)? In the absence of unbiased empirical evidence these conflicts cannot be resolved without invoking basic value judgments.

3.5.2 Policy conclusions

The Harvard School's vision, which emphasises the relationship between market power, business conduct and market results, considerably extends the scope of liability based on competition law. In its simplest version the paradigm condemns positions of strength and barriers to entry if they are not related to economies of scale. In the USA, the Harvard analysis became the cornerstone of competition policy in the 1960s and remained so until the neo-classical and neo-institutional approaches began to win the upper hand in the mid-1970s.

3.5.2.1 Harvard axioms

The principal tenets of the Harvard School of industrial organisation can be summarised as follows:

1. The perfect competition and monopoly models must be supplemented with the more realistic and useful models of imperfect competition (monopolistic competition and oligopoly).

2. Investigation should be concentrated not on individual economic agents but on whole branches of industry or on a group of firms within a given industry.

3. The objective at which antitrust law should aim is not perfect competition but workable competition.

4. The appraisal of the competitiveness of a given activity cannot be the result of logical-theoretical deductive reasoning; it must be a factual judgment. Empirical investigation is essential in order to be able to evaluate the competitiveness of particular branches of industry. Such a factual judgment is based on structural determinism: the structure of the market influences the conduct of firms and the conduct of firms in turn influences performance (the famous Harvard paradigm).

In the 1960s and even more in the 1970s, partly as a response to the emerging opposite views of the Chicago School, the preoccupation with market structure evolved into a wider concern incorporating exclusionary conduct, that is,

---

[55] On this issue, see P.D. Camesasca, *European Merger Control: Getting the Efficiencies Right* (2000).

business behaviour creating market power where it otherwise would not exist or enabling existing market power to sustain super-competitive prices over a period of time. According to the Harvard view, the most onerous of these exclusionary practices is business conduct erecting barriers to entry. Bain identified as barriers to entry scale economies, absolute cost advantages of existing firms, and product differentiation supported by intensive advertising.[56] Later empirical research, conducted by Harvard scholars, showed substantial differences in profit rates between firms with and without differentiated products and concluded that much of this profit rate differential is accounted for by the entry barriers created by advertising expenditure and the resulting achievement of market power.[57] In contemporary writings the old Harvard view on entry barriers is criticised and a more balanced analysis has gained acceptance.[58]

3.5.2.2 Objectives of competition policy

At the policy level the Harvard approach also includes non-economic objectives. In their influential book *Antitrust Policy: An Economic and Legal Analysis*, Kaysen and Turner distinguished four objectives of competition policy: first, to achieve favourable economic results; second, to create and maintain competitive processes; third, to prescribe norms of fair conduct; and, fourth, to restrict the growth of large firms.[59] Their most important views concerning a proper competition policy can be summarised as follows. Efficiency and progress (implying increased sales, the development of new techniques, and the production of new and better products) are considered as the most important economic results which can be substantially influenced by competition policy. Thereafter, stability of employment and a fair distribution of income are stated to be the desired results for the whole economy. For Kaysen and Turner, the second aim which competition policy can achieve is of essential importance. The need to create competitive processes receives special emphasis, namely by promoting competition as an aim in itself instead of as a means of achieving desired economic results. Competition is justified from the point of view of limiting the power of firms. It is therefore linked with the fourth objective of competition policy. The discussion by Kaysen and Turner concerning fair competition is also founded on the importance of competition. Because competition replaces personal control by large firms or by state bureaucracies with impersonal control by the market, it is presented as a means of guaranteeing fairness. According to Kaysen and Turner, it is fairer if restraints on conduct are imposed by the market, rather than through a

---

[56] J. Bain, "Relation of Profit Rate to Industry Concentration: American Manufacturing 1936–1940" (1951) 65 Quart. J. Econ. 293.

[57] W.S. Comanor and T.A. Wilson, "Advertising, Market Structure and Performance" (1967) 49 Rev. Econ. Statist. 437.

[58] See, e.g. D. Harbord and T. Hoehn, "Barriers to Entry and Exit in European Competition Policy" (1994) 14 Int. Rev. Law Econ. 411.

[59] C. Kaysen and D.F. Turner, *Antitrust Policy, An Economic and Legal Analysis* (1959). Compare also E.T. Sullivan, *The Political Economy of the Sherman Act, The First One Hundred Years* (1991), giving a complete and orthodox description of the Harvard views.

dominant position or state regulation.[60] Competitive processes can provide one yardstick for measuring the fairness of business conduct, but it is certainly not the only one. This concept of fairness can thus have various meanings. It can signify similar treatment for firms in similar circumstances. The term can likewise be considered as being synonymous with fair play, which can be interpreted, in the market context, as refraining from the use of market power and thus seeking to achieve reasonable profits rather than maximum profits. According to these views of the concept of fairness, it should be permissible to protect smaller firms at the expense of society as a whole. In the latter case, guaranteeing fairness coincides with the fourth objective of competition policy by spreading economic power through restrictions on large firms. Competition policy can reduce the size of firms both directly (for example, by dismantling dominant positions) and indirectly by restrictions on conduct (for example, through rules prohibiting abuse of a dominant position). It should be noted, however, that Kaysen and Turner admit that the four possible objectives of competition policy are partly inconsistent with each other. In relation to economies of scale, for example, the aims of seeking fairness and redistributing power as between large and small firms are placed on a lower hierarchical level of policy.

3.5.2.3 Practical impact on antitrust law

United States The Harvard view had a substantial impact on American antitrust policy in the 1950s and 1960s. In spite of contemporary criticisms questioning the results of the empirical research, the broad generalisation that price–costs margins and profits vary with the number of rivals and the size of barriers to entry entered US antitrust policy and exerted a noticeable influence upon it, especially in the field of merger control. The original Harvard view, best characterised by Kaysen and Turner's book, was that market power *per se* is harmful and therefore should be illegal.[61] The focus of analysis was on market structure rather than on business conduct as the source of adverse economic performance.[62] The Harvard School emphasised structural solutions. If it is believed that large firms use their market power to earn supernormal profits, then mergers must be closely scrutinised. Bain suggested divestitures in highly concentrated markets. In his view, if the eight largest firms account for two-thirds of production, powerful firms must be broken up so as to produce an oligopoly with only a moderate degree of concentration.[63]

In the US Department of Justice's 1968 Merger Guidelines,[64] it was stated that an analysis of market structure was fully adequate for showing that the

[60] Kaysen and Turner's views should be related to the discussion of the goals of competition law in the second chapter of this book.
[61] Compare the ordoliberal view, described in s.3.4 of this chapter.
[62] C. Kaysen and D.F. Turner, *Antitrust Policy, An Economic and Legal Analysis* (1959), p.82.
[63] J.S. Bain, *Industrial Organisation* (2nd ed., 1968) p.648. For a neo-classical criticism of such break-up programmes, see R.A. Posner, "Problems of a Policy of Deconcentration", in *Industrial Concentration, The New Learning* (H. Goldschmid, H.M. Mann and J.F. Weston ed., 1974), pp.393–400.
[64] US Department of Justice, Antitrust Division, press release, Merger Guidelines, May 30, 1968, reprinted in (1978) Trade Reg. Rep. 4, para.13.101.

effect of a merger, as spelled out in s.7 of the Clayton Act,[65] "may be substantially to lessen competition, or to tend to create a monopoly". The Department announced that its merger policy would focus on market struc- ture "because the conduct of the individual firms in a market tends to be controlled by the structure of that market". An enforcement policy empha- sising a limited number of structural factors would not only produce adequate economic predictions for the showing of anti-competitive effects, but would also facilitate both enforcement decision making and business planning. Only in exceptional circumstances would structural factors alone be inconclusive (for example, in the case of conglomerate mergers). With respect to horizontal mergers, the 1968 Merger Guidelines used the CR4 ratio as a market con- centration measure: when the shares of the four largest firms amounted to approximately 75 per cent or more, the market was regarded as highly con- centrated. The Department stated its intention to challenge mergers when the market shares of both the acquiring firms and the acquired firms exceeded a certain threshold; for example, in highly concentrated markets mergers between firms accounting both for approximately 4 per cent of the market would be challenged; in less highly concentrated markets a 5 per cent market share for both the acquiring and the acquired firms was used as the relevant threshold. The Merger Guidelines were revised several times (in 1982, 1984, 1992 and 1997) to take account of developments in economic thinking con- cerning the competitive effects of mergers. In the 1997 Merger Guidelines,[66] there is no longer an explicit reference to the structure–conduct–performance paradigm; instead, the current Merger Guidelines explicitly allow for an efficiency defence, which clearly reflects the influence of the Chicago School.

Europe   From what is said above, it should be clear that the Harvard School is sympathetic to far-reaching government intervention and extends the scope of liability based on competition law. In addition, the concept of workable competition, which, albeit undefined, is used as a blueprint for competition policy, confers large discretionary powers on the competition authorities. These views still have a clear impact on European competition policy. The competition law of the European Community can best be described as a piece- meal policy which aims at workable competition in the common market. It dramatically reflects the difficult choices that have to be made when the first best solutions are not available. Notwithstanding the fact that it is unlikely that the authors of the Treaty of Rome were aware of the concept of workable

---

[65] Clayton Act, 15 U.S.C. § 17 (1976).
[66] US Department of Justice and Federal Trade Commission, Horizontal Merger Guidelines, April 2, 1992, reprinted in (1978) Trade Reg. Rep. 4, para.13.104; the April 8, 1997 revision to this section may be retrieved from the DoJ website (*www.usdoj.gov/atr/public/guidelines/sec4.htm*); while a fully integrated version of the guidelines is to be found at the FTC homepage (*www.ftc.gov/bc/docs/ horizmer.htm*). Unless specified differently, reference is given to the updated 1992/1997 version.

competition,[67] many of the distinguishing features of European competition policy seem to fit nicely into this theoretical framework. It is noteworthy that the European Court of Justice, in its leading *Metro* judgment, referred to the concept of workable competition as being the type of competition that was necessary to achieve the economic objectives of the EC Treaty.[68] This judgment was concerned with the lawfulness of selective distribution agreements. Once technical and luxury products are sold—for resale—only to recognised distributors, one can no longer discern a market which accords with the model of perfect competition. On the other hand, it is indeed possible to speak of workable competition if the product differentiation, which is thus created, is moderate (see the criteria in Box 3.1). In *Metro*, the European Court of Justice emphasised that price competition is not the only form of competition for wholesalers and retailers. It considered that it was in consumers' interests for prices to be set at a certain level in order to be able to support a network of specialised dealers alongside a parallel system of dealers who themselves provide services and undertake other actions to keep distribution costs down. This choice was made available to certain sectors in which high quality, technically advanced and durable goods are produced and distributed. In its effect, the *Metro* judgment gave the green light to selective distribution systems. The current law on vertical restraints in distribution contracts is described and critically examined in Chapter 6.

The Harvard approach also became very popular in Germany as Kantzenbach published his well-known book on the workability of competition in 1967.[69] In this work Kantzenbach plainly rejected the use of the perfect competition model as a policy guideline and defended the position that workable competition can be achieved in a broadly oligopolistic market structure with a low degree of product differentiation and informational uncertainty. This approach stood in stark contrast to previous policy recommendations made by ordoliberal authors, such as Eucken[70] and Böhm,[71] who proposed a polyopolistic market structure as the ideal market form. The structuralist conception of competition policy was challenged by Hoppmann, who advanced the alternative concept of freedom of competition (*Konzept der Wettbewerbsfreiheit*) as a blueprint for competition policy. This alternative, dynamic view will be presented later in this chapter. Current German competition policy still relies

---

[67] It was mainly political necessity, rather than this or that economic theory, that made an active competition policy necessary in the eyes of the authors of the Treaty. The elimination of market compartmentalisation caused by restrictions on competition was necessary in order to achieve the central objective of integrating national markets. European competition policy was an instrument for opening up new sales territories in order to stimulate economic progress, sustained by the efforts of independent firms from all the Member States. This aim of market integration is essential for an understanding of the principal characteristics of European competition law.

[68] Case 26/76 *Metro SB-Großmärkte GmbH and Co KG v Commission* [1977] ECR 1875, para.20. In another case, however, the Court used the expression "normal competition", which is not based on any economic theory at all: Case 85/76 *Hoffmann-La Roche v Commission (Vitamins)* [1979] ECR 461. One must therefore be cautious when subjecting judgments of the European Court of Justice to an economic analysis.

[69] E. Kantzenbach, *Die Funktionsfähigkeit des Wettbewerbs* (1966).

[70] W. Eucken, *Die Grundlagen der Nationalökonomie* (1965).

[71] F. Böhm, *Wettbewerb und Monopolkampf: Eine Untersuchung zur Frage des wirtschaftlichen Kampfrechts und zur Frage der rechtlichen Strukturen der geltenden Wirtschaftsordnung* (1933).

heavily on the Harvard axioms, though. Competition is mostly seen as a goal in itself, with increasing market concentration being superstitiously guarded. Most illustrative of this approach is the opinion of the Bundeskartellamt's former President Wolf, who considered the proposals to introduce into European merger control an efficiency defence along the lines of the US Merger Guidelines to be "superfluous, if not dangerous".[72]

3.6 The Chicago approach to problems of competition policy

Chicago lawyer-economists caused a revolution in thinking about antitrust issues. The basic ideas of the Chicago approach to competition law originated with the economist Aaron Director who, in the 1950s, taught the antitrust course at Chicago University together with the lawyer Edward Levi.[73] Numerous authors such as Bork,[74] Bowman,[75] McGee[76] and Telser[77] elaborated further on Director's core ideas. The Chicago School's starting point can be found in neo-classical price theory. The confrontation between the classical, legal dogmatic approach to antitrust law and the micro-economic mode of analysis gave rise to an extremely rich, new theory based on efficiency.

3.6.1 Chicago versus Harvard

3.6.1.1 The re-emergence of price theory

The notion that the Chicago approach to competition policy is merely the result of the rejection of government intervention in the economy is a misunderstanding of frequent occurrence. On the contrary, Director reached his conclusions by viewing competition problems through focusing on price theory.[78] Unlike the traditional Harvard economists, who devoted themselves to studying specific industries and examining competition problems on the basis of observable phenomena through empirical research, instead of having recourse to a general economic theory, Director sought an explanation for practices observed in real markets which tallied with economic theory's profit maximisation principle.

The Chicago views are derived from the central tenets of neo-classical price

---

[72] D. Wolf, "The Reform of EU Competition Law: Member State Perspectives" in Fordham Corp. L. Inst. 1996, 169, 171 (B. Hawk ed., 1997).

[73] Director formulated his ideas mainly orally (R.A. Posner, "The Chicago School of Antitrust Analysis" (1979) 127 U. Pa. L. Rev. 925).

[74] R.H. Bork, "Vertical Integration and the Sherman Act: The Legal History of an Economic Misconception" (1954) 22 U. Chi. L. Rev. 157; R.H. Bork, *The Antitrust Paradox: A Policy at War with Itself* (2nd ed., 1993). This book gives the most complete and orthodox overview of the doctrine of the Chicago School.

[75] W.S. Bowman, "Tying Arrangements and the Leverage Problem" (1957) 67 Yale L.J. 19.

[76] J.S. McGee, "Predatory Price Cutting. The Standard Oil (N.J.) Case" (1958) 1 J. Law Econ. 137.

[77] L.G. Telser, "Why Should Manufacturers Want Fair Trade?" (1960) 3 J. Law Econ. 86.

[78] R.A. Posner, "The Chicago School of Antitrust Analysis" (1979) 127 U. Pa. L. Rev. 925.

theory. From this perspective, the Chicago School has developed a powerful, if controversial, philosophy of competition. As stated above, price theory proceeds upon the assumption that firms which behave in a rational economic manner will seek to maximise their profits; firms that do not will not survive over time. Director adds to this the assumption that, failing proof to the contrary, conduct based on the maximisation of profits can be considered as competitive conduct and that, in principle, markets are capable of correcting eventual imperfections by themselves. Most markets are believed to be competitive, even if they contain relatively few firms; if price competition is reduced, other non-price forms of competition will fill the gap. The Chicago School also believes that monopolies will not last forever. High profits earned by dominant firms will attract new entry that will erode the positions of dominance. On the basis of these axioms, it is possible to explain the market conduct of firms and to formulate two guidelines for antitrust policy.[79] The first guideline states that conduct aimed at maximising profits must, in principle, be regarded as lawful. The second guideline states that the question whether a given conduct is or is not competitive should not be answered on the basis of some abstract economic model; what should be examined instead, is whether or not the conduct is economically efficient. As a result, antitrust law should present no hindrance to efficient forms of conduct as the legal rules should be aimed solely at promoting efficiency.

The most remarkable differences between the Harvard and Chicago Schools can be summarised as follows:

1. The Harvard School is criticised for lack of theory.[80] Chicago economists seek explanations for practices observed in real markets which conform to the foundations of economic theory. In this vein, practices that were previously thought to be anti-competitive (such as vertical restraints) are rationalised.

2. The structure–conduct–performance paradigm is rejected. The positive correlation between structure and performance is not seen as a loss of welfare caused by market power, but simply as the consequence of higher efficiency. The allocative efficiencies associated with economies of scale and scope are thought to be of paramount importance.

3. In contrast with the multitude of goals accepted by the Harvard School, productive efficiency and allocative efficiency are advanced as the only objectives to be taken into account in interpreting and applying antitrust law. When markets generate inefficient outcomes (which is considered to

---

[79] R.A. Posner, *Antitrust Law: An Economic Perspective* (1976).

[80] One of the harshest critics is Posner, who argues that Harvard's version of industrial organisation consists of "casual observation of business behavior, colorful characterizations (such as the term 'barriers to entry'), eclectic forays into sociology and psychology, descriptive statistics, and verification by plausibility which took the place of the careful definitions and parsimonious logical structure of economic theory. The result was that industrial organization regularly advanced propositions that contradicted economic theory", see R.A. Posner, "The Chicago School of Antitrust Analysis" (1979) 127 U. Pa. L. Rev. 925 at p.931.

be unlikely) government intervention (which is considered prone to failure) is appropriate only if it improves economic efficiency.

These differences are further explained below by focusing on a number of examples: vertical restraints, merger control and entry barriers.[81]

3.6.1.2 Vertical restraints

Director and Stigler[82] provided industrial organisation with something which the Harvard School did not have: a theory to explain collusion and so-called exclusionary practices. One of the best known examples is the efficiency explanation of minimum resale price maintenance, which traditionally had been seen as a way of keeping prices high to the benefit of traders and to the detriment of consumers. In 1960 Telser published an article on vertical restraints which has since become a classic.[83] In this essay, the so-called free rider problem plays a central role in explaining vertical price fixing, whereto it is important to understand properly a producer's motives in imposing resale price maintenance. If the dealers' margins increase, retail prices will also rise and a drop in the number of products sold will ensue. A fall in the producer's profits should therefore be expected. However, there are also circumstances in which vertical price fixing improves the producer's position because the advantages arising from efficiency exceed the short-term, disadvantageous consequences flowing from the reduction in demand resulting from the (dealers') higher profit margins. An increase in services and in publicity as a result of the fixing of minimum retail prices can enhance the value of the product to a more extensive group of consumers and should be able to generate increased demand. It should, therefore, be potentially advantageous for a rational producer marketing differentiated products to use resale price maintenance with a view to encouraging his retailers to offer special services. Sales promoting publicity in the form of advertisements, displays of goods and demonstrations adds to the retail price. A competitor who does not invest in the same publicity can profit from the advertising of others and will thus be able to sell at a lower price. Without higher prices, however, fewer services would be provided because consumers could buy from low price dealers while still receiving the services elsewhere. Vertical price fixing imposed by the producer thus prevents this sort of free riding and encourages retailers to offer an optimum level of pre-sales service.[84]

The free riding argument is not only used in the analysis of vertical price fixing but has been extended to other intra-brand restraints such as the reservation of exclusive sales territories (exclusive distribution) and exclusive

---

[81] For a more elaborate discussion see Chs 6, 9 and 4, s.4.3.

[82] Stigler emphasised the difficulties in maintaining collusive agreements, rendering them profitable only at the highest levels of concentration, see G. Stigler, "A Theory of Oligopoly" (1964) 72 J. Polit. Economy 44. As a result the Chicago School does not assign much importance to the empirical relationship between concentration and monopoly power, see R.H. Bork, *The Antitrust Paradox: A Policy at War with Itself* (2nd ed., 1993), p.178.

[83] L.G. Telser, "Why Should Manufacturers Want Fair Trade?", (1960) 3 J. Law Econ. 86.

[84] For further elaboration upon this argument see Ch.6, s.6.2.2.

sales channels (selective distribution, franchising). Protection against free riding may also explain inter-brand restraints such as exclusive purchasing. Exclusive distribution agreements address free riding of one dealer on the efforts of another, whereas exclusive purchasing agreements address free riding of one manufacturer on the efforts of another. Exclusive purchasing agreements can be understood as a means of protecting the manufacturer's property rights in cases in which he possesses informational advantages and is therefore better placed to regulate the sale of his own products.[85]

3.6.1.3 The Chicago School and merger control

It is in the field of merger control that the approaches of the Chicago School and the Harvard School diverge most strongly. The nub of this difference lies in the explanations for the positive relationship, established in many empirical investigations, between concentration and price–cost margins and profits. Policy makers who lean towards the Harvard School refer to studies which are alleged to prove that concentrations lead to the acquisition of market strength which facilitates collusion, which, in turn, makes it possible to set prices above the competitive level. It is claimed that leading firms in highly concentrated industries knowingly develop parallel conduct aimed at achieving super-normal profits. Writers of the Chicago School have initiated an intense debate about the linkage between structure and performance and its implications for competition policy. They argue that large firms are more efficient than smaller ones and will therefore grow more rapidly at a given price level, thus strengthening the tendency towards a higher degree of concentration without thereby causing problems of abuse of market power. If the efficient firms are given room to grow, consumers will profit in the end because scarce resources are then set free to satisfy consumers' wishes in other sectors of the economy.

The trend of the Chicago School's thinking is that the positive relationship between structure and performance is not necessarily indicative of a loss of welfare caused by market power, but is simply the consequence of higher efficiency. Demsetz[86] argued that some products are more efficiently produced by large firms, while in other industries large market shares are not necessary for efficiency. Industries in which large firms have cost advantages will become more concentrated than industries where scale economies are less important. Large firms will have higher profit rates than small firms because their costs are lower, not because they are able to hold the price above the level needed to cover the costs of smaller, less efficient firms. Market concentration and high industry average rates of return both result from efficiency savings

[85] See H.P. Marvel, "Exclusive Dealing" (1982) 25 J. Law Econ. 6.
[86] H. Demsetz, "Industry Structure, Market Rivalry and Public Policy" (1973) 16 J. Law Econ. 1; Demsetz, *The Market Concentration Doctrine* (1973); Demsetz, "Two Systems of Belief about Monopoly", in *Industrial Concentration: The New Learning* (H.J. Goldschmid, H. M. Mann and J.F. Weston ed., 1974), pp.164–184.

realised by large firms. According to Demsetz and Brozen,[87] the empirical studies of the Harvard School discussed above[88] did not justify the conclusion that the profitability of firms in concentrated sectors is significantly higher than that of firms in sectors where there is no concentration. Rather, the correlation coefficients were very low; there was no linear relationship between concentration and profitability; the samples were too limited and the studies were carried out over too short a period. In concentrated branches of industry profitability is higher in the short term, while in the long term profits fall again. This is simply the result of the operation of the market. More important than the criticisms relating to the methodology employed in empirical studies is the Chicago School's assertion that branches of industry become concentrated because larger firms are more efficient than smaller ones. The market selects the best adapted form of organisation for each branch of industry, and the degree of concentration thus reflects the most efficient form of organisation. To test this thesis empirically, Harvard's study of structure–conduct–performance relationships across fairly large groups of industries was found to be inadequate. Following Demsetz[89] the appropriate empirical test for examining whether collusion or efficiency causes the link between sector performance and concentration consists in comparing the rates of return of large and small firms in specific concentrated industries. If concentration represents collusion, both small and large firms will profit. By contrast, if concentration is the consequence of the greater efficiency of large firms, only the rates of return of the latter will be high.

The lesson for competition policy is clear: market concentration as such is not a problem. In the Chicago view of things, there is only one justifiable objective for competition policy, namely the elimination of inefficiencies resulting from collusive price increases and output restrictions. Even though this danger can materialise above a certain level of concentration, what should be forbidden is not concentration itself but collusion, since the latter has a negative impact on total welfare. In the early 1970s, members of the Chicago School were already sharply criticising an antitrust policy that was based on prejudice against the market results associated with high levels of concentration. Posner stressed that persistent market concentration is not at all synonymous with market power. It is the result of either large scale economies or the ability of some firms to attain economic profits persistently thanks to cost reductions and product improvements. The relevant inquiry is not how

[87] Y. Brozen, "The Antitrust Taskforce Deconcentration Recommendation" (1970) 13 J. Law Econ. 279; Brozen, "Bain's Concentration and Rates of Return Revisited" (1971) 14 J. Law Econ. 351; Brozen, "Deconcentration Reconsidered: Comment" (1971) 14 J. Law Econ. 489; Brozen, "The Persistence of 'High Rates of Return' in High-Stable Concentration Industries" (1971) 14 J. Law Econ. 501; Brozen, "Concentration and Profits: Does Concentration Matter?", in *The Competitive Economy—Selected Readings* (Y. Brozen ed., 1978), pp.135–144; Brozen, "Concentration and Structural Market Disequilibria", in *The Competitive Economy—Selected Readings* (Y. Brozen ed., 1978), pp.259–263.
[88] J.S. Bain, "Relation of Profit Rate to Industry Concentration: American Manufacturing 1936–40" (1951) 65 Quart. J. Econ. 293; H.M. Mann, "Seller Concentration, Barriers to Entry and Rates of Return in Thirty Industries, 1950–60" (1966) 48 Rev. Econ. Statist. 296.
[89] H. Demsetz, "Industry Structure, Market Rivalry and Public Policy" (1973) 16 J. Law Econ. 1 at pp.1–9.

concentration can cause collusion, but rather how economic rents can persist over a period of time without being eroded by new entry.[90]

3.6.1.4 The Chicago view on entry barriers

In the vision of Harvard scholars, barriers to entry are an alternative explanation for continuing concentration and above-normal profits. Following Stigler's attacks on the Harvard School's intellectual foundations, some of the force of this argument has been lost.[91] In the Chicago view, there are no significant barriers to entry except those created by government (licensing laws). Stigler defined a barrier to entry as "a cost of producing (at some or every rate of output) that must be borne by a firm which seeks to enter the industry but is not borne by firms already in the industry".[92] Barriers to entry are present only if the costs for firms entering the market turn out to be higher than the costs for the existing firms. If, for example, it costs US$ 10 million to build the smallest possible efficient factory having an economic life of ten years, then the annual costs for a new entrant will be only US$ 1 million. The existing firms will be confronted with the same annual costs, at least if it is assumed that they also intend to replace their factories. Accordingly, there is no cost disadvantage for the new entrant.[93] In Stigler's approach the importance of barriers to entry is reduced. If his approach is followed, classic barriers to entry such as, for example, significant capital requirements, will present no serious hindrance to market entry. If monopoly profits are achieved and the capital markets are functioning efficiently, it is presumably possible to raise the necessary capital in order to start up in competition. In this approach, advertising potential and product differentiation will likewise not constitute serious barriers to entry. Whereas the Harvard School qualified a great many things as barriers to entry, the Chicago School stressed that one must distinguish between forms of efficiency, such as product differentiation, and artificial entry barriers.[94] The question for antitrust policy is then limited to finding out whether there are any artificial impediments apart from government regulations (licensing requirements) which restrict entry into the market.

3.6.2 Policy conclusions

3.6.2.1 Chicago's guide on antitrust

Where the Harvard School assigned a multitude of goals to competition law, providing the basis for a more interventionist policy, Chicago scholars

---

[90] R.A. Posner, "The Chicago School of Antitrust Analysis" (1979) 127 U. Pa. L. Rev. 925, at p.945.
[91] G. Stigler, *The Organisation of Industry* (1968), pp.67, 94.
[92] *ibid.*, p.67. Compare with J.S. Bain, *Barriers to New Competition* (1956), p.3, defining entry barriers as "the advantages of established sellers in an industry over potential entrants, these advantages being reflected in the extent to which established sellers can persistently raise their prices above a competitive level without attracting new firms to enter the industry".
[93] R.A. Posner, "The Chicago School of Antitrust Analysis" (1979) 127 U. Pa. L. Rev. 925.
[94] R.H. Bork, *The Antitrust Paradox: A Policy at War with Itself* (2nd ed., 1993), pp.311–312.

acknowledged only one goal of antitrust policy: the pursuit of economic efficiency. The orthodox Chicago approach heavily criticises a policy that protects individual (small) competitors at the expense of competition (and of large competitors). A firm becomes large because it is efficiently organised: "big is beautiful".[95] A policy that attacks the big firms for fear of growing concentration can be disastrous for economic welfare. Disciples of the Chicago School warn against a competition policy that ignores considerations of efficiency. Vertical restraints, for example, may cope with free riding and provide incentives for dealers to optimally invest in sales efforts. Also mergers may achieve perceivable efficiencies such as economies of scale, better integration of production facilities, specialisation, lower transportation costs and reduction of administrative expenses.

Chicagoans, moreover, stress that the fear that the market will be dominated by efficient firms which abuse their market power is often exaggerated. Should a dominant firm try to exploit consumers by increasing its prices far above the level of its costs, smaller firms will extend their market shares beneath the price umbrella of the dominant firm. In the improbable event that mergers drive all the other firms out of the market, new firms from other geographical markets will enter the monopolised market. Potential competition then becomes actual competition. Newcomers will seize the opportunity to reap monopoly profits. They will enter the market and undermine the high prices when these overshoot the level that is necessary to exclude less efficient firms. Concentration can persist only if economies of scale preclude the existence of a multiplicity of firms or if monopoly profits are a just reward for having achieved a higher degree of efficiency by means of price reductions or product improvements which the competing firms and new entrants were unable to achieve. Also, the view that monopolistic firms may leverage their monopoly power in related markets and achieve two monopoly profits is rejected. In the next chapters of this book, the Chicago views will be contrasted with modern industrial organisation theories.

3.6.2.2 Practical impact on antitrust

United States   The Chicago School acquired a strong influence on US antitrust policy from the 1970s onwards and reached the apogee of its influence in the 1980s. Many competition theorists and jurisdictions accepted Chicago's competition philosophy. Several examples could be given to appropriately illustrate the altered judgment on forms of market conduct which, until the Chicago School emerged, seemed to cause competition problems but which, through the renewed application of price theory, no longer give rise to problems.[96] Later chapters of this book will show how the Chicago learning influenced the assessment of vertical restraints, predatory pricing and mergers.[97] Even though it would be inappropriate to qualify the 1997 Merger

---

[95] A suitable answer to Schumacher's "small is beautiful" theory; see E.F. Schumacher, *Small is Beautiful: A Study of Economics as if People Mattered* (8th ed., 1993).
[96] See H. Hovenkamp, "Antitrust Policy after Chicago" (1985) 84 Mich. L. Rev. 213.
[97] See, for a further elaboration, Chs 6, 7, s.7.5 and Ch.10.

Guidelines as a Chicago document, a comparison with the earlier 1968 Merger Guidelines shows that the old Harvard approach has been adapted by taking into account some of Chicago's findings. A more complete overview of the assessment of mergers will be provided in Chapter 9. Here, a few examples must suffice to illustrate the Chicago School's impact. Throughout the 1997 Merger Guidelines the analysis is focused on whether consumers or producers "likely would" take certain actions, that is, whether the action is in the player's economic interest. This reflects the Chicago concern to explain, rather than to merely describe—as Harvard economists do—behaviour in (concentrated) markets, in order to be able to avoid inappropriate regulatory interventions. Chicagoans stress that the possibility of market entry may prevent the post-merger firm from earning above-normal profits. Following this view, the 1997 Merger Guidelines state that mergers in markets where entry is easy raise no antitrust concern.[98] Finally, the Guidelines explicitly say that the primary benefit of mergers to the economy is their efficiency enhancing potential, which can increase the competitiveness of firms and result in lower prices for consumers: "as a consequence, in the majority of cases, the Guidelines will allow firms to achieve available efficiencies through mergers". Efficiency gains of mergers will be assessed and may serve as a defence for the benefit of the merging firms.[99]

Europe   In Europe the substantive rules of competition law and practice of the European Commission remained largely unchanged during the antitrust revolution in the USA. The Chicago views hardly affected European competition law which, in the 1970s and 1980s, was still based on the Harvard insights. This, together with the emphasis on the market integration goal, still explains remaining differences between US antitrust law and European competition law. A few examples may suffice at this point to show that Brussels (and Luxembourg) is still relatively far away from Chicago. Absolute territorial protection for distributors, which could be justified as a remedy against free riding, is outlawed by Regulation 2790/1999 on vertical agreements.[1] In contrast with the US Supreme Court which, in accordance with the Chicago view, considered predatory pricing as an irrational strategy, the European Court of Justice has adopted a strict attitude towards price wars as a result of which dominant firms selling below average variable costs will be heavily fined for infringement of Article 82 EC. However, there are signs in recent European Commission practice that the tide may be turning. For example, in *Wanadoo*, the European Commission reviewed recoupment of losses as an aspect of predation[2] and the EC Horizontal Merger Guidelines now contain an explicit efficiency defence.[3]

---

[98] Section 3 of the 1997 Merger Guidelines.
[99] Section 4 of the 1997 Merger Guidelines.
[1] See Ch.6, s.6.3.2.
[2] See Ch.7, s.7.5.2.2.
[3] See Ch.9, s.9.2.3.

3.7 Competition as a dynamic process

The Harvard approach has been characterised as the structuralist conception of competition policy. The particular attention which disciples of the Harvard School devote to market structure stands in sharp contrast to the central concern of competition theories which analyse competition not as a structure but as a process. The opinions of prominent economists such as Schumpeter, writers of the Austrian School, including von Hayek, von Mises, and Kirzner, and disciples of the concept of free competition (*Konzept der Wettbewerbsfreiheit*), such as Hoppmann and Schmidtchen, are diametrically opposed to the structuralist theories of competition which have been discussed above. The importance of this largely German literature in the field of competition theory should not be underestimated, even if it is less well known than the Harvard–Chicago controversy.

3.7.1 Schumpeter and dynamic innovation

The first important author in the series of competition theoreticians who advocate a dynamic vision of competition is Schumpeter. In Schumpeter's work[4] competition is regarded as a dynamic process of "creative destruction". Pioneer firms introduce new products and new production methods, thereby opening up new markets. The dynamism of these firms initially gives them a temporary monopoly position in the market, but at the same time stimulates others to imitate them. These successive innovations and imitations promote economic progress. Seen from the perspective of competition as a dynamic process, deviations from the perfect competition model, such as product differentiation and lack of market transparency, are prerequisites for the "workability" of that process.

The ensuing rejection of market structure as a fixed point of reference by which competition should be judged has worked its way through to competition policy. Whereas in price theory monopoly was unambiguously considered to be something bad, this is no longer the case in a dynamic view. Indeed, monopolies are seen as a decisive factor in promoting competition. Schumpeter argued that a monopoly might be necessary in order to finance research and development (R&D) costs. Under perfect competition firms will not dare to undertake expensive research because of the associated costs and risks. Large expenditures on R&D without any results to show for can be enough to eliminate a firm from a competitive market. Large firms can more readily indulge in research and development because for them it is cheaper and less risky.[5]

The relationship between R&D expenditure and monopoly is a bone of

[4] J. Schumpeter, *Capitalism, Socialism and Democracy* (3rd ed., 1950).
[5] *ibid.*, p.160.

contention in current industrial economics. Apart from cost reductions, dynamic issues may indicate a preference for more concentrated market structures—even though in static terms this is allocatively inefficient. A more fragmented market structure may be allocatively efficient, but at the same time inhospitable to innovation. The economic discussion of how to take technological progress into account is one of the most frequently undertaken in industrial organisation. Ever since Schumpeter presented the issue of a possible link between market structure and the rate of innovation, as well as firm size and innovation, implying that it would be advisable to allow for higher market shares in innovation markets, this has been a prolonged field of controversy.[6] Arrow showed that, theoretically, a monopolist has less incentive to invest in innovation than a new entrant or a firm in a competitive industry.[7] Empirical evidence, however, still fails to demonstrate any definitive relationship between firm size, market concentration and the pace of innovation.[8] General conclusions to be drawn from a structural innovation markets analysis are thus reduced to long-shot value for the purpose of antitrust.[9] Instead, the individual circumstances of the industry under scrutiny will weigh heavily on the final outcome.[10]

3.7.2 Austrian economics

The dynamic vision of competition was advanced in its most extreme form by the disciples of the Austrian School. Neither von Mises nor von Hayek is particularly interested in market equilibrium, which can never be achieved in any case; instead, they stress the tendency towards market equilibrium. Emphasis is placed on the time factor, which is absent from price theory models. Unlike Schumpeter, the Austrians do not accept the tendency towards market equilibrium as being axiomatic. According to von Hayek, this tendency

[6] Passionately argued by J.K. Galbraith, *American Capitalism: The Concept of Countervailing Power* (1952), p.92; and dismissed with similar vigour by W.R. MacLaurin, "The Sequence from Invention to Innovation" (1953) 67 Quart. J. Econ. 107. Empirical research highlights the importance of big and small for innovative activity; see E. Mansfield, "Technological Change and Market Structure: An Empirical Study" (1983) 73 Amer. Econ. Rev., P&P 205. See more recently on the issue: R.J. Gilbert and S.C. Sunshine, "Incorporating Dynamic Efficiency Concerns in Merger Analysis: The Use of Innovation Markets" (1995) 63 Antitrust L.J. 567, and the numerous offspring of this article.
[7] See K.J. Arrow, "Economic Welfare and the Allocation of Resources for Invention", in *The Rate and Direction of Inventive Activity* (Nber ed., 1962), p.609. His findings have in the meantime been refined: see J.F. Reinganum, "The Timing of Innovation: Research, Development and Diffusion", in *The Handbook of Industrial Organization I* (R. Schmalensee and R.D. Willig ed., 1989), p.849.
[8] F.M. Scherer, "Schumpeter and Plausible Capitalism" (1992) 30 J. Econ. Lit. 1416, provides for a survey of numerous studies; see W.M. Cohen and R.C. Levin, "Empirical Studies of Innovation and Market Structure", in *The Handbook of Industrial Organization II* (R. Schmalensee and R.D. Willig eds., 1989), pp.1059, 1066–1079. Recent empirical work arguing a positive correlation between product market competition and productivity growth include S. Nickell, "Competition and Corporate Performance" (1996) 104 J. Polit. Economy 724.
[9] See R.T. Rapp, "The Misapplication of the Innovation Market Approach to Merger Analysis" (1995) 64 Antitrust L.J. 19 at pp.26–33.
[10] See, e.g. G.L. Roberts and S.C. Salop, "Dynamic Analysis of Efficiency Benefits" (1995/1996) 19 W. Comp. 5 at pp.13–17.

is an empirical matter;[11] and for von Mises it is the result of entrepreneurial activity.[12] Building on this notion, Kirzner has emphasised that it is the entrepreneur who establishes and consolidates the market.[13] Competition, for the Austrian School, is a process of continual interaction between the entrepreneur and the environment. It is the entrepreneur, as coordinator of the market, who makes the market.

The start point in the analysis of Nobel Prize laureate von Hayek is that—contrary to the assumptions of the model of perfect competition—suppliers only have imperfect, subjective knowledge of buyers' preferences. It is the task of the competitive process itself to find out the best products and production methods. The price system provides market participants with important signals that enable them to adapt to events and circumstances of which they are unaware. This basic insight, which initiated a Copernican revolution in economics, has far-reaching consequences for competition policy. Von Hayek defended the position that numerous interventions by competition law, such as determining the optimum size for firms, or the degree of workable competition, and the requirement that costs be justified, are vacuous and erroneous. Costs, prices and results cannot be determined by market simulations but are revealed by the competitive process itself. To remain in business, firms must constantly obtain information about market conditions and how they change. Individuals hold important economic information in an extremely non-aggregated way. No single economist, administrator or judge can answer the relevant questions of competition policy better than the competitive process itself. Von Hayek rejects both a prohibition against cartels and the surveillance of abuses by firms in a dominant position because of their negative effects on the dynamic competitive process.[14] Kirzner likewise considers even the extreme case of an entrepreneur getting permanent control over the whole supply of a particular raw material as being the result of the imaginativeness of a pioneer firm.[15] According to the Austrian view of things, interference by competition law must be avoided because of its potentially negative effects on the competitive incentive system.

These theories, by concentrating on competitive processes, place great emphasis on potential competition. Traditional competitive concepts relate to actual competition. According to dynamic views, competition can also exist in a latent or potential form. Although Schumpeter had already recognised the concept of potential competition, it was above all the economists of the Austrian School who elaborated the concept.[16] This School's approach implies that the exploitation of monopolistic positions is rendered impossible by the existence of potential competition (new firms, or pre-existing large firms in competing countries), at least in the long run. The attention which Schumpeter

---

[11] F.A. von Hayek, *Wettbewerb als Entdeckungsverfahren* (1968).
[12] L. von Mises, "Artikel: Markt" (1968) 7 HdSW 131.
[13] J.M. Kirzner, *Wettbewerb und Unternehmertum* (1978), p.168.
[14] F.A. von Hayek, "Grundsätze einer liberalen Gesellschaftsordnung" (1967) 18 ORDO 11.
[15] J.M. Kirzner, *Wettbewerb und Unternehmertum* (1978), p.168.
[16] See for example, D.W. Reekie, *Industry, Prices and Market* (1979). For the US, compare D.T. Armentano, *Antitrust and Monopoly: Anatomy of a Policy Failure* (1982).

and the Austrians devoted to potential competition has recently taken formal shape in the theory of contestable markets.[17]

3.7.3 The German concept of freedom of competition (*Konzept der Wettbewerbsfreiheit*)

Among the German theoreticians rejecting the structure–conduct–performance paradigm, a prominent author is Erich Hoppmann, who has advanced the concept of freedom of competition (*Konzept der Wettbewerbsfreiheit*) as an alternative approach for assessing restrictions on competition.[18] Instead of focusing on structural solutions, Hoppmann emphasises individual freedom of action, which reflects the ordoliberal foundations of his approach. Authors, such as Kantzenbach,[19] who suggest optimal market structures, are sharply criticised by Hoppmann. In Hoppmann's writings, competition is seen as a dynamic market process and not as a state (a rejection of static approaches). Freedom of competition is also regarded as the guarantor of economic advantages (*ökonomische Vorteilhaftigkeit*), which manifests itself in two ways: spontaneous coordination of business plans, and evolution. As mentioned earlier, Clark, in his later writings, criticised the concept of perfect competition on account of its static nature. Consequently, economic progress was accepted as an important indicator of good market performance. However, the need to accept restrictions on competition (like patents limiting the number of suppliers and thus negatively affecting market structure) in order to improve competition in terms of market performance was therefore seen as a dilemma. Hoppmann rejects this finding, as, in his view, no conclusions about market performance can be drawn from market structure criteria. Competition is defined as a process of spontaneous coordination and evolution, which creates economic advantages.[20] The rejection of market performance tests also makes it clear that the idea of competition as a learning process is taken seriously.

The conceptual approach of freedom of competition also addresses the notion of restrictions of competition. In Hoppmann's view, only forms of conduct which significantly restrict freedom of competition by fostering unreasonable market power should be prohibited by competition law. According to Hoppmann, freedom of competition embraces two components: on the one hand, the freedom to emulate the performance of competitors and to introduce innovations (*Wettbewerb im Parallelprozess*) and, on the other hand, the freedom to choose one's trading partners (*Wettbewerb im Austauschprozess*).

---

[17] See s.3.8.
[18] E. Hoppmann, "Zum Problem einer wirtschaftspolitisch praktikabelen Definition des Wettbewerbs", in *Grundlagen der Wettbewerbspolitik* (H.K. Schneider ed., 1968), p.9; and E. Hoppmann, "Das Konzept der optimalen Wettbewerbsintensität. Rivalität und Freiheit des Wettbewerbs: Zum Problem eines wettbewerbspolitisch adäquaten Ansatzes der Wettbewerbstheorie" (1966) 180 *Jahrbuch für Nationalökonomie und Statistik* 286.
[19] E. Kantzenbach, *Die Funktionsfähigkeit des Wettbewerbs* (1966).
[20] E. Hoppmann, "Zum Problem einer wirtschaftspolitisch praktikabelen Definition des Wettbewerbs", in *Grundlagen der Wettbewerbspolitik* (H.K. Schneider ed., 1968), p.27.

Legal prohibitions should, according to Hoppmann, be formulated as *per se* rules in order to minimise legal uncertainty for firms. Hoppmann's advocacy of *per se* rules is criticised by other German authors because it is difficult to give a description of practices which are, by their very nature, restrictive of competition.[21] Other proponents of the concept of freedom of competition have argued that the requirements of justice and legal certainty do not require *per se* rules, but can also be satisfied by the formulation of abstract rules that apply in a general way and are sufficiently stable.[22] Taking account of the requirement in current European competition law to define a relevant market on which the prohibited restrictions of competition materialise, a striking feature of the German conceptual approach of freedom of competition is that the market system is seen as unique and indivisible.[23] All products and services compete with each other and competition cannot be divided in different market segments. Consequently, the concept of a relevant market is meaningless.

3.8 The theory of contestable markets

3.8.1 Contestability as a theoretical yardstick

Among the recent economic approaches toward competition law and policy, contestability theory[24] is closely related to the general thrust and effects of the Chicago School. An important distinction between the structuralist theories of competition and the theory of contestable markets has already been indicated by the emphasis which the latter places on potential competition. Under the theory of contestable markets, market performance is judged without any regard at all to market structure. If contestability is taken as a yardstick, the fact that the market structure is concentrated says nothing, by itself, about the degree of efficiency. Even with a high degree of concentration, allocative efficiency is not excluded because potential entrants exercise a controlling discipline over monopolists and oligopolists. In contestable markets abnormally high profits are not achieved and inefficiencies are likewise not possible in the long run. Perfect contestability produces a similar outcome to perfect competition. Perfect contestability can be seen as a new ideal of welfare economics. In the extreme case of a perfectly contestable market, the performance of the incumbent firms is the same as those operating in a perfectly competitive market and there is no need for competition law.

---

[21] For an overview, R. Clapham, "Das wettbewerbspolitische Konzept der Wettbewerbsfreiheit", in *Handbuch des Wettbewerbs* (H. Cox, U. Jens and K. Markert ed., 1981).
[22] D. Schmidtchen, "Fehlurteile über das Konzept der Wettbewerbsfreiheit" in ORDO *Jahrbuch für die Ordnung von Wirtschaft und Gesellschaft* (1988), p.113.
[23] E. Hoppmann, *Marktmacht und Wettbewerb* (1977), p.9.
[24] The most complete, but also very technical, description of the theory is given by W.J. Baumol, J.C. Panzar and R.D. Willig, *Contestable Markets and the Theory of Industry Structure* (1982).

A perfectly contestable market is characterised by completely free entry and the absence of exit costs. Free entry does not imply that entry costs absolutely nothing, or that it is easy, but rather that the entrant has no relative cost disadvantages compared with participants who are already active in the market. Potential entrants find it appropriate to judge the profitability of market entry on the basis of the entry costs of the firms which are already present in the market. Costless exit implies that a firm can leave the market without hindrance and, in so doing, also recoup any entry costs incurred. Sunk costs must be zero. Contestable market theory therefore makes an important distinction between fixed costs and sunk costs: fixed costs do not vary with output but are recoverable if the firm leaves the market; sunk costs are costs that cannot be recouped if the firm leaves the market.

Firms which operate in a perfectly contestable market are exposed to hit-and-run competition.[25] If market price increases beyond marginal costs, a potential entrant can effectively enter, make significant profits by setting his price somewhat below the market price, and leave the market again before the market price changes. The threat of a hit-and-run strategy makes above normal profits impossible, even in a monopolistic market.[26] The only equilibrium which can be maintained is that at which prices are equal to average costs. It must be stressed that vulnerability to hit-and-run competition implies that entrants can establish their operations and undercut incumbents before the latter respond to the entry with price cuts.

At the policy level, the theory of contestable markets leads to conclusions minimising the need for competition law. First, the degree of concentration yields no decisive conclusion as to the degree of efficiency. Unlike the theory of perfect competition which is applicable only to markets with a large number of sellers, the doctrine of contestable markets applies equally to oligopolistic markets. A market may even be contestable with one single seller and can operate just as competitively as a market with perfect competition. Monopolies and oligopolies are not objectionable *per se* from the welfare economics point of view. A high degree of concentration can even be a healthy sign. Second, in contestable markets the existing monopolies and oligopolies can prevent market entry only by asking competitive prices. Any prices which exceed that level will attract hit-and-run entrants. The argument that the US airline industry was perfectly contestable was at least part of the justification for its deregulation in that country.[27] In a deregulated market, so it was argued, airline companies can simply fly planes into airports to compete with existing companies already serving the routes from that airport. Because potential entrants have cheap access to the market, since capital assets—*i.e.* planes—are perfectly mobile and can likewise be withdrawn from the market at practically

---

[25] W.J. Baumol "Contestable Markets: An Uprising in the Theory of Industry Structure" (1982) 72 Amer. Econ. Rev. 1.

[26] If two or more firms operate in the market, price will be equal to marginal costs. If the market is a natural monopoly, price will only be sufficient to cover average costs; compare M.A. Utton, *Market Dominance and Antitrust* (2nd ed., 2003), p.128.

[27] See J.F. Brodley, "Antitrust Policy under Deregulation: Airline Mergers and the Theory of Contestable Markets" (1981) 61 B.U.L. Rev. 823.

no cost, natural monopoly[28] routes were considered to be contestable. Mergers between large carriers (rising market share from around 50 per cent to practically 75 per cent) were not considered anti-competitive because airline markets were readily contested.[29]

Many authors are sceptical of the claims of the contestability theory and its resulting policy recommendations.[30] In their view, the theory is not robust. Small departures from its assumptions cause major alterations to the predictions. As long as the entrants are able to realise their investments without suffering a loss before the producers already present in the market can react, the market can be regarded as contestable and intervention by the antitrust authorities will be superfluous. In a more realistic scenario, however, where the incumbent can respond before the entrant is sufficiently established to start production and supply the market, some sunk costs would deter all entry.[31] If small departures from perfect contestability produce dramatically different results, it may not make sense to analyse markets according to the degree to which they are contestable (or "workably" contestable). The airline example illustrates the danger of slipping from theory to the real world. Entry conditions in the airline market are indeed far from easy. The airport is a major sunk facility and guaranteeing equal access to competing airlines has proved to be difficult. Environmental concerns make it troublesome to increase the availability of runways; likewise, political considerations lead to the protection of national airlines and cause discrimination in the allocation of slots. Given the non-robust nature of the theory, in practice there is no reason to expect outcomes which resemble the theoretical results.

3.8.2 Policy conclusions

In spite of these criticisms the contestability theory has some merit. First, the Contestability School assumes that firms adjust their strategy to what market structures could become, rather than determining a strategy on the basis of what market structures actually exist. Firms, in this view, follow a sort of pre-emptive or entry deterring strategy. Hence, the issue to be tackled by competition law is not concentration, as is the case in the structuralist view, but lack of contestability. In perfectly contestable markets competition problems are excluded. Such problems are caused precisely by obstacles which hinder free entry to, and withdrawal from, the market and thus make the market incontestable. All business practices which erect such barriers must therefore be resisted with the aid of competition law. From this perspective, both the

[28] A natural monopoly is an industry in which economies of scale are so large (average costs decline as output increases) that the efficient level of production for one firm satisfies the entire market demand.
[29] E. Bailey, "Contestability and the Design of Regulatory and Antitrust Policy" (1981) 71 Amer. Econ. Rev. 178 at p.181.
[30] S. Martin, *Industrial Economics: Economic Analysis and Public Policy* (1994), pp.223–224; M.A. Utton, *Market Dominance and Antitrust* (2nd ed., 2003), pp.132–135.
[31] M.A. Utton, *Market Dominance and Antitrust* (2nd ed., 2003), p.129.

existence of vertical restraints in concentrated markets and the creation of excess capacity can justifiably be subjected to antitrust surveillance. Also, contestable market theory illustrates the fundamental importance of sunk costs in the analysis of barriers to entry. Incumbent firms may possess strategic (first mover) advantages in the presence of sunk costs: advertising expenditures, which are not recoverable in case of exit, provide an example.

Second, the theory of contestable markets emphasises that not only firms but also, and above all, governments can adopt measures which are detrimental to market contestability. Government action restricting freedom of entry to (and withdrawal from) the market goes against a competition policy which attaches great significance to contestability. It follows from the theory of contestable markets that states ought not to enact any regulations hindering competitive entry to the market, but should, instead, create precisely those conditions promoting contestability. Unfortunately, the reality is often different. It is remarkable that the attainment of efficient results in relatively contestable markets is, on numerous occasions, hindered by regulatory activity which protects existing firms. On the basis of the theory of contestable markets there must be serious doubt as to the desirability of state interventions such as licensing laws which make market entry difficult for newcomers. Indeed, rules regarding the establishment of firms, which cannot be justified as appropriate measures to cure informational asymmetries,[32] regularly turn out to have as their principal economic consequence the provision of interest groups with economic rents, while, in so doing, transforming relatively contestable markets into protected monopolies. In spite of deregulation efforts, examples remain numerous. It suffices to mention the disproportionate rules of the licensing laws in the sector of the liberal professions in many European countries,[33] the Belgian restrictions regarding travelling salespersons,[34] and the Austrian regulations concerning the exploitation of taxi services.[35] These rules cause inefficiencies instead of reducing them. Several competition laws have created unique possibilities of repealing provisions which hinder market contestability. According to Article 21 of the Italian Competition Act,[36] the Italian Competition Authority (*Autorità Garante della Concorrenza e del Mercato*) can judge what steps are necessary in order to eliminate distortions of competition caused by laws, regulations and general administrative decisions and can make appropriate recommendations for reform.[37] In Belgium there are no such

---

[32] On information remedies in cases of market failure, see A.I. Ogus, *Regulation. Legal Form and Economic Theory* (1994), Ch.7.

[33] R.J. Van den Bergh, "Self-Regulation of the Medical and Legal Professions: Remaining Barriers to Competition and EC Law", in *Organized Interests and Self-Regulation* (B. Bortolotti and G. Fiorentini ed., 1999), p.89.

[34] See R.J. Van den Bergh, "Belgian Public Policy towards the Retailing Trade" in *Law and Economics and the Economics of Legal Regulation* (M. Graf von der Schulenburg and G. Skogh ed., 1986), p.185.

[35] See P. Lewisch, "The Political Economy of Barriers to Entry: The Example of the Amendment for Taxicab Regulation in Austria", in *Economic Analysis of Law: A Collection of Applications* (W. Weigel ed., 1991), pp.292–334.

[36] Law No.287, October 10, 1990, *Gazzetta ufficiale*, October 13, 1990, No.240.

[37] See further A. Frignani, R. Pardolesi, A. Patroni Griffi and L.C. Ubertazzi (eds), *Diritto Antitrust Italiano* (1993).

express provisions, but similar problems may nevertheless be indicated in a report by the Competition Council (*Raad voor de Mededinging*).[38] As far as European law is concerned, reference must be made to the consistent case law of the European Court of Justice[39] which prohibits Member States from adopting measures which could deprive the European competition rules of their practical effect (Articles 3g and 10 EC in conjunction with Articles 81 and 82 EC). In this way national provisions that threaten the contestability of the markets in question are fought.

Third, the theory of contestable markets likewise focuses policy makers' attention on the necessity of competition *for* a given market and stresses the limitations of a policy which concentrates exclusively on competition within that market. Even if a market only has room for one firm (a natural monopoly), competition can play an important role in deciding which firm is entitled to enter the market, how long that firm may remain in the market, and what prices it will ask. These insights also have proved to be useful for assessing the possibilities of liberalising traditional energy sectors, such as gas and electricity. For example, avoiding the high costs of duplication arising as a result of the establishment of new networks, competition may be served equally well by granting newcomers access to existing networks.[40]

3.9 The transaction cost approach

3.9.1 Minimising transaction costs

In his classical contribution *The Nature of the Firm*, Nobel Prize winner Coase[41] laid the foundations for the new institutional economics[42] by offering an explanation for the choice between the market and the firm as alternative decision-making mechanisms for completing transactions. Although there are no traditional cost differences in the form of production costs and transportation costs between these two institutions, there can still be cost differences which may be described as transaction costs. Transaction costs are search and information costs, negotiation costs and the costs of implementing and enforcing the resulting agreements. The extent of these transaction costs in the alternative institutions (the market or the firm) can explain the choice in favour of the market as an instrument of coordination, or in favour of the firm with its distinctive, hierarchical, organisational structure. In managerial terms, this

---

[38] Arts 16(2) and 21, Law August 5, 1991.
[39] Case 311/85 *Vereniging van Vlaamse Reisbureaus ASBL v Sociale Dienst van de Plaatselijke en Gewestelijke Overheidsdiensten* [1987] ECR 3801.
[40] See D.M. Newbery, *Privatization, Restructuring, and Regulation of Network Utilities* (1999).
[41] R.H. Coase, "The Nature of the Firm" (1937) 4 *Economica* 386.
[42] On the "new institutional economics", consult E.G. Furubotn and R. Richter, "The New Institutional Economics: An Assessment", in *The New Institutional Economics: A Collection of Articles from the Journal of Institutional and Theoretical Economics* (E.G. Furubotn and R. Richter ed., 1991), pp.1–32.

choice may be referred to as the make-or-buy decision. When transactions between contract parties are too expensive and an organisation could coordinate them at a lower cost than if they were market transactions, then firms emerge as organisational structures. As a result, such transactions will not be carried out in ordinary markets, but will be internalised within the firm. The reason is that making (a product) is cheaper than buying (this product). According to this approach, the reason for the establishment of firms lies precisely in the existence of transaction costs.

The transaction costs approach has now developed into an important element of the new institutional economics. In Williamson's work[43] emphasis is placed in particular on the need to take into account considerations concerning transaction costs in the analysis of competition problems. The transaction costs approach superimposes transaction costs considerations upon micro-economic price theory, thus being more of a complement to, instead of a substitute for, price theory. The starting point in Williamson's analysis is not the subject matter of the sale–purchase transaction of goods or services, but the transaction itself. The transaction is an exchange between two or more individuals whereby they transfer property rights, that is, rights to dispose of scarce resources, which may be limited not only by other individuals' ownership rights but also by rules of legal liability and the provisions of competition law.[44] Transactions differ perceptibly so far as costs are concerned and these differences in transaction costs influence the choice of the right organisational form or governance structure. Markets and firms are regarded as alternative instruments for implementing transactions.[45] The transaction costs across markets and within firms are affected by human and environmental (market) factors. The transaction costs of writing contracts vary with the characteristics of the human decision makers (bounded rationality, danger of opportunism) and the objective properties of the market (degree of uncertainty, frequency of the transactions, grade of asset specificity).

Whether a set of transactions is carried out via the market (by entering into agreements) or through a single firm depends on the relative efficiency of these two institutions. A hierarchical form of organisation may be superior to a market-based solution. The relative efficiency of the two forms is determined, on the one hand, by the costs of entering into, and carrying out, agreements in a market (market factors or transactional factors) and, on the other hand, by the characteristics of the individuals who are affected by the transaction (human factors). Transactions differ from each other in a number of respects: the uncertainty to which the transactions are exposed, the frequency with

---

[43] On transaction-cost economics, see Williamson's review article—O.E. Williamson, "Transaction Cost Economics", in *Handbook of Industrial Organisation I* (R. Schmalensee and R.D. Willig eds., 1989), pp.135–182. See also Williamson, *The Economic Institutions of Capitalism: Firms, Markets, Relational Contracting* (1985); Williamson, "Assessing Vertical Market Restrictions: Antitrust Ramifications of the Transaction Cost Approach" (1979) 127 U. Pa. L. Rev. 953; Williamson, *Markets and Hierarchies: Analysis and Antitrust Implications: a Study in the Economics of Internal Organisation* (1975).

[44] "Property rights" in economics carries a much broader meaning than the legal concept of property; compare R.D. Cooter and T. Ulen, *Law and Economics* (4th ed., 2004).

[45] O.E. Williamson, *Economic Organisation, Firms, Markets and Policy Control* (1986), pp.199–202.

which market participants repeat the transactions (once, occasionally, or regularly), and the extent to which transactions must be supported by transaction-specific investments (asset specificity). By asset specificity Williamson means the extent to which suppliers and customers must make relation-specific investments in order to be able to carry out transactions. The value of these investments exceeds the value of the best alternative use and thus creates a quasi-rent. Asset specificity refers to either physical or human elements in the transaction. Examples include the location of plants close to the site of the principal customer or the building up of human capital to exercise a specific occupation. Asset specificity follows from the fact that there is no second-hand market for the investments in question, as these investments are idiosyncratic to particular transactions (for example, particular skills in an employer–employee contract). Transaction-specific investments bind the supplier and the customer closely together. If the supplier cannot readily exploit his specific investments elsewhere, and the purchaser, because of his specific investments, cannot readily place his order elsewhere, the supplier and the purchaser are bound to each other for a substantial period of time. In cases of "small numbers exchange", where market participants are very much dependent upon each other, serious lock-in effects will emerge. Circumstances not contracted upon *ex ante* allow one party possessing *ex post* bargaining power to decide over the division of the quasi-rents, to the counterparty's disadvantage. This is the hold-up problem arising from contractual incompleteness. The more specific the asset, the greater the need for continuity, and the more likely it will be that internal governance will replace market governance.

Besides the transactional factors Williamson emphasises a number of human factors which influence the level of transaction costs. Accordingly, bounded rationality and opportunism distinguish the individuals who implement a transaction. Bounded rationality refers to the limited capacity of the human mind to formulate and solve highly complex problems.[46] Opportunistic conduct alludes to the lack of honesty in transactions, as the pursuit of self-interest can be disastrous for the success of a transaction.

The combination of a number of transactional and human factors can impede the conclusion of an exchange. In particular, the combination of uncertainty and bounded rationality and the linking of small numbers exchange with opportunistic conduct increases transaction costs significantly. In the case of small numbers exchange, the opportunistic tendency to pursue self-interest will generate serious risks for the trading partners. Within a firm the transactional factors and the human factors which hinder exchanges between firms manifest themselves in different ways. Because hierarchical forms of organisation reduce transaction costs, a firm can thus be a better governance structure than the market. Box 3.2 provides an overview of efficient governance structures depending on the frequency of the transactions and the degree of asset specificity.

---

[46] The concept is described by H.A. Simon, *Models of Man* (1957), p.198.

Box 3.2: Transaction costs and optimal governance structures

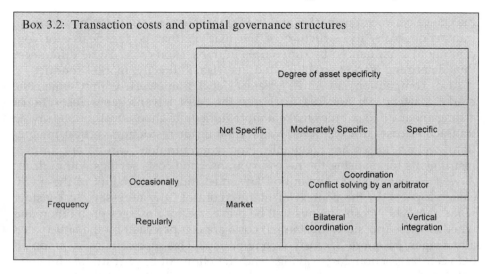

		Degree of asset specificity		
		Not Specific	Moderately Specific	Specific
Frequency	Occasionally	Market	Coordination Conflict solving by an arbitrator	
	Regularly		Bilateral coordination	Vertical integration

The market is the appropriate structure for standardised transactions (on which uncertainty has no bearing) or for transactions which require no specific investments, irrespective of their frequency. By contrast, if non-standard transactions are frequent and characterised by asset specificity, a transaction-specific structure will be the most appropriate form. In this way, Williamson distinguishes between bilateral structures and hierarchy. Bilateral structures lend themselves to transactions which are repeated regularly and for which moderate specific investments are needed. Franchising is an example of such transactions. In cases of frequent transactions a high degree of asset specificity will necessitate a hierarchical form of organisation (vertical integration). Lastly, hybrid forms are appropriate if transactions which require moderate specific investments occur on an occasional basis (trilateral coordination).

3.9.2 Policy conclusions

The transaction cost approach affects older competition theory and competition policy. Conclusions derived from models of perfect competition or monopoly, without taking account of transaction costs, are often premature and misleading.[47] Most importantly, Coase's point of view provides an explanation for changes in market structure. His insights are therefore of great importance for competition policy and law.[48] Price theory analyses stating how allocative efficiency can be realised lose their validity when high transaction costs have to be incurred in order to achieve an efficient outcome. These transaction costs must be taken into account explicitly before any welfare judgment can be pronounced. The Harvard approach, which draws conclusions as to market conduct and market results from data on market structure, must be critically examined anew in the light of transaction cost economics. If

---

[47] O.E. Williamson, *Economic Organisation, Firms, Markets and Policy Control* (1986), pp.202–237.
[48] See C. Kirchner, "Wettbewerbstheoretische Ansätze bei Ronald Coase" (1992) 42 WuW 584.

the choice between the market and the firm is made as a function of savings in transaction costs, the structure of the market (that is, the degree of concentration) is influenced by differences in transaction costs. These differences thus determine market structure and likewise, indirectly, market conduct.

Also, competition law must create a legal framework within which the market participants are free to choose the most advantageous institutional arrangements. If legal rules make it more difficult to choose institutions saving transaction costs (for example, by prohibiting or restricting vertical integration), welfare losses are inevitable. First, concentrations can be appropriate instruments for realising the necessary transaction costs savings within firms. A welfare-maximising competition law must thus take account of these efficiency aspects. In the context of merger control, it is necessary to consider what transaction costs savings will be prevented by a merger prohibition and whether these (possibly substantial) costs are compensated by the anticipated advantages of more intensive competition. This necessitates a trade-off between transaction costs savings and the elimination of restraints on competition. Second, one of the most important contributions of the transaction costs approach is the fundamental change which it has brought about in the thinking regarding vertical restraints as a competition problem. Vertical restraints—not just territorial restrictions but also restrictions on the circle of purchasers and vertical price fixing—reduce transaction costs. And, finally, the transaction costs approach also makes clear that the problem of oligopoly cannot be equated with the problem of monopoly. The transaction costs, which go hand in hand with negotiating and implementing an extensive cartel agreement, will jeopardise the achievement of a profit-maximising outcome. A firm in a dominant position need take no account of these problems in its internal organisation. An economically rational competition law must therefore address first of all the industries in which dominant firms operate before dealing with oligopolies. It is apparent from these examples that transaction costs analysis is an important complement to the Chicago view. The need to save on transaction costs may provide an additional explanation (and, possibly, justification) for mergers and practices which, in the old Harvard view, were seen as exclusionary conduct.

3.10 Modern industrial organisation

In spite of the differences between them, many of the theories discussed earlier can in many respects be considered to have become part of current mainstream industrial organisation. In contrast with a widespread belief in Europe, Chicago economics are not necessarily seen by US researchers as biased, ideological or inappropriate. Many of the Chicago views have been adopted in modern industrial organisation and the Chicago research has established itself as central to the entire discipline. Obviously, the initial excesses of the Chicago approach have been mitigated, as is also the case with the immoderations of the Harvard approach. The debate over the size of the firm and its profitability and the related issues of concentration, market power and efficiency continues. Thanks to the Harvard–Chicago controversy a balanced view of these issues has found its way into modern industrial organisation and a consensus has been reached on large number of issues, even though opinions may continue to differ on the assessment of the competitive impact of certain practices in some real-life cases. The consensus among economists does not, however, extend to the radical Austrian approach, which remains outside the mainstream of industrial organisation.

How do the modern views of new industrial organisation theory relate to the structuralist Harvard view and the efficiency philosophy of the Chicago School? First, the linearity of the structuralist view has come into question. Structure, conduct and performance may indeed be interdependent; the possibility has been identified of behaviour affecting market structure. This modern insight has, for example, shed a new light on the Harvard–Chicago debate with respect to the existence of entry barriers. Whereas the dominant Chicago view accepted only entry barriers resulting from government regulation and qualified other barriers as the consequence of the higher efficiency of incumbent firms, the modern view accepts that entry barriers may be created by strategic behaviour of market participants. Second, in the structuralist view, collusion increases profits so that firms can be expected to collude and collusion is deemed most likely in concentrated markets. The Chicago criticisms of this view stressed that collusion is difficult for firms to enforce and thus unlikely; consequently, collusion would occur only in industries with government regulation or protection. The modern view asserts that collusion is possible when competitors are repeat players and most likely in industries with repeated encounters and easy monitoring, as well as in regulated and protected industries. Third, as to the relationship between the number of competitors and market performance, it is no longer argued that more competitors automatically implies more competition and it is accepted that competition can be effective with a small number of competitors. Fourth, as to the sources of market power, the modern view is that market power not only arises from horizontal factors (as was argued by the Chicago School) but that it can be extended through vertical arrangements and strategic behaviour.[49] Fifth, the debate has stilled concerning the interpretation of the relationship between concentration and profits. Most economists will probably accept Demsetz's compromise that market concentration can reflect both elements of efficiency and market power. It is now accepted that high profits for large firms may be explained not only by greater market power, but also by the greater efficiency of the large firms. Large efficient firms may succeed in colluding and set prices at a level which yields high rates of return for them but not for less efficient, more moderately sized firms.[50] Policy makers should take

---

[49] This summary is based on the overview of the differences between the structural view, the Chicago School and new industrial organisation theory in D.P. Baron, *Business and its Environment*, (5th ed., 2006), p.292.

[50] H. Demsetz, "Two Systems of Belief about Monopoly", in *Industrial Concentration: The New Learning*, (H.J. Goldschmid, H.M. Mann and J.F. Weston ed., 1974), pp.164, 178–179.

both efficiency savings (scale economies or other advantages of large firms) and market power (high profit rates) into account.

Modern industrial organisation stresses the need for an analysis of strategic interaction to understand industry structure and concentration. Whereas the Harvard paradigm analysed industries in terms of a causative chain from structure to conduct to performance, the new approach emphasises that conduct (strategic interaction) affects industry structure and performance. Game theory[51] offers formal tools helping to understand strategic interactions.[52] Strategic behaviour arises when two or more individuals interact and the behaviour of each individual turns on what this individual expects other individuals to do. Game theory offers important insights with respect to the need for competition rules as it makes clear under what conditions (assumptions) strategic behaviour may cause welfare losses. Competition rules may subsequently limit the scope for strategic interaction by outlawing certain types of conduct revealed by game theory as detrimental. Game theory may thus help in shaping competition rules that give parties an incentive to act in ways that enhance economic welfare. Game theoretic insights are particularly relevant for assessing the degree of competition in oligopolistic markets. Since the examination of oligopolistic interdependencies is made more difficult by the mutual expectations of the oligopolists with respect to the reactions of their competitors, the game theoretic toolbox is very appropriate to analyse such markets. Aside from the analysis of strategic behaviour on oligopolistic markets, game theory has also been able to show—contrary to the thesis of the Chicago School—that firms enjoying market power may be able to erect private barriers to entry, by raising the costs of their rivals.[53] Game theoretic theories are becoming increasingly important in competition policy discussions and have also been given particular emphasis in assessing competition in high technology and network industries.[54]

Compared to traditional price theory, game theory allows a more precise and differentiated analysis of different market forms. The equilibrium concept in game theory does not relate to the structure of a market (as in the theory of perfect competition) but to the conduct of firms. An equilibrium is a combination of strategies that the players of a game are likely to adopt. The aim in game theory is to identify each player's best strategy, that is, the strategy that will maximise the player's pay-off, taking the other player's strategy into account. The most important instrument to analyse strategic interaction is the concept of a Nash equilibrium. Such an equilibrium is reached when no player

---

[51] Games are a scientific metaphor for human interactions, where the outcomes depend on the interactive strategies of two or more human players. It is a mathematical theory of bargaining and an interdisciplinary approach to human behaviour. The first work is J. von Neumann and O. Morgenstern, *The theory of games and economic behaviour* (1944).

[52] See G. Norman and M. La Manna (eds) *The New Industrial Economics* (1992); or D. Fudenberg and J. Tirole, *Game Theory* (1991).

[53] S. Salop and D. Scheffman, "Cost-Raising Strategies" (1987) 36 J. Ind. Econ. 19.

[54] See, e.g. D. Rubinfeld, "Antitrust Enforcement in Dynamic Network Industries" (1998) 43 Antitrust Bull. 859, at p.882; J. Ordover and R.D. Willig, "Access and Bundling in High Technology Markets" in *Competition, Innovation and the Microsoft Monopoly: Antitrust in the Digital Marketplace* (J. A. Eisenach and T. M. Lenard ed., 1999), pp.103, 128.

has the possibility of profiting from a unilateral change of conduct, given the conduct of the other player. In the context of competition, it is the combination of output levels chosen by firms so that no firm can increase its profit by changing its level of output given the outputs chosen by its rivals (Nash–Cournot equilibrium[55]). Game theory has been able to provide a theoretical explanation for the instability of cartels, which is caused by the incentive for individual cartel members to deviate from the collusive price. This insight may be derived from the so-called prisoners' dilemma, in which the strategy combination that is in the joint interests of both players is not played. Oligopolists would prefer an outcome in which both charge a high price to that in which they both charge a low price. However, the incentive to charge a low price, while the rival firm charges a high price, results in both firms charging a low price.[56]

The tools of game theory are highly technical and many of them have been developed only in recent years.[57] Given that this body of literature is close to pure theory and not yet meaningfully verified by empirical research, some commentators warn against drawing generalised conclusions to be implemented by competition law.[58] On the sceptical side, it is argued that the results of the game theoretic research are insufficiently complete to provide firm conclusions or to allow an assessment of what will happen in particular cases.[59] On the optimistic side, it is argued that game theory allows the analysis of a much broader range of business competitive strategies than before.[60] Within the limited format of this book it is not possible to introduce lawyers to the complexities of game theory; those interested in such an introduction are invited to read other publications.[61] In Chapters 5 and 7 of this book, the lessons of game theory with respect to two hot issues in competition law (collusion and predatory pricing, respectively) will be summarised. Within the confines of this book this is to be seen as a modest attempt to illustrate how game theory may be helpful in solving complex problems of competition law.

Modern industrial organisation also offers advances on the empirical side. Several sector-specific models that simulate the effects of mergers and detect

---

[55] A Nash equilibrium is the central solution concept in game theory. It is named after John Nash who, together with Harsanyi and Selten, was awarded the Nobel Prize in 1994. Compare J. Nash, *Equilibrium Points in N-Person Games* (1950), p.36. If the decision variable is price, the equilibrium will be called a Nash–Bertrand equilibrium after another French economist.

[56] D.W. Carlton and J.M. Perloff, *Modern Industrial Organization* (2nd ed., 1994), pp.254–259. See, for further elaboration, Ch.5.

[57] For definitions and concise explanations of concepts of Game Theory, see E. Rasmusen, *Games and Information: an Introduction to Game Theory* (3rd ed., 2001).

[58] See B.H. Kobayashi, "Game Theory and Antitrust: A Post-Mortem" (1997) 5 Geo. Mason L. Rev. 411; and S. Peltzman, "The Handbook of Industrial Organisation: A Review Article" (1991) 99 J. Polit. Economy 201.

[59] F.M. Fisher, "Games Economists Play: A Noncooperative View" (1989) 20 Rand J. Econ. 113 at p.124.

[60] C. Shapiro, "The Theory of Business Strategy" (1989) 20 Rand J. Econ. 125.

[61] An excellent introduction for lawyers is: D. Baird, R. Gertner and R. Picker, *Game Theory and the Law* (1994). This book applies game theory to a large number of classic legal problems, ranging from contract law and tort law to labour law, environmental regulations and antitrust law. On a more advanced level, see L. Phlips, *Competition Policy: A Game-Theoretic Perspective* (1995).

collusive behaviour have been developed.[62] The problem with this approach is that models do not yet exist for every sector. Moreover, these studies often rely on historical data and so not allowing conclusions for today's markets. Efforts to find robust results that can be applied to every industry have been made in the pioneering contributions by Panzar and Rosse,[63] and Porter,[64] but above all by Sutton.[65] The latter approach appears to indicate an upper and lower bound to concentration: predictions are possible as to within which boundaries a sector will move without providing precise evidence on market structural changes. The new empirical literature shows how shaky the traditional Harvard approach was when it claimed it could make exact predictions.

3.11 Conclusions

This chapter has revealed different schools of thought in the field of competition policy. Even though most current industrial organisation research is grounded in the same formal economic theory, differences of opinion among economists exist when it comes to policy issues. A simple chronological overview is extremely helpful in revealing both common grounds and lines along which economists may disagree. In classical economics, competition was a behavioural concept. It was defined as a price-determining force (Adam Smith's "invisible hand"), which guided business decisions towards economic welfare, and not as a market structure. In neo-classical price theory, the formal models of perfect competition and monopoly were developed. These models focus on the properties of the market equilibrium and describe competition as a market structure. They show that perfect competition is Pareto efficient, whereas monopoly causes a welfare loss. The models, in spite of their elegance, focus exclusively on the effects of competition and lose sight of the behavioural processes leading to these results. Most real markets cannot be characterised by either perfect competition or monopoly. This insight has led to the development of more sophisticated economic approaches. This evolution was not without cost, though, as consensus among economists disappeared.

Looking at the evolution of economic thinking on competition policy in the USA in the past century, it becomes clear that the discussion mainly centred around two different approaches: the structuralist view of the Harvard School

---

[62] F. Verboven, "International Price Discrimination in the European Car Market" (1996) 17 Rand J. Econ. 240; S. Berry, J. Levinsohn and A. Pakes, "Automobile Prices in Market Equilibrium" (1995) 63 Econometrica 841; F. Gasmi, J.-J. Laffont and Q.H. Vuong, "Econometric Analysis of Collusive Behavior in a Soft Drink Market" (1992) 1 J. Econ. Management Strat. 277; J.B. Baker, "Identifying Cartel Policy under Uncertainty: The U.S. Steel Industry: 1933–1939" (1989) 32 J. Law Econ. 547; D. Sullivan, "Testing Hypotheses about Firm Behaviour in the Cigarette Industry" (1985) 93 J. Polit. Economy 586.

[63] J.C. Panzar and J.N. Rosse, "Testing for Monopoly Equilibrium" (1987) 35 J. Ind. Econ. 443.

[64] R.H. Porter, "A Study of Cartel Stability: The Joint Executive Committee 1880–1886" (1983) 14 Bell J. Econ. 301.

[65] J. Sutton, *Sunk Costs and Market Structure* (1991); Sutton, *Technology and Market Structure* (1998).

and the efficiency theories of the Chicago School. The structuralist approach argues that market performance is dependent on the conduct of firms which in turn is dependent on the market structure of the industry under investigation. This vision of things has become known as the structure–conduct–performance paradigm. The Harvard writers argued that high concentration in markets enables the exercise of market power (collusion) and the achievement of high profits to the detriment of consumers. This view led to a very interventionist antitrust policy, including *per se* rules on anti-competitive behaviour and divestitures in highly concentrated markets. From the 1940s onwards, perfect competition as a blueprint for competition policy was replaced by the concept of "workable competition". The latter notion accepts that different market imperfections may neutralise each other and that restrictions of (certain forms of) competition may be necessary to further (other forms of) competition. Consequently, there can be different ideas about the ideal market structure (and ultimate performance) for different sectors of the industry and large discretionary powers are given to antitrust authorities.

The views of the Harvard School were severely criticised by scholars belonging to the Chicago School. In the writings of the latter School, the empirical studies showing a mono-causal and mono-dimensional relation between market concentration and profits were challenged by a different approach comparing profits of large and small firms in specific concentrated industries. If concentration is the consequence of greater efficiency, only the profits of large firms will be high. The structure–conduct–performance paradigm was rejected by the Chicagoans and the loose concept of "workable competition" had to give way to the view that productive and allocative efficiency are the only acceptable goals for competition policy. To explain business practices in real-life markets, use was again made of price theory. The vision of things of the Chicagoans led to dramatically different policy conclusions. Vertical restraints of competition (in particular resale price maintenance) were rationalised as mechanisms to cure "free riding" and considered legal. High profits were not seen as the consequence of collusion but as the result of higher efficiency (economies of scale and scope). Persistent market concentration was seen as the result of minimum efficient firm size and a merger policy not taking account of efficiency savings was rejected. In the US, the Chicago revolution led to a number of changes in the antitrust policy during the 1970s and 1980s, which softened the previous more interventionist antitrust laws.

In Europe, the views of the Chicago School never had a direct impact on policy making. Up until the end of the 20th century, much of European competition policy remained affected by the structuralist view. However, to fully understand the underlying principles of European competition law and the precise meaning of the cartel prohibition and the ban on abuses of a dominant firm, it is important to realise that the wording of Articles 81 and 82 EC was influenced by the ordoliberal ideas of the Freiburg School. The latter approach favoured a strong competition policy to protect individual economic freedom. Moreover, European competition rules have been used as instruments to achieve market integration, and this also explains a number of persisting differences with American antitrust law. As to the schools of thought, it must be added that—aside from the outdated ordoliberalism— dynamic approaches to competition policy have continued to play an important role in economic writings. The Austrian School questions the feasibility of a competition policy due to the lack of knowledge on the part of competition authorities. In the view of Hayek, only competitive processes themselves can reveal the necessary information on costs, prices and market results. The German concept of freedom of competition (*Konzept der Wettbewerbsfreiheit*) rejects a structuralist approach and favours behavioural rules that protect competition in both horizontal and vertical relations. In sum, the overview in this chapter has made clear that there is no such thing as *the* economic approach to competition. This important insight should always be kept in mind when rules of current European competition law, which are presented by the European Commission as economics-based, have to be assessed.

In modern industrial organisation, the immoderations of both the structuralist view (Harvard School) and the Chicago School have been mitigated. Current European competition law and US antitrust law profit from this modern learning. Modern industrial organisation teaches that a positive correlation between concentration can have different causes: market power, lower costs or strategic opportunities. Three important extensions of the Chicago approach have gained importance in the more recent literature: the theory of contestable markets, the transaction cost approach, and insights from game theory. As to the goals of competition policy, the focus now rests on both static and dynamic efficiency. Contestable markets theory has provided the important insight that potential competition may be an effective deterrent to anti-competitive behaviour if there is free market entry and free market exit. The structuralist view must also be reassessed on the basis of transaction cost theory. Vertical mergers (and vertical restraints in long-term contracts) may achieve important transaction cost savings that should be traded off against potential restrictions of competition. Finally, with respect to the discussion on the possibility of collusion in oligopolistic markets and barriers to entry, insights from game theory have appeared to be very enlightening. Harvard scholars described markets as fragile and prone to failure, whereas the Chicago scholars argued that markets can largely correct themselves. Modern industrial organisation accepts that most markets are resilient but imperfections may be caused by strategic behaviour limiting efficiency. The Harvard School identified many barriers to entry (also erected by private firms), whereas the Chicago School qualified private entry barriers as the result of the higher efficiency of incumbent firms. The modern insights on sunk costs (contestable markets theory) and strategic behaviour (game theory) have revitalised the debate on entry barriers and made clear that they can be more persistent than Chicagoans thought.

Obviously, competition law can largely profit from the theoretical and empirical work in the field of industrial organisation. The following chapters of this book will investigate to what extent there is a (dis)harmony between modern economic insights and current competition law.

Chapter 4

··

MARKET POWER, MARKET DEFINITION AND ENTRY BARRIERS

4.1 Introduction

This book subscribes to the view that the crucial concern of competition policy and law is the possible inefficiencies of market power. Before addressing the ways in which market power is acquired and exploited, the preliminary question of how market power may be identified must be addressed. The definition of market power is the central issue of this chapter. Definitions of market power, which may be found in the economic literature on industrial organisation, are clearly influenced by the characteristics of the model of perfect competition. For example, Carlton and Perloff define market power as ''the ability of a firm to set price profitably above competitive levels (marginal costs)''.[1] Many industrial economics books equally refer to discretion over price (the extent to which firms can hold price above marginal costs, measured

---

[1] D.W. Carlton and J.M. Perloff, *Modern Industrial Organisation* (4th ed., 2005), p.642.

by the Lerner index) as the relevant test for market power.[2] This economic literature further emphasises that market power only causes concerns from a competition policy viewpoint if prices can be kept above the competitive level (through output restrictions) for a sustained period of time because of the existence of entry barriers. If firms cannot easily enter and exit a market, incumbent firms enjoying market power may deploy forms of anti-competitive behaviour enabling them to earn supra-normal economic profits by hindering the growth of other firms and impeding the entry of newcomers.

The economic definition, which focuses on an individual firm's pricing discretion in the absence of entry barriers, differs from the traditional definition of a dominant firm found in competition law. The relevant case law of the European Court of Justice defines market power in terms of independent behaviour in markets as:

"...a position of economic strength enjoyed by an undertaking which enables it to prevent effective competition being maintained on the relevant market by giving it the power to behave to an appreciable extent independently of its competitors, customers, and, ultimately, consumers".[3]

Whereas the economic definition emphasises the ability of a firm to keep prices above competitive levels for the foreseeable future, the legal definition focuses on the degree of independence and thus equally includes concerns about limitations of the market participants' economic freedom.[4]

Another difference between economic and legal discussions of market power is the emphasis on market definition issues in the latter writings. Application of the relevant competition rules requires the lawyers to define the boundaries of the relevant market where market power is exercised. Defining the relevant market is the first and, in many respects, the most important question in legal analysis. In many competition law cases, the outcome falls neatly from the resolution of the market definition issue. In narrowly defined markets, mergers may be blocked and business practices may be prohibited which, if a wider market definition had been adopted, could have been cleared. Ill-defined relevant markets will have the consequence that the prohibitions of competition law are either under-inclusive or over-inclusive (type I and type II errors).[5] The quality of the study of industrial organisation is not similarly dependent on market definition decisions. This may explain why the economists' profession has, for a long time, not offered much practical help to

---

[2] S. Martin, *Industrial Economics: Economic Analysis and Public Policy* (1994), p.14.

[3] Case 27/76 *United Brands v Commission* [1978] ECR 207; see also Case 85/76 *Hoffmann-La Roche v Commission (Vitamins)* [1979] ECR 461.

[4] This can be related to the discussion on the goals of competition law: allocative efficiency and/or protection of individual economic freedom. See, for an elaboration, Ch.2, s.2.4.5 of this book.

[5] Unfortunately, the terms "type I error" and "type II error" as well as the expressions "false positives" and "false negatives" are not used in a consistent way in the legal and economic literature. In this book, the authors follow the classification proposed by A. Polinsky and S. Shavell, "Legal Error, Litigation and the Incentive to Obey the Law" (1989) 5 J. Law Econ. Organ. 99. Consequently, a type I error (false positive) refers to a conduct generating negative welfare effects which is wrongly allowed. Conversely, a type II error (false negative) denotes an erroneous prohibition of a conduct which would have increased welfare.

the competition lawyers' community in establishing reliable economic criteria allowing a delineation of relevant markets for legal purposes. Together with a greater openness towards economic arguments on the lawyers' side, economic input in competition law cases is now becoming increasingly important.

The economic definition makes it clear that the degree of market power may be measured directly if the relevant figures about marginal costs, price and residual demand elasticity are known. If the figures needed for direct measurement are not available, market power must be assessed in an indirect way. In competition law two consecutive steps are common. First, a relevant market is defined. Second, the competitive surroundings of this market are analysed, paying particular attention to the number of suppliers, which allows us to see how market shares are distributed over competitors. If information about market shares is available, concentration indices (such as the CR4 and the HHI[6]) can also be calculated. It is important to realise that market shares derived from relevant markets are an indirect way of assessing market power. If market power can be measured directly by measuring the relevant residual demand elasticity, the exercise of market definition may be superfluous.

Following the indirect method of assessing market power, the next issue to be assessed, after the calculation of market shares, is the analysis of entry barriers. The traditional legal definition does not explicitly mention entry barriers as a constitutive element of dominance. Consequently, the prohibitions of competition law will usually apply if high market shares have been established. Economic theory makes clear that market power can be exercised for a significant period only if barriers to market entry exist. The theory of contestable markets,[7] which is the most dramatic exponent of this view, even questions the desirability of antitrust intervention in cases of monopoly. Generally, if markets are easily accessible and if new entrants can leave without impediments, the threat of new entry will withhold incumbent firms from raising prices above competitive levels. Economists agree that government regulation making market entrance dependent on the possession of a licence is an important entry barrier. Opinions differ, however, on the extent to which private firms themselves may create entry barriers through exclusionary behaviour by raising rivals' costs. Also, the question of whether product differentiation and advertising may be used to deter market entry is a subject of great controversy.

This chapter is structured as follows. In the next section methods of market definition for antitrust purposes (hence, for establishing market shares) are discussed and related to the concept of market power. Old-fashioned legal definitions focusing on products' characteristics will be contrasted with the more recent SSNIP[8] methodology, which claims to give a better reflection of current economic learning. Particular attention will be devoted to the

---

[6] It may be recalled that the CR4 is computed by summing up the market shares of the four largest firms in the relevant market, whereas the Herfindahl–Hirschmann index (HHI) is the sum of the squares of the market shares held by all firms. For further discussion and comments, see Ch.3, s.3.5.1.1 and Ch.9, s.9.2.1.

[7] See Ch.3, s.3.8.

[8] Abbreviation of "Small but Significant and Non-transitory Increase in Price".

European Commission's Notice on market definition[9]: it will be investigated in how far the guidance offered in this Notice coincides with economic theory and to what extent the Notice embraces modern econometric techniques to measure market power. Comparisons with US antitrust law will be made to allow an overall assessment of the (dis)harmony between the state of the art in economics and the current rules of competition law. In the third section, the emphasis shifts to the analysis of entry barriers. As indicated above, market power may be exercised in the long run only if firms face difficulties in entering markets and incumbents are thus protected from competition by newcomers. Empirical research grounded in the structure–conduct–performance paradigm indicated a great number of entry barriers, including economies of scale, product differentiation and advertising. It will be investigated how modern industrial organisation has reshaped thinking on these issues and how current competition law assesses alleged barriers to entry.

4.2 Market definition and market power

The economic concern with market power has traditionally been translated into an indirect structuralist approach to competition law based on market shares and starting from the definition of relevant markets. In recent years, market definition issues have been given an ever increasing importance since low market shares may guarantee antitrust immunity to firms (see, for example, the "safe harbours" in the Guidelines on horizontal cooperation, the Regulation on vertical restraints, and the Merger Regulation[10]). The increasing reliance on market shares is presented as an economically oriented approach, to contrast it with the legalistic tradition of competition law. However, in the view of the authors of this book, it may be misleading to present rules based on market shares as *the* economic approach to all kinds of competition law problems. In the following, the main economic insights on market definition will be presented.

The crucial economic concept for market definition purposes is the so-called SSNIP test, also known as the hypothetical monopolist test.[11] This market identification process seeks to recognise the smallest group of products and geographic areas, for which a hypothetical monopolist could impose a profitable price increase, ranging between 5 and 10 per cent, lasting for the foreseeable future (at least one year).[12] This examination is clearly different from

---

[9] Commission Notice on the definition of the relevant market for the purposes of Community competition law [1997] O.J. C 372/1.

[10] For discussion, see Ch.5, s.5.3.2, Ch.6, s.6.3.2 and Ch.9, s.9.2 respectively. All other "modern" block exemptions also contain market share safe harbours. At the time of writing, the Commission is in the process of phasing out the remaining premodernisation block exemptions; for references, see Ch.5, s.5.3.4.

[11] See P. Crocioni, "*The Hypothetical Monopolist Test: What It Can and Cannot Tell You*" (2002) 23 E.C.L.R. 354.

[12] These figures are based on a normative judgment, according to which price increases exceeding these limits are deemed unacceptable from a competition policy perspective.

the traditional legal approach, which seeks to define relevant markets upon the basis of a comparison of the characteristics of goods and geographic areas. It will be argued below (section 4.3.2) that the Guidelines of the European Commission on market definition are not in perfect harmony with the economic insights flowing from the SSNIP test. Both the theoretical framework and the use of quantitative techniques to delineate relevant markets will be critically assessed. Before focusing on the Commission's Notice, section 4.2.1 will first summarise the relevant theoretical economic insights on market definition and then warn of possible misconceptions of the notion of a relevant market.

4.2.1 Market power and the concept of a relevant market

There are several reasons why it may be misleading to present market share analysis as *the* economic approach to problems of competition policy and law. To start with, there are economic approaches to competition law that reject market definition as a tool of decision making. At this point, the German theory of freedom of competition (*Konzept der Wettbewerbsfreiheit*) must be recalled.[13] In this conceptual approach, both the market and the process of competition are seen as unique and indivisible. Every euro the consumer spends on buying a certain product cannot be spent on other purchases; consequently, all firms compete with each other to get the largest possible share of the consumer's purchases. The exercise of market definition is meaningless since all products compete with all remaining products. The definition of the relevant market is a concept that builds upon the structure–conduct–performance paradigm, but is superfluous in an approach—such as the German concept of freedom of competition—that makes only a distinction between permitted and prohibited practices.[14]

This section will not further elaborate on the German concept of *Wettbewerbsfreiheit*, that rejects market share analysis altogether. Rather, the focus will be on the risks that a misguided use of market share analysis poses for antitrust law. Obviously, before these risks—that are manifold—can be addressed, it is necessary to first explain the prevailing economic approach to market power and market definition, which has become universally known as the SSNIP test (section 4.2.1.1). After the discussion of the SSNIP test, this section will address the inherent restrictions of market share analysis. It will first be argued that the definition of the relevant market may in itself be misleading. The relevant antitrust market should not be confused with other concepts of markets, such as industries, economic markets and strategic markets (section 4.2.1.2). This chapter will also warn against too far reaching conclusions based on a simple calculation of market shares. Obviously, the quality of the

---

[13] The *Konzept der Wettbewerbsfreiheit* was discussed in Ch.3, s.3.7.3.
[14] See E. Hoppmann, *Marktmacht und Wettbewerb* (1977); and D. Schmidtchen, *"Fehlurteile über das Konzept der Wettbewerbsfreiheit"* in ORDO *Jahrbuch für die Ordnung von Wirtschaft und Gesellschaft* (1988), pp.113, 130–132.

decisions based on market shares is crucially dependent on the value of the market definition exercise. There is a risk that the market definition may be biased towards finding an infringement of the competition laws. But even if markets are appropriately defined, one should be careful not to underestimate or overestimate the conclusions that can be drawn from market share analysis (section 4.2.1.3). Finally, in recent economic literature, it is asserted that problems of competition law may also be solved without going to the trouble of delineating relevant markets. This view should not be confused with the German concept of freedom of competition, discussed above. However, it also questions not only the market share analysis but the entire market definition exercise on grounds derived from mainstream economic analysis (section 4.2.1.4).

4.2.1.1 The Lerner index and the SSNIP test

The standard theoretical economic approach assesses the degree of market power as an increase in the Lerner index.[15] A firm in a perfectly competitive market faces a perfectly elastic (horizontal) demand curve and is said to possess no market power, since it can only act as a price-taker. By contrast, a monopolist sets his price at the point on his demand curve where marginal costs equal marginal revenues. The Lerner index formalises this concept of market power as the setting of price in excess of marginal costs by measuring the proportional deviation of price at the firm's profit-maximising output from the firm's marginal costs at that output. Its simplest formulation is: $L = (P - MC) / P$.

The Lerner index thus measures the difference between price and marginal costs; the greater the deviation between these standards of measurement, the greater the market power of the firm and the ensuing allocative inefficiency. By re-arranging the above formula, the mark-up factor can be defined as $1 / (1 - L)$.

Due to the traditionally limited applicability of the marginal cost concept, antitrust economics has focused mainly on the elasticities of demand to determine market power.[16] It is important to distinguish between the elasticity of demand for a product[17] and the elasticity of demand faced by a firm: the former referring to the impact of the change in price on the market's demand, the latter also including any changes in demand for the product after a price rise as a result of any induced changes in the price of competing products. Since the Lerner index is a measure of the firm's market power, the relevant elasticity is the firm's elasticity of demand, for it is the response to the firm's output to a change in price that determines the degree to which it has market

---

[15] See A.P. Lerner, "The Concept of Monopoly and the Measurement of Monopoly Power" (1934) 1 Rev. Econ. Studies 157.

[16] W.M. Landes and R.A. Posner, "Market Power in Antitrust Cases" (1981) 94 Harv. L. Rev. 937 at p.941.

[17] In general, the elasticity of demand for a product describes what happens when the price of that product changes, holding constant the prices of all other products.

power.[18] It may be shown[19] that the proportionate price–cost margin charged by a profit maximising firm will be equal to the reciprocal of the absolute value of the own-price elasticity of demand faced by that firm, and that this elasticity itself has two components: first, the (direct) own-price elasticity of demand for the product(s) produced by the firm, and, second, the (indirect) sum of the cross-price elasticities with respect to competing products as a result of changes in the prices set by other firms.[20] The higher the elasticity of demand for the firm's product at the firm's profit maximising price, the closer that price will be to the competitive price, and the less, therefore, the monopoly over-charge will be. If the elasticity of demand is infinite at the firm's profit max-imising price, then the Lerner index will equal zero. An infinite elasticity in demand means that the slightest increase in price will cause the quantity demanded to fall to zero. Conversely, as long as the firm is in the inelastic region of its demand curve (where the elasticity of demand is less than one), prices may be profitably raised.

The Lerner index makes clear that the market power of a firm (or group of firms) is limited by the degree of both demand substitution and supply sub-stitution. The residual demand elasticity captures both competitive con-straints. Unfortunately, its direct measurement by advanced econometric techniques requires extensive, reliable data and is therefore difficult.[21] As mentioned above, in daily antitrust practice the most common way to define market power is by calculating market shares on a relevant market. To gear the use of market shares to the economic concept of market power, the so-called SSNIP test has been developed. Only if this test is followed will market shares be a reliable indicator for the degree of market power of the firm(s) under investigation.

The SSNIP test was adopted by the US antitrust agencies in the 1982 Merger Guidelines.[22] This method of defining the product and geographic dimension of the market starts with a narrowly defined product (or geographic area) of one of the merging firms and judges the profitability of at least a "Small but Significant and Non-transitory Increase in Price" (SSNIP, normally 5 per cent lasting for the foreseeable future) by a hypothetical monopolist of the product in question. Products are included at each stage of the next best substitute, until a group of products is formed so that, at least, a SSNIP for a product of

---

[18] See W.M. Landes and R.A. Posner, "Market Power in Antitrust Cases" (1981) 94 Harv. L. Rev. 937 at pp.940–941.

[19] See, for example, D. Neven, R. Nuttall and P. Seabright, *Merger in Daylight: The Economics and Politics of European Merger Control* (1993), pp.20–21.

[20] Own-price product demand elasticity is negative, and measures the extent to which a firm can raise the price of its product without experiencing a decline in total revenue. In the following, own-price elasticity of demand and price elasticity of demand are used as synonyms. The cross-elasticities measure the extent to which changes in the prices of related products affect the sales of the product in question, and will be positive if products are substitutes. The induced changes in price of competing products will be positive if firms coordinate their behaviour, and negative if they compete aggressively.

[21] W. Kerber and U. Schwalbe, "Ökonomische Grundlagen des Wettbewerbsrechts" in *Münchener Kommentar zum Europäischen und Deutschen Wettbewerbsrecht*, Bd I, nrs. 184 (2006, forthcoming), pp.196–199.

[22] US Department of Justice, Antitrust Division, Merger Guidelines, August 9, 1982, Fed. Reg. 47, 1982, 28,493, reprinted in: Trade Reg. Rep. 4, Chicago, CCH, 1978, para.13,102; at s.1.

one of the merging firms would be maximally profitable for the hypothetical monopolist of that group. The relevant product market is the smallest set of products for which a hypothetical monopolist would find it profitable to increase prices by 5 per cent. The analysis continues until markets are delineated around each of the products of each of the merging firms. The two sets of product markets are then compared to determine whether the two merging firms are participants in any of the same product markets. An identical procedure is used to define the geographic market. The present 1997 Merger Guidelines[23] thus define the relevant market as:

"... a product or group of products and a geographic area in which it is produced or sold so that a hypothetical profit maximising firm, not subject to price regulation, that was the only present and future producer or seller of those products in that area would likely impose at least a 'small but significant and non-transitory' increase in price, assuming the terms of sale of all other products are held constant."

The reduction in demand for a hypothetical monopolist's products in response to a projected price increase has three components: (1) demand-side substitution; (2) supply-side substitution of existing products outside the relevant market; and (3) supply-side substitution of new products (*viz.* potential competition).[24] According to s.1.11 of the 1997 Merger Guidelines, the US antitrust agencies take into account "all relevant evidence", including, but not limited to, evidence that buyers have shifted purchases between products in response to relative changes in price or other competitive variables, evidence that sellers base business decisions on the prospect of buyer substitution between products in response to relative changes in price or other competitive variables, the influence of downstream competition faced by buyers in their output markets, and the timing and costs of switching products. Apart from the inherent arbitrariness of choosing the appropriate level for a SSNIP (the range is usually between 5 and 10 per cent and the time period at least one year), the procedure as contained in the Merger Guidelines provides for a tightly focused technique on how to define the market, thereby providing consistency among cases. The Guidelines present a comprehensive approach to the question of an integrated product and geographic market definition. Econometric estimations of demand and supply relations are, if present,

---

[23] s.1.11. of the 1997 Merger Guidelines.
[24] Compare D. Neven, R. Nuttall and P. Seabright, *Merger in Daylight: The Economics and Politics of European Merger Control* (1993), pp.47–50; and H. Hovenkamp, *Federal Antitrust Policy: The Law of Competition and its Practice* (1994) p.89: "no grouping of sales is a relevant market unless both the elasticity of demand and the elasticity of supply are sufficiently low to warrant a conclusion that the sole seller of that grouping could profitably raise price substantially above the competitive level". Demand-side substitution takes place when buyers switch from one product to another in response to a change in price; supply-side substitution refers to competing producers reacting to a price increase; while potential competition takes into account competitive constraints under assessing entry; see S. Bishop and M. Walker, *Economics of EC Competition Law: Concepts, Application and Measurement* (2nd ed., 2002), paras 4.20–4.32.

closely analysed, as are econometric studies relating price to concentration in the industry under scrutiny.[25]

The SSNIP's European presence was upstaged in the Commission's *Nestlé/ Perrier* decision,[26] subsequently formalised in *Saint-Gobain/Wacker-Chemie/ NOM*,[27] and eventually adopted as the common standard for defining relevant antitrust markets in the European Commission's 1997 Notice. Notable even at this point is the Notice's general reference to the SSNIP test, not only in cases of controlling concentrative activity as in the USA, but also related to findings of dominance. Applying, however, the SSNIP test in instances already characterised by existing market power may lead to unwanted results, as will be further elaborated upon later.

Since the SSNIP test has been adopted both by the European and American competition authorities, the question naturally arises how this approach relates to the economic insights on market definition. Among economists there is a consensus that the critical concept underlying the definition of an antitrust market is the residual demand facing a given group of producers.[28] Such residual demand denotes the demand function specifying the level of sales made by the group as a function of the price they charge, thereby taking into account competitors' reactions. The residual demand elasticity measures the extent to which a firm would be able to raise a price by reducing output, after taking into account the demand responses of buyers and the supply responses of rivals.[29] It thus combines demand-side and supply-side substitution. In practice, the US 1982 Merger Guidelines applied a similar estimation technique to define markets.[30] Residual demand methodology raises a particular firm's costs without raising the costs of its competitors, and this induces the firm to exercise market power over price if it can, and this, in turn, enables the measurement of market power.[31] For the purpose of delineating markets, costs are hence raised simultaneously for all the firms selling inside the proposed market without raising costs for firms selling possible demand substitutes initially outside the proposed market.[32] If the residual demand elasticity is sufficiently high so that the price increase is unprofitable, then the market must be expanded to include the next best substitute. Under the 1982 Merger

[25] Compare D.L. Kaserman and H. Zeisel, "Market Definition: Implementing the Department of Justice Merger Guidelines" (1996) 41 Antitrust Bull. 665; and J.R. Morris and G.R. Mosteller, "Defining Markets for Merger Analysis" (1991) 36 Antitrust Bull. 599.

[26] Case IV/M.190 *Nestlé/Perrier* [1992] O.J. L 356/1.

[27] Case IV/M.774 *Saint-Gobain/Wacker-Chemie/NOM* [1997] O.J. L 247/1, para.220.

[28] Introduced by W.M. Landes and R.A. Posner, "Market Power in Antitrust Cases" (1981) 94 Harv. L. Rev. 937; and elaborated in D.T. Scheffmann and P.T. Spiller, "Geographic Market Definition under the US Department of Justice Merger Guidelines" (1987) 30 J. Law Econ. 123 at pp.130–131.

[29] See J.B. Baker and T.F. Bresnahan, "Estimating the Residual Demand Curve Facing a Single Firm" (1988) 6 Int. J. Ind. Org. 283.

[30] Section 2.11 of the 1982 Merger Guidelines. Compare J.J. Simons and M.A. Williams, "The Renaissance of Market Definition" (1993) 39 Antitrust Bull. 799 at 823–828.

[31] J.B. Baker and T.F. Bresnahan, "Empirical Methods of Identifying and Measuring Market Power" (1992) 61 Antitrust L.J. 3 at pp.7–8.

[32] Translated to the SSNIP approach residual demand elasticities measure the percentage change in the price charged by the hypothetical monopolist. Products with a high residual demand elasticity would lose a large proportion of their sales in response to a small increase in price.

Guidelines' approach, cross-price elasticity (or interchangeability for that matter) thus remains useful for identifying the range of substitutes thereto.[33] The residual demand elasticity subsequently needs to be remeasured for the hypothetical monopolist of a new and larger candidate market. If, however, the producers in the proposed market react collectively to an industry costs increase by raising prices, despite the threat of loss of sales to the producers outside this proposed market, then it is likely that the proposed market would form a relevant antitrust product market.[34]

Unfortunately, the 1992/1997 Merger Guidelines deviate from their predecessors in qualifying s.1.0 so that now the terms of sale of all other products are to be held constant when applying the SSNIP. In so doing, it is assumed that all potential substitutes have infinitely elastic supply at current prices, and this principally removes the assessment of competitors' reactions from the market delineation stage.[35] This supposition suggests that the econometric estimation underlying market definition is to proceed solely through the estimation of own-price elasticities of demand and cross-price elasticities of demand. Properly considered, both concepts of elasticity are of course important for incorporation into the antitrust process of market definition.[36] This approach, however, needs to be traced back to the original goal of conducting market delineation in the first place, to wit the identification of market power. Accordingly, the inclusion of supply-side considerations at some point of the assessment is essential. In the USA, this is undertaken at the competitive effects stage of the analysis. Similar to the current version of the US Merger Guidelines, the European Commission has opted for a combination of product price elasticities of demand and cross-price elasticities of demand.[37] Given that the Notice's structural quantitative estimation tools only account for demand-side considerations, the market delineation exercise remains incomplete. In line with the Notice's theoretical framework, it thus becomes very important to assure that supply-side considerations are indeed withheld at a later stage of the assessment before conclusions on market power are reached.

4.2.1.2 Possible misconceptions about the relevant antitrust market

As it has become clear from our discussion of the SSNIP methodology, the exercise of defining a relevant market has as its ultimate goal identifying the most important competitive constraints that exist between products and regions. The following rule of thumb can always be helpful as a guide in

---

[33] See J.J. Simons and M.A. Williams, "The Renaissance of Market Definition" (1993) 39 Antitrust Bull. 799 at pp.825–826.

[34] Although attractive in many ways, the residual demand analysis does have its own difficulties, summarised in: D.L. Kaserman and H. Zeisel, "Market Definition: Implementing the Department of Justice Merger Guidelines" (1996) 41 Antitrust Bull. 665 at pp.677–678.

[35] ss.1.0 and 1.3 of the 1997 Merger Guidelines.

[36] Compare W.F. Shughart, II, R.D. Tollison and E.C. Reed, "Breakfast at the Federal Trade Commission", in *Economic Inputs, Legal Outputs* (F. McChesney ed., 1996) pp.85, 86; and G.J. Werden, "Demand Elasticities in Antitrust Analysis" (1998) 66 Antitrust L.J. 363, containing an overview of the different concepts of elasticities as mentioned.

[37] s.39 of the 1997 Notice, n.5.

decision making: the relevant market is where the battle is. Consequently, concepts of markets that do not capture the limitations on profitable lasting price increases are misleading. In this section, three such concepts will be presented: industries, economic markets and strategic markets.[38]

Industries The notion of a relevant market has its roots in the US Supreme Court's precedent law, which in turn was based on economic theory common during the first major antitrust proceedings.[39] In this context, however, the indication of economic theory is somewhat euphemistic, given that Harvard economists were setting the tone, using the structure–conduct–performance approach that may be described as fundamentally *a*theoretical. As discussed earlier,[40] Harvard scholars tended to base their investigations upon assessing whole industries, which Bain defined in 1951 as a group of products featuring high cross-price elasticities with each other, but low cross-price elasticities with other products.[41] This definition of an industry may not be confused with the "relevant market" in competition law, since the cross-price elasticities brought up by Bain may be inappropriate to decide pending antitrust cases. What can be learned from cross-price elasticities will be documented in the discussion of the Commission's Notice later. Here, it may suffice to say that cross-price elasticities allow a ranking of substitutes but that, on the basis of these figures alone, it remains unclear where the border line between the different substitutes must be drawn to delineate the relevant antitrust market. Only the (critical) residual demand elasticity allows for a direct delineation of the relevant market for antitrust purposes.

Hence, industry classifications as forwarded by Harvard scholars may best be applied for statistical aims; they do not carry practical information for pending antitrust cases. The level of concentration in an industry as such is not to be unequivocally equated with the level of market power in the relevant antitrust market. In 1956, however, the US Supreme Court referred to Bain in its *Cellophane* ruling,[42] stressing the importance of assessing whether buyers could switch to substitute products and indicating cross-price elasticities as the standard of measurement to be determined econometrically. Two decades later, the European Court of Justice, in its notorious *Chiquita* judgment (see Box 4.1) similarly applied the concept of cross-price elasticities, and defined the relevant product market as comprising:

"... the totality of products which, with respect to their characteristics, are particularly suitable for satisfying constant needs, and are only to a limited extent

---

[38] See also P.A. Geroski, "Thinking Creatively about Markets" (1998) 16 Int. J. Ind. Org. 77.

[39] On the US, compare J.J. Simons and M.A. Williams, "The Renaissance of Market Definition" (1993) 39 Antitrust Bull. 799; or R. Pitofsky, "New Definitions of Relevant Market and the Assault on Antitrust" (1990) 90 Colum. L. Rev. 1805.

[40] See Ch.3, s.3.5.

[41] J.S. Bain, "Relation of Profit Rate to Industry Concentration: American Manufacturing" (1951) 65 Quart. J. Econ. 293.

[42] *United States v E.I. DuPont de Nemours and Co (Cellophane)*, 351 US 377 (1956), para.400.

interchangeable with other products in terms of price, usage, and consumer preference".[43]

As will be further explained below, one should be cautious in drawing conclusions as to market definition on the basis of figures on cross-price elasticities.

Box 4.1: The banana case

Among Europe's classics *United Brands (Chiquita)*[44] still manages to hold its own. Concerning the relevant product market, the European Court of Justice stated that this was to be formed by bananas (as distinguished from the wider market of fresh fruit in general). The Court reached this conclusion in alluding to the banana's special product attributes (such as appearance, taste, softness, seedlessness and easy handling) which enables it to satisfy the constant needs of an important section of the population consisting of "the very young, the old, and the sick".[45] Furthermore, bananas are characterised by an uninterrupted level of production, leading to limited effects on price competition from other fresh fruit (such as grapes and peaches) at the banana's seasonal peak periods. These considerations, so the Court infers, outweighed others such as the fall in price of, and the demand for, bananas at times when more fruits are available, as the latter showed merely a limited interchangeability.[46]

By ruling out the existence of significant cross-price elasticities between bananas and other summer fruits, this case depicts well the risks attached to delineating markets based solely on product characteristics. There is no convincing economic reason for a market defined so narrowly as to exclude melons, strawberries, plums and the like. Besides, *United Brands* highlights the limited applicability of the cross-elasticity concept as a stand-alone device for defining relevant antitrust markets. The issue is not whether certain groups of customers have strong preferences for the product in question, but if, for a 5 or 10 per cent increase above the competitive price, generally significant interproduct substitution would take place. The fact that particular groups of consumers (in the Court's vision of things the "toothless", being the very young, the old and the sick) will perceive

---

[43] Case 27/76 *United Brands v Commission* [1978] ECR 207, paras 12 and 31.
[44] *ibid.*; The issue before the European Court of Justice was whether United Brands' pricing and distribution policy for bananas was in breach of Art. 82 EC.
[45] *ibid.*, para.34.
[46] Indeed, "[F]or the banana to be regarded as forming a market which is sufficiently differentiated from other fruit markets it must be possible for it to be singled out by such special factors distinguishing it from other fruits that it is only to a limited extent interchangeable with them and is only exposed to their competition in a way that is hardly perceptible"; see *ibid.*, para.22. Compare C.W. Bellamy and G. Child, *Common Market Law of Competition*, (5th ed., 2001) para.9–010.

differences in product characteristics when comparing bananas, peaches, pears and other types of fresh fruit does not allow for the conclusion that price increases for bananas will be profitable. Identifying a distinct sub-group of consumers is only possible in those cases where it may be established that producers can effectively distinguish between such sub-groups (*in casu* between those consumers able to chew, and the toothless), thus barring arbitrage. If this would seem an impossible task, then United Brands' alleged position of dominance could not be abused. In its Notice on market definition, the European Commission has acknowledged that the scope for narrow markets is dependent on the feasibility of price discrimination: "A distinct group of customers for the relevant product may constitute a narrower, distinct market when such a group could be subject to price discrimination. This will usually be the case when two conditions are met: first, it is possible to identify clearly which group an individual customer belongs to at the moment of selling the relevant products to him, and, second, trade among customers or arbitrage by third parties should not be feasible."[47] This is an important innovative aspect as the European Commission nowadays seems less inclined to conclude upon separate narrow sub-markets.[48]

Economic markets The Bainian notion of an industry (and the related measurement of cross-price elasticities) is not the only potential cause of confusion surrounding the notion of a relevant market. The relevant market for antitrust purposes should equally not be confused with an economic market (or a strategic market). Economic markets (as defined in economics textbooks) are markets for goods (and/or geographic areas) where supply and demand lead to equilibrium. Economic markets are areas where the law of one price holds.[49] In an economic market, if producer A increases his price, this may cause buyers to switch to producer B. As a result of this arbitrage, price differences will become smaller and B's output will increase. This possibility of arbitrage tempers but does not necessarily eliminate the exercise of market power. It is not excluded that A increases his prices—in other words, applies an SSNIP—profitably if not too many sales are lost to producer B (because B's output is relatively small and supply elasticity is low). In the example given, the relevant antitrust market is smaller than the economic market. Conversely, the relevant antitrust market may also be larger than the economic market. Two distant geographic areas, where homogeneous goods (produced competitively under constant marginal costs) are sold, may form two separate economic markets (since price levels are similar in each market considered individually) but constitute a single antitrust market. Even if there is no

---

[47] Section 43 of the 1997 Notice.
[48] In the *Veba/Degussa* merger, for example, the Commission declined to separate isophoron diamines from the overall market of diamines (hardeners for epoxy resin systems used in varnishes, steel and concrete coatings), although they make up 30% of the value of the total market and it had been established that up to 20% of the applied isophoron diamines are limited in their substitutability. (Case IV/M.942 *Veba/Degussa* [1998] O.J. L 201/102, para.33).
[49] A. Marshall, *Principles of Economics* (9th ed., 1961), p.325.

similarity of price levels across both markets, an increase of prices in territory A may incite a producer in territory B to enter territory A if the transportation costs are lower than the price increase. This risk of entry may refrain producer A from raising his prices. In the latter case, the relevant antitrust market will comprise two territories with different price levels and thus consist of two separate economic markets.[50]

Strategic markets   Another source of confusion is the concept of a strategic market, which can be found in marketing literature.[51] Strategic markets comprise consumer groups and geographic territories at which marketing activities are targeted. It is quite possible that the marketing techniques used in different geographic areas are largely similar. This similarity does not, however, indicate a single relevant antitrust market. For example, the sales methods, distribution techniques and promotion schemes (in particular advertising) of clothes may be the same in distant parts of the European Community, but these parts will form separate antitrust markets if lasting profitable price increases are possible in each of them. As a consequence, the strategic market will be much wider than the relevant antitrust market.[52]

The distinction between strategic markets and relevant antitrust market shows that competition authorities should be cautious in interpreting economic evidence. Marketing specialists may not be the right experts to be consulted in antitrust cases. Marketing studies are often quite informative but they are designed for the purpose of understanding consumer buying patterns and do not ask the crucial question of how buying behaviour changes in response to changes in price. Hence, the information provided by such studies must be interpreted with care: it is not directly relevant for the issue of market definition and is useful only in as far as that information complements econometric evidence about demand elasticities.[53]

Not only marketing studies, but also studies by econometricians showing positive price correlations between two or more products should be treated with care. Similarity of price movements over time allows the identification of an economic market, but does not automatically justify the conclusion that this economic market is also the relevant antitrust market. This last point will be further elaborated upon in section 4.2.2.2. on econometric evidence.

---

[50] D. Scheffman and P. Spiller, "Geographic Market Definition under the U.S. Department of Justice Merger Guidelines" (1987) 30 J. Law Econ. 123 at p.127.
[51] The standard textbook is P. Kotler, *Principles of Marketing, International Edition* (9th ed., 2001).
[52] The Dutch Competition Authority (NMa) may be criticised for having used a definition of a strategic market in the *KBB/Vendex* merger case. See R. Van den Bergh, "Dante, Calimero en de rechter-econoom" (2003) 51 S.E.W. 10.
[53] See D. Rubinfeld, "Market Definition with Differentiated Products: The Post/Nabisco Cereal Merger" (2000) 68 Antitrust L.J. 163 at p.167. The author provides the following clarifying example. If 80% of the average adult's cereal consumption is of adult cereals and 70% of the average child's consumption is of children's cereals, both products may still be in the same relevant antitrust market if a 10% increase in price of adult cereals would be unprofitable because consumers of all ages switch to children's cereals.

4.2.1.3 Market share analysis: risks and limitations[54]

Quite regularly the use of an indirect approach leads to focusing the attention on market definition, not on the fundamental question of the effects of market power. Whatever market shares may mean, their interpretation depends on how the market is defined. In a market too narrowly defined, a high share does not carry much information. In a market defined overly broadly, a low share does not. The concept of a relevant market, in the end, is but a deliberate attempt, for the sake of workability, to oversimplify the very complex inter-actions between a number of diversely situated buyers and sellers, each of whom has in reality different costs, needs, and substitutes. It is definitely not an end in itself.

Risk of subjective decisions Market definition only provides a foundation on which it is possible to evaluate likely competitive effects. If market defi-nition becomes the goal of the assessment by the competition authority, rather than an instrument to better understand the antitrust problems at hand, decisions in real-world cases may be biased. This risk is particularly severe when the old-fashioned legal definition focusing on product characteristics is used. The policy problems which may then arise are numerous: lack of transparency leading to large discretionary power of competition authorities, danger of regulatory capture, and lack of objectivity (how much substitution is necessary?). In the literature serious concerns have been expressed with respect to the risk of subjective decisions. It has been noted that the European Commission did not always establish dominance independently, but tended to determine that an abuse had occurred and then defined the market in such a way that dominance became unquestionable. These concerns are substantiated by examples of market definitions clearly including non-substitutable goods (such as the market for "vitamins"[55]) or findings of dominance in cases of quite modest firms (see the discussion of the *Hugin* case in Box 4.2). Obviously, the boundaries of the market should not be expanded or contracted in such a way that the accused firm can be identified as a dominant producer within it.[56]

---

[54] See also G.J. Werden, "Assigning Market Shares" (2002) 70 Antitrust L.J. 67.

[55] In *Hoffmann-La Roche*, the complaint was directed against fidelity rebates based on aggregate purchases of the whole range of vitamins produced by the company. The Court of Justice relied on the company's share of particular vitamins to prohibit a strategy which applied to the whole range. Clearly, the relevant market cannot include all vitamins because they are not substitutable by either consumers or producers. Consequently, the Court's decision thus ultimately rests on fud-ging the market concept. See M.A. Utton, *Market Dominance and Antitrust Policy* (2nd ed., 2003), p.79.

[56] J.A. Fairburn, J.A. Kay and T.A.E. Sharpe, "The Economics of Article 86", in *European Industrial Policy* (G. Hall ed., 1986), p.41.

Box 4.2: Hugin and aftermarkets

In *Hugin*, the European Court of Justice looked into Hugin's refusal to supply spare parts for its cash registers to a London based servicing and maintenance company, Liptons.[57] The facts of the case are somewhat unusual, since the relevant product market as identified by the Court consisted of "spare parts for cash registers manufactured by Hugin required by independent undertakings". Hugin, a Swedish company having at the time 13 per cent of the United Kingdom market for such registers, had argued that the relevant market was to be "cash registers" as a whole, a "very competitive" market.[58] An argumentation thereto based on the technical complexity of the product was rejected by the Court in terms of its characteristics,[59] however, and Hugin, as a consequence, was found to constitute a monopolist in the supply of its own spare parts.[60] Subsequent cases further established that spare parts can form a market separate from the products for which they are needed.[61] Although touching the fascinating issue of aftermarkets neither the European Court of Justice nor the European Commission in the underlying decision[62] posed the relevant questions in the matter. An aftermarket can only be considered as a relevant antitrust market if the producer of the complementary product is able to increase prices profitably, because consumers are locked-in and cannot turn to substitutes.

By limiting itself to a (rather brief) appraisal of the product's characteristics, the Court failed to assess whether Hugin as a producer of its spare parts could permanently raise its prices 5 to 10 per cent without losing so many customers as to make this price increase unprofitable. Effectively, the essence of an aftermarket arises in those cases where a consumer, having chosen a specific brand at one point in time, may find it costly later on to switch to other brands. The key elements to an aftermarket are the following: (a) the provision of practical consumer value to the product at hand requires several purchases of complementary components working together as a system; (b) purchases are spread over different points in time, and

---

[57] Case 22/78 *Hugin v Commission* [1979] ECR 1869. Following disagreements between the parties, further supply of spare parts was refused, preventing Liptons from carrying on its independent business of servicing registers of that kind. Brought before the European Court of Justice, it was argued that the ensuing elimination of Liptons would remove a major competitor of Hugin in the servicing and repair of Hugin cash registers. Ultimately, the Court held that trade between Member States of the Community was not affected, thus preventing the application of Art. 82 EC. The servicing and repair facilities of cash registers and ancillary activities, so the argument went, were essentially local in character and could not be operated profitably beyond a certain area around the commercial base of an undertaking. There is, however, "no reason to suppose that the [underlying] Commission's decision would have been annulled on the question of abuse"; compare C.W. Bellamy and G. Child, *Common Market Law of Competition* (5th ed., 2001) para.9–096.
[58] *Hugin*, paras 3–4.
[59] *Hugin*, paras 6–7. It was found that cash registers are of such a technical nature that the user cannot fit the spare parts into the machine but requires the service of a specialised technician; also, independent undertakings which specialise in the maintenance and repair of cash registers make up a specific group of customers for Hugin spare parts, as those parts are not interchangeable with spare parts for cash registers of other brands.
[60] *Hugin*, para.9.
[61] Compare the references contained in R. Whish, *Competition Law* (3rd ed., 1994), p.252.
[62] Case IV/29.132 *Hugin/Liptons* [1978] O.J. L 22/23.

(c) there is some degree of sunk costs in the sense that at least some of the initial expenditure cannot be recovered if the consumer later decides to switch brands.[63] In the case of cash registers, the initial investment is in the machine itself, while the components purchased later are the spare parts and the maintenance necessary to keep the machine operable. Under certain limited circumstances economic theory does offer some indicators on when manufacturers in competitive equipment markets might profitably harm consumers by changing their policies with regard to the sale of replacement parts to independent service providers. A firm like Hugin selling both equipment and associated proprietary aftermarket products faces a trade-off when setting its aftermarket price. A higher price will, on the one hand, allow it to earn more profits on aftermarket sales to consumers who have already purchased the equipment (the lock-in effect). On the other hand, however, it will also reduce sales of the primary equipment because potential buyers will take into account this higher expected cost of pur-chasing the aftermarket products and maintenance (the reputation effect).

Defendants in antitrust aftermarket cases such as *Hugin*, or the dissenting opinion of the US Supreme Court in *Kodak*[64] for that matter, have often argued that, if the equipment market is sufficiently competitive, then the reputation effect will overwhelm the lock-in effect and firms will set prices for the proprietary aftermarket goods at competitive levels. Some econo-mists are indeed very sceptical about the possibility of an aftermarket hold-up. According to other commentators, the economic basis for such a conclusion is limited to specific cases.[65] A manufacturer's anti-competitive aftermarket strategies can reduce its future profits in two ways: first, by reducing sales to new customers and, second, by losing incumbent owners of the equipment when it is replaced or upgraded. However, the equipment manufacturer does not easily lose profits on new customers because it can lower the equipment's price to compensate these customers for higher aftermarket prices. With existing customers, then, the manufacturer can make more profits as they have already bought the equipment and are not

---

[63] C. Shapiro, "Aftermarkets and Consumer Welfare: Making Sense of Kodak" (1995) 63 Antitrust L.J. 483 at 486; B. Klein, "Market Power in Aftermarkets", in *Economic Inputs, Legal Outputs: The Role of Economics in Modern Antitrust* (F. McChesney ed., 1998), p.47. For a detailed discussion of Klein's arguments, see Ch.7, s.7.4.2.

[64] *Eastman Kodak Co v Image Technical Services, Inc*, 112 S. Ct. 2072 (1992), para.2097. The majority ruled that a manufacturer could, as a matter of law, have monopoly power in the servicing of its own equipment, even if it had no such power in the sale of that equipment. Compare B. Klein, "Market Power in Aftermarkets", in *Economic Inputs, Legal Outputs: The Role of Economics in Modern Antitrust* (F. McChesney ed., 1998), p.47; or H. Hovenkamp, *Federal Antitrust Policy: The Law of Competition and its Practice* (1994), pp.91–96.

[65] Compare B. Klein, "Market Power in Aftermarkets", in *Economic Inputs, Legal Outputs: The Role of Economics in Modern Antitrust* (F. McChesney ed., 1998), p.47; or H. Hovenkamp, *Federal Antitrust Policy: The Law of Competition and its Practice* (1994), pp.91–96; and S. Borenstein, J.K. MacKie-Mason and J.S. Netz, "Antitrust Policy in Aftermarkets" (1995) 63 Antitrust L.J. 455.

compensated for the higher aftermarket price. Future profits due to reputation-building are consequently balanced against the cost in foregone profits from customers already owning the equipment.[66]

Essentially, aftermarkets need to be carefully assessed on a case-by-case basis. In following the earlier *Pelikan* decision,[67] the European Commission's Notice points towards a reconciliation with a more sophisticated analysis in this regard, conceding that a narrow definition of markets for secondary products (hereto spare parts are explicitly mentioned) should only result when compatibility with the primary product is important, together with the existence of high prices and a long lifetime of the primary product. In addition, the method of defining markets in aftermarket cases has been pointedly brought in line with the Notice's general approach inspired on the SSNIP test where it is referred to as assessing the responses of customers based on their purchasing decisions to relative price changes.[68]

Limitations of market share analysis The relevance of market shares and concentration indices is not only dependent upon the objectivity of the definition of the market in question. It also depends on the type of the anticompetitive effects encountered. Market shares may give reliable indications as to whether markets for homogeneous goods, which are under scrutiny, are conducive to collusion, but will be less reliable indicators of antitrust worries when unilateral effects in differentiated product markets arise.

Market share analysis which shows low market shares may overestimate the competitive constraints between products. As will be further explained in Chapter 9, antitrust intervention is not only needed in an environment of fewer competitors, which is more favourable to collusion (giving rise to oligopolistic or collective dominance). The concept of unilateral effects makes clear that firms can also increase prices without taking into account competitors' responses or coordinating behaviour. The loss of localised competition may make post-merger price increases profitable. Also, when mergers do not lead to high market shares, competitive constraints may thus be substantially weakened and necessitate antitrust intervention to avoid lasting supra-normal profits. This has been acknowledged by the European Commission in its Horizontal Merger Guidelines.

Market shares do not only give an imperfect indication of the intensity of competition in differentiated product markets. Moreover, the market definition exercise may be inherently complex and difficult in such settings. There is no obvious chain of substitutes and a number of rules of thumb could be used to add products sequentially to the candidate market until a profitable price increase becomes possible, as it is required by the SSNIP methodology. The

---

[66] C. Shapiro and D.J. Teece, "Systems Competition and Aftermarkets: An Economic Analysis of Kodak" (1994) 39 Antitrust Bull. 135.
[67] Case IV/34.330 *Pelikan/Kyocera*, September 22, 1995, unpublished decision discussed in European Commission, *Fifteenth Annual Report on Competition Policy 1995* (1996), p.140 and paras 86–87.
[68] Section 56 of the 1997 Notice.

result could be multiple competing market definitions.[69] Both the criticism that market share analysis does not fully capture anti-competitive effects and the complexity of the market definition exercise are arguments that favour direct assessments of market power in differentiated product markets.

4.2.1.4 Is market definition really necessary? More direct measures of market power

Theoretical as well as empirical developments in the USA have initiated an evolution that could lead to putting less emphasis on the role traditional methods of market definition play in determining the market players' positions and, ultimately, market power. Indeed, while the structuralist approach based on market shares may bring forth convincing conclusions in markets distinguished by homogeneous goods, this no longer holds when goods are differentiated or branded[70] and market shares do not confer trustworthy information on the market's competitiveness.[71] Initially cultivated as a means of assessing merged companies' incentives to raise differentiated goods' prices post-merger, the unilateral effects theory mentioned above comprehensively diminishes the need for delineating relevant markets. As noted by Stigler and Sherwin, the hypothetical monopolist test coupled with a judgment concerning the level and changes in concentration is not in any way easier than asking directly whether the merger under investigation will result in an increased price.[72] Hereinafter, two of the more commonly applied techniques for directly assessing market power will be briefly discussed: price–concentration analysis and simulation analysis. These and other techniques, mainly used in the merger context, will be further discussed in Chapter 9, s.9.3.

Price–concentration analysis Price–concentration analysis, which explores the relationship between concentration and prices, may provide important information about the likely effects of a merger. This econometric technique is particularly useful in a cross-section analysis (for example comparison of price levels in different geographic markets) where one market is under scrutiny. If higher concentration levels are associated with higher prices, this suggests that a merger will lead to higher prices. One example is the *Kleenex* merger case, discussed in Box 4.3. Another example is the investigation of the American Federal Trade Commission (FTC) into the effects of the merger between Staples and Office Depot, two superstores selling office products. The FTC

[69] D. Rubinfeld, "Market Definition with Differentiated Products: The Post/Nabisco Cereal Merger" (2000) 68 Antitrust L.J. 163 at p.177.
[70] Products can be differentiated in a number of ways, including characteristics relating to the product itself (such as by brands, physical characteristics or utility for the end user), or relating to how and to whom the product is sold (such as by channel of distribution, customers, or being sold as a cluster). See, for an overview, J.A. Keyte, "Market Definition and Differentiated Products: The Need for a Workable Standard" (1995) 63 Antitrust L.J. 697 at pp.701–703.
[71] Compare R. Schmalensee, "Another Look at Market Power" (1982) 95 Harv. L. Rev. 1780 at 1800; and E.H. Chamberlin, "Product Heterogeneity and Public Policy" (1950) 40 Amer. Econ. Rev. 85 at pp.86–87.
[72] G. Stigler and R. Sherwin, "The Extent of the Market" (1985) J. Law Econ. at pp.555–585.

collected data on concentration and prices in different geographic areas and used different econometric studies, which tried to assess market power directly. This showed that Staples and Office Depot could charge significantly higher prices in the monopolised markets than in markets with two or three competitors (respectively 13 and 15 per cent). These results were an important factor in the ultimate decision to reject the merger.[73]

Two additional remarks on the value of price–concentration analysis may be added. First, price–concentration analysis can also be a useful instrument in dominance cases. If there is no price–concentration relationship in a given market, this suggests that a high market share does not confer market power. In Article 82 EC cases, the need for market definition also diminishes if the challenged conduct itself proves both the existence of a dominant position and its abuse. At this point, the German concept of *Wettbewerbsfreiheit* should be recalled. This approach rejects the need for market definition and prefers *per se* rules. A prohibition of systematic price discrimination (seen as a constellation where market power and abuse co-exist and reinforce each other) has been suggested as an appropriate *per se* prohibition.[74]

Second, econometric studies relating price to the degree of concentration in a certain industry can be useful to check a proposed market definition. If the relevant market is well defined, prices must be higher when market shares are elevated. If, by contrast, prices are higher in markets with a lower degree of concentration, high prices must be caused by other factors. For example, suppose that firms complain about high prices for advertising space in regional newspapers. The latter will not constitute a relevant market if prices are higher in regions where these newspapers have a lower market share and meet substantial competition by national newspapers. High prices will then not be caused by exploitation of market power by regional newspapers, but rather by other factors such as the population density of the geographic area.[75] If there is no relation between concentration and price, there is no evidence that market power can be exploited. Since the relevant market is precisely the area where profitable price increases are possible, in the example given limiting the market to regional newspapers and excluding national newspapers is an ill-conceived decision.

Simulation analysis An alternative technique is direct assessment of market power through a structural oligopoly model describing the conduct of consumers and producers. On the basis of information on observed prices and sales, price-elasticities and the intensity of competition can be estimated. Through simulation analysis the market power may be deduced or the change

---

[73] *FTC v Staples, Inc and Office Depot, Inc* (Case 1: 97CV00701 (District of Columbia)).
[74] E. Hoppmann, *Behinderungsmissbrauch* (1980); O. Wilde, *Wettbewerbsverzerrungen und Wettbewerbsbeschränkungen durch Nachfragemacht* (1979).
[75] This example also illustrates that it may be crucially important to define the relevant product market and geographic market simultaneously.

in market power through a merger may be calculated.[76] Chapter 9 provides a case example: *Volvo/Scania*.[77] The direct identification of market power has several benefits. It is no longer necessary to make the detour of the SSNIP test with its inherent complexities to reach a decision. Another advantage is that also other factors can be incorporated in the analysis. A simulation analysis may allow an answer to the question whether the costs savings resulting from a merger will be sufficiently passed on to consumers, which allows the competition authority to judge whether the anti-competitive effects will be compensated. Also, in this way decisions can be reached without going first through the market definition exercise.

Given their potential to alleviate the coercive character of market definition, unilateral theories and simulation techniques are prone to controversy. Competition policy will have to reconsider how to treat findings linking the demonstration of negative effects on post-merger prices only to estimates of consumer substitution patterns of a limited number of branded products when spatial differentiation is extreme.[78] In addition, it follows that a dominant role for market shares in the decision making process no longer appears warranted in all cases. Hence, also, the "certainty" linking low market shares to the absence of market power disappears. Low concentration, safe harbours in merger control may thus become less of a haven.[79] And on top of all this, the preceding by no means should imply that differentiated goods mergers are to be rated negatively *per se*, as the efficiency gains made possible through such mergers can outdo the anti-competitive effects attached, leading to lower prices for consumers.[80] Similarly, (the threat of) new entry may be able to counterbalance the increase in market power.[81]

4.2.2 The European Commission's Notice

4.2.2.1 The theoretical framework

Economic insights injected into a legal straight-jacket The European Commission's Notice is a somewhat peculiar document in that one is left with

---

[76] Examples of simulation analyses include the telecommunications industry (J.G. Hausman and G. Leonard, "Econometric Analysis of Differentiated Products Mergers Using Real World Data" (1997) 5 Geo. Mason L. Rev. 321) and the trucks market (M. Ivaldi and F. Verboven, *Quantifying the effects from horizontal mergers in European competition policy* (2000)).

[77] See Ch.9, s.9.3.2.

[78] See, for example, J.B. Baker, "Product Differentiation through Space and Time: Some Antitrust Policy Issues" (1997) 42 Antitrust Bull. 177 at p.188, concluding that in such cases, the output of the standard market definition exercise can be "unnecessary" and "distracting".

[79] J.A. Hausman and G.K. Leonard, "Economic Analysis of Differentiated Products Mergers Using Real World Data" (1997) 5 Geo. Mason L. Rev. 321. See below, Ch.9 on the concept of safe harbours in merger control, arising when concentration indices are low.

[80] Which still holds even under most dire conditions; see G.J. Werden, "A Robust Test for Consumer Welfare Enhancing Mergers among Sellers of Differentiated Products" (1996) 44 J. Ind. Econ. 409.

[81] Compare R.J. Gilbert, "Mobility Barriers and the Value of Incumbency", in *The Handbook of Industrial Organisation I* (R. Schmalensee and R.D. Willig ed., 1989), p.475.

the impression of new theories and techniques being injected into an orthodox legal straight-jacket.[82] At the outset the European Commission repeats the traditional legal definition of the relevant market, related to functionable interchangeability.[83] According to the European Court of Justice in *Hoffmann-La Roche*, this amounts to determining which products are sufficiently similar in function, price and attributes to be regarded by consumers as reasonable substitutes for each other, concluding that:

> "The concept of the relevant product market in fact implies that there can be effective competition between the products which form part of it and this presupposes that there is a sufficient degree of interchangeability between all the products forming part of the same market insofar as a specific use of such products is concerned".[84]

Subsequently, the European Commission states that companies are restrained in their competitive scope of action by three factors, namely demand-side substitution, supply-side substitution and potential competition.[85] Of these, demand-side substitution focusing on consumer preferences is considered the most relevant and important. The delineation of the relevant market is therefore brought into line with the more advanced economic insights where the Notice alludes to "postulating a small, non-transitory change in relative prices"[86] and is now formalised by referring to the SSNIP approach as used under the US Merger Guidelines. The Notice thus states:

> "The exercise of market definition focuses ... on demand substitution arising from small, permanent changes in relative prices.... Conceptually, this approach means that, starting from the type of products that the undertakings involved sell and the area in which they sell them, additional products and areas will be included in, or excluded from, the market definition depending on whether competition from these or other products and areas affect or restrain sufficiently the pricing of the parties' products in the short term. The question to be answered is whether the parties' customers would switch to readily available substitutes or to suppliers located elsewhere in response to a hypothetical small (in the range of 5 to 10 per cent) but permanent relative price increase in the products and areas being considered. If substitution were enough to make the price increase unprofitable because of the resulting loss of sales, the additional substitutes and areas are included in the relevant market. This will be done until the set of products and geographic areas is such that small, permanent increases in relative prices would be profitable."[87]

---

[82] This cannot really surprise, however, as the Notice dates back to 1997 and came at a pivotal moment where the European Commission was commencing a real push away from old-fashioned legalistic thinking.

[83] Commission Notice on the definition of the relevant market for the purposes of Community competition law [1997] O.J. C 372/5, paras 7–8.

[84] Case 85/76 *Hoffmann-La Roche v Commission (Vitamins)* [1979] ECR 461, para.24.

[85] s.13 of the 1997 Notice.

[86] s.15 of the 1997 Notice.

[87] ss.15–17 of the 1997 Notice. The European Commission does indicate that the price increase should be in the range of 5 to 10%, being "nontransitory" and leading to a "permanent relative price increase" (as compared to the "foreseeable future" in the US Merger Guidelines). It does not clarify, though, which percentage of customers is required to switch demand; compare K.S. Desai, "The European Commission's Draft Notice on Market Definition: A Brief Guide to the Economics" (1997) 18 E.C.L.R. 473 at pp.473–474.

The explicit adoption of the hypothetical monopolist test should thus imply that the European Commission intends to put more weight behind the market delineation endeavour's economic analysis. The passage on the realms of economical foundations was not entirely completed, however, as the old-style definition based on product characteristics clearly remains a prominent feature in the Notice's textual build-up. The criterion of functionable interchangeability does not carry as its central aim the ultimate task of identifying market power, as the products' attributes only contain relevance in inasmuch as they influence the extent of competition in-between commodities and locations. A comparison of product characteristics does not allow one to judge whether products belong to the same relevant market. Products with different characteristics may constitute the same relevant market (for example, beer and wine, trains and buses or small and large trucks[88]). Conversely, products having the same characteristics may constitute different relevant markets (for example, branded products and non-branded products that are physically identical). The same criticism applies to products in the same price range[89] or products with a similar intended use. Consequently, a market definition based upon irrelevant product characteristics, similarity of price levels or intended uses may lead to distorted conclusions on the firms' market power.[90] What antitrust authorities should be figuring out instead, is whether the companies under investigation can significantly and lastingly raise their prices because buyers do not have substitutes to turn to. Further, if it is thought that a price increase of 5 to 10 per cent as compared to the competitive price is unacceptable, then the regulators have to determine which products and geographic areas the hypothetical monopolist has to control in order to be able to sustain such a price increase profitably, as it is precisely those products and areas that its buyers would transfer to in response to the increase in price. That way, reasonable judgments become possible on the potential exercise of market power.

Inconsistencies Where new insights find themselves bottled in old definitions, there is clearly a risk of overall inconsistency. Unfortunately, this is also the case with the Notice which suffers from ill-conceived attempts at dealing with supply-side substitution, the neglect of potential competition at the stage

---

[88] In *Mercedes-Benz/Kässbohrer*, the European Commission distinguished different markets according to the loading capacity of trucks: between 5 and 6 tons and above 16 tons (Case IV/M.477 *Mercedes-Benz/Kässbohrer* [1995] O.J. L 211/1).
[89] In *Orkla/Volvo*, the European Commission argued that the price of beer is only one fourth of the price of a similar quantity of wine and distinguished two separate markets accordingly (Case IV/M.582 *Orkla/Volvo* [1996] O.J. L 66/17). This decision may be criticised, since the relevant question is whether a sufficient number of consumers would switch to beer in case of a 5 to 10% increase of the price of wine, so that the price increase would be unprofitable.
[90] Compare K.S. Desai, "The European Commission's Draft Notice on Market Definition: A Brief Guide to the Economics" (1997) 18 E.C.L.R. 473 at p.476; and R.J. Van den Bergh, "Modern Industrial Organisation versus Old-fashioned European Competition Law" (1996) 17 E.C.L.R. 75 at pp.82–83. S.36 of the 1997 Notice does contain a nuance to the importance of product characteristics in that "product characteristics and intended use are insufficient to show whether two products are demand substitutes". If one accepts this statement at face value, the question remains why the traditional definition was not scrapped completely.

of market definition, and consecutive (instead of simultaneous) delineation of the relevant product and geographic market areas.

First, the hypothetical monopolist test is indeed about assessing the profitability of a price increase. Apart from taking into account demand-side substitution, however, this also requires considering supply-side substitution (competing firms' reactions inside the relevant market) and potential competition (competing firms' reactions outside the relevant market). In the Notice supply-side substitution is recognised as being equivalent to demand-side substitution.[91] The European Commission envisions this to be the case when suppliers are "able to switch production to the relevant product and market it without incurring significant additional costs or risks". Such a situation would typically occur when companies market a wide range of qualities and grades of one product. Supply-side substitution is consequently accepted when its "effectiveness" and "immediacy" is similar to demand-side substitution, whereto it must be timely and occur without significant additional costs or risks in response to small and permanent changes in relative prices. Nowhere, however, is there a clear line drawn, nor an explicit allusion made to applying the SSNIP test also to supply-side substitution. It has already been noted that identifying these costs or risks and quantifying how much is "significant" will be a contentious issue.[92] On top of this, the European Commission's own example relating to the paper market does not bring enlightenment; rather, it provides for additional confusion. From a demand point of view it is stated that different qualities of paper cannot be used for any given function, as the example of an art book printed on low quality paper illustrates. On the supply-side, the European Commission "would not define a separate market for each quality of paper and its respective use", as paper manufacturers are able to compete for orders of the various qualities, given the absence of particular distribution hurdles and sufficient lead time to allow for modification of production plants.[93] Therefore, the question of whether producers of low-quality paper (such as for newspapers) could profitably and permanently raise their prices by 5 to 10 per cent is not even posed—although this may very well be the case. Producers of high-quality paper (such as for art books) may have good reasons not to switch production to manufacturing low quality paper (such as the higher profitability of the up-scale market segment, its faster rate of growth, or the existence of long-term contracts for delivering high-quality paper). Hence, the different types of paper can each constitute a relevant product market.

Second, the Notice clarifies that the analysis of potential competition and the assessment of barriers to entry, if required, will be carried out—but only after

---

[91] Section 20 of the 1997 Notice; see also M. Furse, "Market Definition—The Draft Commission Notice" (1997) 18 E.C.L.R. 378 at p.380. In the USA supply-side substitution is separated from the market delineation when controlling merger activity; see thereto ss.1.0 and 1.3 of the 1997 Merger Guidelines.

[92] See S. Baker and L. Wu, "Applying the Market Definition Guidelines of the European Commission" (1998) 19 E.C.L.R. 273 at p.275.

[93] Section 22 of the 1997 Notice.

the relevant market has been defined.[94] At the stage of market definition the European Commission intends not to consider strategic decisions surpassing the short term (elucidated as "a period that does not entail a significant adjustment of existing tangible and intangible assets"[95]). Concluding *ab initio* upon a relevant market without taking into account the reactions of competitors operating outside this market, however, will prevent the taking into account of such companies' incentives to switch into the initial market, after this has become profitable because of the price rise. When deciding upon increasing prices, firms have to take notice of their market surroundings. If their customers anticipate a medium term response by related producers, a temporary fall in quantity demanded will ensue. As this loss in sales might also influence the profitability of the envisioned price increase, it needs to be included in some way during the market definition stage. If, instead, one follows the European Commission's approach of assessing such potential competition only on a market where market power is already ascertained, it is implicitly acknowledged that its starting point was not correctly defined. Again, heightened transparency would have been opportune, as now one needs to distinguish between market definition-stage supply-side substitution and subsequent stage potential competition according to the ductile criterion of "significant adjustments".

Third, the techniques attached to defining the geographic area are distinct from their product market counterparts. The conventional definition relating to the homogeneity of competitive conditions remains the determinative factor for delineating the geographic market[96] with no reference being made to consumers' behaviour in switching locations as a reaction to a price increase. Additionally, the evidential material relied on to define relevant product and geographic markets differs.[97] As a result, the Notice preserves European practice defining both areas consecutively (instead of simultaneously as under the US Merger Guidelines[98]), and this heightens the risk of a market being defined too narrowly, as total demand substitution towards both other products and other locations will normally exceed that in either dimension separately.[99] A price increase that is just about profitable under the sequential procedure may no longer be profitable under the simultaneous procedure. As long as consumers who switch to other products are not exactly the same as those consumers who switch towards other locations, the total substitution effect will always be larger than under a sequential definition of the product and geographic market area. In extreme cases, in which none of the consumers

---

[94] Section 24 of the 1997 Notice. On the underlying rationale, see K. Mehta, "Market Definition", in *The EC Law of Competition* (J. Faull and A. Nikpay ed., 1999), para.1.141.
[95] Section 23 *juncto* 20 of the 1997 Notice.
[96] Section 8 of the 1997 Notice.
[97] Compare ss.36–43 and 44–52 of the 1997 Notice.
[98] Compare s.1.0 of the 1997 Merger Guidelines.
[99] Compare R.D. Willig, "Merger Analysis, Industrial Theory, and Merger Guidelines" (1991) Brookings Pap. Econ. Act., Microeconomics 281 at p.284. This has been equally recognised in Europe: see J. Sedemund, "Zwei Jahre europäische Fusionskontrolle: ausgewählte Zentralfragen und Ausblick", in *Europarecht, Kartellrecht, Wirtschaftsrecht, Festschrift für Arved Deringer* (U. Everling, K.-H. Narjes and J. Sedemund ed., 1993) pp.379, 388; J. Jickeli, "Marktzutrittsschranken im EG-Kartellrecht" (1992) 42 WuW 101 at pp.195, 203.

who would have substituted towards other products belonged to the group of consumers who would have substituted towards other locations, for example, the elasticity of demand would be halved.

One last remark on the Notice's theoretical framework concerns the application of the SSNIP test to Article 82 EC cases. In such disputes the use of prevailing prices[1] to define markets will cause considerable problems because of what has become known as the "cellophane fallacy".[2] In the *Du Pont (Cellophane)* case, the US Supreme Court had enunciated the standard for market definition so that two products are in the same market only if they are "reasonably interchangeable".[3] Unfortunately, the percentage of interchangeability required has never been set (nor would this seem possible), while the presence of substitutes is not necessarily an indication of the absence of market power (as was held in *Du Pont*). *In casu* the Court argued that cellophane is only one of a number of products making up the market of flexible packing materials, as a high level of cross-price elasticity of demand was determined between cellophane and other wrapping materials. Cellophane could thus not constitute a separate market as, obviously, consumers would switch to substitute products when confronted with monopoly prices for cellophane. The key issue remaining untouched, however, is whether consumers treat the products as close substitutes under competitive prices. In *Cellophane*, Du Pont, being the sole producer of cellophane, had already set prices at levels where alternative products provided an effective competitive constraint on the pricing of its product, implying, in fact, that the high cross-price elasticities indicated *Du Pont* was exercising monopoly power. Similarly, it may be difficult for a competition authority to apply the SSNIP test (as a deviation of 5 to 10 per cent from competitive market prices), since information about what would be a competitive price is not easily available. In markets not yet highly concentrated pre-merger prices may, however, be an appropriate point of reference for the SSNIP test. By contrast, if market concentration is high and collusion is already a problem, this approach to market definition will be biased in favour of permitting mergers. To counter such an effect s.1.11 of the 1997 Merger Guidelines specifically states that the prevailing price will be used "unless pre-merger circumstances are strongly suggestive of coordinated interaction". In Article 82 EC investigations the problem is pervasive. Although the European Commission is aware of the issue,[4] nowhere is there a solution offered. When thus drawing a general conclusion on the Notice's theoretical framework, an overall commendation may be conferred to the adoption of the SSNIP, conditioned, however, by the inconsistencies and inherent limitations attached.

---

[1] Section 19 of the 1997 Notice.
[2] See G.W. Stocking and W.F. Mueller, "The Cellophane Case and the New Competition" (1955) 45 Amer. Econ. Rev. 29 and many subsequent articles. An overview is presented in H. Hovenkamp, *Federal Antitrust Policy: The Law of Competition and its Practice* (1994), pp.98–102.
[3] See *United States v E.I. DuPont de Nemours and Co (Cellophane)*, 351 US 377 (1956), 394–395.
[4] Section 19 of the 1997 Notice.

4.2.2.2 Empirical evidence

The so-called SSNIP test is not a test in itself but a conceptual framework, within which several quantitative tests can be employed to address the market delineation question. Consequently, the real added value of the Notice's stipulations needs to be determined by assessing whether its hypothetical monopolist-settings may actually be put into antitrust practice, which relates to the availability of empirical evidence and econometric techniques. The Notice[5] is fairly confirmatory in this respect by registering quantitative tests, next to probative evidence and views of customers and competitors, to be used to determine the hypothetical price increase. Probative evidence consists of circumstantial evidence of substitution in the recent past which may consist of: (a) sudden events or shocks indicating substitution, (b) changes in relative prices in the past and reactions in quantities demanded, and (c) launches of new products and resultant lost sales to established products.[6] As for quantitative tests, the Notice also lists three, namely: (a) price elasticities of demand, (b) cross-price elasticities of demand, and (c) price movements over a period of time.[7]

Unfortunately, the Notice does not make clear how the quantitative techniques mentioned relate to the SSNIP test and what conclusions can be drawn from such data. Some of the techniques mentioned by the European Commission carry an intuitive appeal but suffer from serious shortcomings, which may distort the definition of the relevant market. Cross-price elasticities and price correlation tests may provide some piece of evidence, but only own-price elasticities' estimates based on a demand function estimation can address the market definition question directly. A low own-price elasticity indicates the existence of a separate relevant product market.[8] The choice of the demand model to investigate the relationship between prices charged and quantities sold is a technical question that cannot be discussed within the confines of this

---

[5] Refreshingly enough, though, it may be noted that this more substantial approach is not a complete novelty; in 1994, the European Commission had already declared that it may make use of both qualitative and quantitative methods for the purpose of analysing demand substitutability: see European Commission, *Fourteenth Annual Report on Competition Policy 1994* (1995), para.280.

[6] Section 38 of the 1997 Notice. On the probative evidence of demand substitutability, see K.S. Desai, "The European Commission's Draft Notice on Market Definition: A Brief Guide to the Economics" (1997) 18 E.C.L.R. 473 at pp.474–475; on interpreting competitors' and customers' views, see S. Baker and L. Wu, "Applying the Market Definition Guidelines of the European Commission" (1998) 19 E.C.L.R. 273 at pp.279–280.

[7] Section 39 of the 1997 Notice. While looking at prices of goods over time has obvious advantages over price elasticities because of higher availability of information, the causality between price movements and the relevant market as presupposed may be unrelated; compare K.S. Desai, "The European Commission's Draft Notice on Market Definition: A Brief Guide to the Economics" (1997) 18 E.C.L.R. 473 at pp.476–477.

[8] An example may further illustrate this. An own price-elasticity of -0.5% implies that a price increase of 10% will lead to a loss of sales not higher than 5%. If 100 products are sold at a price of 80, the total income is 8000. In case of a 10% price increase, demand will drop by 5%, but the remaining products will be sold at the higher price of 88. This leads to an increased gain of 4.5%: 95 $\times$ 88 = 8360.

introductory book.[9] The crucial challenge for the econometric delineation of the relevant market is to compare the actual elasticity with the threshold elasticity (critical elasticity) above which a price increase is no longer profitable. The Notice does not elaborate on the concept of critical demand elasticity and the technique of critical loss analysis, which puts this concept into practice. It also omits a discussion of the Elzinga–Hogarty test, which is the most widely used empirical method for delineating a relevant geographic market. In sum, the Notice does not provide a complete picture of the available econometric techniques for defining relevant markets and carries the risk that disproportionate attention will be focused on data that are easily available but not always reliable to delineate antitrust markets. These criticisms are further elaborated upon below.

Cross-price elasticities   To determine cross-price elasticities it is asked whether certain products (for example, pears, melons, strawberries) are in the same market as the product under investigation (for example, bananas). This enquiry focuses on the significance of individual substitutes rather than on the collective competitive significance of all substitutes. Cross-price elasticities do not address the market definition question directly, since they do not indicate how much substitution is enough to constrain the profitability of an SSNIP. Nevertheless, cross-price elasticities may provide useful information in antitrust proceedings. They may confirm that there is demand-side substitution between products inside and outside the proposed market. This can be a powerful defence in cases where the investigating competition authority proposes a narrow market definition (for example, corn flakes), which neglects substantial demand-side substitution (for example, other breakfast products).[10]

Figures on cross-price elasticities also allow us to make a ranking of substitutes. However, information about the critical (residual) demand elasticity, which is the threshold elasticity above which a price increase by the hypothetical monopolist is no longer profitable, is needed to define the boundaries of the relevant market. For example, the cross-price elasticities of products B, C and D with respect to product A may amount to 2, 1.8 and 1.4 respectively. These figures allow a ranking of substitutes but do not allow us to decide whether A constitutes a market in itself or the market also includes product B and eventually also products C and D. To define the market, information is needed about the critical demand elasticity. If the latter elasticity amounts to 5, a 10 per cent price increase for A will not be profitable, since 52 per cent of

---

[9] A widely adopted model among antitrust practitioners is the Almost Ideal Demand System (AIDS). See: A. Deaton and J. Muelbauer, "An Almost Ideal Demand System" (1980) 70 Amer. Econ. Rev. 312.

[10] W.F. Shughart, II, R. D. Tollison and E.C. Reed, "Breakfast at the Federal Trade Commission", in *Economic Inputs, Legal Outputs* (F. McChesney ed., 1996), pp.85–92. See also: *State of New York v Kraft General Foods, Inc*, 926 F. Supp. 321, 356 (S.D.N.Y. 1995). The latter case shows that demand elasticities can have a considerable impact on assessing the sensibility of further subdivisions of the antitrust market. While the State of New York proposed a relevant market containing only adult cereals, defence convincingly argued the market should comprise all ready-to-eat cereals, based in part on evidence of relatively high cross-price elasticities between adult and children's cereals.

sales will be lost. By contrast, if the hypothetical monopolist producing product A also controls the market for product B, the price increase will pay since only 32 per cent of sales will be diverted to products C and D. Consequently, in this example the relevant product market comprises products A and B. Figures about cross-price elasticities must thus be complemented with figures on critical demand elasticities to define the relevant antitrust market. In sum, cross-price elasticities are a useful device for determining an appropriate chain of substitutes and showing why a proposed market definition cannot be valid. The proper role of cross-price elasticities in antitrust cases will vary depending on the nature of the product market being studied and on the issues raised in a particular case.

Similarity of price levels and price-correlation analysis   The choice of the empirical techniques used in antitrust proceedings often depends on the data that are available.[11] Ideally, which technique is to be preferred rests upon the question asked: econometric evidence must be related to the antitrust issue at hand. In practice, there is a risk that particular quantitative techniques will be used more often because the data needed to perform the analysis are more easily available and that the choice of the methodology will thus be biased. It may be the case that data on price movements are available, while data on demand elasticities are lacking. Here, one should keep in mind that, as evidential sources, price parallelism tests and price-correlation analyses do not enjoy the same analytical rigour as econometric estimates of demand elasticity and are not fully trustworthy techniques to define antitrust markets.

In several high-profile decisions, the European Commission relied on differences in absolute price levels to delineate product markets.[12] Unfortunately, similarity of price levels is not necessarily a reliable criterion to define relevant antitrust markets since price differences do not need to imply that products cannot be considered substitutes. Inferring that products with substantially different prices are not close substitutes overlooks the relevant question for competition law analysis, which remains whether an increase in the price of the candidate market's product will induce enough consumers to switch, so that the price increase would be unprofitable. Defining relevant markets based on observed differences in absolute prices may be misleading if price differentials reflect actual or perceived quality differences. To capture the consumers' price–quality trade-off, the inquiry should focus on the degree to which the pricing of the high quality or the branded product is constrained by the existence of lower quality or unbranded (private label) products.[13] For example, branded and unbranded products may be in the same market

---

[11] Compare generally: J.B. Baker and D.L. Rubinfeld, "Empirical Methods Used in Antitrust Litigation: Review and a Critique" (1999) 1 A.L.E.R. 386.
[12] For example Case IV/M.53 *Aerospatiale/Alenia/de Havilland* [1991] O.J. L 334/42 (price differences between different types of aircraft); Case IV/M.190 *Nestlé/Perrier* [1992] O.J. L 356/1 (price gap between retail prices of source water and other soft drinks); Case IV/M.2609 *HP/Compaq* [2002] O.J. C 39/23 (division of market for computer servers according to price ranges).
[13] S. Bishop and M. Walker, *Economics of EC Competition Law: Concepts, Application and Measurement* (2nd ed., 2002), pp.108–110.

despite obvious price differences, if the cross-price elasticities between the products are high (see the discussion of the *Kimberley-Clark* case in Box 4.3)

Box 4.3: Kimberly-Clark and quantitative analysis

In its 1996 decision declaring compatible under certain conditions Kimberly-Clark's acquisition of Scott,[14] the Commission made extensive use of toilet tissue market studies submitted by both the parties and major competitors which addressed the impact of the operation on competition in the UK. Albeit featured only when discussing the parties' positions on markets already defined, the studies focused on whether prices of branded products are constrained by prices of private-label products, drawing direct inference from price quantity data.[15] The price elasticities of demand estimated for the whole market, comprising both branded and private-label segments, showed overall market demand for toilet tissue to be inelastic (i.e. demand elasticity lower than 1). Hence, the relevant market was certainly not wider than all toilet tissues, since a 5 per cent price increase will be followed by a less than 5 per cent drop in sales. Concerning the cross-price elasticity estimates, the studies submitted by the parties led to quite different results and the Commission reached the conclusion that there existed "a certain price competition" between the differentiated private-label and branded segments. Yet, accounting for the high market shares of the parties and the strong brand loyalty, the inelastic total demand for toilet tissues was seen as creating scope for the parties to abuse their position on the British market for toilet tissues after the merger.

Hampered by the decision's deletion of data for reasons of business confidentiality, some deductions may still be made when comparing the European case with the parallel consent settlement issued in the USA in *Kimberly-Clark*.[16] The likely price effects of the proposed merger on the toilet tissue market were econometrically estimated using Nielsen supermarket scanner data from five major US cities for five years. Contrary to the Department of Justice's preliminary imputations (based on the parties' substantial market share) showing a substantial increase in concentration in a market already considered highly concentrated according to the Merger Guidelines' standards,[17] the figures presented by defence allowed the clearing of the merger. First, evidence showed two separated market segments[18]: the premium (designated branded in the European counterpart) market and the economy (private-label in the European counterpart)

[14] Case IV/M.623 *Kimberly-Clark/Scott Paper* [1996] O.J. L 183/1. The two companies are among the largest world producers of hygienic paper products.
[15] *ibid.*, paras 172–177.
[16] *United States and State of Texas v Kimberly-Clark Corp and Scott Paper Co* Civil No.3:95 CV 3055-P (D.C. Texas). See the case discussion by its expert witness in J.A. Hausman and G.K. Leonard, "Economic Analysis of Differentiated Products Mergers Using Real World Data" (1997) 5 Geo. Mason L. Rev. 321 at pp.335–336 also including a detailed description of the price-concentration analysis applied.
[17] Compare s.1.51 of the 1997 Merger Guidelines.
[18] See the tables in J.A. Hausman and G.K. Leonard, "Economic Analysis of Differentiated Products Mergers Using Real World Data" (1997) 5 Geo. Mason L. Rev. 321 at pp.344–346.

market. Kimberly-Clark produced the premium "Kleenex", while Scott produced a premium, "Cottonelle", and an economy brand, "ScotTissue". The premium segment was dominated by "Charmin", a competing Procter and Gamble brand, with a 30.9 per cent share of the whole tissue market. The share of the second and third brands, Northern and Angel Soft, were 12.4 and 8.8 per cent respectively; Kleenex held a share of 7.5 per cent, and Cottonelle 6.7 per cent. The economy brands were dominated by ScotTissue with a 16.7 per cent share of the total market, followed by other brands (together 9.4 per cent) and Private Label with 7.6 per cent. Hausman and Leonard's estimated demand system found that the own-price elasticity for Kleenex, Cottonelle and ScotTissue were −3.4, −4.5 and −2.9 respectively, implying sales reduction of 34, 45 and 29 per cent in response to a 10 per cent increase in their price. The estimated cross-price elasticities were very low; the largest Kleenex cross-elasticity was with Charmin at 0.69, indicating Charmin to be the closest substitute for Kleenex (and implying that sales of Kleenex would go up by 6.9 per cent in response to a 10 per cent increase in the price of Charmin). The next largest cross-price elasticities were all estimated to be with other premium brands.

Second, the relevant products' cross-price elasticities were all different from each other and asymmetric. Using the estimated elasticities of demand, the parties predicted the price effects from the merger of Kimberly-Clark's and Scott's toilet tissue activities to constitute a price increase of 2.4 per cent for Kleenex, 1.4 per cent for Cottonelle and 1.2 per cent for ScotTissue (the parties' respective products), assuming no cost efficiencies. As these are very low figures the merger was consequently approved. The toilet tissue case reaffirms the decreasing significance to be attached to pre-merger computations of market shares in heterogeneous product markets (see ss.4.2.1.3 and 4.2.1.4).

The European Commission mentions price movements over a period of time as one of the possible empirical methods to define relevant markets.[19] The statistical technique used to measure the degree of interdependence between prices of two different products is called price-correlation analysis. The underlying idea is that if two products are in the same relevant product market, then the price of each will constrain the other. So prices of products in the same relevant product market should move together over time.[20] To conduct a price-correlation analysis, time series data are essential. Correlation coefficients express quantitatively the scale of the relationship between the two price series. The relevant numbers are between + 1 (perfect positive correlation: the prices series move perfectly together) and − 1 (negative correlation: the price series move perfectly inversely to one another). High positive correlations indicate that two products belong to the same relevant product market. Price correlation studies are widely used as a tool for market

---

[19] Section 39 of the 1997 Notice.
[20] S. Bishop and M. Walker, *Economics of EC Competition Law: Concepts, Application and Measurement* (2nd ed., 2002), p.382.

delineation in many European competition law investigations, particularly in merger cases, due to the simple intuition behind the technique and the relatively modest data requirements. An example is the *Nestlé/Perrier* case, in which price-correlation analysis played a central role in reaching the conclusion that different water brands are in the same relevant product market, because their prices are highly correlated with one another (between 0.85 and 1) regardless of whether they are still or sparkling. Correlations between the water brands and soft drinks appeared to be much weaker and sometimes negative, which seemed to justify the conclusion that soft drinks and waters constitute different product markets.[21]

How should the use of price-correlation studies be assessed? Price-correlation analysis as a sole means for defining relevant antitrust markets is no longer considered a robust tool, since the technique suffers from a number of inherent shortcomings that undermine its reliability. While looking at prices of goods over a period of time may have obvious advantages over investigating demand elasticities because of higher availability of information, the causality between price movements and the relevant market as presupposed may be unrelated.[22] The risk of spurious correlations must be overcome: parallel prices are neither a necessary nor sufficient condition for products being substitutes. Spurious correlation results when the relationship between two price series is not driven by competitive interaction but caused by common factors that are not held constant in the analysis.[23] For example, similarity in price movements may arise because firms have the same input costs so that price decreases or increases reflect the changing input costs,[24] rather than competitive interaction between products or regions. Similarly, low correlations need not always indicate that two products are not in the same market. To avoid spurious correlations the price series should be adjusted to remove the common costs or

---

[21] Case IV/M.190 *Nestlé/Perrier* [1992] O.J. L 356/1. For another example, see Case IV/M.1939 *Rexam/American National Can* [2001] O.J. C 325/11.

[22] K.S. Desai, "The European Commission's Draft Notice on Market Definition: A Brief Guide to the Economics" (1997) 18 E.C.L.R. 473 at pp.476–477.

[23] D.L. Kaserman and H. Zeisel, "Market Definition: Implementing the Department of Justice Merger Guidelines" (1996) 41 Antitrust Bull. 673; M. Slade, "Exogeneity Tests of Market Boundaries applied to Petroleum Products" (1986) 34 J. Ind. Econ. 291 at p.293; P. Massey, "Market Definition and Market Power in Competition Analysis: Some Practical Issues" (2000) 31 Econ. Soc. Rev. 315.

[24] Prices of petrol and toothbrushes might display high correlation because both are produced using oil, thus falsely suggesting that the products compete with each other. See S. Bishop and M. Walker, *Economics of EC Competition Law: Concepts, Application and Measurement* (2nd ed., 2002, p.392). An alternative cause for a distorted price correlation analysis can be seasonality; for example, similar price movements for ice creams and bathing suits, both sold independently of one another but at similar times.

take account of other common components in prices.[25] Another problematic issue with price correlation studies is how high the correlation coefficient needs to be to trigger off the conclusion that different products are within the same relevant market. A high correlation coefficient between two products which are accepted as being in the same relevant market (for example Coca-Cola and Pepsi-Cola) could be used as a benchmark against which lower correlation results (other colas or soft drinks) are estimated. However, some degree of subjectivity will remain in the final assessment and biased decisions cannot be excluded. Finally, price-correlation analyses remain an imperfect method of market definition. In the case of a price increase of product A, a competing firm with a high elasticity of supply can expand production and render the price increase unprofitable. Yet, if the price of the substitute product is not raised, price correlation analysis will indicate a low correlation coefficient. Price correlation studies thus define economic markets instead of relevant antitrust markets, since supply substitution is not taken into account. For example, producers of soft drinks (cola, lemonade, fruit juices) could find it profitable to enter the market for mineral water in cases of price increases for the latter product. A price correlation analysis that excluded soft drinks from the market definition because of too low correlation coefficients will not provide an adequate foundation upon which the competitive effects of an agreement or a merger can be assessed.

Critical loss analysis As indicated above, economists generally prefer residual demand analysis to define relevant markets. The informational requirements for the latter type of analysis are more bothersome, however. Only if figures about the (critical) residual demand elasticity faced by a (group of) firm(s) are available will it be possible to judge whether a price increase in the range of the SSNIP test will be profitable. A technique which enjoys increasing popularity in the USA is critical (sales) loss analysis. The elasticity above which a price increase becomes unprofitable is called critical elasticity of demand. If the prevailing elasticity of demand in the candidate market is lower than the critical value, the hypothetical monopolist will not refrain from increasing prices above the current level.

Corresponding to any critical elasticity of demand is a critical sales loss, which is the amount of sales to be lost in order to make a price increase unprofitable. If the actual loss is less than the critical loss, the price increase will be profitable. Conversely, if the actual loss is greater than the critical loss, a broader definition of the market is called for. To calculate the critical loss, the

---

[25] More sophisticated econometric techniques, such as Granger causality and cointegration tests, can be used to complement the correlations and may solve the problem of spurious correlations. Granger causality is used to assess the degree of causality between the variables under investigation. A variable X is said to Granger-cause a variable Y, if taking into account past values of variable X leads to improvements in the predictions of variable Y (C. Granger, "Investigating Causal Relations by Econometric Models and Cross-Spectral Methods" (1969) 37 Econometrica 424). Cointegration analysis examines whether two variables have a stable long run relationship by comparing two price series and checking whether they are stationary (R.F. Engle and C. Granger, "Co-integration and Error Correction: Representation, Estimation and Testing" (1987) 18 Antitrust Bull. 45).

effects of a price increase must be balanced. On the one hand, a price increase raises the profit margin on all units sold, but, on the other hand, it also reduces the overall quantity demanded. The critical loss values depend on the initial price costs margins and the size of the price increase (see Box 4.4). Price costs margins can be calculated from accounting data on the industry under investigation. Information about actual elasticities and actual losses can be obtained in several ways: through econometric estimations (regression analysis), figures on diversion ratios, shock analyses[26] or qualitative evidence (surveys and third-party sources) that buyers shifted their purchases between alternative products or locations in response to a price increase.

Box 4.4: Critical loss analysis in practice: cruise mergers
The following table illustrates how critical loss values change for various price increases and initial price–cost margins:

Price Increase

Initial Margin	5%	10%	15%	20%
0.1	0.33	0.5	0.6	0.67
0.2	0.2	0.33	0.43	0.5
0.3	0.14	0.25	0.33	0.4
0.4	0.11	0.20	0.27	0.33
0.5	0.09	0.17	0.23	0.29
0.6	0.08	0.14	0.20	0.25
0.7	0.07	0.13	0.18	0.22
0.8	0.06	0.11	0.16	0.2
0.9	0.05	0.10	0.14	0.18

For example, if the pre-merger margin is 60 per cent, the critical sales loss following a 5 per cent price increase should be about 8 per cent. Intuitively, the larger the margin, the greater the profit lost from a given reduction in quantity, so the smaller the reduction in quantity (i.e. critical loss) required for a given price increase to be unprofitable. If the price costs margin is quite high (e.g. 80–100 per cent) a loss in sales of only about 5 per cent would be sufficient to deter the hypothetical monopolist from increasing price by 5 per cent. If the margin is quite low (e.g. less then 20 per cent), a loss in sales of more than 20 per cent would be necessary to dissuade the monopolist from increasing price by 5 per cent.[27]

---

[26] In a regression analysis the demand for a good (dependent variable) is defined as a function of several independent variables (such as the price of the good, the price of substitute products and complements) and the demand function is econometrically estimated. Such an analysis requires high quality data for a sufficiently long period and can be carried out only by experts in econometrics. A diversion ratio indicates the effects of a price increase on the demand of a given product (for example, a diversion ratio of 0.60 for product 1 with respect to product 2 indicates that the seller of product 1 will loose 60% of its sales to the seller of product 2). A shock analysis investigates the effects of a sudden and unexpected event on the demand for a product.

[27] G.J. Werden, "Four Suggestions on Market Delineation" (1992) 37 Antitrust Bull. 107 at p.116.

The investigations undertaken by three different competition authorities (European Commission, Federal Trade Commission, UK Competition Commission) into mergers in the cruise industry illustrate the importance attached to critical loss analysis in differentiated product markets.[28] The merger of P&O Princess with either Carnival Corporation or Royal Caribbean cruises would have created an operator with a market share above 60 per cent in the UK market. The British Competition Commission, which analysed the latter operation, presented the critical loss methodology stating that the fall in passenger numbers would be "around 9.5 to 11.5 per cent if prices were raised by 5 per cent, and to be around 17 to 21 per cent for a hypothesised 10 per cent price increase". The concept of critical loss was, however, merely used to launch the discussion on the boundaries of the relevant market. The market definition was ultimately simply left open since the Competition Commission was "not able to come to a single view".[29] In contrast with the UK approach, the European Commission did not attempt to quantify the impact of a hypothetical price increase. The European Commission noted the possibility of unilateral effects within a narrow sub-set of cruises and examined these as a part of the competitive assessment. The European Commission argued that a mix of demand and supply substitution justified a broad prohibition. In this way, the European Commission recognised that market definition is not an end in itself but just an intermediate stage in the evaluation that must be augmented by consideration of the specific impact of the merger, given the nature of the competition in the differentiated cruise market. Finally, the American Federal Trade Commission investigated both transactions for their impact on the US market. In the discussion on market definition, the FTC used reviews of prices revealing that the cruise industry's critical loss was extremely low, corresponding to a very high overall industry elasticity of demand. It was found that in order for a hypothetical monopolist to increase price profitably, its margins would have to be below 50 per cent, much lower than short-run cruise ship margins. Even though these figures made clear that an across-the-board price increase would be unprofitable and defining the relevant market as a broader vacation market would have been appropriate, the FTC identified cruises as a separate relevant market. In sum, all three competition authorities differed in their approaches toward market definition in general and to the use of econometric analysis in particular. Since they all decided not to challenge the mergers, no lasting damage was done. In this respect, it was crucial that none of the authorities decided on a narrow market definition, such as luxury oceanic cruises. Also the importance given to supply-side responses at the stage of the

---

[28] See also the discussion by H. Nevo, "Current Uses of Quantitative Techniques in Defining Relevant Markets", (2004) Paper presented at the 21st Conference of the European Association of Law and Economics (*http://efzg.globalnet.hr/UserDocsImages/zsr/eale_nevo.pdf*).
[29] Competition Commission, *P&O Princess plc and Royal Caribbean Cruises Ltd* (2002), paras 2.64 and 5.6.

competitive assessment shows that a market definition inspired by demand-side factors alone would have been deficient.[30]

The Elzinga–Hogarty test for defining the relevant geographic market   The most widely used empirical method for defining relevant geographic markets has been named after the authors who initially proposed it.[31] The Elzinga–Hogarty test specifies two criteria that are based on shipments data: LIFO (little in from outside) and LOFI (little out from inside). A high LIFO indicates that the demand is primarily served by local production (few imports), whereas a high LOFI indicates that the majority of the local production is used to serve the local market (few exports). If trade patterns observed in a region fail either the LIFO or LOFI conditions, this testifies that the region is subjected to external competition. The candidate geographic market is expanded until the inflow and export rate (calculated over the total number of sales) is sufficiently low, for example 10 per cent.

This test has provoked several criticisms. First, the choice of the threshold (for example 0.9 as the critical value for both LIFO and LOFI) is arbitrary and not always appropriate for each individual case.[32] Second, conclusions on the geographic size of the entire market are taken by referring to the purchasing behaviour of a minority of consumers. If the silent majority of consumers faces high transportation costs and if the demand for the products concerned is rather inelastic, suppliers may enjoy strong market power. If a broader market definition is chosen on the basis of the low number of purchases outside the geographic area, the result of the Elzinga–Hogarty test will be unreliable.[33] Third, on a more general level, the criteria proposed by Elzinga and Hogarty are inappropriate since they are independent of the supply elasticity of the exporting region. As a consequence an economic market is defined instead of a relevant antitrust market.[34]

4.3 Barriers to entry as a prerequisite for market power

The analysis of barriers to entry is another fundamental component of the assessment of market power. A firm may exercise market power for a

---

[30] RBB Economics, "Goldilocks and the Three Bears—the Story of Market Definition and the Cruise Mergers" (2003) RBB Brief 11.
[31] K.G. Elzinga and T.F. Hogarty, "The Problem of Geographic Market Delineation in Antimerger Suits" (1973) 18 Antitrust Bul. 45.
[32] S. Bishop and M. Walker, *Economics of EC Competition Law: Concepts, Application and Measurement* (2nd ed., 2002), p.408.
[33] C. Capps, D. Dranove and S. Greenstein, "The Silent Majority Fallacy of the Elzinga-Hogarty Criteria: A Critique and New Approach to Analysing Hospital Mergers", Working Paper (2001), cited by: E.E. van Damme and F. Verboven, "Het nieuwe toezicht op ondernemingen: Economische aspecten van marktwerking en regulering", in *Preadviezen van de Koninklijke Vereniging voor Staathuishoudkunde* (2001); *Herpositionering van Ondernemingen* (2001), pp.139, 151.
[34] D.T. Scheffmann and P.T. Spiller, "Geographic Market Definition under the US Department of Justice Merger Guidelines" (1987) 30 J. Law Econ. 123 at p.129.

significant period of time only if barriers to new entry exist. When one decides whether a firm is abusing market power or a merger will cause welfare losses, analysis of entry conditions is thus of major importance. This is acknowledged by the European Commission in its Horizontal Merger Guidelines, where it states: "When entering a market is sufficiently easy, a merger is unlikely to pose any significant anti-competitive risk".[35] Entry barriers may result from a wide variety of factors and may be present at the supplier's or buyer's level, or both.

In the past, economists conducted an intense debate on the contribution to entry barriers of determinants such as economies of scale, product differentiation and capital requirements. Together with absolute cost advantages, Bain mentioned those factors in his seminal 1956 book as entry barriers.[36] Bain laid the foundations for what became known as the Harvard School of industrial organisation: followers of this approach qualify a great many things as barriers to entry. Conversely, the Chicago School, represented in the writings of Stigler, Bork and Posner, argues that most factors qualified by Harvard scholars as barriers to entry are, in fact, natural barriers and that antitrust law should be concerned only with artificial barriers to entry. Recent work in industrial organisation has clarified to a great extent the approach that should be taken in the analysis of entry conditions in general, and product differentiation and advertising in particular. A description of the Harvard–Chicago controversy, however, remains useful to help us understand the issues at hand. An important contribution to the current understanding of entry barriers has been made by the recent theory of contestable markets. The latter approach has revealed the fundamental importance of sunk costs. In assessing the feasibility of market entry, exit conditions are equally important as entry conditions. Relying on this insight, the European Commission states that entry is particularly likely if suppliers in other markets already possess production facilities that could be used to enter the market, thus reducing the sunk costs of entry.[37] Conversely, firms may abstain from entering if barriers to exit, prohibiting them from recouping entry costs, exist. Hence, barriers to exit are crucial in assessing market power. Finally, game theory has shown that incumbent firms may engage in strategic behaviour to alter the perceptions of rivals concerning industry conditions in such a way as to deter entry. For example, strategic behaviour may raise rivals' costs by foreclosing important inputs to production (for example, through exclusive dealing agreements),[38] or incumbent firms may build a reputation for aggressive responses to entry. Such strategies may successfully deter entry or at least minimise its competitive impact.

---

[35] Guidelines on the assessment of horizontal mergers under the Council Regulation on the control of concentrations between undertakings [2004] O.J. C 31/5, para.68.

[36] J. Bain, *Barriers to New Competition* (1956).

[37] Guidelines on the assessment of horizontal mergers under the Council Regulation on the control of concentrations between undertakings, [2004] O.J. C 31/5, para.73.

[38] S. Salop and D. Scheffman, "Cost-Raising Strategies" (1987) 36 J. Ind. Econ. 19.

The scope of this introductory book does not allow for an in-depth discussion of entry barriers.[39] Common views and points of disagreement are only briefly sketched. There is agreement among economists that government regulation creates entry barriers.[40] Opinions differ with respect to non-regulatory entry barriers: some economists take a critical view of private market participants' possibilities to erect entry barriers. A useful distinction can be made between absolute advantages and strategic advantages that derive from the asymmetry of timing between incumbent firms and entrants (so-called first mover advantages of incumbents). The latter category includes scale economies and product differentiation (supported by advertising) as the most prominent examples. In addition, recent literature also discusses vertical foreclosure and predatory pricing as entry barriers caused by strategic behaviour of incumbent firms.[41] Apart from entry barriers, there may be entry impediments that afford only temporary protection for a limited period of time. Barriers to entry allow incumbent firms to make long-run super-normal profits without being more efficient than potential rivals. Only barriers to entry benefiting incumbent firms that are not more efficient than newcomers should raise antitrust concerns.

4.3.1 Absolute advantages

Absolute cost advantages for incumbents arise if some factor of production is denied to the potential entrant and, but for this omitted factor, the latter firm would be as efficient as incumbent firms.[42] Absolute advantages are easy to identify by looking at government regulation. Monopoly rights granted to a single trader or a group of professionals constitute entry barriers for potential competitors who are not allowed to sell similar goods or perform similar services. Monopoly rights that were granted to public utilities to supply customers with gas, electricity and water are clear examples of legal barriers to entry. The same conclusion holds with respect to licensing systems in the sector of the liberal professions and entry regulation in retailing. In each of these sectors of industry, deregulation measures have been taken to promote competition. It would be premature, however, to conclude that the recent deregulation has created the conditions to guarantee efficient outcomes.[43]

Intellectual property rights (patents, copyright) belong to the same category

---

[39] See Office of Fair Trading, *Barriers to Entry and Exit in Competition Policy* (1994); D. Harbord and T. Hoehn, "Barriers to Entry and Exit in European Competition Policy" (1994) 14 Int. Rev. Law Econ. 411.

[40] See also Guidelines on the assessment of horizontal mergers under the Council Regulation on the control of concentrations between undertakings [2004] O.J. C 31/5, para.71(a).

[41] For a discussion of these issues, see Chs 6 (vertical foreclosure) and 7 (predatory pricing) respectively.

[42] R.J. Gilbert, "Mobility Barriers and the Value of Incumbency", in *The Handbook of Industrial Organisation I* (R. Schmalensee and R.D. Willig ed., 1989), p.475.

[43] R.J. Van den Bergh, "Self-regulation of the Medical and Legal Professions: Remaining Barriers to Competition and EC law", in *Organized Interests and Self-Regulation* (B. Bortolotti and G. Fiorentini, ed., 1999), p.89.

of absolute cost advantages, but they require a different evaluation because of their potential to generate dynamic efficiencies. The economic rationale of patent protection is to promote competition in innovation by making sure that firms are able to reap the profits from their investments in research and development. Similarly, copyright protection grants monopoly rights to authors to protect them from free riding and guarantee an optimal level of literary and artistic production. Here, it is not the place to go into the discussion of whether intellectual property rights do indeed provide incentives for innovation and how broad their scope, in particular their duration, should be to balance optimally the anti-competitive effects (losses of allocative efficiency) and the gains in innovation (dynamic efficiencies). Interested readers are invited to consult other publications.[44]

4.3.2 Strategic advantages, sunk costs, product differentiation and advertising

In Bain's view, scale economies were considered as an important source of barriers to entry. Bain argued that minimum efficient scale may impede entry; coming in at less than the minimum efficient scale would not be feasible if it involved average costs substantially higher than those of established firms. In Bain's view, economies of multi-plant operation and economies of scale in distribution equally limit entry. In the former case an entrant may have to enter several geographic markets at once; in the latter an entrant may have to come in on a vertically integrated basis.

The modern view is that scale economies can constitute a barrier to entry if they are combined with sunk costs.[45] The more costs are sunk, the more potential entrants have to weigh the risks of entering. Incumbents will be able to deter potential entrants if sunk costs are high: for the former it is costly to leave the market and for the latter the sum of fixed and sunk costs acts as a deterrent.

Another bone of contention concerns product differentiation and advertising. In the perfect competition model, firms sell homogeneous products. They have no incentives to use non-price strategies (such as physical differentiation and services provided with the product) to increase sales, since they can sell as much as they want without such extra effort. In real-world markets firms use product differentiation and advertising to make their product(s) special to more and more consumers so that sales increase. The view that product differentiation and advertising must be qualified as first mover advantages and, hence, fall into the group of strategic entry barriers, is not universally accepted. There are, broadly speaking, two conflicting approaches.

---

[44] W.K. Viscusi, J.M. Vernon and J.E. Harrington, Jr, *Economics of Regulation and Antitrust* (2nd ed., 1995), pp.831–870.
[45] The Commission's Horizontal Merger Guidelines still mention economies of scale without this qualification. See Guidelines on the assessment of horizontal mergers under the Council Regulation on the control of concentrations between undertakings, [2004] O.J. C 31/5, para.71(b).

Some commentators have argued that product differentiation alters the public's perception of the product. According to Bain, product differentiation "refers to the extent to which buyers differentiate, distinguish, or have specific preferences among the competing outputs of the various sellers".[46] A lot of product differentiation is perceived rather than real. Real differences include those in product reliability and performance as well as the quality of connected services (delivery time, pre- and post-sales services). Perceived product differentiation refers to the subjective appreciation of a product. Examples include colour, packaging, design, and prestige brand names. In the tradition of Bain, Harvard scholars see advertising as persuasion: by changing the consumers' preferences firms may increase their market power. If advertising campaigns are successful, consumers will perceive the advertised brand(s) as the best and most reliable. Since advertising is a means of building up consumer loyalty, it may make entry by new firms into the market difficult. Hence, firms that were the first to introduce changes in the product enjoy a first mover advantage. Rival firms then have the choice of offering similar products or implementing their own strategies to make their products special to consumers. In industries where products are differentiated, advertising may be used as a means of establishing brand loyalty as a result of which there will be barriers to entry. With an inferior image new entrants may be condemned more or less permanently to charge lower prices than the incumbent(s) and may have to spend more on promotion to change the consumers' brand loyalty or inertia. If the presence of the incumbent raises the marketing entry costs of the second firm, then the first firm has a permanent advantage (a long-run barrier to entry) and can maintain high prices.

Bork stressed the fact that many barriers to entry are inherent in the nature of different industries and thus natural. Anybody understands that it is more difficult to enter the computer industry than to open a sweet shop. Hence, it is necessary to distinguish carefully between forms of efficiency and artificial entry barriers. The key question for antitrust policy is to find out whether there are any artificial entry barriers.[47] Regarding product differentiation, Bork disagreed with the Bainian approach which assesses this as a barrier to entry. Sellers differentiate their products to increase their appeal to consumers and such differentiation is only profitable if consumers value it. Hence, successful product differentiation must be classified as a form of efficiency. Even though an incumbent firm's product differentiation policy may create an entry barrier when consumers prefer established products to new rival products, entrants remain free to design their products as they wish. It all comes down to consumers' preferences.

Further disagreement with the Bainian approach is found in advertising. The Chicago view on advertising originated with George Stigler and sees advertising as information. Stigler showed that if consumers lack information about the prices charged by different sellers of a product, then the sellers

---

[46] J.S. Bain, *Industrial Organisation* (2nd ed., 1968), p.223.
[47] R.H. Bork, *The Antitrust Paradox: A Policy at War with Itself* (2nd ed., 1993), p.311.

would be able to charge higher prices than if the consumers had been perfectly informed.[48] Advertising reduces search costs of consumers and is pro-competitive. The scope of this section does not allow us to elaborate on the question of whether and to what extent advertising is informative. But even if advertisements are seen as merely persuasive, the informative value of advertising does not automatically fall to zero. Nelson argued that high expenditure on advertising is in fact a signal of the high quality of the product: the advertiser's confidence in the product is such that he is willing to spend money on it.[49] Under some circumstances the amount of persuasive advertising may indeed be a signal of quality. High-quality firms selling experience goods will earn high confidence premiums; as a consequence they have a greater incentive to advertise than low-quality firms. Obviously, this argument only holds if high-quality and low-quality firms have the same variable costs. If low quality firms (fly-by-night firms) can easily enter the market, sell worthless products that are almost costless to produce, and leave the market before consumers are able to retaliate, the amount of the premiums for opportunistic behaviour may be higher than the amount of the confidence premiums. The fly-by-night firm makes larger profits on its initial sales (opportunism premiums) since it has no intention of being around for very long; earning confidence premiums is not an objective. Low-quality firms may thus mimic the actions of high quality firms by raising advertising to high levels. A related problem is false advertising. In markets in which opportunism premiums exceed confidence premiums false advertising should be combated by appropriate legal rules. From an efficiency point of view, in cases where there is a danger of opportunistic behaviour confidence is to be protected if information costs are reduced and a confidence premium is paid.[50] Both conditions are satisfied here: advertising reduces the search costs of consumers and the costs of advertising are passed on to consumers via higher resale prices. Hence, a prohibition of false advertising is warranted to cope with the danger of opportunistic behaviour. Even though there is thus a clear economic rationale for a prohibition of false advertising, in practice the law faces serious difficulties in adequately dealing with deception. A major problem is how to formulate a prohibition of misleading advertising without banning true advertising.

Recent work in modern industrial organisation has further contributed to our understanding of product differentiation and advertising as entry barriers. It now appears that a cautious approach is warranted. Product differentiation and advertising can, under certain conditions, reduce consumer welfare. Advertising may be used either to increase the objective knowledge of

---

[48] G.J. Stigler, "The Economics of Information" (1961) 69 J. Polit. Economy 213.

[49] P. Nelson, "Advertising as Information" (1974) 81 J. Polit. Economy 729. Building on Nelson's work, Bagwell and Ramey argue that even where advertising is ostensibly uninformative, it may achieve coordination economies if it directs consumers towards the firms that offer the best deals (K. Bagwell and G. Ramey, "Coordination Economies, Advertising and Search Behaviour in Retail Markets" (1994) 84 Amer. Econ. Rev. 498).

[50] Further requirements are that the advertiser is the cheapest information producer and that the information provided through advertising is productive. See H.B. Schäfer and C. Ott, *The Economic Analysis of Civil Law* (2004), p.380.

products or to create consumers' preferences for a particular brand, thereby making the demand for those products less elastic and market entry by newcomers more difficult. However, to qualify as an entry barrier and not just as an entry impediment, the effects of advertising must last sufficiently long to enable incumbent firms to earn super-normal profits persistently. On the latter point the relevant empirical evidence is mixed: some researchers found that the effects of advertising lasted for several years, whereas others found that advertising effects are gone within a year.[51] Modern industrial organisation stresses the importance of sunk costs in assessing whether advertising may function as a barrier to entry. Sunk costs are central to the calculations of potential entrants: advertising costs to build consumer loyalty are normally sunk costs unless an exiting firm could either sell its brand name or use it somewhere else without a loss. The higher advertising and promotion expenditures that cannot be recovered on exiting a particular market, the more entry will be deterred.[52] Recent literature in industrial organisation on product differentiation also includes the view that it may be used as an instrument to obstruct market entry. To deter entrants looking for unfilled product design or brand image niches, established sellers might seek to crowd product space with enough brands (brand proliferation) so that no room for profitable new entry remains.[53] Consumer switching costs are a closely related topic. Goods or services which are perfect substitutes prior to the first purchase may become differentiated for a consumer who has already purchased because of *ex post* switching costs. Examples include bank accounts and airlines with frequent flyer programmes. Consumers who have already purchased from incumbent firms are locked in to a greater or lesser extent and hence are less available to entrants than uncommitted consumers.[54] A competitive assessment of product differentiation thus requires careful weighing of the following: the duration of advertising effects, the magnitude of sunk costs and the use of product differentiation in a strategic way (brand proliferation, switching costs).

To conclude this section a few comments on European case law seems appropriate. Decisions of the European Commission and judgments of the European Court of Justice show that European competition law may run the risk of protecting competitors willing to enter the market, even if they may be less efficient than the incumbents and their entry would not necessarily benefit consumers. Successful product differentiation is seen as an important factor in establishing market dominance but it is not always made clear how this makes market entry more difficult. In *United Brands* the price differential between Chiquita and unbranded bananas was seen as evidence of a successful advertising campaign which resulted in the Chiquita banana being considered

---

[51] Compare R. Ayanian, "The Advertising Capital Controversy" (1983) 56 J. Bus. 349; and R. Boyd and B.J. Seldon, "The Fleeting Effect of Advertising" (1990) 24 Econ. Letters 375.

[52] Sutton classifies advertising as endogenous sunk costs, as opposed to exogenous sunk costs such as investments in production capacity, see J. Sutton, *Sunk Costs and Market Structure: Price Competition, Advertising, and the Evolution of Concentration* (1991).

[53] R. Schmalensee, "Entry Deterrence in the Ready-to-Eat Breakfast Cereal Industry" (1978) 9 Bell J. Econ. 305.

[54] P. Klemperer, "Markets with Consumer Switching Costs" (1987) 102 Quart. J. Econ. 375; P. Klemperer, "The Competitiveness of Markets with Switching Costs" (1987) 18 RAND J. Econ. 138.

by the public to be of high quality. It was, however, not determined whether the high quality of the bananas (efficiency) or the advertising campaign (entry barrier) was the determinant force in achieving this result. In the *Nestlé/Perrier* case merger, the Commission pointed out the high degree of brand recognition in the mineral water industry that was due to intensive advertising campaigns and the difficulties for new entrants to compete in the market because of the large number of existing brands already introduced by the top three firms. This decision implicitly endorsed both the view that advertising is an entry barrier in the sense of being a sunk cost and the brand proliferation argument. The recent Horizontal Merger Guidelines confirm that advertising and other advantages relating to reputation may be qualified as entry barriers.[55]

4.4 Conclusions

Competition law is an instrument to avoid companies enjoying market power imposing lasting price increases surpassing the competitive level. The first task of competition authorities thus consists of identifying market power. The economic definition of market power, which focuses on the difference between market prices and marginal costs and the existence of entry barriers, differs from the legal concept of dominance, which focuses mainly on the degree of independence of a powerful firm limiting the individual economic freedom of competitors and consumers. Figures about firms' residual demand elasticities are immediately relevant for defining their degree of market power. Conversely, calculating market shares on a previously determined relevant market is only an indirect approach for assessing market power. As Richard Posner had already written in 1976: "It is only because we lack confidence in our ability to measure elasticities, or perhaps because we do not think of adopting so explicitly an economic approach that we have to define markets instead."[56] Quite often, the use of an indirect approach leads to focusing attention on market definition, not on the fundamental question of market power. This may lead to biased decisions, in which the market is defined in such a way that an infringement of the competition rules becomes unquestionable.

According to the traditional legal definition, a relevant product market comprises all those products, which are regarded as interchangeable or substitutable by the consumers, by reason of the product's characteristics, their prices and their intended use. The relevant geographic market is defined by assessing whether the conditions of competition in a given region are sufficiently homogeneous. Conversely, the SSNIP test defines the relevant market as a product or group of products and a geographic area in which it is sold so that a hypothetical profit maximising firm, that was the only present and future seller of those products in that area, would impose a profitable Small

---

[55] See Guidelines on the assessment of horizontal mergers under the Council Regulation on the control of concentrations between undertakings [2004] O.J. C 31/5, para.71(c).
[56] R.A. Posner, *Antitrust Law: An Economic Perspective* (1976), p.125.

but Significant and Non-transitory Increase in Price above prevailing or likely future levels. In contrast with the traditional legal definition, the SSNIP test gears the delineation of the market to the crucial question of market power. It takes into account three forces that might simultaneously discipline market power: demand-substitution, supply-substitution and potential competition. The SSNIP test also defines the product market and the geographic market simultaneously instead of sequentially.

The concept of the relevant antitrust market is sometimes confused with other notions of markets. Industry classifications do not provide a sound basis for assessing the competitive impact of agreements, practices or mergers. Economic markets are markets for goods or geographic areas where supply and demand lead to equilibrium prices. Strategic markets are groups of consumers and geographic areas at which marketing activities are targeted. By contrast, the relevant antitrust markets are markets where profitable price increases are possible. Consequently, the concept of an economic market and the notion of a strategic market provide no sound foundation on which it is possible to evaluate likely competitive effects, since they do not allow identification of the group of products and geographic areas that are worth monopolising.

Market share analysis does not always capture the relevant concerns of competition law enforcement. Market shares are less reliable indicators of antitrust worries when, as a consequence of mergers, unilateral effects in differentiated product markets arise. In such cases, a simulation analysis or a price–concentration study may allow a direct assessment of market power and avoid burdensome market definition debates. Direct measurement of market power may also be possible in cases of abuse of a dominant position if the conduct under investigation itself proves the existence of a dominant position or if a price–concentration relationship is absent in the market under scrutiny.

The Notice of the European Commission on market definition is not fully consistent with insights from the economic analysis. As was pointed out in this chapter, the Notice is a somewhat peculiar document since modern economic views are injected into an orthodox legal straight-jacket. This causes several inconsistencies: the focus on product characteristics leads to inappropriate decisions if they do not influence the extent of competition in-between commodities and locations; there is no clear indication whether the SSNIP test should apply to supply substitution; there is no emphasis on the need to define product markets and geographic markets simultaneously; and there is no solution for the specific problem of applying an SSNIP test in dominance cases (to avoid the *Cellophane* fallacy, the test should start from competitive prices that cannot easily be established). Apart from these inconsistencies, the Notice may also be criticised for not offering sufficient guidance concerning the use of quantitative techniques for defining a relevant market.

In the past decades, the necessary data for quantitative analysis have become available on a wider scale and direct econometric inferences on the relevant elasticities to define market power have thus come within the reach of day-to-day competition law practice. As a result, the US judiciary seems to have accepted that price elasticities of demand are a better way of establishing market power when compared to a pure market share approach.[57] Hence European competition law also should intensify its employment of advanced econometrics in determining market power, as long, of course, as European competition authorities are really serious about increasing the momentum of economic analysis.

In antitrust cases, econometric techniques may be used for two separate purposes: either to reject a definition suggested by a party or the competition authority, or to define the boundaries of the relevant market. The data needed to perform the second task are more comprehensive than the information requirements for the first job. Even though the data available may be insufficient to define the boundaries of the relevant market, they may be enough to reject the definition suggested by a party in the legal proceedings. For example, if the price elasticity of a particular product shows a high negative value and the cross-price elasticities with other products are high, it is unlikely that this product will constitute, in itself, a relevant product market. Judges may also reject the definition of the relevant market proposed by the competition authority, if it is not based on satisfactory economic evidence.

A direct delineation of the relevant market by means of econometric techniques is more burdensome. Cross-price elasticities of demand allow a ranking of substitutes and may provide sufficient proof of substitution to reject a proposed (narrow) market definition. However, it is not possible to define the relevant market on the basis of figures on cross-price elasticities without information about the critical demand elasticity. Price correlations are a widely applied empirical tool, since the data required may be easily available. Unfortunately, they are also an imperfect method of market definition. It remains unclear how high a correlation coefficient needs to be for allowing any conclusion on the boundaries of the relevant market. Furthermore, positive correlations may be spurious, for example by indicating an interdependency that is not caused by competitive constraints. And on top of this, price correlation studies define economic markets and not relevant antitrust markets, since supply substitution is not taken into account. The same criticism applies to the Elzinga–Hogarty test for delineating the relevant geographic market.

The most direct approach to market definition focuses on the own-price elasticity of demand for the product(s) in the potential relevant market. Comparing the critical demand elasticity (that is, the threshold above which a price increase becomes unprofitable) with the actual demand elasticity, brings the SSNIP test from the world of theoretical economics into daily antitrust practice. A technique to directly define a relevant market, which is becoming

---

[57] In, for example, *Eastman Kodak*, it was found that "price elasticities are better measures of market power [as compared to market shares]"; see *United States v Eastman Kodak Co*, 853 F. Supp. 1454 (W.D.N.Y. 1994); aff'd, 63 F.3d 95 (2d Cir. 1995); at 1472. After having established Kodak's market shares in the USA to be 67% of unit sales and 75% of dollar sales, the Court followed the econometric analysis conducted (based on the analysis of scanner data of film purchases), which revealed film purchasers to be price sensitive, in concluding that Kodak does not possess market power. Earlier on, see *State of New York by Abrams v Anheuser-Busch, Inc*, 811 F. Supp. 848 (E.D.N.Y. 1993); at 873; the Court finding that "if market power is the ability to raise prices and maintain such prices above competitive levels, than a high degree of price sensitivity in a market exemplifies a lack of market power".

increasingly popular, is critical loss analysis. In this approach the critical loss is calculated taking into account the initial profit margin and then compared with the actual loss. If the latter exceeds the former, a broader definition of the market is called for until the borderline is reached, where the critical value is no longer exceeded.

This chapter concluded with an analysis of entry barriers. After having recalled the Harvard–Chicago debate on this topic, the most important insights from modern industrial organisation theory were summarised. Sunk costs and strategic behaviour are crucial factors in assessing the existence of entry barriers. In addition, a distinction can be made between absolute costs advantages (licensing laws, intellectual property rights) and strategic or first mover advantages (economies of scale combined with sunk costs, lasting effects of advertising and brand proliferation through product differentiation). Competition authorities should carefully distinguish between both categories of entry barriers, on the one hand, and obstacles to entry that are caused by higher efficiency, on the other hand.

Chapter 5

....

COMPETITOR COOPERATION AND HORIZONTAL RESTRICTIONS

5.1 Introduction

This chapter deals with competitor cooperation and horizontal restrictions of competition; vertical restrictions are the subject of the next chapter. The EC Treaty sets out the general rules relevant to horizontal restrictions in Article 81 EC. According to Article 81(1) EC, all agreements, decisions of associations of undertakings, or concerted practices between undertakings[1] that restrict competition and affect trade between Member States are prohibited. The prohibition may, however, be declared inapplicable if the four cumulative conditions of Article 81(3) EC are fulfilled: to qualify for an exemption the cartel agreement must achieve efficiencies benefiting consumers without imposing restrictions that are disproportionate to the advantages achieved or which eliminate competition in respect of a substantial part of the products in question. Regulation 1/2003 makes both Articles 81(1) and 81(3) EC directly applicable by the European Commission, National Competition Authorities (NCAs) and national courts.[2] Clauses in agreements violating the prohibition and not qualifying for an exemption are null and void by way of Article 81(2) EC.[3] In addition, under Regulation 1/2003, substantial fines can be imposed, up to a maximum of 10 per cent of the turnover of the companies which infringe the cartel prohibition.[4] Some remaining sector-specific rules notwithstanding,[5] the cartel prohibition of Article 81(1) EC covers all horizontal cooperation concerning products and services.[6]

Article 81 EC applies only to agreements, decisions of associations of undertakings, and concerted practices. In general, only collusive behaviour is prohibited. Unilateral measures and exclusionary behaviour are not covered by the cartel prohibition but may constitute an abuse of a dominant position governed by Article 82 EC; the latter prohibition will be discussed in Chapter 7 of this book. Mergers, although also originating from agreements between firms, have different competitive effects. First, most mergers end competition completely between the parties involved. Cooperation, in contrast, preserves some sort of competition. Second, mergers are designed to be permanent, while competitor collaboration is typically of a more limited duration. The formers' potential for excluding future competition necessitates a modified

---

[1] On the notion of undertaking, see W.P. Wils, "The Undertaking as Subject of EC Competition Law and the Imputation of Infringements to Natural or Legal Persons" (2000) 25 E.L. Rev. 99.

[2] [2003] O.J. L 1/1, Art.3. For a discussion of the new system of enforcement, see Ch.8.

[3] Whether the sanction of nullity affects the entire agreement is to be decided under the relevant rules of national private law.

[4] Even though these fines seem high at first sight, it is quite possible that they are inadequate to deter the more harmful types of horizontal agreements. See Ch.8, s.8.2.2.3.

[5] The European Commission's stated aim under Regulation 1/2003 is to bring in line all sector-specific rules: at the time of writing, remaining exceptions such as Regulation 4056/86 (Liner Conferences) and Regulation 1617/93 (IATA) are under review.

[6] See Case T–66/92 *Herlitz v Commission (Parker Pen I)* [1994] ECR II–531, paras 29–34.

antitrust approach.[7] Mergers are thus covered by a separate set of rules[8] which will be discussed in Chapter 9. Instead of opting for a full merger, firms may also bring together capital, production assets, technology and knowledge to create a joint venture which will produce a new product or take over activities (for example, research and marketing) from the founding companies. Legally, joint ventures are also treated separately; their treatment depends on the degree of integration achieved.

It is noteworthy that Article 81 EC bans not only hard core cartels (explicit agreements between competitors having as their object the restriction of competition), but also agreements whose effects are anti-competitive and concerted practices where the collusive agreement is merely implicit (soft cartels). When a set of one or more agreements or concerted practices is entered into among companies operating at the same level of the production and distribution chain, Article 81 EC aims at preventing both actual and potential harm to competition. Agreements on prices and output or market sharing whereby companies want to eliminate competition among them are a clear example of harmful cartels. Collusive behaviour may also take different forms: agreements may aim at harming rivals not party to the collusion (for example, boycotts) or changing the conditions under which competition in the market is to take place (for example, restrictions on advertising).

In contrast with these anti-competitive effects, horizontal cooperation among competitors may also generate benefits. It often covers areas such as research and development (R&D), common schemes of production, purchasing, marketing or expanding into foreign markets. Companies need to respond to the increasing dynamism of the globalising marketplace and its growing complexity. Cooperation thereto can offer a means of sharing risks, saving costs, pooling know-how and stepping up innovative activity. Contrary to agreements on prices and output or collusion to change the competitive market surroundings, the latter form of cooperation is benign. The efficiencies achieved notwithstanding, horizontal cooperation of the benevolent kind may also lead to anti-competitive concerns, as the firms involved can simultaneously agree to fix prices or output, share markets, or generally try to obtain or increase collective market power. The actuality of this trade-off between benefits and drawbacks to cooperation has been explicitly recognised by antitrust authorities both in the USA and Europe.[9] In the following section, it will be assessed whether Article 81 EC provides the legal platform for an

---

[7] Antitrust authorities recognise these differences; compare the European Horizontal Guidelines, paras 12–13; and US antitrust guidelines for collaborations among competitors, April 2000 (hereinafter the "US Horizontal Guidelines"), para.1.3.

[8] On the Merger Regulation and merger control, see Ch.9 of this book, the residuary applicability of Art. 81 EC in the wake of the ECJ's *Philip Morris* decision notwithstanding (Joined Cases 142/84 and 156/84 *British American Tobacco Company Ltd and R.J. Reynolds Industries, Inc v Commission* [1987] ECR 4487).

[9] Compare the EC Horizontal Guidelines, paras 2–4; and the US Horizontal Guidelines, at the Preamble.

economically balanced consideration of both the anti-competitive effects and the efficiencies of horizontal cooperation.[10]

The rest of this chapter is structured as follows. The next section summarises the most important insights of economic theory relating to horizontal restrictions of competition. The welfare losses that may be caused by different types of collusion will be described. Particular attention will be devoted to the incentives for firms to enter into cartel agreements. Economic theory can assist in detecting whether collusion is more likely to occur and cartels are likely to succeed or fail. Factors that may make collusion either harder or easier will be highlighted. A major factor inhibiting successful cartelisation is the risk of cheating. Therefore, the section discusses how cartels may detect and punish deviations from the collusive outcome. Competitor cooperation may also have benign effects. The section ends with an overview of the efficiencies that may be generated by horizontal cooperation. Reference to the relevant case law will be included where this is helpful for a better understanding of the economic criteria that determine the (lack of) success of cartels. The third section then discusses the legal structure of Article 81 EC in force and simultaneously provides for an economic assessment of the current law.[11] It subsequently focuses on the benchmark for cartelisation, the need for proof of explicit or implicit coordination and on the assessment of efficiencies. Particular attention will be paid to the treatment of efficiencies, in reference to the Article 81(3) Notice.[12] In the fourth section, joint ventures will be explored. These types of strategic alliances are on the dividing line between horizontal cooperation and full merger, depending on the degree of integration involved. Legally, they are treated separately according to a complex set of rules which will be commented upon from an economic perspective.

As in the other chapters of this book, comparisons with US antitrust law[13] will be made to provide for a clearer understanding of the most debated legal and economic issues of the cartel prohibition as contained in Article 81 EC. Issues of enforcement—such as allocation of cases in the Network consisting of the European Commission, the NCAs and the national courts, leniency programs and fining—will be discussed in Chapter 8.

---

[10] Regulators, too, stress the need to base the analysis on economic criteria; compare the Art. 81(3) Notice [2004] O.J. C 101/97; the EC Horizontal Guidelines, paras 6–7; and the US Horizontal Guidelines, para.1.2.

[11] In line with the scope of this book, Art. 81 EC is to be highlighted from a legal and economic perspective. For a more comprehensive legal analysis, the reader may consult L. Ritter, W.D. Braun and F. Rawlinson, *European Competition Law: A Practitioner's Guide* (3rd ed., 2004), chs 2, 3 and 6; or J. Faull, A. Nikpay (eds), *The EC Law of Competition* (1999) chs 2 and 6. For a more elaborate (but technical) economic analysis, see L. Phlips, *Competition Policy: A Game-Theoretic Perspective* (1995).

[12] Guidelines on the application of Art. 81(3) of the Treaty [2004] O.J. C 101/97.

[13] For an overview of the relevant issues, see H. Hovenkamp, *Federal Antitrust Policy: The Law of Competition and its Practice* (2000), ch. 4; or W.E. Kovacic, "The Identification and Proof of Horizontal Agreements under the Antitrust Laws" (1993) 38 Antitrust Bull. 5. The applicable statutory material is contained in s.1 Sherman Act (15 U.S.C. 1), prohibiting contracts, combinations or conspiracies that unreasonably restrain trade, and in s.7 Clayton Act (15 U.S.C. 18), relating to coordinated effects in merger situations. The key document covering the horizontal issues are the US Horizontal Guidelines.

5.2 Lessons from economics

5.2.1 General insights[14]

5.2.1.1 Forms of collusion

Economic theory is helpful in explaining why competitors have incentives to cooperate and why cartels are formed. On oligopolistic markets firms may increase their profits by cooperating. Potentially anti-competitive collusion can take three forms:

1. Firms may agree to fix prices, restrict output, freeze market shares, or divide markets. Such agreements allow cartel members to maximise their profits directly. In practice the horizontal fixing of minimum prices also requires agreements on limiting production capacities and a concomitant discipline among cartel members not to exceed the production limits agreed upon. Most far-reaching is the founding of a common sales office (also called syndicate) which represents the cartel in its relations with clients and divides the orders as well as the resulting profits among the cartel members.

2. A second category of collusion consists of agreements to take action to harm rivals who are not party to the collusion. Firms can reduce their rivals' revenues through boycotts or raise rivals' costs by forcing the latter to increase prices (allowing the cartel members to sell under the rivals' price umbrella).

3. Finally, firms can collude to change the rules of competition in a manner that will lessen forms of competition other than price competition. The latter category includes agreements to limit advertising or raising consumers' search costs in another way (for example, restricting opening hours of shops).

5.2.1.2 Welfare effects of collusion

Collusion of the first type directly raises price and causes a wealth transfer from consumers to the cartel as well as a deadweight loss (allocative inefficiency). From society's perspective, the costs of forming and enforcing the cartel ("rent seeking") are also welfare-reducing. In addition, the prospect of profits that are easy to make may reduce incentives to keep production costs low (productive inefficiency) or to innovate (dynamic inefficiencies). Since cartels of the second category lead to supra-competitive pricing, they can also cause all these types of detrimental effects. In addition, collusion to

---

[14] See also, for a general overview: G. Hewitt, "Oligopoly: Background Note" (2002) 3 *OECD Journal of Competition Law and Policy* 143.

disadvantage rivals causes wasteful defensive measures by the victims and wasteful expenditure of resources by the cartel members to accomplish the cartel's objectives. The welfare effects of cartel agreements of the third type are even more numerous and complex. Since consumer prices will be higher— because of the restrictions on advertising (or other sales methods)—losses in terms of allocative efficiency and rent seeking will again ensue. In addition, the latter cartels will cause increased consumer search costs and lower the quality or variety of products offered in the market. The number and possible magnitude of these losses certainly seems to justify the costs of enforcing a cartel prohibition.[15]

5.2.2 Collusion and the game theoretic literature on oligopolies[16]

5.2.2.1 The problem of oligopolistic markets

As soon as the number of suppliers is limited and the products sold are not homogeneous, perfect competition no longer exists. Deviations give rise to different types of markets, of which monopoly is only one alternative. When products are differentiated, a distinction can be made between a pure multi-product monopoly (where there is only one seller), a differentiated oligopoly (where there are a few sellers), and monopolistic competition (where a large number of sellers offer differentiated products). The latter market form does not give rise to significant competitive concerns. Although it allows for price discrimination, this is not to be equated with the monopoly problem.[17] The gains from product diversity can be large and may easily outweigh the inefficiencies resulting from small monopoly power.[18] When products are homogeneous, there are once again three types of markets: a pure monopoly, a homogeneous oligopoly, and perfect competition. In this section, the focus will be on oligopolistic markets.

The formation of cartels is easier if the firms involved are few and the industry concerned is concentrated (although the opposite may also be true, as some of the most notorious cartels consisted of numerous participants[19]). However, it would be premature to characterise all oligopolistic markets as prone to causing substantial welfare losses. The most important element distinguishing oligopolistic markets from monopoly and/or perfect competition is that an oligopolistic firm's profits are strongly dependent on the actions chosen by its competitors. A monopolist can maximise his profits by producing exactly the output where marginal revenues equal marginal costs. A firm

---

[15] See the figures mentioned in Ch.2, s.2.2.3.
[16] For an overview, see G.J. Werden, "Economic Evidence on the Existence of Collusion: Reconciling Antitrust Law with Oligopoly Theory" (2004) 71 Antitrust L.J. 719.
[17] See Ch.7, s.7.2.
[18] R.S. Pindyck and D.L. Rubinfeld, *Microeconomics* (6th ed., 2005), pp.439–440.
[19] For example, see Cases IV/33.126 and IV/33.322 *Ciment* [1994] O.J. L 343/1; Case IV/33.833 *Cartonboard* [1994] O.J. L 243/1.

in a perfectly competitive market must take price as a given since it is too small to have an impact on the market price; hence price equals marginal costs. In oligopolistic markets firms face a choice between cooperating (entering into cartel agreements) and competing (staying out of the cartel or cheating). In choosing one of these alternatives, an oligopolist will have to consider the plausible reactions of his competitors.

5.2.2.2 Basic insights from game theory

In game theory, models have been developed which describe behavioural choices of firms in an oligopolistic market which have to take reactions by competitors into account. Game theory is a powerful tool to explain and predict the behaviour of oligopolistic firms. It supplements and refines the traditional insights of micro-economics with respect to welfare losses caused by oligopolies, by stressing that both cooperative and non-cooperative outcomes can be achieved.[20]

The relevant economic, and in particular game-theoretic, literature on oligopolies is most extensive and cannot be covered within the scope of this introductory book.[21] Economists have developed different models of oligopolistic industries, each carrying its own assumptions. The conclusions from this theoretical literature are highly dependent upon the underlying assumptions made. For the purposes of this book, it suffices to highlight the mainstream economic insights into the typical competitive problems encountered in oligopolistic markets. Game theory is helpful for revealing under which conditions price levels in oligopolistic markets may be above the competitive price.

Game theory distinguishes between cooperative and non-cooperative games. Under the former the parties can make binding agreements. In the latter this is not possible and strategic interaction may lead to an outcome which is suboptimal in comparison to what would be feasible if agreements were allowed. The game providing the most relevant insights thereto is the classic one-shot prisoners' dilemma. Two criminals, who together committed a crime, are caught and put in separate cells. Not having enough direct evidence, the police needs a confession from one of them in order to convict both of them for the crime and impose a high sentence. The criminals are questioned separately and each prisoner is told that if he or she testifies against the other, he or she will receive a lighter sentence. Neither prisoner can speak with the other before making the decision whether to talk or remain silent. The best solution for both prisoners is that neither of them testifies. Having insufficient evidence, the public prosecutor will not be able to ask for a high sentence. However, if one prisoner talks, it is better for the other to testify as well in order to escape a more severe punishment. If the other remains silent, testifying is also the best choice since it once again guarantees a lighter

---

[20] See in general L. Phlips, *Competition Policy: A Game-Theoretic Perspective* (1995).
[21] Compare, e.g. J. Tirole, *The Theory of Industrial Organization* (1988). An overview is presented by D.W. Carlton and J. M. Perloff, *Modern Industrial Organization* (3rd ed., 1999), pp.153–186; or R.S. Pindyck and D.L. Rubinfeld, *Microeconomics* (6th ed., 2005), pp.452 *et seq.*

punishment. In the jargon of game theory, testifying is the dominant strategy.[22] As a result, both prisoners will be severely punished. The optimal outcome from the prisoners' perspective would have been a lighter sentence because of lack of evidence; but this will not be obtained, as the two criminals cannot make a prior binding agreement.

5.2.2.3 The prisoners' dilemma in oligopolistic markets

The above analysis can be extended to the study of oligopolies. Given the existing interdependencies as a result of which a firm's actions depend on a rival's decisions, oligopolistic markets are characterised by strategic behaviour. Firms will face a choice between cooperative and non-cooperative strategies (collusion or cheating). On the one hand, they will recognise the possibility of earning higher profits jointly through coordinating their activities. Price agreements or joint decisions to restrict output will achieve this goal. On the other hand, though, the collective incentive to collude will be opposed by the strong private incentives of each individual firm to cheat on its fellow cartel members. If other firms respect the price agreement, the cheating firm will achieve additional profits. The example in Box 5.1 shows the different pay-offs for two firms which both face a choice between collusion (obeying the cartel agreement) and cheating (price undercutting or output expansion to attract additional customers). The numbers in each box denote the profits resulting from the outcome of the two firms' decisions. The first number shows the profits which Firm A makes and the second the profits which Firm B obtains. Considering the various outcomes, both firms would prefer an outcome in which both charged a high price (top left quadrant) to that in which they both charged a low price (bottom right quadrant). However, the duopoly is characterised by a prisoner's dilemma so that the outcome (Nash equilibrium) will be that both firms cheat.

Box 5.1: The prisoners' dilemma: profit opportunities in a duopoly

		Firm B	
		Collude	Cheat
Firm A	Collude	20, 20	15, 22
	Cheat	22, 15	17, 17

If both firms coordinate their behaviour and collude, they will charge higher prices (or restrict output) and obtain joined profits amounting to €40 with each firm individually earning €20. If one firm cheats on the other by price undercutting (or expanding production) while the other firm adheres to the cartel agreement, the cheating firm will earn €22 while the other firm's profit

---

[22] A strategy that is a best choice for a player in a game for every possible choice by the other player is called a dominant strategy. See for further clarification: D.G. Baird, R.H. Gertner and R.C. Picker, *Game Theory and the Law* (2nd ed., 1998), p.306.

declines to €15. Clearly, both firms are better off collectively if they collude. The joint collusive profits equal €40 and exceed the joined profits of €34 in case of price undercutting (or output expansion) by both firms. It is equally clear, however, that each firm has an incentive to forsake collusion and improve its own position through cheating. On the one hand, the latter option will increase profits by an additional €2 (22 compared with 20) if the second duopolist does not cheat as well. On the other hand, if the rival cheats, adhering to the cartel agreement reduces profits by €3 (17 compared with 20). Given the extra profit in the case of cheating and the fear of losing money if the rival cheats, each duopolist will decide to cheat. In game-theoretic terms, the non-cooperative strategy will be dominant. To the duopolists the final outcome of the game (joined profits of €34) is worse than the cooperative outcome (joined profits of €40). To avoid this non-cooperative outcome the duopolists must be able to detect and punish cheating.[23]

The fact that firms do meet in practice makes a collusive outcome more likely. Even in the absence of explicit agreements, non-cooperative games that are subject to repeated interaction (suggesting an infinite repetition of the prisoners' dilemma) may lead to a collusive outcome. In industries where only a few firms compete over a long period under stable demand and costs conditions cooperation prevails, even though no contractual arrangements are entered into.[24] Thus, if antitrust laws require hard evidence to show the existence of concerted practices, they may fall short of adequately controlling serious anti-competitive concerns.[25]

In the remainder of this section, three issues will be addressed in more detail: the prerequisites for successful cartel agreements, the problem of cheating, and the efficiency savings from horizontal cooperation.

5.2.3 Conditions for successful collusion

An important insight, often neglected by over-zealous competition authorities and antitrust lawyers, is that oligopolistic markets do not necessarily lead to collusive outcomes. Some cartels will succeed, while others will fail. In this section, three requirements for cartel success will be discussed: (1) the potential for monopoly power, given the characteristics of the market, (2) expected high gains, and (3) the need to overcome the organisational problems of cartels.[26] A major factor inhibiting successful cartelisation is the risk of cheating. The next section will discuss how deviations from the collusive outcome can be detected and punished.

---

[23] For a further elaboration on methods to detect and punish cheating, see ss.5.2.4.2 and 5.2.4.3.
[24] For the more specific concepts of Cournot competition and their relation with the basic prisoners' dilemma, the reader may refer to R.S. Pindyck and D.L. Rubinfeld, *Microeconomics* (6th ed., 2005), p.474 *et seq.*
[25] See H. Hovenkamp, *Federal Antitrust Policy: The Law of Competition and its Practice* (2nd ed., 1999), p.157.
[26] R.S. Pindyck and D.L. Rubinfeld, *Microeconomics* (6th ed., 2005), p.463.

5.2.3.1 Market characteristics

A number of market characteristics complicate collusion and thus decrease the potential for monopoly power: they may be apportioned among demand, supply and other factors.[27]

Anticipated complicating elements on the demand side include:

- an elastic demand at the competitive price;

- the existence of large and sophisticated buyers;

- differentiated products;

- volatile demand; and

- demand booms.

The more inelastic the demand curve facing a cartel, the higher the price the cartel can set and the higher its profits. Examples of markets where cartels can be profit-maximising thus include cigarettes and services provided by utilities. Buying power might counteract the cartel's power to increase prices: large buyers may succeed in obtaining secret discounts causing the cartel to unravel. Heterogeneous products make traditional price fixing unlikely; most cartels involve homogeneous products, such as cement, glass, salt and cartons.[28] Cartels are also facilitated if the market is mature, rather than dynamic. If the technology used is well known and widespread, no major innovations are to be expected and demand is relatively stable or declining, negative effects are more likely than in more dynamic markets.

On the supply side, factors complicating collusion include:

- low seller concentration;

- the existence of a competitive fringe with elastic supply;

- ease of entry; and

- cost asymmetries.

Entry by non-member firms or close substitutes produced in other industries prevents cartels from increasing prices. By contrast, collusion will be facilitated if the number of suppliers is limited and entry barriers exist. Finally, other factors complicating collusion include the absence of prior collusion and one-shot competition.

It should be noted, though, that some of these complicating factors will often

---

[27] For an overview of the relevant literature, both theoretical and empirical, see M. Knight and A.R. Dick, *Tacit Collusion* (1998), p.17; and D.W. Carlton and J.M. Perloff, *Modern Industrial Organization* (4th ed., 2005), Ch.5. Some of the relevant factors have been listed by the European Commission (EC Horizontal Guidelines, para.30). For additional discussion in the context of mergers, see Ch.9, s.9.2.2.

[28] For example, see Cases IV/33.126 and IV/33.322 *Ciment* [1994] O.J. L 343/1; Case IV/33.833 *Cartonboard* [1994] O.J. L 243/1; Case IV/29.869 *Italian Cast Glass* [1980] O.J. L 383/19.

be present without posing a serious risk to collusion. There is indeed no need for collusion to be perfect in order to work; firms only need to figure out convincingly that they are better off when coordinating instead of competing by independent pricing. Firms may also be able to adopt facilitating practices that help to offset or mitigate complicating factors. Moreover, empirical evidence of where collusion arises and persists identifies some complicating factors which are actually more reliable predictors.[29] In general, though, caution should reign when making predictions, as studies vary widely by methodologies and samples.[30]

5.2.3.2 Expected high gains

If the potential gains from monopoly power achieved through cooperation are large, firms will have more incentive to form cartels and develop devices to make them effective instruments for raising prices persistently above competitive levels. If competition authorities strictly enforce the cartel prohibition, the expected penalties effectively reduce the expected value of collusion and fewer cartels will be formed.[31] During periods when the US Department of Justice was relatively lax in enforcing the antitrust laws, price fixing conspiracies were more prevalent.[32] In Europe, in the period between both World Wars governments took a positive attitude towards cartels in an attempt to protect national industry from foreign competition. Since the creation of the Common Market, government-aided collusion has become a clear infringement of the Member States' duty not to take action inhibiting the achievement of the internal market goals.[33]

Cartels will not succeed if their members can and want to cheat on the agreement because the expected gains from cheating exceed the profits generated by the price fixing agreement. In this respect the moment at which deviation is detected and punished is crucial: the longer a firm can cheat without being detected, the more profitable this becomes. If cartel members can undermine the price fixing agreement by granting secret discounts and are able to continue this practice for a sufficiently long period, cheating can be more profitable than respecting a price fixing agreement. In order to succeed, a cartel must detect deviations from the collusive outcome and effectively and severely punish the firms who cheat. Devices that can be used to enforce cartels successfully will be discussed in s.5.2.4.3 of this chapter.

---

[29] See A.R. Dick, "When Are Cartels Stable Contracts?" (1996) 39 J. Law Econ. 241.

[30] Compare *ibid.*; as well as P. Asch and J.J. Seneca, "Is Collusion Profitable?" (1976) 58 Rev. Econ. Statist. 1.

[31] This does not imply that enforcement will be socially optimal. See on this issue, Ch.8.

[32] R.A. Posner, "A Statistical Study of Antitrust Enforcement" (1970) 13 J. Law Econ. 365.

[33] An example of a clear infringement is to be found in Case 311/85 *Vereniging van Vlaamse Reisbureaus ASBL v Sociale Dienst van de Plaatselijke en Gewestelijke Overheidsdiensten* [1987] ECR 3801 (the Belgian government endorsed a price fixing agreement by travel agents and made it compulsory for outsiders by enacting a royal decree, which explicitly prohibited the granting of discounts). Recent case law has made it clear that national judges must disapply national rules; see Case C–198/01 *Consorzio Industrie Fiammiferi v Autorità Garante della Concorrenza e del Mercato* [1993] ECR I–8055.

5.2.3.3 Low organisational costs

The transaction cost approach has made it clear that antitrust law should first address distortions of competition caused by dominant firms, since agreements among oligopolists may face great difficulties in minimising the costs of negotiating and enforcing agreements. The greater the number of firms, the higher the transaction costs will be. Firms will also face more difficulty in agreeing on prices when each firm's product has different qualities or properties; this strengthens the argument already advanced that successful cartelisation is more likely in homogeneous goods markets.

In general it is thought that cartels are to be found in concentrated industries where competitors are few. Economists will hesitate to give a clear number indicating precisely what "few" in this context means. A theoretical model developed by Nobel Prize winner Reinhard Selten[34] implies that if there are fewer than five competitors, they will all find it profitable to collude explicitly; if there are more than five competitors, however, it becomes more attractive to be an outsider to the cartel. The subtitle of Selten's article neatly summarises the main insight: "four are few and six are many". However, as is the case with all economic models, the outcome is dependent on the assumptions made and antitrust practice also shows examples of high numbered cartels. It must also be added that in Selten's model there is no room for cheating or untruthful costs reporting; his point is thus very different from the transaction costs argument.[35] This difference draws attention again to the cartel members' need to communicate with each other. Cartels collapse if their members are trapped in a prisoners' dilemma. It was shown earlier that duopolists who cannot influence each other's decision will choose not to cooperate and thus achieve a result which is worse than the one in case of collusion. A non-cooperative outcome[36] can be avoided if firms are able to control each other's behaviour; in other words: cartels will be profit-maximising strategies if cheating can be detected and prevented.

Even before transaction costs theory had developed, the view was held that cartels did not raise significant concerns for competition policy.[37] A cartel is inherently more fragile than a monopoly, as the interest of the cartel as a whole diverges substantially from the interests of its individual members.[38] With explicit coordination between firms (and thus the possibility of communication and negotiation) being prohibited, cooperative strategies can only be designed with considerable difficulty as a result of which their implementation will remain unstable. The view that cartels will not be formed because of

---

[34] R. Selten, "A Simple Model of Imperfect Competition, where 4 are Few and 6 are Many" (1973) 2 Int. J. Game Theory 141; and reinforced in L. Phlips, *Competition Policy: A Game-Theoretic Perspective* (1995), pp.56–66. It should be noted that in Selten's model there are no statements made on the impact the number of competitors has on the enforcement of a cartel agreement, as there is no room for cheating in the chosen non-cooperative Nash equilibria with perfect information.

[35] See also L. Phlips, *Competition Policy: A Game-Theoretic Perspective* (1995), p.24.

[36] In technical terms: a "non-cooperative Nash equilibrium".

[37] See G.J. Stigler, "A Theory of Oligopoly" (1964) 72 J. Polit. Economy 44.

[38] The formal treatment may be retrieved from L. Phlips, *Competition Policy: A Game-Theoretic Perspective* (1995), pp.49–66.

high transaction costs is too optimistic, however. The collective exercise of market power does not always require elaborate explicit coordination. If firms interact with each other on a prolonged basis, then the pursuit of individual interests—without any communication or negotiation between firms—may be consistent with the collective exercise of market power. The formal theory of repeated games describes how firms might resist taking advantage of their competitors in the short term because they would otherwise risk endangering a profitable long-term arrangement.[39] Deviation from an established equilibrium situation will require a profitable trade-off between the resulting short-term gains and the long-term consequences. The outcome of this trade-off will depend on the market circumstances as well as on whether the competitors can credibly announce that short-term deviations will be severely punished. If repeated interactions thus provide adequate surroundings for enforcing outcomes with substantial market power, then soft cartels may become a concern of competition policy as serious as hardcore cartels—their intrinsic volatility notwithstanding. In short, from a welfare point of view, prohibiting explicit coordination does not solve all problems. Coordination may also take the form of tacit collusion. In oligopolistic markets, there may be a situation of "joint dominance" under which prices are kept high out of fear of retaliation.

5.2.4 Enforcement of cartels: reaching agreements to restrict competition, cheating and punishing deviations

Collusion requires that (a) competitors reach an understanding on prices, output or another factor of competition; that (b) they can detect deviations from the common understanding; and that (c) they can credibly punish deviations from the collusive outcome. The ease of cheating varies considerably with the type of market. Cartels are most successful (cheating is most difficult) when markets are characterised by large-scale, infrequent sales and determined through secret bids with publicly announced results.[40]

5.2.4.1 The meeting of the minds

The successful formation of a cartel requires a "meeting of the minds". As has already been indicated, however, the repeated interaction of firms in an oligopolistic market leads by no means voluntarily to a coordinated outcome. Rather, multiple equilibria frequently exist, with the firms' profits differing accordingly. It is thus essential for firms to indicate to their potential fellow conspirators which strategy to pick. Two strategies for reaching an understanding on the parameters of competition will be discussed: cheap talk and focal points, and basing point pricing.

[39] J. Friedman, "A Non-cooperative Equilibrium for Supergames" (1971) 38 Rev. Econ. Stud. 1.
[40] Compare H. Hovenkamp, *Federal Antitrust Policy: The Law of Competition and its Practice* (1994), pp.145–146.

Cheap talk and focal points Providing rivals with advance notice of intended prices may allow time to gauge the other firms' willingness to respond as well as to adjust prices if necessary. One way of doing so is so-called "cheap talk", such as preannouncing a price.[41] A prominent example is the *Wood Pulp* cartel case, which was built on evidence of parallel quarterly announcements of prospective price rises.[42] A variant is posed by referring to "focal points", such as preserving existing price differentials or existing market shares.[43]

Implicit coordination through repeated interaction may be ineffective because it is a non-exclusive strategy. This makes it complicated for firms to focus on a particular cooperative outcome, finding instead that a given market's non-collusive focal points can often provide similar outcomes. For example, one firm's announcement of a precise percentage price increase may serve as a sufficiently self-evident way for its competitors to behave. As such, any exercise of collective market power, if solely based on the observation of market interactions in the absence of explicit coordination, will be highly imperfect.

Under antitrust constraints, the identification of implicit anti-competitive collaboration would often be similarly haphazard. Given the limited feasibility of exercising market power through implicit coordination and the costs of potentially wrong convictions, proceedings should be conducted with great caution. For example, in *UPM Kymmene/Haindl*,[44] a merger case, the theory of cheap talk was actually used to demonstrate the absence of collusion.

Basing point pricing A second strategy for making accomplices behave in unison is by "basing point pricing".[45] This scheme implies that sellers who produce at geographically dispersed locations set their prices according to a common price for delivered goods (thereby negating transportation as variable costs), typically designating a major production hub as a basing point. The price thus becomes independent of the actual distance between the seller and the buyer. An example is the price system explicitly imposed by the now defunct Article 60 of the Treaty of the European Community for Coal and Steel (ECSC Treaty).[46] When the Common Market for Steel between the Benelux countries, France, Germany and Italy was envisaged, the point arose as to how to define a common pricing policy without endangering the prevailing allocation of geographic markets between countries or raising the probability of price wars. The solution opted for in the ECSC consisted of creating a multiple basing point system characterised by an alignment rule, ensuring that

[41] Compare J. Farrell, "Cheap Talk, Co-ordination, and Entry" (1987) 18 Rand J. Econ. 34.
[42] Joined Cases C–89/85, C–104/85, C–114/85, C–116/85, C–117/85 and C–125–129/85 *A. Åhlström Osakeyhtio and others v Commission (Wood Pulp II)* [1993] ECR I–1307. A discussion is provided by L. Phlips, *Competition Policy: A Game-Theoretic Perspective* (1995), pp.131–136
[43] The theory of focal points was first devised by T.C. Schelling, *The Strategy of Conflict* (1960); and later formalised by R. Sugden, "A Theory of Focal Points" (1995) 105 Econ. J. 535.
[44] Case COMP/M.2498 *UPM-Kymmene/Haindl* [2002] O.J. L 233/38.
[45] Compare D.D. Haddock, "Basing Point Pricing: Competitive v. Collusive Theories" (1982) 72 Amer. Econ. Rev. 289.
[46] L. Phlips, "Basing Point Pricing, Competition and Market Integration", in *Does Economic Space Matter?* (H. Ohta and J.F. Thisse ed., 1987), pp.303–315.

at any given geographic location the delivered price to be quoted by all the competitors was equal to the lowest combination of a base price plus freight (to that location) calculated from all basing points existing in the system. As a result a single delivered price was charged at every location, in effect tying pre-Common Market customers to their traditional sellers.

5.2.4.2 Detecting deviations from the collusive outcome

Reaching a collusive agreement by no means guarantees its smooth running. Successful collusion is by no means self-enforcing. The profit opportunities created by collusion will attract entry into the market which the established members of the collusion must prevent, or else they have to persuade the new entrants to abide by the established code of conduct. As a consequence, members of a successful cartel often have to spend substantial resources to monitor their fellow accomplices' actions and restore discipline should cheating be detected. Monitoring will be more difficult when information deficiencies exist or if the number of buyers is high. Conversely, monitoring may be alleviated when firms interact repeatedly. Three devices for detecting violations from the collusive outcome will be described: information sharing, meeting competition clauses, and repeated interaction.

Information sharing   Imperfect or incomplete information available to firms can impede coordination if they hold divergent views about demand conditions. This makes it more difficult to agree upon a common price and, once a common understanding is reached, makes it harder to sustain the agreement. Detecting the ensuing cheats may be facilitated if information is shared.[47] Information sharing presents antitrust with a dilemma. On the one hand, pooling information is a good thing as long as firms behave competitively but, on the other hand, shared information makes anti-competitive agreements easier to construct.[48]

A case-by-case analysis is generally required, as the European Commission highlighted in the *Fatty Acids* case, the first time an agreement on the exchange of information in itself constituted an infringement of European competition law.[49] The exchange of information can—depending on the underlying facts— also be seen as neutral (see, e.g. parts of the information sharing discussed in

---

[47] Compare D.A. Malueg and S.O. Tsutsui, "Coalition-proof Information Exchanges" (1997) 63 J. Econ. (Z. Nationalökon.) 259; and K.-U. Kühn and X. Vives, *Information Exchange among Firms and their Impact on Competition* (1994).
[48] R.N. Clarke, "Collusion and the Incentives for Information Sharing" (1983) 14 Bell J. Econ. 383.
[49] Case IV/31.128 *Fatty Acids* [1987] O.J. L 3/17. On the antitrust treatment of information exchange agreements, see F.E. Gonzales Diaz, D. Kirk, F. Perez Flores and C. Verkleij, "Horizontal Agreements", in *The EC Law of Competition* (J. Faull and A. Nikpay ed., 1999), paras 6.343–6.366; A. Capobianco, "Information Exchange under EC Competition Law" (2004) 41 C.M.L. Rev. 1247; and K.-U. Kühn, "Fighting Collusion: Regulation of Communication between Firms" (2001) 16 Economic Policy 167.

the *UK Tractor* cases[50]) or benign (see, e.g. *European Wastepaper Information Service*[51]). In general, the economics of information sharing require careful assessment before any conclusions can be drawn from the competitive effects entailed.[52]

Meeting competition   A second impediment to an unruffled collusive cohabitation is given when firms sell to many buyers, making it difficult to detect all instances of price undercutting. By adopting a "meet competition" clause, however, their buyers are guaranteed that, should they find another firm offering a lower price, the selling firm will match it or release the buyer from the contract. The latter part of a "meeting competition" clause may arguably serve the (pro-competitive) goal of giving a potential buyer more freedom when entering into a long-term contract which they might otherwise be hesitant to sign. The clause without the release option is a singularly powerful device to deter firms from cheating on their conspirators: they now know that this firm will retaliate against any detected price reduction and that customers will report any such price reduction to it.[53]

Repeated interaction   Monitoring as such may be alleviated when firms interact repeatedly, as firms will find it easier to observe the other cartel members' behaviour. Therefore elaborate measures have been devised to prevent cheating by making it more observable. Reporting and book-keeping are only as valuable as the individual cartel member's honesty, however. Consequently, most cartels have turned to alternative methods of verification, by, for example:

- agreeing on a standard product and its accompanying services as a benchmark;

- destroying all faulty merchandise (which in a truly competitive market could be used for rebates);

- publicising all prices;

- imposing output restrictions (this works well in markets where the government requires detailed reporting of output or where the number of units sold is easy to verify);

---

[50] Cases IV/31.370 & IV/31.446 *UK Agricultural Tractor Registration Exchange* [1992] O.J. L 68/19; decision upheld in CFI and ECJ, Case T–35/92 *John Deere v Commission* [1994] ECR II–957, upheld in Case C–7/95P [1998] ECR I–3111; and Case T–34/92 *Fiatagri and New Holland v Commission* [1994] ECR II–905, upheld in Case C–8/95P [1998] ECR I–3175.
[51] *European Wastepaper Information Service* [1987] O.J. C 399/7.
[52] See R. Nitsche and N. von Hinten-Reed, *Competitive Impacts of Information Exchange* (2004).
[53] Compare S.C. Salop, "Practices that (Credibly) Facilitate Oligopoly Co-ordination", in *New Developments in the Analysis of Market Structure* (J.E. Stiglitz and G.F. Mathewson ed., 1986). This conclusion is qualified by J.W. Logan and R.W. Lutter, "Guaranteed Lowest Prices: Do They Facilitate Collusion?" (1989) 31 Econ. Letters 189.

- alternatively, agreeing on market shares with penalties for firms that exceed their allotment (preventing firms from bidding aggressively for new customers);

- dividing territory horizontally (leaving each territorial "monopoly" to equate its own marginal costs and revenues without any incentive to cheat on its fellow cartel members).

5.2.4.3 Punishing deviations from the collusive outcome

The detection of deviations from collusion must be reinforced by some credible threat of punishment to serve as a meaningful deterrent. If secret price cuts or output reductions are traceable, the introduction of punishment causes a further series of problems. Given that competition law prohibits cartelisation and anti-competitive collusion, punishment must make cheating unprofitable without causing the cartel or collusion to be detected. Even if this is possible, the disciplinary measure will only be effective if its expected costs to the cheating member exceed the additional profits to be made. Ideally, cheating should be detected immediately and punished without exception, rendering it unprofitable. Among the more credible intimidations is threatening the offender with the loss of (part of the) collusive profits once their misbehaviour is discovered. A common punishment is for the non-cheating cartel members to revert to the non-collusive price by raising output for some time.[54] The longer a firm can cheat without being detected, though, the more profitable this becomes. Another problem with cheating is that the costs of punishment are regularly higher for the imposing cartel members than for the offender. But, if this method of punishment can be presented as a convincing strategy, then it becomes possible to sustain the collusive equilibrium. Below, attention is focused on three devices for achieving adequate punishment of deviations from the collusive outcome: first, most favoured customer clauses, second multi-market contacts, and third, cross-ownership among rivals.

Most favoured customer clauses   One way of ensuring punishment is by embracing a "most favoured customer" clause (often to be found in combination with a "meet competition" clause). As cheating on a collusive price is generally profitable in the short run—until it is detected and punished—a "most favoured customer" clause guarantees the buyer any discount offered to another buyer by the same seller under the terms of the contract. Thereby, uncertainty about rivals' prices is reduced, allowing firms to track just one or two buyers' prices to monitor rivals' reliability.[55] By their nature, "most favoured customer" clauses tend to have mainly vertical implications, as illustrated by the European Commission's Notice on vertical restraints[56] or the Bundeskartellamt's reservations in the *Metro*-merger.[57] Another prominent

---

[54] M.J. Osborne and C. Pitchik, "Cartels, Profits and Excess Capacity" (1987) 28 Int. Econ. Rev. 413.
[55] For details, see L. Phlips, *Competition Policy: A Game-Theoretic Perspective* (1995), pp.91–93.
[56] Commission Notice—Guidelines on vertical restraints [2000] O.J. C 291/1, para.47.
[57] BKartA, WuW , DE-V 94 (*Metro MGE Einkaufs GmbH*).

example, from the US case law, is *General Electric*,[58] illustrating how a duo-poly's members had connived to protect their prices by promising buyers of electric turbines that if any one of them received a discount, all buyers from the last six months would receive that same discount retrospectively.

Multi-market contacts   Another complicating factor in reducing the con-spirators' incentives to cheat is that the maximum punishment credibly imposable (i.e. reverting to the competitive price) is often inadequate or more detrimental to the firms imposing the punishment. Multi-market contacts may make mutual forbearance more likely, though, with firms having a large range of outcomes that may find support as equilibrium and the maximum possible punishment across markets becoming more than sufficient to enforce collu-sion.[59] In the *Soda Ash* case[60] Solvay (concentrating its sale of soda ash on the continent) and ICI (having a near monopoly in the United Kingdom) had agreed in 1945 to maintain the actual market sharing arrangements prevailing at the time. After the agreement was suspended the European Commission suspected the companies of continuing to coordinate their behaviour, arguing that the total absence of any market interpenetration could only be explained by a tacit agreement to maintain the formerly explicit cartel. To justify its reasoning the European Commission pointed to the price gap between the two markets which had existed for a long time until the prices rose dramatically in the United Kingdom in the 1980s, ICI even resorting to buying soda ash from Solvay. When Solvay still did not enter the lucrative British market the Eur-opean Commission acted accordingly.

Cross-ownership   An alternative way of bolstering collusive agreements is by increasing cross-ownership among rivals, as this creates greater similarity of interests. Whether partial ownership actually hinders or facilitates collusion depends on the industry demand conditions, given that some of the penalty is borne by the rivals through their stake in the punished firm.[61] A case-by-case analysis appears warranted, and this is also stressed under the *Philip Morris*-doctrine[62] on minority shareholdings as an instrument for influencing com-mercial conduct.

---

[58] *United States v General Electric Corp*, 1977 Trade Cas. (CCH) 61,659 (E.D. Pa. 1976); at 72,715. For a discussion, see T.E. Cooper, "Most Favoured Customer Pricing and Tacit Collusion" (1986) 17 Rand J. Econ. 377.
[59] B.D. Bernheim and M.D. Whinston, "Multimarket Contact and Collusive Behaviour" (1990) 21 Rand J. Econ. 1.
[60] Case IV/33.133 *Imperial Chemical Industries Ltd/Solvay (Soda Ash II)* [1991] O.J. L 152/1. On appeal: Case T–36/91 *Imperial Chemical Industries Ltd v Commission (Soda Ash)* [1995] ECR II–1847. For a discussion of the case and a competitive explanation for the firms' behaviour, see B. Böhnlein, *The Soda-ash Market in Europe: Multi-market Contact with Collusive and Competitive Equilibria* (1994).
[61] D. Reitman, "Partial Ownership Arrangements and the Potential for Collusion" (1994) 42 J. Ind. Econ. 313; and J. Farrell and C. Shapiro, "Asset Ownership and Market Structure in Oligopoly" (1990) 21 Rand J. Econ. 275.
[62] Joined Cases 142/84 and 156/84 *BAT and Reynolds v Commission* [1987] ECR 4487. On the doctrine, L. Ritter, W.D. Braun and F. Rawlinson, *European Competition Law: A Practitioner's Guide* (2nd ed., 2000), pp 548–554.

5.2.5 Efficiency savings from horizontal cooperation

Cooperation between firms may be motivated by goals which are beneficial to societal welfare. Competition law should, therefore, take into account these benign effects of competitor collaboration rather than solely focusing on the anti-competitive effects. Different types of cooperation can lead to a range of efficiencies, such as economies of scale and scope, better planning of production, advantages in marketing and distribution, and in research and development. These are also recognised in the European Commission's Article 81(3) Notice, as well as in the Technology Transfer, Specialisation and R&D Block Exemption Regulations. In the following, the different types of efficiency savings will be discussed in turn. The discussion is not intended to be exhaustive, but only aims at giving the reader a general picture of the different categories of efficiencies.[63]

5.2.5.1 Economies of scale

Economies of scale are reductions in average unit costs attributable to increases in the scale of output at the plant level. As a more general matter, economies of scale exist when the production cost of a single product decreases with the number of units produced. These costs savings can, *inter alia*, accrue from a better division of labour within the production unit, the spreading of fixed costs and longer production runs. There can also be scale economies in functions such as transport, distribution and research. Lowering costs will, of course, give the opportunity to increase profitability. The size of the economies achieved will depend on the slope of the average costs curve for outputs below the optimum scale.[64] Besides these static scale economies there is the phenomenon of learning effects associated with the increasing experience of production of a product or service. This means that the cost of producing each extra unit decreases as the cumulative previous output increases. The minimum efficient scale is the size of a plant at which all economies of scale are exhausted and beyond which the long-term average costs curve either turns upward or remains flat (if returns to scale remain constant).

Types of economies of scale Potential economies of scale vary widely between different countries, industries and time periods. Chandler[65] has argued that these distinctions result from differences in technologies of production and distribution as well as of sizes and locations of markets. This is particularly relevant at a time of rapid technological change and changing market characteristics.

Typical economies of scale include:

---

[63] It is not intended to draw clear and firm distinctions between the different categories, since there may be considerable overlap between the various types of efficiencies.
[64] A. Jacquemin, P. Buigues and F. Ilzkovitz, "Horizontal Mergers and Competition Policy in the European Community" (1989) 40 European Economy 16.
[65] A.D. Chandler, Jr, *Scale and Scope: The Dynamics of Industrial Capitalism* (1990).

- Indivisibilities: many costs are wholly or partly indivisible with respect to output and as such independent of the scale of output (fixed set-up costs). When output is increased indivisible costs can be spread over larger numbers, reducing thereby the costs per unit.[66]

- Increase in dimension: for many types of capital equipment both the initial and operating costs increase less rapidly than capacity.

- Economies of specialisation: the larger the output of a product, plant or firm, the greater will be the opportunities for, and advantages of, specialisation of the labour force and the machinery. Increased output may enable a firm to employ specialised staff or buy equipment for a particular purpose.

- Economies of massed reserves: a larger sized firm may enjoy certain benefits that come with being big. This statistical law holds that random events tend to cancel out if there are enough of them.[67] Operating a line of identical machines instead of just one may result in relatively fewer spare parts to be stocked, as it is unlikely that all machines would develop the same malfunction at the same time. There may be similar economies for emergency stocks of raw materials as well as for certain types of labour and monetary resources. Through its diversity a large firm may be better placed to spread its risks.

- Superior organisation: from a certain size onward automatic machinery may be used instead of manually operated tools, guaranteeing more efficient production as scale increases.

- The learning effect: the essence of the "learning by doing" matter is that one learns how to reduce production costs through actual production experience. The more a firm produces, the lower its production costs will be (all things being equal).[68]

Diseconomies of scale   Even if economies of scale characterise some functions of a firm, diseconomies of scale may characterise others. Whether the firm experiences economies overall depends on the contribution of each function to total costs. Increases in unit costs may occur as scale increases for the following reasons:

- Factor limitations: the supply of a factor of production is fixed or the costs of a factor increase with rising demand for that factor.

- Decline in the efficient use of a factor: the efficiency in use of factors of

---

[66] In its Guidelines on Art. 81(3) EC, the European Commission gives the example of the cost of operating a truck. This is almost the same regardless of whether it is almost empty, half-full or full [2004] O.J. C 101/97, para.66.

[67] For an example of how a relatively large number of customers can offset random demand in the bakery industry, see D.W. Carlton and J.M. Perloff, *Modern Industrial Organization* (1994), pp.60–61.

[68] For examples and further applications, see P.D. Camesasca, *European Merger Control: Getting the Efficiencies Right* (2000), pp.137–139.

production may decline with increases in scale for a number of reasons. First of all, there are some technical forces which cause diseconomies of scale. As the capacity of a unit is increased, stresses and strains may result. In most cases it will be possible to counter these by using stronger materials or innovative techniques, but the costs of doing so might increase faster than the increase of scale—often, the simple duplication of an existing production line will do. In this regard, strains are a limitation on the sources of economies of scale rather than a source for diseconomies in their own right.

- Motivation of managers: they might want to shelter behind the (technical) efficiencies achieved by their firms, as the determination to maximise profits at the expense of other objectives may decline. Also, as scale increases, the costs of organising and coordinating production may rise out of proportion. This problem is aggravated when the firm operates in a complex or rapidly changing environment.[69] The chain of management grows longer and it will be more difficult to focus financial incentives accurately.

- Selling and distribution costs: possible sources of increased costs arise at higher scales of output, for instance, if the scale of a plant is increased; this might also apply to the geographic spread of markets, and thus the average length of haulage and the unit costs of transport. The costs of delivering output to customers (or bringing customers to the place where service is provided) will then limit the size-increasing effect of scale economies. However, one can argue that, on the contrary, transportation costs rise less than proportionately with the distance shipped.[70] Transportation costs absorbed by the producer rise with output when prices are uniform in all markets or when the prices in the more distant markets are set by rival producers located more advantageously.

5.2.5.2 Economies of scope

Economies of scope are another field where cooperation can be beneficial for firms that engage in different but complementary activities, as it is less costly for one firm to perform two activities than for two specialised firms to perform them separately.[71] Economies of scope imply that it is efficient to produce two or more different products together on the basis of the same input. They do not necessarily imply that these products should be produced in a single plant. Economies of scope may also arise in distribution, when producers combine their operations. For example, several types of goods (frozen pizzas and frozen vegetables) can be distributed in the same vehicles (refrigerated trucks) and

---

[69] D. Schwarzman, "Uncertainty and the Size of the Firm" (1963) 30 Economica 287.
[70] D.W. Carlton and J.M. Perloff, *Modern Industrial Organization* (4th ed., 2005), pp.38–39.
[71] See W.J. Baumol, J.C. Panzar and R.D. Willig, *Contestable Markets and the Theory of Industry Structure* (1982); and compare R.H. Coase, "The Nature of the Firm" (1937) 4 Economica 386 at p.389, who observed, "the distinguishing mark of a firm is the suppression of the price mechanism".

economies of scope may be substantial if there are customer groups that are largely similar.[72] In complex goods industries such as cars or computers there are appreciable economies of scale in several aspects of sales promotion and product differentiation.

5.2.5.3 Better planning of production and distribution

The research and development, production and distribution process can be divided into a number of stages. Before a final product reaches the consumer, several actions must be performed by one or more firms. At each stage, firms must make a choice between performing the activity themselves (or together with other firms) or outsourcing the activity. Several efficiencies can be realised by improving the planning of production and distribution:

- Transaction costs: if firms have to rely heavily upon each other, transaction costs tend to be high and each firm is liable to be exploited.[73] A firm may lower its transaction costs by integrating vertically. Such costs include the initial costs of negotiating an agreement as well as the ongoing costs of enforcing it. Because no agreement can specify all possible contingencies, modifying agreements to deal with unforeseen events also causes important transaction costs. Every time two unrelated parties agree to a transaction to be completed in the future, each may engage in opportunistic behaviour, taking advantage of the other whenever circumstances allow them to do so. If contracts are simple, then such circumstances are unlikely; in complicated contracts, however, the threat is very real. The incentive for opportunistic behaviour changes if activities are organised within a firm rather than between firms in the marketplace, as disagreements can be resolved differently. Transaction costs are likely to be high in cases of asset specificity and changing market conditions.

- Externalities: vertical cooperation may offer the means to correct market failures due to externalities by integrating those externalities, as this provides management with more effective ways to monitor and improve performance, ensuring, for example, that customer service departments fulfil the firm's warranty commitments, or guaranteeing market-wide uniform quality by controlling all retail or restaurant outlets, as one bad store can harm the business of all distributors. A good example may be found in any big international hotel chain, where a consumer who likes the outlets knows that the others are similar.

- Integration to ensure supply: a common reason for integration is to ensure the supply of important inputs, as timely delivery is of crucial concern to business, especially in markets where prices are not the sole device used to allocate goods. In times of supply shortages or rationing, good customers often get the product first. Just-in-time deliveries (i.e. an obligation

---

[72] Guidelines on Art. 81(3) EC, para.67.
[73] See Ch.3, s.3.9.

on a supplier to continuously supply the buyer according to his needs) minimise inventory costs while ensuring timely delivery. Under these circumstances, closer cooperation improves the probability of meeting the deadlines.

- Synergies resulting from an integration of existing assets: the establishment of a production joint venture combining the production assets of two parties may allow the attainment of a higher level of output with a lower input of raw materials per unit of output.[74]

5.2.5.4 Advantages in marketing and distribution

Competitor collaboration may also confer advantages in marketing, for instance through the pooling and streamlining of sales forces, the ability to offer distributors a broader product line, the use of common advertising themes, and the sharing of advertising media discounts. One has to differentiate carefully between the origins of economies, as a range of savings will be pecuniary and, as such, associated with decreased outlays per advertising exposure purchased by large firms. Such pecuniary economies may result from discriminatory pricing by advertising media, from declining average costs of producing and distributing advertising messages and from economies of joint advertising of several products. For example, efficiencies may be derived from discount offers for combining a large volume of advertisements. Larger firms may be better positioned to take advantage of such offers, as they will be able, for instance, to pack two different brand advertisements into a longer, and thus overall cheaper, commercial.
   Examples include:

- The need to obtain a certain level of advertising messages before they reach their maximum effectiveness. The message might have to be repeated over a period of time, or have to reach a broad segment of population. Larger firms have an advantage here, in stemming consumer inertia or from physical barriers to the rapid expansion of sales. The response functions facing firms of varying size may also differ because advertising has cumulative as well as current effects. It takes a long time to build an image of this order; to counter this phenomenon a small firm would have to advertise vigorously before it has achieved the size of the well-established sellers.

- Multi-brand interaction can occur if a favourable reputation from one set of products spills over to other products with the same brand name.

- Consumer advertising may also influence trade, leading to more intense distribution, more prominent display of more sizes, and fewer shortages. Such effects may be reinforced by advertising and may cause the

---

[74] Guidelines on Art. 81(3) EC, para.65.

proportion of buyers to increase.[75] Promotional economies, however, pose severe analytical problems, especially as the element of chance plays an important part in sales promotion. A more streamlined advertisement campaign might enable firms to charge higher prices than smaller firms with comparable products. Also, it is not quite clear to what extent market structure is affected by the private advantages of sales promotion.

5.2.5.5 Economies of research and development

Substantial cost savings can result from the joint undertaking of research and development (R&D) and other innovative activity, either through contractual arrangements, joint ventures or mergers. In its Article 81(3) Notice, the European Commission distinguishes between cost efficiencies (development of new production technologies and methods) and qualitative efficiencies (whereby value is created in the form of new or improved products and greater product variety). Since clear and firm distinctions between the different types of efficiencies are not appropriate,[76] both costs efficiencies and dynamic efficiencies resulting from research and development and other innovative activity are subsumed here under the same heading. In the field of knowledge transfer and innovation, a range of particularly elusive synergies may be presented. Quite often these efficiencies represent a special case of those already mentioned.[77]

Types of economies of research and development A series of synergies in research and development may be distinguished:

- Spreading costs and risks: R&D efforts are often expensive and almost always risky, so arrangements that spread the costs and risks of the undertaking among two or more companies can be very attractive. These risks can arise because of the unproven nature of certain technologies, the uncertain nature of demand for unfamiliar products, and the short life cycle for many high technology products. This point is closely related to Schumpeter's view, namely, that a monopolistic surrounding may provide a more secure platform to engage in risky R&D investment, as a large firm's access to capital may be an advantage in obtaining the necessary financing for costly R&D.[78]

---

[75] K.D. Boyer and K.M. Lancaster, "Are there Scale Economies in Advertising?" (1986) 59 J. Bus. 509 at p.512.

[76] Guidelines on Art. 81(3) EC, para.59.

[77] On the traditional rationale for innovative firms to attain economies of scale and scope, see T.M. Jorde and D.J. Teece, "Innovation and Cooperation: Implications for Competition and Antitrust" (1990) 4 J. Econ. Perspect. 75 at p.81; J.A. Ordover and W.J. Baumol, "Antitrust Policy and High Technology Industries" (1988) 4 Oxf. Rev. Econ. Pol. 13 at p.27; G.M. Grossman and C. Shapiro, "Research Joint Ventures: An Antitrust Analysis" (1986) 2 J. L. Econ. Org. 315 at pp.321–322.

[78] J. Schumpeter, *Capitalism, Socialism and Democracy* (3rd ed., 1950), pp.81–106. In attaining the requisite knowledge and putting it to practical use, extensive sunk costs may be encountered. See W.J. Baumol and J.A. Ordover, "Antitrust: Source of Dynamic and Static Inefficiencies?", in *Antitrust, Innovation, and Competitiveness* (T.M. Jorde and D.J. Teece ed., 1992), pp.82, 84.

- Complementary assets: there are many situations in which companies have complementary, but only partially overlapping, technological abilities. It is highly unlikely that all firms are equal in the effectiveness of their innovative efforts. A company may possess private information about R&D opportunities or may have unique assets indispensable for innovative success. This type of synergy is commonplace when the venture participants are firms from different industries or different niches of an industry. Moreover, the transfer of technology among the various activities that constitute innovation is not without cost. This is especially true if the know-how to be transferred cannot easily be bundled—this will be the case for simultaneous development activity where knowledge has a high secrecy component. One solution would be the transfer of personnel, which is easier to realise within a company than under a contractual relationship.[79]

- Elimination of redundant R&D efforts: the same holds if the combined firm is able to eliminate redundant R&D activities and thus lower costs without significantly reducing innovation.[80] Some firms fail to manage the complexities of the innovative race so their disappearance will not slow the innovative pace; rather, the resources entangled in such obsolete projects will be freed for use elsewhere.[81] Independent research activities often proceed down (near) identical technological paths (unnoticed because of the pressures of the competitive surroundings),[82] while a given research finding can be used for many applications at little extra cost. This duplication may be wasteful and can be minimised if research plans are coordinated.[83] On the other hand, independent research programmes may hide important differences. Combining such programmes may risk the elimination of an alternative path of discovery. Nonetheless, the public-good nature of information suggests that cooperation is more likely to promote efficiency. In this context, research joint ventures or mergers can be seen as promoting the *ex post* dissemination of innovations, for example if they include firms that otherwise would neither conduct the research independently nor purchase the requisite know-how through a

[79] T.M. Jorde and D.J. Teece, "Innovation and Cooperation: Implications for Competition and Antitrust" (1990) 4 J. Econ. Perspect. 75.

[80] R.J. Gilbert and S.C. Sunshine, "Incorporating Dynamic Efficiency Concerns in Merger Analysis: The Use of Innovation Markets" (1995) 63 Antitrust L.J. 567 at p.594. This illustrates Schumpeter's hypothesis that the average productivity of R&D increases with firm size. See F.M. Fisher and P. Temin, "Returns to Scale in Research and Development: What Does the Schumpeterian Hypothesis Imply?" (1973) 81 J. Polit. Economy 56.

[81] D. Fudenberg, "Pre-emption, Leapfrogging and Competition in Patent Races" (1983) 22 Eur. Econ. Rev. 3.

[82] Leading to an over-investment in R&D relative to the social optimum; see S. Bhattacharya and D. Mookerjee, "Portfolio Choice in Research and Development" (1986) 17 RAND J. Econ. 594.

[83] C. Shapiro and R.D. Willig, "On the Antitrust Treatment of Production Joint Ventures" (1990) 4 J. Econ. Perspect. 113 at p.120; J.A. Ordover and W.J. Baumol, "Antitrust Policy and High Technology Industries" (1988) 4 Oxf. Rev. Econ. Pol. 13 at p.27; B.J. Nalebuff, and J.E. Stiglitz, "Information, Competition and Markets" (1983) 73 Amer. Econ. Rev. 278 at p.284; P. Dasgupta and J.E. Stiglitz, "Industrial Structure and the Nature of Innovative Activity" (1980) 90 Econ. J. 266 at p.289.

licensing agreement. To the extent that diffusion is promoted such cooperation increases downstream competition.

- Technology transfer and networking: the transfer of technology among the various production stages that constitute innovation, development, manufacture and marketing is not costless. These expenses will be increased considerably when the knowledge involved has a high tacit component, and this is often the case in high technology markets. Additionally, the combining activities proceed in part simultaneously. Both characteristics require a tighter basis than that which can be offered by an arms-length and non-exclusive contractual relationship in the marketplace.[84] Once innovation has occurred consumers have to be willing to switch from their current appliance. Especially when network effects are high, more concentrated market structures can help to disperse new and beneficial technology.

- Rent dissipation: there is a severe free rider problem in the R&D and innovation field.[85] Often intellectual property rights will offer no, or only inadequate, legal protection,[86] while reverse engineering is normally cheaper, quicker and less risky than innovation.[87] As a consequence, knowledge which cannot be directly protected diffuses to competitors and allows them to share in the benefits of an innovation. Firms are reluctant to invest huge amounts of money in the development of new products or processes for fear that other firms will be able simply to copy their efforts without making a comparable investment. Therefore, there are typically large positive spillovers from innovation and a corresponding underinvestment in innovative activities. A large share of the market in which an innovation would be used may enable a firm to appropriate more fully the value of its innovative efforts, giving a greater incentive to innovate. The free rider argumentation has to be balanced carefully. Even without adequate legal protection a lead start may often result in enormous financial rewards.[88] Then again, this advantage may not necessarily hold in markets characterised by rapid technological change or markets in which dominant firms are well situated to enter quickly with imitations of smaller rivals' innovations.

---

[84] S.J. Winter, "Knowledge and Competence as Strategic Assets", in *The Competitive Challenge: Strategies for Industrial Innovation and Renewal* (D.J. Teece ed., 1987); N. Rosenberg, *Technology and American Economic Growth* (1972).

[85] W.J. Baumol and J.A. Ordover, "Antitrust: Source of Dynamic and Static Inefficiencies?", in *Antitrust, Innovation, and Competitiveness* (T.M. Jorde and D.J. Teece ed., 1992), pp.82, 83.

[86] E. Von Hippel, *The Sources of Innovation* (1988), pp.47–55.

[87] W. Baldwin and G. Childs, "The Fast Second and Rivalry in Research and Development" (1969) 36 Southern Econ. J. 18 at p.21. See also E. Mansfield, A. Romeo, M. Schwarz, D.J. Teece, S. Wagner and P. Brach, *Technology Transfer, Productivity, and Economic Policy* (1982), p.217, concluding that "it is a myth that a patent nearly always results in a seventeen-year monopoly over the relevant information".

[88] On the advantages of the "first mover", see C.A. Conrad, "The Advantage of Being First and Competition between Firms" (1983) 1 Int. J. Ind. Organ. 353. Conversely, first mover advantages may serve as a barrier to entry; see Ch.4, s.4.3.

Diseconomies in research and development Again, a number of disadvantages must also be discussed regarding cooperation in the field of research and development:

- Dynamic inefficiency: the greatest danger attached to research cooperation lies in the fact that the participating firms may use the venture to collude in slowing the pace of technological innovation.[89] The potential for collusion to slow down technological progress is more likely to be present in an ongoing venture with ill-defined objectives than in a short-term venture with a well-specified project goal. By preventing a patent race, research collaborations can slow innovation if they do not significantly reduce R&D costs but combine the research efforts of significant competitors. Indeed, rivals may collaborate precisely because they wish to reduce the risk of being left behind in the technology race.[90]

- Multiple owners in research joint ventures: R&D collaboration often takes place under the organisational model of a joint venture. These, however, may suffer from a number of shortcomings which originate in the fact that joint ventures have multiple owners who, without the existence of the joint venture, would be competitors.[91] Decision-making may suffer if the objectives of the venture differ and also if there is a problem of trust.

5.3 Article 81 EC and competitor cooperation

European competition law seeks to restrain anti-competitive coordination of companies' behaviour. In a first step, Article 81(1) EC bans cartel agreements, decisions of associations of undertakings and concerted practices that harm competition. In a second step, Article 81(3) EC grants an exemption when the benefits of the agreement in terms of efficiencies and consumer welfare are deemed to prevail without causing disproportionate restrictions or eliminating competition for a substantial part of the products in question.[92]

Since Regulation 1/2003 on the modernisation of European competition law[93] has entered into force, Article 81(3) EC sets out an exception rule, which provides a defence for undertakings against a finding of an infringement of Article 81(1) EC. Agreements, decisions of associations of undertakings and

[89] C. Shapiro and R.D. Willig, "On the Antitrust Treatment of Production Joint Ventures" (1990) 4 J. Econ. Perspect. 113 at p.120.

[90] J. Kattan, "Antitrust Analysis of Technology Joint Ventures: Allocative Efficiency and the Rewards of Innovation" (1993) 61 Antitrust L.J. 937 at p.944; J.A. Ordover and R.D. Willig, "Antitrust for High Technology Industries: Assessing Research Joint Ventures and Mergers" (1985) 28 J. Law Econ. 311 at p.317.

[91] J.D. Lewis and M. Huber, *Strategische Allianzen* (1991), pp.289 *et seq.*

[92] See, for a legal analysis: J. Bourgeois and J. Boecken, "Guidelines on the Application of Article 81(3) of the EC Treaty or How to Restrict a Restriction?" (2005) 32 Leg. Issues Eur. Integ. 111. For an economic analysis, see P. Nicolaides, "The Balancing Myth: The Economics of Article 81(1) & (3)" (2005) 32 Leg. Issues Eur. Integr. 123.

[93] For a discussion of the new system of enforcement, see Ch.8.

concerted practices caught by Article 81(1) EC which satisfy the conditions of Article 81(3) EC are valid and enforceable, no prior decision to that effect being required. Concerning the adjudication of such agreements the European Commission, in its Regulation 1/2003, has effectively switched to a directly applicable exception system,[94] allowing companies to self-assess whether they are caught by Article 81 EC. This interpretation, which led to the complete abolishment of the notification system as contained in the old Regulation 17, has the consequence of making restrictive practices, which are prohibited by Article 81(1) EC but meet the trade-off contained in Article 81(3) EC, lawful without the need for any prior decision.

As part of the extended legislative framework considered of "primary importance"[95] to ensure the application of the rules to be sufficiently reliable and consistent to allow businesses to assess whether their respective practices are lawful, the European Commission's Guidelines on the applicability of Article 81 EC to horizontal cooperation already provided the general framework. As part of the modernisation package, the European Commission has further issued Guidelines on the application of Article 81(3) EC ("the Article 81(3) Notice").[96] The Article 81(3) Notice explicitly states that the existing Guidelines on vertical restraints, horizontal cooperation agreements and technology transfer agreements continue to apply, as the purpose of those Guidelines is to set out the European Commission's view of the substantive assessment criteria applied to the various types of agreements and practices. The Article 81(3) Notice provides more detailed guidance on the application of the four conditions of Article 81(3) EC, also with regard to agreements already covered by the existing Guidelines (compare Sections 3 and 5 of the Article 81(3) Notice). Their aim—in line with the wider goals of the European Community's competition policy—is "to provide an analytical framework for the most common types of horizontal cooperation", which is to be "based on criteria that help to analyse the economic context of a cooperation agreement".[97] In the remainder of this section, the constitutive elements of the cartel prohibition and the conditions for exemption are summarised and commented upon from an economic perspective.

5.3.1 Restriction of competition as the object of cooperation

Although economic analysis does not provide support for a clear distinction between hard and soft cartels, European competition law differentiates between agreements having restriction of competition as their object and agreements or concerted practices which, also implicitly, may have anti-competitive consequences. Economic analysis stresses the need to examine the

---

[94] See the White Paper, paras 69–73.
[95] *ibid.*, para.84.
[96] [2004] O.J. C 101/97.
[97] See the EC Horizontal Guidelines, para.7; and compare H. Schröter, "Aktuelle Probleme der Anwendung von Artikel 81 EG," Speech, St Gallen, April 27, 2000.

real-life consequences of both explicit and tacit collusion. Even though restriction of competition may be the proven object of cooperation, market evidence may show that prices are not substantially above competitive levels, which makes antitrust intervention less compelling or even unnecessary. In general, agreements such as price fixing, market sharing, quotas and rigging bids having as their object the restriction of competition will mainly entail enforcement-related issues such as leniency, fines and damages. These are dealt with in Chapter 8. In such cases—entailing a *per se* infringement of Article 81 EC—the Horizontal Guidelines do not require further evidence to establish that an explicit agreement can cause negative market effects. The prohibition thus applies without the need for taking into account the agreement's economic context.

Not all competitor agreements restricting competition deserve the same degree of censure. Ideally, sanctions should differ according to the seriousness of the competitive harm that is caused. Article 81 EC does not differentiate as far as legal consequences are concerned: all agreements are equally void.[98] However, fines imposed on the basis of Regulation 1/2003 and the EC Fining Guidelines[99] will reflect the seriousness and duration of the infringement.

5.3.1.1 Price fixing, market sharing, quotas, bid rigging

Horizontal agreements having as their object a restriction of competition are considered by the nature of the cooperation to indicate the applicability of Article 81(1) EC *per se*, as they are presumed to have negative market effects.[1] The European Commission considers this to be the case even if such agreements fall under its *de minimis* Notice's less-than-5-per cent market share hurdle.[2] The European Courts, like their US counterparts, ruled that for agreements fixing prices,[3] concerning market sharing,[4] quotas[5] and rigging bids,[6] it is thus unnecessary to take into account the actual effects of that agreement. As a result, prohibition often ensues virtually *per se* with the issues at stake in prolonged hard core cartel proceedings (for an example in the

---

[98] Compare F.E. Gonzales Diaz, D. Kirk, F. Perez Flores and C. Verkleij, "Horizontal Agreements", in *The EC Law of Competition* (J. Faull and A. Nikpay ed., 1999), para.6.07.
[99] [1998] O.J. C 9/3; see also Ch.8 on enforcement.
[1] Compare the EC Horizontal Guidelines, para.18; equally, see the US Horizontal Guidelines, para.3.1.
[2] Commission Notice on agreements of minor importance, [2001] O.J. C 368/13.
[3] For Europe, see Case 123/83 *Bureau National Interprofessionnel du Cognac (BNIC I) v Guy Clair* [1985] ECR 391. For the USA, see *United States v Trenton Potteries Co*, 273 U.S. 392 (1927).
[4] For Europe, see Case 41/69 *ACF Chemiefarma NV v Commission* [1970] ECR 661, para.128. For the USA, see *Palmer v BRG of Georgia, Inc*, 498 U.S. 46 (1990).
[5] For Europe, see Case T–142/89 *Usines Gustave Boël SA v Commission (Welded Steel Mesh)* [1995] ECR II–867, 871.
[6] For Europe, see Case T–29/92 *Vereniging van samenwerkende prijsregelende organisaties in de bouwnijverheid (SPO I) and others v Commission* [1995] ECR II–289.

banking industry, see Box 5.2) thus evolving mostly around the standard of proof adhered to and the fines to be imposed.[7] Given the strict antitrust prohibition, firms will often try to keep price agreements secret. Sometimes a cartel is organised under the cover of an ostensibly legitimate trade association. In *Cartonboard* the undertakings concerned had set up the so-called Product Group Paperboard which, in reality, implemented a series of regular concerted price initiatives across western Europe. Directors from the leading producers took the important decisions and marketing managers from all producers implemented the chosen strategy. In order to disguise the concerted price initiatives as natural price leadership the producers decided in advance who would be the first to announce the agreed price increase on what date, and the precise order in which, and dates on which, the rest would purport to follow. The European Commission imposed high fines taking into account the seriousness and the long duration of the infringement, but distinguished between the ringleaders and the ordinary members of the cartel.

Box 5.2: The Lombard case: price fixing in the Austrian banking sector[8]

On June 11, 2002, the European Commission imposed fines (totalling €124.3 million) on eight Austrian banks for participating in a price cartel. The penalty punished some members of the Lombard Club for fixing interest rates for loans and savings for private as well as commercial customers and other fees between 1995 and 1998. Furthermore, the cartel also extended to money transfers and export financing. During the presentation of the decision, European Commissioner Monti stated: "The institutional set-up of this cartel and its comprehensiveness, both in terms of the banking services covered and geographical scope, makes it one of the most shocking cartels ever discovered by the Commission. Banks should be in no doubt that they are subject to European Union competition rules just like any other sector".

In the aftermath of the Second World War, the Nationalbank, the Austrian central bank, took the initiative to form the Lombard club in order to prevent cut-throat competition between commercial banks and steer credit into sectors favoured by state planners. Although competition was restricted for several years it did not lead to higher profitability in the banking sector. To the contrary, poor profitability in the early 1980s elicited a reaction from the legislator in the form of an amendment to the 1986 Banking Act and from the banks themselves in the form of the establishment of a target-rate cartel for lending and deposit rates. Although the regulative agreements were annulled in the summer of 1989, the banks found it difficult to set their rates without recourse to binding agreements.

---

[7] A prime example constitutes the numerous appeals against the European Commission's decision in Case IV/33.833 *Cartonboard* [1994] O.J. L 243/1; see Cases T–295/94, T–304/94, T–308/94, T–309/94, T–310/94, T–311/94, T–317/94, T–319/94, T–327/94, T–334/94, T–337/94, T–338/94, T–339/94, T–340/94, T–341/94, T–342/94, T–347/94, T–348/94, T–352/94 and T–354/94 *Cartonboard* [1998] ECR II–813.

[8] Case COMP/D–1/36.571 *Austrian banks—"Lombard Club"* [2004] O.J. L 56/1. Thanks go to Luit Bakker, author of this box.

The participating banks even continued to conclude agreements on lending and deposit rates after Austria's accession to the European Economic Area on January 1, 1994 and Austria's membership of the European Union on January 1, 1995. The banks took the view that: "cartel agreements had always been part of banking and they therefore did not in the least intend to change this now simply because of the applicability of European antitrust law".[9] The object of the Lombard cartel was expressed clearly by the host of the illicit meetings in February 1995, when he welcomed the participants with the words: "The exchange of experience between banks' in relation to interest rates has repeatedly proved to be a useful means of avoiding uncontrolled price competition. In this vein today's meeting should likewise ensure a focused and reasonable approach by all banks with regard to pricing. The way in which interest rates are currently being set shows that is again necessary for us to sit down together and counteract problematic price developments".

In the meantime, the Austrian public became more and more suspicious, and in connection with changes to rates and charges, accusations of cartel-like pricing policies and of manifest agreements were repeatedly being made in public, especially in the press. Eventually, this culminated in simultaneous surprise inspections by investigators of the European Commission, assisted by officials of the Austrian Ministry of Economic Affairs, in June 1998. The hundreds of documents found unveiled a network of cartel committees which covered the entire country "down to the smallest village", as one of the participants put it. It was discovered that between January 1994 and the end of June 1998 in Vienna alone at least 300 meetings were held. Furthermore, the European Commission found that most, if not all, Austrian banks participated.

Given the overwhelming evidence of documents, the highly institutionalised and closely interconnected cartel network, and the geographic coverage, it comes as no surprise that the European Commission considered the price fixing behaviour of the Austrian banks to constitute a very serious infringement of Article 81 EC. In accordance with this the fine was substantial, i.e. the sixth-largest fine ever levied. The European Commission reduced the fine by 10 per cent to take into account the cooperation afforded by the banks during the investigation.

The strict illegality of hard core cartels does not imply that they disqualify for an exemption through Article 81(3) EC because of their anti-competitive nature; at the time of writing, even explicit price fixing is still exempted under Article 3 of the Liner Conference block exemption.[10] Still, the European Commission and Courts are quite wary of allowing agreements which are considered to carry few efficiencies while being generally deemed most

---

[9] All quotes are taken from documents seized during the raid by the European Commission's officials at the banks' premises in June 1998.
[10] Regulation 4056/86 [1986] O.J. L 378/4; the review was commenced in March 2003 with the stated aim of abolishing this exemption.

restrictive of competition, as they "directly lead to customers paying higher prices or not receiving the desired quantities"[11]—thus implying a decrease in welfare. It is for this reason that the conditions for exemption laid down in Article 81(3) EC are interpreted strictly. Under the old system, as contained in Regulation 17, the Courts required hard core cartels to be "properly notified to the Commission"[12] in order to be eligible for exemption. This was rarely ever the case as they are normally kept secret;[13] after modernisation this option has disappeared, together with the overall notification system.

In short, price fixing cartels or other agreements having as their object the restriction of competition are virtually illegal *per se*. On this point, there is no perfect harmony between legal rules and economic insights. A full scale economic analysis could show that prices are not above competitive levels, making antitrust intervention redundant. Even in markets that lend themselves to successful cartelisation (homogeneous products, mature market, predictable demand, no huge advances in technology, and high barriers to entry), price fixing agreements may prove to be ineffective because of the presence of large buyers on the market and plenty of cheating on the cartel price. Even though their explicit objective is to raise prices, under these circumstances cartels will be imperfect and thus not able to push through the prices agreed effectively. Another example is recommended fees in the sector of the liberal professions. Since the number of practitioners in these markets is high, cartel discipline is difficult to maintain and cheating very attractive. The non-sustainability of price cartels under such circumstances is also confirmed by empirical evidence.[14] (The specific problems caused by introducing competition in markets for professional services are discussed in Box 5.3.) Current European competition law, however, allows the relevant economic evidence to be pushed aside if the objective to fix prices or control output can be proven, and the (lack of) economic impact on the market will only be taken into account when determining the ultimate fine.[15]

> Box 5.3: Application of the European competition rules to the liberal professions
> The sector of the liberal professions (such as lawyers, notaries, architects, accountants and engineers) is characterised by high levels of regulation, which are often a mix of state regulation and self-regulation. The regulatory

---

[11] See the EC Horizontal Guidelines, para.25. Similar remarks may be made about the USA; compare the US Horizontal Guidelines, para.3.2.; as well as *Arizona v Maricopa County Medical Society*, 457 U.S. 332, 339 and 356–357 (1982).

[12] Case T–17/93 *Matra Hachette SA v Commission and Ford-Volkswagen (Matra II)* [1994] ECR II–595, para.85.

[13] Compare L. Ritter, W.D. Braun and F. Rawlinson, *European Competition Law: A Practitioner's Guide* (2nd ed., 2000), p.141; and F.E. Gonzales Diaz, D. Kirk, F. Perez Flores and C. Verkleij, "Horizontal agreements", in *The EC Law of Competition* (J. Faull and A. Nikpay ed., 1999), para.6.09.

[14] See F. Stephen, "Effects of Deregulation in Professional Services Markets: Scottish Conveyancing Markets" (1993) 9 *Strathclyde Economic Papers*; E. Shinnick, "The Market for Legal Serices in Ireland" (1995), quoted by F. Stephen and J. Love, "Regulation of the Legal Profession", in *Encyclopedia of Law and Economics* No.5860 (B. Bouckaert and G. De Geest ed., 2000), p.999

[15] See Ch.8, s.8.2.1.2.

framework includes exclusive rights to perform certain professional services, regulation of fees, restrictions on advertising and regulations governing business structure and multidisciplinary practices. The European Commission is of the opinion that many of these rules unnecessarily restrict competition. It has invited regulatory authorities in the Member States and professional bodies to review existing rules, taking into consideration whether those rules are beneficial for society in general and proportionate to the public interest goal to be achieved. The European Commission accepts that some carefully targeted regulation of professional services can be necessary. However, restrictions on prices and advertising restrictions should be removed quickly. The analysis here will show that this is too rapid a conclusion. The specific characteristics of the markets for professional services make the design of the "optimal" regulation, which not unnecessarily restricts competition, very difficult. Consequently, all limitations of competition, including fee and advertising restrictions, must be more carefully assessed.

A vast economic literature has shown that free markets for professional services will not produce efficient outcomes. There are three market failures that may impede a full satisfaction of consumers' wishes. A first major problem is asymmetric information. Professional services require a high level of technical knowledge that many consumers do not have. Free markets will only achieve efficient outcomes if a significant number of consumers is able to make purchase decisions on the basis of complete and undistorted price–quality judgments. Many consumers cannot judge the quality of the services offered by the professions before purchase (no search qualities). At most, some quality assessment may be possible after the services have been bought (experience qualities), but in many cases the buyers will never be able to perform a reliable quality judgment (credence qualities).[16] As a consequence, free markets for professional services will fail due to adverse selection (overall deterioration of quality) and moral hazard (supplier induced demand).[17] Regulation of quality is a response to this problem. A second problem is that bad performance of contracts between sellers and buyers of professional services will cause negative externalities to third parties and society at large. For example, an inaccurately drafted will will harm the heirs of the testator and a poorly constructed bridge will jeopardise traffic safety. In a free market, these negative externalities are not internalised in the decision-making process of the suppliers. The third market failure is known as the "public good" problem. Professional services generate important positive externalities that are of great value for

---

[16] The distinction between search goods and experience goods was first made by P. Nelson, "Information and Consumer Behaviour" (1970) 78 J. Polit. Economy 311. On credence goods, see M. Darby and S. Karni, "Free Competition and the Optimal Amount of Fraud" (1973) 16 J. Law Econ. 67.

[17] It should be added, however, that in some markets consumers may be professional buyers who regularly purchase the professional services, so that markets may function efficiently.

society in general. Examples include a proper administration of justice (lawyers) and increased legal certainty (notaries), as well as a high quality urban environment (architects). In a free market, suppliers of services who do not get any reward from persons (other than the contract parties) profiting from these benefits may not supply or inadequately supply public goods.

From these arguments, it becomes clear that introducing competition in the sector of the liberal professions will not necessarily be welfare increasing. If there are no limitations on price fixing and advertising, the risk exists that competition will be mainly on price and quality dimensions that buyers of services can easily access, such as the location of the offices and the friendliness of the professionals. By contrast, in markets plagued by severe information asymmetries, professionals will not be able to credibly signal the intrinsic high quality of the services provided. The consequence of price advertising may thus be a process of adverse selection leading to an overall deterioration of quality. Introducing price competition may be counterproductive if it is not accompanied by adequate measures to improve the quality assessment in markets for professional services. Also, the provision of public goods may be jeopardised by increasing competitive pressures. In a regulated market, less profitable services may be cross-subsidised by gains on more lucrative market segments. Deregulation will cause prices to sink in the profitable market segments ("cream skimming") but lead to price increases for the previously cross-subsidised services. The deregulation of the market for notaries in the Netherlands confirms this outcome: whereas prices decreased for authenticating transfers of property, prices in the family practice (wills, matrimonial contracts) increased.[18] As a consequence, fewer people will ask the notary's assistance, which in turn will decrease legal certainty and harm society at large. In sum, competition between professionals may be counterproductive if no accompanying measures to improve quality assessment and guarantee provision of public goods are taken.

Guaranteeing quality may be a difficult task for government agencies lacking specific knowledge of the professions. An important benefit of self-regulation is the possibility of using the information advantage of the professions. Other benefits include greater flexibility, allowing easy adaptations to changed consumer preferences, and the internalisation of regulatory costs within the profession. Disadvantages of self-regulation are its lack of democratic legitimacy and the risk that professions may abuse their self-regulatory powers to restrict competition. Self-regulatory bodies are not accountable through normal democratic channels and third parties do not

---

[18] R. Van den Bergh and Y. Montangie, "Competition in Professional Services Markets: Are Latin Notaries Different?" (2006) 2 J.C.L.E., forthcoming.

usually participate in establishing the self-regulatory regime. On top of these problems, self-regulatory rules may create entry barriers and enable the professions to achieve super-competitive profits. The problem of disproportionate regulation, which is stressed by the European Commission, can be seen as an example of an anti-competitive entry barrier. It thus seems to be the case that curing one market imperfection (information asymmetry) creates another market imperfection (super-competitive prices). A possible way out of this conundrum may be to create scope for competition between self-regulatory bodies (competitive self-regulation).[19] In this way, the information advantage of the professions is kept intact and competition between the professional bodies impedes excessive profits. Under a system of competitive self-regulation, there remains a role for the state as a referee. Professional bodies may be required to get approval of their rules (accreditation) before they are allowed to enter the market; in this way the risk of a "race to the bottom" is contained. Aside from a few exceptions (for example, competition between English barristers and solicitors to plead cases in the higher courts), the regulatory framework of the EC Member States provides no scope for competitive self-regulation. Also, the European Commission seems to have set the wrong priorities. Abolishing restrictions on fees and advertising may be counterproductive in markets characterised by serious information asymmetries. By contrast, abolishing reserved rights and creating scope for competition between accredited professional groups may be the best available method to guarantee quality at competitive prices.

5.3.2 Restriction of competition as the effect of cooperation

Most competitor cooperation does not have as its object a restriction of competition, though. For gauging the applicability of Article 81(1) EC in such cases an analysis of the agreement's effects is required. Thereto the agreement must be able to limit competition between the parties involved and it must be likely to affect competition in the market to such an extent that negative market effects as to prices, output, innovation or the variety or quality of goods and services can be expected. The European Commission's Horizontal Guidelines (like their US counterpart under the "rule of reason" assessment[20]) explicitly admit that this depends on the economic context of the agreement, taking into account both (a) the nature of the agreement and (b) the parties' combined market power, as this (together with other structural factors) determines the ability of the cooperation to affect overall competition.[21] The "economic

---

[19] See: R. Van den Bergh, "Towards Efficient Self-regulation in Markets for Professional Services", in *The Relationship between Competition Law and (Liberal) Professions* (C.D. Ehlermann and I. Atanasiu ed., 2006), pp.157–178.
[20] See the US Horizontal Guidelines, para.3.3.
[21] See the EC Horizontal Guidelines, paras 19–20.

analysis" thus prescribed by the European Commission is basically a two-tier test: first, one has to decide what characteristics the parties' cooperation has and, second, the amount of market shares the parties hold in their competitive surroundings must be investigated.

Historically, Article 81(1) EC has been interpreted widely—almost any agreement that restricted commercial freedoms was deemed to distort competition.[22] This meant that substantive analysis was largely confined to the Article 81(3) EC question, which in turn led to an excessive burden on the European Commission. Nowadays, both the European Commission and Courts recognise that this formalistic approach has no place in a modern effects-based competition regime, and post modernisation, the need for a detailed substantive analysis of the impact of an agreement under Article 81(1) EC has become ever more important.

5.3.2.1 The nature of the agreement

The characteristics of a cooperation agreement relate to factors such as the business purpose of the cooperation, the competitive relationship between parties, and the extent to which they intend to integrate their activities. As such, competitor cooperation may take place under a multitude of possible arrangements, whereto the antitrust laws aim to provide a common framework that applies to all types of agreements. Under the EC Horizontal Guidelines, although no single element is found decisive for inferring whether, overall, the coordination will be likely to raise competitive concerns, the parties' commonality in total cost is listed as indicative.[23] Whether a significant degree of such shared costs exists will depend on two conditions: (a) the area of cooperation (such as production or purchasing) has to account for a high proportion of the total costs in a given market; and (b) the parties' need to combine their activities in that area of cooperation to a significant extent. Both requirements will be discussed in turn.

Area of cooperation This first component of the analysis of cooperation agreements between horizontal competitors is designed to exclude from further antitrust scrutiny those arrangements which bring together firms that could not carry out the envisioned project by themselves or those that concern cooperation relating to an activity far removed from the commercial marketing level (such as R&D cooperation). The Horizontal Guidelines, after a general overview,[24] are divided into chapters relating to certain types of agreements, with specific guidance provided accordingly. A distinction is made between

---

[22] Here the impact of the Freiburg School on European competition law must be recalled; see Ch.3, s.3.4.
[23] See the EC Horizontal Guidelines, para.23.
[24] *ibid.*, paras 21–26.

cooperation on research and development,[25] production and specialisation,[26] purchasing,[27] commercialisation,[28] standards[29] and the environment.[30] The US Guidelines distinguish a (non-exhaustive) range of agreements that might harm competition and then continue the overall assessment. Mention is made of research and development, production, buying and marketing collaborations.[31]

Extent of cooperation   The parties' commonality in (total) costs constitutes the benchmark for determining whether agreements on production or purchasing may coordinate market prices and output.

How can this approach be assessed economically? In order to coordinate behaviour and install a credible enforcement mechanism, firms must be able to observe each other's behaviour. This often poses intricate hurdles, though, as individual actions of deviation are often impossible to discover, and firms have, instead, to rely on information regarding aggregate variables only, as prices are subject to random shocks in demand. A drop in price can, however, result from a drop in demand and the ensuing competitive reaction of reducing output, or from a competitor's deviation from the collusive equilibrium as he expands output and engages in a price war.[32] Consequently, this makes the hurdles to prove a violation even more challenging, while on the other hand raising the compulsion to carefully observe the circumstances surrounding a price war.[33] Cramton and Palfrey show that if the uncertainty in cartel enforcement is about a common cost, so that all firms are equally efficient, the problem is simply to determine aggregate production on the basis of the information reported by the cartel members about their common costs.[34] All members of the cartel then produce an equal share of that total. As a result of such an agreement on costs a large cartel can successfully attain a monopolistic outcome. The distinction drawn in Section 22 of the Horizontal Guidelines

---

[25] See the EC Horizontal Guidelines, paras 39–77. Compare also the Commission Regulation (EC) No.2659/2000 on the application of Art.81(3) of the Treaty to categories of research and development agreements [2000] O.J. L 304/7; as well as its predecessor, the Commission regulation (EEC) No.418/85 on the application of Art.81(3) of the Treaty to categories of research and development agreements [1985] O.J. L 53/5; as amended by the Commission Regulations (EEC) No.151/93 [1993] O.J. L 21/8; and No.2236/97 [1997] O.J. L 306/12.

[26] See the EC Horizontal Guidelines, paras 78–114. Compare also Commission Regulation (EC) No.2658/2000 on the application of Art.81(3) of the Treaty to categories of specialisation agreements [2000] O.J. L 304/3; as well as its predecessor, the Commission Regulation (EEC) No.417/85 on the application of Art.81(3) of the Treaty to categories of specialisation agreements [1985] O.J. L 53/1; as amended by the Commission Regulations (EEC) No.151/93 [1993] O.J. L 21/8; and No.2236/97 [1997] O.J. L 306/12.

[27] See the EC Horizontal Guidelines, paras 115–138.

[28] *ibid.*, paras 139–158.

[29] *ibid.*, paras 159–178.

[30] *ibid.*, paras 179–198.

[31] See the US Horizontal Guidelines, para.3.31(a).

[32] E.J. Green and R.H. Porter, "Noncooperative Collusion under Imperfect Price Information" (1984) 52 *Econometrica* 87.

[33] J.B. Baker, "Identifying Cartel Policing under Uncertainty: The U.S. Steel Industry, 1933–1939" (1989) 32 J. Law Econ. 47.

[34] P.C. Cramton and T.R. Palfrey, "Cartel Enforcement with Uncertainty about Costs" (1990) 31 Int. Econ. Rev. 17.

between firm-specific (private) costs and common costs is therefore an important one.

5.3.2.2 The market circumstances: market power and market share thresholds

If the nature of the agreement points towards a potential competitive worry, then the second component of the test for deliberating whether the effect of a cooperation may serve to restrict competition (by raising prices, restricting output, hampering innovation, or limiting the quality or variety of goods and services available) will assess the market power of the parties involved.

At least preliminarily, the market share of the firms is often considered determinative to make inferences about market power.[35] Since the European Court of Justice's ruling in *Delimitis*,[36] a full market analysis is already required under Article 81 EC in all those cases not representing *per se* infringements.[37] In the *Flat Glass* case, the Court of First Instance stated that the definition of the relevant market in a more systematic way is a "necessary precondition of any judgment concerning allegedly anti-competitive behaviour".[38] This position was further refined in *European Night Services* where it was held that

> "...in assessing an agreement under Article [81](1) of the Treaty, account must be taken of the actual conditions in which it functions, in particular the economic context in which the undertakings operate, the products or services covered by the agreement, and the actual structure of the markets concerned".[39]

For a long time, the market power of the parties involved was gauged according to the (negative) test of noticeability formulated in *Völk v Vervaecke*[40] investigating whether the possible effect on competition was appreciable. The European Commission's practice thereon translated into issuing the afore-mentioned *de minimis* Notice creating relatively safe harbours based on low market shares[41] to which the Horizontal Guidelines now extend. Similarly, the EC Fines Guidelines and Commission's practice in this field reflect that market impact is crucial to determine liability and the level of the fines if an infringement is found.[42]

Since many forms of coordination indeed appear ineffective in establishing market power, some argue in favour of a market power test to be added to the evidence of coordination before a violation takes place. In the light of the obstacles encountered when measuring market power, however, as well as

[35] See the EC Horizontal Guidelines, para.27.

[36] Case C–234/89 *Delimitis v Henniger Bräu AG* [1991] ECR I–935.

[37] Made explicit in Case T–14/89 *Montedipe/Anic SpA v Commission (Polypropylene—Montedipe)* [1992] ECR II–1155.

[38] Joined Cases T–68/89, T–77/89, T–78/89 *Societa Italiana Vetro SpA, Fabrica Pisana SpA, Vernante Pennitalia v EC Commission (Italian Flat Glass)* [1992] ECR II–1403.

[39] Joined Cases T–374/94, T–375/94, T–384/94, T–388/94 *European Night Services Ltd and others v Commission* [1998] ECR II–3141, para.136.

[40] Case 5/69 *Völk v Vervaecke* [1969] ECR 295.

[41] See above. For a discussion, see L. Ritter, W.D. Braun and F. Rawlinson, *European Competition Law: A Practitioner's Guide* (2nd ed., 2000), pp.103–109.

[42] See Ch.8, s.8.2.1.2.

the limited confidence in an approach based on market shares to indicate the market actors' relative power,[43] and the likelihood that conclusions are mistakenly drawn that no market power exists in a coordination setting, a prohibition of cartels involving such a test will entail only a limited deterrence effect.[44] To carry out this analysis the relevant market has to be defined according to the Notice on the definition of the relevant market.[45] With market shares available, the Horizontal Guidelines create a range of relatively safe harbours, depending in scope on the nature of the agreement (as do most block exemptions). For example, if the parties together hold less than 25 per cent of the market for agreements on R&D, less than 20 per cent for production and specialisation agreements, or less than 15 per cent for purchasing agreements and commercialisation agreements,[46] then a restrictive effect of the cooperation is considered unlikely. With agreements on standards or the environment,[47] high market shares are not considered to reflect a deciding factor for antitrust purposes. In addition to the combined market shares, the parties' individual shares must be taken into consideration in order to account for cooperation with insignificant partners. If the overall market position of the firms involved is strong, then the positions of their competitors are to be assessed, too, according to the Herfindahl–Hirschman index (HHI) as a concentration measure.[48] Other factors, such as the stability of market shares over a period of time, entry barriers, countervailing buyer power, the nature of the products, and specific characteristics relating to innovation are also to be withheld.[49] Further specific conditions relating to each individual type of agreement are highlighted throughout the EC Guidelines.

The US Guidelines follow a similar overall structure, less related to the individual types of competitor cooperation, though.[50] A general safety zone is created for competitor cooperation where the parties together account for less than 20 per cent of the relevant market. Innovation markets benefit from a wider safe harbour based on the existence of substitute efforts by rivals.[51] Overall, both the European and the US regulators thus present a flexible analysis that varies in focus and detail depending on the nature of the agreement and market circumstances.

---

[43] See Ch.4, s.4.2.2.
[44] For a discussion, see D. Neven, P. Papandropoulos and P. Seabright, *Trawling for Minnows: European Competition Policy and Agreements between Firms* (1998), pp.51–53.
[45] See Ch.4, s.4.2.2.
[46] See the EC Horizontal Guidelines, paras 62, 93, 130 and 150, respectively.
[47] *ibid.*, paras 168 and 183, respectively.
[48] *ibid.*, para.29; an HHI below 1000 characterises a low market concentration, between 1000 and 1800 is moderate and above 1800 is high. On the HHI in general, compare below, Ch.9, s.9.2.1.
[49] See the EC Horizontal Guidelines, para.30.
[50] See the US Horizontal Guidelines, paras 3.32–3.35. Explicit reference is made to the 1997 Horizontal Merger Guidelines para.3.33 and the range of HHI's contained.
[51] *ibid.*, paras 4.2.–4.3.

5.3.3 Evidence of anti-competitive effects

Not all restrictions of competition resulting from agreements or concerted practices between competitors may be identified with the same degree of certainty. For the time being, the legal distinction between hardcore cartels (explicit collusive agreements to fix prices or share markets between producers and sellers of substitute products) and soft cartels (implicit collusive agreements) will be utilised.[52] Article 81(1) EC specifically prohibits hardcore cartels; the range of soft cartels and other forms of competitor cooperation covered by the prohibition is unclear. The legal debate thus mostly deals with inferring the existence of concerted practices deemed illegal from the evidence available.

5.3.3.1 Explicit coordination

Article 81(1) EC is addressed broadly in scope[53] to both formal and informal agreements and concerted practices among all forms of business enterprise, qualifying it to be sufficient for an agreement to exist "if the undertakings in question have expressed their joint intention to conduct themselves on the market in a specific way".[54] Documentation of explicit coordination can be established through direct material evidence or from evidence of firms' behaviour. Thereto more often than not the standard of proof for explicit coordination should not be too stringent, as firms have ample opportunity to conceal cartelisation from the antitrust authorities. In practice, direct evidence is deduced from documents, handwritten notes, confidential business information of one company found at another company, and minutes of meetings.

5.3.3.2 Implicit coordination

Proving the existence of illegal cartel agreements when only indirect evidence is available poses greater difficulties. Under European competition law, a concerted practice relates to coordination where firms "knowingly substitute practical cooperation between them for the risk of competition,"[55] thus requiring (a) contact between firms, (b) subsequent behaviour on the market and (c) causality between the two.[56] As a result, it emerges that, in principle, the legal standard is based on some form of explicit contact between firms, which, according to Neven, Papandropoulos and Seabright is "preferable"[57] when compared with a standard endeavouring to also include implicit

---

[52] See also D. Neven, P. Papandropoulos and P. Seabright, *Trawling for Minnows: European Competition Policy and Agreements between Firms* (1998), p.45.

[53] L. Ritter, W.D. Braun and F. Rawlinson, *European Competition Law: A Practitioner's Guide* (2nd ed., 2000), pp.40–41, 77.

[54] Case T–7/89 *S.A. Hercules Chemicals NV v Commission* [1991] ECR II–1711, para.2.

[55] Case 48/69 *Imperial Chemical Industries Ltd v Commission (Dyestuffs—ICI)* [1972] ECR 619.

[56] Case C–49/92P *Commission v Anic Partecipazioni SpA* [1999] ECR I–4125.

[57] D. Neven, P. Papandropoulos and P. Seabright, *Trawling for Minnows: European Competition Policy and Agreements between Firms* (1998), pp.45, 76.

coordination. The cost of type II errors (implying false convictions), associated with the implementation of the former standard, is likely to be relatively small.

Implicit coordination—solely based on the firms' observations of market interactions—does not hence feature as a standard of evidence in the European case law. Rather, parallel conduct in itself "cannot be regarded as furnishing proof of concerted action unless concerted action constitutes the only plausible explanation for such conduct",[58] a test so "strict and hard to meet"[59] it is safe to maintain that repeated interaction without any communication or negotiation among firms will seldom suffice to lead to a prohibition under European competition law.

5.3.3.3 Economic evidence and damages from competitor coordination

Economic science, similarly, will stress the difficulties of drawing conclusions with any certainty. In line with the above observations relating to the complications firms encounter when trying to provide an adequate mechanism to enforce repeated interactions without knowing for sure each other's behaviour and motives, the common lack of formal treatment of non-cooperative games is thus not altogether unsurprising.[60] The risk lies in misinterpreting the firms' legitimate competitive interactions in the market with them consciously trying to support some form of implicit coordination. Thereto the European Courts have indeed acknowledged that the law does not deprive firms of the right to "adapt themselves intelligently to the conduct of their competitors".[61] Furthermore, it may be noted that the European Commission intends to intensify its *ex post* control to ensure that the competition rules are respected by strengthening its powers of inquiry, making it easier to lodge complaints, and reorganising the system of penalties.[62] Whether a more refined rule would not be more suitable, is something one is consequently left to wonder about.[63] Soon, as the economic analysis of repeated games further develops, firms might argue that it would be irrational to leave any material traces of concerted action in the first place, given that the observation of market interactions suffices anyway to collude. Accordingly, they could argue for a much stricter standard of proof.[64] This becomes of great importance when taking into account damages from cartelisation. When focusing on the legal standard of

---

[58] Joined Cases C–89/85, C–104/85, C–114/85, C–116/85, C–117/85 and C–125–129/85 *A. Åhlström Osakeyhtio and others v Commission (Wood Pulp II)* [1993] ECR I–1307.
[59] A. Nikpay and J. Faull, "Article 81", in *The EC Law of Competition* (J. Faull and A. Nikpay ed., 1999), para.2.51.
[60] A formal treatise of focal point selection is provided for by R. Sugden, "A Theory of Focal Points" (1995) 105 Econ. J. 535.
[61] Joined Cases 40–48/73, 50/73, 54–56/73, 111/73, 113/73 and 114/73 *Coöperative Vereniging "Suiker Unie" VA and others v Commission* [1975] ECR 1663.
[62] The White Paper, paras 108–128.
[63] Already noted by D. Neven, P. Papandropoulos and P. Seabright, *Trawling for Minnows: European Competition Policy and Agreements between Firms* (1998), p.77.
[64] Already predicted by J.B. Baker, "Two Sherman Act Section 1 Dilemmas: Parallel Pricing, the Oligopoly Problem, and Contemporary Economic Theory" (1993) 38 Antitrust Bull. 143 at pp.146–147.

proof and the standard for intervention, a certain disparity thus emerges with the way game theory would handle issues of concerted action.

5.3.4 Taking into account efficiencies—the functioning of Article 81(3) EC

5.3.4.1 Self-assessment of agreements restricting competition

Article 81(3) EC expressly endorses the efficiencies collaboration among competitors may generate, if the following four cumulative[65] conditions are met:

1. the agreement must contribute to improving the production or distribution of goods (or services), or to promoting technical or economic progress;

2. consumers must be allowed a fair share of the resulting benefits;

3. any restrictions imposed must be indispensable to attaining the preceding objectives;

4. the agreement must not be capable of eliminating competition in relation to a substantial part of the products in question.

If the four conditions of Article 81(3) EC are satisfied, agreements that come under Article 81(1) EC are exempted. Thereto, the net effect of the agreement must thus be beneficial to consumer welfare, not just to the parties involved. The burden of proof is on the parties and subject to the general requirement of proportionality: only indispensable restrictions of competition may be exempted and only if they are devised for the minimum period of time necessary to enable the parties to achieve the benefits justifying the exemption.[66]

Up to May 2004, the European Commission held the sole authority and broad discretion to grant exemptions under Article 9(1) of Regulation 17 by individual decisions or by block exemption regulations.[67] By contrast, Regulation 1/2003 has introduced a system of self-assessment that leaves it mostly up to companies and their advisors to determine whether or not their

---

[65] Joined Cases 43/82 and 63/82 *VBVB and VBBB v Commission* [1984] ECR 19, para.61. Compare also L. Ritter, W.D. Braun and F. Rawlinson, *European Competition Law: A Practitioner's Guide* (2nd ed., 2000), pp.115–116; A. Nikpay and J. Faull, "Article 81", in *The EC Law of Competition* (J. Faull and A. Nikpay ed., 1999), paras 2.124–2.172.

[66] Joined Cases T–374/94, T–375/94, T–384/94 and T–388/94, *European Night Services Ltd and others v Commission* [1998] ECR II–3141, para.230. Similarly, the US Horizontal Guidelines, para.3.36(a) and (b) require efficiencies to be cognisable, reasonably necessary and unattainable by less restrictive alternatives.

[67] See generally on exemptions L. Ritter, W.D. Braun and F. Rawlinson, *European Competition Law: A Practitioner's Guide* (2nd ed., 2000) pp.113–137; and, particularly on Block Exemptions, *idem.*, 703–718; A. Jones and B. Sufrin, *EC Competition Law: Text, Cases and Materials* (2nd ed., 2004), 654–677.

agreements lead to anti-competitive effects under Article 81(1) EC, and, if so, whether pro-competitive effects—under the four cumulative conditions of Article 81(3) EC—can offset any welfare loss entailed.

It is important to stress that the assessment under Article 81(3) EC only becomes relevant if Article 81(1) EC determines an infringement of competition. In the absence of restrictions of competition, it is not necessary to determine the benefits of an agreement. Sections 13 to 31 of the Article 81(3) Notice contain some general guidance on the application of Article 81(1) EC.

Where in an individual case a restriction of competition within the meaning of Article 81(1) EC has been proven, Article 81(3) EC can be invoked as a defence. When the four cumulative conditions of Article 81(3) EC are fulfilled, it is assumed that the agreement enhances competition within the relevant market, because it leads the undertakings concerned to offer cheaper or better products to consumers, compensating the latter for the adverse effects of the restrictions of competition (Sections 34 and 41 of the Article 81(3) Notice).

Article 81(3) EC can be applied either to individual agreements or to categories of agreements by way of a block exemption regulation.[68] When an agreement is covered by a block exemption the parties to the restrictive agreement are relieved of their burden under Article 2 of Regulation 1/2003 of showing that their individual agreement satisfies each of the conditions of Article 81(3) EC. They only have to prove that the restrictive agreement benefits from a block exemption. The application of Article 81(3) EC to categories of agreements by way of a block exemption regulation is based on the presumption that restrictive agreements that fall within their scope fulfil each of the four conditions laid down in Article 81(3) EC (see Section 35 of the Article 81(3) Notice). Where no block exemption applies, the Article 81(3) Notice indicates a methodology to assess the pro-competitive effects of an agreement.

5.3.4.2 Towards a "rule of reason" in EC competition law?

Under the old enforcement regime, both stages of the assessment were not entrusted to the same authority. The concentration of the power of exemption in the hands of the European Commission entailed either rejecting *in toto* the rule of reason approach or reducing its breadth to the four conditions listed in Article 81(3) EC. Regulation 1/2003 has re-invigorated the debate on the possibility of a "rule of reason" approach, as in force in the USA. Since both the evaluation of anti-competitive effects and the assessment of efficiencies are now in the hands of the same authority, the practical importance of the distinction between prohibition and exemption fades away. Indeed, under US antitrust law, the general evaluation of all the relevant facts already includes

---

[68] Examples are contained in Regulation (EC) No.823/2000 (Consortia) [2000] O.J. L 100/24, as amended by Regulation (EC) No.611/2005 [2005] O.J. L 101/10; Regulation (EC) No.772/2004 (Technology transfer agreements) [2004] O.J. L 123/11; Regulation (EC) No.358/2003 (Insurance) [2003] O.J. L 53/8; Regulation (EC) No.2658/2000 (Specialisation agreements) [2000] O.J. L 304/3; Regulation (EC) No.2659/2000 (R&D agreements) [2000] O.J. L 304/7; Regulation (EC) No.1400/2002 (Motor vehicles) [2002] O.J. L 203/30; Regulation (EC) No.1105/2002 amending Regulation 1617/1993 (Passenger tariffs and slot allocations at airports), [2002] O.J. L 167/6; and Regulation (EC) No.2790/99 (Vertical agreements) [1999] O.J. L 336/21.

the assessment of what under European law would only be part of the appraisal as initiated under Article 81(3) EC.[69] To make the requisite determination of a competitor agreement's overall competitive effect, the US antitrust authorities also consider whether cognisable efficiencies would be sufficient to offset the potential of the agreement to harm consumers.[70] Also in Europe, the contested conduct will be prohibited as anti-competitive whenever it appears, from the enforcing authority's viewpoint as lacking the redeeming virtues needed to pass the overall scrutiny. As put by Pardolesi: "not yet a rule of reason, but an important step in that direction".[71]

Further arguments to support the emergence of a rule of reason in European competition law can be deduced from the case law of the European Courts. Under European competition law, agreements which have as their object a hardcore restriction of competition are considered *per se* illegal. In such cases, as the Court of First Instance held in *European Night Services*,[72] "the restrictions of competition may be weighed against their claimed pro-competitive effects only in the context of Article [81](3)". Whether efficiencies may be withheld under Article 81(1) EC, instead of only under Article 81(3) EC, when assessing agreements which have as their effect a restriction of competition, has been left open by the Court, however, thereby leaving open the possibility of a "rule of reason" approach.[73]

5.3.4.3 The European Commission's Guidelines on Article 81(3) EC

Summary of the Notice The framework of the Article 81(3) EC Notice relating to the four conditions of Article 81(3) EC is as follows.

First, Section 51 of the Article 81(3) EC Notice determines that all efficiency claims must be substantiated so that the following can be verified:

- the nature of the claimed efficiencies;

- the link between the agreement and the efficiencies;

- the likelihood and magnitude of each claimed efficiency; and

- how and when each claimed efficiency would be achieved.

To do so, the Article 81(3) EC Notice contains a detailed description of two "types" of efficiencies: (a) cost efficiencies (Sections 64–68, including

---

[69] See the US Horizontal Guidelines, para.3.36. On the USA in general, compare the articles contained in the Symposium on the future course of the rule of reason, published in (2002) 68 Antitrust L.J. 331–539.

[70] This is necessarily an approximate judgement only. See the US Horizontal Guidelines, para.3.37.

[71] R. Pardolesi, "Modernization: The 'new mantra' of transatlantic competition law", Speech given at Harvard University on February 11, 2005.

[72] Joined Cases T–374/94, T–375/94, T–384/94 and T–388/94 *European Night Services Ltd and others v Commission* [1998] ECR II–3141, para.136.

[73] See L. Ritter, W.D. Braun and F. Rawlinson, *European Competition Law: A Practitioner's Guide* (2nd ed., 2000), pp.103–104; A. Nikpay and J. Faull, "Article 81", in *The EC Law of Competition* (J. Faull and A. Nikpay ed., 1999), para.2.98; O. Black, "Per Se Rules and Rules of Reason: What are They" (1997) 18 E.C.L.R. 145.

economies of scale and scope, as well as improved planning), and (b) qualitative efficiencies (Sections 69–72, including dynamic efficiencies related to
improvements in innovation and distribution).

Second, Sections 73–74 of the Article 81(3) EC Notice explain that this
condition of Article 81(3) EC implies a two-fold test: (a) the restrictive agreement as such must be reasonably necessary in order to achieve the efficiencies;
and (b) the individual restrictions of competition that flow from the agreement
must also be reasonably necessary for the attainment of the efficiencies.
According to the European Commission, the decisive factor is whether or not
the restrictive agreement and individual restrictions make it possible to perform the activity in question more efficiently than would likely have been the
case in the absence of the agreement or the restriction concerned.

Third, Sections 83 *et seq.* of the Article 81(3) EC Notice explain that the pass-
on of benefits must at least compensate consumers for any actual or likely
negative effect caused them by the restriction of competition found under
Article 81(1) EC. Moreover, the European Commission holds that society as a
whole benefits where the efficiencies lead either to fewer resources being used
to produce the output consumed or to the production of more valuable products and thus to a more efficient allocation of resources. In line with the
overall objective of Article 81 EC to prevent anti-competitive agreements, the
net effect of the agreement must at least be neutral from the point of view of
those consumers likely to be or directly affected by the agreement. If such
consumers are worse off following the agreement, this condition of Article
81(3) EC is not fulfilled. The positive effects of an agreement must be balanced
against and compensate for its negative effects on consumers. When that is the
case, consumers are not harmed by the agreement. A certain time lag between
the emergence of the efficiencies and the pass-on to consumers is acceptable.
However, the greater the time lag, the greater also must be the efficiencies to
compensate for the loss to consumers during the period preceding the pass-on.

In order to deal with the difficulties relating to the accurate calculation of the
consumer pass-on rate, the Article 81(3) EC Notice refers to a number of
characteristics to be taken into account as far as costs efficiencies are concerned
(such as the market structure; the nature and magnitude of the efficiency
gains; elasticities of demand; and the nature of the restriction of competition).
As far as qualitative efficiencies are concerned, the European Commission
notes that it is difficult to attach a precise value, and more generically states
that it must be "carefully assessed whether the claimed efficiencies create real
value for consumers in that market so as to compensate for the adverse effects
of the restriction of competition" (Sections 103 and 104 of the Article 81(3) EC
Notice).

Fourth, Sections 105–115 of the Article 81(3) Notice deal with the final
condition of Article 81(3) EC, and focus on the various sources of (actual and
potential) competition in the market, the level of competitive constraint that
they impose on the parties to the agreement, and the impact of the agreement
on this competitive constraint. Entry, the presence of mavericks and the
impact of product differentiation are singled out.

Preliminary assessment of the Article 81(3) Notice The Article 81(3) EC Notice greatly improves the methodological foundations for the application of Article 81 EC and contains numerous examples and illustrations of the principles the European Commission intends to apply to the assessment of restrictive agreements. Hence, it should be of guidance to companies and their advisors when conducting the self-assessment which is at the core of the modernisation of EC competition law. Nevertheless, the conformity of the Article 81(3) Notice with economic insights is subject to criticisms.[74]

The Article 81(3) Notice is to apply to all types of agreements, that is horizontal agreements, vertical agreements, technology transfer, and so on. The main problem with this approach obviously relates to the nature of horizontal and vertical agreements. While vertical agreements concern mostly complementary products, horizontal agreements deal with competing products. This not only makes the incentives to cooperate—and the effects of cooperation—very different, but also affects the principle sources of pro-competitive effects. While horizontal agreements could give rise to economies of scale (often in combination with an increase of market power), vertical agreements are often pro-competitive to start with (by, for example, reducing prices and improving coordination). By failing to distinguish explicitly between horizontal and vertical coordination, the framework contained in the Article 81(3) Notice is seriously hampered from an analytical perspective.

The measurement of efficiencies relating to horizontal agreements boils down to a trade-off between the competition-reducing impact that the restrictive agreement has on price–cost margins (which become more significant as competition is further eliminated), and the price-reducing impact that the efficiencies have on marginal costs. As Section 98 of the Article 81(3) Notice recognises, reductions in marginal costs (as opposed to fixed costs) are likely to be required in order to convince the competition authority (be it the European Commission, an NCA or a national court) that savings, once achieved, will be passed on to customers. Lower marginal costs provide incentives for firms to seek increased sales volumes, and this makes them likely to transform some of their efficiency gains into price reductions (that will, in turn, induce extra sales). In contrast, simple theories of the firm predict that savings in fixed costs will not affect competitive behaviour. Hence, their benefit accrues to the firm rather than its customers, which is not in line with the consumer welfare standard underlying the Article 81(3) Notice.[75]

Vertical agreements require a different analysis; as such agreements may lead to efficiency gains other than cost savings. For example, vertical agreements may eliminate free riding or alleviate the double mark up problem (see Chapter 6 for a detailed discussion).[76] Methodologies exist for quantifying the consumer welfare gains that arise from quality improvements. However, estimating such pro-competitive effects is significantly more complex than the

---

[74] See also L. Kjølbye, "The New Commission Guidelines on the Application of Article 81(3): An Economic Approach to Article 81" (2004) 25 E.C.L.R. 566; and P. Nicolaides, "The Balancing Myth: The Economics of Article 81(1) and (3)" (2005) 33 Leg. Issues Econ.Integr. 123.
[75] See Ch.2, s.2.1.3.3.
[76] See Ch.6, s.6.2.2.2.

assessment of marginal costs reductions applicable to horizontal agreements, especially where customers place different subjective valuations on product attributes (thus creating a mix of winners and losers). The Article 81(3) EC Notice chooses not to deal with such issues.

It is somewhat early into modernisation to fully gauge the impact of these preliminary comments on the practical application of the Article 81(3) EC Notice, and it remains to be seen how the precedents will evolve. The authors are aware of only one fully argued and econometrically substantiated Article 81 EC assessment publicly available, which was performed by the ELAA (European Liner Affairs Association, grouping the world's liner shipping companies) to argue its case for replacement of Regulation 4056/86 containing the Liner Shipping block exemption. The economic evidence provided prompted the European Commission to order its own economic expert study to rebut the industry's arguments concerning the benefit of stability of supply, the need for information exchange, meetings between carriers and their customers, a price index, and so on. At the time of writing, the outcome of the review process was still open.[77]

One way or another, however, the European Commission has undertaken a laudable effort to bring together the various aspects of Article 81(3) EC into one comprehensible set of guidelines, which should (hopefully) assist in further increasing the consistent application of economic analysis in Article 81 EC-type situations.

5.4 The efficiency of coordination and joint ventures

5.4.1 The hybrid standard applying to joint ventures

As almost any agreement integrating two or more firms' operations could be described as a joint venture, competition law has focused on a number of factors discerning the distinctive efficiency advantages and particular anti-competitive risks. Brodley[78] thereto lists four conditions:

- the enterprise is under the joint control of the parent firms which are not under related influence;

- each parent makes a substantial contribution to the joint enterprise;

- the enterprise exists as a business entity separate from its parents; and

- the joint venture creates a significant new business capability in terms of new productive capacity, new technology, a new product, or entry into a new market.

---

[77] All material concerning the review of Regulation 4056/86 is available on the DG Comp website.
[78] J.F. Brodley, "Joint Ventures and Antitrust Policy" (1982) 95 Harv. L. Rev. 1523 at pp.1526–1529.

Similar contingencies have been developed by the European Court of Justice in its *Philip Morris* judgment.[79] As a result, a joint venture is broader than a simple contractual arrangement, as it involves the creation of a new firm or business rather than being merely a cooperation between the parties. Yet it also differs from a merger because it typically involves the creation of a separate, limited-purpose firm, not a full union of two previously independent firms. Reflecting their hybrid status in-between simple coordination and full merger, joint ventures are exposed to a special competition law regime. Since the 1997 amendments to the Merger Regulation came into force, all full function joint ventures are subject to a system which draws mainly from the procedures and timelines as instituted by the Merger Regulation[80]—as indeed it does not make sense to treat joint ventures any more harshly than the more far-reaching alternative of merger. The joint ventures' distinct organisational form and its characteristics are acknowledged by their special position, which is explicitly provided for in Article 2(4) of the Merger Regulation. Article 81 EC remains applicable to cases of coordination of the parent companies' behaviour. The substantial provisions contained in Article 81(3) EC are well-honed to deal with the efficiencies generated by joint ventures.

Joint ventures offer a means of achieving many of the transactional efficiencies related to integrating activities within a single firm, without encountering the disadvantages of mergers:

- Joint ventures can achieve economies of scale in research and distribution not reachable through single firm operations.

- Shared profits and managerial responsibilities alleviate the risk of opportunism and informational imbalance, while offering a means to monitor the use of the parties' input in the project.

- Evaluating the parties' respective input to the project is mitigated, because this can await determination on the market over the course of the joint ventures' running time.

- Joint ownership also provides a way of spreading the costs of producing valuable information that is normally protected from appropriation only by contractual undertakings which are difficult to enforce.

Joint ventures thus represent the tool of choice for projects involving high risk, high information costs or innovation activities for which there are no equally efficient substitutes. The following section will focus in particular on these efficiencies and the way European competition law takes them into account under Article 81(3) EC.

---

[79] Joined Cases 142/84 and 156/84 *British American Tobacco Company Ltd and R.J. Reynolds Industries, Inc v Commission* [1987] ECR 4487.

[80] For an overview of the evolution the treatment of joint ventures underwent, the reader may refer to J. Venit, "The Treatment of Joint Ventures under the EC Merger Regulation—Almost through the Ticket", in Fordham Corp. L. Inst. 1999, 465 (B. Hawk ed., 2000). On the treatment of mergers and the Merger Regulation, see below, Ch.9.

5.4.2 Quantifying efficiencies?

Under the self-assessment imposed by Regulation 1/2003, and the guidance contained in the Article 81(3) Notice, efficiencies have to counterbalance any anti-competitive effects that joint ventures may entail that are, similar to regular cases of coordinated behaviour, mainly related to collusion.[81] Thereto the four requirements prescribed by Article 81(3) EC will be assessed in turn.

Article 81(3) EC states that all kinds of improvements in production, distribution, and technical and economic progress are to be taken into account. Regarding joint ventures, the European Commission has held the following benefits as relevant:[82]

- the likelihood of producing a new or greatly improved product resulting in increased choice for consumers;

- the contribution and sharing by the parents of complementary technology or experience;

- objective technical difficulties which are insurmountable for the individual parent companies;

- speeding up the entry of a new competitor, in comparison with the market situation without the joint venture, as well as the penetration of new markets;

- the need to share the costs and risks of research and development, or where the capital costs of long term investment are particularly high;

- the need to supply customers with a range of products or services as well as the joint venture's ability to provide speedy and efficient after sales services in the case of large equipment manufacturers;

- the advantages of an associated specialisation arrangement;

- the lowering of prices;

- improved capacity utilisation, rationalisation and capacity reduction.

Although this listing of potential benefits associated with cooperative agreements (and joint ventures in particular) appears extensive, a more profound study of the case law leads to the conclusion that such efficiencies are hardly ever quantified in practice.[83] Given the limited practical feasibility of such quantification, it may suffice to point out that the resulting level of discretion

---

[81] On the particularities of collusive interdependencies and joint ventures, compare J.F. Brodley, "Joint Ventures and Antitrust Policy" (1982) 95 Harv. L. Rev. 1523 at pp.1530–1531. An analysis based on the European case law is to be found in J. Temple Lang, "International Joint Ventures under Community Law", in Fordham Corp. L. Inst. 1999, 381, 395–410 (B. Hawk ed. 2000).

[82] For an overview of the relevant case law, see J. Temple Lang, "International Joint Ventures under Community Law", in: Fordham Corp. L. Inst. 1999, 381, 415–417 (B. Hawk ed. 2000).

[83] D. Neven, P. Papandropoulos and P. Seabright, *Trawling for Minnows: European Competition Policy and Agreements between Firms* (1998).

the European Commission enjoys under Article 81(3) EC is substantial. Because of the restricted supervision exercised by the European Courts, the perception of some form of industrial policy meddling was never entirely subdued,[84] and it remains to be seen to what extent modernised European competition law will be able to change this.

Article 81(3) EC requires that the restriction of competition resulting from the agreement must be indispensable for the synergies to materialise. Thereto the European Court of First Instance determined in *European Broadcasting Union*[85] that the provisions of the agreement in question must be "objectively and sufficiently determinate so as to enable [its provisions] to be applied uniformly and in a non-discriminatory manner". To decide whether the restrictive clauses contained in the joint venture agreement (such as non-competition clauses) are indispensable the Court's *Matra* ruling obliges the European Commission to consider whether the parent companies were capable of entering the market on their own and had substantial reason for doing so.[86] If similar or greater benefits would have been obtained if the parent companies had entered the market separately, or the adverse effects of competition are disproportionate, then the efficiency gains are to be refused as countervailing benefits. More generally, if less restrictive alternatives are economically feasible, then the European Commission may rule that close cooperation structures are unnecessary for reaching the stated goals.[87]

A fair share of the benefits associated with the joint venture is to be passed on to consumers, in line with the general goals of European competition law as discussed in the second chapter of this book. In the case of joint ventures falling under Article 81 EC, the European Commission assumes this to be the case if the relevant market is competitive or if the buyers are powerful and sophisticated companies.[88]

Finally, Article 81(3) EC and Article 2(3) of the Merger Regulation state that no exemption may be given for an agreement which gives the parties the possibility of eliminating competition over a substantial part of the products or services. As such the European Commission strives to ensure that there is still "sufficient external competition to guarantee the maintenance of an effective competitive structure on the markets concerned".[89]

Joint ventures thus provide a good illustration of what the system of self-assessment envisaged under Regulation 1/2003 may amount to. Complex economic activities involving multiple firms (such as a joint R&D project), which are governed by individual contracts, encounter substantial transactional problems, especially when they run for an extended time. Specifying the terms of the arrangement, bringing together the parties' disparate economic goals and fixing the rate of future contributions by participants will often pose

---

[84] See V. Emmerich, *Kartellrecht* (8th ed., 1999), p.442.
[85] Joined Cases T–528/93, T–542/93, T–543/93 and T–546/93 *Métropole Télévision and others v Commission (Eurovision II)* [1996] ECR II–649.
[86] Case T–17/93 *Matra Hachette SA v Commission and Ford-Volkswagen (Matra II)* [1994] ECR II–595, 637.
[87] Compare Case IV/32.006 *Alcatel/ANT* [1990] O.J. L 32/19, para.20.
[88] European Commission, *14th Annual Report on Competition Policy 1994* (1995), para.177.
[89] Case COMP/36.253 *P&O Stena Line* [1999] O.J. L 163/61, paras 67–135.

insurmountable difficulties for the parties. One apparent solution thereto is to internalise all activities in one firm by way of a full merger.[90] However, this may raise problems of its own in terms of the parties' differing desires for future development, as well as because of the antitrust implications mergers tend to raise.

5.5 Conclusions

Economic theory is helpful in explaining why competitors have incentives to cooperate and why cartels are formed. As soon as the number of suppliers is limited and the products sold are not homogeneous, perfect competition no longer exists. In game theory, models have been developed which describe behavioural choices of firms in an oligopolistic market which have to take reactions by competitors into account. It was shown that game theory is a powerful tool to explain and predict the behaviour of oligopolistic firms.

In discussing the three requisites for cartel success, (a) the potential for monopoly power, given the characteristics of the market, (b) expected high gains, and (c) the need to overcome the organisational problems of cartels, this chapter found that oligopolistic markets do not necessarily lead to collusive outcomes. Some cartels will succeed, while others will fail.

At the same time, economic insights demonstrate that cooperation between firms may be motivated by goals which are beneficial to societal welfare. Competition law should also take into account these benign effects of competitor collaboration rather than solely focusing on the anti-competitive effects. Different types of cooperation can lead to a range of efficiencies, such as economies of scale and scope, better planning of production, advantages in marketing and distribution, and in research and development.

Turning to the applicable law, this chapter explained how European competition law seeks to regulate competitor cooperation and restrain anti-competitive coordination of companies' behaviour. Article 81(1) EC bans cartel agreements, decisions of associations of undertakings, and concerted practices that harm competition. Article 81(3) EC grants an exemption when the benefits of the agreement in terms of efficiencies and consumer welfare are deemed to prevail without causing disproportionate restrictions or eliminating competition for a substantial part of the products in question.

Since Regulation 1/2003 on the modernisation of European competition law has entered into force, Article 81(3) EC now consists of an exception rule, which provides a defence for undertakings against a finding of an infringement of Article 81(1) EC. In so doing, the European Commission has effectively switched to a directly applicable exception system, allowing companies to self-assess whether they are caught by Article 81 EC. The Article 81(3) EC Notice provides more detailed guidance thereto.

---

[90] R.H. Coase, "The Nature of the Firm" (1937) 4 *Economica* 386.

European competition law differentiates between agreements having restriction of competition as their object and agreements or concerted practices which, also implicitly, may have anti-competitive consequences. Economic analysis stresses the need to examine the real-life consequences of both explicit and tacit collusion. Even though restriction of competition may be the proven object of cooperation, market evidence may show that prices are not substantially above competitive levels, which makes antitrust intervention less compelling or even unnecessary. In general, agreements such as price fixing, market sharing, quotas and rigging bids having as their object the restriction of competition will mainly entail enforcement related issues such as leniency, fines and damages.

Having said that, horizontal agreements having as their object a restriction of competition are considered by the nature of the cooperation to indicate the applicability of Article 81(1) EC *per se* as they are presumed to have negative market effects, and current European competition law seemingly allows economically relevant evidence to be pushed aside if the objective to fix prices or control output can be proven (viz. the example of liberal professions); (lack of) economic impact will only be taken into account when determining the ultimate fine.

Most competitor cooperation does not have as its object a restriction of competition, though. The applicability of Article 81(1) EC in such cases requires an analysis of the agreement's effects. Thereto the agreement must be able to limit competition between the parties involved and it must be likely to affect competition in the market to such an extent that negative market effects as to prices, output, innovation or the variety or quality of goods and services can be expected. The European Commission's Horizontal Guidelines hold that this depends on the economic context of the agreement, taking into account both (a) the nature of the agreement and (b) the parties' combined market power, as this (together with other structural factors) determines the capability of the cooperation to affect overall competition.

The "economic analysis" thus prescribed by the European Commission is basically a two-tier test: first, one has to decide what characteristics the parties' cooperation has and, second, what amount of market shares the parties hold in their competitive surroundings must be investigated. For a critical analysis of the market share approach, the reader may refer to the fourth chapter of this book.

This chapter described how, historically, Article 81(1) EC has been interpreted widely. Nowadays, both the European Commission and Courts recognise that this formalistic approach has no place in a modern effects-based competition regime and, post-modernisation, the need for a detailed substantive analysis of the impact of an agreement under Article 81(1) EC has become ever more important. The legal distinction between hardcore cartels (explicit collusive agreements to fix prices or share markets between producers and sellers of substitute products) and soft cartels (implicit collusive agreements) is useful to show that Article 81(1) EC specifically prohibits hardcore cartels; the range of soft cartels and other forms of competitor cooperation covered by the prohibition is unclear. The legal debate mostly deals with inferring the existence of concerted practices deemed illegal from the evidence available.

In terms of assessment methodology, the Article 81(3) EC Notice greatly improves the methodological foundations for the application of Article 81 EC and contains helpful examples and illustrations of the principles the European Commission intends to apply to the assessment of restrictive agreements. At the time of writing, it is somewhat early into modernisation to fully measure the impact of the Article 81(3) EC Notice on the practical application of Article 81 EC, and it remains to be seen how the precedents will evolve. One way or another, however, the European Commission has undertaken a laudable effort to bring together the various aspects of Article 81 EC into one comprehensible set of Guidelines, which should (hopefully) assist in further increasing the consistent application of economic analysis in Article 81 EC-type situations.

Chapter 6

···

VERTICAL RESTRAINTS

6.1 Introduction

Manufacturers may impose conditions on the distributors with whom they deal beyond requiring them to pay the wholesale price for their products. In contracts with dealers, manufacturers may specify the retail price at which the products must be resold, other business terms or forms of behaviour. Apart from price restraints, territorial restrictions limiting the places where dealers may resell products (location clauses) and customer restrictions limiting the group(s) of buyers to which products can be resold (customer clauses) are widespread in distribution agreements. Such contractual terms are commonly called vertical restraints.

For the purposes of legal and economic analysis, vertical restraints are often divided into price and non-price restraints. Price restraints can take different forms. Manufacturers may require distributors to charge a fixed price or limit their freedom to determine prices by setting a minimum or maximum retail price. This practice is variously termed resale price maintenance, vertical price fixing, or fair trade.[1] An important variant of resale price maintenance is the communication by the manufacturer of non-binding recommended prices or advertised prices.

Non-price restraints include requirements that distributors do not locate near each other, so that each dealer enjoys some degree of territorial protection (exclusive distribution), that they do not sell competing products (exclusive purchasing[2]), that they sell a fixed quantity or a minimum number of units (quantity fixing), that they satisfy a number of quality requirements (selective distribution), or that they operate within a standardised and highly detailed promotional framework (franchising).[3] Franchising bundles several restraints. In European law a franchise was defined as:

"... a package of industrial or intellectual property rights relating to trademarks, trade names, shop signs, utility models, designs, copyrights, know-how or patents to be exploited for the resale of goods or the provision of services to end users".[4]

Franchisers may provide franchisees with a total system of doing business, thus decreasing the likelihood of failure compared to the bankruptcy rate of other independent retailers. In order to protect the parties' specific investments various clauses are inserted into the franchise contracts. On the one hand, exclusive territories are granted to franchisees to ensure that they will earn a return on the investments they sink. On the other hand, exclusive dealing provisions and non-competition clauses are inserted into the contract to safeguard the franchiser's incentives to invest in know-how.

Vertical restraints may limit both intra- and inter-brand competition. The manufacturer and its retail network may be considered as a unique vertical structure. If the brand name of a product offered by a vertical structure is attached to the corresponding manufacturer, intra-brand competition refers to competition between retailers offering the product of a given manufacturer within a given vertical structure. Inter-brand competition involves the interaction between vertical structures. Intra-brand competition is typically limited by resale price maintenance: retailers selling the same brand will not compete on price (even though there may be strong incentives to improve pre- and post-sales services to attract buyers of products for which prices have been fixed). Conversely, in-store inter-brand competition will be weakened if

---

[1] Antitrust laws (dating from the 1950s) allowing for resale price maintenance in some American states were called "fair trade laws". This explains the title of Telser's seminal article on vertical minimum price fixing: L. Telser, "Why Should Manufacturers Want Fair Trade?" (1960) 3 J. Law Econ. 86.

[2] Hereinafter also called exclusive dealing.

[3] The terminology used is taken from the EC Regulations which were in force until May 31, 2000 (Regulation 1983/83 [1983] O.J. L 173/1; Regulation 1984/83 [1983] O.J. L 173/5). Exclusive distribution is also termed exclusive territories, whereas exclusive dealing is synonymous with exclusive purchasing. In this chapter these terms are used interchangeably.

[4] Art. 1(3)(a) of Regulation 4087/88 [1988] O.J. L 359/46. The Franchising Regulation has been replaced by Regulation 2790/1999 on vertical agreements [1999] O.J. L 336/21 (hereinafter Regulation 2790/1999).

retailers are tied to manufacturers by means of exclusive purchasing agreements.

In the next section of this chapter, an attempt will be made to answer the question why manufacturers may find it profitable to place vertical restraints on the distributors' actions. Positive economic analysis seeks to explain why some manufacturers establish vertical restraints. There are several economic theories of vertical restraints, which all provide useful information for the policy maker who has to design a welfare improving competition law. In the third section, a brief comparative overview of the competition rules governing vertical restrictions will be given. Both European competition law and US antitrust law will be discussed and contrasted with each other; a brief comparison with national competition rules in some of the EC Member States will equally be included. The following section then provides an economic assessment of these diverging competition laws. It will be shown that current competition rules are not entirely consistent with the goal of allocative efficiency. In recent decades vertical restraints have received a great deal of attention from economic literature. An extensive amount of new thinking has led to a substantial revision of the policy implications, but competition law has not been revised so rapidly (and frequently) as the economic theories on vertical restraints. In addition, political reasons have inhibited a full reception of the economic analysis of vertical restraints. As a consequence there is no perfect harmony between economic insights and competition law. Finally, the most important conclusions are summarised.

6.2 Economic analysis of vertical restraints

6.2.1 Overview

Economic theories can be broadly divided into two categories: theories stressing the danger of anti-competitive effects (such as collusion and the erection of entry barriers) on the one hand, and efficiency theories explaining vertical restraints as remedies to principal–agent problems and opportunistic behaviour on the other. Initially, economists were uneasy about vertical restraints because several restrictions, such as prohibiting distributors from lowering prices or selling competing products, appear to restrain competition and harm consumers by increasing product prices. However, the early assessments of vertical restraints ignored the costs of distribution. Obviously, the model of perfect competition that takes distribution as a costless activity does not provide good insight into markets that rely on substantial sales expenditures. Every manufacturer must pay dealers for their sales efforts and check them to make sure that products are distributed in a manner that is best for the manufacturer's interests.

The evolution of economic thinking on vertical restraints has thus led to the emergence of more benign views. Nowadays economists describe the relation between a manufacturer and a distributor as a principal–agent dependence. The principal hires the agent to perform an action in a manner that the principal cannot fully control.[5] Principal–agent problems create a variety of both horizontal and vertical externalities[6] that can be addressed with vertical restraints. Each vertical structure faces a number of decision variables: fixing of wholesale and retail prices, quantities to be purchased by distributors, quantities to be sold to consumers, sellers' efforts, location of stores, and so on. Neither the manufacturer nor the distributor can control all these variables directly: some are controlled by the producer only, while others are monitored only by the distributors. Some decisions affect the total profits of the vertical structure; other decisions affect the distribution of profits between the manufacturer and the distributor. The decentralisation of decision making generates externalities, since one firm's decisions affect the other firm's profits. It is thus natural for the manufacturer and the distributor to look for some means of aligning both parties' interests and in that respect vertical restraints can help. A large part of the economic literature discusses vertical restraints as instruments to solve coordination problems in vertical structures.[7]

In addition, the transaction costs approach to problems of competition law has made it clear that the costs of distribution will determine the choice to be made by the manufacturer between setting up his own distribution system (a firm) or to sign contracts with independent distributors (the market solution). If the latter option is chosen, vertical restraints may cope with lock-in effects, which are the consequence of specific investments and the resulting risk of appropriating profits through opportunistic behaviour. Once a long-term investment that involves substantial sunk costs (for example in specialist equipment or training) is made, the investing firm's bargaining position is weakened. Accordingly, it will not want to make this investment before particular arrangements to avoid a hold-up by the other contract party are agreed upon. The transaction costs approach reaffirms and refines some of the insights flowing from the principal–agent models.[8] Transaction-specific investments bind the supplier and the distributor closely together (small numbers exchange); in such circumstances vertical restraints may limit the scope for opportunistic behaviour. These insights will be further commented on later.

In the early days of antitrust, vertical restraints (in particular price restraints) were seen as detrimental to competition. In the 1980s, as a consequence of the development of the efficiency theories, economists generally considered vertical restraints as relatively innocuous for competition. The

---

[5] D.W. Carlton and J.M. Perloff, *Modern Industrial Organization* (4th ed., 2005), p.414.
[6] An externality is a negative or positive consequence of an action by an individual (or firm) on another person (or firm).
[7] For an overview, see P. Rey and F. Caballero-Sanz, *The Policy Implications of the Economic Analysis of Vertical Restraints* (1996), pp.11–21.
[8] See Ch.3, s.3.9.

benign view towards vertical restraints found its most clear formulation in the US Guidelines of 1985 issued by the Antitrust Division of the Department of Justice,[9] which were repealed by the Clinton administration. Nowadays economists tend to be much more cautious in the assessment of the welfare effects of vertical restraints. This has resulted in policy recommendations rejecting simple rules such as *per se* (il)legality of (certain types of) vertical restraints. An optimal legal rule must take into account the fact that vertical restraints have ambiguous effects on economic welfare, depending on the context in which they are used (effects-based approach). This section first addresses economic explanations for price restraints and then proceeds with the analysis of non-price restraints.

6.2.2 Price restraints

Vertical minimum price fixing has often been hypothesised to function primarily as an aid to collusion by suppliers or dealers. However, starting from the publication of Telser's seminal article in 1960,[10] there has been considerable development of other economic theories of vertical restraints that recognise the principal–agent nature of the manufacturer–distributor relationship. In addition, current economic thinking on vertical price fixing distinguishes between minimum retail prices and maximum retail prices. Whereas the former may enhance efficiency in distribution by preventing "free riding" and solving coordination problems among distributors, the latter may serve the interests of both manufacturers and consumers by preventing the charging of successive monopoly prices. Before exploring the efficiency savings brought about by resale price maintenance in more detail, it will be investigated whether vertical price fixing has an important potential to limit competition.

6.2.2.1 Theories explaining vertical price fixing as anti-competitive practices

Collusion theories refer to the possibility that vertical minimum price fixing may be used to sustain a dealers' cartel or facilitate upstream collusion by reducing the manufacturers' incentives to lower wholesale prices. There are two main effects of minimum and fixed retail prices on competition. First, the dealers can no longer compete on price and this leads to a total elimination of intra-brand price competition. Second, there is increased transparency on price and responsibility for price changes. The latter effect makes horizontal collusion easier, at least in concentrated markets.

In the manufacturer-collusion theory, vertical price fixing is used to set retail prices to reflect the collusive wholesale price. Vertical price fixing is said to

---

[9] 50 Fed. Reg. 62, 663 (February 14, 1985). The DOJ Guidelines outlined both the pro-competitive (increased inter-brand competition, new entry and elimination of free riding) and anti-competitive (reduction of intra-brand competition, exclusion of competitors and facilitation of collusion) consequences and advocated a rule of reason balancing both effects.
[10] L. Telser, "Why Should Manufacturers Want Fair Trade?" (1960) 3 J. Law Econ. 86.

prevent cheating since retail price cuts are easier to detect. It also makes wholesale price cuts less desirable, since such a price cut at the upstream level cannot be passed on to the downstream level.[11] In the distributor-collusion theory, dealers acting as a group induce the supplier to enforce a collusive price through vertical price fixing. The goal pursued is either to discipline price cutting among the distributors or to prevent the evolution of more efficient forms of distribution. Vertical restrictions are thus used to circumvent the prohibition of horizontal price fixing; clearly this is a misuse of vertical restraints and is banned by the competition laws of most countries.

Competition lawyers tend to overemphasise the risk that manufacturers can be persuaded by retailers to introduce and monitor resale price maintenance. There are two reasons why this emphasis may be misplaced.[12] First, the collusive price desired by dealers conflicts with the manufacturer's interest of making maximum sales, given the wholesale price. A manufacturer may gain more by reporting collusion between dealers to the antitrust authorities than by enforcing minimum retail prices. The gain to a manufacturer of maintaining a resale price may not be worth the costs of foreclosing the sector of discount stores. Second, given that entry is relatively easy in many retail markets, abnormally high profits resulting from vertical price fixing are likely to attract new entrants. For these reasons, although there may be instances where retailers have put pressure on manufacturers to impose minimum resale prices, it seems unlikely that dealers' collusion is a major explanation for vertical price fixing. The opposite conclusion is tenable only in as far as retailing markets are not competitive and fit the description of a local small-numbers oligopoly.[13]

6.2.2.2 Principal–agent theories of vertical price fixing

Principal–agent theories of vertical price fixing include: (a) the double monopoly mark-up theory, (b) the free rider or special services theory, (c) the demand risk theory, (d) the quality assurance theory, and (e) the outlets theory. With the exception of the monopoly mark-up theory, which offers an explanation for vertical maximum price fixing, all theories provide an economic rationale for fixing minimum resale prices.

Efficiency explanation for maximum retail prices   The successive monopoly mark-up problem offers an efficiency explanation for the fixing of maximum retail prices. If the manufacturer and the distributor are both monopolies, each adds a monopoly mark-up so that consumers face two mark-ups instead of one. The manufacturer charges the distributor a wholesale price which is

---

[11] See L. Telser, "Why Should Manufacturers Want Fair Trade?" (1960) 3 J. Law Econ. 86; and R. Posner, "The Rule of Reason and the Economic Approach: Reflections on the Sylvania Decision" (1977) 45 U. Chi. L. Rev. 1 for a discussion of these issues.
[12] See also M.A. Utton, *Market Dominance and Antitrust Policy* (2nd ed., 2003), pp.239–240.
[13] Such a view is taken by M.E. Porter, *Interbrand Choice, Strategy, and Bilateral Market Power* (1976), p.13. See also B.S. Sharp, "Comments on Marvel: How Fair is Fair Trade?" (1985) 111 *Contemporary Policy Issues* 37.

above marginal cost. The distributor treats this price as his marginal cost and adds a second monopoly mark-up. As a consequence of this "double marginalisation",[14] output is lower and price is higher than in the case of a vertically integrated firm which takes care of both manufacturing and distribution. Both consumers and manufacturers are worse off with successive monopolies. Consumers facing the double mark-up buy less output. Profits under successive monopolies are also lower.[15] The coordination problem comes from the fact that each firm, when setting its own price, does not take into account the effect of this price on the other firm's profit. (The distributor "forgets" that reducing quantity adversely affects the manufacturer's profit.) Vertical restraints can be used to prevent losses due to successive monopoly mark-ups. If vertical price fixing is legal, the manufacturer may contractually impose a maximum retail price and thus prevent the distributor from raising his price much above the wholesale price. Avoiding the successive addition of margins by the manufacturer and the retailer will ensure that retail sales volume is as large as possible. Vertical maximum price fixing used for the sole purpose of eliminating the problem of double marginalisation leads to lower prices and thus benefits both firms and consumers.

Efficiency explanation for minimum retail prices: the "free rider" theory
Of the economic theories providing an explanation for fixing minimum retail prices the "free rider" or special services theory is most well-known. In 1960 Telser published an article on vertical restraints which has since become a classic.[16] In his essay, the free rider problem played a central role in explaining minimum resale price maintenance. Free riding, which is an externality, occurs when one firm benefits from the actions of another without paying for it. This problem is very relevant in the context of distribution agreements. It is important that a manufacturer's motives for imposing vertical restraints be well understood. If the distributors' margins increase, retail prices will also rise and a drop in the number of products sold will ensue. A fall in the manufacturer's profits should therefore be expected. However, there are circumstances in which vertical price fixing improves the producer's position, because the long term advantages arising from more efficient distribution exceed the short term, disadvantageous consequences flowing from the reduction in demand resulting from the distributors' higher profit margins. An increase in advertising and pre-sales services as a result of vertical minimum price fixing can enhance the value of the product to a more extensive group of consumers and should be able to generate increased demand. It should, therefore, be potentially advantageous for a rational manufacturer marketing differentiated products to fix minimum retail prices with a view to encouraging his retailers to offer special services. Sales promotion in the form of advertisements, displays of goods, knowledgeable sales help and customer

---

[14] Double marginalisation was the first coordination problem in vertical structures formally analysed. See J.J. Spengler, "Vertical Integration and Antitrust Policy" (1950) 58 J. Polit. Economy 347.
[15] For a graphical representation, see D.W. Carlton and J.M. Perloff, *Modern Industrial Organization* (4th ed., 2005), p.416.
[16] L. Telser, "Why Should Manufacturers Want Fair Trade?" (1960) 3 J. Law Econ. 86.

demonstrations obviously add to the retail price. Here the free riding problem emerges. Consumers could go to a store providing a full service (explanation of how to use the product, free tests, detailed information about alternative offers and so on) and, having obtained the information and weighed the various available options, go to the nearest discount store which provides no service but offers the desired product at a cheaper price. Consumers would thus free ride on the full service. Similarly, distributors who do not invest in the same promotion efforts can profit from the advertising and selling services of others and free ride on the labour of their competitors. Vertical minimum price fixing imposed by the manufacturer prevents this sort of free riding. It encourages retailers to offer an optimum level of sales services.

Before jumping to the conclusion that it should simply be legal for manufacturers to fix minimum retail prices to cope with the free riding problem, the limits of the special services argument should be stressed. The free rider theory is fundamentally grounded in the value of pre-purchase information to consumers. Free riding between retailers can take place only on pre-sales services and not on after-sales services.[17] For the special services theory to apply, consumers must be able to benefit from the services without purchasing the product. Moreover, the free rider problem occurs only in cases where services are necessarily linked to the product; it does not arise if distributors can sell the goods and services separately. The problem is based on two factors. First, sales must be taken away from distributors who offer a complete service and must go, instead, to suppliers of low grade services. Second, the provision of services, including those provided by the first category of distributors, must be reduced as a result of the free riding.[18]

In addition, it must be emphasised that the welfare effects of minimum retail prices are ambiguous. In sharp contrast with the case of pure double marginalisation, solving vertical coordination problems by means of minimum resale price maintenance is not necessarily socially desirable. Firms and consumers may disagree on the optimal amount of retail services or, more precisely, on the right mix between retail services and prices. Manufacturers are interested in the marginal consumers they can attract through increased sales efforts and they tend to neglect the impact of their decisions on infra-marginal consumers. Whereas the former are just willing to pay for the product at its prevailing price, the latter are willing to pay significantly more. The marginal consumers will purchase more products only if the value they derive from the services is higher than the increase in price. By contrast, infra-marginal consumers are relatively insensitive to a price increase caused by the provision of retail services and will continue to buy the product even if the additional services are valued less than the increase in price. As a result, manufacturers will profit from imposing minimum resale price maintenance when the marginal consumers value the additional services more than their costs, regardless of the infra-marginal consumers' preferences. If marginal consumers are

---

[17] In the latter hypothesis the quality assurance theory may explain minimum retail prices; see later.

[18] See W.S. Comanor, "Vertical Price Fixing, Vertical Market Restrictions, and the New Antitrust Policy" (1985) 98 Harv. L. Rev. 983.

willing to pay more to benefit from additional services whereas infra-marginal consumers would prefer to have lower services and prices, then it may be in the interest of the vertical structure to increase the level of effort and the retail price, even though it hurts the majority of consumers and decreases total welfare. In technical terms, the consequences for economic welfare depend on the shifts of the demand curve as a result of the provision of services. Increased demand may generate both additional profits for the manufacturer and an increase in consumer surplus, but this is not the inevitable outcome.[19] The divergence between the objectives of the manufacturer and the dealer, on the one hand, and the objectives of the consumers, on the other, is likely to be important when the vertical structure enjoys market power. If consumers can easily switch to alternate solutions, vertical minimum price fixing is unlikely to hurt consumers.

Telser's original free rider theory has been broadened to include other more general information services such as the fashion or quality certification implicit in high reputation outlets carrying the product.[20] If the distributor/retailer has developed a reputation for selling only high quality products (for example, by being a fashion trendsetter), other dealers can free ride on the investments made by the "certifying" store by stocking the same goods. Consequently, the theory not only explains vertical minimum price fixing for complex goods, such as computers, electrical appliances and consumer durables, but also for simple products that fit the fashion and quality certification version of the theory. Examples include clothing,[21] packaged foods, household goods, cosmetics and perfume. The quality of some of these goods cannot perfectly be observed prior to purchase; when they are sold in high reputation outlets information asymmetries on the part of consumers may be overcome by quality certification. For example, in the case of clothes, shops that do not hire qualified staff who are able to spot trends in fashion and recognise high quality clothes could free ride on the reputation of high quality stores. Minimum retail prices may prevent this.

Apart from curing information asymmetries, vertical minimum price fixing may also add to the prestige of the brand name, which may be a valuable asset to (some) consumers. Manufacturers may thus wish to maintain prices as a means of ensuring that their products are carried by outlets with the highest reputation for quality. This view is also connected to a more traditional justification for limitations of price competition often stressed in legal literature,

---

[19] For graphical representations, see F.M. Scherer and D. Ross, *Industrial Market Structure and Economic Performance* (3rd ed., 1990), pp.541–548; and M.A. Utton, *Market Dominance and Antitrust Policy*, (2nd ed., 2003), pp.235–238.

[20] H.P. Marvel and S. McCafferty, "Resale Price Maintenance and Quality Certification" (1984) 15 RAND J. Econ. 346.

[21] Compare *FTC v Levi Strauss and Co*, 433 U.S. 36 (1977). It is indeed questionable which kind of services can affect the demand for jeans but quality certification may very well explain the use of minimum resale price maintenance.

that it prevents the practice of "loss leaders".[22] A distributor may decide to cut the price of a popular leading brand in order to attract customers to his store. Manufacturers may legitimately feel that, if consumers frequently judge quality by price, the widespread use of their products as loss leaders will negatively affect sales as consumers lose confidence in their quality.[23]

Other efficiency explanations for minimum retail prices For the sake of completeness, three additional efficiency explanations for minimum retail prices are briefly sketched below. Klein and Murphy have advanced a quality assurance theory, which sees vertical minimum price fixing as a contract enforcement mechanism.[24] Whereas the special services theory is an example of a principal–agent problem created by horizontal externalities, the quality assurance theory involves vertical externalities. For some products the distributor can influence the final quality of the good received by the consumer. Examples include products for which post-sale services are important, such as cars and electronic equipment. In some circumstances, the distributor may have the incentive to provide a lower quality level than the manufacturer would like, thus creating a vertical externality for the manufacturer. Minimum retail prices, together with control over the number of dealers and the right to terminate dealers, can resolve this problem. Vertical minimum price fixing is thus used to create incentives for distributors to provide the quality of post-sale services that the manufacturer wants. The potential future flow of rents assures that retailers will not engage in shirking and will follow the manufacturer's wishes with respect to the amount of services needed. For the theory to apply, the distributor must be able to affect the consumer's satisfaction in a non-trivial way. If distributors' behaviour is unimportant to quality, such as with petrol, beer, ice cream or cosmetics, other explanations for vertical price fixing must be sought.

According to the outlets theory, vertical minimum price fixing is used to increase the number of outlets willing to carry the product.[25] If competition between retailers is too intense, then too few retailers from the manufacturer's perspective may stock the product. Minimum resale price maintenance may thus function as a substitute for a direct limitation of the number of retailers. It can be added that the interests of manufacturers and retailers may also diverge with regard to the location of the outlets. For example, retailers may choose to locate sufficiently far from other retailers so as to ensure that they achieve high profits. By eliminating competition between retailers, minimum retail prices

---

[22] In some European countries, such as France and Belgium, sales at loss prices or with an exceptionally reduced profit margin are prohibited. The prohibition is justified, *inter alia*, by the fear that large retail stores may attract consumers by lowering prices for popular brands, while at the same time keeping prices constant for other goods needed in everyday life. The practice is also nicely described as "the island of losses in the ocean of profits".

[23] M.A. Utton, *Market Dominance and Antitrust Policy* (2nd ed., 2003), p.238.

[24] B. Klein and K.M. Murphy, "Vertical Restraints as Contract Enforcement Mechanisms" (1988) 31 J. Law Econ. 265.

[25] J.R. Gould and L.E. Preston, "Resale Price Maintenance and Retail Outlets" (1965) 32 *Economica* 302.

may contribute to an optimal density of the retail network. From the latter perspective, vertical minimum price fixing is an alternative to location clauses.

Finally, Rey and Tirole have advanced the demand risk theory which sees vertical price fixing as a means of reducing the risk faced by differentiated distributors when consumer demand is uncertain. Exclusive distribution contracts have the effect of transferring all demand risk to distributors. If distributors are more risk averse than the manufacturer, it may be optimal to share some of the risk between the parties. Vertical minimum price fixing, which limits the extent of discounting if demand turns out to be low, has this effect.[26] Even though resale price maintenance may provide benefits to retailers by reducing the extent to which their profits vary with sales, this use of the practice may not be socially desirable due to the adverse effects on consumers.

6.2.2.3 Empirical studies

After the description of different theories on minimum resale price maintenance, the question about the relative importance of these theories in real-life markets naturally emerges. Empirical research in the USA showed that principal–agent theories have a greater potential to explain vertical price fixing than collusion theories. Research by Ornstein showed that less than a third of the resale price maintenance cases involved hints of a cartel, and claims that further restraints need to be imposed in order to sustain a cartel.[27] Ippolito's investigation of reported cases litigated between 1975 and 1982 revealed that only 13 per cent of the overall sample and 10 per cent in the private-case sample contained allegations of any horizontal collusion. By contrast, the free rider theory could provide an explanation for 65 per cent of the private litigation sample.[28] At the margin the American *per se* rule prohibiting minimum vertical price fixing thus appears likely to deter resale price maintenance used to solve principal–agent problems between manufacturers and distributors rather than to prohibit collusion.

6.2.3 Non-price restraints

As is the case with price restraints, both theories arguing anti-competitive effects and efficiency theories are advanced to explain why manufacturers may wish to impose vertical restraints upon their distributors. The first group of theories stresses that vertical restraints may be used to erect entry barriers or dampen competition at the upstream level. Conversely, principal–agent theories regard non-price restraints as methods to cope with problems of successive monopolies or to prevent free riding. In addition, the transaction costs theory explains vertical restraints as remedies for the danger of

[26] P. Rey and J. Tirole, "The Logic of Vertical Restraints" (1986) 76 Amer. Econ. Rev. 921.
[27] S. Ornstein, "Resale Price Maintenance and Cartels" (1985) 30 Antitrust Bull. 401.
[28] P.M. Ippolito, "Resale Price Maintenance: Empirical Evidence from Litigation" (1991) 34 J. Law Econ. 263.

opportunistic behaviour in cases where manufacturers and distributors are dependent upon each other because of the specific investments made to carry out the transactions (asset-specificity).

6.2.3.1 Theories explaining vertical restraints as anti-competitive practices

In the first place, theories arguing anti-competitive effects have been advanced to explain exclusive purchasing contracts. Exclusive dealing can raise search costs for consumers in relation to comparing prices and obtaining price information in the first place.[29] This adverse effect is particularly likely to be an issue for low value goods, such as impulse purchase of ice cream.[30] Professional buyers may afford specialist purchasing departments because their decisions relate to sizeable transactions. By contrast, for final consumers search costs in time and effort will often be high relative to the value of the good. A more general argument, which is particularly popular in the legal literature on antitrust, is that exclusive dealing leads to market foreclosure. If some distributors agree to handle the products of only one supplier, those outlets are foreclosed to other manufacturers. In the economic jargon, long term exclusive dealing contracts foreclose markets by raising rivals' costs. However, one should not immediately jump to the conclusion that exclusive purchasing arrangements raise barriers to entry. First, exclusive purchasing arrangements must last for longer than the normal contractual period, otherwise competing manufacturers have equal opportunities to win distributors at contract renewal time. Second, to condemn exclusive dealing as an entry barrier, a close examination of the market structures involved is needed. An incumbent with market power can make it difficult or impossible for a rival to enter by tying up scarce distribution channels.[31] If the manufacturer attempting to enforce exclusive dealing has a modest market share, the foreclosure effect is minimal. Even if the manufacturer has a substantial market share, an exclusive distribution contract is likely to have little effect on competition if entry into distribution is easy. In this respect zoning or licensing laws are particularly relevant.[32] In short, as Utton rightly concludes: "Exclusive dealing may be a means of applying pre-existing market power, but does not in itself create it".[33]

Not only exclusive purchasing agreements, but also exclusive distribution agreements may limit inter-brand competition. In the short run, exclusive territories can be used to dampen competition among rivals. In the long run, such restraints may be used by incumbent firms to deter entry. In both cases,

---

[29] D. Neven, P. Papandropoulos and P. Seabright, *Trawling for Minnows: European Competition Policy and Agreements between Firms* (1998), p.31, with further references.
[30] See Case IV/34.072 *Langnese-Iglo GmbH* [1993] O.J. L 183/19.
[31] J.R. Segal and M. Whinston, "Naked Exclusion: A Comment" (2000) 90 Amer. Econ. Rev. at pp.296–309; E. Rasmusen, J.M. Ramseyer and J. Wiley, "Naked Exclusion: A Reply" (2000) 90 Amer. Econ. Rev. at pp.310–311.
[32] In some European countries (e.g. France and Belgium), the opening of retail stores of a certain size is subject to the holding of a licence.
[33] M.A. Utton, *Market Dominance and Antitrust Policy*, (2nd ed., 2003), p.242.

these anti-competitive effects rely on a strategic use of the delegation of price decisions to distributors.[34] In markets where inter-brand competition is initially imperfect, vertical restraints can exacerbate existing imperfections and reduce further the degree of inter-brand competition. If dealers possess market power, cuts in wholesale prices will only be partly passed on to consumers. In addition, if one manufacturer's dealer cuts its retail price following a reduction in the wholesale price, then the other dealers may also react by cutting their retail prices. Both of these effects reduce the expected increase in sales that can be generated by reducing wholesale prices and discourage manufacturers from doing so. Reducing intra-brand competition through the use of exclusive territories thus makes the demand perceived by the manufacturer less elastic to its own wholesale price.[35]

A related argument is that incumbent firms may use both exclusive purchasing and exclusive distribution agreements to commit themselves to a tough attitude in the event of entry by modifying the partners' attitude towards competitors.[36] Exclusive purchasing agreements entered into for long periods induce the dealers to engage in fierce competition if competing products appear. Similarly, exclusive territories may be allocated to induce a tougher response on the part of the distributor in the event of geographically limited entry. In the absence of exclusive distribution agreements, manufacturers may be reluctant to engage in price wars that could also affect neighbouring areas. In contrast, an exclusive distributor would be likely to engage in tougher competition with the local entrant.[37] Finally, franchising also may generate negative effects on inter-brand competition. In the short run incumbents' know-how may reinforce their position, facilitate horizontal collusion and dampen competition among existing rivals. In the long run, the existence of (networks of) franchise agreements may make it more difficult for potential competitors to enter the market.[38]

The above theories stressing the anti-competitive effects of non-price vertical restraints should not detract from the important insight that inter-brand competition may be equally enlivened by the use of such restrictions. The allocation of exclusive territories may induce manufacturers to enter new markets and persuade competent and aggressive retailers to make the investments required in the distribution of products not yet known to the consumers. By raising profits and allowing greater efficiency to be achieved, exclusive territories (and vertical price fixing) can attract more entrants. Franchise agreements, in turn, increase the incentives to invest in (commercial) know-how and promote the entry of innovative technologies. The positive

---

[34] As a consequence resale price maintenance which rules out any freedom in the distributor's choices of prices cannot be used to dampen inter-brand competition. Vertical price fixing will favour rather than limit inter-brand competition.

[35] P. Rey and F. Caballero-Sanz, *The Policy Implications of the Economic Analysis of Vertical Restraints* (1996), p.18.

[36] *ibid.*, p.20.

[37] For a formal analysis, see P. Rey and G. Stiglitz, "The Role of Exclusive Territories in Producers' Competition" (1985) 16 Rand J. Econ. 431.

[38] P. Rey and F. Caballero-Sanz, *The Policy Implications of the Economic Analysis of Vertical Restraints* (1996), p.39.

effects of vertical restraints on inter-brand competition deserve particular attention in a non-integrated market, where entrants might need to make large investments to gain ground.

6.2.3.2 Efficiency theories

Efficiency theories of non-price restraints may be loosely divided into two groups: on the one hand, principal–agent theories, including the double monopoly mark-up theory and the free rider theory, and the transaction cost theory, on the other. If there are successive monopolies in manufacturing and distribution, the double monopoly mark-up theory may also explain vertical restraints other than resale price maintenance. Both sales quotas and franchising may reduce inefficiencies flowing from successive monopolies in manufacturing and distribution.[39] Manufacturers may require distributors to sell a minimum number of products. Sales quotas induce distributors to expand their output by lowering their prices, so that the magnitude of the second monopoly mark-up is reduced. Also, franchising may serve as a device to cope with the double monopoly mark-up problem. As indicated above, a manufacturer may charge the distributor one price for the product and a second price for the right to sell the product. While charging the marginal costs for his product, the manufacturer may make positive profits from the payment of a franchise fee, which grants the right to sell the product under a brand name in the promotional framework set up by the franchiser. The problem of the double monopoly mark-up is thus overcome and profits will be equal to the ones earned by an integrated manufacturer–distributor.[40]

The free rider theory may also explain vertical restraints other than resale price maintenance. The argument has been extended by Chicago School commentators to different intra-brand restraints, such as the reservation of exclusive sales territories and exclusive sales channels (selective distribution, franchising). From the manufacturer's point of view, the advantage of an exclusive territory arrangement is that the offer of a wider margin to the distributors will encourage them to maintain a high quality of service. If the territorial restraint is coupled with exclusive dealing, the manufacturer can also expect the maximum effort on the part of the distributor to sell the product. Protection against free riding may also explain inter-brand restraints, such as exclusive dealing. Exclusive territories address the free riding of one dealer on the efforts of another, whereas exclusive dealing addresses the free riding of one manufacturer on the efforts of another. Exclusive purchasing agreements can be understood as means of protecting the manufacturer's property rights in cases in which he possesses informational advantages and is therefore better placed to organise the distribution of his own products.[41] If a manufacturer conducts a massive advertising campaign to entice consumers to go to the distributor to buy his products, other manufacturers using the same

---

[39] D.W. Carlton and J.M. Perloff, *Modern Industrial Organization* (4th ed., 2005), p.415.
[40] *ibid.*, p.416.
[41] See H.P. Marvel, "Exclusive Dealing" (1982) 25 J. Law Econ. 6.

distributor also benefit from the increased customer flow. The free riding manufacturer who does not advertise has lower costs and can sell at a lower price. Customers may view the free riding manufacturer's product as a better deal at a lower price. Other examples of free riding among manufacturers using the same dealer occur when one manufacturer trains its dealers to repair or sell its product, or provides a list of potential customers to a dealer. In both cases, other manufacturers can take a free ride on the training expenditures or on the first manufacturer's customer list. A common solution to these free rider problems is exclusive dealing. If a manufacturer forbids his distributors from carrying products of competing manufacturers, he will be able to obtain the full reward of his sales efforts.[42]

The free rider justification also plays a prominent role in explaining vertical restraints in franchising contracts. Know-how is very sensitive to free riding: once it is transferred to a third party, this party may use it and even diffuse it at will. Franchisers' incentives to invest in know-how will, in general, be insufficient if they cannot appropriate the full returns for their efforts. Hence, they may wish to stop franchisees from selling competing products (to prevent competitors gaining from the commercial training offered to the franchisees) or from opening stores outside the franchised network or starting up a similar business after the termination of the agreement.

One of the most important contributions of the transaction costs approach to problems of competition law is the fundamental change that it has brought about in thinking regarding vertical restraints as a competition problem. Vertical restraints—not just territorial restrictions but also restrictions on the circle of purchasers, and also vertical price fixing—reduce transaction costs. Manufacturers may place vertical restraints on distributors to approximate the outcome that would occur if the firms vertically integrated. The relevant concepts of the transaction costs approach, such as asset-specificity and opportunistic behaviour, have been explained earlier.[43] Franchising is an example of regularly repeated transactions for which moderate relationship-specific investments are needed. "The crucial economic fact that underlies franchising contracts is that the incentives of the transacting parties do not always coincide".[44] The investments lose much or all of their value if the franchise agreement is ended. Consequently, terms in franchising contracts must cope with the risk of opportunistic behaviour, which may lead both franchiser and franchisee to an under-provision of such investments.

Collectively, all franchisees as well as the franchiser have a strong interest in ensuring that the reputation of the network remains untarnished. Individually, however, some franchise holders may seek to increase sales by reducing the quality of the product and saving on costs. The exclusive franchise provides the incentive structure needed to cope with this "subgoal pursuit" problem. In return for a commitment by the franchisee that the product will always be provided according to the detailed conditions laid down in the contract, the

---

[42] D.W. Carlton and J.M. Perloff, *Modern Industrial Organization* (4th ed., 2005), p.424.
[43] See Ch.3, s.3.9.
[44] See further B. Klein, "The Economics of Franchise Contracts" (1995) 2 J. Corp. Finan. 12.

franchiser guarantees that no one else will be granted a franchise in the area specified. A franchisee would be reluctant to make specific investments if nothing prevents the franchiser from locating another franchisee next to him once the investment has been sunk. Territorial protection thus serves the efficiency goal by reducing the risk of opportunistic behaviour.

6.3 Vertical restraints from a comparative legal perspective

In this section, the treatment of vertical restraints in European competition law is contrasted with their legal status under US antitrust law.[45] In addition, a brief overview of the competition rules that applied until recently in Germany is given in Box 6.2. A comparison with the previous German regime for vertical restraints remains useful to broaden the scope of comparison and enrich the efficiency analysis in this chapter.

6.3.1 US antitrust law

Under Section 1 of the Sherman Act "every contract (combination ... or conspiracy) in restraint of trade" is illegal. In practice, this very broad prohibition is substantially relaxed, since only few types of conduct are deemed *per se* illegal and most antitrust claims are analysed under "a rule of reason".[46] A chronological review of the case law of the Supreme Court equally shows a changing attitude towards the desirability of *per se* rules with regard to vertical restraints. First, the case law on price restraints will be analysed, starting with minimum resale price maintenance and continuing with the setting of maximum prices at retail level. Second, attention will be focused on the case law dealing with other vertical restraints, in particular territorial or customer restrictions.

6.3.1.1 Price restraints

For a long time all price fixing agreements were seen as *per se* illegal. Beginning with *Dr Miles* in 1911, the Supreme Court recognised the illegality of agreements under which suppliers set the minimum resale price to be charged by their distributors. John D. Park, a distributor, refused to enter into a contract that established minimum prices at which Dr Miles' drug products had to be sold. The Supreme Court ruled that this pricing agreement was illegal because it suppressed competition among distributors and was equivalent to

---

[45] A more extensive treatment of American antitrust law on vertical restraints can be found in: K.N. Hylton, *Antitrust Law: Economic Theory and Common Law Evolution* (2003), pp.252–278.
[46] For the explanation of the distinction between *per se* rules and the "rule of reason", see Ch.1, s.1.1.2.

price fixing.[47] Eight years later in *Colgate* the Supreme Court, however, decided that a manufacturer could unilaterally determine its retail price and refuse to sell to discounters.[48] Colgate refused to supply dealers who sold below suggested prices and cut off dealers who did so, but there was no evidence of a contract or conspiracy between Colgate and its dealers.[49] By making a distinction between (legal) unilateral action and (illegal) mutual agreement, the Court in fact softened the prohibition of minimum resale price maintenance.

As a result of political pressure by retailers' trade associations through the 1930s various states passed minimum resale price maintenance laws, called fair trade laws. Minimum retail prices were seen as a way of impeding the growth of large, low-cost retail chains.[50] In 1937, Congress passed the Miller–Tydings Act, which made resale price maintenance legal under the federal Sherman Act where it was legal under state law. In the early 1950s minimum resale price maintenance laws were enforced in all states except Alaska, Missouri, Texas and Vermont. The effect of the Miller–Tydings Act was strengthened by the 1952 McGuire Act, which reversed case law of the Supreme Court and made it possible to enforce minimum retail prices even against dealers who had not signed the resale price maintenance agreement. The laws allowing "fair" prices—that is, minimum prices set by the manufacturer—were repealed in 1975.[51] At this point the original *per se* prohibition resumed its full force.

In recent years the Supreme Court has kept the *per se* prohibition of minimum resale price maintenance intact. In 1984 it did not profit from the opportunity offered in the *Monsanto* case to reverse the *Dr Miles* rule.[52] However, at the same time the Colgate doctrine was revitalised, requiring "a conscious commitment to a common scheme designed to achieve an unlawful objective".[53] Consequently, unwilling compliance with a unilaterally announced policy is not seen as concerted action within the meaning of the Sherman Act. In a later case the Supreme Court held that, even in the presence of an explicit agreement between manufacturer and retailer, the manufacturer will not be charged with infringement of the Sherman Act unless a specific resale price was set.[54] Generally, while persisting with the *per se* prohibition,

---

[47] *Dr Miles Medical Company v John D. Park and Sons Company*, 220 U.S. 373 (1911), para.400.
[48] *US v Colgate and Co*, 250 U.S. 300 (1919).
[49] More recent case law has confirmed the need to show a conspiracy. Complaints by dealers about price cutting by a discounter are not sufficient proof of a conspiracy. It must be shown that the manufacturer and others "had a conscious commitment to a common scheme designed to achieve an unlawful objective." *Monsanto Co v Spray-Rite Service Corp*, 104 S.Ct. 1464 (1984), para.1469.
[50] S. Martin, *Industrial Economics: Economic Analysis and Public Policy* (2nd ed., 1994), p.511.
[51] It may be mentioned that by the time of repeal of the Miller–Tydings Act and the related McGuire Act, only 36 states had fair trade laws, and the laws were not actively enforced in many; D.W. Carlton and J.M. Perloff, *Modern Industrial Organization* (4th ed., 2005), p.670.
[52] *Monsanto Co v Spray-Rite Service Corp*, 104 S. Ct. 1464 (1984), paras 1469–1470, n.7. Eleven years earlier, in *Sylvania*, the Court declined to comment on the *per se* treatment of vertical price restrictions, noting that the issue involved significantly different questions of analysis and policy (*Continental TV, Inc v GTE Sylvania* (433 U.S. 36 (1977), para.51, n.18).
[53] *Monsanto Co v Spray-Rite Service Corp*, 465 U.S. 752 (1984), para.1469.
[54] In the Court's words "a vertical restraint is not illegal per se unless it includes some agreement on price or price levels" (*Business Electronics Corp v Sharp Electronics Corp*, 485 U.S. 717 (1988), para.728).

the range of practices that are judged to be resale price maintenance has been substantially narrowed and limited to concerted vertical price fixing.

In 1951 the Supreme Court condemned an agreement between two affiliated liquor distillers to limit the maximum resale price charged by retailers.[55] Remarkably, at that time the Court did not distinguish between minimum prices and maximum prices, even though the economic effects of these practices are different. The Supreme Court held that both types of restraints limit the freedom of retailers to sell products in accordance with their own judgment, and this was considered sufficient to establish a *per se* violation. In *Albrecht* the Supreme Court again had to deal with price fixing agreements. This case involved a newspaper publisher who had granted exclusive territories to independent carriers subject to their adherence to a maximum price on resale of the newspapers to the public. The Court decided that the imposition of a maximum price by a supplier upon his distributors was *per se* prohibited.[56] It took almost 30 years until *Albrecht* was overruled. In 1997 the Supreme Court delivered its opinion in the case *State Oil v Khan*.[57] Operators of a gas station had entered into an agreement with an oil company which fixed maximum gasoline prices by making it worthless for the operators to exceed the suggested retail prices. Under the agreement it was allowed to charge any amount for gasoline sold to the station's customers, but if the price charged was higher than the suggested retail price, the excess was to be rebated to the oil company. The Supreme Court found it difficult to maintain that vertically imposed maximum prices could harm competition to the extent necessary to justify their *per se* invalidation. The theoretical justification supporting *Albrecht*, such as the fear that vertical price fixing interferes with dealer freedom or the concern that maximum prices may be set too low for dealers to offer consumers essential or desired services, was considered insufficient. In addition, the Court stressed that the *per se* rule could exacerbate problems related to the unrestrained exercise of monopoly power by dealers who have exclusive rights within certain territories. As a consequence, since 1997 maximum resale price maintenance is judged under the "rule of reason".

6.3.1.2 Non-price restraints

The case law on non-price restraints has evolved from *per se* prohibitions to treatment under the "rule of reason". In 1963 the Supreme Court addressed the issue of territorial restrictions in *White Motor Co*.[58] A truck manufacturer limited the territory in which its distributors could sell the product. A majority of the Supreme Court held that too little was known about the impact of such vertical restraints to warrant treating them as *per se* unlawful.[59] Four years later the Supreme Court suddenly changed direction and enunciated in *Schwinn*[60] a

---

[55] *Kiefer-Stewart Co v Joseph E. Seagram and Sons, Inc*, 340 U.S. 211 (1951).
[56] *Albrecht v Herald Co*, 390 U.S. 145 (1968).
[57] *State Oil Co v Barkat U. Khan and Khan and Associates Inc*, 118 S.Ct. 275 (1997).
[58] *White Motor Co v US*, 372 U.S. 253 (1963).
[59] ibid., para.263.
[60] *US v Arnold, Schwinn and Co*, 388 U.S. 365 (1967).

clear-cut but formalistic distinction between restraints imposed by a manufacturer who retained ownership of the goods in question, and those imposed
by a manufacturer after parting with ownership. In an effort to combat the
erosion of his market share, Schwinn, a manufacturer of bicycles, set up a
complex distribution system. It sold less than half of its bikes to distributors,
each of which was instructed to resell only within designated territories and
only to retailers franchised by Schwinn. It also consigned a small portion of its
bikes to these distributors under similar restrictions. The rest of the bikes,
more than half, were sold and shipped to franchised retailers upon orders
taken by distributors acting as sales agents who received a commission on
these sales. The Supreme Court decided that the rule of reason applied to the
merchandise handled by distributors solely as consignees or as sales agents,
whereas restrictions concerning the merchandise sold were held illegal *per se*.
The latter restrictions were considered as obviously destructive of competition. If a manufacturer parts with ownership of his product or transfers risk of
loss to another, he may not reserve control over its destiny or the conditions of
its resale. The very same restraints, unlawful as to bikes sold, were held valid
when incident to consigned bikes or bikes for which the distributors acted as
sales agents. Even though the Court acknowledged that some vertical
restrictions could have pro-competitive effects by allowing smaller enterprises
to compete and that such restrictions may avert vertical integration in the
distribution process, it concluded that manufacturers may no longer control
product marketing once dominion over the goods had passed to dealers.[61]

Under current US antitrust law, territorial restrictions and customer
restrictions are no longer invalid *per se*. In 1977 *Schwinn* was overruled in the
Sylvania case.[62] Sylvania, a TV manufacturer, imposed territorial restrictions on
its distributors who were allowed to resell only from store locations approved
by the TV manufacturer. The restrictions imposed on the retailers were less
strict than in *Schwinn*: retailers were left free to sell to any type of customer,
including discounters and other non-franchised dealers. The majority, however, indicated that it could find no distinction between the customer
restrictions in *Schwinn* and the territory restrictions in *Sylvania*. To demonstrate the economic efficiency of exclusive territories, the US Supreme Court
emphasised their desirable impacts on inter-brand competition in the long
run:

> "Vertical restrictions promote inter-brand competition by allowing the manufacturer
> to achieve certain efficiencies in the distribution of his products. These 'redeeming
> virtues' are implicit in every decision sustaining vertical restrictions under the rule of
> reason. Economists have identified a number of ways in which manufacturers can
> use such restrictions to compete more effectively against other manufacturers. For
> example, newcomers and manufacturers entering new markets can use the restric-
> tions in order to induce competent and aggressive retailers to make the kind of
> investment of capital and labour that is often required in the distribution of products
> unknown to the consumers".[63]

---

[61] *US v Arnold, Schwinn and Co*, 388 U.S. 365 (1967), paras 379–380.
[62] *Continental TV Inc v GTE Sylvania Inc*, 433 U.S. 36 (1977).
[63] *ibid.*, paras 54–55.

The Supreme Court then emphasised that "departure from the rule-of-reason standard must be based upon demonstrable economic effect rather than ... upon formalistic line drawing." After having acknowledged that exclusive territories reduce intra-brand competition, the Supreme Court advocated a rule of reason because of the possible benefits of these restrictions on inter-brand competition.[64]

6.3.2 European competition law[65]

Ever since the landmark *Grundig* case (see Box 6.1), it has been clear that the prohibition of restrictive agreements contained in Article 81(1) EC covers both horizontal and vertical agreements. The consequence of the Court's decision was that conferring absolute territorial protection upon a distributor became one of the "mortal sins",[66] for which there is no chance of an exemption under EC competition rules. In addition, the requirement that inter-state trade must be affected has been interpreted very broadly.[67] Also, agreements between undertakings located in the same Member State may thus come within the scope of the prohibition. Consequently, exemptions became necessary to clear vertical restraints which are not *de minimis*.[68] The European Commission used the block exemption procedure in order to avoid the need for individual appraisal of a multitude of agreements. Until May 31, 2000, different group exemption regulations covered exclusive distribution agreements,[69] exclusive purchasing agreements,[70] motor vehicle distribution and servicing agreements,[71] and franchising agreements.[72] In spite of the Court's case law, asking for a full consideration of the factual, legal and economic context in which the

---

[64] As decided in *Sylvania*, the rule of reason applies to all territorial restrictions, including the stricter variants of the *Schwinn* case (compare the dissenting opinion by Justice White).
[65] For a more detailed overview of European competition law on vertical restraints, see V. Korah and D. O'Sullivan, *Distribution Agreements under the EC Competition Rules* (2002); A. Jones and B. Sufrin, *EC Competition Law: Text, Cases and Materials* (2nd ed., 2005), pp.596–686.
[66] Another sin is vertical price fixing, even though the new Block Exemption has limited the strict ban on the setting of retail prices, allowing the possibility of maximum retail prices.
[67] Case 23/67 *Brasserie de Haecht v Wilkin* [1967] ECR 407. See also the discussion in Ch.10, s.10.3.2.1.
[68] Agreements of minor importance generally fall outside Art. 81(1) EC. The relevant threshold is the parties' market share; it is set at 10% in a vertical case, while being only 5% for horizontal agreements; see Notice on agreements of minor importance [2001] O.J. C 368/13.
[69] Commission Regulation (EEC) No 1983/83 of June 22, 1983 on the application of Art. 85(3) of the Treaty to categories of exclusive distribution agreements [1983] O.J. L 173/1; corrigendum [1983] O.J. L 281/24.
[70] Commission Regulation (EEC) No. 1984/83 of June 22, 1983 on the application of Art. 85(3) of the Treaty to categories of exclusive purchasing agreements [1983] O.J. L 173/5; corrigendum [1983] O.J. L 281/24.
[71] Commission Regulation (EC) No. 1475/95 of June 28, 1995 on the application of Art. 85(3) of the Treaty to certain categories of motor vehicle distribution and servicing agreements [1995] O.J. L 145/25.
[72] Commission Regulation (EEC) No. 4087/88 of November 30, 1988 on the application of Art. 85(3) of the Treaty to categories of franchise agreements [1988] O.J. L 359/46.

distribution agreement operates,[73] the European Commission opted in favour of group exemptions that were all drafted in formal legalistic terms and were often based on distinctions for which there is no economic reason. The old regulations contained both a "white list" of clauses, which could be inserted into contractual agreements without losing the benefit of the block exemption, and a "black list" of clauses that, when inserted, have the effect of bringing the agreement within the scope of the cartel prohibition. The white list had a "strait-jacketing" effect: to avoid problems of compatibility with the European competition rules firms were given an incentive not to include "grey" clauses which were not explicitly exempted. In an exercise of rationalisation and modernisation of its policy concerning vertical restraints, the European Commission adopted a new general block exemption in 1999,[74] replacing three of the previous block exemptions. From the very outset of its reform of vertical restraints, the Commission specified that the new regulation would not cover the distribution of motor vehicles.[75]

Box 6.1: The landmark Grundig case: 40 years later

Any analysis of the legality of vertical restraints under European law must still start with the landmark case *Grundig/Consten*.[76] Grundig, a German supplier, decided to enter the French market in 1957 (before the creation of the Common Market) and agreed with the French distributor Consten to supply only Consten within France with specified products. Consten agreed not to handle competing goods and not to supply the contract goods outside its territory. The same restrictions, including the export ban, applied for dealers in Germany and distributors in other states which became members of the newly established European Economic Community. Distributors in each country owned the trademark Gint, which was placed on each item, and were thus able to sue parallel importers for infringement of the mark. With the establishment of the Common Market and the entering into force of the European competition rules in 1963, price differentials across the Member States created scope for parallel imports. Parallel importers can be seen as "free riders" because they profit from the efforts of the distributor in the import country without contributing to the promotional expenses incurred by the distributor and other dealer(s). The agreements between Grundig and its distributors aimed precisely at the exclusion of this free riding. Nevertheless, the European Commission held the restrictions contrary to Article 81(1) EC (at that time Article 85(1) EC)

---

[73] Except in the case of export bans; see: Cases T–175/95 and T–176/95 *BASF Lacke + Farben Ag v Commission* [1999] ECR II–1581. In favour of a full analysis of the factual, legal and economic context, see: Case 56/65 *Société Technique Minière v Maschinenbau Ulm GmbH* [1965] ECR 235, para.249; Case 23/67 *Brasserie de Haecht SA v Wilkin* [1967] ECR 407, para.415; Case C–234/89 *Delimitis v Henninger Bräu* [1991] ECR I–935, para.984.

[74] Commission Regulation (EC) No. 2790/1999 of December 22, 1999 on the application of Art. 81(3) of the Treaty to categories of vertical agreements and concerted practices [1999] O.J. L 336/21, hereafter referred to as the "new block exemption on vertical restraints".

[75] Green Paper on vertical restraints in EC competition policy, COM(96)721—executive summary, p.ii, n.2.

[76] Case IV/3344 *Grundig-Consten* [1964] O.J. 2545. It was the first decision on an issue of competition law to reach the European Court of Justice.

without paying attention to the problem. The European Commission's decision was clearly influenced by the primary purpose of the European competition rules to prevent market segregation along national borders by private firms. The European Court of Justice confirmed the European Commission's decision.[77]

In reaching its decision, the European Commission adopted an *ex post* approach. When distributors are already active in different Member States, absolute territorial protection may hinder market penetration that seeks to take advantage of price differentials. The picture changes in an *ex ante* perspective, when the investments are not yet made and parties are still negotiating their agreements. In contrast to lawyers who tend to adopt an *ex post* approach, economists evaluate agreements from an *ex ante* perspective. The *Grundig/Consten* case could have had a rather different outcome, if an *ex ante* perspective had been used: would it have been possible for Consten to penetrate the French market without the granting of an exclusive sales territory, ensuring that the distributor would reap any harvest resulting from his investment? If lack of protection from free riding deters firms from becoming distributors, European competition rules may reach exactly the opposite effect to that intended.[78] Counterproductive results may also occur when companies decide to integrate vertically (as happened in the *Grundig/Consten* case) to realise the same efficiencies that could be achieved in a less anti-competitive way by means of vertical restrictions in distribution contracts.

Forty years later the problems created by the *Grundig/Consten* judgment have become crystal clear and the question as to whether market integration should continue to be a goal of European competition law is becoming ever more pressing. In the recent *Adalat* case,[79] the Court of Justice has shown itself to be much more critical concerning the use of competition law for the purpose of sustaining parallel trade. Also, the European Commission, in its recent Guidelines on the application of Article 81(3) EC, no longer advances market integration as a goal of competition policy, but only as an alternative method of achieving an efficient allocation of resources and enhancing consumer welfare.[80] As a consequence, it seems that after 40 years the foundations of the *Grundig/Consten* judgment have been seriously shaken.

On June 1, 2000 a general regulation on vertical restraints entered into force. In contrast with the old regulations, there is now one broad umbrella block exemption regulation that covers all vertical restraints in distribution agreements, excluding only the sale of motor cars. In the "new style" exemption the European Commission works with two parameters: the nature of the vertical

---

[77] Joined Cases 56/64 and 58/64 *Consten and Grundig v Commission* [1966] ECR 299.
[78] After the prohibition of their dual pricing system (different prices for home and export sales to take account of the additional promotional costs borne by foreign distributors), Scottish whisky manufacturers decided to withdraw their most popular brands from the UK market. See V. Korah, "Goodbye Red Label: Condemnation of Dual Pricing by Distillers" (1978) 3 E.L. Rev. 62.
[79] Case T–41/96 *Bayer AG v Commission* [2000] ECR II–3383.
[80] See for a more elaborate discussion, Ch.2, s.2.4.4.

restraint and the level of market power involved. The new regulation introduces a presumption of legality (safe harbour) to the benefit of manufacturers with a market share not exceeding 30 per cent, provided they do not include a number of blacklisted clauses in their distribution agreements. The exemption applies to restrictions of competition contained in agreements or concerted practices entered into between two or more undertakings each of which operates at a different level of the production or distribution chain, and relating to the conditions under which the parties may purchase, sell or resell certain goods or services (Article 2(1) Regulation 2790/99).[81] If the manufacturer hires his own workers, Article 81(1) EC does not apply since employees are not independent undertakings. Also, the mere appointment of an agent does not involve Article 81 EC. However, restrictions relating to the appointment of other agents and the agent's restriction to represent his principal exclusively come within the scope of Article 81(1) EC if the agent has to bear any responsibility for the financial risks connected with the performance of his obligations.[82] It is the market share of the supplier, who inserts vertical restraints into distribution agreements with its dealers, that is to be taken into account in determining whether an agreement benefits from the block exemption (Article 3(1) Regulation 2790/99). Only in the case of an exclusive supply obligation that covers the situation where there is one supplier inside the Community for the purposes of a specific use or resale is the buyer's market share relevant (Article 3(2) in combination with Article 1(c) Regulation 2790/99). It must be stressed that the block exemption does not apply to certain hardcore restraints such as minimum resale price maintenance and market partitioning by territory. These restrictions are included in the black list; they do not profit from the benefit of the group exemption and it is unlikely that they will be permitted by way of individual exemptions. The black list also mentions a number of combinations of vertical restraints: territorial sales restrictions combined with selective distribution at the same level of distribution, exclusive distribution combined with exclusive purchasing and selective distribution combined with exclusive purchasing. In addition, it should be noted that the European Commission has the power to disapply or withdraw the benefit of the group exemption, for instance where similar vertical restraints cover more than 50 per cent of the relevant market.

The market share cap, together with the list of hardcore restraints, creates a safe harbour for manufacturers whose market share does not exceed 30 per cent. As long as they make no use of blacklisted clauses they can be sure that their distribution agreements will not be declared void because of incompatibility with European competition law. Above the threshold (market share higher than 30 per cent) two situations may arise: distribution agreements may be granted an individual exemption; or a prohibition of the vertical restraints will follow if the conditions of Article 81(3) EC are not fulfilled. The

[81] For technical comments on the precise meaning of the words used in the new block exemption, see R. Whish, "Regulation 2790/99: The Commission's 'New Style' Block Exemption for Vertical Agreements" (2000) 37 C.M.L. Rev. 896.

[82] Commission Notice—Guidelines on Vertical Restraints [2000] O.J. C 291/1 (hereinafter referred to as "Guidelines on Vertical Restraints"), paras 12–20.

functioning of the block exemption is graphically depicted in Figure 6.1. The European Commission has published Guidelines discussing its policy above the thresholds and possible withdrawal of the block exemption.[83]

Figure 6.1: Block Exemption Vertical Restraints

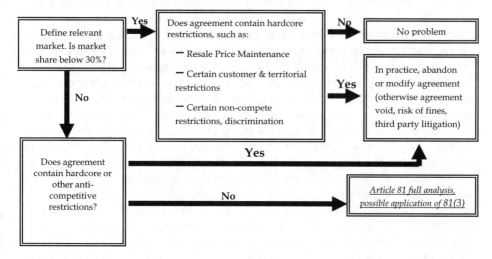

In legal literature the new regulation is seen as a considerable improvement on the "old style" system. Since the new block exemption no longer contains a white list, the strait-jacketing effect is avoided. If the regulation does not prohibit something, it is permitted.[84] In spite of the uncertainties flowing from the definition of relevant markets, the use of a market share cap is seen as in line with an "economics-based approach in order to escape from the discredited and formalistic regulations of the past".[85] A more critical view on the new regulation which takes full account of the relevant economic insights is presented in the fourth section of this chapter.

Box 6.2: The German law on vertical restraints: the better approach that could not survive?

An interesting alternative approach to the European competition rules on vertical restraints was contained in the former version of the German competition law (*Gesetz gegen Wettbewerbsbeschränkungen*, hereinafter abbreviated: GWB). In contrast with Article 81(1) EC, which covers both horizontal and vertical restraints, German competition law distinguished between horizontal restraints (Sections 1–13 old GWB on cartels and concerted practices) and vertical restraints (Sections 14–18 old GWB). Section 1 old GWB banned all horizontal restraints, but this general prohibition was

---

[83] Guidelines on Vertical Restraints [2000] O.J. C 291/1.
[84] R. Whish, "Regulation 2790/99: The Commission's 'New Style' Block Exemption for Vertical Agreements" (2000) 37 C.M.L. Rev. 896 at 898.
[85] *ibid.* at 907.

followed by a number of specific provisions (*Ausnahmetatbestände*) with respect to some types of cartels which could become effective if certain requirements were met (prior notification, failing objection by the cartel authorities, or permission). With respect to vertical restraints, German competition law made a distinction between agreements on prices and business terms (Section 14 old GWB) and agreements by which one party limits the freedom of the other party to enter into contracts with third parties (Section 16 old GWB). In agreements between enterprises on goods or commercial services no restraints could be imposed with respect to prices and business terms in reselling the goods or performing the commercial services. Price agreements were invalid *per se* and the cartel authorities were not empowered to provide exemptions. Exceptions to the ban on resale price maintenance could only flow from the competition law itself. Consequently, Section 15(1) old GWB exempted published materials (*Verlagserzeugnisse*) from the prohibition for reasons of cultural policy. Other vertical restraints (such as exclusive dealing and customer restrictions) were subject to an abuse control only. The seventh amendment of the GWB has aligned the German regime on vertical restraints with European competition law. The new GWB no longer limits the prohibition of Section 1 GWB to companies which compete with each other. Consequently, under the new German regime—as per its European counterpart—vertical restraints have to be judged according to the general cartel prohibition. The *Ausnahmetatbestände* allowing for specific exceptions have also been deleted and replaced by a general clause similar to Article 81(3) EC.

The harmonisation of the German GWB and European competition law in the field of vertical restraints may be perceived as a missed opportunity for beneficial competition of competition laws.[86] There are convincing economic reasons to distinguish between horizontal and vertical restraints. Therefore, the old GWB was more in line with an economics-based approach than European competition law. In contrast with the more interventionist EC approach, former German competition law (Section 16 old GWB) gave preference to an abuse control rather than a prohibition principle for restraints conferring exclusivity rights on firms (territorial and customer restrictions, exclusive purchasing agreements, tying clauses). An abuse principle was deemed to be sufficient to prevent significant competitive distortions. Under an abuse principle vertical restraints may be found illegal by a competition authority but with prospective effect only. According to the prohibition principle (horizontal and) vertical restrictions of competition are directly prohibited and can be invalidated with retroactive effect without the need for a previous decision of a competition authority. In order to conform with European competition law, in many EC countries (not only in Germany but also in Belgium, the Netherlands, Denmark and the United Kingdom) vertical restraints have been subjected to the prohibition principle. The "new style" EC block exemption remains different from the old German solution. Under current European

---

[86] See Ch.10.

competition law, the range of directly prohibited vertical restraints has become smaller. Since there is no longer a white list, all clauses are allowed if they are not expressly mentioned on the black list. This benefit extends to suppliers having a market share not exceeding 30 per cent. Above this threshold a full analysis of the real-world effects of vertical restraints is needed. Compared to the old regulations the "new style" EC block exemption on vertical restraints thus provides a degree of comfort to firms, and this comes closer to an abuse control. There is, however, no presumption of illegality for vertical restraints falling outside the block exemption. All in all, an abuse control seems more in line with the important economic insight that vertical restraints can be used to realise efficiencies and only pose a problem if third parties are harmed because of insufficient inter-brand competition. It must be added, however, that the economic wisdom of the old German GWB did not extend to vertical price fixing, even though it was less strict than European competition law because of the possibility of legal exceptions.

6.4 Towards a real economics-based approach

For a long time antitrust policy towards vertical restraints was dominated by technical legal distinctions rather than economic analysis.[87] Both in the US and Europe the picture is now gradually changing but the quality of decision making must still be improved substantially to coincide better with the goal of allocative efficiency. In the US the rule of reason, which allows for the taking into account of the economic effects of practices challenged under the antitrust laws, now governs all vertical restraints with one notable exception: vertical minimum price fixing. In contrast to the tolerant attitude towards other types of vertical restraints, such as territorial restrictions and customer restrictions, minimum resale price maintenance remains subject to a *per se* prohibition. In Europe, competition law in the field of vertical restraints has always been characterised by a high degree of regulatory intervention. The outcome of the recent revision (1999) has been re-regulation rather than deregulation. In its Green Paper the European Commission announced a "more economics-based approach"[88] towards vertical restraints, but immediately made an exception for absolute territorial protection and vertical minimum price fixing, which will both continue to be seen as a very serious infringement of the European competition rules with practically no chance of being exempted from the prohibition of Article 81(1) EC.

The price to be paid for this stubborn unwillingness to revise the strict prohibitions of absolute territorial protection and vertical minimum price fixing is high: it excludes the design of a legal regime for vertical restraints which is consistent with economic theory. The European Commission,

---

[87] See V. Verouden, "Vertical Agreements and Article 81 (1) EC: The Evolving Role of Economic Analysis" (2004) 71 Antitrust L.J. 525.
[88] Green Paper on vertical restraints in EC competition policy, COM(96)721.

however, argued that "economic theory cannot be the only factor in the design of policy. ... Strict economic theory must take place in the context of existing legal texts and jurisprudence".[89] As a consequence many of the criticisms directed towards the old regulations[90] will remain valid after the legal reform. Given the boundaries set by the new block exemption, the following discussion of an economically optimal legal regime for vertical restraints is necessarily *de lege ferenda*.

It must be acknowledged that the design of an optimal legal regime for vertical restraints is not an easy task because of the ambiguous effects of these restrictions. In spite of these difficulties the following lessons may be derived from the above analysis:

- First, the economic consequences of vertical restraints, and not their legal form, should be decisive in judging their conformity with the competition rules. Under current European competition law, technical legal distinctions continue to play an excessively important role. This may not only cause inefficiencies; it may also make some of the prohibitions ineffective.

- Second, different types of vertical restraints can be substitutes for each other so that there is no economic reason for distinct rules. Hence, economic analysis does not provide a justification for the different treatment of price and non-price restraints. In past decades competition lawyers have become so accustomed to the ban on vertical minimum price fixing that it has achieved the status of a legal dogma, even though there are powerful efficiency arguments for allowing minimum resale prices in individual cases.

- Third, the effect, if not the intention, of the recent legal reform is essentially to call into question the firmly established rule against granting absolute territorial protection to dealers.

- Fourth, competition law should not hinder the achievement of efficiencies through vertical agreements; only if there is a serious risk of anti-competitive consequences should antitrust authorities and judges intervene.

- Finally, European competition law should not impose a mortgage on national competition laws. The strict attitude towards vertical minimum price fixing and absolute territorial protection flows from the aim of achieving market integration, a goal which is absent in the competition laws of the Member States.

---

[89] Green Paper on vertical restraints in EC competition policy, COM(96)721, para.86.
[90] See, e.g. B. Hawk, "System Failure: Vertical Restraints and EC Competition Law" (1995) 32 C.M.L. Rev. 973; and R.J. Van den Bergh, "Modern Industrial Organisation versus Old-fashioned European Competition Law" (1996) 17 E.C.L.R. 75.

6.4.1 Technical legal distinctions

Even though economic arguments are becoming increasingly important, technical legal distinctions remain and often determine the outcome of cases. This has the unfortunate consequence that similar practices are treated differently. If the goal is to improve welfare, the economic effects of the vertical restraint and not the legal form should be decisive. From this perspective serious doubts arise with respect to: (a) the different legal status of full vertical integration and vertical restraints in long term contracts, and (b) the different treatment of agents and distributors.

6.4.1.1 Full vertical integration as an alternative

Any manufacturer considering how to distribute products in the internal market or any of its Member States has a wide range of choices. The main decision to be taken relates to the extent to which its distribution system is to be integrated with the remainder of its organisation. The greatest degree of control is given by making use of its own employees. In many cases, however, direct representation may not be the best method of ensuring effective distribution in foreign countries. The distribution outlets may be far apart, making it costly for managers to travel to them and spend time becoming familiar enough with local market conditions to be able to judge the efficiency of a particular distribution outlet. Local agents or distributors will be more familiar with local markets, languages and conditions. Agents bring principals into contractual relations with customers and receive a percentage commission for sales. Distributors purchase goods at their own risk and resell them either directly to the public or through (selected) wholesalers and dealers. As will be shown below, the choice in favour of a particular distribution method may be distorted by a different legal treatment of alternative solutions that are all similar from an economic perspective. In this and the next subsection attention will be paid to two alternatives for contracts between manufacturers and distributors: vertical integration and agency agreements.

Full vertical integration falls outside the scope of the cartel prohibition,[91] while similar restraints in long term vertical agreements receive a more critical treatment. Under the old legal regime firms had a strong incentive to integrate vertically rather than to appoint distributors. It is most relevant to note that Grundig and Consten ultimately integrated vertically (see Box 6.1). It was (and still is) not unusual for a brand owner to have a wholly owned subsidiary operating as distributor for each Member State.[92] The difference in legal status is not understandable from an economic point of view: it must not be forgotten that vertical restraints are imposed by manufacturers on distributors with the aim of approximating the outcome that would occur if the firms vertically

---

[91] Agreements within a group are free from attack as long as they aim merely at an internal distribution of tasks. See Case 22/71 *Béguelin v SAGL* [1971] ECR 949.

[92] V. Korah and M. Horspool, "Competition" (1992) 37 Antitrust Bull. 337 at pp.347–348.

integrated. In the case of full vertical integration a hierarchical structure is set up to minimise exactly the same costs vertical restraints aim to reduce.[93] Control of opportunistic behaviour by dealers is possible either by inserting clauses into long term contracts or by substituting an employer–employee dependence for the contractual relationship.

Obviously, vertical integration achieved through merger can be challenged under the Merger Regulation if the effect is to significantly impede effective competition in the common market. Therefore, in a full economics-based approach, the treatment of vertical restraints in long term contracts and vertical mergers should be the same. At present, however, there is no explicit presumption of legality of vertical mergers leading to a market share not exceeding 30 per cent.[94] In addition, there are no guidelines for assessing vertical mergers above that threshold. It must be admitted that, compared to the old regulations, the safe harbour created by the new block exemption has reduced the risk of inefficiencies. As long as the market share of the supplier or the buyer does not exceed the threshold of 30 per cent vertical integration does not bring any legal benefit if the contracts do not contain blacklisted clauses. However, parties who consider hardcore restraints essential for the viability of their commercial relationship may decide in favour of a vertical merger if the costs of vertical integration are lower than the benefits of the blacklisted vertical restraints. For this reason the trend to change the legal form of the transactions may continue. This is worrying if distribution through employees (full vertical integration) is less efficient than the appointment of independent distributors. If firms decide to integrate vertically rather than to appoint distributors efficiency losses may be substantial: distributors may be more aware of local market conditions, costs to control and monitor the employees may be high, and distributors may have better incentives to promote the products since they themselves bear the risk for the transactions. This brings one to the conclusion that the current treatment of vertical restraints not only carries the risk of inefficiencies but is also ineffective. Only where the cost of vertical integration is higher than the cost of imposing vertical restraints does a ban on particular vertical restraints such as minimum resale price maintenance effectively end such practices.[95]

---

[93] This basic insight is derived from R.H. Coase's seminal work; see R.H. Coase, "The Nature of the Firm" (1937) 4 *Economica* 386. Coase's ideas have been further elaborated upon in: O.E. Williamson, *Markets and Hierarchies: Analysis and Antitrust Implications* (1975).

[94] A Communication of the European Commission mentions a factual *de minimis* rule benefiting vertical mergers achieving a market share of not more than 25% ([2000] O.J. C 217/32). This market share is lower than the one used in the new Block Exemption on vertical restraints. It should be added, however, that a Communication does not have the binding character of a Regulation.

[95] D.W. Carlton and J.M. Perloff, *Modern Industrial Organization* (4th ed., 2005), pp.430–431.

6.4.1.2 Distributors or agents?

Agency agreements fall outside the scope of the cartel prohibition contained in Article 81(1) EC if the agents[96] bear no, or only insignificant, financial and commercial risks. In the opposite situation agents will be treated as independent dealers who must remain free in determining their marketing strategy. The European Commission considers that Article 81(1) EC will generally not be applicable when property in the contract goods bought or sold does not vest in the agent and the latter does not incur commercial risks or costs.[97] Hence, under European competition law principals may control agents' behaviour (Article 81 EC does not apply) but limitations on a distributor's freedom are carefully scrutinised.

This distinction based on the transfer of the property title is remarkably close to the old-fashioned US *Schwinn* rule.[98] According to the principle of alienation, which was the basis for the *Schwinn* decision of the US Supreme Court, an individual who relinquished possession of goods does not retain any rights whatsoever over the goods.[99] The Supreme Court ruled that vertical restraints are illegitimate *per se*, because they violate the retailer's freedom by subjecting him to the manufacturer like an employee. The manufacturer cannot exercise any power over the resale of goods that have left the sphere of his ownership. Before the 1977 *Sylvania* judgment of the US Supreme Court,[1] which introduced an effects-based analysis, vertical restrictions imposed on independent dealers were seen as illegal *per se*, whereas restrictions in agency agreements were judged under the rule of reason. Under current US antitrust law, the distinction between distributors and agents is no longer relevant for the assessment of customer and territorial restrictions. The European regulator missed the opportunity to get rid of this old-fashioned peculiarity. In short, similar conclusions as in the case of vertical integration emerge: the current rules are both inefficient and ineffective. Agency agreements rather than distributorships may be used to circumvent the burdensome provisions of the block exemption. Distorted business decisions will follow if a legal form is chosen because of the more lenient treatment of a less efficient alternative.[2] Moreover, changes of the legal form mainly benefit specialised competition lawyers and significantly add to the indirect costs of the cartel prohibition.

---

[96] In legal literature the term agent has a meaning that is different from the one used in economic analysis. The economic concept is much broader than the legal concept: it covers all sales persons performing tasks for a manufacturer. Legally, only sales agents not bearing financial and commercial risks can be qualified as agents.

[97] Guidelines on Vertical Restraints, [2000] O.J. C 291/1, para.15.

[98] *US v Arnold, Schwinn & Co*, 388 U.S. 365 (1967).

[99] If possession and ownership are not equated, the latter may be understood as a bundle of property rights. This bundle can be split up and only some of the rights can be exchanged with the physical transfer of the product into the hands of a downstream agent.

[1] *Continental TV Inc v GTE Sylvania Inc*, 433 U.S. 36 (1977).

[2] The latter distribution structure causes efficiency losses if independent distributors are more aware of local market conditions, the costs to control and monitor the employees are high, and distributors have better incentives to promote the products since they bear themselves the risk of the transactions.

6.4.2 Different legal treatment of price and non-price restraints

It is striking to contrast the difference in the attitudes towards price and non-price restraints with the findings of economic analysis. Both types of restraints (price restrictions and non-price restrictions) appear to have both positive and negative impacts on economic efficiency, depending on the context and their purposes. Great parts of the economic analysis apply, word for word, to both types of restraints. As far as price restraints are used to protect dealers from free riding, there is no economic reason to distinguish minimum resale price maintenance from other types of vertical restraints. Hence, the absolute ban in European competition law cannot be reconciled with the tolerant attitude towards selective distribution and franchising.

One of the most important lessons for antitrust policy that can be drawn from the economic analysis is that the nature of the restraint on its own does not allow us to predict whether it will always have good or bad effects on economic efficiency and welfare. Consequently, there is no sound economic reason for a different treatment of price restraints. A part of this economic wisdom was absorbed slightly earlier in US antitrust law. Since the 1977 *State Oil v Khan* judgment, the rule of reason has applied with respect to vertical maximum price fixing. Since June 2001 European competition rules also distinguish between the legal assessment of minimum resale prices and that of maximum resale prices. Maximum resale price maintenance may be efficiency enhancing since it is a device to fight against problems of double marginalisation arising under conditions of successive monopoly. Since the elimination of double monopoly mark-ups benefits consumers as well as firms, the antitrust prohibition should not be applied to price ceilings used to fight double marginalisation problems. The double monopoly mark-up is particularly relevant in exclusive distribution agreements. Distributors who have been granted an exclusive territory will enjoy market power which may enable them to increase prices above competitive levels.

Political reasons may explain why efficiency arguments relating to minimum prices fixed by manufacturers are not easily accepted. It follows from the economic literature that resale price maintenance in the form of price floors is desirable if the risk of free riding is important and inter-brand competition is strong. Hence, rather than prohibiting minimum resale price maintenance *per se*, a real economics-based approach should pay attention to the motives underlying vertical price fixing and the existence of market power at one or both stages of the industry. If no market power limiting inter-brand competition exists, the issues of vertical price restraints are unlikely to be of much importance. Nevertheless, policy makers may be reluctant to accept arguments justifying minimum resale price maintenance, since the practice seems to have a direct negative effect on retail prices. Also, other vertical restraints (selective distribution, franchising) may increase price levels, but that effect is indirect and its precise intensity may remain hidden to consumers. Both in the USA and in Europe, associations of small retailers supporting minimum resale price maintenance have lost political momentum to the benefit of the consumer movement. This may explain why minimum prices remain politically unpopular. Additionally, in the European context, setting of minimum prices at the retail level can be used as an instrument to achieve market partitioning along national borders. In such circumstances the market integration goal will again take precedence over efficiency considerations.

6.4.3 The ban on absolute territorial protection and other inconsistencies

Economic analysis makes it clear that different types of vertical restraints serve the same goal and may therefore be used as substitutes for each other. On the positive side, the allocation of exclusive territories, the limitation of the number of dealers and minimum resale price maintenance all deal with the free riding problem.[3] These restraints are designed so that dealers may reap the benefits from their sales efforts. The effect of the limitation of the number of dealers is similar to that of absolute territorial protection. Price competition is limited and more of the gain from sales efforts accrues to the dealer who makes the efforts. The effect of minimum vertical price fixing is equally similar. On the negative side all vertical restraints may generate anti-competitive effects. There is no economic reason to distinguish between different types of vertical restraints; such a differentiation inevitably causes inconsistencies.

Compared to the previous legal regime, the new rules that entered into force on June 1, 2000 contain a substantial number of improvements. The old block exemptions were form-based instead of effects-based and as a result were extremely legalistic. For example, restraints considered legal in a franchised network were outlawed when inserted into an exclusive (or selective) distribution agreement.[4] As a general rule limitation of the number of dealers was not allowed in a selective distribution network for which there was, by the

---

[3] Another example is the problem of double marginalisation (see s.6.2.2.2), which can be eliminated both by vertical price fixing and the imposition of minimum quantities, which is equivalent to a price ceiling.

[4] A nice example of the old double-thinking is the treatment of distribution networks for cosmetics and perfumes. Compare joined Cases IV/31.428–IV/31.432 *Yves Rocher* [1987] O.J. L 8/49 on franchising; and Case IV/33.242 *Yves Saint Laurent* [1992] O.J. L 12/24, as well as Case IV/33.542 *Givenchy* [1992] O.J. L 236/11, on selective distribution. On the one hand, in the decision concerning the franchised network of Yves Rocher (a popular brand for cosmetics), the European Commission argued that making the opening of a new Yves Rocher Centre dependent on the results of a market study is not to be considered as a limitation of competition, because the choice of a bad location would lead to commercial failure and could damage the reputation of the franchised network. On the other hand, in decisions concerning selective distribution of rival cosmetics (*Yves Saint Laurent* and *Givenchy*), a limitation of the number of retail outlets in function of the economic potential of the geographic area was not allowed. Conversely, the European Commission accepted substantial minimum supply figures because an unlimited recognition of dealers who are not able to buy minimum quantities (not exceeding 40% of the average turnover of all retail shops in a Member State) would destabilise the selective distribution system. The acceptance of minimum purchasing quantities comes very close to the degree of territorial protection granted to franchisees. Except from increasing income for competition lawyers, these distinctions brought no benefits.

way, no group exemption. Systems of selective distribution were cleared only if the selection criteria were related to quality and did not impose a quantitative restriction on dealer outlets. The prohibition of quantitative restrictions on the number of dealers in selective distribution systems could be circumvented by increasing the quality requirements for admission. In contrast with the strict attitude towards selective distribution, a limited territorial protection for franchisees by means of location clauses was deemed necessary to protect the investments to be made.[5] Under the new block exemption, exclusive distribution, selective distribution (with the exception of motor vehicle distribution agreements) and franchising are all covered by the same regulation. Since each of these distribution systems causes similar concerns about their impact on competition and, at the same time, shares a potential to generate efficiency improvements, there is indeed no reason for a separate legal treatment. If legal categories are the legislator's crucial concern, parties will be given an incentive to change the legal form of the transaction in order to escape from antitrust liability. The increased popularity of franchising compared to exclusive or selective distribution might also be attributed to the earlier more favourable antitrust treatment of the former distribution formula. It is to be welcomed that the many economically irrelevant distinctions are no longer part of the list of inconsistencies in European competition law. It would be premature, however, to characterise the new rules as a complete victory for economics and effects-based law making.

The most remarkable remaining inconsistency of the new block exemption is the prohibition of absolute territorial protection. Together with minimum resale price maintenance such arrangements are put on the black list with practically no chance of being exempted from Article 81(1) EC. In a passage of the Guidelines, the European Commission states that it is not required to assess the actual effects on the market of the hardcore restrictions.[6] This amounts to a formulation of prohibitions *per se*, and this is not conducive to economic analysis. As shown above, it is easy to see how the distributor's incentives to make investments for the promotion of the manufacturer's products would be undermined if distributors in other Member States where the brand has already been introduced could free ride on those investments. To avoid free riding distributors active in other markets should then be restrained from selling in the new market.

The European Commission is aware of the problem,[7] but remains reluctant to accept its consequences to their full extent. On the positive side, a manufacturer may appoint an exclusive distributor in certain territories provided that "passive sales" to such territories are permitted.[8] This means that distributors must be free to sell and deliver goods in response to unsolicited requests from individual consumers, including, generally, over the internet. In addition, the Guidelines on vertical restraints do not consider it anti-

---

[5] See the earlier criticisms in: R.J. Van den Bergh, "Modern Industrial Organisation versus Old-fashioned European Competition Law" (1996) 17 E.C.L.R. 75.
[6] Guidelines on Vertical Restraints, para.7.
[7] *ibid.*, para.116, 2.
[8] Art. 4(b) of Regulation 2790/1999.

competitive if, in the case of entering a new geographic market, restrictions on active and passive sales to intermediaries in the new market are imposed on the direct buyers of the supplier located in other markets for a period of two years.[9] On the negative side, an absolute territorial protection excluding equally active and passive sales to consumers without time limitation cannot be organised. Given the growth of internet trading and website marketing, direct orders by consumers may gain in importance. If the protection from free riding is not watertight, distributors may be dissuaded from launching products in new geographic markets. In addition, free riding is not necessarily a temporary problem; temporary territorial protection is thus no guarantee that distribution efficiencies will be preserved. It is to be deplored that the existence of a trade-off between market integration and competition is not explicitly acknowledged. At best, the current Guidelines may be seen as an unspoken compromise between the conflicting objectives of market integration and the desirability of efficiency enhancing vertical restraints.

6.4.4 The unavoidable trade-off: efficiency savings versus anti-competitive effects[10]

Current mainstream industrial organisation accepts the analysis of the first part of this chapter showing that vertical restraints have both desirable and undesirable effects. This inevitably leads to a trade-off balancing the efficiency gains against the anti-competitive effects. Competition lawyers recognise this trade-off only to a limited extent. In line with US case law, courts and policy makers sometimes phrase the evaluation of a vertical restraint in terms of the promotion of inter-brand competition versus the restriction of intra-brand competition. However, this is not the relevant balancing act. Benefits in terms of efficiency savings must be weighed against costs in terms of restrictions of competition. Even in the absence of inter-brand competition, sales efforts can stimulate trade and benefit consumers. From an economic perspective an "efficiency defence" must therefore also be available for firms enjoying market power. The block exemption is without prejudice to the application of Article 82 EC;[11] individual exemption for practices considered to be an abuse of dominant position is not possible.

It has been stressed in the second chapter of this book that Article 81 EC does not allow the phrasing of the goal of competition law solely in terms of maximising the sum of consumer and producer surplus. Consumer surplus is given particular importance: according to the wording of Article 81(3) EC, consumers must receive a fair share of the efficiency savings. This does not imply that traditional economic analysis becomes irrelevant; it merely requires the broadening of the scope of the analysis by paying particular attention to

---

[9] Guidelines on Vertical Restraints, para.119, 10.
[10] This paragraph draws on P.W. Dobson and M. Waterson, *Vertical Restraints and Competition Policy* (1996).
[11] Regulation 2790/1999, recital 16.

the effects of vertical restraints for consumers. Obviously, close antitrust scrutiny of vertical restraints is needed only if inter-brand competition is restricted, so that the anti-competitive effects of vertical restraints are potentially serious. Therefore, the first key question for consideration in an investigation of vertical restraints is whether there is significant horizontal market power at the manufacturers' or retailers' level, or both.

The block exemption applies when the market share of the supplier does not exceed 30 per cent. The European Commission has chosen this market share cap both for reasons of legal certainty and to bring the legal treatment of vertical restraints more in line with the economic approach. It is doubtful whether these goals have been reached. In the absence of horizontal market power it is unlikely that the issues of vertical restraints are important. Unfortunately, as shown in Chapter 4 of this book, market shares are not a completely reliable indicator of market power. A major problem is that relevant markets may be ill-defined, and this will lead to biased conclusions. This raises the question whether there is other relevant evidence for market power. In this respect Dobson and Waterson advance the following factors: substantial mark-ups at either or both stages of the industry by comparison with products having similar characteristics, high profits, stable and substantial market shares, and high and stable concentration.[12] The latter view is consistent with definitions of market power in textbooks on industrial organisation (Lerner index) and stresses that a dynamic analysis of evolution of market shares is usually more relevant than a static approach. By limiting the evaluation solely to market share and ignoring other highly probative evidence, accurate outcomes cannot be guaranteed. Limiting the analysis to the supplier's market share exacerbates the difficulties. Vertical restraints involve the analysis of many markets. Distributors may buy intermediate or final goods: whereas in the former case it may be sufficient to analyse the market where manufacturers and distributors meet, in the latter case it will usually be necessary to analyse also the competitive effects on the downstream market (where consumers buy). In addition, the proper relevant market depends on the type of anti-competitive allegation that is considered. A decision that a firm has a low market share might be relevant to restraints that could permit prices to rise. However, it would not be relevant to restraints that would raise entry barriers and prevent post-entry prices from falling.[13] In short, an analysis of the effects on all relevant markets at each level of trade affected by the restraints is excluded for reasons of "legal certainty" and reserved for individual exemptions above the 30 per cent threshold. Obviously, legal certainty comes at the expense of accuracy, if at all.

If no market power may be established the investigation of the real-world effects of vertical restraints can already stop here. In the opposite case the next key issue relates to the seriousness of the competitive distortions to the consumer. To give consumer welfare the particular attention it deserves within

[12] P.W. Dobson and M. Waterson, *Vertical Restraints and Competition Policy* (1996), p.58.
[13] S. Salop, "Analysis of Foreclosure in the EC Guidelines on Vertical Restraints", in Fordham Corp. L. Inst. 2000, 177 (B. Hawk ed. 2001).

the legal framework of Article 81 EC, the question must then be asked whether the reduction in intra-brand or inter-brand competition harms consumers. If consumers can easily switch to other products and/or retailers, vertical restraints are less likely to be harmful. By contrast, moderate or low cross-elasticities of demand indicate that the anti-competitive effects may be important to consumers. If market power at one or both stages of the industry can be established and if the resulting competitive distortions are likely to harm consumers, there is a *prima facie* case against the vertical arrangements in the market under investigation. Prohibition of the vertical restraints may then be avoided only by proving substantial efficiency savings which outweigh the anti-competitive effects. If there are significant indications of efficiency gains associated with restricting the number of dealers, there may be an efficiency justification for exclusive or selective distribution. If efficiency gains flow from a restriction of the dealer's product range, there may be a justification for exclusive purchasing agreements. Minimum resale price maintenance may equally be justified if the gains to marginal consumers, who benefit from improved service, exceed the losses of infra-marginal consumers who are willing to pay high prices surpassing the value of the services offered (see section 6.2.2.1 of this chapter). An important issue in arguing efficiencies relates to substantial search costs which consumers might face to allow an informed purchase. The strongest case for efficiency gains is when retailers provide an input into the perceived quality of the goods and/or important reliable information which the consumers, in the absence of the vertical restraints, would miss. Box 6.3[14] illustrates that the strength of the efficiency argument depends on the type of product and the nature of the distribution system.

Box 6.3: The strength of the efficiency argument for vertical restraints		
Product/ Distribution Nature	**Strongest Case**	**Weakest Case**
Product complexity	Highly complex or technical	Simply or non-technical
Costs for consumer	Expensive—large part of budget	Inexpensive
Consumer buying habits	One-off purchases	Repeat purchases
Shopping format	Non-convenience outlet	Convenience outlet
Consumers' product information	Limited knowledge	Details/features widely known
Price/quality comparability	Experience or credence goods	Search goods
Perceived product differentiation	Unclear—weak branding	Clear—strong branding

[14] Source: P.W. Dobson and M. Waterson, *Vertical Restraints and Competition Policy* (1996).

Position in product life cycle	New	Established or mature
Entry barriers in retailing	Low	High
Economies of scope in retailing	Insignificant	Substantial

Against the economic background sketched above, the new block exemption and the related guidelines can be evaluated as follows. The market share cap of 30 per cent may be judged too static an approach for allowing a full-scale welfare analysis of dynamic distribution markets. In addition, criteria for judging both the effects on efficiency and the possible anti-competitive consequences are still either too legalistic or insufficiently accurate. In short, the trade-off between the goals of legal certainty and limiting the number of ill-conceived decisions does not seem appropriate from an economist's perspective.

6.4.5 Market integration as a goal in itself

The objective of market integration, which is crucial under European competition law, may explain the harsh treatment of minimum retail prices and absolute territorial restrictions. On the one hand, all (combinations of) vertical restraints making inter-state trade either by final customers or by distributors more difficult, if not impossible, are negative from a market integration perspective. On the other hand, these vertical restraints may generate efficiencies in the organisation of distribution networks within the internal market. This trade-off is not explicitly recognised; market integration tends to be pursued as a goal in itself. Two remarks are appropriate.

First, the number of conflicts between the goal of market integration and the aim of curing principal–agent problems and lowering transaction costs will be lower than expected if an *ex ante* perspective is used, rather than an *ex post* appraisal. If distributors are already active in various Member States, consumers will profit if they can shop around and buy the products in the Member State where prices are lowest. Prohibiting parallel imports then seems to interfere with market integration, causing substantial losses for consumers. The picture changes, however, if an *ex ante* perspective is adopted. In order to persuade a local distributor to make investments to establish a brand in a new geographic market, it may be necessary to provide territorial protection to the distributor so that those investments can be recouped by charging a higher price. Unfortunately, in the classic *Grundig* case the European Commission adopted an *ex post* approach. Under an *ex ante* approach different questions would have arisen (see Box 6.1). If lack of protection from free riding deters firms from becoming distributors in some of the Member States, European competition rules may have exactly the opposite effect of that for which they were enacted. These adverse effects may be overcome by taking account of economic insights. If no protection from free riding is possible, future distributors may decide not to start up distribution systems in the first place. If distributors are deterred from conquering new markets, the legal regime for vertical restraints may harm, rather than further, market integration. Economic analysis also warns against such perverse effects.

Second, European competition rules should not affect the contents of national competition laws, since the goal of market integration is absent in the Member States. In the past economically sound rules, such as the old German rule (which remained valid until 1973) to permit vertical price fixing as long as there is inter-brand competition, were changed because of the need to conform to European competition law. Since parallel importers could not be forced to respect prices imposed by German manufacturers the system could not be kept watertight.[15] Recently, the distinction between horizontal and vertical restrictions was eliminated from the German competition law (see Box 6.2) in order to align the legal regime of vertical restraints closely to the European competition rules. Unfortunately, many Member States decided to copy the European competition rules for reasons of legal certainty. By analogy with European competition law, only contractual terms, which are exempted by an EC block exemption, are equally valid under national competition law. The peculiarities of the situation in the Member States do not call for such an approach, for the central aim of European competition law, namely market integration, is absent from the national statutes.

The competition laws of the Member States should be interpreted on the basis of an economic analysis which is free of all the dogmas and precedents of European law. National legislators are better placed to elaborate economically justified and legally consistent rules for contract terms that do not fall within the scope of Article 81 EC.[16] The aim of market integration, which is the cause of the conspicuous inconsistencies in the treatment of vertical restraints at European level, should not also afflict national law. What was there to prevent the national legislators from affording equal treatment both to complete vertical integration and to integration by means of clauses in long term contracts, such as territorial restraints, customer restraints (selective distribution, franchising) and even vertical minimum price fixing? In so far as these restraints provide gains in efficiency and do not cause any significant restrictions on competition—and this will be the case in the markets for most products and services, given that there is a sufficient degree of inter-brand competition—there is no antitrust problem and detailed legal rules are superfluous. In such circumstances competition law only entails administrative costs without any compensatory welfare advantage. For the limited number of cases where inter-brand competition is substantially restricted, an abuse control (as contained in the former version of the German competition law, see Box 6.2) seems to be

---

[15] Under old German competition law the legality of resale price maintenance was subjected to the requirement of *Lückenlosigkeit*.
[16] If Art. 81 EC applies, there is no scope for divergent national competition rules because of the supremacy of European law.

more appropriate than a prohibition tempered by a complex set of exceptions. It is a mistake to incorporate European competition rules without first analysing their relevance to domestic competition concerns.[17] Only political reasons may explain the massive adoption of the inefficiencies and inconsistencies of the European competition rules on vertical restraints in the Member States. Several pressure groups that have a clear interest in the adoption of those rules have been active: large firms and specialised competition lawyers urged for this solution emphasising the need for legal certainty. In contrast with small and medium-sized enterprises which might profit from certain prohibited restrictions, the former have an interest in harmonised laws, since it lowers the costs of inter-state trade. The latter also obviously profit: the value of human capital built up at a period when national competition laws were non-existent (or hardly implemented) increases substantially when national competition laws are a copy of the European rules.

Box 6.4: The Block Exemption Regulation on Car Distribution and Servicing Agreements

Car manufacturers distribute their cars and provide after sales services through networks of authorised dealers. In the past, several group exemptions were enacted which, under certain conditions, legalised some of the vertical restrictions of competition contained in the dealership agreements.[18] These group exemptions were justified by the specific nature of a car (expensive, durable, complex and movable consumer good with a relatively long lifespan, requiring an efficient level of pre- and after-sales services) and the need to provide legal certainty to the contract parties. However, the old rules were criticised for not achieving the objective of guaranteeing consumers the possibility of profiting from the benefits of market integration. The new Regulation 1400/2002[19] has changed the previously existing white list of exempted restrictions. Particularly, the combination of selective and exclusive distribution within the same market was identified as the major factor for persisting price differences across the Member States. Henceforth, manufacturers must choose between two distribution systems: (a) exclusive distribution, whereby the dealer is granted an exclusive sales territory, or (b) selective distribution based on qualitative or quantitative criteria (without territorial protection). In the case of exclusive distribution the agreement is exempted if the manufacturer's

---

[17] For a critical analysis of the White Paper and other suggested reforms in the United Kingdom, see P. Freeman and R. Whish, *Butterworths Competition Law* (2001), Div. I, paras 810–864.
[18] Commission Regulation (EEC) No.123/85 of December 12, 1984 on the application of Art. 85(3) of the Treaty to certain categories of motor vehicle distribution and servicing agreements, [1985] O.J. L 15/16; Commission Regulation (EC) No.1475/95 of June 28, 1995 on the application of Article 85(3) of the Treaty to certain categories of motor vehicle distribution and servicing agreements, [1995] O.J. L 145/25.
[19] Commission Regulation (EC) No.1400/2002 of July 31, 2002 on the application of Art. 81(3) of the Treaty to categories of vertical agreements and concerted practices in the motor vehicle sector, [2002] O.J. L 203/30.

market share does not exceed 30 per cent of the relevant market. It is further required that unauthorised dealers are free to buy and resell the contract goods. In the case of quantitative selective distribution, the Regulation provides a safe harbour if the market share of the car manufacturer does not exceed 40 per cent. By contrast, systems of selective distribution based upon qualitative criteria profit from the exemption irrespective of the market share of the manufacturer. (The European Commission is of the opinion that the latter agreements normally do not have anti-competitive effects.) In both cases of selective distribution, territorial protection from sales by other authorised dealers cannot be granted, so that active or passive sales to end users cannot be restricted. Moreover, from October 1, 2005, the distributors have had to be able to establish additional sales outlets at other locations within the common market where selective distribution is applied (prohibition of location clauses).

An important objective of the new Regulation is to increase the economic freedom and commercial autonomy of the dealer. This goal is pursued in two ways: through allowing the sale of different brands of cars by the same dealer (multi-branding), and by the duty to insert in the contract a set of clauses protecting the dealer from manipulation by the manufacturer, who is supposed to be the stronger contract party. The list of required clauses includes the right to cede the contract, the duty to give notice of termination in writing, a minimum duration of the agreement for five years or an indefinite period (with a period of notice of two years, reduced to one year if appropriate compensation is paid or the network is reorganised) and the right to refer disputes to an independent arbitrator. Another major change is that the new block exemption does not allow tying of sales and after-sales services. The distributor must be left free to subcontract the provision of repair and maintenance services to authorised repairers. Finally, minimum prices and fixed prices remain on the list of the hardcore restrictions and are consequently blacklisted.

Regulation 1400/2002 seems to be the last bastion of the "old regime" governing vertical restraints. Even though a move was made in the direction of a so-called economic approach (limiting the scope of the prohibitions to cases where the car manufacturer has a substantial market share),[20] the legalistic style of the block exemption and its imminent strait-jacketing effects are striking. Profiting from the discussion in Chapter 2 on the goals of competition law, it becomes immediately clear that market integration and protection of individual business freedom have been the major objectives of the new Regulation. The goal of market integration has inspired rules protecting intra-brand competition and furthering parallel trade. From an efficiency perspective, there are powerful arguments to prohibit multi-branding and to allow location clauses. Both devices may be appropriate remedies to combat free riding and cure principal–agent problems in

---

[20] On the limitations of a market share-based analysis, see Ch.4, s.4.2.

distribution agreements. The complete prohibition of non-competition clauses[21] may also have a counterproductive impact on inter-brand competition by making it impossible for newcomers to use exclusive dealing arrangements to penetrate the market and by impeding the development of potentially more efficient distribution channels. The rules aiming at protecting the commercial freedom of the weak contract parties (car dealers) recall German ordoliberal thinking. The block exemption contains a set of requirements that restrict the contractual freedom even where inter-brand competition is sufficiently working. In sum, Regulation 1400/2002 is not really economics based but largely inspired by the political goal of market integration and concerns about the commercial independence of car dealers.

6.5 Conclusions

In the economic literature, different reasons have been advanced for explaining why firms make use of vertical restraints in distribution contracts, such as price-fixing, location clauses or customer clauses. On the one hand, there are efficiency explanations which analyse the relation between manufacturers and dealers as principal–agent problems. On the other hand, there are theories arguing that vertical restraints may be used to support collusion, create entry barriers and restrict inter-brand competition. Given these divergent theories, the explanation of vertical restraints remains ultimately an empirical issue. An efficient competition law regime should allow manufacturers and dealers to reap the efficiency benefits of vertical restraints as long as these exceed the costs of reduced competition. In markets with sufficient inter-brand competition, legal prohibitions will cause substantial administrative costs without compensating benefits.

The efficiency explanations for vertical restraints include both price restraints and non-price restraints. A large part of the economic literature discusses vertical restraints as instruments to solve coordination problems in vertical structures. Maximum prices prevent a double monopoly mark-up in cases of successive monopolies and thus increase the output of the distributor to the benefit of both the manufacturer, who will sell more products, and the consumers who will pay lower prices. Minimum prices may achieve efficiency savings in three different ways. First, they may prevent free riding among distributors in cases where pre-sales services are important. Second, they may guarantee that contractual obligations will be respected if after sales services are important. Third, vertical minimum price fixing may improve risk distribution if distributors are more risk averse than manufacturers. Fourth, minimum prices may assure a sufficient number and optimal density of sales outlets. In contrast with maximum prices, minimum prices are not unequivocally desirable from a global welfare perspective. If the gains of the marginal

---

[21] Compare Regulation 2790/1999 which prohibits non-competition clauses only if they have an unlimited duration or exceed five years.

consumers, who value the pre-sales services, are lower than the losses of infra-marginal consumers, who prefer lower prices to increased service, the overall effect on consumer surplus will be negative.

Also with respect to non-price restraints, several efficiency explanations have been advanced. Exclusive distribution (territorial protection) prevents free riding among distributors active in different geographic areas. In turn, exclusive purchasing prevents a free ride on the advertising or training expenditures of a manufacturer by a rival supplier. Also, the transaction costs approach may rationalise vertical non-price restraints. If relation-specific investments were made, some degree of exclusivity will be necessary to pro-tect the dealers from opportunistic behaviour (hold-up) by the manufacturer.

The efficiency explanations of vertical restraints are challenged by an alternative view which stresses their anti-competitive potential. It is argued that vertical restraints may facilitate collusion between producers or dealers. Vertical restraints may also restrict inter-brand competition by increasing higher search costs for consumers and causing price rigidity. Finally, vertical restraints may create entry barriers, in particular in cases of exclusive pur-chasing agreements and franchised networks. Empirical research has shown that the efficiency explanation is more relevant than the alternative view that vertical restraints cause anti-competitive harm. Therefore, competi-tion authorities should be careful not to prohibit vertical restraints if anti-competitive effects cannot be convincingly shown.

In the past, the legality of vertical restraints had to be judged on the basis of several group exemptions covering different types of vertical restraints and the case law of the European Court of Justice on selective distribution. The old regime was heavily based on technical legal distinctions (form of the agree-ments), the exemptions had a strait-jacketing effect and the law contained a number of inconsistencies (such as the contrasting favourable treatment of franchising and ban on quantitative selective distribution). The new Regula-tion 2790/1999 has been presented as an economics-based approach, which is effects-based rather than form-based. It provides a safe harbour for manu-facturers wishing to impose vertical restraints provided their market share does not exceed 30 per cent. To profit from the group exemption, manu-facturers should not use blacklisted clauses, such as minimum vertical price fixing and clauses guaranteeing an absolute territorial protection. If the market share of the manufacturer exceeds 30 per cent, a full economic analysis under Article 81(3) EC is required.

An evaluation of the new block exemption shows that there is no complete harmony between economic theory and competition law. First, legal distinc-tions remain a hindrance for a full integration of economic insights. Full vertical integration (through a merger) is an alternative for long term contracts containing vertical restraints, but not subject to the same legal treatment. Also, the preservation of the distinction between an agent and a distributor is form-based and not effects-based. Second, the strict prohibitions of minimum prices and absolute territorial protection are equally inconsistent with economic theory. Different forms of vertical restraints are mutually interchangeable, so that legal prohibitions create a substituting effect. If minimum prices are outlawed, other devices will be used to cope with free riding: limitations of the number of dealers, exclusive territories, contractual obligations to provide services, refusals to deal, subsidising dealers' efforts or marketing by manufacturers. There is no economically sound reason for a different treatment of these interchangeable devices. Competition problems arise only when there is insufficient inter-brand competition in the affected markets. From a competition policy perspective, the crucial question is whether vertical restraints cause (substantial) restrictions of competition that are not made good by efficiency savings. Under current European law, the seriousness of the restrictions is judged by looking at the market share of the manufacturer. Apart from the difficulties in defining the relevant markets (and the ensuing unreliability of market share analysis), the problem remains that distortions of competition are possible also at the distribution stage. A real economics-based approach would ask for a complete analysis of the efficiency savings and require a balancing of these benefits against the restrictions of competition. The current legal regime on vertical restraints is not sufficiently hospitable to such an economic assessment.

Chapter 7

....

EXCLUSIONARY BEHAVIOUR OF
DOMINANT FIRMS

7.1 Introduction

This chapter discusses some types of behaviour often considered to be anti-competitive when practised by firms enjoying substantial market power (dominance). The topics covered are price discrimination (in particular the granting of rebates), tying and bundling, refusals to deal (of which refusing access to essential facilities is a subcategory) and predatory pricing. These modes of conduct may be considered exclusionary practices.[1] The main focus

---

[1] Price discrimination may also harm some (sub)groups of customers and can, therefore, equally be considered an exploitative practice. Other exclusionary practices indirectly harm consumers by excluding competition in the long run.

will be on Article 82 EC, which prohibits abuses by dominant firms, but comparisons with its US counterparts, Section 2 of the Sherman Act and the provisions of the Robinson–Patman Act on price discrimination, will be included to allow for a more profound comparative economic analysis of the European competition rules on abuse of dominance.

From the economic theory of monopoly one could deduce that exploitative practices, most prominently charging too high prices, would be the major concern of the prohibition of abuses by dominant firms. Article 82 EC does indeed mention "directly or indirectly imposing unfair purchase or selling prices or unfair trading conditions" as the first example of abuse (Article 82(a) EC). This formulation, which clearly expresses fairness as a policy consideration, stands in marked contrast with Section 2 of the Sherman Act, which focuses on monopolising conduct and thus more easily enables an economics-oriented welfare analysis. In practice, however, it is unclear under European competition law on the basis of which criteria it should be assessed whether a price is "fair". As a measurement technique for market power the Lerner index[2] does not provide any direct guidance. Data to calculate marginal costs are not easily available and, even if they were, it would still be unclear where the border line between fair and unfair deviations of marginal costs must be drawn. European competition authorities have been using comparisons with some measure of costs, prices charged by competitors or prices in other markets to challenge excessive prices under the abuse of dominance provision. These attempts may remain largely unsuccessful due to information problems[3] and difficulties of finding comparable markets where prices are not above competitive levels. The problem of assessing abusively high prices is further discussed in Box 7.1. The main text of this chapter will deal solely with the four types of exclusionary behaviour mentioned here.

The European Court of Justice has stated that an abuse is

"...an objective concept relating to the behaviour of an undertaking in a dominant position which is such as to influence the structure of a market where, as a result of the very presence of the undertaking, the degree of competition is weakened and which, through recourse to methods different from those which condition normal competition in products or services on the basis of the transactions of commercial operators, has the effect of hindering the maintenance of the degree of competition still existing in the market or the growth of that competition".[4]

Apart from introducing the vague and slippery concept of "normal competition",[5] this definition also provides the basis for condemning so-called

---

[2] See Ch.4, s.4.2.1.1.

[3] Price–cost comparisons are also very costly to undertake. For this reason both firms and competition authorities may abstain from such exercises.

[4] Case 85/76 *Hoffmann-La Roche v Commission (Vitamins)* [1979] ECR 461, para.6.

[5] Kallaugher and Sher remark that the ensuing confusion about what is "normal" or "abnormal" competition has been caused by a translation error. It is clear from the German and the French versions that the Court of Justice adopted the German concept of *Leistungswettbewerb* (competition on the basis of performance). See J. Kallaugher and B. Sher, "Rebates Revisited: Anti-Competitive Effects and Exclusionary Abuse under Article 82" (2004) 25 E C.L.R. 263 at p.270.

structural abuses which exclude actual or potential rivals from the market (exclusionary behaviour).

Exclusionary behaviour can take three different forms.[6] First, an incumbent firm may force the exit or prevent the entry of a rival firm or discipline its competitive behaviour (exclusion within one market). Exclusion of this first type can be achieved through, *inter alia*, predatory pricing, targeted rebates and tying the sale of complementary products. Second, the exclusionary effects may materialise in a market which is related to the home market of the dominant firm in the sense that the competitive conditions in the former market depend on the competitive conditions in the latter market (exclusion in adjacent markets). Exclusion of this second type can be achieved through a variety of practices, the most important of which are bundling and tying. Third, exclusion may take place at different stages of the production process, either upstream or downstream (exclusion in vertically related markets). A prominent example is a refusal to deal through which a dominant firm refuses access to a "bottleneck", i.e. an input in the production process that is necessary for upstream or downstream firms to exert their economic activity (essential facilities).

At the time of writing, a discussion is taking place as to the desirability of an economics-based approach towards Article 82 EC. The prohibition of abuse of dominance may be seen as the last bulwark of legal formalism in European competition law.[7] Economists argue that the European Commission should adopt an effects-based rather than a form-based approach to Article 82 EC.[8] Under the latter approach, categories of conduct are identified that it can be judged whether a certain practice is unlawful.[9] Under the former approach, it must be shown that certain practices generate anti-competitive effects, such as exclusion of competitors in the same market or in a horizontally or vertically related market, that inflict harm on consumers. Within the confines of this chapter, a full discussion of the feasibility and desirability of an economic approach to Article 82 EC is not possible. The following remarks seem, however, appropriate.

In contrast with Article 81 EC, an economics-based approach to abuse of dominance does not seem in tune with the text of Article 82 EC, which does not require proof of anti-competitive effects and does not provide for an efficiency defence. The formulation of Article 82 EC is clearly inspired by German ordoliberalist thinking[10] and fairness considerations. Ordoliberalism

---

[6] This distinction is also made by the expert group of European industrial economists advising on European competition policy issues (consisting of J. Gual, M. Hellwig, A. Perot, M. Polo, P. Rey, coordinator, K. Schmidt and R. Stenbacka). See EAGCP, *An Economic Approach to Article 82* (2005).
[7] Even though, as was made clear in former chapters, leftovers of legal formalism can still be found in the field of horizontal and vertical restraints (see Ch.5, s.5.3 and Ch.6, s.6.4).
[8] EAGCP, *An Economic Approach to Article 82* (2005).
[9] See T. Eilmansberger, "How to Distinguish Good from Bad Competition under Article 82 EC: In Search of Clearer and More Coherent Standards for Anti-Competitive Abuses" (2005) 42 C.M.L. Rev. 129. This author favours a *per se* prohibition of market power leveraging abuses (tying and refusals to grant access to essential facilities) and suggests that market structure abuses (achievement of a high market share through normal commercial techniques) be subjected to a proof of both effect and intent.
[10] See Ch.3, s.3.4.

aims at protecting the individual's economic freedom as a value in itself against any impairment of excessive market power.[11] Consequently, the philosophy underlying the prohibition of abuse of dominance is very different from US law (Section 2 Sherman Act). In an ordoliberal approach, it is neither necessary to investigate foreclosure effects nor possible to justify conduct in terms of efficiency savings and increased consumer welfare. Rather, ordoliberal writers adopted the concept of *Leistungswettbewerb* (derived from early 20th-century rules on unfair competition), which bans conduct that is not performance-based. A prominent example is the prohibition of a fidelity rebate, since it cannot be linked to the firm's performance (i.e. lower prices, better service, better quality).[12] Clearly, from a welfare economics perspective, an effects-based analysis is preferable to legal formalism. A form-based approach carries the risk that dominant firms may substitute prohibited types of conduct by permissible forms of anti-competitive behaviour (for example, price discrimination as a substitute for a refusal to grant access to a bottleneck facility). By focusing on considerations of fairness and protection of individual economic freedom, a form-based approach also tends to favour individual competitors rather than competition (and consumer welfare). Conversely, an effects-based approach guarantees that alternative practices that serve the same purpose are treated in the same way. Moreover, since competitive harm must be assessed with reference to consumer welfare, protection of individual competitors may be avoided. However, given the ordoliberalist foundations of Article 82 EC, an economics-based approach must involve a major policy change that will shake the foundations of European competition law much more seriously than any of the several recent reforms in this field (including vertical restraints, merger control and enforcement).

This chapter is structured as follows. In the next section, current rules of European competition law on price discrimination will be summarised and assessed from an economic perspective. The economic analysis of price discrimination warrants a cautious approach towards this practice, since its effects on welfare are ambiguous. Rebates granted by dominant firms are the most debated issue. Small competitors may initiate proceedings against the dominant firm, arguing that they are excluded from the market when rebates are limited to the most important customers and thus "targeted" at competitors. It will be shown that rebates may have both harmful and beneficial effects on competition. In the third section, the analysis will shift to bundling and tying. The wording of Article 82(d) EC[13] reflects the idea that tying contracts create an artificial connection between the availability of two distinct products. However, tying may serve legitimate business goals and enhance efficiency. As is often the case in competition law, a more balanced judgment

---

[11] W. Möschel, "Competition Policy from an Ordo Point of View" in *German Neo-Liberals and the Social Market Economy* (A. Peacock and H. Willgerodt ed., 1989), p.147.

[12] J. Kallaugher and B. Sher, "Rebates Revisited: Anti-Competitive Effects and Exclusionary Abuse under Article 82" (2004) 25 E.C.L.R. 263 at p.270.

[13] "Making the conclusion of contracts subject to acceptance by the other parties of supplementary obligations which, by their nature or according to commercial usage, have no connection with the subject of such contracts".

requires a consideration of both the efficiency savings brought about by tying and its potential anti-competitive consequences. Similar to the structure of the other sections of this chapter, the economic analysis of tying will first be described and then compared with its current legal treatment. In the fourth section, refusals to deal will be discussed. If such a practice is considered an abuse of dominance according to Article 82 EC, the obligation to deal may be imposed on the dominant firm. The most prominent cases are those where small competitors require access to facilities of the dominant firm deemed to be "essential". Finally, the fifth section of this chapter is devoted to the exclusionary practice which has provoked the most extensive discussion among economic commentators: predatory pricing. Dominant firms may grant substantial price discounts to a (selected) group of customers with the aim of excluding smaller rival suppliers from the market. Contrary to the point of view of the Chicago School, modern industrial organisation teaches that predatory pricing may be rational. Game theory has elaborated the conditions under which dominant firms may engage in price wars to drive smaller competitors out of the market. In the last section of this chapter, current European and US antitrust law on predatory pricing will be contrasted with the findings of the economic analysis.

Box 7.1: Excessive prices

Excessive prices compared to the underlying costs of providing a good or service are prohibited by Article 82 EC when charged by a firm in a dominant position. The following rules can be deduced from the precedent case law. In principle, a dominant company can participate in price competition with its competitors; it cannot, however, charge excessive prices. A number of methodologies can be used for gauging whether or not prices charged are excessive. These include a comparison of the selling price of the product or service with: (a) its costs of production and the resulting revenue/profit margin[14] (comparison A); (b) the selling price of the same products or services sold by competitors (comparison B); and/or (c) prices charged on similar markets which are open to competition (either in closely related product areas, or in different geographic markets)[15] (comparison C).

In *Deutsche Post*, the European Commission applied the above methodologies cumulatively, expressly stating, however, that it did not intend to act as a price regulator for dominant firms. The European Commission also wants to avoid any finding implying that prices of a dominant company would need to go beyond costs and some reasonable mark-up.[16] In fact, the European Commission's decisions in this area reveal that only truly exorbitant pricing has triggered regulatory intervention. The following examples are illustrative. In *General Motors*, up to 400 times the "actual costs" is

---

[14] On option (a) in particular, see Case IV/26.699 *Chiquita* [1976] O.J. L 95/1; Case 27/76 *United Brands v Commission* [1978] ECR 207; and Case 66/86 *Ahmed Saeed* [1989] ECR 803.
[15] On options (b) and (c) in particular, see Case 395/87 *Ministère Public v Tournier* [1989] ECR 2521; Joined Cases 110/88, 241/88 and 242/88 *Lucazeau v SACEM* [1989] ECR 2811; and Case 30/87 *Bodson v Pompes Funèbres* [1988] ECR 2479.
[16] *Deutsche Telekom, XXVII Annual Report on Competition Policy* (1997), p.77.

deemed excessive while up to 8 times the "effective costs" is held acceptable.[17] In *Chiquita*, a margin in excess of 100 per cent is found to be excessive, although this may be remedied by a price reduction of 15 per cent.[18] In *British Leyland*, a margin in excess of 100 per cent is found to be excessive.[19] Finally, in *Deutsche Telekom*, price comparisons showed differences up to 100 per cent, but the European Commission has decided that this may be remedied by price reductions between 38 and 78 per cent.[20]

The decision practice of competition authorities of the Member States also shows the typical difficulties that arise from attempts to control excessive prices charged by dominant firms:

- Under German competition law, an *Als-Ob* argumentation (comparison C) was used to conclude that prices charged by a dominant firm deviated substantially from so-called normal prices in competitive markets. To make comparisons between prices in the latter market and those charged in a monopolised market, a lot of factors that influence prices (differences in market characteristics) must be discounted; it must equally remain possible for the dominant firm to justify price differences on economic grounds (cost savings). The *Als-Ob* method was largely unsuccessful because of the difficulty of finding a similar market, where prices are not above competitive levels and the large number of adjustments that must be made when comparing competitive with non-competitive prices.[21]

- In the United Kingdom, the level of pricing and profitability in directories services (yellow pages and the like) was recently investigated by the OFT.[22] In its review of the profitability levels[23] of the two UK directories suppliers, Yell and Thompson, the OFT compared the two companies' profitability against each other (comparison B). However, since there was a risk that prices in this already highly-concentrated market would not be at a competitive level, the OFT benchmarked the profitability levels against those of "comparator firms" in other

---

[17] Case IV/28.851 *General Motors* [1975] O.J. L 29/14.
[18] Case IV/26.699 *Chiquita* [1976] O.J. L 95/1.
[19] Case IV/30.615 *British Leyland* [1984] O.J. L 207/11.
[20] *Deutsche Telekom*, XXVII *Annual Report on Competition Policy* (1997), p.77.
[21] See, e.g. BGH, WuW/E, BGH, 1454; BGH, WRP, 1980, 259.
[22] See *OFT Report* on Classified Directories Advertising Services (2001). The issue is currently under review by the UK Competition Commission.
[23] In the *OFT Report* (2001), the OFT measured profitability based on Return on Sales ("ROS"). ROS was found to be a more accurate indicator of profitability than Return on Capital Employed ("ROCE") because ROS excludes goodwill (which is potentially high in this market but is also very difficult to value). In 2003, Yell's ROS was 37% (for print directories only), whereas Thompson in the same year had a ROS of 27% but covering all lines of business; however, the OFT viewed confidential information and reported that Thompson's Return on Sales on print alone did not change the OFT's view on its overall profitability. See UK Competition Commission, Issues Statement (2005).

industries, chosen either because they were involved in the similar activity of newspaper publishing and advertising, or because they had a similar ratio of tangible assets to turnover to Yell (Comparison C).[24]

- The most aggressive application of the abuse of dominance provision in prohibiting excessive prices can be found in the Netherlands. The Dutch Competition Authority has gone further than the European Commission but has been criticised for having acted as a price regulator.[25]

In marked contrast with Article 82 EC, excessive pricing claims have been rejected in principle under Section 2 of the Sherman Act.[26] Several arguments underlie the more liberal US approach.[27] First, it is feared that prohibiting excessive prices may penalise dominant firms that have reached that position through efficient means, thus reducing the incentives to compete and hurting dynamic efficiency. As forcefully stated by Judge Learned Hand: "The successful competitor, having been urged to compete, must not be turned upon when he wins".[28] Second, it is expected that monopoly profits attract new competitors whose entry will drive prices back to competitive levels. Finally, in practice it is very difficult to determine the borderline between a reasonable and an abusive price. The US authorities seem more concerned with over-deterrence (type II errors, false negatives) and less concerned with under-deterrence (type I errors, false positives) than their European counterparts.[29] This is neatly reflected in the recent *Trinko* case, where the Supreme Court has stated: "the mere possession of monopoly power, and the concomitant charging of monopoly prices, is not only not unlawful; it is an important element of the free-market system. The opportunity to charge monopoly prices—at least for a short period—is what attracts 'business acumen' in the first place, it induces risk taking that produces innovation and economic growth".[30]

---

[24] See *OFT Report* (2001), cited above, paras 34 *et seq.*
[25] E. Pijnacker Hordijk, "Excessive Pricing under EC Competition Law: An Update in the Light of Dutch Developments", in 2001 Fordham Corp. L. Inst. 463 (B. Hawk ed., 2002).
[26] For a comparison of European and US law, also from an economic perspective, see generally: M. Gal, "Monopoly Pricing as an Antitrust Offense in the U.S. and the EC. Two Systems of Belief about Monopoly?" (2004) 49 Antitrust Bull 343.
[27] See B.E. Hawk, "Article 82 and Section 2: Abuse and Monopolizing Conduct" (Forthcoming ABA-Antitrust Section publication).
[28] *United States v Aluminium Co of America*, 148 F.2d 416 (2d Cir., 1945) at 430.
[29] Evans and Padilla argue in favour of no *ex post* intervention, given the size of the error costs. See D. S. Evans and A. Padilla, "Excessive Prices: Using Economics to Define Administrable Legal Rules" (2005) 1 J.C.L.E. 97.
[30] *Verizon Communications Inc. v Law Offices of Curtis V. Trinko, LLP*, 124 S. Ct. 872, 879 (2004). For a critical comment, see A.I. Gavil, "Exclusionary Distribution Strategies by Dominant Firms: Striking a Better Balance" (2004) 72 Antitrust L.J. 3.

7.2 Price discrimination

7.2.1 Lessons from economic theory

Price discrimination occurs when identical products are sold at different prices under identical costs conditions or when non-identical but similar goods are sold at prices which are in different ratios to their marginal costs. At the same time, price discrimination in an economic sense occurs if identical units of a product are sold at a common price under different costs conditions. It must be stressed that different prices for identical or similar goods do not necessarily imply price discrimination. A bulk buyer obtaining large quantities of goods will be charged lower prices than a small-scale consumer. This should not be labelled discriminatory pricing if costs savings (administrative costs, costs of transportation and other handling costs) can justify differences in price. Competition laws banning price discrimination usually allow for a costs justification defence, either explicitly or implicitly.[31] Physically identical units of goods are different articles in an economic sense if they are sold in different markets.[32] This again illustrates the importance of adequately defining the relevant antitrust market.[33] Moreover, to avoid hasty conclusions on the existence of price discrimination, persistent costs differences in marketing should also be taken into account. A final introductory remark seems appropriate. The central concern of competition law must be systematic price discrimination by firms with substantial market power. Sporadic price discrimination is characteristic of the adjustment of competitive markets towards equilibrium.[34]

Three necessary conditions must be satisfied to enable a firm to engage in price discrimination and make it a profitable strategy.[35] First, the firm must possess some market power. In perfectly competitive markets firms have to take the market price as given and cannot practice price discrimination. It must be stressed that price discrimination requires power only over one's own prices, not necessarily a monopoly. Discriminatory prices on their own are not

---

[31] Section 2(a) Clayton Act, as amended by the Robinson–Patman Act reads as follows: "that nothing herein contained shall prevent differentials which make only due allowance for differences in the cost of manufacture, sale, or delivery resulting from the differing methods or quantities in which such commodities are to such purchasers sold or delivered". Under European competition law the term "equivalent transactions" in Art. 82(c) EC is sufficiently broad to allow for a costs justification defence. It is worth noting that the Federal Trade Commission enforced the Robinson–Patman Act rather vigorously until the late 1970s, but has since lost enthusiasm. This policy change came about after increasingly sharp economic criticisms were directed towards the prohibition of price discrimination which is far too general and also bans pro-competitive price discrimination. Cases that arise today are private actions by firms which have lost their market position to new competitors. See also s.7.5.

[32] S. Martin, *Industrial Economics: Economic Analysis and Public Policy* (1994), p.418.

[33] For an example of physically identical goods that constitute separate antitrust markets (i.e. branded and non-branded toilet tissues), see the discussion of the *Kimberley-Clark* case in Ch.4, Box 4.3.

[34] S. Martin, *Industrial Economics: Economic Analysis and Public Policy* (1994), p.418.

[35] F.M. Scherer and D. Ross, *Industrial Market Structure and Economic Performance* (1990), p.489.

evidence of antitrust market power. All that is necessary is that the firm faces a negatively sloped demand for its products, as do all firms selling unique products (monopolistic competition). Second, the firm must have information about the maximum prices (different groups of) consumers are willing to pay (i.e. information about the reservation prices). Third, arbitrage must be prevented. Buyers paying low prices must not be able to transfer the products easily to other groups of buyers paying higher prices, since this would prevent the producer from maintaining price differences between classes of buyers. Price discrimination will be a profitable strategy only if a firm is able to group consumers together around their different reservation prices and to prevent resale by low price consumers to high price consumers. For this reason price discrimination often occurs for goods that cannot be stored (such as electric power) and for services (for example, in the sector of the liberal professions[36]).

Following the work of Pigou[37] it is customary to distinguish three types of price discrimination: first, second and third degree price discrimination. First degree price discrimination occurs when each single unit of output is sold at the highest possible price. It is difficult to imagine a situation in which this type of price discrimination could be implemented, and it is generally considered to be of theoretical interest only. Perfect price discrimination leads to an outcome which is allocatively efficient, since the firm is able to sell its entire output at prices covering marginal costs and each unit of output is sold at its maximum demand price (given that different consumers have different "reservation prices"). Under monopoly without price discrimination some of the consumer surplus is transferred to the producer and there is a deadweight loss which represents a true decrease in welfare.[38] This is due to the fact that the monopolist operates at an inefficient level of output. Even though some consumers are willing to pay more for additional units of output (than it costs to produce them), the monopolist is not willing to generate additional output since this would lead to a general decrease of the price for all of its output and thus reduce profits. By contrast, if the monopolist can perfectly price discriminate, consumers with high reservation prices will be charged more than consumers with lower reservation prices. First degree price discrimination eliminates the deadweight loss associated with single-price monopoly.[39] If the goal of competition policy is the minimisation of deadweight loss, first degree price discrimination is clearly a good thing. Compared to the situation of a monopolised market where a single price is charged, consumers with higher reservation prices are offered additional output and consumers with lower reservation prices are better off since they can now afford to buy the good. However, consumer surplus is entirely captured and transferred to the monopolist. Even though the sum of producer and consumer surplus is

---

[36] For an empirical study on the use of discriminatory prices in a legal services' market, see F.H. Stephen, J.H. Love, D.D. Gillanders and A.A. Paterson, "Testing for Price Discrimination in the Market for Conveyancing Services" (1992) 12 Int. Rev. Law Econ. 397.

[37] A.C. Pigou, *The Economics of Welfare* (1920), pp.240–256.

[38] See Ch.2 s.2.2.2.

[39] Abstraction is made from the transaction costs involved in implementing a discriminatory scheme. From a total welfare point of view price discrimination is beneficial only if the deadweight loss is larger than the sum of transaction costs.

maximised, this result does not eliminate other objections to monopoly, such as the distributional effects and the social costs resulting from "rent seeking".[40]

Whereas first degree price discrimination is mainly a theoretical case, both second and third degree price discrimination regularly occur in practice since they require less information about demand. Second degree price discrimination takes place when a firm sells different units of output for different prices, even though every individual buying the same amount of the goods pays the same price. Output is divided into successive batches which are sold for the highest price customers are willing to pay. Hence, prices differ across the units of the goods but not across people, so that some buyers enjoy a consumer surplus. Block pricing (i.e. charging a decreasing average price with increasing use), often practised by public utilities, and quantity discounts are two forms of second degree price discrimination. If average and marginal costs decrease by expanding output, block pricing may be encouraged. Consumer welfare can thus be increased, even though allowing for greater profit to the company. The reason is that prices are reduced overall, while the savings from the lower costs per unit allow a reasonable profit.[41]

Third degree price discrimination occurs when a firm segregates consumers into distinctive groups characterised by different elasticities of demand which are explained by exogenous criteria such as location, age, sex or occupation. Different (groups of) buyers pay different prices, but every unit of output sold to a given buyer (or a given group) is sold at the same price. Thus, prices do not differ across the units of the good (as is the case under second degree price discrimination) but between individual (or groups of) consumers. Third degree price discrimination is the most common form of discriminatory marketing. Firms charge different prices in different segments of their markets; deviations of prices from marginal costs will be highest in markets with the least elastic demand. In various industries, pricing above marginal costs is needed to recover fixed costs and provide incentives for firms to make investments in the future.[42] Examples of third degree price discrimination permeate a large variety of industries, ranging from cement producers to record companies and law firms; they include student discounts, cheaper train tickets for aged people and the sale of identical or virtually identical products under different brands in various Member States. Clearly, the practice is not confined to dominant firms.

The welfare analysis of third degree price discrimination is not as clear-cut as the above analysis of first degree price discrimination. In a classic article, Schmalensee shows that the impact of price discrimination by a monopolist on welfare is indeterminate: welfare may be increased if price discrimination succeeds in increasing the output level, for example by allowing the firm to enter a new market segment. In general, however, unless a prohibition of price

---

[40] See also R.A. Posner, "The Social Costs of Monopoly and Regulation" (1975) 83 J. Polit. Economy 807.

[41] R.S. Pindyck and D.L. Rubinfeld, *Microeconomics* (4th ed., 1998), p.381.

[42] D. Ridyard, *Recent Article 82 Cases and Pricing Abuses—An Economic Perspective* (2000). D. Ridyard, "Exclusionary Pricing and Price Discrimination Abuses under Article 82 EC: An Economic Analysis" (2002) 23 E.C.L.R. at pp.286–287.

discrimination results in a substantial reduction in output, price uniformity will be superior to price discrimination.[43] In non-monopolised markets, price discrimination may raise concerns about competition at the downstream level (for example, if retailers who are customers of a price discriminating supplier compete on the basis of different input costs[44]) and issues of predation.[45] Most commentators agree that it must be possible for costs differences to be reflected in price differentials and that price discrimination may have beneficial effects in oligopolistic markets. Rigid oligopolistic price structures may be enlivened by secret rebates.[46] Secret price cuts are the Achilles' heel of tacit or overt collusion. If price discrimination is prohibited, price discipline in oligopolistic markets may be tighter than it might otherwise have been. Apart from this beneficial effect, the welfare analysis of third degree price discrimination in general leads to ambiguous results.

The ambiguity of the economic analysis also makes the results of the removal of price discrimination ambiguous.[47] The most important lessons for competition policy and law seem to be the following. First, price discrimination is not a phenomenon confined to firms with dominant market power[48] and is as such not anti-competitive. From an efficiency perspective, intervention by competition authorities to guarantee price uniformity may be defended only if the firm engaged in price discrimination possesses substantial market power. Second, in fixed costs recovery industries firms must be able to charge prices in excess of marginal costs, in order to keep incentives to invest intact. Third, if a result of the introduction of uniform pricing is that a large group of low price consumers no longer receives supplies, price discrimination is preferable from a welfare point of view.[49] In addition, it must be noted that uniform prices may have adverse distributional effects if lower income groups are forced to pay higher prices.

[43] R. Schmalensee, "Output and Welfare Implications of Monopolistic Third-Degree Price Discrimination" (1981) 71 Amer. Econ. Rev. 242.

[44] See on different types of price discrimination and their effects on competition: F. Machlup, "Characteristics and Types of Price Discrimination", in *Business Concentration and Price Policy* (1955), p.397

[45] See s.7.5.

[46] F.M. Scherer and D. Ross, *Industrial Market Structure and Economic Performance* (1990), p.308. In particular, large retail firms may use their countervailing power to enliven price competition among manufacturers of consumer goods. See J. Galbraith, *American Capitalism: The Concept of Countervailing Power* (1956), p.119. On the condition that they are not based on costs savings associated with large deliveries, rebates that were originally granted on a secret basis may thereafter spread to the benefit of all (also small) retailers.

[47] M. Armstrong and J. Vickers, "Price Discrimination, Competition and Regulation" (1993) 41 J. Ind. Econ. 335.

[48] As a consequence, complaints are also lodged against non-dominant firms. In Germany, due to political pressures exerted by small retailers' groups, the threshold of market dominance has been lowered for price discrimination cases (s.20 GWB). In addition, price discrimination is sometimes held illegal on the basis of laws banning unfair trade practices (in Germany: s.1 UWG; in Belgium: Art.93 Loi sur les pratiques du commerce). These rules are clearly over-inclusive since they also outlaw competitive uses of price discrimination and thus lead to type II errors (false negatives).

[49] S.K. Layson, "Market Opening under Third-degree Price Discrimination" (1994) 42 J. Ind. Org. 335.

7.2.2 The prohibition of price discrimination in Article 82 EC

7.2.2.1 The conditions of the prohibition

Article 82(c) EC states that it is prohibited to "apply dissimilar conditions to equivalent transactions with other trading parties, thereby placing them at a competitive disadvantage". For this prohibition to apply, three conditions must be satisfied. First, for transactions to be equivalent, the product or service provided must be substitutable taking into account all relevant market factors.[50] If substantial differences arise in terms of costs, quality and type of service provided, then services are not equivalent.[51] Also the trading parties must be equivalent (i.e. comparable).[52] Second, whether or not conditions are dissimilar can be assessed by reviewing (a) the nature of the transaction; (b) the differences in the nature of the products (or services) sold; and (c) the costs of supply.[53] Third, there may be objective justifications for the different treatment (for example, technical or commercial grounds), but these must be demonstrated by the dominant company.[54] A well-known case example is *United Brands (Chiquita)*.[55] In this case, the economic requirements for third degree price discrimination were neatly satisfied. In spite of this, the prohibition of the practice under Article 82(c) EC may be criticised for its counter-productive effects on both allocative efficiency and distributive goals (see Box 7.2).

Box 7.2: Prohibition of price discrimination: the banana case revisited
The United Brands Corporation (UBC) imported bananas from Latin America and was selling bananas under the brand name Chiquita to distributors at different prices in various Member States. The European Commission found UBC guilty of four abuses: (a) prohibiting its distributors from reselling green (unripened) bananas; (b) charging discriminatory prices; (c) charging excessive prices in some European countries; and (d) refusing to supply Olesen, a Danish importer. UBC had refused to supply Olesen because the latter had participated in an advertising campaign by a rival brand. On appeal, the European Court of Justice upheld the European Commission's decision on all but the third charge. This case offers a school example of third degree price discrimination: all conditions for profitable price discrimination were remarkably satisfied.

---

[50] Case IV/33.941 *HOV-SVZ/MCN* [1994] O.J. L 104/34, para.47.
[51] Case 27/76 *United Brands v Commission* [1978] ECR 207, para.302. See also Opinion of Advocate General Jacobs in Case 395/87 *Ministère Public v Tournier* [1989] ECR 521.
[52] Case C–62/86 *AKZO Chemie v Commission* [1991] ECR I–3359.
[53] Cases IV/34.621 and IV/35.059 *Irish Sugar* [1997] O.J. L 258/1, para.138.
[54] Case 311/84 *CBEM v CLT and IPB (Télémarketing)* [1985] ECR 3261, para.26.
[55] Case 27/76 *United Brands v Commission* [1978] ECR 305.

First, UBC enjoyed sufficient market power to be able to control prices: the popular brand name Chiquita is a unique product feature. Once companies produce products that are distinguishable from their competitors' products, they face a downward sloping demand and, hence, have the ability to engage in price discrimination. Second, consumers were grouped together around the highest price they were prepared to pay. The facts of the case show that the highest prices were charged in Belgium, Denmark and Germany, whereas the lowest prices were charged in Ireland. The differences in price could not be explained by transport costs, since it is actually more expensive to transport goods to the Irish market than to any other Member State. Basic economics teaches that markets where higher prices are charged must have a lower price elasticity of demand. A price discriminating firm will set low prices for a price-sensitive group and high prices for the groups that are relatively price-insensitive. The Irish consumers who were willing to pay less because their incomes were lower typically belong to the former group, whereas the Belgian, Danish and German consumers—because of their higher willingness and ability to pay—belong to the latter groups. UBC, by way of a defence, argued that it was only "charging what the market can bear". The European Court of Justice rejected this argument by means of the following circular reasoning: "Although the responsibility for establishing the single banana market does not lie with the applicant, it can only endeavour to take what the market can bear provided that it complies with the rules for the regulation and coordination of the market laid down by the Treaty".[56] Looking at the conditions for profitable price discrimination, it becomes clear that UBC simply confirmed that it was able successfully to divide consumers into groups with different reservation prices. Third degree price discrimination is nothing other than carving up the market according to price elasticity of demand and then charging what the market can bear. Lastly, arbitrage was prevented by prohibiting the distributors in various Member States from reselling green bananas. The first abuse was nothing other than a necessary condition to make the second abuse (price discrimination) feasible. From an economic point of view the explicit prohibition of the sale of green bananas was redundant, since the practice of price discrimination can only be profitable if arbitrage is successfully prevented.

The finding that all requirements for profitable third degree geographic price discrimination were satisfied in the *Chiquita* case does not allow one to jump to the conclusion that the prohibition under Article 82 EC was justified. The European Commission objected to different prices at the distributors level but acknowledged that differences in marketing conditions might justify different levels in price or sale at the retail level.[57] The European Court of Justice added that: "The mechanisms of the market are

---

[56] Case 27/76 *United Brands v Commission* [1978] ECR 305.
[57] Case IV/26.699 *Chiquita* [1976] O.J. L 95/1.

adversely affected if the price is calculated by leaving out one stage of the market and taking into account the law of supply and demand as between the vendor and the ultimate consumer and not as between the vendor (United Brands) and the purchaser (the distributors)".[58] This consideration seems to imply that if UBC had been vertically integrated into distribution, the Court would not have objected to making assessment of retail demand conditions in different markets and then fixing the prices accordingly. Conversely, when a dominant firm operates through independent wholesalers or retailers, it must act as if it is pricing in a single market. If a firm must supply the goods at the same import prices and demand conditions in various Member States differ, the only result is that retailers will discriminate. This may provoke non-integrated firms to make inefficient integration decisions in order to practice price discrimination without incurring antitrust penalties. Another objection relates to equity which was adversely affected. Both the European Commission and the European Court of Justice seem to have been concerned only with market integration and to have pursued this goal at any cost. In the *Chiquita* case, uniform prices come at the expense of a more equitable income distribution.[59] Price uniformity implied price increases in a poor country and price decreases in richer countries. Poor consumers who could afford to buy bananas at lower prices may be unable to do so if prices are uniform, but higher.

7.2.2.2 Rebates granted by dominant firms: legal rules

The European Court of Justice had to judge the validity of rebate schemes granted by a dominant company in the leading *Michelin I* case.[60] Three essential principles can be drawn from the European Court of Justice's findings in this and subsequent cases. When assessing a rebate scheme, all relevant circumstances need to be taken into account.[61] Rebates granted by a dominant company must be justified by showing that they are based on an economic benefit for the dominant firm. This is the case with (a) quantity rebates in exchange for economies of scale achieved through higher turnover, (b) functional discounts (i.e. discounts corresponding to the customer rendering additional promotional activities), (c) discounts given for cash payments, or (d) discounts given because of quality defects.[62] The rebate must not distort competition by (a) excluding competitors from the market, and/or (b) effectively tying customers to the dominant supplier,[63] and/or (c) discriminating between customers.[64]

[58] Case 27/76 *United Brands v Commission* [1978] ECR 305.
[59] See also W. Bishop, "Price Discrimination under Article 86: Political Economy in the European Court" (1981) 44 MLR 282.
[60] Case 322/81 *Michelin v Commission* [1983] ECR 3461, para.71.
[61] See also Case T–228/97 *Irish Sugar v Commission* [1999] ECR II–2969, para.214.
[62] Case IV/32.186 *Gosme/Martell-DMP* [1991] O.J. L 185/23, paras 11 and 34.
[63] Case 322/81 *Michelin v Commission* [1983] ECR 3461, para.73.
[64] Case IV/29.020 *Vitamines* [1976] O.J. L 223/27, paras 24 and 26; Case 85/76 *Hoffmann-La Roche v Commission (Vitamins)* [1979] ECR 461, para.90; Case T–228/97 *Irish Sugar v Commission* [1999] ECR II–2969, paras 213 and 218; Case COMP/34.780 *Virgin/BA* [2000] O.J. L 30/1, paras 97–111.

In developing the European Court of Justice's precedent, the European Commission has strictly limited the type of rebate scheme that can be operated by a dominant firm. The restrictive nature of the Commission's practice is demonstrated in the decisions *Virgin/BA*[65] and *Michelin II*,[66] where the Commission came down heavily on rebate schemes. In *Virgin/BA*, the Commission stated that the earlier *Michelin I* and *Hoffman-La Roche* cases establish a general principle that "a dominant supplier can give discounts that relate to efficiencies … but cannot give discounts or incentives to encourage loyalty, that is for avoiding purchases from a competitor of the dominant supplier" (para.101). The European Commission has emphasised several factors as distorting competition, and hence subject to a *per se* prohibition:[67] (a) a rebate system which is equivalent to an exclusivity requirement, implying that the discount should not be conditional on the customer's obtaining all or most of its supplies from the dominant supplier, thus functioning as a loyalty and/or fidelity rebate;[68] (b) a rebate system which is discriminatory among customers of the dominant supplier in applying dissimilar conditions to equivalent transactions;[69] a rebate system can be found discriminatory if discounts are granted on the basis of subjective criteria;[70] (c) a rebate system which is discriminatory among customers of the dominant supplier in making discounts granted dependent upon orders placed in a certain period, thus functioning as a target rebate.[71]

Other types of rebates and discounts have been found to infringe European competition law, depending upon their discriminatory character and the degree to which they bind buyers to the dominant supplier. Regarding quantity discounts, the absence of linear progression in the increase of quantity discounts may constitute evidence of discriminatory treatment.[72] The reference period on the basis of which the discount is calculated should not be too long. While the European Commission in *British Gypsum Super Stockist Scheme* still accepted a one-year reference period,[73] six months is seen as the maximum in the air transport issues raised in *Virgin/BA*, three months was

---

[65] Case COMP/34.780 *Virgin/BA* [2000] O.J. L 30/1; confirmed under appeal in Case T–219/99 *BA v Commission* [2003] ECR II–5917; subject to further appeal, see Case C–95/04P.
[66] Case COMP/36.041 *Michelin II* [2002] O.J. L 143/1; confirmed under appeal in Case T–203/01 *Michelin v Commission (Michelin II)* [2003] ECR II–4071.
[67] Case COMP/34.780 *Virgin/BA* [2000] O.J. L 30/1, paras 97–111.
[68] Case T–219/99 *BA v Commission* [2003] ECR II–5917, para.244. See also Case 85/76 *Hoffmann-La Roche v Commission (Vitamins)* [1979] ECR 461, para.89; and compare Case COMP/35.141 *Deutsche Post* [2001] O.J. L 125/27, where exclusivity provisions are held to constitute a direct incentive to shut out competitors. Most recently, in Case COMP/39.116 *Coca-Cola* [2005] O.J. L 253/21, all exclusivity arrangements were given up.
[69] Case T–219/99 *BA v Commission* [2003] ECR II–5917, para.240. See also Case IV/35.703 *Portuguese Airports* [1999] O.J. L 69/31, para.35; Case COMP/36.041 *Michelin II* [2002] O.J. L 143/1, paras 250–253.
[70] Case T–203/01 *Michelin v Commission (Michelin II)* [2003] ECR II–4071, paras 145–150. *In casu*, Michelin's general manual—the "Instructions for Using the Service Bonus Form"—was found to be, in fact, subjective.
[71] Case COMP/34.780 *Virgin/BA* [2000] O.J. L 30/1, para.109; see also Case T–219/99 *BA v Commission* [2003] ECR II–5917, para.245. Most recently, in Case COMP/39.116 *Coca-Cola*, all target rebates were given up.
[72] Case C–163/99 *Portuguese Republic v Commission* [2001] ECR I–2613, paras 52–53.
[73] Case IV/32.929 *British Gypsum Super Stockist Scheme* [1992] O.J. C 321/9.

accepted in the 1989 *Coca-Cola case*,[74] and three months was viewed a reasonable period in *Michelin II*.[75] In *Michelin II*, the Court of First Instance concluded that a progressive volume discounting scheme in which (a) there is a significant variation in the discount rates between the lower and the higher steps, which (b) has a reference period of one year, and in which (c) the discount is fixed on the basis of total turnover achieved during the reference period, has the characteristics of loyalty rebates.[76] Loyalty and/or fidelity rebates—the offering of rebates on the condition that the customer will obtain all or most of their requirements from the dominant supplier—will be contrary to Article 82 EC, as such a scheme effectively rewards customers for not buying from the supplier's competitors.[77] The offering of target rebates that are payable retrospectively, conditional upon customers conducting a high proportion of their business with the dominant supplier ("payments rolled back to zero"), will also be contrary to Article 82 EC.[78]

7.2.2.3 Rebates granted by dominant firms: economic assessment

The principles, which may be derived from the above case law, and the outcomes of the individual proceedings are not in harmony with basic insights from economic analysis. First, the general rule requiring that rebates must be based on cost differences is ill-conceived. Rebates are offered not only to reflect costs savings, but also to gain more customers. The latter goal says nothing about the pro- or anti-competitive impact of the discount scheme. On the one hand, discount schemes may enliven competition and benefit consumers. The overall effect on consumer welfare is *a priori* ambiguous, since consumers with a high elasticity of demand benefit from price differentiation, whereas consumers with a low elasticity may suffer from it. However, if output increases (more consumers are served), pro-competitive effects of discount schemes will dominate over anti-competitive ones. Efficiency gains can also be achieved when discount schemes are used as an incentive mechanism to induce efficient behaviour by retailers (solving adverse selection and moral hazard problems). Moreover, discount schemes may also enable the dominant firm to achieve economies of scale and enable transaction costs savings for the buyers.[79]

On the other hand, rebates may exclude rival suppliers and lead to market foreclosure. Discount schemes may generate any of the three types of exclusionary effects indicated in the introduction to this chapter: (a) selective rebates offered to consumers considering switching to a new entrant may lead to exclusion within one market; (b) rebates offered if the products on an adjacent market are bought together with products on the main market may

---

[74] Case COMP/36.041 *Coca-Cola*, Commission Press Release IP/90/7.
[75] Case COMP/36.041 *Michelin II* [2002] O.J. L 143/1, para.216.
[76] Case T–203/01 *Michelin v Commission (Michelin II)* [2003] ECR II–4071, paras 67–80 and 95.
[77] Case COMP/34.780 *Virgin/BA* [2000] O.J. L 30/1, para.3. Rebates granted purely to encourage loyalty are assumed to be illegal. See Case COMP/34.780 *Virgin/BA* [2000] O.J. L 30/1, para.101; Case T–219/99 *BA v Commission* [2003] ECR II–5917, paras 246–247. See, earlier, also Case COMP/ 39.116 *Coca-Cola*, Commission Press Release MEMO/99/42.
[78] Case COMP/34.780 *Virgin/BA* [2000] O.J. L 30/1, paras 30 and 102.
[79] EAGCP, *An Economic Approach to Article 82* (2005).

lead to exclusion in a horizontally related market; and (c) rebates offered to retailers in order to discourage them from selling competitors' products may lead to exclusion in a vertically related market. Only a case-by-case approach is able to distinguish competitive and anti-competitive uses of discount schemes. A necessary condition for a finding of exclusionary pricing behaviour is that rival firms have been forced to leave the market or that their market share is in such decline that their continued existence as effective rivals is in doubt.[80] Under these conditions, competitive harm and a lowering of consumer welfare will result.

Second, the European Commission may be criticised for choosing a form-based rather than an effects-based approach. This weakness is exacerbated by the view of the Court of First Instance, according to which it is sufficient to show that a rebate is loyalty-enhancing to bring it within the scope of the prohibition of Article 82 EC. Even though quantity discounts are more likely to be motivated by efficiency considerations than fidelity rebates, the distinction is prone to enforcement errors. Indeed, the form of the discount does not constitute a clear indicator of the motivations underlying the rebate scheme. Efficiency considerations might require personalised schemes, tailored to the size of the retailer, which could take the form of target rebates or fidelity discounts.[81] The European Commission may be criticised for not carrying out a market effect test determining whether discount schemes enable dominant firms to exclude rivals and raise prices afterwards. The major weakness of current European competition law is that it is not required to show that rebates are likely to cause a reduction in output or an increase in prices harming consumers.[82]

Third, the European Commission's decision in *British Airways* neglects the insight that price discrimination may be objectively justified in industries where there are large fixed costs and low marginal costs (such as airlines).[83] In *British Airways*, the European Commission objected to extra commission payments to travel agents for meeting or exceeding the previous year's sales of British Airways tickets in the United Kingdom. In the European Commission's view the extra sales commissions were not related to savings in distribution costs. Instead, by rewarding customer loyalty, they made the travel agents loyal to British Airways and discouraged them from providing services to

---

[80] In *British Airways* no evidence supporting exclusionary behaviour was furnished. By contrast, British Airways' market share was in constant decline (from around 46% to less than 40%). The counterargument that competitors had been able to gain market share was discarded by the European Commission, arguing that "It can only be assumed that competitors would have had more success in the absence of these abusive commission schemes" (Case COMP/34.780 *British Airways* [2000] O.J. L 30/1, para.107). The latter statement is typical of the European Commission's lack of understanding of the relevant economics; it is at best a tautology; see D. Ridyard, "Exclusionary Pricing and Price Discrimination Abuses Under Art. 82—An Economic Analysis" (2002) 23 E.C.L.R. 286.

[81] EAGCP, *An Economic Approach to Article 82* (2005), p.37.

[82] J. Kallaugher and B. Sher, "Rebates Revisited: Anti-Competitive Effects and Exclusionary Abuse under Article 82" (2004) 25 E.C.L.R. 263.

[83] OFT, *Assessment of Individual Agreements and Conduct* (1999).

other airlines; a substantial fine of €6.8 million was imposed.[84] The requirement that rebates to dealers must reflect savings in distribution costs or an
increase in the value of services provided by the distributor is too simplistic.
Not only distribution costs, but also production costs matter. For firms with
high fixed costs it is important to be able to offer high discounts on incremental sales to recoup the fixed costs investments. Even if the price–costs
margin on sales to infra-marginal consumers substantially exceeds the margin
earned on the incremental sale, this does not mean that the latter sale is
abusive or that the former sales were made at an excessive price. From a
viewpoint of economic efficiency large price rebates are cost justified if they
are intended to increase sales with the purpose of recouping large fixed costs
as long as they exceed the marginal costs of supply.[85] Therefore, the European
Commission's view that rebates infringe Article 82 EC if they are discriminatory is not based on sound economics.

7.3 Tying and bundling

Practices of dominant firms may generate anti-competitive effects in related or
adjacent markets. A dominant firm may establish a link between its home
market and a horizontally related market through bundling and tying.
Bundling may be pure or mixed. In the case of pure bundling, two or more
products are sold together for a single price. Pure bundling may be achieved
through contractual agreements or through technological links, which make it
physically impossible for the consumer to buy the products separately (technological bundling; a well-known example is Microsoft's technological integration of its operating system Windows and its browser Internet Explorer). In
a pure bundle, as in the case of Microsoft, the products are offered only in
fixed proportions, such as A–B or 2A–2B. In mixed bundling, consumers have
the choice of buying the products separately or as a package (the bundle),
which is sold at a discount (for example, all-in holiday packages).

With respect to "tying" a distinction can be made between a static and a
dynamic tie. The static tie can be considered as half of a mixed bundle or an
exclusivity arrangement. In such a case, the customer who wants to buy
product A must also buy product B, although it is possible to acquire product
B separately. Consequently, the products offered for sale are B or A–B as a
package. Hence, in the case of a static tie, the sale of the "tying product" is
contingent on the purchase of the "tied product", both products belonging to
different relevant product markets.[86] The difference between pure bundling
and a static tie is that under the latter the tied product may be bought alone.
The difference between mixed bundling and a static tie is that in the former
case both products are available separately. The second type of tying is a

---

[84] Case COMP/34.780 *British Airways* [2000] O.J. L 30/1.
[85] D. Ridyard, "Exclusionary Pricing and Price Discrimination Abuses Under Art. 82—An Economic Analysis" (2002) 23 E.C.L.R. 286.
[86] Commission Guidelines on Vertical Restraints [2000] O.J. C 291/1, para.106.

dynamic form of a pure bundle, i.e. a dynamic tie. In order to be able to buy product A, a customer is also required to buy product B, but the quantity of product B may differ from customer to customer. The combinations for sale may be A–B, A–2B, A–3B, and so on. Hence, a dynamic tie has the feature of exclusivity of a static tie, but the amount of the tied product may differ. The products are sold in variable proportions. A dynamic tie is also labelled "requirements tying"[87] (for example the sale of a photocopier on the condition that the purchaser also buys toner and paper from the same manufacturer). The older legal and economic literature uses tying as a general denominator for each of the described practices.

7.3.1 Economic analysis of tying and bundling

Tying and bundling will be anti-competitive if these practices exclude competitors and hurt consumers. Conversely, tying and bundling will be benign if they increase efficiency. The Chicago School criticised the traditional leverage argument, according to which a monopolist in the market for product A (home market) may use tying in order to reduce competition for a complementary product B (adjacent market) and thus achieve two monopoly profits. Recent theoretical economic research has revealed the limitations of the Chicago critique and shown that dominant firms may strategically use bundling or tying in order to leverage market power in adjacent markets. However, given the strict assumptions of these new theories, the number of cases where the practice is anti-competitive will be relatively low. By contrast, bundling and tying may generate different types of efficiencies (costs savings, quality assurance) and be used as a price discrimination device. The different economic explanations for bundling and tying will be successively presented later in this chapter.

7.3.1.1 Tying and bundling as an anti-competitive practice: leveraging market power

The overwhelmingly negative attitude towards tying in competition law has its origin in the "leverage theory", which was popular in the early days of antitrust. The basic argument is that a firm having a dominant position in the market for the tying product (possibly as the consequence of patent protection) uses tying arrangements to extend its dominant position into the market for the tied product. As a consequence there are two deadweight losses and a dominant firm obtains a monopoly profit twice. In the 1970s, Chicago economists attacked this theory and argued that it is not possible for a firm to leverage monopoly power from one activity into another. Even if the firm is a monopolist in the market for the tying product, it cannot achieve a second monopoly profit in the market for the tied product (single monopoly profit

[87] M. Motta, *Competition Policy—Theory and Practice* (2004), p.460.

theorem). Assume two complementary products: the first product is sold at the profit-maximising monopoly price (€200) and the second product is competitively priced (€30). To achieve a double monopoly profit the sale of the first product must be made contingent upon the purchase of the second product and the price for the latter product must be increased (to, let's say, €50). However, if the price of the tied product is higher than the competitive price, consumers will perceive the package price as being too high and will buy less of the tying product.[88] Since consumers are not willing to pay €250 for the first product sold in combination with the second product, which they value at €30, the firm will have to reduce its package price to maximise its profits (in the example €230). Hence, achieving a double monopoly profit through tying is not possible. By contrast, the dominant firm will profit from competition in the market of the second product since any monopoly profit earned by others will reduce its own.[89]

Recent research in industrial organisation has made it clear that the Chicago approach is only valid on its own assumptions. The Chicago critique only applies if the tied market is perfectly competitive. Obviously a crucial assumption is that consumers are perfectly informed: if they are not able to calculate the full package price, the risk that they may be exploited cannot be excluded. This is the reason why the American Supreme Court decided in the *Kodak* case that buyers of photocopying machines, who are required to purchase maintenance services from the same manufacturer, may be exploited if they cannot calculate the lifetime costs of using the machine (see Box 7.3).

Box 7.3: Leveraging market power and aftermarkets: the US Kodak case
The facts of the *Kodak* case[90] can be summarised as follows. Kodak sells photocopiers in competition with numerous other sellers. At the time of the litigation Kodak had a 23 per cent share of the high-volume copier market and less than a 20 per cent share of the micrographic equipment market. Kodak effectively tied sales of machinery and repair and maintenance services by refusing to supply independent service organisations with spare parts. The latter complained that Kodak had limited the availability of its proprietary spare parts in order to monopolise the market for the servicing of Kodak photocopiers and other equipment. The independent service organisations conceded that Kodak did not have market power in the original equipment market, but claimed that the tying product was Kodak replacement parts. Kodak was alleged to have used its monopoly power in

---

[88] R. Bork, *The Antitrust Paradox* (1978), p.140; R. Posner, *Antitrust Law: An Economic Perspective* (1976), p.173.
[89] D.S. Evans and A.J. Padilla, "Designing Antitrust Rules for Assessing Unilateral Practices: A Neo-Chicago Approach" (2005) 72 U. Chi. L. Rev. 73 at p.77.
[90] *Eastman Kodak Co v Image Technical Services, Inc*, 112 S.Ct 2072 (1992).

the Kodak parts aftermarket where it essentially had a 100 per cent market share to gain control of the Kodak service aftermarket by means of illegal tying. Kodak's defence was primarily based on the argument that if there is competition in the primary market of equipment, aftermarket power cannot negatively affect consumers. The Supreme Court, however, ruled that it was possible for a manufacturer to have monopoly power in the servicing of its equipment, even if it did not have market power in the original sale of that equipment. The Supreme Court recognised that the manufacturer's ability to raise prices in aftermarkets will in all cases be constrained by the possibility of consumers purchasing alternative equipment from another manufacturer. However, if consumers lack the necessary information to calculate the likely lifetime costs of competing producers' machines, they may find themselves locked-in to a particular brand of equipment after they have made their initial equipment purchase. Consumers should look at the package price covering the initial purchase price of the machine and all maintenance costs during its lifetime. If consumers are fully informed at the time of the initial purchase decision, manufacturers can raise the price of the maintenance services only at the expense of lowering the initial purchase price of the equipment. Conversely, information deficits on the part of the consumers enable manufacturers to raise prices in aftermarkets, thus exploiting consumers who are locked-in to the original products due to high switching costs.

The Supreme Court's judgment in *Kodak* may be criticised. The Supreme Court rejected the defendant's economic theory of fully informed consumers considering full package prices before making purchases and accepted the plaintiff's economic theory of an aftermarket hold-up of imperfectly informed consumers. It is, however, doubtful whether the assumption of imperfect information coincided with reality. Many of Kodak's customers were large sophisticated businesses that may be expected to explicitly consider full lifetime costs before making their purchasing decisions.

Further criticisms have been advanced by Klein.[91] This author argues that an aftermarket hold-up is not possible even if consumers are totally uninformed, as long as there is competition among informed sellers in the primary market. Sellers know that they will be able to increase aftermarket prices up to the amount of the consumers' switching costs (not by a higher amount since consumers will switch to competing suppliers after they learn about the high repair parts and maintenance prices). Vigorous competition in the primary market will force manufacturers to reduce equipment prices to avoid loss of sales to competing suppliers. In the view of Klein, hold-ups require that sellers also possess imperfect information of future market

---

[91] C. Klein, "Market Power in Aftermarkets", in *Economic Inputs, Legal Outputs: The Role of Economics in Modern Antitrust* (F. McChesney ed., 1998), p.47. See also C. Shapiro, "Aftermarkets and Consumer Welfare: Making Sense of Kodak" (1995) 63 Antitrust L.J. 483.

conditions. Unanticipated changes in market conditions determine whether a manufacturer will find it profitable to engage in a hold-up. Opportunism will be in the private interests of a manufacturer if the benefit to be gained from exploiting locked-in consumers by asking super-competitive prices for maintenance services exceeds the resultant loss of future demand for the primary good. Short term gains from opportunistic behaviour may exceed long term reputational costs caused to the brand name if there is an unexpectedly large increase in demand for services or an unexpectedly large decrease in demand for equipment. In the former case hold-ups are profitable given the substantial gains from a strategy of installed base opportunism. In the latter case long run reputational disadvantages become less important and the costs of a hold-up may become less than the gains of such an action. This is particularly true for firms who have decided to exit the primary market. In a "last period" situation the brand name costs associated with the lost premium on future sales become an unimportant constraint on seller behaviour. Klein stresses that hold-ups, even if they do occur, are not evidence of market power. Manufacturers may decide to engage in a hold-up even if they face competition from many alternative suppliers. Many contract disputes are the consequence of changes in market conditions not anticipated when the original contractual agreement was reached. Contract law is superior to antitrust law in hold-up cases because it explicitly takes account of the contractual environment.

Other commentators have advanced arguments in support of a greater scope for aftermarket hold-ups. In their view, profit maximisation can be realised by adjusting two variables: the equipment price and the after-market product price. The equipment price affects the firm's competitiveness in attracting new (and repeat) buyers, but is not relevant to incumbent owners of the equipment who purchase only the aftermarket product. The aftermarket price, however, affects both potential new buyers and incumbent owners of the equipment who purchase only the aftermarket product. The latter price may thus be used to strike the ideal balance between profiting from customers who have already bought the equipment and maintaining a reputation for low aftermarket prices, necessary to continue attracting new customers. As a consequence, the level of competition in the equipment market has little or no impact on the mark-up of proprietary aftermarket products.[92]

The *Kodak* case bears close resemblance to the older European *Hugin* case.[93] A manufacturer of cash registers refused to supply spare parts to competing suppliers of servicing, thus tying the supply of maintenance and repair services to the purchase of spare parts for the machines. Even though Hugin's market share in the market for cash registers was low (not exceeding 13 per cent), the refusal to supply independent service organisations was qualified as an abuse. In the European Commission's view, the

---

[92] S. Borenstein, J.K. MacKie-Mason and J.S. Netz, "Antitrust Policy in Aftermarkets" (1995) 63 Antitrust L.J. 455 at p.463.
[93] Case 22/78 *Hugin v Commission* [1979] ECR 1869.

refusal to supply had the result of removing a major competitor (Liptons) in the matter of service, maintenance, repair and the supply of reconditioned machines. In the early days of European competition law the relevant competition problems of aftermarkets were not touched upon. The Court of Justice annulled the decision for a different reason, namely the absence of impact on interstate trade.

In recent theoretical economic literature, a number of models has been developed which show that—contrary to the Chicago learning—dominant firms may strategically leverage market power in adjacent markets. Within the scope of this book, a complete overview of this literature cannot be provided. Two different scenarios of anti-competitive effects will be briefly presented. First, bundling may lead to entry deterrence in the market of the bundled product if this market is subject to economies of scale. Second, tying and bundling may affect the future competitiveness of rivals in the market of the tied/bundled product and deter them from competing in the home market. The first scenario involves independent products.[94] By credibly committing itself to sell the products only as a bundle (for example, technological bundling), the dominant firm signals to competitors in the market of the bundled good that pricing will be aggressive. Fierce competition in the bundled good market may decrease the rivals' profits and force them to exit. However, if the dominant firm is unable to commit itself to the bundling strategy (if it cannot credibly threaten to refuse supplies to customers who do not want to purchase the bundle), re-entry may be expected if the price of the bundled good is increased. The second scenario involves complementary products. Tying can be a profitable strategy in markets where firms compete through upfront R&D investments and entry is, therefore, risky. By tying the two products, the prospects of recouping an investment (by new entrants) are made less certain. The reason is that innovations by newcomers must be simultaneously successful in both markets, because the tying and tied good are complements. Since successful entry requires that newcomers enter two markets instead of one, the entrants' incentives for investment and innovation will be reduced.[95] Bundling may also be anti-competitive if it allows the achievement of economies of scale and scope. In such a case, the incumbent may deny entrants the possibility of achieving the minimum efficient scale in the adjacent market and thus prevent entry also into the complementary home market.[96] These models show under which conditions tying and bundling may cause anti-competitive

---

[94] M.D. Whinston, "Tying, Foreclosure and Exclusion" (1990) 80 Amer. Econ. Rev. 837. It should be noted that a recent variant of the Whinston model shows similar exclusion effects in the case of complementary goods (B. Nalebuff, "Bundling as an Entry Barrier" (1999) 114 Quart. J. Bus. Econ. 283). However, the latter model is of limited practical relevance since it assumes monopoly power in both markets.

[95] J.P. Choi and C. Stefanadis, "Tying, Investment and the Dynamic Leverage Theory" (2001) 32 Rand J. Econ. 52.

[96] D.W. Carlton and M. Waldman, "The Strategic Use of Tying to Preserve and Create Market Power in Evolving Industries" (2002) 33 Rand J. Econ. 194. It may be noted that some Chicagoans continue to argue that neither independent nor complementary goods allow for leveraging. See K. Hylton, *Antitrust Law* (2003), p.280.

effects, but their practical value is limited because the available data are rarely adequate to determine whether the practice will actually reduce welfare (weighing any potential efficiencies with possible losses due to foreclosure).

7.3.1.2 Efficiency explanations of bundling and tying

If the only purpose of bundling and tying was to hinder the entry of or to induce the exit of an equally efficient competitor, a flat prohibition would be defensible. In reality, however, market foreclosure is not the entire story. The foreclosure explanation is challenged by efficiency theories. Bundling and tying may reflect consumers' preferences, achieve costs savings and/or be used for reasons of quality assurance. Other explanations for tying include the wish to practice price discrimination or to increase the sales of the tying product. Firms may thus advance several reasonable business rationales for tying in order to defend themselves against the "abuse of dominance" or monopolisation claim.[97]

Tie-in sales are benign if they generate efficiencies. Many products are naturally and efficiently tied together or bundled. There is no reason for antitrust intervention when consumers desire assembled products such as laced shoes, radios and cars.[98] Besides reflecting consumer preferences, bundling and tying may generate costs efficiencies. Costs savings resulting from economies of scope arise if consumers purchase complementary goods from the same producer. Also the suppliers' costs of producing and distributing those products are reduced through bundling or tying.

Another reason to engage in tying is quality assurance and the related protection from opportunistic behaviour.[99] Generally, a firm may assure quality by forcing customers to buy another of its products or services and not to use substitutes. A manufacturer of durable goods may decide to operate through a network of exclusive dealerships forcing customers to purchase servicing from the network. The refusal to supply independent service organisations may be motivated by the concern that the low quality of the servicing provided by the latter may harm the reputation of the network.

A prominent explanation for bundling and tying is that it permits profitable price discrimination.[1] Once an intermediate durable good is sold, control of its rate of utilisation passes to the downstream purchaser. Manufacturers of such

---

[97] Another non-benign reason of tie-in sales is to circumvent price regulation. If the price for the tying product is regulated, a high price for tied products can completely circumvent the price regulation unless also the price for the latter products is regulated. In most European countries price controls for consumer goods have been abolished. The hypothesis of evasion of price regulation, which is not further elaborated upon in the text, may remain relevant as long as price controls exist (e.g. in the sector of utilities) and tie-in sales are commercially feasible.

[98] D.W. Carlton and J.M. Perloff, *Modern Industrial Organization* (4th ed., 2005), p.319.

[99] R.H. Bork, *The Antitrust Paradox* (1978), pp.379–380.

[1] Stigler explained a single-package price for films (block booking) as a method to price discriminate according to the implicit valuation of different films within the package by individual buyers (G. Stigler, "United States v Loew's Inc: a Note on Block Booking" (1963) 152 Sup. Ct. Rev. 153). In current economic literature, price discrimination is advanced as a prominent efficiency rationale for bundling and tying. See M. Motta, *Competition Policy—Theory and Practice* (2004), pp.462–463; J. Tirole, *The Theory of Industrial Organization* (2001), p.146.

durable goods may tie the purchase of relatively low-valued commodities to the sale of the primary goods. Hence, tying arrangements (in particular a dynamic tie or "requirements tying") may be motivated by the goal of gaining control over the rate of utilisation of durable goods.[2] Tied sales of machines and complementary products may enable manufacturers to charge higher prices to high intensity users.[3] The same is true for tied sales of machines and maintenance services. If the purpose of the tying firm is to discriminate in price, other alternatives such as attaching a meter to measure the intensity of use are available. These alternatives may, however, involve greater policing and monitoring costs than a tying scheme. The welfare effects of price discrimination were discussed in section 7.2.1.

The foreclosure explanation of tying is also challenged by the possibility of using repair parts tying arrangements in order to increase the sales of the original equipment. By increasing prices for maintenance services and reducing the prices of the original equipment,[4] manufacturers may wish to prevent customers from opportunistically extending the useful lives of the machines and, hence, buying fewer of them than would be consistent with the firm's profit-maximising objectives. The welfare effects of such arrangements are ambiguous. A larger output of high quality durable goods must be balanced against a reduction of the output of repair parts below competitive levels.

7.3.2 Legal treatment of bundling and tying

In the old days of US antitrust, judges regarded tying as merely anti-competitive. In *Standard Oil*, Justice Frankfurter wrote that tying agreements "serve hardly any purpose beyond the suppression of competition".[5] In the *Northern Pacific* case (1958) the Supreme Court held that tying denies competitors free access to the market for the tied product not because the party imposing the tying requirements has a better product or a lower price but

---

[2] See J. Bowman, "Tying Arrangements and the Leverage Problem" (1957) 67 Yale L.J. 19 at p.24, noting that "the use of a tie-in sale as a counting device is consistent with the facts of a large number of tying cases".

[3] A clear example is the *Vaessen-Moris* case decided by the European Commission in 1979 (Case IV/29.290 *Vaessen-Moris* [1979] OJ. L 19/32). A firm acquired a patent on a machine to make sausages. The use of the machine was free to users who agreed to buy skins from the supplier of the machine. A competing skin manufacturer complained that he was foreclosed from the market of the secondary product. The European Commission argued that the patent owner had extended monopoly power into a second market without checking whether the package price for the machine and the skins was higher than the sum of the prices when the goods were sold separately. High intensity customers who place a relatively high value on the particular features of the specific manufacturer's product will be willing to pay relatively high prices for the use of the machine. Competing manufacturers cannot supply a perfect substitute. This does not mean that the price discrimination is anti-competitive. Creation of features is exactly what the competitive process should encourage.

[4] In competitive markets overpricing of service implies the corresponding underpricing of equipment.

[5] *Standard Oil Co v United States*, 337 U.S. 293, 305–306 (1949).

because of his "power leverage in another market".[6] In *Jefferson Parish*,[7] the majority decided to keep the *per se* prohibition intact, but required that the tying allegation has to pass several screens before being considered illegal on its appearance. This test (modified *per se* illegality) consists of four steps: (a) the tying and tied goods are two separate products; (b) the defendant has market power in the tying product market; (c) the defendant forces consumers to purchase the tied product; and (d) the tying arrangement forecloses a substantial volume of commerce. Modern US antitrust shows the impact of the Chicago School and its rejection of the leverage argument. In the recent *US Microsoft* case, the leverage theory does not appear in the DC Circuit Court of Appeals' opinion.[8] Rather, the Court caused a Copernican revolution in the antitrust treatment of tying by endorsing a "rule of reason" approach to "technological tying" (bundling). Under a rule of reason standard, it must be shown that tying harms the competitive process and thereby harms consumers; in addition, there is scope for the monopolist to argue a pro-competitive justification (for example greater efficiency or enhanced consumer appeal).[9] This approach allows the assessment of whether the integrated product is more valuable to end users than the sum of its parts, so that technological bundling can be accepted if it leads to an increase of consumer welfare.

The American Supreme Court's view that tying agreements serve hardly any purpose beyond the suppression of competition has inspired European competition law and has laid the basis for a sceptical treatment of tying which comes close to a *per se* prohibition. The formulation of Article 82(d) EC tends to remain a major obstacle to an analysis focusing on allocative efficiency and consumer welfare. The idea of a superficial link between products is more hospitable to protection of competitors from (unsubstantiated) leveraging of market power than to a careful analysis of competitive harm damaging consumers.

In European competition law, the leverage argument is prominently present in the leading *Tetra Pak* case,[10] which identifies five leveraging categories that may be abusive, two of which are particularly relevant: (a) the abuse takes place on the dominated market but its effects are felt on another market on which the company does not hold a dominant position; and (b) the abuse takes place on a market separate from, but related to and connected with, the market dominated by the company.[11]

---

[6] *Northern Pacific Railway Company v United States*, 356 U.S. 1 (1958).
[7] *Jefferson Parish*, 46 U.S. 9 (1984).
[8] In the US, the *Microsoft* case has kicked off a lively debate among economists. The main contenders have issued their views in D.S. Evans, F.M. Fisher, D.L. Rubinfeld and R.L. Schmalensee, *Did Microsoft Harm Consumers? Two Opposing Views* (2000).
[9] *US v Microsoft*, 253 F.3d 34 (D.C. Cir.2001), at 95–97.
[10] Case T–83/91 *Tetra Pak International v Commission* [1994] ECR II–755, paras 118 *et seq.*, as confirmed on appeal in Case C–333/94P *Tetra Pak International SA v Commission* [1996] ECR I–5951.
[11] Compare, for an overview, Opinion of Advocate General Colomer in Case C–333/94P *Tetra Pak International SA v Commission* [1996] ECR I–5951, para.38.

Consequently, tying is likely to infringe Article 82 EC if the supplier is dominant in the market of the tying product.[12] The only way to avoid the prohibition is by showing that tying can be objectively justified. It should be noted that there is no scope for an efficiency defence. An objective justification requires that the dominant firm pursues a legitimate objective and that tying is a reasonable and proportionate means to achieve that objective.[13] Up until now, there have been no Article 82 EC proceedings in which tying has been permitted. This does not automatically mean that tying can never be objectively justified. Indeed, there were only a few cases in which the Court of Justice dealt with tying and in these cases there was no clear (economic) justification of the practice (see the case discussions in Box 7.4).

Box 7.4: Two European tying cases: Hilti and Tetra Pak

Two pivotal tying cases under European competition law are *Hilti* and *Tetra Pak*. In *Hilti*[14] a manufacturer supplying nail guns to the construction industry was found to be abusing its dominant position by tying the purchase of nails and cartridges to the purchase of guns. Both the Hilti nail gun and its cartridge strips were protected by patent. Hilti had a 55 per cent market share in the market for nail guns but a much lower market share in the market for Hilti-compatible nails and cartridge strips. The European Commission, upheld by the European Court of Justice, found Hilti guilty of abusing its dominant position by commercial practices that hindered the entry into the market for Hilti-compatible nails of independent nail producers. The *Tetra Pak* case[15] concerned the world leader in the field of packaging liquid foods (such as milk and fruit juices) in cartons. Tetra Pak produces both packaging machinery and cartons. At the time of the decision Tetra Pak's market share in aseptic packaging (i.e. for long-life products) was between 90 and 95 per cent, while its market share in non-aseptic packaging (i.e. for fresh products) was between 50 and 55 per cent. Tetra Pak required exclusive use of Tetra Pak cartons on its machines. Moreover, Tetra Pak sold cartons on the Italian market for non-aseptic packaging at prices below average variable costs. The first practice was condemned as illegal tying and the price reductions were seen as evidence of "predatory pricing" prohibited by Article 82 EC. Tetra Pak was condemned to pay a fine of no less than 75 million ECU for having abused its dominant position.[16]

---

[12] Exceptionally, the European Commission has also found an infringement of Article 82 EC when the undertaking was only dominant in the tied product. See *Digital*, Commission Press Release IP/97/868.

[13] See P.-J. Loewenthal, "The Defence of 'Objective Justification' in the Application of Article 82 EC" (2005) 28 World Competition 455.

[14] Case IV/31.488 *Eurofix-Bauco/Hilti* [1988] O.J. L 65/19.

[15] Case T–83/91 *Tetra Pak II* [1994] ECR II–755.

[16] The fine was reduced by the European Court of Justice, see Case C–333/94P *Tetra Pak International SA v Commission* [1996] ECR I–5951.

It is not easy to determine which explanation for tying is the most convincing in the above cases. The firms may have engaged in tying to foreclose competitors on an adjacent market, but also for the purpose of price discrimination or with the aim of guaranteeing the quality of their products. In *Hilti* the defendant's argument that the reliability and safety of its nail gun system was enhanced by tying the sale of nail guns to nails seemed more plausible than the European Commission's theory of anti-competitive behaviour.[17] When tying is seen only as a way to expand monopoly power into another market, many relevant issues will remain unanswered. Even if anti-competitive effects materialise, from an economic perspective efficiency defences for tying must be allowed. However, the latter may not fit into the existing legal framework or may conflict with the broader goals of European competition policy. According to the ordoliberal ideas underlying Article 82 EC, practices that are perfectly legal when practiced by firms not possessing market power may be considered an abuse when carried out by a dominant firm.[18] In addition, tying for the purpose of price discrimination (between Member States) flies in the face of the goal of market integration and will thus be banned in spite of possible ensuing efficiencies.

Tying is often used as a means of entering a relatively fast-moving "new" market, into which a dominant player wishes to establish itself by drawing from its existing market position. The European Commission's recent *Microsoft* decision confirms that Article 82 EC fully applies to practices exercised on such markets[19]—if dominance can be established either on such a new market or a related market. The fact that a dominant company merely reacts to competitive pressure does not ward off a potential infringement aiming at a restriction of competition.[20] In *Microsoft*,[21] the European Commission outlined four conditions under which tying is incompatible with Article 82 EC: (a) the tying and tied goods are two separate products;[22] (b) the company concerned is dominant in the tying product market; (c) the company concerned does not give customers a choice to obtain the tying product without the tied product;

---

[17] B. Nalebuff and D. Majerus, "Bundling, Tying, and Portfolio Effects: Part 2—Case Studies" (2003) 1 DTI *Economics Paper* 19.

[18] According to the European Court of Justice, dominant firms have a "special responsibility not to allow their conduct to impair genuine undistorted competition on the common market". See Case 322/81 *Michelin v Commission* [1983] ECR 3461, para.57.

[19] See, for example, Case COMP/37.792 *Microsoft*, case not yet reported, paras 694, 725, 781, 842, 897, 969, 973–983 and 1067.

[20] Case T–203/01 *Michelin v Commission (Michelin II)* [2003] ECR II–4071, para.245; and Case COMP/38.233 *Wanadoo Interactive*, case not yet reported, paras 315 *et seq.*

[21] Case COMP/37.792 *Microsoft*, case not yet reported, para.794.

[22] This implies distinct demand and different levels of supply; complementary usage is not a sufficient defence.

and (d) tying forecloses competition. If these conditions are satisfied, tying will be illegal unless it can be objectively justified. Instead of subjecting tying to a "rule of reason" standard, these requirements boil down to a modified *per se* illegality test,[23] which was rejected in the US *Microsoft* case by the DC Circuit Court of Appeals (see above). The European Commission concluded that Microsoft had illegally tied (bundled) the sale of its operating system (Windows) with that of its streaming media software (Windows Media Player). The requirement imposed on Microsoft to untie Windows Media Player from Windows recognises the leveraging power of Microsoft's operating system's dominant position.

The European case law also offers some indications as to the permissibility of mixed bundling, where the different products are still available to the customer separately. Article 82 EC may apply when a dominant undertaking offers a bonus or discounts if the customers acquire different products.[24] This conduct can be viewed as abusive, in particular when the large size of the discounts provides powerful incentives to buy the bundle of goods.[25] It may be added that, in a merger case, it was held that mixed bundling is usually compatible with European competition law, except in cases where the financial reserves are used to subsidise the sales of product A or B in the mixed bundle (see *GE/Honeywell*[26]).

Looking at the case law and taking into account the different economic explanations for bundling and tying, current European competition law seems too simplistic. Even though leveraging market power cannot be excluded, the conditions under which anti-competitive effects may occur require careful consideration. The requirement of foreclosure, mentioned in *Microsoft*, implies that the competition authority must prove the anti-competitive effects of tying. Critics have argued that the European Commission failed to do so. To bring their streaming media software to the market, competitors have many alternative channels at their disposal, the most common of which is certainly direct download from the web.[27] In addition, a full economic analysis requires consideration of potential efficiencies and an analysis of effects of the practice on consumers. Technological tying may reduce the deadweight loss by allowing for price discrimination, it can reduce consumer risk and respond to a need to control the quality of a system good. By contrast, the anti-competitive effects seem negligible since software integration normally does not impose any additional charge on end users.[28] In sum, a more careful analysis of anti-

---

[23] As is correctly noticed by Evans and Padilla in a reaction to a contribution by Dolmans and Graf. See M. Dolmans and T. Graf, "Analysis of Tying Under Article 82 EC: The European Commission's Microsoft Decision in Perspective" (2004) 27 *World Competition* 225; D.S. Evans and A.J. Padilla, "Tying Under Article 82 EC and the Microsoft Decision: A Comment on Dolmans and Graf" (2004) 27 *World Competition* 503.

[24] Case 322/81 *Michelin v Commission* [1983] ECR 3461.

[25] Case T–203/01 *Michelin v Commission (Michelin II)* [2003] ECR II–4071, paras 161–164. Most recently, in Case COMP/39.116 *Coca-Cola* [2005] O.J. L 253/21, tying provisions were explicitly targeted.

[26] Case COMP/M.2220 *General Electric/Honeywell* [2004] O.J. L 48/1, para.353.

[27] See for this and other criticisms R. Pardolesi and A. Renda, "The European Commission's Case Against Microsoft: Kill Bill?" (2004) 27 *World Competition* 558.

[28] *ibid.* at 563.

competitive effects and a full consideration of efficiency gains benefiting consumers are needed to bring the current European competition law on tying in line with sound economic principles.

7.4 Refusals to deal and essential facilities

Firms enjoying a dominant position have a duty to supply on a non-discriminatory basis. In *Commercial Solvents*, the Court of Justice held that refusing to supply a downstream competitor in order to restrict competition in the market for the final product must be considered an abuse within the meaning of Article 82 (then 86) EC.[29] From this case law has developed the notion of essential (or bottleneck) facilities which has had a significant and increasing role in the Community's liberalisation programmes in network industries such as telecommunications, gas, electricity and transport.[30] Essential facilities cases involve refusals to deal of a special type: the firm holding the facility refuses to provide other firms with access to something that is vitally important to competitive viability in a particular market.[31] Usually, the situation is one in which two related activities consisting of an upstream and a downstream component are necessary to generate the final product, as may be the case for providing electricity services through a net-work and the services themselves. A competition problem can then arise if a vertically integrated firm owns an input (the facility) to compete in the final market and denies request for access to that input by other firms.[32] In the following, two questions will be dealt with: what are the welfare effects of refusals to deal, and under which conditions may an essential facilities doc-trine in competition law be economically justified?

7.4.1 Economic analysis of refusals to deal

When a dominant firm is vertically integrated and refuses to deal with a competitor in a downstream market, various factors, dependent on the char-acteristics of the industry involved, affect the welfare analysis.[33] Economic theory teaches that vertical integration by a monopolist has no effect on wel-fare in a world of complete information and no uncertainty, where the upstream monopoly is uncontested and sells to identical downstream buyers who use these inputs in fixed proportions and employ a constant return to

---

[29] Joined Cases 6/73 and 7/73 *Istituto Chemioterapico Italiano Spa and Commercial Solvents Corp v Commission* [1974] ECR 223.
[30] D.M. Newbery, *Privatization, Restructuring, and Regulation of Network Utilities* (1999).
[31] S. Bishop and M. Walker, *Economics of E.C. Competition Law: Concepts, Application and Measure-ment*, (2nd ed 2002) para.6.104.
[32] OECD, *The Essential Facilities Concept* (1996), p.87.
[33] Compare OECD, *The Essential Facilities Concept* (1996), p.87; and see also G.J. Werden, "The Law and Economics of the Essential Facilities Doctrine" (1987) 32 St. Louis U.L.J. 433 at 473.

scale production technology. Whether the monopolist charges prices at the stage of production or decides to integrate downstream, he will be able to appropriate all monopoly profits in either scenario.[34] This insight is in accordance with the Chicago view that there is only one monopoly profit to be gained without there being any need for the monopolist to take recourse to foreclosing competitors in the downstream market.[35] The argument no longer holds, however, when there is scope for the monopolist to charge different profit-maximising prices to different customers, and this will be the case when contracts are secret. The upstream monopolist may then use vertical restraints to foreclose a market so as to reduce intra-brand competition downstream, even when the downstream market is competitive.[36] What type of effects this entails for social welfare can only be determined through a case-by-case assessment. At this point it may suffice to say that those cases where the anti-competitive effects are of such magnitude as to require firms to provide competitors with access to their monopoly assets should be rare. Therefore, an eminent commentator concluded on essential facilities that they are "less a doctrine than an epithet indicating some exceptions to the right to keep one's creations to oneself, but not telling us what those exceptions are".[37]

As regards competition policy and law, caution is warranted when access to essential facilities is claimed. During the appraisal two observations must be firmly kept in mind. First, competition law protects competition, not competitors. A generous application of the essential facilities doctrine will lead to unsatisfactory results when aiding only competitors in catching up on their more efficient counterparts, since it will discourage them from investing in the development of competing facilities themselves and so truly benefit consumers.[38] Second, it has been argued that granting access through essential facilities should be limited to natural monopolies.[39] In other industries which are not characterised by natural monopoly the application of the essential facilities doctrine will undermine the incentives for dynamic efficiency. Innovation activities by the dominant firm may be discouraged since giving its competitors access to the bottleneck is an expropriation of the return on the firm's efforts. If the bottleneck is due to an intellectual property right (for example, in high technology markets), competition authorities should be particularly reluctant to intervene.[40] More generally, the implication of

---

[34] J.A. Ordover and G. Saloner, "Predation, Monopolisation and Antitrust", in *The Handbook of Industrial Organization I* (R. Schmalensee and R.D. Willig ed., 1989), p.564.

[35] See s.7.3.1.1.

[36] O.D. Hart and J. Tirole, "Vertical Integration and Market Foreclosure" (1990) Brookings Pap. Econ. Act., Microeconomics 205.

[37] P.E. Areeda, "The Essential Facilities Doctrine: An Epithet in Need of Limiting Principles" (1989) 58 Antitrust L.J. 841.

[38] This has been pointedly noted by the Advocate General Jacobs in his Opinion to Case C–7/97 *Oscar Bronner GmbH & Co KG v Mediaprint (Bronner)* [1998] ECR I–7791, paras 57–58.

[39] G.J. Werden, "The Law and Economics of the Essential Facilities Doctrine" (1987) 32 St. Louis U.L.J. 433 at p.476.

[40] EAGCP, *An Economic Approach to Article 82* (2005), p.44. For the opposite view that dynamic efficiency is not necessarily negatively affected by a duty to license, see C. Ritter, "Refusal to Deal and 'Essential Facilities': Does Intellectual Property Require Special Deference Compared to Tangibile Property?" (2005) 28 World Competition 281.

requiring dominant firms to provide access to their assets will be a need to impose price regulation on access terms to that monopoly asset,[41] and this may require sector-specific regulation to complement general competition law.

7.4.2 An economic assessment of the case law on refusals to deal under Article 82 EC[42]

In early decisions, the application of Article 82 EC to grant access to facilities deemed essential witnessed substantial proliferation. The European Commission was apparently willing to intervene in a host of industries ranging from telecommunications and transmission of energy to transport on most diverse grounds.[43] Notwithstanding lack of consensus even on which cases constitute an essential facility,[44] the European Commission created a broad principle holding that companies in a dominant position must not refuse to supply their goods or services to either competitors or customers if the refusal would have a significant effect on competition which cannot be legitimately justified.[45] Essential facilities thus became an acronym for forcing access by new competitors on recently deregulated markets, often based on competitors' complaints alleging that their economic survival was on the line. Not questioning the general drive of liberalisation, it does look as if the essential facilities tool was used somewhat haphazardly. Frequently, the factual analysis—starting with the definition of the relevant market—was conducted in a rather patchy manner, and this then resulted in an overt summary appraisal of the essential character of the facility at hand. The *Sea Containers v Stena Sealink*[46] case may serve as an example. Concerning the Holyhead harbour in Wales, the Commission concluded that Stena Sealink had abused its dominant position "in the provision of an essential facility" as the harbour's operator by refusing access without objective justification or by granting other companies access only on terms less favourable than those which it gives to its own services. In so doing Stena Sealink protected its position as a ferry operator

[41] S. Bishop and M. Walker, *Economics of E.C. Competition Law: Concepts, Application and Measurement* (1999), para.5.32.

[42] For an overview of the current state of EC law on refusals to deal and essential facilities, see J. Temple Lang, "The Principle of Essential Facilities in European Community Competition Law—The Position since Bronner" (2000) 1 Journal of Network Industries 375.

[43] A full listing of Commission interventions on such grounds is to be found in: L. Ritter, W.D. Braun and F. Rawlinson, *European Competition Law: A Practitioner's Guide* (2nd ed., 2000), pp.382–383; as well as in J. Temple Lang, "Defining Legitimate Competition: Companies' Duties to Supply Competitors and Access to Essential Facilities" (1994) 18 Fordham Int'l L.J. 245 at pp.319–321.

[44] OECD, *The Essential Facilities Concept* (1996), p.7.

[45] In Case IV/34.689 *Sea Containers v Stena Line* [1994] O.J. L 15/8, the Commission stated that the facility is considered essential where access is necessary for competitors to provide services to their customers, imposing an "insuperable barrier to entry" or creating a "serious, permanent and inescapable handicap" to their activities (further elaborated upon in Case IV/32.318 *London European/Sabena* [1988] O.J. L 317/47) and that, in the absence of legitimate business reasons, access may not be denied or granted on terms less favorable than those which the dominant firm gives to its own services (*Sealink/B&I* (1992) 9 C.M.L.R. 255).

[46] Case IV/34.689 *Sea Containers v Stena Line* [1994] O.J. L 15/8, para.66.

from Holyhead. Picking a particular route as the relevant market following Sea Container's contentions and without conducting an in-depth analysis thereon, however, artificially narrowed down the assessment to start off with. As a result the European Commission's approach found itself open to allegations of protecting competitors rather than competition.[47] In the meantime, the evolution of this particular market may have proved the European Commission wrong in defining such a harbour as an essential facility:[48] competition on the route indicated had meanwhile been promoted from Liverpool harbour, which had not been considered in the original decision to be part of the relevant market.[49]

That a more cautious approach would be warranted became perceptible in the *Tiercé Ladbroke* case[50] and in *European Night Services*,[51] leading ultimately to the adoption by the European Court of Justice of the *Bronner* test which has substantially limited the scope of the essential facilities doctrine under European law. The facts of the latter case can be briefly summarised as follows. Mediaprint has a very large share of the daily newspaper market in Austria[52] and operates the only nationwide newspaper home-delivery scheme in that country. Bronner, the publisher of a rival newspaper which, by reason of its small circulation,[53] is unable either alone or in cooperation with other publishers to set up and operate its own home-delivery scheme in economically reasonable conditions, asked to have access to Mediaprint's scheme for appropriate remuneration. The Court held that refusing access does not constitute an abuse of a dominant position within the meaning of Article 82 EC. The Bronner conditions for a facility to be essential and Article 82 EC to be infringed can be summarised as follows:[54]

1. the facility is controlled by a monopolist;

2. the facility is considered essential because it is indispensable in order to compete on the market with the controller of the facility;

3. access is denied or granted on unreasonable terms;

4. no legitimate business reason is given for objectively justifying the denied access (as to the feasibility of providing the facility);

---

[47] J.S. Venit and J.J. Kallaugher, "Essential Facilities: A Comparative Law Approach", in Fordham Corp. L. Inst. 1994, 315, 333 (B. E. Hawk ed., 1995).
[48] Quoting from the Commission officials' commentary; see C. Esteva Mosso and S. Ryan, "Article 82—Abuse of a Dominant Position", in *The EC Law of Competition* (J. Faull and A. Nikpay ed., 1999), para.3.176, fn.157.
[49] NERA, Competition Brief No.4, 1999. Other examples may be found in L. Hancher and H.H.P. Lugard, "De essential facilities doctrine" (1999) 47 S.E.W. 323 at pp.326–327.
[50] Case T–504/93 *Tiercé Ladbroke v Commission* [1997] ECR II–923, para.131. On appeal, see Joined Cases C–359/95P and C–379/95P *Tiercé Ladbroke v Commission* [1997] ECR I–6265.
[51] Case IV/34.600 *Night Services* [1994] O.J. L 259/20; Joined Cases T–374/94, T–375/94, T–384/94 and T–388/94 *European Nights Services Ltd and others v Commission* [1998] ECR II–3141.
[52] 46.8% in terms of circulation and 42% in terms of advertising revenues. See *Bronner*, para.6.
[53] 3.6% in terms of circulation and 6% in terms of advertising revenues. See *Bronner*, para.4.
[54] Compare thereto the references to *Bronner* contained in L. Ritter, W.D. Braun and F. Rawlinson, *European Competition Law: A Practitioner's Guide* (2nd ed., 2000), p.381.

5. a competitor is unable (practically or reasonably) to duplicate the essential facility.

It thus seems that the exceptional circumstances requiring the application of the essential facilities doctrine as bypassing the regular rulings on the refusal to deal (formulated in *Commercial Solvents*[55]) exist only if the monopolist's refusal to deal eliminates all competition in a downstream market and if this service is indispensable to carrying out the competitor's business.[56] The crux to answering the latter is contained in the condition requiring duplication of the facility to be "unpractical" or "unreasonable", as, in Advocate General Jacobs' wording, it is only under such circumstances that the holder of the facility has a "genuine stranglehold" on the related market and not just a legitimate "competitive advantage".[57] Natural monopolies seem to be a clear case where access to essential facilities could be supported both by economic arguments and the legal criteria advanced by the European Court. In other market settings, the scope for imposing a duty to deal has been made subject to very strict requirements. The company claiming access will have to prove that it is either physically impossible or economically too expensive to duplicate the alleged "essential facility". This is to be welcomed, given the potential negative effects on dynamic efficiency and consumer welfare of a too lenient rule.

7.5 Predatory pricing

Predatory pricing constitutes a type of behaviour where prices are so low that the competitive process itself is damaged. Since low prices are also a virtue of the competitive process, competition authorities face a difficult task in distinguishing predatory pricing from healthy price competition. The elimination of inefficient firms is the natural consequence of the competitive process, but competition will be damaged if efficient rivals are also driven out of the market through price reductions by dominant firms. The basic idea is that a dominant firm, called the predator, incurs short term losses in a particular market in order to induce the exit or deter the entry of a rival firm, called the prey, so that super-normal profits can be earned in the future, either in the same market or in other markets. The stylised story goes as follows. A dominant firm active in many geographic markets (or selling many brands of a differentiated product) sets a price below costs in one geographic market where its actions are constrained by a fringe of small competitors (or cuts the price for one brand which faces competition), while holding a price above costs in other markets. Small competitors that are not sustained by their operations in other markets suffer losses in the short run and exit in the long

---

[55] Joined Cases 6/73 and 7/73 *Instituto Chemioterapico Italiano SpA and Commercial Solvents Corp v Commission* [1974] ECR 223.
[56] *Bronner*, para.41.
[57] See Advocate General Jacobs in his Opinion to Case C–7/97 *Bronner*, para.65. Compare *Bronner*, para.44.

run. After the elimination of the target firms, the dominant firm inherits a monopoly, restricts output, increases prices and earns supra-competitive profits.

The price reduction is profitable only because of the added market power the predator gains from eliminating, disciplining or otherwise inhibiting the competitive conduct of a rival or potential rival. Several factors have an impact on the profitability of predatory pricing: chances that losses can be recovered by future gains are higher if demand is inelastic, if the price war is of short duration and the price reductions relatively small, if the predator is able to gain additional market share, and if entry barriers are high. In this respect one should also take into account that the goal of the predatory campaign may be to discipline a rival's pricing behaviour rather than to totally eliminate him from the market. In the latter scenario, predatory pricing will more often be profitable and it may thus be expected that most cases of predation will involve inducements of collusion or merger.[58] Apart from low prices predatory behaviour may take other forms such as expansion of capacity, excessive advertising or the introduction of new products for strategic purposes.[59] There are two related debates on predatory behaviour: a theoretical debate focusing on the question of whether it may actually occur and a practical debate concerning the optimal legal rule for predatory pricing. Both problems will be successively dealt with below.

7.5.1 The economic debate: is predatory pricing a rational strategy?

7.5.1.1 The Chicago argument: predatory pricing is irrational

Traditionally Chicago economists have argued that predation is unlikely to occur because it is a very costly strategy for the predator to undertake. Predatory pricing is costly both to the incumbent and its rivals, and the more so if the incumbent is larger than the rivals and unable to price discriminate by cutting price only where the rivals challenge. In the long run, sales at below costs prices can be profitable only if the price cutter, after eliminating its target competitor, can make good its losses by means of a price increase. In most cases this will be impossible because the increased price will attract new entrants. The price will therefore be forced down towards a competitive level

---

[58] This is confirmed by empirical evidence. Koller investigated 26 decisions and found evidence of predatory pricing in only four cases, three of which were motivated by the goal of enforcing a horizontal price agreement or inducing a merger (R.H. Koller, "The Myth of Predatory Pricing: An Empirical Study" (1971) 4 Antitrust Law Econ. 105. See also: R.O. Zerbe and D.S. Cooper, "An Empirical and Theoretical Comparison of Alternative Predation Rules" (1982) 61 Tex. L. Rev. 704).
[59] P.E. Areeda and D. Turner, "Predatory Pricing and Related Practices under Section 2 of the Sherman Act" (1975) 88 Harv. L. Rev. 164; S. Martin, *Industrial Economics: Economic Analysis and Public Policy* (1994), pp.484–488.

and there will be no recouping of losses. In a seminal paper, McGee suggested that the predator would find it more profitable to merge with the prey.[60]

In the Chicago view there are three reasons why dominant firms will not engage in predatory pricing. First, a dominant firm cutting prices below costs will lose money in the short run (even though it may hope to drive rivals out of business and increase its power to control prices afterwards). The predator may lose substantially more than the target firm: as a consequence of the low prices market demand for his products may significantly increase and the costs of the overall price reductions may be larger than the losses incurred by the prey to meet competition.[61] The magnitude of the losses will depend on how long the predatory campaign must last to induce the exit of the prey. If the assets employed in an industry are sunk, the costs to a new entrant of leaving the market are greater[62] and the price war will be of long duration.[63] Generally speaking, the losses from predation do not make predatory pricing a profitable strategy. It should be added, however, that the predator might be able to lower prices selectively in particular regions or for particular types of customers, thus targeting predatory discounts at the market segments in which the prey is most heavily committed. Under the latter scenario losses will be lower and can be recouped more easily.

Second, even if the predator succeeds in driving the target firm out of the market, in the absence of barriers to entry, a monopolist will not be able to earn super-competitive profits. If markets are contestable, the target firms will re-enter or new firms will be attracted by the prospect of creaming off monopoly profits. If it is profitable for the target firm to re-enter, it will, so it is argued by Chicagoans, be able to find the financial resources needed to survive the price war.[64] Also customers who are the ultimate victims of the predator's future monopoly prices will come to the aid of target firms. The prey may offer long term contracts at a price which would be less than the price the predator would charge if it obtained a monopoly.[65] In short, predatory pricing is only a profitable strategy if the monopoly profits from predation in the second stage of the predation process exceed the losses during the first stage of predation when prices were below costs. To make predation credible, there must thus be

---

[60] J.S. McGee, "Predatory Price Cutting: The Standard Oil (N.J.) Case" (1958) 1 J. Law Econ. 37. See also: R.H. Bork, *The Antitrust Paradox: A Policy at War with Itself* (1993), p.144. Granitz and Klein criticise the original findings by Mc Gee; they conclude that Standard Oil had indeed used predatory tactics, though not by predatory pricing but by raising rivals' costs to facilitate their acquisition. See: E. Granitz and B. Klein, "Monopolisation by Raising Rivals' Costs: The Standard Oil Case" (1996) 39 J. Law Econ. 1.

[61] For a graphical representation, see S. Martin, *Industrial Economics: Economic Analysis and Public Policy* (1994), pp.454–456.

[62] An incumbent firm will rationally disregard sunk costs. An entrant, however, will want to recoup the costs of investments and this is impossible if it leaves the market when faced with the risk of below-cost pricing by an aggressive competitor.

[63] S. Martin, *Industrial Economics: Economic Analysis and Public Policy* (1994), p.458.

[64] R.H. Bork, *The Antitrust Paradox: A Policy at War with Itself* (1993), pp.147–148.

[65] F. Easterbrook, "Predatory Strategies and Counterstrategies" (1981) 48 U. Chi. L. Rev. 270.

the possibility of recoupment which precludes the possibility of predatory pricing in markets that are relatively easy to enter.[66]

Third, even if—because of the existence of entry barriers—the strict condition of recoupment is satisfied, predatory pricing is not necessarily the most profitable alternative. From a profit-maximising point of view, mergers are better since the revenues to be gained during the predatory price war will always be less than those that could be obtained immediately through purchase and will not be higher after the war is concluded.[67] The latter point needs a qualification, however. Acquiring a competitor may be unlawful under the Merger Regulation so that the purchase of a rival firm is ruled out as an option. If mergers are illegal, a predator will have to carry a price war to the bitter end, and this is more costly (both in terms of incurred losses and risk of being detected by antitrust authorities) than instigating a price war to drive down the purchase price of a rival.[68] If there is a good chance that the merger will be cleared, the latter strategy may be the driving motive for predatory pricing. Indeed, mergers and predatory pricing need not be mutually exclusive. Predatory pricing or other predatory tactics could soften up a potential acquisition making the prey more willing to deal or to lower the acquisition price.

If the Chicago School's arguments are accepted, the antitrust offence of predatory pricing may simply be forgotten. However, there are good reasons to think that predatory pricing can be entirely rational, and the threat of it credible. In addition to the possibility of price discrimination making price wars less costly, two crucial assumptions of the Chicago analysis warrant careful consideration: free entry and perfect information. First, entry is rarely completely free. If barriers to entry (in particular, high sunk costs) exist, then the dominant firm will be able to raise prices after eliminating competition. The extent to which super-normal profits can be extracted will be directly related to the height of the entry barriers. Even if entry barriers are low, the expectation of low profits because of vigorous competition in the market place will deter entry if the associated costs are seen as irrecoverable.[69] Second, and even more importantly, the Chicago theory only holds in markets characterised by perfect information. If this assumption is relaxed, it becomes possible to show that predatory pricing may be an entirely rational strategy. Under conditions of imperfect information victims of predatory pricing will not easily receive financial aid in the capital market or convince customers who are the ultimate victims of the predator's future monopoly prices to support them.[70] The prey may give too optimistic a picture of his chances of

---

[66] Recall that the Chicago School uses a very narrow notion of entry barriers: apart from government regulation most market impeding factors are seen as "natural" barriers. See the discussion in Ch.4, s.4.3.

[67] J.S. McGee, "Predatory Price Cutting: The Standard Oil (N.J.) Case" (1958) 1 J. Law Econ. 37 at p.140.

[68] *ibid.* at 298. A formal model was developed by G. Saloner, "Predation, Mergers, and Incomplete Information" (1987) 18 RAND J. Econ. 165.

[69] S. Bishop and M. Walker, *Economics of E.C. Competition Law: Concepts, Application and Measurement* (2nd ed., 2002), p.60.

[70] The argument that consumers will come to the aid of target firms is made by F. Easterbrook, "Predatory Strategies and Counterstrategies" (1981) 48 U. Chi. L. Rev. 270 at p.271.

surviving the price war. Potential financial lenders who are aware of this danger may therefore ask a higher risk premium disadvantaging the target firm. Long term contracts between the prey and its customers may also be difficult to agree upon because of the same reason and the magnitude of transaction costs involved.[71] Therefore, contrary to what is assumed by Chicago scholars, financial markets and coalitions of customers will not always provide support to firms that are targets of predatory campaigns. This equally implies that predation cannot be ruled out as a rational strategy.

7.5.1.2 Game theory: predatory pricing as a rational strategy

Modern economic literature on predation has relaxed the Chicago assumptions and made clear under what conditions predatory pricing may be a profitable strategy. Stimulated by the growing number of observed instances of predatory pricing and the emergence of game theory providing the necessary tools to analyse complex strategic situations, the economic discipline developed new theories of predatory pricing beginning in the early 1980s. The new body of research has challenged McGee's static framework of perfect information, although in the early days game theory seemed to provide support for the Chicago School's reasoning. Nobel Prize laureate Reinhard Selten developed a formal model showing that accommodating new entrants is a rational strategy for a dominant firm operating in several geographic markets; in equilibrium threats of predation are not credible.[72] He called this a "paradox" because logic game-theoretical reasoning did not seem to coincide with intuition and observations of reality. Later studies, however, showed that the paradox may be resolved by relaxing Selten's assumptions of perfect information on the prey's side and a finite number of markets. Predatory pricing can be rationalised for its demonstration effect, insulating the dominant firm from competition in all or some of the markets in which it operates. In a dynamic world of imperfect and asymmetric information the predator seeks to influence the expectations of rivals by convincing them that continued competition or future entry into the market would be unprofitable.

Three main types of formal economic models have been constructed in which predatory behaviour emerges in equilibrium as a rational strategy for the predator: deep pocket models (including capital market imperfections), signalling models and reputation models. The game-theoretical models do not mean that predatory pricing is widespread. The contribution to competition policy from these models is to recognise the strategic and dynamic nature of predation. They lead to the important insight that the traditional Chicago analysis is only correct under conditions of perfect information.

Deep pocket models (capital market imperfections) The traditional deep pocket model contrasted a dominant firm having easy access to capital or able to cross-subsidise from other markets, where it meets relatively little

---

[71] S. Martin, *Advanced Industrial Economics* (1993), p.463.
[72] R. Selten, "The Chain Store Paradox" (1978) 9 *Theory and Decision* 127.

competition ("deep pocket" or "long purse"), and a rival facing tighter financial constraints. The former (the predator) could decrease prices below the level of the latter's variable costs and thus exhaust the financial resources of the prey. If losses of the price war can be recovered by monopoly profits afterwards, the deep pocket scenario shows predatory pricing as a feasible and rational strategy.[73] However, in game-theoretical terms, instigating a price war is not an equilibrium strategy since the informed prey will leave the market after the first signs of predation or not enter in the first place. In such circumstances price reductions need not even be effected to deter rivals. More recent theoretical research has overcome this problem by relying on developments in the theory of finance, discussing situations of imperfect imperfection. In its newer version the deep pocket models—or more appropriately, the capital market imperfection models—present predatory pricing as a rational, profitable strategy under equilibrium. Deep pocket models now rest upon imperfections in the capital market. Capital market imperfections are the consequence of principal–agent problems, for instance when lenders cannot observe the level of effort or risk chosen by borrowers. Under conditions of imperfect information, target firms will not receive funds or, at least, will face higher interest rates because the risk of bankruptcy is greater. Incumbents facing potential entrants may exacerbate existing capital market imperfections. Predatory pricing in the first period may impair the target firm's access to capital in the second period.[74] If the prey depends on outside financing, capital providers must know that the victim's losses are due to predation, and not to poor management or unfavourable market conditions. In addition, suppliers of financial capital will have only limited information about the prey's ability to survive a period of predatory pricing and about the predator's resources and the determination of its management to pursue a predatory strategy to the bitter end. In another model it is shown that under imperfect information predatory pricing can raise rivals' costs by reducing their equity and hence raise their capital costs.[75] As a consequence, a predatory campaign by a dominant firm may cause rival firms to exit the market in order to escape from bankruptcy.

Many commentators believe that, in general, capital markets are relatively efficient and that it can be safely assumed that there are no capital market imperfections. Hence, victims of predatory pricing will be able to raise the necessary finance in the same way that firms finance start-up costs: short term losses are accepted by the financial markets because of the expectation of future gains.[76] This scepticism about the assumptions underlying deep pocket and capital market imperfection models invites discussion of alternative game-theoretical models.

[73] The "long purse" story was first told by L. Telser, "Cutthroat Competition and the Long Purse" (1966) 8 J. Law Econ. 259; and later formalised by J. Benoit, "Financially Constrained Entry into a Game with Incomplete Information" (1984) 15 RAND J. Econ. 490.
[74] See the formal model by P. Bolton and D.S. Scharfstein, "A Theory of Predation Based on Agency Problems in Financial Contracting" (1990) 80 Amer. Econ. Rev. 93.
[75] For a formal analysis, see J. Tirole, *The Theory of Industrial Organization* (1988), pp.378–379.
[76] S. Bishop and M. Walker, *Economics of E.C. Competition Law: Concepts, Application and Measurement* (2nd ed., 2002), pp.221–222.

Reputation models In reputation models of predatory pricing[77] the predator develops and maintains a reputation for preferring to fight entry. The reputation acts as an entry barrier because it leads potential entrants to the belief that entry would be vigorously resisted and so is unlikely to be profitable. Reputation motives for predatory behaviour are particularly important if the incumbent operates in many markets, because predation in one market can spill over into a reputation for aggressive responses against entry in all its markets. In game theory a scenario of predatory pricing has provided the basis for the analysis of repeated games of finite length using backwards induction.[78] Selten introduced what has become known as the chain store paradox to examine a situation in which a firm in a number of markets faces possible entrants in each of them.[79] He showed that the outcome in every game was the same as it would be if the game were played in isolation.

The following example illustrates the game-theoretical reasoning (see Box 7.5).[80] An incumbent monopolist owns a chain of stores in many towns and faces potential entrants in each town. The different towns make up separate geographical markets. Prior to the entry of competition the firm was making monopoly profits of €20,000 in the first market. Following entry it has the choice between price cutting to resist the entrant (deterrence strategy) and cooperating (i.e. accommodating the entrant). In the former case both the incumbent and the entrant will lose €10,000. In the latter case when the potential entrant enters and the incumbent firm accommodates entry both will make profits of €10,000 (Figure 1 in Box 7.5).

---

[77] D.M. Kreps and R. Wilson, "Reputation and Imperfect Information" (1982) 27 J. Econ. Theory 253; P. Milgrom and J. Roberts, "Predation, Reputation and Entry Deterrence" (1982) 27 J. Econ. Theory 280.

[78] Backwards induction consists of examining the actions available to a player at the decision nodes immediately preceding the terminal nodes. The action bringing the player the highest pay-off is identified and the decision node is then replaced with the terminal node associated with that pay-off. The process is repeated until a single terminal node remains; this is the outcome of the game.

[79] R. Selten, "The Chain Store Paradox" (1978) 9 Theory and Decision 127.

[80] The example is based on S. Bishop and M. Walker, Economics of E.C. Competition Law: Concepts, Application and Measurement (2nd ed., 2002), pp.222–223.

Box 7.5: The reputation game

Figure 1

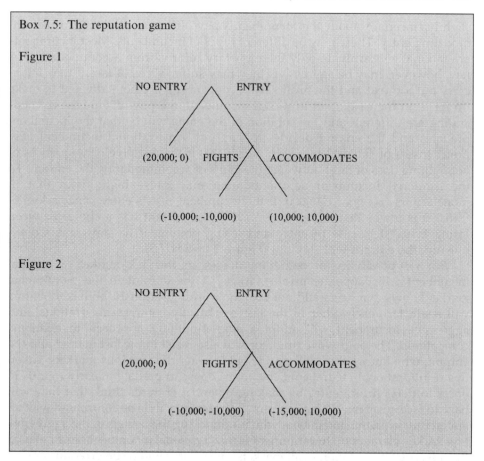

Figure 2

Faced with these pay-offs the entrant will enter and the incumbent will cooperate. Once the entrant enters the incumbent faces a pay-off of €10,000 from cooperating and loses a pay-off of €10,000 from choosing a deterrence strategy. Hence, the entrant believes at the start that the incumbent accommodates when the former enters. Clearly, a strategy to deter entry will not work in the final market. It would cost the incumbent a pay-off of €10,000 with no possibility of later gain; thus the incumbent would certainly cooperate in the final market. Selten showed that when this game is repeated a finite number of times, this outcome holds for each of the geographical markets. If the entrant in the penultimate market is clever enough, he will realise that if a pay-off-maximising incumbent must cooperate in the final market, then such an incumbent would have nothing to gain by playing a deterrence strategy in the penultimate market. Selten called this a paradox because, he argued, in reality the incumbent firm would be much more likely to adopt a deterrence strategy from the beginning in the first market. The main condition for this result is that the entrants know with certainty that the incumbent has an incentive to accommodate entry.

However, the outcome may be entirely different if the entrant is only slightly uncertain about the incumbent's pay-offs from predating or accommodating entry. There may be different types of incumbents. Most incumbents are rational and evaluate only the monetary returns from accommodating. A few, however, may be aggressive: they may suffer a loss of face if they fail to carry out a threat and the profits from cooperating are not sufficient to make up for it. In the case of an irrational incumbent, the pay-offs in case of cooperating are different and the solution of the game will be that the incumbent predates and the entrant decides to stay out. An irrational incumbent may prefer losses of €10,000 to a gain of €10,000 if the negative consequences of not fighting (loss of face) outweigh the gains of accommodating the entrant. To the irrational incumbent accommodating may cause high losses that in monetary terms equal €15,000. If the incumbent resists entry (since a loss of €10,000 is lower than a loss of €15,000), the entrant has a choice between losing €10,000 in case of entry and losing nothing if he stays out. Consequently, the entrant will stay out (Figure 2 in Box 7.5).

With no possibility of recouping losses in the last market, a rational incumbent will cooperate in all markets. If the entrant in the penultimate market knows that he should not take the warning seriously, both competitors will again face each other in the last market. By contrast, an irrational and aggressive incumbent will adopt a stop-at-nothing approach to eliminate competition. The aggressive predator will also resist in the last market and the entrant, who knows this, will decide not to enter the previous markets. Given this result, rational incumbents, too, may choose to predate in early rounds in order to deter future entry by making potential entrants think that they will have to face an aggressive incumbent. Entrants may thus be confronted with an apparently irrational incumbent who is mimicking the actions of the aggressive type. A key element of this argument is that a rational incumbent need not bear the full costs of predation in all markets, since entry will be deterred in some of them. In the example given, accommodating entry in ten markets brings the incumbent profits amounting to €100,000 (10 × €10,000). Predatory pricing in three markets (losses of 3 × €10,000 = €30,000) and being a monopolist in the other seven markets (gains of 7 × €20,000 = €140,000) leads to a higher profit of €110,000 (€140,000 − €30,000 = €110,000).

If the incumbent wants to develop a reputation for aggressive responses to competition, the entrant must be certain whether the incumbent is rational or not. Entrants observe the previous actions of the incumbent. When there is some uncertainty in the pay-offs, predation may be a sensible strategy for both rational and aggressive incumbents. Even a tiny amount of fear on the part of potential entrants that the incumbent might be aggressive could make it rational for incumbents of all types to fight entry to deter future entrants. Aggressive incumbents will predate because they suffer a loss of face if they fail to carry out a threat, but also rational incumbents may choose to predate in early rounds in order to deter entry by making potential entrants believe that they are aggressive incumbents.[81] In short, the inability of entrants to

---

[81] See the discussion by D.G. Baird, R.H. Gertner and R.C. Picker, *Game Theory and the Law* (1994), pp.178–183.

distinguish different types of incumbents may deter entry and, contrary to what Chicago economists believed, predatory pricing might be a rational strategy.

Signalling models Finally, signalling models equally lead to the conclusion that predatory pricing can be a profitable strategy. The latter models start from the assumption that the predator has an informational advantage over the prey and is, therefore, able to influence the target firm's expectations about future profits. It is possible that an entrant does not have complete information about the production costs of the predator or is unable to predict whether demand for his (new) product will be either high or low. Under such circumstances a better informed incumbent firm has an incentive to charge low prices. In this way the predator signals that competing with him will not be profitable, perhaps by conveying false information that market demand is low or that he has lower costs than the prey. By signalling to rivals that the predator has low costs, firms may be induced to exit. If the predator signals its low costs, staying in or entering a market requires that the prey perceives the price as predatory and not as normal price competition.

Signalling models have been developed by Milgrom and Roberts who assume better information about costs and market demand on the side of the predator[82] and by Saloner, who shows that signalling may lower the acquisition costs of the target firm.[83] Apart from the above assumption these models also suppose that the less informed prey deduces the incumbent's information advantage from its price and output decisions and correctly interprets the predator's choices. Even if the latter assumption is not satisfied, predation will cause the prey's exit and, therefore, warrant even stricter antitrust scrutiny. Related game-theoretical approaches towards predatory pricing, which are known as signal-jamming models,[84] assume no better information on the part of the predator but rather his ability to exert an impact on prices or demand which cannot be correctly observed by the prey. A test market offers an example. If the prey is testing demand for his new product in a market where the predator is already active, then the latter may disturb the tests in a non-perceptible way by lowering prices to distributors or increasing promotional efforts. Also signal-jamming models show that predation may deter entry (or induce exit) even in cases where the strategy would not be successful if the prey decided to stay in the market.

[82] J. Roberts, "A Signalling Model of Predatory Pricing" (1986) 38 Oxford Econ. Pap. (Supplement) 75; P. Milgrom and J. Roberts, "Limit Pricing and Entry under Incomplete Information: An Equilibrium Analysis" (1982) 50 Econometrica 443.

[83] G. Saloner, "Predation, Mergers, and Incomplete Information" (1987) 18 RAND J. Econ. 165.

[84] See M.H. Riordan, "Imperfect Information and Dynamic Conjectural Variations" (1985) 16 RAND J. Econ. 41; D. Fudenberg and J. Tirole, "A 'Signal-jamming' Theory of Predation" (1986) 17 RAND J. Econ. 366.

7.5.2 The legal debate: towards an optimal legal rule for predatory pricing

Even though the theoretical literature has succeeded in describing the conditions under which predatory pricing may occur, it has not simplified the choice of an optimal legal rule. Those who consider allocative efficiency as the main goal of competition law may urge a detailed economic analysis of allegations of predatory pricing. Complex analyses will inevitably provoke criticisms from the side of traditional competition lawyers, because such analyses neither provide judges with workable rules nor firms with legal certainty. From an economic welfare perspective, two kinds of mistakes may be made. If the legal rule is under-inclusive (type I errors/false positives) types of anti-competitive behaviour will not always be recognised as predatory pricing. Conversely, if the legal rule is over-inclusive (type II errors/false negatives) competitive behaviour may be outlawed. Type II errors will be particularly worrisome in the European context, since they are counterproductive to achieving market integration. Cutting prices is an important means of entering markets; entry into new geographical markets in the EC may be unnecessarily deterred if an over-inclusive rule regarding predatory pricing prevails. In addition to the error costs described above, enforcement costs of different rules for predatory pricing must equally be taken into account. An optimal rule should minimise error costs without causing enforcement costs that outbalance the former savings.

A particular difficulty for competition authorities and courts is that claims that pricing is predatory are made in the first stage of the predation process when prices have supposedly been lowered to drive rivals out of the market. The problem is that prices may fall for many reasons and that most of them reflect increased competition rather than predation. Different rules have been suggested to allow competition authorities to decide if the price reduction is the result of competitive forces or simply the first stage of a predatory scheme. Among the different policy suggestions made by lawyers and economists the rule that has had the greatest impact on competition authorities and judges is the Areeda–Turner test.[85] These authors propose a test based on average variable costs: prices below average variable costs are seen as illegal. Average variable costs are a surrogate for short run marginal costs which are difficult to determine. The underlying rationale of the Areeda–Turner rule is that pricing below marginal costs is inconsistent with short term profit maximisation and must therefore be predatory, since the losses can only be justified by recoupment via higher prices at a later time. The initial success of this rule in the USA (until the *Matsushita* case, which is discussed below) may be

---

[85] P.E. Areeda and D. Turner, "Predatory Pricing and Related Practices under Section 2 of the Sherman Act" (1975) 88 Harv. L. Rev. 697. An alternative costs test using marginal costs in the long run as its benchmark was proposed by R. Posner, *Antitrust Law: An Economic Perspective* (1976), pp.184–196.

explained by the manageability of the proposed costs criterion, rather than by its merits from a viewpoint of allocative efficiency.[86] Other policy proposals include the "no post-entry output increase" rule and the "no post-exit price increase" rule. In contrast with the static Areeda–Turner approach, the latter rules emphasise the strategic aspects of predatory pricing. Williamson proposes forbidding a dominant firm increasing output in response to entry for a period ranging from 12 to 18 months.[87] Baumol suggests allowing a firm to cut price in response to entry, but to forbid raising price if at some later date the entrant decides to exit.[88] The two-tier test suggested by Joskow and Klevorick should also be mentioned.[89] According to their approach, in a first stage those markets that are most suitable for successful predatory pricing must be isolated. To this end an examination of market structure and of the market power of the alleged predator is needed.[90] Only if this test is met, a second tier of analysis (behavioural test) should be applied. At the second stage of the inquiry Joskow and Klevorick draw on the rules proposed by Areeda–Turner and Baumol. If predatory pricing turns out to be a feasible strategy, prices below average costs should be prohibited and price reductions reversed within two years should equally be condemned. Finally, a recent contribution by Bolton, Brodley and Riordan suggests how game-theoretical insights can be inserted into a legal framework which outlaws predatory pricing if possible recoupment of the incurred losses can be proven.[91]

7.5.2.1 US antitrust law

Predatory pricing cases were infrequent (*Standard Oil*[92] being a noticeable exception) until after the passage of the Robinson–Patman Act in 1936. Under this Act, discriminatory price cutting by large interstate sellers injuring small local businesses was virtually *per se* unlawful. The most dramatic example of the strong enforcement efforts by the Federal Trade Commission was the *Utah Pie* case.[93] The plaintiff sold frozen pies and had over 65 per cent of sales in one regional market. Three national firms entered that market and constantly sold at lower prices than in other regional markets. For a period of four years Utah Pie's sales and profits increased considerably but its market share fell to about 45 per cent. The Supreme Court held that a firm operating in two or more markets cannot engage in price competition in one of those markets without

---

[86] See the criticisms by F.M. Scherer, "Predatory Pricing and the Sherman Act: A Comment" (1976) 89 Harv. L. Rev. 869.
[87] O.E. Williamson, "Predatory Pricing: A Strategic and Welfare Analysis" (1977) 87 Yale L.J. 284.
[88] W. Baumol, "Quasi-Permanence of Price Reductions: A Policy for Prevention of Predatory Pricing" (1979) 89 Yale L.J. 1.
[89] P.L. Joskow and A.K. Klevorick, "A Framework for Analyzing Predatory Pricing Policy" (1979) 89 Yale L.J. 213.
[90] This "structural filter" or "structural requirements test" is supposed to reduce litigation and simplify legal work in predatory pricing cases.
[91] P. Bolton, J.F. Brodley and M.H. Riordan, "Predatory Pricing: Strategic Theory and Legal Policy" (2000) 88 Geo. L.J. 2239.
[92] *Standard Oil Co v United States*, 221 U.S. 1 (1911).
[93] *Utah Pie Co v Continental Baking Co*, 386 U.S. 685 (1967).

doing so in all. The *Utah Pie* decision was heavily criticised for not considering consumers' interest in low prices.[94]

In the USA the enforcement climate changed radically with the publication of the Areeda–Turner article in 1975. Their rule suggesting the illegality of prices below average variable costs had an immediate and dramatic impact on the courts. In the five years following the publication of the seminal article no plaintiff prevailed. Given the latter effect and the difficulties of cost determination, the courts augmented the Areeda–Turner rule with other factors, including intent and market structure. While there were variations, most courts held that a price below average variable costs was presumptively unlawful, while a price above average total costs was conclusively lawful. A price falling between both benchmarks was presumptively lawful, but the presumption could be rebutted by evidence of intent and market structure.

In the 1980s Chicago analysts gained a noticeable influence upon US case law on the subject of predatory pricing. In the *Matsushita* case (in which US manufacturers of consumer electronic products accused Matsushita of combining with other Japanese manufacturers to monopolise the US market through predatory pricing), the Supreme Court quoted a number of publications by disciples of the Chicago view in support of its rejection of predatory pricing as a rational (i.e. profit-maximising) economic strategy.[95] The Supreme Court emphasised that a campaign of predatory pricing can be rational only if, after the elimination of the target, there remains sufficient market power to raise prices and thus generate additional income. Given that in the *Matsushita* case it was unlikely that the purpose of the predatory pricing could be achieved, the majority concluded that the price undercutting firms "competed for business rather than to implement an economically senseless conspiracy".[96]

The *Brooke* case is the Supreme Court's most important predatory pricing decision in modern times. The alleged predation occurred in response to the plaintiff's introduction of non-branded, low cost cigarettes. The defendant, who had a 12 per cent market share, introduced its own, similar non-branded cigarettes and undersold its rival in a series of ever-steeper price cuts. For 18 months it held prices below average variable costs, thus sustaining losses of millions of dollars. At the end of this period the plaintiff raised the price and the price war came to an end. The Court rejected the possibility of predatory pricing. Since the defendant was relatively small, predation could occur only through the joint action of the leading firms engaged in oligopolistic price coordination. The latter was considered implausible given the market conditions on the oligopolistic manufacturers' market.

In *Brooke* the Supreme Court required pricing below costs and a sufficiently high probability of recoupment. The Court did not clearly specify how costs

---

[94] W.S. Bowman, "Restraint of Trade by the Supreme Court: The Utah Pie Case" (1968) 77 Yale L.J. 70. The Utah Pie Company went bankrupt in 1972 because of poor management (see: K.G. Elzinga and T.F. Hogarty, "Utah Pie and the Consequences of Robinson–Patman" (1978) 20 J. Law Econ. 427).

[95] "There is a consensus among commentators that predatory pricing schemes are rarely tried, and even more rarely successful". *Matsushita Elec. Indus. Co v Zenith Radio Co*, 475 U.S. 574, 598 (1986).

[96] *Matsushita* 475 U.S. 597–598 (1968).

are to be measured. In the Court's terminology, a price cannot be predatory unless it is below "some measure of cost" or even "some measure of incremental cost". Proof of recoupment requires that the predator will be able to raise price above the competitive level sufficient to compensate the predator for its predatory investment.

7.5.2.2 European competition law

The fact that the economic doctrine of the Chicago School has not had the same influence on European competition law is clearly apparent from the decisions in *AKZO* and *Tetra Pak II*.[97] The *AKZO* case is summarised and critically assessed in Box 7.6. In this case, the Court of Justice accepted a price–costs comparison as the yardstick by which to establish the permissibility of price undercutting. In its decision, the European Commission had rejected the position that the test for compliance with Article 86 (now 82) EC is completely dependent on the mechanical application of a *per se* criterion based on marginal or variable costs; such a criterion would take no account of the broad aims of the European competition rules as manifested in Article 3(g) EC.[98] By contrast the Court of Justice specified more precisely which cost-based criteria are applicable in order to establish an abuse of a dominant position. Abuse of dominant position must be deemed to be present once prices fall below the level of average variable costs. According to the Court of Justice, a firm with a dominant position will always suffer losses if it charges such prices and it will have an interest in doing so only if it is aiming to exclude competitors in order to profit thereafter by means of price increases from the monopoly it has achieved. Furthermore, the Court of Justice considered that prices which are higher than average variable costs but lower than average total costs must be considered as unlawful to the extent that the fixing of prices at that level forms part of a strategy of excluding competitors. According to the Court of Justice, such prices can exclude from the market firms that are just as efficient as the dominant firm but do not possess sufficient financial resources to enter such a price war.[99] One can detect in this last argument the old fashioned deep pocket reasoning.[1] In the event that the prices of the defendant firm are lower than average variable costs there is an irrefutable presumption of prohibited predatory pricing. The European Court therefore has adopted a stricter attitude towards price wars than the US judges did before *Matsushita*. Once prices are higher than average variable costs but lower than average total costs, supplementary evidence must be adduced in order to establish incontrovertibly the existence of a strategy aimed at the exclusion of competitors. From the Court's further reasoning it seems that making threats, asking "unreasonably low prices", maintaining artificially low prices over long periods and granting

---

[97] Case 62/86 *AKZO v Commission* [1991] ECR I–3359; Case T–83/91 *Tetra Pak International SA v Commission* [1994] ECR II–755.
[98] Case IV/30.698 *ECS/Akzo Chemie* [1985] O.J. L 374/1 (Art.3f EC has been renumbered Art. 3g EC by the Treaty on the European Union).
[99] Case 62/86 *AKZO v Commission* [1986] ECR 1503, paras 71–72.
[1] See s.7.5.1.2.

fidelity rebates can, one and all, provide the necessary supplementary evidence. The Court relied heavily on the subjective evidence of intention on AKZO's part.[2] According to the Court, AKZO's intention was clearly to annihilate ECS (the target of the price war) because AKZO's prices were not fixed in order to meet competition from ECS but in fact turned out to be significantly lower.

In 1994 the European Court of First Instance had an opportunity to reconsider the legality of predatory pricing in *Tetra Pak II*,[3] for the European Commission's finding that Tetra Pak had practiced predatory pricing was specifically challenged by reference to the economic theory accepted in the most recent US case law.[4] Tetra Pak argued that, even if it had priced its products under costs, it could not have been indulging in predatory pricing because it had no reasonable hope of recouping its losses in the long term. The Court, however, upheld the European Commission's finding without any serious examination of this argument, maintaining that where a producer charged AKZO-type loss-making prices, a breach of Article 82 (then 86) EC was established *ipso facto* without any need to consider specifically whether the company concerned had any reasonable prospect of recouping the losses which it had incurred.[5]

It would be appropriate for the European Commission and the European Court of Justice to adopt a more cautious rule with regard to predatory pricing. In so doing they should benefit from economic theory. In particular, greater stress should be placed on the requirement that there be a serious threat of price increases after the disappearance of the target. A cost test, as suggested by the European Court of Justice, is easy to use but it should be applied only when predatory pricing is a feasible strategy. When analysing a complaint of predatory pricing, the extent of monopoly power, the conditions for market entry, and the effects that a dynamic competitive process has on costs should be carefully examined in order to determine whether a sufficient degree of monopoly power could be acquired in the long run.[6] Only if this is the case will predatory pricing be a realistic—and welfare damaging—strategy. If the evaluation of the above-mentioned market characteristics indicates that monopoly power is probable in the long run, a costs-based rule can be applied in the second phase of the decision-making process. Such a rule will not, however, prohibit every form of anti-competitive pricing conduct because strategic conduct is still excluded from its scope. The game-theoretical models show that the success of a predatory campaign is not related to whether the predator charges prices above or below average variable costs. Rather, the long term average total costs of the prey are relevant: if target firms believe that entry (or staying in the market) will not be profitable because of high costs, weak market demand, overcapacity in the industry or aggressive

---

[2] Case 62/86 *AKZO v Commission* [1986] ECR 1503.
[3] Case T–83/91 *Tetra Pak International SA v Commission* [1994] ECR II–755.
[4] *Brooke Group v Brown and Williamson Tobacco* 125 L Ed 2d 168 (1993).
[5] Case 62/86 *AKZO v Commission* [1986] ECR 1503, para.150.
[6] See the two-tier approach presented in P.L. Joskow and A.K. Klevorick, "A Framework for Analysing Predatory Pricing Policy" (1979) 89 Yale L.J. 213.

behaviour by a strong competitor, predatory pricing may be a feasible and profitable strategy. In order to bring strategic conduct within the scope of the rule it should also be possible to deduce predatory pricing by showing that the assumptions formulated by the game-theoretical models are satisfied. In this way it can be shown that recoupment of the incurred losses will be possible.[7] Furthermore, to avoid an over-inclusive prohibition and thereby reducing type II errors (false negatives), a broader scope for defences should be created. Apart from meeting the competition of a rival, an efficiency defence should be available to justify the price reductions challenged.[8] Efficiency reasons may include below costs prices to induce sufficient demand in case of network externalities, sales of perishable goods and sales below costs to induce the purchase of a complementary good.

Even though current European competition law is not in line with economic insights on predation, there are some signs that the tide may be turning. In *Wanadoo*,[9] the European Commission was confronted with the argument (based on the work by Bolton *et al.*[10]) that a strategy of predation may be considered viable and realistic only if the structure of the market and the presence of sufficient barriers to entry enable the dominant undertaking subsequently to enjoy high, stable margins on the relevant market and thus to recoup any losses initially incurred. The European Commission stresses that neither the case law of the European Court of Justice, nor its own decision-making practice requires proof of recoupment of losses as a condition for a finding of abuse through predatory pricing. Nevertheless, in the following paragraphs the European Commission examines the entry barriers and entry costs which characterise the relevant market and which render plausible the recoupment of the losses of the dominant firm in the long run. After this examination the European Commission concludes that "The recoupment by Wanadoo Interactive of its initial losses is therefore a likely scenario. The predatory strategy introduced in 2000 appears pertinent in this context".[11] In spite of *Wanadoo*, the most recent policy document on Article 82 EC remains overtly restrictive. The European Commission states that once it has been established that the price is below average avoidable costs (AAC),[12] it is not necessary to investigate any further the actual or likely exclusion of the target firm (prey). Separate proof of recoupment is not considered necessary "as

---

[7] For a view arguing against the adoption of a recoupment test in European competition law, see C. Ritter, "Does the Law of Predatory Pricing and Cross-Subsidisation Need a Radical Rethink?" (2004) 27 *World Competition* 613.

[8] Compare the proposal by P. Bolton, J.F. Brodley and M.H. Riordan, "Predatory Pricing: Strategic Theory and Legal Policy" (2000) 88 Geo. L.J. 2239.

[9] Case COMP/38.233 *Wanadoo Interactive*, case not yet reported, paras 332–367.

[10] P. Bolton, J.F. Brodley and M.H. Riordan, "Predatory Pricing: Strategic Theory and Legal Policy" (2000) 88 Geo. L.J. 2239; P. Bolton, J. Brodley and M. Riordan, "Predatory Pricing: Response to Critique and Further Elaboration" (2001) 89 Geo. L.J. 2512.

[11] Case COMP/38.233 *Wanadoo Interactive*, case not yet reported, para.367.

[12] The relevant question is whether the dominant company, by charging a lower price for its output over the relevant time period, incurred losses that could have been avoided by not producing that output.

dominance is already established which implies that entry barriers are sufficiently high."[13]

Box 7.6: The AKZO case: predatory pricing or competition?

AKZO was the major European producer of organic peroxides, one of which, benzoyl peroxide, was used as a flour additive in the United Kingdom and Ireland. There were three large buyers (flourmills) of roughly comparable size with a combined market share of 85 per cent next to a number of smaller flourmills. Most sales of organic peroxide were in the European plastics market where AKZO was a dominant supplier. ECS, a British firm, which was initially one of AKZO's customers, began to produce benzoyl peroxide for its own use and, later on, started to expand into the plastics market. AKZO responded with threats of overall price reductions and price cuts targeted at ECS' main customers in order to induce its rival to exit the plastics sector.

There are several possible explanations for the *AKZO* case: one of them is predatory pricing; another is the breakdown of a cooperative oligopoly. To conclude in favour of predation the European Commission relied heavily on the proven intent of AKZO to eliminate ECS and also pointed to previous predatory episodes (the elimination of Scado after which AKZO raised prices again). Both assessments were based solely on internal documents of AKZO. Therefore, some scepticism is justified: it is sufficiently known that firms tend to exaggerate in their own documents the success of their destruction campaigns.[14] As mentioned by Posner, a rule based on proven improper intent is often a function of luck and of the defendant's legal sophistication: firms with executives sensitive to antitrust problems will not leave any documentary trail of predatory intent.[15] The alternative explanation is that the European Commission's intervention put an early end to a competitive price war in a bilateral oligopoly.[16] Prior to the conflict between ECS and AKZO, the three producers of flour additives granted each other assistance in the form of mutual deliveries and collective production. Initially, ECS was supplied by AKZO but, in 1977, after a series of substantial price increases, ECS started its own production. AKZO was dissatisfied with the decision of its former buyer, but it was prepared to endure this evolution provided that the interests of AKZO were not threatened. Price agreements existed between AKZO and

---

[13] DG Competition Discussion Paper on the application of Art.82 of the Treaty to exclusionary abuses, para.122 (*http://europa.eu.int/comm/competition/antitrust/others/article_82_review.html*).

[14] Harbord and Hoehn, however, support the predatory pricing explanation. Apart from the factors mentioned, they also stress that prices were below average variable costs in targeted market segments (price discrimination reduces the costs of a predatory campaign) and that ECS was financially constrained. (D. Harbord and T. Hoehn, "Barriers to Entry and Exit in European Competition Policy" (1994) 14 Int. Rev. Law Econ. 430).

[15] R. Posner, *Antitrust Law: An Economic Perspective* (1976), pp.189–190.

[16] See also L. Phlips and I.M. Moras, "The AKZO Decision: A Case of Predatory Pricing?" (1993) 41 J. Ind. Econ. 315.

Diaflex, the third supplier in the market. These facts reveal how perfectly the market was divided between the three suppliers before the start of the price war. The initial plan of AKZO to buy ECS out is also indicative of the end of a cooperative oligopoly. The European Commission minimised the role of the large buyers in this process, since they were considered not to be price-sensitive.[17] The outbreak of the price war would have made them quickly aware of their market power, however.

It will be clear to the reader that the decision in the *AKZO* case is not entirely consistent with economic theory. The weakest point both in the European Commission's reasoning and in that of the Court of Justice is that in neither of them was it adequately demonstrated that AKZO's so-called predatory pricing could have succeeded. An essential condition for considering predatory pricing as a rational competitive strategy is that the price undercutter can recoup his losses after driving the target out of the market. Even though Chicago economists may have underestimated the danger of predatory pricing in real-life markets, economists generally agree that any approach to the identification of predation must begin with an analysis of market conditions and the characteristics of the alleged predator to see whether predation is a feasible strategy. The longer the price undercutting lasts, the larger the accumulated losses will be. Also, it will be very difficult or impossible to recoup the losses if potential new entrants to the market have to be borne in mind. Neither the European Commission nor the Court of Justice gave sufficient consideration to these factors. The facts of the case do indeed raise some serious doubts as to the feasibility of the alleged predatory pricing campaign. Taking into account the considerable market share of ECS, the losses that AKZO would have had to suffer in order to drive ECS out of the flour additives market would have been prohibitively high. The facts of the case show that after a two-year price war the market share of ECS decreased from 35 to 32 per cent; in the same period the share of AKZO increased only by 2 per cent. In spite of these figures, the European Commission argued that AKZO's policy would have resulted in the withdrawal of ECS from both the flour additives market and the plastics market.[18] This conclusion must be doubted taking into account the haracteristics of the flour additives market where the price war was fought. The ease with which ECS entered the UK organic peroxide market suggests low entry barriers.[19] Moreover, large buyers could have elaborated a counterstrategy aiming at keeping ECS in the market since disappearance of the latter would have made it impossible to induce price competition between the oligopolists. In oligopolistic markets price competition often takes the form of secret discounts. To safeguard possibilities of price discrimination large

---

[17] Case IV/30.698 *ECS/Akzo Chemie* [1985] O.J. L 374/1.

[18] *ibid.*, paras 91–94.

[19] R. Rapp, ''Predatory Pricing and Entry Deterring Strategies: The Economics of AKZO'' (1986) 7 E.C.L.R. 233.

buyers could have entered into long term contracts with ECS.[20] Taking into account these facts, the only indisputable conclusion seems to be that AKZO was guilty of behaviour aiming at causing commercial harm to ECS.[21] If undertakings in dominant positions can be accused of abusing their power merely when they put competitors at a disadvantage, Article 82 EC will outlaw much more than anti-competitive predatory pricing.

7.6 Conclusions

This chapter discussed several types of exclusionary behaviour by dominant firms. It was shown that the welfare effects of these practices (such as price discrimination, tying and bundling) are inherently difficult to assess. All forms of so-called exclusionary behaviour may also generate efficiencies and benefit consumers. This leaves competition authorities and judges who take economic analysis seriously with a difficult task: they have to carefully analyse the reasons why firms engage in such practices and assess their effects on allocative efficiency and consumer welfare in real-life markets.

Economic analysis shows that price discrimination can be beneficial if the deadweight loss is reduced by increasing output, in particular when the practice allows the dominant firm to serve additional market segments. It was also shown that there are no firm economic grounds to flatly prohibit non-cost-related rebates granted by dominant firms. Such rebates may have both beneficial and harmful effects on competition. The need to recover fixed costs can provide considerable scope for robust justification of discriminatory pricing. In sum, a sound economic approach towards rebates requires proof of anti-competitive effects (likely exclusion of rivals) and harm to consumers (increased prices, reduced output).

Also tying and bundling may both cause competitive harm and serve legitimate business goals, which enhance efficiency. Even though the single monopoly profit theorem of the Chicago School has limited the relevance of the traditional leverage theory, it cannot be totally excluded that firms make a strategic use of bundling and tying to prevent entry in the market of either the tying or the tied product. Conversely, bundling and tying may be used to increase efficiency: the practice may allow the achievement of costs savings, guarantee quality or enable price discrimination (and increase output). Again, an effects-based analysis is necessary to distinguish beneficial and harmful instances of bundling and tying.

To assess the effects of refusals to deal, a trade-off between short and long term competition is needed. This is particularly acute in cases where small competitors require access to facilities of the dominant firm deemed to be "essential". On the one hand, stepping in to guarantee a small firm's dealings

[20] M.A. Utton, *The Economics of Regulating Industry* (1986), p.113.
[21] This is the weakest alternative from Art.1 of the Decision at [1985] O.J. L 374/1.

may be justified by the need to protect short term competition in the relevant market. On the other hand, if firms have to fear that they might be coerced into giving competitors access to their assets, such as the facilities they have built, the incentive to engage in useful economic activities (innovation) might be reduced in the first place.

The welfare effects of low prices practiced by dominant firms are also ambiguous. Low prices may be a sign of both healthy competition and predation. Contrary to the work of the Chicago School, smaller rival suppliers may be excluded from the market if the dominant firm is able to profit from imperfections in capital markets (financial predation), establish a reputation of aggressive behaviour or signal that market entry will not be profitable. An economically sound competition law should again carefully analyse whether anti-competitive effects (exclusion) really may materialise.

Current European competition law is not in harmony with the above economic insights. The burden of proof under Article 82 EC does not require evidence of likely competitive harm (exclusion of rivals) and reduction of consumer welfare. Non-costs related discounts and tying are subject to what comes down to almost a *per se* prohibition. Also, the case law on predatory pricing is overtly restrictive since it contains no requirement that recoupment of the losses suffered during the price war is possible. So far, only the approach towards granting access to essential facilities is more in line with a sound economic approach. As compared to the European approach, US antitrust law is steadily moving towards a more economically sound approach (requirement of recoupment in predation cases, rule of reason with respect to technological tying). A similar evolution may be expected in Europe if the European Commission will opt for an effects-based approach. However, such a reform does not easily fit with the current text and case law of Article 82 EC which are clearly inspired by ordoliberal thinking (protection of individual economic freedom of action) and goals of fairness.

Chapter 8

......

ENFORCEMENT OF ARTICLES 81 AND 82 OF THE EC TREATY

8.1 Introduction

In a significant number of industries, cartels continue both to form and succeed in maintaining discipline over a long period of time. A major problem of the cartel prohibition (Article 81 EC) thus seems to be an implementation issue. The purpose of this chapter is to investigate the strengths and weaknesses of the current enforcement regime, contained in Regulation 1/2003. In economic terms, the enforcement of European competition law may be qualified as optimal if welfare-reducing anti-competitive practices can be deterred, no enforcement errors are made and enforcement costs are minimised. Full deterrence is achieved when all firms abstain from engaging in welfare-reducing anti-competitive practices, since the gains from doing so are lower than the costs of the sanctions that are imposed for violating the competition rules. Error costs may occur when harmful practices are allowed (type I errors/false positives) or anti-competitive practices that do not harm economic welfare are falsely prohibited (type II errors/false negatives). Enforcement costs are not minimised when the benefits of the competitive processes that are preserved do not outweigh the administrative costs of detection and sanctioning violations of the competition rules. These administrative costs include both the expenses of the public sector (costs of competition authorities, prosecutors and courts) and the costs borne by the businesses or individuals concerned (management costs, costs of external lawyers and experts). Full deterrence will not be efficient if the latter costs are higher than the benefits resulting from prohibiting harmful practices. An optimal enforcement system minimises the sum of social costs resulting from the infringements and the costs of enforcement.

In designing enforcement mechanisms, policy makers face difficult choices. All decisions made will have an impact on the level of deterrence and on the risks that errors are made or that enforcement costs are not minimised. The relevant policy questions are even more complex since, besides the deterrence objective, goals of corrective and proportional justice have to be taken into account as well. This chapter highlights the relevant insights on the enforcement of the European competition rules from an economic perspective, without neglecting their relation with the justice goals. In recent years, the analysis of enforcement mechanisms has been focused mainly on Article 81 EC, in particular the hardcore cartels (price fixing, market sharing, bid rigging). A large part of this chapter is devoted to this discussion, but a number of questions concerning the optimal enforcement of the prohibition of vertical restraints and abuses of a dominant position under Article 82 EC are also dealt with. Since a comparison of European competition law and US antitrust law is useful to illustrate the consequences of the different choices of enforcement mechanisms that can be made, the economic analysis hereafter uses a comparative perspective. The merger review process is not described in this chapter, but some detail is provided below.[1]

In this chapter three questions are addressed. The structure of the chapter follows Shavell's distinction of the three basic dimensions according to which methods of law enforcement can differ: the form of the sanctions, the role of private parties versus public agents in enforcement, and the timing of legal intervention.[2] In a federal or quasi-federal context, such as the European Union, a fourth dimension must be added: the division of competences

---

[1] See Ch.10, ss.10.2 and 10.3.

[2] S. Shavell, "The Optimal Structure of Law Enforcement" (1993) 36 J. Law Econ. 255. See more specifically with respect to enforcement of antitrust law W.F. Schwartz, "An Overview of the Economics of Antitrust Enforcement" (1980) 68 Geo. L.J. 1075; W.M. Landes, "Optimal Sanctions for Antitrust Violations" (1983) 50 U. Chi. L. Rev. 652; K.N. Hylton, *Antitrust Law: Economic Theory and Common Law Revolution* (2003), pp.43–67.

between the central competition authority and decentralised enforcement agencies (competition authorities and judges of the Member States). The modernisation[3] debate on the enforcement of European competition law[3] was largely limited to the third and fourth dimension of the choice between different enforcement systems. The discussion was focused on the following two questions: should there be an *ex ante* control of anti-competitive practices (notification and authorisation regime) or is it sufficient to have an *ex post* control (legal exception regime)? And: should enforcement of the European competition rules be decentralised by giving more powers to national competition authorities and judges, thereby alleviating the burden of a single central enforcement agency (European Commission)? Economic analysis can be helpful in answering these two questions and providing criteria to evaluate the enforcement regime that has been chosen. Even though the importance of the modernisation debate should be acknowledged, the first two questions on the type of sanctions and the role of private parties in the enforcement of the competition rules merit equal attention and have recently gained importance. The major factors influencing the level of deterrence are monetary sanctions for companies and individuals, and prison sentences for individuals. Public and private enforcement combined determine the level of the former. However, for didactical reasons, this chapter discusses first public enforcement and then turns to the role of private enforcement. The discussion of these issues precedes the analysis of the timing of the antitrust intervention in the fourth section. The fourth question relating to the choice between a centralised enforcement system by a single antitrust authority and decentralised enforcement by different agencies at lower levels of government is discussed in Chapter 10.

The structure of this chapter is as follows. The question addressed in the next section relates to the sanctions. The main choice is between administrative fines and criminal sanctions. In cases of infringement of competition rules, fines can be imposed on companies only. It is, however, also possible to supplement those fines with individual sanctions imposed on the responsible decision makers within the companies; such sanctions may include fines, imprisonment or disqualification of directors who committed an antitrust violation. Both in US antitrust law and European competition law, the heaviest fines are reserved for very serious infringements which effectively harm consumers (hardcore cartels, such as price fixing, market sharing and bid rigging). Generally, if sanctions are too low, the expected benefits from

---

[3] This debate started with the publication of the White Paper on Modernisation of the Rules Implementing Articles 81 and 82 (Formerly Articles 85 and 86) of the EC Treaty ([1999] O.J. C 132/1) and resulted in the enactment of Regulation 1/2003 ([2003] O.J. L 1/1). This Regulation replaced the old enforcement system contained in Regulation 17, which was enacted back in 1962 (Council Regulation No.17 [1962] O.J. 13/204). Together with Regulation 1/2003 the Commission has published a total of six Notices: two on cooperation (within the Network of Competition Authorities [2004] O.J. C 101/43 and between the Commission and the courts of the EU Members States [2004] O.J. C 101/54), one on the handling of complaints [2004] O.J. C 101/65, one on informal guidance relating to novel questions concerning Arts 81 and 82 [2004] O.J. C 101/78 and two Guidelines on the interpretation of concepts of competition law: the effect on trade concept [2004] O.J. C 101/81 and the application of Art.81(3) of the Treaty [2004] O.J. C 101/97.

violating the competition rules may exceed the expected costs of infringing the law and underdeterrence will result. Also, deterrence will not be achieved if the financial means of the company are insufficient to pay the imposed fine. In the latter case, imprisonment may be considered as a remedy to the judgment proof problem. The next section of this chapter gives an overview of the sanctions as contained in both European and US antitrust law and provides an economic assessment of the divergent regimes from a comparative perspective. It also provides an evaluation of the different sanctions from the viewpoint of corrective and proportional justice. Optimal sanctions should both deter welfare-reducing anti-competitive practices and conform to the requirements of fairness and proportionality.

The third section discusses the question relating to enforcement agents: not only public agents but also private parties can play an important role in the enforcement of the competition rules. In the case of public enforcement, antitrust authorities may put an end to infringements in administrative law procedures.[4] Private enforcement involves actions to obtain injunctive relief or damages brought by private parties in civil courts. By claiming damages for the harm suffered as a consequence of the violation of the competition rules, private parties may contribute to the achievement of both deterrence and compensatory objectives (efficiency and corrective justice). Again, the European and the US situation differ. Whereas private parties so far have played a rather modest role in enforcing the European competition rules, they have been much more active in the USA, and this has had an impact on both the number and type of cases under antitrust investigation. The third section of this chapter discusses the advantages and disadvantages of private enforcement to find out whether, from an efficiency perspective, private court actions are an alternative for or a desirable supplement to enforcement by administrative agencies. The role of private enforcement in reaching corrective justice (compensation) is also assessed.

The question discussed in the fourth section relates to the timing of the legal intervention. Intervention may take place before an undesirable act is committed or after the harm has occurred. Under a notification regime, firms may be required to inform the competition authorities of practices they are contemplating, so that antitrust authorities may screen agreements before they are put into practice. The alternative regime tries to achieve deterrence by imposing sanctions if competition is harmed and no exception to the prohibition of anti-competitive practices applies. In European competition law, one may observe a shift from an *ex ante* to an *ex post* control. Until May 2004, undertakings could notify their agreements to the European Commission, asking for a formal decision implying that the agreement did not constitute a restriction of competition (negative clearance) or that it did, but could benefit from an exemption. The Commission was the only agency empowered to grant individual exemptions. This notification system was abolished and has been replaced by a directly applicable legal exception regime. Under the new

---

[4] This is the case in Europe. In the USA, public enforcement agencies may have to bring cases to court in order to have antitrust infringements prohibited. See s.8.3.2.

enforcement system, the European Commission as well as all competent national competition authorities and judges conduct a full evaluation of the agreements, including the conditions to grant an exemption. It may be assumed that firms react differently to these divergent regimes and that this will have an impact on the type of agreements entered into. If the system change entails the risk that more harmful agreements are implemented or that some beneficial agreements are no longer signed (type I and type II errors), the new regime will be far from optimal. The fourth section of this chapter gives an overview of the theoretical economic literature, which sheds some light on these questions, and attempts a preliminary economic evaluation of the system change.

8.2 The choice of sanctions

8.2.1 A brief comparison of European and US sanctions

8.2.1.1 Differences in type and severity of sanctions

As far as sanctions for infringement of competition rules are concerned, there are remarkable differences between European competition law and US antitrust law.[5] These differences relate to the range of antitrust offenders that can be fined, the type of the sanctions and their magnitude. The first difference is that European competition law—at European Commission level—is enforced by imposing fines on undertakings, whereas in US antitrust law such penalties are combined with fines on individuals as well as imprisonment. The European Court of Justice has defined undertakings as economic units, even if in law the economic unit may consist of several natural or legal persons.[6] In practice, for reasons of enforceability, the European Commission imposes fines on companies (or other legal persons), to which the violation committed by the undertaking is imputed. The situation in the USA is different, since antitrust law is also enforced by means of criminal liability of individuals, including corporate directors, officers and employees.

A second difference relates to the type of the sanctions. Fines can be criminal, civil or administrative. Criminal fines carry a stigma, showing that society morally disapproves of a certain behaviour. Whereas with respect to the most serious violations of the Sherman Act (price fixing and bid rigging) such a censure is clearly present in US antitrust law, the fines imposed under

---

[5] For a comparison, also from an economic perspective, see W. Wils, "Does the Effective Enforcement of Articles 81 and 82 EC Require not Only Fines on Undertakings but also Individual Penalties, in Particular Imprisonment?" in *European Competition Law Annual 2001: Effective Private Enforcement of EC Antitrust Law* (C.D. Ehlermann and I Atanasiu ed., 2002), reprinted in: W. Wils, *The Optimal Enforcement of EC Antitrust Law* (2002), p.188. The discussion in this chapter has benefited from this contribution.

[6] Case 170/83 *Hydroterm v Compact* [1984] ECR 2999, para.11.

European competition law for similar infringements are not of a criminal law nature.[7] It should be added, however, that competition laws of some EC Member States also allow for criminal sanctions, imposed both on companies and individuals (see Box 8.1). Clearly, the parallel provisions of administrative-type sanctions at EC level and criminal-type sanctions at Member State level lead to tensions in determining the desirability of leniency applications and the appropriate level of fines (see the following subsections).

Box 8.1: Criminal sanctions in national competition laws

In the United Kingdom, the Enterprise Act 2002 introduced prison sanctions, fines and director disqualifications for infringements of the national competition law. Cartel offences will be the subject of trial by jury in a criminal court. To impose criminal sanctions, a narrowly focused prohibition is needed. Hence, the UK cartel offence is not a copy of Article 81 of the EC Treaty, since the wording of this article (referring to all restrictions of competition) is much too broad and not appropriate for criminalisation. The cartel offence (Section 188 Enterprise Act) is a separate crime and applies only to obvious, hardcore agreements (price fixing, limitation of supply or production, market sharing, bid rigging). Conversely, the UK cartel offence does not apply to vertical agreements. Also, abuses of a dominant position are not criminalised. A commission of the cartel crime requires dishonesty, a concept which has two elements. As an objective matter, the jury will have to assess whether the defendant acted dishonestly according to the standards of reasonable people. As a subjective matter, it must be investigated whether the defendant realised that his behaviour was dishonest by those standards. Individuals who are found guilty of a cartel offence may be penalised with prison sentences of up to five years and unlimited fines. Aside from the cartel offence, the Enterprise Act has also introduced company director disqualification for any infringement of the national competition law (Section 200).

Also in other European Member States, infringements of competition law have been (partly) criminalised. In Ireland, price fixing and related hardcore cartel behaviour have been criminalised.[8] Conviction on indictment may result in a maximum corporate and individual fine of €4,000,000 or 10 per cent of the turnover during the prior financial year. Individuals may also be sentenced to a maximum of five years imprisonment (section 8, Competition Act 2002). Economically, these sanctions can be seen as additional sanctions for hardcore violations of Article 81 EC. In Germany, restrictions of competition in relation to tenders (bid rigging) are punished with criminal sanctions and professional disqualifications (paragraph 298 *Strafgesetzbuch*, the German Penal Code).

---

[7] Art.23(5) of Regulation 1/2003.
[8] See P. Massey, "Criminal Sanctions for Competition Law: A Review of Irish Experience" (2004) 1 Comp. Law Rev. 23.

A third difference is the severity of sanctions. The European Commission is empowered to impose on undertakings or associations of undertakings fines not exceeding 10 per cent of the worldwide turnover in the preceding business year of each of the undertakings participating in the violation. The criminal sanctions in the USA are more severe. Corporations risk heavy criminal fines. After two amendments of the Sherman Act (in 1974 and 1990) and the passing of an alternative Fine Statute, the maximum fine has been ultimately increased by the Antitrust Criminal Penalty Enhancement and Reform Act of 2004. The fine that can be imposed on an organisation now amounts to US$100 million or, alternatively, twice the gross gain to the offender or twice the gross loss to the victims of the conspiracy.[9] In the years 2000–2003 the fines obtained by the Antitrust Division exceeded US$150 million, US$280 million, US$75 million and US$107 million respectively. The fines obtained in 2004 totalled over US$350 million. Relying on the twice the gain/loss formula, the Antitrust Division of the Department of Justice imposed a maximum criminal fine of US$500 million on a single company. The maximum sentence for individuals is ten years' imprisonment and a fine that is the greatest of US$1 million, twice the gain to the cartel, or twice the loss suffered by the victims. In the years 2000–2004, over 80 antitrust offenders (including 18 foreign nationals in international cartel cases) were sent to jail. In the 1990s the average actual prison term was almost nine months; since then a record jail sentence of ten years was imposed.[10] In Europe, administrative fines imposed on single companies, which participated in hardcore cartels, are often of similar levels as in the USA.[11] However, criminal sanctions on individuals are only possible in some Member States (United Kingdom, Ireland) and the divide with the USA becomes even greater once civil (often "treble") damages are taken into account. While the latter are well established in the USA at both federal and state level, they are a relatively recent phenomenon in Europe—again, however, only at Member State level, see for example the *Provimi* case in the United Kingdom (see Box 8.3) and the recent changes to German competition law.

8.2.1.2 Guidelines on imposing fines

For a long time, the European Commission's fining policy was not based on specific criteria. In practice a certain percentage of turnover in one year of the different participants in the relevant market, usually the sales of the product in the Community, was taken as the basis for administrative fines in cartel cases. One author found that the fines varied roughly between 2 and 4 per cent of the

---

[9] Antitrust Procedures and Penalties Act of 1974 § 3, Pub. L No.93–528, 88 Stat. 1706; Antitrust Amendments Act of 1990 § 4, Pub. L No.101–588, 104 Stat. 2879, 18 U.S.C. § 3571(d).

[10] See: S.D. Hammond, "An Overview of Recent Developments in the Antitrust Division's Criminal Enforcement Program", speech Kona (Hawaii), January 10, 2005. For figures on total fines obtained in the years 2001–2003, see J.S. Magney and R.C. Anderson, "Recent Developments in Criminal Enforcement of US Antitrust Laws" (2004) 27 *World Competition* 101.

[11] Remarkably, the largest fine (€497 million) was imposed for abuse of a dominant position (Case Comp/C-3/37.792 *Microsoft*, not yet reported).

turnover in the European Community;[12] more recent cases showed fines amounting to 9 per cent for the ringleaders and 6 per cent for the foot soldiers.[13] In 1998, to ensure "transparency and impartiality" the Commission published Guidelines for calculating fines.[14] The method of determining the fine starts from a "basic amount" fixed by reference to the gravity and duration of the infringement. Infringements are put into one of three categories: minor infringements (vertical restrictions with a limited impact), serious infringements (horizontal restrictions, vertical restrictions with a wider impact, abuses of a dominant position), and very serious infringements (price cartels and market sharing quotas, partitioning of national markets, clear-cut abuses by virtual monopolists). Likely fines for minor infringements vary from €1000 to €1 million; they amount to a figure between €1 million and €20 million for serious infringements, and will be above €20 million for very serious infringements. The Guidelines do not provide precise indications of how the start point for the calculation is determined; the amounts of likely fines are indications of the overall fine.[15] The start point is chosen in assessing the gravity of the infringement by taking account of "its nature, its actual impact on the market, where this can be measured, and the size of the relevant geographic market", a flexible description allowing the Commission large discretionary powers to set the fine. The Commission may use the product turnover in setting the fine base and amend this figure through a multiplier to make sure that it has a sufficient deterrent effect, taking account of the firms' size and resources.[16] The fine base, which reflects the gravity of the infringement, must be adjusted to mirror the duration of the infringement: for example, the amount set for gravity may be increased up to 50 per cent for infringements of between one and five years. The "basic amount" (determined by taking into account the gravity and duration of the infringement) may be adjusted upwards for aggravating circumstances (for example, leading role in a cartel or repeated infringement) or downwards for attenuating circumstances (for example, passive role in a cartel set-up or termination of the infringement as soon as the Commission intervenes). Further adjustments may have to be made to ensure that the imposed fine does not exceed the maximum ceiling of 10 per cent of the worldwide turnover of the company or the "ability to pay in a specific social context". Eventually, the last step in the calculation of the fine is the application of the percentage reduction as provided for in the Leniency Notice if the requirements of the latter (see 8.2.1.3) are satisfied.

The case law of the European Courts fudges the issue whether total turnover or the turnover on the relevant market (i.e. the affected commerce) is an

---

[12] M. Reynolds, "EC Competition Policy on Fines" (1992) 3 E.B.L. Rev. 263.
[13] Case IV/C/33.833 *Cartonboard* [1994] O.J. L 243/1.
[14] Guidelines on the method of setting fines, [1998] O.J. C 9/3.
[15] J.M. Joshua and P.D. Camesasca, "EC Fining Policy against Cartels after the Lysine Rulings: The Subtle Secrets of X" (2004) *The European Antitrust Review* 6.
[16] The Court of First Instance has recently stated that in fixing the multiplier the Commission may take into account the deterrent effect that fines must have. See Case T–31/99 *ABB Asea Brown Boveri Ltd v Commission* [2002] ECR II–1881.

appropriate benchmark to assess the gravity of the infringement.[17] Whereas the former figure indicates the size of the firm and its economic power, the latter gives a proxy of the seriousness of the infringement. The European Court of Justice did express the principle that a fine must be proportionate to the level of sales of the product which is the subject of the infringement.[18] However, in various other judgments alternative measures of the appropriate turnover were referred to. Moreover, in complex cartel cases involving many firms, the specific weight of each firm on the infringement has to be assessed. The scale of the infringement cannot be assessed by relying on the total turnover figure (which is an imprecise guide) but rather by calculating the share of the affected commerce held by each undertaking.[19] The ultimate fine imposed should be a function of the impact on the market of the infringement. It is important to stress the Court of First Instance's finding in *Lysine* that concerning the latter it is indeed market impact and not impact on the individual firm concerned. In this case, one of the parties to the cartel, ADM, had argued that the fine imposed by the European Commission should be significantly lowered as it had submitted economic evidence demonstrating it had acted as a "cheat" to the cartel (hence, diminishing its role in the infringement). The Court of First Instance dismissed ADM's claim, confirming that what matters is overall impact on the market and not an individual firm's conduct.[20]

In the USA, figures relating to the volume of the affected commerce are crucial for calculating fines that are proportionate to the impact of the prohibited cartel agreement. The US Sentencing Guidelines use 20 per cent of the volume of affected commerce as the base fine level for convicted organisations.[21] In drafting these Guidelines, the Sentencing Commission relied on estimates that the average overcharge from price fixing is 10 per cent of the selling price.[22] Since the Sentencing Commission believed that the loss to society is larger than the excess profits gained by the cartel members, this percentage was doubled to set the start point for the fine calculation. Depending on culpability factors and other circumstances, the fines for organisations may be increased up to 80 per cent of the volume of affected commerce and thus reach a level that is 8 times the assumed overcharge from price fixing.

---

[17] Case T–61/99 *Adriatica di Navigazione SpA v Commission* [2003] ECR II–5349.
[18] *ibid.*
[19] Case T–224/00 *Archer Daniels Midland Company v Commission (Lysine)* [2003] ECR II–2597, para.196.
[20] J.M. Joshua and P.D. Camesasca, "EC Fining Policy against Cartels after the Lysine Rulings: The Subtle Secrets of X" (2004) *The European Antitrust Review* 6.
[21] See US Sentencing Commission, *Guidelines Manual*, November 2003, § 2R1.1 (d) 1, p.275. For a complete description of the application of the US Sentencing Guidelines, see M.O: Wise, "The System of Sanctions and Enforcement Co-operation in US Antitrust Law", in *Competition Law Sanctioning in the European Union: The EU Law Influence on the National Law Systems of Sanctions in the European Area* (G. Dannecker and O. Jansen ed., 2004), p.200.
[22] Recent research has shown that this figure may seriously underestimate the price increases caused by cartels.

8.2.1.3 Leniency programmes

Public enforcers often lack sufficient evidence to prove a violation of the competition rules. This is particularly worrisome in the case of hardcore cartels (such as price fixing and agreements to share markets), which may result in increased prices and reduced choices for consumers without any redeeming virtue. Leniency programmes aim at increasing the rate of detection by granting favourable treatment to companies willing to inform the antitrust authorities about serious infringements and to put an end to their participation in these secret cartels. In order to improve the chances that secret cartels are detected and punished, the Antitrust Division of the US Department of Justice started an amnesty programme in 1978. Under that programme, cartel members who reported their illegal activity before an investigation was underway were eligible for complete immunity from criminal sanctions. The grant of amnesty, however, was not automatic and the Antitrust Division retained a large margin of discretion. This first programme was not successful: only few amnesty applications were filed and no single international cartel was detected.

In 1993, three major revisions were made to the US Leniency Programme. First, amnesty is now certain when a corporation comes forward prior to an investigation and meets the programme's requirements. These conditions include duties to promptly terminate the participation in the illegal activity, to fully cooperate with the Antitrust Division and to make restitution to injured parties. Amnesty will only be granted if, at the time the corporation comes forward with evidence, the Antitrust Division has not yet received information about the illegal activity from another source. Second, amnesty may still be available even if cooperation with the Antitrust Division starts after the investigation is underway. Third, if a corporation qualifies for automatic amnesty, then all officers, directors and employees who cooperate are equally protected from criminal prosecution. These dramatic extensions of the Amnesty Programme[23] have clearly raised the incentives for companies and individuals to report criminal activities. In recent years, the US Corporate Leniency Programme has been responsible for detecting and cracking many hardcore violations, in particular international price fixing cartels.

The European Commission started a leniency programme in 1996. In spite of the US experience that was available at that time, the European amnesty programme had a timid start. Under the first Leniency Notice, full immunity from fines was not guaranteed. Even the first firm willing to cooperate with the Commission by providing information about the infringement could nevertheless be penalised up to 25 per cent of the otherwise imposed fine. It was also required that the leniency applicant came forward with "decisive

---

[23] Here, it may be added that the recent Antitrust Criminal Penalty Enhancement and Reform Act of 2004 has further increased the effectiveness of the Leniency Program by excluding the possibility that, if the conditions for amnesty are satisfied, individual claimants may collect treble damages for infringements of the antitrust laws (see on treble damages, s.8.3.3). This "detrebling" provision in the case of a company that cooperates with private litigants against other members of a cartel has removed a major disincentive for submitting amnesty applications.

evidence" proving the existence of the cartel. The 2002 Notice[24] has made cooperation with the Commission much more attractive by making it possible to grant full immunity from fines for the first company which cooperates with the Commission and by replacing the "decisive evidence" requirement by two different evidential thresholds for obtaining full leniency in different situations. In addition, firms that were not the first to come forward with the required evidence and, therefore, cannot profit from full immunity, are still eligible for a reduction of the fine.

The European Commission will grant an undertaking immunity from any fine if the undertaking is the first to submit either (a) evidence which may enable the Commission to adopt a decision to carry out an investigation procedure (commonly a surprise investigation: a so-called dawn raid), or (b) enable it to find an infringement of Article 81 EC. Immunity will only be granted if the Commission did not have, at the time of the submission, sufficient evidence to take one of both mentioned actions. A company will receive a conditional grant of full immunity as soon as it discloses the required evidence. This conditional grant will be confirmed at the end of the procedure (assuming a decision is eventually adopted) if the company fulfils three additional requirements: (a) it must fully and continuously cooperate with the Commission, (b) it must have ended its involvement in the cartel at the time when it submitted the required evidence, and (c) it may not have coerced other undertakings to join the cartel. It should be noted that US antitrust law does not require that the applicant meets an evidential burden to be conditionally admitted to the US Justice Department's Programme, provided the "illegal activity" is reported with candour and completeness.[25]

Another novelty of the 2002 Notice (not existing under the US leniency programme) is the sliding scale, whereby companies that do not qualify for full amnesty are still eligible for reduction in fines ranging from 20 to 50 per cent. In contrast with the US "winner takes all" approach, undertakings may be granted a reduction of fines if they submit evidence which represents "significant added value" with respect to the suspected infringement, provided they end their involvement in the cartel no later than the time at which the evidence is submitted. The reductions in fines may reach a maximum of 50 per cent. Timing is crucial: the first company to cooperate may obtain a reduction in fines of between 30 and 50 per cent, the second will be able to obtain a reduction of between 20 and 30 per cent, and the reduction for all others is limited to a maximum of 20 per cent. The precise percentage

---

[24] Notice on immunity from fines and reduction of fines in cartel cases [2002] O.J. C 45/3.
[25] To grant leniency before an investigation has begun, six conditions must be met: (1) the Antitrust Division has not received information about the illegal activity from any other source; (2) the corporation took prompt and effective action to terminate its part in the activity; (3) the corporation reports the wrongdoing with candour and completeness and provides full cooperation; (4) the confession is truly a corporate act; (5) where possible, the corporation makes restitution to injured parties; and (6) the corporation did not coerce another party to participate in the illegal activity and clearly was not the leader in, or originator of, the activity. Leniency may also be granted after an investigation has begun to the corporation that is the first to come forward at the time when the Antitrust Division has not yet evidence that is likely to result in a sustainable conviction, and granting leniency is not unfair to others. In the latter case, conditions 2–5 equally apply. See Department of Justice, Corporate Leniency Policy (*www.usdoj.gov/atr/publc/guidelines/lencorp.htm*).

reduction a company will obtain within the category to which it is allocated will depend on the nature of the submitted evidence—the European Commission prefers evidence originating from the period to which the facts pertain to evidence subsequently established or to circumstantial evidence—and the extent and continuity of the cooperation.

8.2.2 An economic assessment

8.2.2.1 Introductory remarks: different enforcement goals and ways to achieve them

The most relevant feature of an enforcement system from an economic point of view is its ability to deter violations of the law. Consequently, an economic analysis of the sanctions described above necessarily requires an assessment of whether they will be effective in preventing infringements of Articles 81 and 82 of the EC Treaty. Fines imposed for reasons of deterrence should be sufficiently high to make it unprofitable for firms to engage in anti-competitive practices. For antitrust conspiracies where the probability of detection is low (such as price fixing), it is necessary to require the payment of the multiple of profits to achieve deterrence. If a multiplier in inverse proportion to the probability of detection and punishment of the violation needs to be applied, the resulting fine may be extremely high and exceed the ability to pay of the antitrust offender. When such a "judgment proof" problem arises, competition law should provide for the possibility of alternative sanctions, such as imprisonment of the individual decision makers (e.g. directors of companies) who decided to commit an antitrust violation.

Besides the focus on deterrence, the analysis below will also investigate whether the current sanctioning policy achieves non-economic goals, in particular corrective and proportional justice. This extension of the analysis is necessary to obtain a more complete understanding of the current enforcement mechanisms, which are not exclusively based on deterrence goals. Sending corporate managers to jail may seem a very harsh sanction in countries lacking a competition culture. Even though such an approach may be necessary to achieve deterrence, it may conflict with other notions of adequate punishment, such as proportional justice. Under the latter approach, only fines may be considered as appropriate sanctions. These fines may be lower than the amount required for effective deterrence if their purpose is only to guarantee that a committed wrong is corrected by forcing the wrongdoer to pay a sum of money that is an adequate compensation for the harm caused. Alternatively—from a perspective of corrective justice—one may also consider it "just" to disgorge the profits realised by the infringement of the law. Again, this will have an impact on the amount of the monetary sanction, implying that it may be lower than the sum needed to achieve deterrence. A simple example can illustrate that fines imposed for reasons of deterrence may be (much) higher than sanctions imposed for reasons of corrective justice. If the profit achieved by a price fixing cartel equals 10, the harm caused to society in terms of deadweight loss amounts to 20, and the probability of detection is 15 per cent, the fine to achieve deterrence should be above 66. Conversely, the fines to compensate for the harm (20) or to make sure that profits are disgorged (10) are both considerably lower.

From the preceding discussion, it should be clear that policy makers must make a number of choices, depending on the goals they are willing to achieve. In making these choices, they should realise that different policy goals may be inconsistent with each other and should find ways to reduce the ensuing tensions or carefully make inevitable trade-offs. The policy choices relate to the type and severity of sanctions and the resources to be spent on detection. These decisions will have an effect on the expected fine. Since the pursuit of deterrence will always imply administrative costs for both law enforcers and offenders, an optimal enforcement regime will investigate possible antitrust violations only as long as the goal of deterrence is worth the costs of attaining it. Optimal enforcement requires an efficient mix of enforcement expenditures and fines (and/or imprisonment). The choice of a sanction and the way in which it is determined have an effect on the enforcement costs. For example, imprisonment is clearly more costly than imposing fines; for the calculation of the fines, it is easier to estimate the gains of an antitrust violation than to assess the harm caused. Because enforcement is costly, full deterrence may not be efficient.[26] The upper ceiling of the enforcement costs is given by the dead-weight loss and the losses of dynamic efficiency and rent seeking; beyond this limit the enforcement of antitrust rules is welfare-reducing. Consequently, a low level of collusive activity will remain and will not be challenged by the enforcement agencies because it would be too costly compared to the social benefits that can be obtained. Similar conclusions will be reached when the goal of enforcement is corrective justice through compensation; again the presence of enforcement costs will imply that full compensation is not optimal.

8.2.2.2 Enforcement mechanisms to achieve deterrence

In a deterrence approach, the sanctions imposed for infringements of the competition rules must achieve a genuine dissuasive effect and ensure that firms have an incentive to avoid any kind of unlawful anti-competitive agreement or practice. In a seminal contribution, Nobel Prize laureate Gary Becker has shown that criminal fines can be understood as prices attached to certain forms of undesirable conduct. If the price is too high, rational people will refrain from engaging in such behaviour. Alternatively, crimes will be committed if the expected benefits exceed the expected costs, which equal the statutory fine discounted by the probability of detection and punishment.[27] Becker's view on criminal sanctions is most relevant for the enforcement of the cartel prohibition. Whereas the assumption of rational behaviour may be

---

[26] K.G. Elzinga and W. Breit, *The Antitrust Penalties: A Study of Law and Economics* (1976), p.9; S. Souam, "Optimal Antitrust Policy with Different Regimes of Fines" (2001) 19 Int. J. Ind. Organ. 1.
[27] G.S. Becker, "Crime and Punishment: An Economic Approach" (1968) 76 J. Polit. Economy 169.

criticised with regard to irrational crimes (such as murder), calculating behaviour is a rather realistic scenario for white-collar crimes. Antitrust violations generally result from calculating business decisions.[28] Firms will engage in price fixing if the gains derived from this activity are higher than the costs, both adjusted for the probability that they will materialise. From a viewpoint of deterrence, the relevant parameters are the expected fine and the expected gain from an antitrust violation. The expected gain is the additional profit the lawbreakers will obtain, compared to the situation if no infringement of the competition rules is committed. The expected fine is the fine imposed if the violation is detected and punished, discounted by the probability of detection and punishment. In cases of *per se* prohibitions and easy qualification of the act as an infringement of the law, the main enforcement problem is the detection of the infringement. In other cases, the standard of proof allowing the imposition of punishment will be more burdensome. For the latter reason, it seems that the Becker model of the rational criminal is most suitable for naked cartel abuses.

A standard argument in the Law and Economics literature is that a combination of a low probability of detection and high fines is best in terms of efficiency.[29] According to Becker's model, which assumes that monetary sanctions can be increased without costs (since they simply amount to a transfer of wealth from the offender to the society), fines should be increased up to the highest feasible level, which is up to the ability to pay of the offender.[30] By keeping at the same time the probability of detection at the lowest level, the highest level of deterrence can be reached with the lowest use of scarce resources. For competition authorities, it is indeed very costly to control all kinds of behaviour in order to detect infringements and important resources can be saved by keeping the probability of detection low. Moreover, the scope for raising the European Commission's resources is limited in practice, since enforcement budgets are fixed and cannot be easily changed. It follows from the economic analysis that optimality can still be achieved when fines are increased so as to compensate for a low probability of detection. Nevertheless, it is difficult to choose an increase in fines that is exactly proportionate to the decrease in the optimal amount of resources spent on detection.

The comparison of the European and US enforcement regimes has shown that fines can be calculated either on the basis of turnover or by referring to the gains of the lawbreakers or the losses caused by the infringement of the competition rules. From a deterrence perspective, the turnover is not a sound basis for calculating the fine if it does not allow the reversal of the gains of the infringement. It is clear that cartels cause more harm to society than gain for

---

[28] The results of a survey by Feinberg confirm that disregard for the law in pursuit of profits is an important source of EC antitrust violations. See R.M. Feinberg, "The Enforcement and Effects of European Competition Policy: Results of a Survey of Legal Opinion" (1985) 23 J. Common Mkt. Stud. 373.

[29] E. Eide, "Economics of Criminal Behaviour", in *Encyclopedia of Law and Economics* (B. Bouckaert and G. De Geest ed., 1999), p.8100.

[30] The EC Fine Guidelines seem to have taken this point on board ([1998] O.J. C 9/3).

the participants, since only part of the losses are recovered through transfer to the cartels. The harm of such antitrust infringements is difficult to assess, since it does not simply equal the consumer surplus transferred to the producer but also consists of the additional loss of consumer welfare (deadweight loss), the harm in terms of productive and dynamic efficiencies as well as the costs of the rent seeking efforts. To achieve deterrence, however, it is sufficient to know the size of the gains, since this amount multiplied in inverse proportion to the probability of detection and punishment enables the enforcement agency to set the fine above the expected profit.[31] The gain equals the mark-up times the volume of the affected commerce. Figures on sales are not difficult to obtain given the broad availability of market studies. It is more difficult to determine the mark-up, since this requires either econometric calculation or the identification of a benchmark of the competitive price in the absence of collusion. The first method requires data on costs, prices and quantities that must be interpreted by using a credible model of interaction without collusion. The second method requires the use of reference prices, like foreign prices (corrected according to national differences in the level of costs) or historical prices (before and after method). Both methods pose theoretical difficulties and empirical complexities. Still, compared to the problems in determining the harm (which, *inter alia*, requires information on the elasticity of demand and supply and the size of the rent seeking efforts), the determination of the gain is easier to assess. This explains why with regard to the determination of sanctions more attention is paid to the financial benefits of the infringement than to the harm caused.[32]

8.2.2.3 The European sanctions: limited deterrence

Both the choice of sanctions (in particular the exclusive use of fines on companies) and the Guidelines of the European Commission for calculating the fines have been criticised from different angles. Competition lawyers have argued that the goal of legal certainty is not achieved: in particular, the European Commission has not clarified the way in which the starting point of the calculation (gravity of the infringement) is chosen.[33] From the standpoint of economic analysis of law, the central question is whether the goal of deterrence is achieved. This question will be addressed later. In section 8.2.2.4, some comments will be made from other perspectives: both issues of corrective justice and proportionality will then be briefly addressed. Thereafter, the European Leniency Programme will be assessed.

To better address and understand the issues that are raised by the "amnesty game", it seems crucial to highlight directly the major difference between the

---

[31] Compare A.M. Polinsky and S. Shavell, "Should the Liability be Based on the Harm to the Victim or the Gain to the Injurer?" (1994) 10 J. Law, Econ., Organ. 436.

[32] M. Van Oers and B. Van der Meulen, "The Netherlands Competition Authority and its Policy on Fines and Leniency" (2003) 26 *World Competition* 28 with reference to enforcement systems making use of a gain based sanction.

[33] J.M. Joshua and P.D. Camesasca, "EC Fining Policy against Cartels after the Lysine Rulings: The Subtle Secrets of X" (2004) *The European Antitrust Review* 6.

US enforcement system and its European counterpart. In the USA, the enforcement agencies are able to bring in the "big gun" of jail time to force cartelists into submission (and, hence, bludgeoning both companies and individuals into cooperation with the government). The first company to come in and provide evidence of a cartel receives full amnesty. Subsequently, the US enforcement agencies build their case by picking off the various remaining cartelists one by one, extracting more information on the other members of the cartel in exchange for agreed upon "pleas", effectively settling the criminal investigation for the company concerned (as well as its executives, except those who have been carved out to serve prison sentences).[34] Depending on one's point of view, the relative brutality of the US system may be questioned; what is beyond doubt, however, is its rigorous effectiveness in unearthing and terminating cartels.

The European Commission does not have criminal sanctions at its disposal and, instead, needs to rely on a more subtle "game of poker" through the mechanisms contained in the 2002 Leniency Notice, nudging companies—not executives—to cooperate through the uncertainty surrounding the ultimate fine. In so doing, the Commission needs to rely on its discretion to inform applicants of the fine reduction granted at a relatively late stage, by pushing the requirement of "significant added value" when requesting incriminating evidence as the basis for accepting leniency applications and granting fine reductions, and "continuous cooperation" throughout the investigation. There are no—or, at the time of writing, not yet—agreed settlements available in Europe,[35] and even with all members of a cartel fully cooperating with the Commission, all stages of the administrative process (including the Statement of Objections and oral hearing) need to be trudged through before an investigation comes to its formal end when the Commission issues its final decision.

In addition to the lack of criminal sanctions to force cartelists to confess and cease their activities, further reasons may be advanced why the current enforcement of European competition rules is not optimal from a deterrence perspective. First, the use of qualitative criteria to classify infringements in different categories (very serious, serious and minor) impedes an easy calculation of the expected fine. Although this is material to the Commission's strategic use of uncertainty while investigating an alleged infringement, it may be counterproductive in less clear-cut cases. Where companies are in doubt about their exposure (for example, as their involvement was not clear, or in cases where there is a perceived lack of contemporaneous documents to prove an infringement), their incentives to cooperate with the Commission may be hampered by a perception that they may "get away with it", or, if not, that they may face only a minor fine. Second, in as far as total turnover is used as a

---

[34] Civil damages cases will, obviously, continue—and more often than not—intensify after a plea has been reached with the government. We note that full amnesty in the government's criminal proceedings does not shield the company from such civil damages.

[35] We note that DG Comp is currently reviewing its position on this point, and contemplating changes to the EC fines guidelines to, *inter alia*, align the European system with the US plea bargains. Given the relatively early stages of this review, a discussion of the potential implications would go beyond the scope of this edition.

criterion to fix the maximum fine (it is noted the legal uncertainty on this point as discussed above), this is not related to the gains of the infringement. Third, the maximum administrative fine imposed may be too low to deter by itself (it is recalled that piled-on civil damages are nowhere near as "institutionalised" in Europe as in the US, where they are a near-natural component of any cartelist's calculation of the exposure faced). Fourth, in case the lawbreakers cannot pay the fine (judgment proof problem), no alternative sanctions are available. If one compares the European with the US system of enforcement, it seems that the latter is better able to achieve a sufficient level of deterrence.

To achieve the goal of deterrence, quantitative criteria are more appropriate than qualitative criteria. By reference to objective elements in assessing the sanction, the discretion of the competition authority is greatly reduced. Consequently, it becomes easier to assess the amount of the expected fine and this will increase the level of deterrence. According to its 1998 Notice, the European Commission takes into account the gravity and duration of the infringement, as well as aggravating or attenuating circumstances. The Guidelines on calculating fines are rather opaque concerning the criteria to assess the gravity of the violation. They state that "account must be taken of its nature, its actual impact on the market, where this can be measured, and the size of the relevant geographic market". In the past the Commission calculated fines as a percentage of turnover of products involved in the infringement within the European Community. Consequently, the annual sales volume of the goods affected by the price increase was a relevant criterion. From a viewpoint of deterrence, the new approach, as contained in the Guidelines, seems to be a step in the wrong direction. Since there is no clear reference to the quantity of goods affected by the price increase imposed by the cartel members, there is a risk that the fine is chosen regardless of the position of the companies in the relevant market. Consequently, the profitability of potential infringements will not be the decisive criterion whether to engage in anti-competitive practices or not. It is noteworthy that the European Court of Justice has censured decisions of the Commission that did not take account of the affected commerce and has reduced the fines imposed. Although the subsequent case law by the European Commission and the European Court of First Instance is not entirely clear on this point (see above), the European Court of Justice has, in so doing, provided important guidance in fixing fines that will ultimately lead to more effective deterrence.

Indeed, total turnover is not an appropriate benchmark for the determination of the fines, since it indicates the absolute size of the firm rather than the volume of affected commerce, i.e. the quantity of goods whose prices are influenced by the infringement. To determine the efficient fine, that is the fine bringing the highest deterrent effect at the lowest cost, one must calculate the gain brought about by the infringement of the competition rules and then multiply this amount in inverse proportion to the probability of detection and punishment. To calculate the gain, not the overall turnover but the share of the affected commerce held by each participant is the suitable criterion. Market share is mentioned in the European Fine Guidelines as one of the factors to be taken into account. The affected commerce, however, is one that needs to be determined through a precise application of the European Court of Justice's guidance.[36]

Another feature of the current enforcement regime limiting its deterrent effect is the maximum fine that can be imposed for a violation of the competition rules. Taking a price cartel as an example, the gain which the cartel members obtain will depend on the turnover in the products concerned by the violation, the price increase caused by the cartel, the price elasticity of demand faced by the cartel members, and the duration of the cartel. In the literature, calculations of the efficient fine were based on the assumptions that, on average, cartels raise prices by 10 per cent and that the cartel duration is 5 years.[37] If a price increase of 10 per cent leads to an increase in profits of 5 per cent of turnover, the cartel lasts 5 years, and the probability of detection and punishment is 16 per cent,[38] a fine in the order of no less than 150 per cent of the annual turnover would be needed to effectively deter a price cartel from being implemented.[39] The most recent research shows that the appropriate multiplier may be much higher than the last figure. Focusing on the period post-1990, Connor and Lande found that the overcharge is 15–16 per cent for domestic US cartels and 25 per cent for international cartels. In addition, they note that cartel duration is likely to be longer than 5 years: cartels may last between 7 and 8 years. If only the adjustment for the underestimated overcharge is made, fines would have to be in the range of 225–375 per cent of annual turnover to deter. Such high fines are far above the percentage figures that can be deduced from the Commission's sanctioning practice. Up until 1998, fines were in the range of between 2 and 9 per cent of the turnover in the products concerned by the violation. Fines have considerably increased after the publication of the Guidelines,[40] but—since the maximum level of 10 per cent of the annual world-wide turnover has not been adjusted upwards—may still be too low to effectively deter serious infringements of the European competition rules.

Finally, the European enforcement regime does not provide a remedy for the judgment proof problem. There is indeed a risk that the financial position of firms that violated the competition rules will not allow them to pay the fines imposed.[41] The deterrence goal will not be achieved if no alternative sanctions to cure the judgment proof problem, such as imprisonment, are available.

---

[36] Again, we note the ongoing review of the EC fines guidelines. Also on this point, the European Commission contemplates to move to alignment with the US and adopt a "volume of commerce" based standard.

[37] These figures are based on US studies. Figures on road building bid rigging cases suggest that the conspiracies increased price by at least 10%. See W. Wils, *The Optimal Enforcement of EC Antitrust Law* (2002), with further references. Own-price elasticity of demand is supposed to be −2.

[38] This figure is again based on a US study, estimating the probability of a successful prosecution of a price cartel at most between 13 and 17%. See: P.G. Bryant and E.W. Eckhard, "Price Fixing: The Probability of Getting Caught" (1991) 73 Rev. Econ. Statist. 531.

[39] W. Wils, *The Optimal Enforcement of EC Antitrust Law* (2002), p.201.

[40] Record fines have been imposed for hard core cartels, such as Case IV/31.149 *Polypropylene* [1986] O.J. L 230/1; Case IV/33.833 *Cartonboard* [1994] O.J. L 243/1; and Case COMP/37.512 *Vitamins* [2003] O.J. L 6/1.

[41] In fact, the EC fines guidelines already provide for a possible reduction of the fine to take into account a company's (in)ability to pay.

Comparing the US and European enforcement systems, it becomes clear that deterrence goals can be better realised in the former than in the latter jurisdiction.[42] The first reason is the level of sanctions. The changes to the Sherman Act, increasing the fines up to US$100 million or twice the gain/loss resulting from the conspiracy, clearly reflect a goal of deterrence.[43] Conversely, an increase of the level of sanctions has been left out of the European debate on the modernisation of the enforcement system. Even though the Guidelines mention that fines for very serious infringements can be above €20 million, there will be no possibility of imposing such very high fines if the limit of 10 per cent of overall turnover is exceeded. Moreover, there is no guarantee that the fines that can be imposed on multi-billion euro corporations within the limit of 10 per cent of overall turnover will be sufficiently high to achieve deterrence. In addition, imprisonment of corporate directors is not available as an alternative sanction in cases where the imposed fine exceeds the offender's ability to pay. (Proposals to criminalise European competition law are discussed in Box 8.2). The second reason is that the European criteria for calculating sanctions are not linked to the deterrence goal. The Guidelines pursue a qualitative approach, stressing that this "will make it possible to apply differential treatment to undertakings according to the nature of the infringement committed".[44] By contrast, the US Sentencing Guidelines accept that it is possible to estimate the gains achieved by a cartel as a percentage of the selling price. The price increase caused by the cartel can thus be estimated and multiplied by the volume of affected business. If it is assumed that 10 per cent of the price is the price increase caused by the cartel, the gain to the cartel can be estimated as 10 per cent of the turnover (quantity times price increase). This amount should then be multiplied to account for low probabilities of detection. The US Federal Sentencing Commission model takes as the start point 20 per cent of the total volume of affected commerce, but allows adjusting this upwards to no less than 80 per cent. This is ten times the percentage of turnover which was imposed by the European Commission in the period before the Guidelines were issued. A further difference between the European and US Guidelines is that the effect of attenuating and aggravating circumstances on the multiplier of basic fine is predetermined in the latter system, whereas the European Commission enjoys a great margin of discretion to adapt the fine in an individual case.

---

[42] It is also to be noted that the USA is agressively exporting its antitrust enforcement system through a network of Mutual Legal Assistance Treaties (MLATs), which in tandem with dual criminality provisions tend to impose US antitrust globally.

[43] The goal of deterrence was also clearly embraced by the American Congress: "The committee believes that increasing the maximum fines for criminal violations of section 1 is necessary and appropriate to deter the most flagrant and abusive forms of antitrust crimes. ... Particularly with respect to corporate offenders, fine levels are simply too low to deter effectively antitrust conspiracies and courts have been reluctant to impose maximum fines even for wilful violations" (Senate Report to the Antitrust Amendments Act of 1990, Senate Report No.101–287, 1990 U.S. Code Congress. And Admin. News, at p.4111).

[44] Section 1.A, sixth consideration.

Box 8.2: Must European competition law be criminalised?

In a critical evaluation of the current system of enforcement, Wils proposes to make use of individual penalties, including imprisonment, in combination with corporate sanctions.[45] He advances several arguments why increasing the fines on companies above the current limit of 10 per cent of the worldwide turnover will not cure the problem of underdeterrence. First, the fines required for effective deterrence would often exceed the firms' ability to pay. Profits are usually not retained and, in any case, would count for only a fraction of the fine; moreover, liquidating the assets would not generate sufficient revenues if the annual turnover exceeds the assets.[46] Second, imposing very high fines would force companies into bankruptcy, causing undesirable social costs (losses to, among others, employees, creditors and tax authorities). Third, even below the level of inability to pay, the imposition of high fines is administratively costly and may have undesirable side effects. Creditors will suffer a diminution in the value of their securities, salaries of employees may be cut down, tax receipts will be reduced and the costs may be passed on to consumers in the form of higher prices. Finally, the fines required for effective deterrence may raise fundamental objections of proportional justice.

Aside from the fact that fines needed for effective deterrence are impossibly high, corporate sanctions do not always guarantee adequate incentives for responsible individuals within the firm. First, firms have often only a limited ability to discipline their agents: the greatest sanction available (dismissal) may not sufficiently deter and monitoring of employees to avoid antitrust violations can be very costly. Second, firms may be management controlled, so that fines will not sufficiently affect shareholders to give them incentives to control the managers' behaviour. Third, managers may have left the firm by the time their violation is detected.

According to Wils, deterrence can be best increased by threatening the accountable decision makers within the firm with fines. The effectiveness of this sanction may be limited by the individuals' ability to pay, but this problem can be overcome by using prison sanctions as well. Antitrust authorities will be better able than firms to control the individual decision makers by threatening severe punishment. Prison sanctions are a very effective deterrent and carry a strong moral message. Sanctions imposed on individuals should not only be of a monetary kind but include the possibility of imprisonment for an additional reason. Firms may compensate managers *ex ante* for taking the risk of committing antitrust violations or

---

[45] W. Wils, "Does the Effective Enforcement of Articles 81 and 82 EC Require not only Fines on Undertakings but also Individual Penalties, in Particular Imprisonment?", in *European Competition Law Annual 2001: Effective Private Enforcement of EC Antitrust Law* (C.D. Ehlermann and I. Atanasiu ed., 2002); W. Wils, "Is Criminalization of EU Competition Law the Answer?" (2005) 28 *World Competition* 117.

[46] It should be added that the European Commission takes the bad financial situation into account when setting the amount of the fine. See: EC fines guidelines, para.5(b).

indemnify them *ex post*, thus taking away the deterrent effect of fines. Imprisonment avoids such circumventing behaviour.

The next question is for which types of violations imprisonment should be imposed as a sanction. Wils suggests limiting its use to hardcore cartels: horizontal price fixing, bid rigging and market allocation schemes. Imprisonment should not be used for other horizontal agreements, vertical restraints and infringements of Article 82 EC. This proposal invites some comments. Price fixing is a comparably profitable and easy to hide violation. Consequently, it would be unacceptably costly to increase the level of certainty in detection and imprisonment will be an adequate deterrent. Also the risk that errors[47] are made is low: price fixing is a clear-cut violation of the competition rules. The latter is no longer true when it must be assessed whether vertical restraints harm competition or a firm in a dominant position commits an abuse. If deterrence was the only criterion to assess the efficiency of law enforcement, a case could be made for criminalising also the less serious infringements of competition law. However, if imprisonment is used as a sanction, the error costs (in particular type II errors) may be high and outweigh the benefits of deterred anti-competitive practices. In addition, reserving imprisonment for horizontal price fixing, bid rigging and market partitioning is a choice that can be justified on grounds of proportional justice.

8.2.2.4 The European sanctions from a perspective of corrective justice

Contrary to the US vision of things, in European competition law the view that punishment should effectively deter harmful conduct in the future is not explicitly accepted as the major goal of imposing fines. Regulation 1/2003 seems to reflect requirements of proportional justice rather than deterrence. As explained above, the upper ceiling expressed as 10 per cent of the worldwide turnover of the undertaking, which committed an antitrust violation, is ill-suited to achieve deterrence. Its only function seems to be the determination of the limit above which the size of the fine is deemed to be dangerous for the existence itself of the undertaking and, hence, not proportional. The maximum fine reflects the degree of disapproval of the behaviour. In Europe there is not (yet) a competition culture comparable to the US one and people still tend to consider infringements of competition rules less serious than other forms of disapproved conduct sanctioned by criminal fines (although reference must be made to criminalisation of competition law in the UK and Ireland, see Box 8.1). Very high fines (such as 300 per cent of the annual turnover of the products concerned by the violation) imposed to achieve deterrence may be disproportionate to the degree in which society disapproves of the harm caused and thus conflict with goals of proportional justice.[48] A similar concern seems to underlie the Guidelines on the imposition of fines. Deterrence does not strictly require that the calculation of fines conforms with criteria such as the

---

[47] Clearly error costs are higher with imprisonment than with monetary sanctions.
[48] Art. 49(3) CFREU.

culpability of the antitrust offenders and the duration of the infringement. However, such criteria may be seen as indispensable from a corrective justice approach. Also, qualitative criteria (such as the nature of the infringement and the distinction between minor, serious and very serious infringements) are inadequate from a deterrence perspective since they do not allow an easy calculation of the expected fine. However, they may again be appropriate from a perspective of proportional justice. In the 1998 Guidelines, the emphasis seems to be on the latter goal, rather than on deterrence.

However, emphasising justice goals is no easy way to stop the criticisms on the current European system of enforcement. Besides their relative ineffectiveness in deterring violations of the competition rules, the current sanctions may be criticised for not achieving corrective justice either. From a corrective justice perspective, the sanction should be linked to the harm caused. The 1998 Guidelines' criterion of "impact on the market" should be more precisely defined as the losses suffered by consumers (transfer of consumer surplus to the producers), the deadweight loss and the other costs (losses in terms of productive and dynamic efficiency and rent seeking). Again, the relevant start point to calculate the monopoly profits (harm to consumers) is not the total turnover but the volume of business affected by the cartel agreements. The latter amount should be discounted by a percentage reflecting the price increase caused by the cartel. To this effect, empirical estimates of the overall harm (price overcharges) in markets affected by the illegal agreement can be used.[49]

Calculating damages from the perspective of corrective justice is not an easy task. Compensation of the harm poses serious problems since it is very difficult, if not impossible, to identify all victims. The primary victims are those who would have bought the product at a lower price; the costs of identifying these buyers are prohibitive. It is also difficult to identify the secondary victims, who bought at the cartel price, and the customers of these purchasers. There may be several tiers in the distribution chain between the manufacturer and the ultimate consumers and particular buyers should be awarded compensation only if the overcharge was passed on to them.[50] Often this is not an easy inquiry. Not only buyers of the high priced goods but also suppliers of a cartel may be harmed. These tertiary victims should also be entitled to compensation if they can show that they are injured as a result of decreased sales associated with the reduction in output. In sum, compensation of persons injured will be difficult to implement in practice.[51] Besides the harm caused to

---

[49] Assuming availability of data and agreement on the relevant measurement techniques.
[50] It should be added, however, that from a deterrence perspective it may be preferable to deny standing to indirect purchasers and thereby increase the potential payoffs to direct purchasers who will thus have greater incentives to initiate private enforcement actions. See W.M. Landes and R.A. Posner, "Should Indirect Purchasers Have Standing to Sue Under Antitrust Laws? An Economic Analysis of the Rule of Illinois Brick" (1979) 46 U. Chi. L. Rev. 602.
[51] See for further analysis: T. Calvani, "Competition Penalties and Damages in a Cartel Context: Criminalisation and the Case for Custodial Sentences", in *Criminalization of Competition law Enforcement and Legal Implications for the EU Member States* (K.J. Cseres, M.P. Schinkel and F.O.W. Vogelaar ed., 2005). This author also discusses the requirements and limitations that courts have imposed on plaintiffs willing to recover damages for antitrust infringements.

the different categories of victims identified above, also the losses of dynamic efficiency and the costs of rent seeking are part of the social costs of cartels. These costs may exceed the maximum ceiling of 10 per cent of the worldwide turnover, so that the application of Regulation 1/2003 will not achieve the goal of corrective justice. This may be a reason to allow private damages actions besides the infringement proceedings initiated by the competition authorities. Whereas public enforcement may be better suited to achieve deterrence, private enforcement may play a complementary role in achieving corrective justice.[52]

8.2.2.5 Economic assessment of leniency programmes

Leniency programmes may contribute significantly to the efficiency of law enforcement. By guaranteeing lenient treatment for the cheaters and making it profitable to deviate from the collusive path, these programmes aim at destabilising cartels. Leniency programmes not only bring direct benefits, resulting from lowering the costs of detection in cases of hardcore violations, but also indirect benefits. Since antitrust authorities can devote more resources to cartels that are not revealed, the detection rate of the latter may also increase.

The leniency programme has a clear underlying economic logic: it increases the probability of detection and punishment by placing the cartel members in a prisoners' dilemma.[53] All cartel members have an interest that the cartel cannot be proven (not to confess) but mistrust among the cartel members creates a race to be the first to confess. In a prisoners' dilemma, each player can be better off by defecting from the "not confess" to the "confess" strategy. Hence, the cartel members may decide to confess, even though it is in their common interest not to do so. Consider the very common situation when a cartel first learns that it is under investigation. Each member of that cartel knows that any of its co-conspirators can be the first to come forward in exchange for total immunity from fines. Such a decision will seal the fate of all other cartel members. Clearly, it would be in the common interest of the cartel members that nobody decides to cooperate with the antitrust authority, thus depriving the latter of the evidence needed to prove an infringement. However, the amnesty for the first one through the antitrust authority's door creates tension and mistrust among the cartel members.

In the theoretical literature several useful insights for designing optimal leniency programmes can be found. This literature also shows that positive rewards may deter collusion in a more effective way than reduced fines. Motta and Polo have demonstrated that it can be efficient to reduce fines even when an antitrust investigation is already under way, but the competition authority has not yet obtained evidence of an infringement. Reduced fines are a second best instrument in cases where the budget of the competition authority is not

---

[52] See s.8.3.3
[53] See Ch.5, s.5.2.2.3 for a discussion of this concept and its application to cartels.

sufficiently high to intervene often enough to fully deter collusion.[54] The 2002 Notice of the European Commission is in line with this theoretical insight, since it allows cartel members to join the leniency programme even after an investigation has started, when the incentive to cheat is stronger and the cartel more unstable. Another paper by Spagnolo assumes that cartels are convicted after detection and thus allows focusing on cartels that are not already under investigation. Spagnolo shows that an efficient outcome is reached when the competition authority offers a positive award equal to the sum of the fines paid by the convicted firms to the first party that reports. Provided that the maximum fine is high enough, such a reward policy can achieve full deterrence at no cost.[55] Aubert, Rey and Kovacic demonstrate that positive rewards have a larger deterrent effect than reduced fines and that rewards for individuals can be more effective than corporate ones. In particular, rewards to employees can be very effective, provided they are high enough to compensate the employee for the anticipated reduction in future earnings, since being a whistle-blower is likely to end the insider's career with his employer and possibly with the entire industry. These authors also discuss remedies for potential adverse effects of reward programmes, such as introducing fines for false denunciations in order to avoid restrictions of efficient exchanges of information between competing firms.[56] The latter insights from theory have not found their way into antitrust practice; up until now leniency programmes are not complemented by reward programmes.

A potential problem of leniency programmes is that overall fines will be lower, since companies that come forward with relevant evidence will get immunity. In the literature,[57] two different effects of leniency programmes have been identified: on the one hand, there is a negative impact on deterrence *ex ante* since the expected fine will be lower given the possibility of a fine reduction for law offenders who have cooperated with the antitrust authorities. On the other hand, leniency programmes increase law compliance *ex post*, since after its collapse the cartel will not be restored given the loss of confidence among the participants. If *ex ante* deterrence is already achieved, leniency programmes should not be used; otherwise they are an important enforcement mechanism. Possible negative effects on deterrence may be cured by raising the maximum fine and through limiting conditions for full immunity. As to the first response, European competition law seems to be in need of stiffer sanctions (in particular imprisonment) to deter effectively. The second remedy is already included in the European leniency programme since full immunity is only available to the first company who reveals information making it possible to establish an infringement.

The experience with the US amnesty programme teaches that leniency

---

[54] M. Motta and M. Polo, "Leniency Programs and Cartel Prosecution" (2001) 21 Int. J. Ind. Organ. 347.

[55] G. Spagnolo, "Divide et Impera: Optimal Deterrence Mechanisms against Cartels and Organized Crime", Mimeo (2004), available at: *www.cepr.org*.

[56] C. Aubert, P. Rey and W.E. Kovacic, "The Impact of Leniency and Whistle-blowing Programs on Cartels" (2006, forthcoming) Int. J. Ind. Org.

[57] M. Motta and M. Polo, "Leniency Programs and Cartel Prosecution" (2001) 21 Int. J. Ind. Organ. 347.

programmes are successful when three conditions are met. First, antitrust laws must provide the threat of firm sanctions for hardcore infringements. Second, antitrust offenders must perceive a significant risk of detection by antitrust authorities if they engage in illegal conspiracies. Third, antitrust authorities must publish transparent leniency programmes so that prospective cooperating parties can predict with a high degree of certainty whether they will get immunity. Since the first two conditions are met to a lesser extent in Europe, the European Commission's leniency programme risks being less successful than its US counterpart. Exposure to criminal sanctions may be the driving factor in the decision of US firms to cooperate with the antitrust authorities. Also, if competition law infringements are not of a criminal law nature, a number of investigative techniques will not be available, thus reducing the perceived risk of detection. With respect to the third requirement the heavy evidential burden of "decisive evidence" contained in the first European leniency programme has been replaced by less stringent requirements, which bring the European programme more in line with its US counterpart. An evidential hurdle continues to exist for partial amnesty (granted to firms not qualifying for full immunity from fines), which can be granted only if the evidence submitted represents "significant added value". In both the US and European system of enforcement, transparency is still reduced by fairness arguments. In Europe, companies which did "take steps to coerce other undertakings to participate in the infringement" (see the Notice, at 11(c)) do not qualify for full immunity. In the USA, a similar restriction applies if leniency is required before an investigation has begun and no information about the illegal activity has been reported from any other source. In other cases and also after an investigation has begun, the Antitrust Division may decide not to grant leniency if this would be "unfair" to others. Discretionary powers to assess the role of companies in the offence may be defensible for corrective justice reasons. However, if companies cannot predict how "coercion" will be interpreted, they may decide against cooperation and existing cartels will remain unreported and unpunished.

8.3 Public and/or private enforcement

8.3.1 The choice between public and private enforcement

Both in Europe and in the USA, enforcement actions can be initiated by public authorities and private parties. However, the way in which public enforcement of the competition rules is organised differs. At the European (quasi) federal level, a single administrative body (the European Commission) has been empowered to enforce the competition rules. After the modernisation of the system of enforcement introduced by Regulation 1/2003 (which entered into effect on May 1, 2004), Articles 81 and 82 EC are also enforced by a network of national competition authorities and judges. In the USA, the competence to enforce federal antitrust law is shared by the Antitrust Division of the Department of Justice and the Federal Trade Commission. The European Commission is both prosecutor and judge: it combines investigative, prosecutorial and adjudicative powers.[58] Conversely, in the USA the Department of Justice must seek a court judgment to prohibit a violation of Sections 1 and 2 of the Sherman Act. The Federal Trade Commission combines prosecutorial and adjudicative powers, but a complex system of internal checks and balances has been built into the FTC procedure.

In Europe, up until very recently, public enforcement has traditionally played a dominant role, both at the Community level and in national legal systems. Whereas the enforcement in Europe relies heavily on administrative acts, private lawsuits have been playing an important role in the US system of enforcement for a much longer period. In practice, 90 per cent of antitrust cases in the USA are private actions at both federal and state level.[59] The recent change of the European Regulation on enforcement seems to have increased the role of private parties somewhat by granting national judges the power to apply Article 81 EC in its entirety. However, private enforcement through national courts will have effects that will probably remain far behind the impact of private action in the USA. Important institutional differences exist between the two legal systems, which makes private action in the USA much more attractive. In the remainder of this section the differences between the European and US systems of enforcement will be further explained and an economic assessment of the respective strengths and weaknesses of both systems will be provided.

8.3.2 Public enforcement: the combination of investigative, prosecutorial and adjudicative powers

In Europe all stages of the procedure (investigation, negotiation, decision and political review) are assigned to the European Commission. As has been pointed out above,[60] the European Commission enjoys relatively large discretionary powers when deciding on the substance of the infringement, the level of the fines and the fine discount granted through a leniency application. The Commission's ultimate decision is obviously subject to an appeal before the Court of First Instance, whereto it may be noted that in cartel cases the Court of First Instance tends to limit its in-depth review to points of process rather than substance.

In the USA, the Department of Justice has extensive powers to investigate

---

[58] In US antitrust terms "the Commission combines the functions of prosecutor, judge and jury" (I. Van Bael, "The Antitrust Settlement Practice of the EC Commission" (1986)) 23 C.M.L. Rev. 61). In reaction to complaints about this improper combination of functions, a Hearing Officer has been appointed within DG COMP.
[59] European Commission, "The EU gets new competition powers for the 21st century" (2004) *Competition Policy Newsletter—special edition 1.*
[60] See s.8.2.2.3.

potential violations of Sections 1 and 2 of the Sherman Act but has no power to adopt decisions finding an infringement and imposing sanctions. To that effect suits must be brought in court; district courts may impose fines on companies and fines and prison sentences on individuals. Unlike the Department of Justice, which has only investigative and prosecutorial functions, the Federal Trade Commission also has adjudicative powers. Under the Federal Trade Commission Act, it can issue cease and desist orders to stop unfair methods of competition, including violations of Sections 1 and 2 of the Sherman Act. The initial decision, which is taken by an administrative law judge, may be appealed to the Federal Trade Commission (FTC). When deciding on the appeal, the FTC's Commissioners sit as judges and hear directly both sides of the case. This is different from the European enforcement system, since in the latter jurisdiction there is no independent initial adjudicator and the European Commissioners decide on the proposal of the Competition Commissioner, who has been briefed by the DG Competition officials dealing with the case.

The question whether it is preferable to separate the adjudicative function from the investigative and prosecutorial functions should be answered by assessing the strengths and weaknesses of the alternative systems in terms of accuracy and administrative costs. If the European Commission combines all functions, enforcement errors caused by overly active competition officials may be more frequent than in a system in which Community judges take the ultimate decision. Conversely, administrative costs may decrease by combining the investigative, prosecutorial and adjudicative functions. Wils has argued that, theoretically, there are three possible sources of prosecutorial bias.[61] First, competition authorities may hold the initial belief that a violation is likely to be found and search for evidence, which confirms rather than challenges this belief (confirmation bias). Second, officials may be psychologically motivated to avoid discovering that there is no case for a prohibition decision (hindsight bias) or may desire to justify past efforts, thus pre-empting complaints about inefficient use of scarce resources. Third, competition authorities may wish to show a record of numerous infringements and high fines, in order to demonstrate that they are fulfilling their task well (desire to show a high level of enforcement). All these risks can be contained by internal checks and balances (such as a peer review panel or the setting up of a separate entity which plays the role of the devil's advocate) and frequent judicial review; see for an example, the EC system of merger control described in Box 9.1. However, such controlling mechanisms will decrease the savings in administrative costs. Therefore, on balance it seems that an alternative system in which the European Commission would prosecute before the Community courts is superior for Article 81 EC and Article 82 EC cases.[62]

---

[61] W. Wils, "The Combination of the Investigative and Prosecutorial Function and the Adjudicative Function in EC Antitrust Enforcement: A Legal and Economic Analysis" (2004) 27 *World Competition* 205.

[62] In merger cases, only the hindsight bias seems relevant, whereas there is no risk for confirmation basis or a too high level of activity since mergers must be notified by the parties concerned and most mergers are found to be unproblematic.

8.3.3 The role of private parties in enforcing competition law

8.3.3.1 A comparison: USA—Europe

In the USA, the attractiveness of private action is due to a number of factors. The most important reasons include the following.[63] First, successful plaintiffs are entitled to so-called treble damages (which hardly exist in Europe), entitling them to claim three times the actual damages (Section 4 Clayton Act). Such private antitrust lawsuits are likely after a successful criminal prosecution, since a criminal conviction constitutes *prima facie* evidence that the defendant violated the antitrust laws in any subsequent civil litigation.[64] The prospect of collecting treble damages is a powerful incentive for private parties to take legal action against their competitors. In abuse of dominance cases, the fact that the volume of case law on predatory pricing in Europe is minor compared to in the USA may be due to this important institutional difference between both legal systems. Second, contrary to the laws of many Member States of the European Union, in the USA contingency fee arrangements are legal. Attorneys at law may conclude an agreement with their clients stating that the lawyer only has to be paid if he wins the case. The fee is usually a fraction of the awarded damages, but the lawyer receives nothing if the case is lost. Under a contingency fee system, the client thus bears no trial risk. Third, the possibility of antitrust class action suits may be an appropriate remedy if private parties lack incentives to sue because their individual damages are relatively small compared to the costs of litigation (e.g. in price fixing cases). Class actions allow a plaintiff to obtain damages not only for the harm he suffered himself but also for the harm suffered by other victims.[65] Finally, problems of proof faced by private parties are mitigated by US procedural law. Whereas in European civil proceedings the relevant information has to be voluntarily supplied by the parties, US courts generally order the defendant to supply all relevant information in a pre-trial discovery procedure (this is very far-reaching and in a global cartel also covers documents submitted to other agencies, such as the European Commission).[66] In Europe, only competition

---

[63] For a more complete list, see J.S. Venit, "Brave New World: the Modernization and Decentralization of Enforcement under Articles 81 and 82 of the EC Treaty" (2003) 40 CML Rev. 545 at p.572.

[64] See §5(a) Clayton Act, §16(a) 15 U.S.C.

[65] As far as the authors are aware, the first serious attempt in Europe to achieve results similar to a class action concerns the cement cartel. A number of direct purchasers in Germany have pooled their resources in a Belgian company to enable the filing of a suit in Germany and to gain access to their mutual pricing data for assessment by economic experts as evidence of the alleged overcharge.

[66] For an economic analysis of this mechanism, see A. Polinsky and S. Shavell, "The Economic Theory of Public Enforcement of Law" (2000) 38 J. Econ. Lit. 45.

authorities enjoy investigative powers to force companies to submit the relevant evidence.[67]

European law does not provide similar incentives for private parties to become active as antitrust enforcers. The prospective damages award may be too small: there is no right to treble damages and punitive damages are not feasible under national procedural laws. The risk of losing the case may act as a further deterrent, since procedural costs cannot be spread over several victims and information costs to cure problems of proof may be prohibitively high. Up until now, Community law has been largely invoked as a "shield" to justify non-performance of a contractual obligation on the grounds that the contractual provision in question infringes the cartel prohibition (so-called Euro defences). The use of European competition law as a "sword" to obtain injunctive relief to prevent harm or to obtain damages has been limited.[68] This state of things is understandable if one takes into account the lack of incentive mechanisms as far as private enforcement of the competition rules is concerned.

Unlike US antitrust law, the EC Treaty does not include any express provision on the question of damages that successful plaintiffs may receive. Regulation 1/2003 has facilitated the invocation of the nullity defence, since national courts can now apply themselves the four conditions of Article 81(3) EC instead of having to suspend their proceedings and wait for a decision of the European Commission. However, the new Regulation contains no rule that directly encourages the development of damage actions.[69] Rather than from the European legislator, the support for private enforcement has come from the European Court of Justice, which in its *Courage* judgment of 2001 has declared a Community law-based right to damages.[70] The Court has stated that private actions for damages before the national courts will help to ensure the full effectiveness of the competition rules, and in particular the practical effect of the cartel prohibition. Private enforcement can thus "make a significant contribution to the maintenance of effective competition in the Community".[71] Since the modernisation of the Regulation on enforcement does not include any harmonisation of sanctions or remedies at the national level, it remains for the domestic legal systems of each Member State to determine the remedies and procedures for claiming damages, provided that these rules

---

[67] The European Commission and national competition authorities can threaten to impose a fine if not all or incorrect information is supplied (see Art.23(1) of Regulation 1/2003). Furthermore, competition authorities have the right to collect evidence by entering the premises of an undertaking without its consent; these are so-called dawn raids (see Arts 17–22 of Regulation 1/2003).
[68] J.S. Venit, "Brave New World: the Modernization and Decentralization of Enforcement under Articles 81 and 82 of the EC Treaty" (2003) 40 C.M.L. Rev. 545 at pp.570–571.
[69] For reasons of completeness, it must be added that private actions for damages are available through the national courts.
[70] Case C–453/99 *Courage Ltd v Bernard Crehan* [2001] ECR I–6297. For a comment, see A.P. Komninos, "New Prospects for Private Enforcement of EC Competition Law: *Courage v Crehan* and the Community Right to Damages" (2002) 39 C.M.L. Rev. 447.
[71] Case C–453/99 *Courage Ltd v Bernard Crehan* [2001] ECR I–6297, para.34.

meet the requirements of equivalence and effectiveness.[72] A first example is the *Provimi* case in the UK[73] (see Box 8.3). Requirements to successfully claim damages for harm caused by infringements of European competition law should not be stricter than for infringements of national law (principle of equivalence) and the national procedures must allow full protection of the individual rights based on directly applicable provisions of the EC Treaty (principle of effectiveness). In spite of the fact that it seems premature to conclude that private parties will soon become full players in the enforcement of competition rules, the recent case law of the European Court of Justice favours such a development. This raises the question whether private enforcement is desirable.

Box 8.3: The Provimi case

In 2003, the High Court ruled in *Provimi Ltd v Roche Products Ltd*, a ruling which may be of particular interest to large companies with operations across Europe. *Provimi* arose out of the vitamins cartel, which pitted big purchaser groups (foodstuffs producers) against the vitamins manufacturers. Both the producers and buyers of bulk vitamins were large conglomerate groups, but by the nature of the market, each national subsidiary dealt with another national subsidiary. The claimants wanted to consolidate as many claims as possible in a single jurisdiction—ideally the most plaintiff-friendly—while the defendants' litigation strategy was to force the claimants to bring a multiplicity of suits, with every prospect of conflicting outcomes. The High Court allowed all the European subsidiaries of the purchaser to sue parent and subsidiaries of the producers in the same litigation in London (instead of having to bring separate actions in each country across Europe).

Although difficult issues remain unresolved—for example, the measure of damages, the treatment of claims by indirect purchasers, and the validity of what is known as the "pass-on defence" (in essence, that no loss was suffered by the buyers since they simply increased the price to their customers)—English courts post-*Provimi* now recognise that the purchasers from cartels can sue in tort for breach of statutory duty under Article 81 EC. The relevant cause of action in English courts for breach of Article 81 EC is a mixture of EC competition law and domestic laws. What constitutes a breach of Article 81 EC is a matter of European competition law, but a claim for breach could only be made against an entity recognised by domestic law, basically one with legal personality. The claimants would have to show that the entity was (a) in breach of Article 81 EC, and (b) liable to damages to the particular claimant for breach. Aikens J. found it was arguable that by

---

[72] Case C–453/99 *Courage Ltd v Bernard Crehan* [2001] ECR I–6297, para.26.
[73] *Roche Products Ltd v Provimi Ltd* [2003] EWHC 961 (Comm). For a comment, see J.M. Joshua, "After Empagran: Could London Become a One-Stop for Antitrust Litigation?" (2005) 4 Comp L.I. 3.

implementing the cartel price, the various Roche companies had caused the alleged injury. Each infringing company could be a tortfeasor. Interestingly, the judge applied a variant of the "but for" test rejected by the DC Circuit in *Empagran*.[74] Without the cartels, there would (arguably) have been competition between Roche and other producers. Had it not been for the cartel, the—*in casu*—German subsidiary might have been able to buy vitamins from Roche UK or another group at lower prices, although it had actually only ever bought in Germany. Also, provided there is a UK "anchor" action, *Provimi* shows how Regulation 44[75] allows the purchaser's German subsidiary to sue its German supplier company in England.

8.3.3.2 Do we need private enforcement?

It seems clear that private actions can be no substitute for public enforcement by competition authorities but may complement such enforcement if the monetary risk is seen as an aid to deterrence. First, from the viewpoint of deterrence, public enforcement clearly dominates private enforcement. In the view of rational antitrust offenders, the expected benefit of infringements will exceed the expected cost of private enforcement and underdeterrence will result. Second, private interests differ from the general interest.[76] Consequently, private actions will not be initiated even when this would be socially desirable. Private parties may lack financial incentives to bring suit or fear retaliation by the accused parties. Third, the costs of private enforcement tend to be higher than the costs of public enforcement. Private parties may be unaware of the existence and harmful effects of infringements of the competition rules. Also the error costs may be higher under a private enforcement regime, particularly when judges lack the required economic expertise to decide cases. Finally, it must be questioned to what extent private actions are needed to achieve justice objectives. Each of these points will be discussed in turn.

To achieve deterrence, public enforcement is indispensable. In cases of hardcore cartels (such as price fixing) private parties may not even realise that they are harmed. They may also face difficulties in proving the size of the damage and the causal link between the infringement and the harm. Competition authorities are better at discovering and proving antitrust infringements since they have wider investigative powers than private parties. Without the investigative powers of competition authorities, very serious infringements will remain undiscovered and unpunished. Moreover, even if it was possible to identify all victims—including not only consumers who paid above competitive prices but above all those who would have bought the product at a lower price—problems of under-deterrence would persist.

[74] *Empagran SA v Hoffman-La Roche Ltd*, 2005 US App. LEXIS 12743.
[75] Council Regulation (EC) No 44/2001 of 22 December 2000 on jurisdiction and the recognition and enforcement of judgments in civil and commercial matters [2001] O.J. L 12/1.
[76] This problem is exacerbated by US trial lawyers, who usually operate under contingency fees arrangements.

Damages awarded to private parties will be computed by reference to lost profits, which bear no relationship with the offender's gain. Also, multiple damages would be needed to offset the problem that only a limited number of victims decide to go to court. The trebling of damages in the USA could be considered as trying to address this problem, but it remains doubtful that three is the correct multiplier. Applying a multiplier in inverse proportion to the probability of detection and punishment is always difficult in practice, but could be done more easily by public authorities. In sum, deterrence objectives can be better reached by public enforcement.[77]

Private interests diverge from the general interest. Private parties will initiate proceedings only if the private benefits of doing so are higher than the private costs. The private costs consist of the information costs that must be borne to discover the infringement, the costs of the court procedure and the costs to prove the size of the damage and the causal link between the infringement and the harm. The private benefits consist of the sanction imposed on the law offender (assuming that there is no judgment proof problem), as far as this will improve the financial situation and/or the competitive market position of the private claimant. This private cost–benefit calculus has no systematic relation with the social costs and benefits. The social costs also comprise the harm suffered by victims who do not sue and other losses (rent seeking) that cannot be attributed to individual victims. Since potential plaintiffs are driven only by the private gains and expenses of their claims, they will have insufficient incentives to invest in detecting and litigating meritorious cases. In addition, a system of private enforcement also creates a free riding problem. Every victim of an antitrust infringement has an interest in leaving the enforcement efforts to other victims, so that profits can be obtained without having to spend their own resources. The free riding problem will reduce the number of private actions below the level of enforcement that would be socially optimal.

The costs of private enforcement also tend to exceed the costs of public enforcement, so that the latter will be preferable from an efficiency perspective. The relevant cost categories do not only include information costs and costs of procedures in court but also error costs. As indicated above, the costs to private parties of enforcing the prohibition of hardcore cartels are prohibitively high, because of the very serious information deficiencies about their existence and the difficulties of proving both the size of the damage and the causality between the infringement and the harm. Private parties will have better information on the existence and effects of vertical restraints and abuses of a dominant position, but in cases of economic dependency this advantage may be outweighed by fear of retaliation (so that no claims are brought before the courts) and the risk of error costs (type II errors/false negatives). It is likely that the majority of private actions will involve alleged exclusionary practices, which may have a pernicious effect on the development of competition law if judges are unable to draw the borderline between anti-competitive and

---

[77] W. Wils, "Should Private Antitrust Enforcement be Encouraged in Europe?" (2003) 26 *World Competition* 473.

pro-competitive behaviour. In this case, private actions will not only fall short of guaranteeing deterrence but may also be used in a counterproductive way. In the US experience, the problem of unmeritorious actions has been identified as the major counterproductive consequence of private antitrust enforcement.[78] Similar problems have arisen in European countries, where private plaintiffs have used competition rules to protect competitors from competition.

The analysis cannot stop here, since a number of counterarguments have been advanced to support the desirability of private enforcement. Wils takes the strong position that there is no need for supplementary private enforcement to provide additional sanctions or to bring additional cases. This has provoked the comment that the choice to be made is not between public enforcement only and private enforcement only. It has equally been argued that private enforcement is a cornerstone of the protection of individual rights in European competition law.[79] This debate invites two additional considerations on the role of private enforcement: its role in providing additional deterrence when public enforcement is not optimal and its function in guaranteeing that justice goals are equally achieved.

In a perfect public enforcement system, competition authorities initiate an optimal number of proceedings in all types of cases and impose optimal sanctions. In the real world, which is far from perfect, private enforcement may continue to play a role. First, private actions draw private resources into the enforcement process and thus complement public enforcement, which may be unable to deal with all attention-worthy cases. This is particularly important when private parties have better access to information than the public authority: for instance, with respect to the harmful effects of vertical restraints.[80] However, it must be repeated that private parties are not protected from retaliation (such as exclusion from a selective distribution system) and may, therefore, be reluctant to initiate proceedings. Apart from this *caveat*, enabling any civil court in the European Union to deal with a competition law case dramatically increases the number of law enforcers. Private enforcement may thus generate an important additional deterrent effect, particularly if companies are more likely to avoid infringements of the competition rules when they risk having to pay damages to their competitors.

Finally, the role of private enforcement in achieving justice goals must be considered. In this respect, it seems important to distinguish between goals of social justice and corrective justice in individual cases. Public enforcement mechanisms may target (a large part of) the total social costs of antitrust infringements, whereas enforcement by private parties will be concerned only with the much smaller costs in individual cases. Private enforcement is not able to guarantee that law offenders must pay back the excess profits achieved or must compensate the losses caused to society at large. Competition

---

[78] See, e.g. R. Posner, *Antitrust Law* (2nd ed., 2001), p.275; E.A. Snyder and T.E. Kauper, "Misuse of the Antitrust Laws: The Competitor Plaintiff" (1991) 90 Mich. L. Rev. 551.

[79] C.A. Jones, "Private Antitrust Enforcement in Europe: A Policy Analysis and Reality Check" (2004) 27 *World Competition* 13.

[80] G. Di Federico and P. Manzini, "A Law and Economics Approach to the New European Antitrust Enforcing Rules" (2004) 1 Erasmus Law Econ. Rev. 143 at p.158.

authorities may be better able to disgorge profits than private parties. The latter sanction implies that excess profits achieved by infringements of competition law must be transferred to the state budget. National competition laws, which allow for such a sanction, do not leave this task to private parties but provide for specific enforcement mechanisms.[81] Damages awarded to victims do not cover the entire harm caused by restrictive practices: at most, harm to individual consumers is compensated and the deadweight loss remains outside of the calculation of the damage award. The emphasis which the European Court of Justice has put on private enforcement as a significant contribution to maintaining effective competition in the European market can be better explained by the need to provide for corrective justice in individual cases than by the broader social justice goals discussed above. Even if private enforcement does not lead to compensation of the harm suffered by the society at large, it seems difficult to deny citizens the possibility of initiating actions in court if the rules of competition law are infringed. The competition rules of Articles 81–82 EC generate rights that national judges must protect (principle of direct effect). Private enforcement remains necessary to protect individual interests of parties harmed by infringements of the competition rules (*Individualschutzfunktion*).[82] This point of view should not detract from the criticisms of the private enforcement system, such as inadequate compensation and the risk of abuses. The solution to these problems is to improve the quality of judicial decision making with respect to both the establishment of infringements and the calculation of damages. Economic analysis will remain very helpful in finding the correct antitrust doctrines that mitigate these problems.

8.4 *Ex ante* or *ex post* control: authorisation regime or legal exception regime?

8.4.1 From *ex ante* control to *ex post* assessment—Regulation 1/2003

The Treaty itself does not set out how the competition rules are to be enforced. Appropriate regulations have to be laid down by the Council of the European Union on a proposal from the European Commission and after consulting the European Parliament (Article 83 EC). From 1962 until 2004 the relevant provisions concerning enforcement were contained in Regulation No.17.[83] This Regulation was replaced by Regulation No.1/2003, which entered into force on May 1, 2004. With respect to cartel agreements (Article 81 EC), the old notification and authorisation system has been replaced by a directly

---

[81] For example, the German law on unfair competition provides for a procedure of *Vorteilsabschöpfung* by consumer associations (Section 10 UWG). A proposal for a similar provision in the German competition law (Section 34 a GWB—Draft 7. Novelle) was deleted from the draft text.

[82] L. Linder, *Privatklage und Schadensersatz im Kartellrecht* (1980); R. Hempel, *Privater Rechtsschutz im Kartellrecht* (2002).

[83] Council Regulation No.17 [1962] O.J. 13/204.

applicable exception system. In the former regime, a decision on the lawfulness of an agreement, a decision by an association of undertakings or a concerted practice may be taken in advance (*ex ante* control). In the latter regime, no enforcement action is taken in advance; firms are free to decide whether they commit the contemplated action, but they will be sanctioned if a violation of the competition rules is established afterwards (*ex post* control).[84] In the old regime, authorities empowered to apply Article 81 EC of the Treaty were the European Commission, national judges and, to some extent, national competition authorities. However, the Commission had the sole power to grant exemptions (Article 81(3) of the Treaty). As from May 1, 2004, all national competition authorities (including those of the new Member States) and national judges are empowered to apply the Treaty's competition rules. Under the new regime, the Commission, all national competition authorities and national judges will apply Article 81 EC to its full extent, including the possibility of granting individual exemptions.

Enforcement of Article 82 EC has always been essentially *ex post*; exemptions from the ban on abuse of a dominant position are not possible. Undertakings enjoying a dominant position decide, after having sought private legal advice, whether they engage in a certain action or not. If the Commission is of the opinion that the action constitutes an abuse, it can order its termination and impose substantial fines. National competition authorities and judges can also enforce Article 82 EC.

The remainder of this section will explain the system change in somewhat greater detail and will then continue with an examination of the efficiency of the different rules concerning the timing of the intervention. The choice between *ex ante* monitoring and *ex post* control, in particular the desirability of a notification and authorisation system, is the central question of this analysis. The discussion of the desirability of decentralised enforcement (giving more powers to national competition authorities and judges) will follow in Chapter 10.

8.4.2 The "modernisation" of the enforcement regime

To allow for an evaluation of the system change, it is useful to recall the main characteristics of the old enforcement regime. In the past, undertakings could notify their agreements to the European Commission thereby seeking either a negative clearance and/or an individual exemption. Negative clearances were formal decisions (without conditions and obligations) certifying that, on the basis of the facts in its possession, the Commission saw no grounds under Article 81(1) EC for action on its part in respect of an agreement or practice. If a restriction of competition within the meaning of Article 81(1) EC was found, the only way to escape from the prohibition was by benefiting from an

---

[84] W. Wils, "Does the Effective Enforcement of Articles 81 and 82 EC Require not Only Fines on Undertakings but also Individual Penalties, in Particular Imprisonment?", in *European Competition Law Annual 2001: Effective Private Enforcement of EC Antitrust Law* (C.D. Ehlermann and I Atanasiu ed., 2002), p.110.

exemption, provided that the four cumulative conditions of Article 81(3) EC were satisfied. To obtain an individual exemption under Article 81(3) EC, notification was compulsory.[85] Exemption decisions could not take effect at a date earlier than that of notification. Only the Commission had the power to grant exemptions in individual cases. The Commission had full discretion to grant a decision and was—contrary to the strict time schedules that apply in merger cases—not bound by time limits.

According to general principles of European law, Articles 81 and 82 of the EC Treaty produce direct effects in relations between individuals and thus create direct rights in respect of the individuals concerned which the national courts must safeguard.[86] This implies that, together with the European Commission, national courts have jurisdiction to apply these Articles, with European law taking precedence over national law. Under the old regime, the Commission could take one of the following actions: a negative clearance decision if there was no infringement of Article 81(1) EC; an infringement decision by which the undertakings were found in breach of Article 81(1) EC and could be fined; and an individual exemption decision under Article 81(3) EC. Negative clearances did not protect the firms concerned from later contrary decisions by national competition authorities or courts, or even by the European Commission itself when new facts emerged. Exemptions were binding on national courts and national competition authorities. Judicial review of the Commission's decisions was possible before the European Courts (European Court of Justice and Court of First Instance).

When Regulation No.17/62 was adopted, a centralised notification and authorisation system was favoured because it would allow the European Commission to create a culture of competition and to ensure uniform application of the competition rules in order to further the integration of national markets. Even in the early days of European competition law it became clear that the Commission would not be able to deal with the bulk of notifications. The Commission became quickly overwhelmed with cases submitted by parties seeking legal certainty about the validity of their agreements. Only four years after Regulation 17 came into force, more than 37,450 cases were pending. As noted in the White Paper, the *ex ante* control mechanism:

"... resulted in undertakings systematically notifying their restrictive practices to the Commission which, with limited administrative resources, was very soon faced with the impossibility of dealing by formal decision with the thousands of cases submitted."[87]

Numerous steps have been taken to alleviate the burden of notification. First, the concept of "appreciable effect" on competition has been created in order to ignore minor cases. The *de minimis* Notice sets quantitative thresholds below

---

[85] The condition of prior notification did not apply to some relatively unimportant horizontal agreements (Art.4(2) Regulation 17) and all vertical agreements (Council Regulation No.1216/1999 [1999] O.J. L 148/5).
[86] Case 127/73 *BRT v SABAM* [1974] ECR 51, para.16.
[87] White Paper on Modernisation of the Rules Implementing Arts 85 and 86 of the EC Treaty [1999] O.J. C 132/1, para.24.

which horizontal restraints are also assumed to have a negligible effect on competition.[88] Second, an increasing number of interpretative Notices, clarifying the European Commission's view on the validity of agreements, have been published. Third, block exemptions have been enacted for different categories of agreements. To enact such block exemptions, governing entire categories of agreements, the Commission must be empowered by Council Regulations. The respective Regulations determine under which conditions agreements will not violate the cartel prohibition. Agreements that do not come within the scope of a block exemption must be exempted on an individual basis. To reduce the huge administrative workload of individual exemptions, the instrument of block exemptions has become increasingly popular for dealing with categories of agreements that are frequently concluded in business practice. Finally, an informal enforcement practice developed: instead of taking a formal decision, in the majority of cases[89] the Commission instead issued a so-called comfort letter. This was not a formal decision, but merely a letter stating that the Commission considered that the agreement did not restrict competition or was of a type that qualified for exemption. These informal decisions allowed the avoidance of the delays due to the publication of formal decisions in all official languages in the *Official Journal of the European Communities*. However, comfort letters were not binding on national courts,[90] so they could not give parties the legal certainty they were seeking when they decided to notify their agreements. At the end of the 20th century, after more than 35 years of existence, it was considered that Regulation No.17 needed modernisation. Even though the number of notification requests had become relatively stable and formal decisions were increasing, more than 90 per cent of cases were closed in an informal way. Moreover, between 1995 and 2000, only 0.5 per cent of the notifications led to a prohibition, suggesting that the European Commission could use its scarce resources in a better way. All these facts led to dramatic reform.

The new regime is different from its predecessor in many respects. First, the notification and authorisation system is replaced by a system of legal exception. Article 1(1) of Regulation No.1/2003 states:

"Agreements, decisions and concerted practices caught by Article 81(1) of the Treaty which do not satisfy the conditions of Article 81(3) EC shall be prohibited, no prior decision to that effect being required."

The last part of this sentence introduces the legal exception system. Consequently, from May 2004, the system of prior control under which agreements

---

[88] Commission Notice on agreements of minor importance which do not appreciably restrict competition under Art. 81(1) of the Treaty establishing the European Community [2001] O.J. C 368/13.

[89] From 1993 to the end of 1997 no more than 19 exemption decisions were adopted by the European Commission.

[90] The Court of Justice has held that Arts 81(1) and 82 tend by their very nature to produce direct effects in relations between individuals and that they thus create direct rights in respect of the individuals concerned which the national courts must safeguard (Case 127/73 *BRT v SABAM* [1974] ECR 51, para.16).

and restrictive practices are prohibited unless expressly permitted by the European Commission is replaced by a regime under which firms are freed from the necessity of notifying agreements to ensure their legality. In other words, a switch from an *ex ante* to *ex post* control has been implemented. Second, the Commission has lost its monopoly to grant exemptions. All national competition authorities (NCAs) and judges are now empowered to apply Article 81 EC in its entirety, including its third paragraph. Regulation 1/ 2003 is based on a system of parallel competences in which all competition authorities have the power to apply Articles 81–82 EC and are responsible for an efficient division of work. Together the NCAs and the Commission form a network called the European Competition Network (ECN). Under this system of parallel competences, cases can by dealt with by a single NCA, several NCAs acting in parallel or the European Commission. Also, national judges can apply the European competition rules in full. Third, the European Commission's and the national competition authorities' powers of investigation have been extended. Besides requests for information (Article 18), the Commission may take statements from employees during company visits (Article 19) and conduct all necessary inspections (Article 20), including premises different from those of the investigated company and inspections in private homes (Article 21). The competition authority of a Member State may in its own territory carry out investigations on behalf and for the account of the competition authority of another Member State in order to establish infringements of Articles 81–82 EC. In the next paragraphs, the new regime will be discussed in more detail as far as this is necessary for a proper economic assessment of the system change.

8.4.3 Economic analysis of the new enforcement system

An economic analysis of the switch from a centralised notification and authorisation system to a system of legal exception (with decentralised enforcement) requires an investigation of its effects on two types of costs: information costs and incentive costs. A first set of questions relates to the impact on information costs: how will the change affect the information about the existence of harmful cartels? What will be the effect on the level of legal certainty available to the affected parties? A second set of questions relates to the impact on incentive costs. How will the switch affect the incentives of companies to enter into agreements? Will an *ex post* control sufficiently deter welfare-reducing agreements? Will the system change encourage welfare-improving agreements to be signed? Clearly, the effects on information costs and incentive costs are interrelated and the introduction of a more decentralised enforcement system has an effect on the overall costs of the system reform as well. However, for reasons of expositional clarity, in this book the different cost categories will be discussed separately. The discussion of the welfare effects of decentralisation is postponed to Chapter 10.

8.4.3.1 Information costs

Information on contents and effects of restrictive practices In a perfect world, all actors (companies, law enforcers and third parties, including competitors and consumers) have perfect information with respect to both the contents and effects of restrictive practices. Furthermore, if effective sanctions can be imposed on lawbreakers at zero cost, no rational undertaking would commit an infringement of the competition rules since the latter is perfectly observable by the law enforcer. Reality, however, is far from perfect, for the following reasons.[91] First, an information asymmetry exists between companies that enter into restrictive agreements and law enforcement agencies. Only the former have perfect information about the details of their agreements, whereas the latter have to gather this information through a costly procedure. By abolishing the system of notification the European Commission has lost an important source of information on competition in particular markets. Second, a similar information asymmetry exists between the cartel participants and third parties, such as competitors and consumers. In both cases, the information asymmetry does not concern just the precise contents of the agreements but also other issues, such as market characteristics and the availability of substitutes, which may have an impact on the assessment of the legal validity of the concluded agreements. Third, since most substantive legal rules are not clear-cut, a costly information gathering and information processing procedure must be conducted in order to assess whether a certain practice constitutes an infringement or not and whether it may profit from an exemption. These costs fall on both the companies and the law enforcers. The latter may commit two types of error: either they erroneously grant an exemption (type I error) or they prohibit a practice that satisfies the conditions for an exemption (type II error).[92] Since these errors have a negative impact on the incentives to engage in welfare-improving behaviour or abstain from welfare-reducing conduct (incentive costs), optimal law enforcement should reduce the different types of information costs.

What are the effects of the modernisation of the enforcement system on the information costs indicated above?[93] A distinction must be made between hardcore cartels and other anti-competitive practices. Public authorities face information deficiencies with respect to both the existence and effects of restrictive practices. A notification system will lead to lower costs of information gathering for the law enforcers if the undertakings voluntarily reveal the existence and contents of restrictive practices. This will not occur in cases

---

[91] See M. Pirrung, "EU Enlargement Towards Cartel Paradise? An Economic Analysis of the Reform of European Competition Law" (2004) 1 Erasmus Law Econ. Rev. 77 at pp.88–89.

[92] It should be noted that allocative efficiency can be achieved only if all welfare-decreasing agreements and practices are prohibited and companies are not hindered from engaging in welfare-increasing agreements or practices. The way in which the conditions of Art. 81(3) EC are interpreted does not necessarily guarantee such outcomes (see Ch.5, s.5.3.4.3). Hence, if allocative efficiency is accepted as the sole goal of the competition rules, error costs may also occur if Art. 81(3) EC is applied in conformity with leading case law.

[93] See M. Pirrung, "EU Enlargement Towards Cartel Paradise? An Economic analysis of the Reform of European Competition Law" (2004) 1 Erasmus Law Econ. Rev. 77 at pp.90–91, 93.

of hardcore cartels. Therefore, a switch from *ex ante* monitoring to *ex post* control has no detrimental effect on information about the existence of those cartels. In addition, in the case of hardcore restraints *ex post* intervention may be defended since the public authority already has information about their actual effects: horizontal restraints normally produce anti-competitive consequences without redeeming virtues (and may be admitted only when they are ancillary to legitimate goals). Hence, a legal exception regime does not increase the information costs, neither with respect to the existence of hardcore cartels, nor with respect to the analysis of the effects of such restrictive practices.

The picture is different in the grey area, where a great deal of uncertainty exists about whether or not a practice infringes the law. Whereas hardcore cartels will be kept secret, companies may wish to reveal the existence of agreements, the legality of which is difficult to assess in order to obtain legal certainty. Vertical restraints are a good example. Also, the legality of vertical restraints is difficult to assess without having access to information about their likely effects. Again, this information may become more readily available under a notification system. If the antitrust authority has limited information about the actual effects of a certain type of conduct, *ex ante* intervention seems more appropriate since it permits the authority to acquire the relevant data for such an appraisal. A notification system may reveal important information to the competition authorities that is very costly (or impossible) to acquire under a legal exception regime. This loss of information also affects competitors and consumers. If they are informed about the existence of welfare-reducing agreements, they can take more timely and effective action against such harmful practices. For the latter reason, it is to be deplored that the idea of setting up a registration system for restrictive practices, which was contained in the draft of the new Regulation, has been abandoned in the final text.[94]

In sum, the switch from an authorisation system to a legal exception system (modernisation) seems to be efficient for hardcore restraints since an *ex ante* control is not able to provide the competent authority with more information than it already possesses. Conversely, for other restraints of competition having no clear-cut consequences for economic welfare, i.e. mostly the ones which were originally clogging up the authorisation system of Regulation No.17, the system change may increase information costs.

Impact of the system change on legal certainty   In the legal literature, the system change has been criticised because of the loss of legal certainty for undertakings.[95] In economic terms, this argument may be rephrased as an increase in information costs. Under a notification and authorisation regime, undertakings do not have to assess whether anti-competitive agreements satisfy the requirements for exemption. If the antitrust authority grants a formal exemption, companies are entirely freed from the risk that the

---

[94] Compare Art.4, para.2 of the proposal and the final text of Art.4 of Regulation 1/2003.
[95] See for example W. Möschel, "Change of Policy in European Competition Law" (2000) 27 C.M.L. Rev. 495 at p.497; A. Bartosch, "Von der Freistellung zur Legalausnahme—Der Vorschlag der EG-Kommission fur eine neue Verordnung" (2001) 17 EuZW 101 at p.105.

agreement may be considered illegal. Obviously, experience has shown that an authorisation system creates a workload that a competition authority cannot manage. Formal decisions were taken only in a very limited number of cases. However, under the previous regime, companies could at least acquire a relative certainty by obtaining a comfort letter from the European Commission. An additional loss in terms of legal certainty follows from the risk that within the Network of Competition Authorities opinions on the legality of agreements and restrictive practices may differ. Since national competition authorities may act in parallel, there is a risk of conflicting decisions in the same case. Under the new system, national judges may also apply Article 81 EC in its entirety, and this further increases the risk of divergent decisions.

The European Commission has not been insensitive to the concerns about increased legal uncertainty. First, conflicting decisions must be avoided in cases of parallel or consecutive application of the EC competition rules by the Commission and national courts. If a national court comes to a decision before the Commission does, it must avoid adopting a decision that would conflict with a decision contemplated by the Commission. The national court may consider staying its proceedings until the Commission has reached a decision. If the Commission comes to a decision before the national court does, the latter cannot take a decision running counter to that of the Commission.[96] If a national court intends to take an opposite view, it must refer a question to the European Court of Justice for a preliminary ruling. Second, a further relief for such companies that are active in several Member States is the possibility that, if national competition authorities envisage conflicting decisions in the same case, the European Commission may initiate proceedings (after consulting with the NCAs), which relieves the competition authorities of their competence to apply Articles 81 EC and 82 EC.[97] Third, the Commission may issue guidance letters in individual cases, which give rise to genuine uncertainty because they present novel or unresolved questions. However, there is no guarantee that such letters will be provided upon request. The usefulness of a guidance letter will be assessed taking account, *inter alia*, of the economic importance of the agreement and the extent of the investments linked to the transaction in relation to the size of the companies concerned.[98]

For assessing the impact of the system change on legal certainty, again the distinction between hardcore cartels and other anti-competitive practices (which may have redeeming virtues) is useful. In the former case, companies know that they commit a clear violation of the competition rules and risk heavy fines. In the latter case, however, clear answers as to the legality of the agreements are not easily available. The publication of Notices by the European Commission may also have left many questions unanswered.[99] Under the

---

[96] Notice on the cooperation between the Commission and the courts of the EU Member States in the application of Arts 81 and 82 EC [2004] O.J. C 101/56.
[97] Art. 11(6) of Regulation 1/2003; Commission Notice on cooperation within the Network of Competition Authorities [2004] O.J. C 101/3, para.54.
[98] Notice on informal guidance relating to novel questions concerning Arts 81 and 82 of the EC Treaty that arise in individual cases [2004] O.J. C 101/78.
[99] It must be added that national judges are not bound by these Notices.

new regime, companies no longer have the right to obtain an official evaluation and they have to rely purely on their own assessment of their practices.
Given the parallel competences of the Commission and national competition
authorities, this is a serious problem for conducting business, especially in
dynamic industries with high rates of innovation. The external information
concerning market characteristics affecting the effects of their practices on each
of the conditions for exemption required by Article 81(3) EC may be difficult to
acquire for private parties who have no investigative powers of an antitrust
authority and may require costly external advice by economic experts. The
validity of a restrictive practice will only be checked when it is challenged by a
competition authority or by third parties before a court. Even the best legal
and economic experts will have difficulties predicting how law enforcers will
evaluate whether the restrictive practice infringes Article 81 EC. The legal
certainty provided by an individual exemption cannot be perfectly substituted
by expert advice. As a consequence, information costs will be higher under a
legal exception regime than under a notification and authorisation system.

8.4.3.2 Incentive costs

As was explained above, the shift from an authorisation system to a legal
exception system tends to increase information costs. In turn, this change may
be expected to affect firms' incentives to perform certain actions. From an
economic welfare point of view, the system change can only be welcomed if it
neither leads to an increase in the number of harmful agreements nor prevents
firms from implementing beneficial agreements (minimisation of type I and
type II errors).

To assess the efficiency of the alternative regimes the decisive question is
under which system an optimal number of agreements will be signed. A
preventive policy (notification) makes it possible to stop harmful agreements
at an early stage. By contrast, in a repression regime with fines (legal exception) the competition authority analyses the agreements after they have been
signed and partially implemented. Di Federico and Manzini argue that an *ex
post* enforcement system reduces the number of controls by antitrust authorities and therefore requires the possibility to apply higher sanctions.[1]
Unfortunately, as discussed above, Regulation 1/2003 has left the maximum
amount of the fine unchanged. In a theoretical paper, assuming that cartel
authorities do not commit errors, Hahn shows that the system of *ex ante*
control is superior to *ex post* control because law enforcement has a greater
deterrent effect when notification is required.[2] This literature warns that the
system change will decrease welfare if it leads to a higher number of harmful
agreements that are not scrutinised by the competition authorities. Moreover,
the switch to a legal exception regime will decrease welfare if beneficial
agreements are no longer entered into because of the high information costs.

---

[1] G. Di Federico and P. Manzini, "A Law and Economics Approach to the New European Antitrust Enforcing Rules" (2004) 1 Erasmus Law Econ. Rev. 143 at pp.149–151.
[2] V. Hahn, "Antitrust Enforcement: Abuse Control or Notification?" (2000) 10 Eur. J. Law Econ. 69.

Theoretical economic literature, which models the behaviour of firms, allows for a better understanding of the possible outcomes of the system reform. This literature focuses on the impact of the modernisation on the type of agreements that firms might implement. Does the new regime cause firms to enter into more harmful agreements or will only beneficial agreements be signed? A crucial factor having an important effect on the outcome of the analysis is the distribution of information discussed above. If firms are uncertain whether the agreement is harmful or not, the new regime may be welfare reducing. By contrast, if firms are aware of the status of the agreement and the quality of the evaluation by the competition authority is high enough, an optimal outcome can be reached. The systems also differ with respect to the degree of legal certainty, leading to divergent outcomes on welfare due to differences in information costs. Whereas under a notification regime firms may seek an opinion from the competition authority on the validity of their agreements, under a legal exception regime firms have to consider themselves whether their agreements infringe the competition rules but may benefit from an exemption. The consequence may be that firms will take less risk, which may result in a lower number of beneficial agreements. Whether these theoretical outcomes will materialise is ultimately an empirical question: it all depends on the relative importance of the effects predicted by the theoretical literature in real-life markets.

Barros[3] considers identical firms and focuses on the impact of the reduced legal certainty created by the removal of the notification and authorisation regime. He shows that, on the one hand, firms might be tempted to sign more restrictive agreements, since the probability of audit is reduced in the *ex post* regime. On the other hand, as legal uncertainty increases, firms may take fewer risks. Barros shows that the latter effect is more likely to prevail, implying that the reform should result in a lower number of restrictive agreements. Neven[4] considers heterogeneous firms and focuses on the incentives created by the elimination of the notification regime. *Ex post* monitoring leads to higher information costs, thus inducing firms to sign agreements that are more likely to be cleared by the competition authority. The consequence is that some beneficial agreements are no longer implemented. From this perspective, the argument that the notification system was counterproductive because it forces the Commission to spend scarce resources on cases raising only minor if any competition concerns,[5] must be reassessed. The consequence of the reform may be that beneficial agreements are no longer signed, for lack of legal certainty. Moreover, Neven argues that the removal of the notification regime induces some anti-competitive agreements,

---

[3] P. Barros, "Looking Behind the Curtain: Effects from Modernisation of European Competition Policy" (2003) 47 Eur. Econ. Rev. 613.

[4] D.J. Neven, "Removing the Notification of Agreements: Some Consequences for Ex Post Monitoring", in *European Integration and International Co-operation: Studies in International Economic Law in Honour of Claus-Dieter Ehlermann* (A. von Bogdandy ed. 2002).

[5] W. Wils, "Does the Effective Enforcement of Articles 81 and 82 EC Require not Only Fines on Undertakings but also Individual Penalties, in Particular Imprisonment?", in *European Competition Law Annual 2001: Effective Private Enforcement of EC Antitrust Law* (C.D. Ehlermann and I Atanasiu ed., 2002), p.212.

which would otherwise have been notified, to be implemented and not monitored. The level of *ex post* enforcement should be high to limit these errors.

The paper by Bergès-Sennou *et al.*[6] starts from different assumptions: firms are aware of the status of the agreement and the audit gives the competition authority an imperfect signal on this status. They show that the notification regime only dominates when the quality of the assessment by the competition authority is fairly poor. The competition authority has prior beliefs concerning the impact of agreements on welfare, which it may revise when it analyses a case after having received information (signal). Priors may be good (e.g. joint research and development agreements) or bad (e.g. horizontal market sharing or resale price maintenance). The signal may be more or less accurate: when the signal is weakly accurate, the decision of the competition authority will be based on its prior beliefs. The authors show that the notification regime is preferred for intermediate values of the priors when the signal is not accurate, whereas the exception regime dominates when the priors are not too high and the signal is sufficiently accurate. When the priors reach extreme values, either a block exemption regime is preferred when the priors are extremely good or a black list regime dominates when the priors are extremely bad and the signal is not accurate. On the basis of these findings, the authors explain a possible motivation for the change from *ex ante* to *ex post* control. When prior beliefs are not extreme and the signal's accuracy increases, a move away from an authorisation regime to an exception regime is justified. It is reasonable to assume that the European Commission has improved its knowledge and that the quality of the decisions is much higher than in 1962. After this learning period, an *ex post* control is optimal. This is due to the fact that if the signal is sufficiently accurate, the legal exception regime reaches an equilibrium, in which only beneficial agreements are signed.

8.4.3.3 Overall assessment

What are the main results of the economic analysis of the switch from an authorisation system to a legal exception system? Generally a notification and authorisation system (*ex ante* enforcement) will be preferable if firms have limited knowledge about whether or not the action they are contemplating will violate the competition rules. Under such circumstances, a legal exception regime (*ex post* enforcement) will impose information costs on firms, which may prevent beneficial agreements from being signed. The fact that information costs also increase for competition authorities and third parties due to the absence of notifications is a further argument against a legal exception regime. On the contrary, if firms are well informed, *ex post* enforcement may be superior provided that the quality of the assessment by the antitrust authority is high enough. If the second scenario is closer to reality than the first, the

---

[6] F. Bergès-Sennou, F. Loss, E. Malavolti-Grimal and T. Vergé, "The Modernisation of European Competition Policy: From Ex Ante to Ex Post Audit", Paper presented at the 20th EALE Conference, available from *www.eale.org* (2003).

change of enforcement regime may be welcomed. In the opposite case, welfare losses may occur.

To improve upon efficiency, two requirements must thus be satisfied. First, there should be sufficient information on the side of companies that envisage signing agreements. Second, the quality of the assessment of the competition authority must be sufficiently high so that type I and type II errors will be minimised. Are these requirements satisfied in the enlarged European Union?

With respect to the first requirement, it seems clear that firms will only have perfect knowledge about prohibited practices if they are put on a black list (*per se* illegality), which makes further analysis superfluous (and notification redundant). In all other cases, some uncertainty on substantive issues will always remain. Here the system change increases information costs by eliminating the possibility of a "safe harbour notification" for agreements in the grey area (no hardcore restraints). This negative effect will, however, be mitigated when firms can rely on the interpretations given in (an ever increasing number of) Notices. However, these Notices cannot possibly provide an answer to all real-life problems, as the Notice on Vertical Agreements—in spite of its considerable length—illustrates. At this point, the question arises whether it would not have been advisable to keep the notification system for contracts that may generate important benefits and risk not being concluded under a legal exception regime. Examples include vertical restraints above the 30 per cent market share threshold, and agreements on research and development above the thresholds in the respective block exemption Regulation. To minimise the risk that beneficial agreements will not be concluded, reducing the scope of the notification system rather than abolishing it entirely seems to be the preferable option.

A similar reasoning applies with respect to the second condition. It seems reasonable to assume that after more than 40 years of experience, the European Commission has gathered sufficient knowledge to adequately analyse the cases. The new Regulation has also expanded the Commission's fact gathering and inspection powers, even though they still fall far short of those of the US antitrust authorities. For an optimal *ex post* enforcement there must be certainty of detection, prosecution and imposition of a sanction in case of violation, and certainty that no sanction will be imposed in case of non-violation. An *ex ante* intervention coupled with relatively mild sanctions was a reasonable solution at the time Regulation 17 was drafted. However, an *ex post* enforcement regime reduces the overall number of controls by competition authorities and therefore requires higher sanctions to compensate for the lower probability of detection of antitrust infringements. If the level of sanctions is not increased (as is the case with Regulation 1/2003) efficient outcomes can be reached only when detection expenditures are increased in a way that is proportional to the reduction of the expected fines perceived by potential infringers.

A final remark is appropriate. The new Regulation enters into force at the same time as the European Union adds a significant number of new Member States. The conditions for an efficient system change indicated will be satisfied to a (much) lesser extent in the latter States: companies will face greater information problems than their counterparts in the old Member States. Hence, it can also be argued that it would have been better to keep the *ex ante* control in the new Member States, at least during a period of transition until information on the contents and application of the competition rules has become sufficiently widespread. Moreover, it may be doubted whether the quality of assessment by the competition authorities of the new Member States is sufficiently high. Without sufficient experience, competition authorities may not have acquired the relevant knowledge and the quality of control may be jeopardised. In sum, in the new Member States the combination of lack of information on the side of market parties and the relative inexperience of the competition authorities do not seem to support the introduction of a legal exception regime.

8.5 Conclusions

In this chapter an economic framework was used to compare US and European rules on enforcement of competition law. Regulation 1/2003, which is without doubt one of the most important reforms in the history of European competition policy, has aligned the European rules on enforcement with their US counterparts as far as the timing of the antitrust intervention is concerned. In addition, the increased role of national judges brought about by the decentralisation of the enforcement system is another feature that has reduced the differences between the enforcement of European competition law and US antitrust law. Since May 2004, the important role of private enforcement and the imposition of criminal sanctions, including imprisonment of individuals, remain the principal differences between both systems of enforcement. In general it may be doubted whether single system components of one regime can simply be exchanged with the other regime's counterparts without adjusting the other components as well. *Ex post* enforcement reduces the number of controls by antitrust authorities and may lead to underdeterrence if the level of sanctions is not simultaneously increased.

Optimal enforcement of the competition rules requires that companies are deterred from engaging in welfare-reducing restrictive practices and that they keep incentives to sign agreements that are socially desirable. In other words, enforcement can only be optimal if no type I or type II errors are made. Moreover, enforcement costs must be minimised. These costs include information costs of all relevant actors (companies that agree on restrictive practices, antitrust enforcers and third parties, in particular competitors and consumers) and the costs of the legal proceedings (administrative expenses of antitrust authorities and judges).

From a viewpoint of deterrence, the expected fine should exceed the expected benefit resulting from infringements of the competition rules. The expected fine is the probability of a conviction multiplied by the imposed sanction. Several reasons can be indicated as to why the goal of deterrence may not be achieved in the current European enforcement regime: the use of qualitative criteria for fixing fines, which impedes an easy calculation of the expected fine; the too low level of the fines; and the absence of a cure for "judgment proof" problems of companies. Regulation 1/2003 has neither changed the exclusive reliance on corporate sanctions, nor increased the ceiling of the fine and introduced individual sanctions (in particular, imprisonment) to cope with the judgment proof problem. Consequently, the expected fine can be raised only by increasing the rate of detection. It remains to be seen whether the latter goal can be achieved by a more efficient use of the European Commission's resources and cooperation between the Commission and national competition authorities in the framework of the European Competition Network. To achieve an efficient level of deterrence at the lowest possible cost, policy makers should also realise that the different elements of the enforcement system interact with each other in a complex way. For example, the amount of fines and damages must be coordinated with the amnesty grants under leniency programmes. In the absence of such coordination, it will not be possible to strike an optimal balance between the deterrence objective and the detection of hardcore cartels.

A comparison of the European and US systems of enforcement reveals that the dominant role of private enforcement in the latter system is due to a number of institutional differences. Since European law does not encourage private claims by allowing treble damages, contingency fees, class actions and pre-trial discovery procedures, enforcement of competition law in Europe has largely remained a public task. From a viewpoint of deterrence, public enforcement is also clearly preferable. The expected benefits of the law offenders are normally higher than the expected costs of the imposed sanctions (nullity plus damages awards to harmed private parties discounted by the probability of detection and punishment). The costs to private parties of enforcing the prohibition of hardcore cartels are prohibitively high: they face significant information deficiencies about their existence and serious difficulties in proving the size of the harm as well as the causal link with the damage incurred. Even though private parties may have better information about the existence of vertical restraints and their possible anti-competitive effects, they may fear retaliation by the accused firms and decide not to initiate legal proceedings. Also error costs (type II) may be high if enforcement is driven by private parties. From a perspective of corrective justice, private enforcement can be better sustained. The dominant legal argument is that Articles 81 and 82 EC are directly applicable and create rights for individuals, which judges must safeguard. Private claims will not generate payments that adequately compensate the harm to society, however. The deadweight loss caused by cartels, the losses in terms of dynamic efficiencies and the costs of rent seeking will not be covered by awards of damages to private parties. Also the enforcement level will remain too low since the private cost–benefit calculus, which is decisive to the decision to sue, differs from the social costs and benefits of enforcing the cartel prohibition.

The economic evaluation of the switch from an authorisation system to a legal exception system crucially depends on the availability and quality of information possessed by both companies and competition authorities. The general lesson from economics is that decentralisation is the more efficient the less important local law is for the central authority with respect to federal welfare and the more valuable local information is for appropriate rule making. National competition authorities are generally better placed to assess matters that are concentrated on their particular state. On the other hand, the risk of regulatory capture at lower levels of government may be higher. Therefore, efficiency can be achieved only by an optimal mix of centralised and decentralised enforcement.

Regulation 1/2003 has increased the information costs for antitrust authorities, companies and third parties in the grey area of agreements, which have both anti-competitive and beneficial effects. The previous notification system signalled the existence of such agreements and could prevent restrictive practices whose ultimate benefits did not outweigh their costs from being implemented. The information costs and the associated risk costs imposed on private companies may also negatively affect their willingness to engage in welfare-enhancing practices. It is to be deplored that the danger of counter-productive effects has not been contained by reducing, rather than completely abolishing, the notification system and/or the establishment of a Register of agreements, which may reduce competition.

The system change from *ex ante* control to *ex post* assessment can be better supported in the old than in the new Member States. In the latter states, companies will face greater uncertainty with respect to the legality of agreements and the quality of analysis by competition authorities may not yet have reached the same standards of quality as in the old Member States. Decentralisation, which goes hand in hand with a move from *ex ante* to *ex post* control, may be poorly suited for the new Member States.

Chapter 9

···

CONCENTRATIONS AND MERGER CONTROL

Co-authored by Eileen Reed[1]

---

[1] Senior Vice-President, CapAnalysis. Eileen has helpfully assisted in providing the case analysis in s.9.3.

9.1 Introduction

Previous chapters of this book dealt with contractual agreements and other types of concerted behaviour coordinating the interaction between independent firms (Article 81 EC, see Chapters 5 and 6), and unilateral behaviour of dominant firms (Article 82 EC, see Chapter 7). In this chapter, concentrations will be examined, that is, structural changes to a market including mergers and acquisitions, as well as those joint ventures which are captured by Regulation 139/2004 (the Merger Regulation).[2] Mergers describe any consolidation where two original companies cease to exist and a new company is formed, which owns the assets of the two former entities. Acquisitions occur when one company purchases all or part of the stock or assets of another company. In European competition law, mergers and acquisitions are subsumed under the common heading of concentrations, including also so-called full-function joint ventures, where two (parent) companies pool (some of) their assets into a new entity which operates on the market.

A concentration implies that firms integrate their operations more completely and permanently than was the case under the contractual settings discussed in Chapters 5 and 6. Due to internal pressures, cartels tend to disintegrate after a while. By their very nature, however, concentrations inevitably eliminate competition permanently between the participating firms. Since concentrations are more farreaching than cartels, one might expect the former to be condemned by a simple *per se* rule. However, closer study of the motives that lead firms to concentrate suggests a more cautious approach. This chapter will show that concentrations—whether mergers, acquisitions or full-function joint ventures—may have detrimental as well as advantageous results for social welfare, and competition law attempts to distinguish between concentrations accordingly. The word "attempt" has been carefully chosen, as it is important to note upfront that the assessment of concentrations is a forward-looking exercise. Based on information and data available prior to a concentration, competition authorities need to project its impact on a given market structure, which will only become fully established after a transaction has been implemented. This makes the assessment of mergers an inherently more uncertain assignment than the review of Article 81 EC and Article 82

---

[2] Current version is Regulation 139/2004 [2004] O.J. L 24/1. The EC Horizontal Merger Guidelines are contained in [2004] O.J. C 31/5; the Implementing Regulation 802/2004 is published in [2004] O.J. L 133/1.

EC-type issues (as there, through past and present behaviour, the facts are generally well established).

A classification of concentrations in three categories according to the competitive relationships between the parties involved is useful in order to assess the anti-competitive effects and efficiency savings caused by concentrations, although the test applied in European competition law does not make such a distinction.[3] In a horizontal transaction, one firm merges with or acquires another firm that produces or distributes identical or similar products at the same level of production or the distribution chain in the same geographic area (in antitrust terms, the firms would be in the same relevant market), thereby eliminating competition between the two firms. Typically, horizontal concentrations entail the most competitive issues, and will be subject to the closest scrutiny by the antitrust authorities. In a vertical merger, one firm acquires either a customer (so-called forward integration) or a supplier (so-called backward integration), one firm producing the input for the other. This implies that vertical mergers are largely motivated by a desire to minimise transaction costs and cure principal–agent problems. They may also cause competitive concerns, though, which justify antitrust scrutiny.[4] For a discussion of the economic effects of such vertical mergers, the reader is referred to Chapter 6 of this book, as the issues are similar to those encountered with vertical agreements. Conglomerate mergers encompass all other acquisitions, including (a) pure conglomerate transactions where the merging parties have no evident economic relationship (unrelated products); (b) geographic extension mergers where the buyer makes the same product as the target firm, but does so in a different geographic market; and (c) product extension mergers where a firm producing one product buys a firm which makes a different product that requires the application of similar manufacturing or marketing techniques (complementary or neighbouring products). Whatever form it takes, a conglomerate merger involves firms which operated in separate markets, and thus would have—*prima facie*—little direct effect on competition.[5]

---

[3] Confirmed in Case T–5/02 *Tetra Laval v Commission* [2002] ECR II–4381, paras 120 and 146.

[4] J. Church, *The Impact of Vertical and Conglomerate Mergers* (Final Report Prepared for DG Comp, 2004). A substantial review of the vertical issues under US and European merger law may be found in the *24th Fordham Corporate Law Institute Compendium* (B. Hawk ed., 1998) chs 7–11, pp.111–223; as well as in the (1995) 25 *Journal of Reprints for Antitrust Law and Economics* 5–481. Major research from a Law and Economics perspective has been conducted by M.H. Riordan and S.C. Salop, "Evaluating Vertical Mergers: A Post–Chicago Approach" (1995) 63 Antitrust L.J. 513; S.J. Grossman and O.D. Hart, "The Costs and Benefits of Ownership: A Theory of Vertical Integration" (1986) 94 J. Polit. Econonomy 691; P.T. Spiller, "On Vertical Mergers" (1985) 1 J. Law, Econ., Organ. 285; B. Klein, R.G. Crawford and A.A. Alchian, "Vertical Integration, Appropriable Rents, and the Competitive Contracting Process" (1978) 21 J. Law Econ. 297.

[5] At the time of writing, vertical and conglomerate transactions have led to a number of high profile decisions by the European Commission. Post *GE/Honeywell* (Case COMP/M.2220 *GE/Honeywell* [2004] O.J. L 48/1; Case T–209/01 *Honeywell v Commission*; and Case T–210/01 *GE v Commission*, not yet reported) and *Tetra Laval/Sidel* (Case COMP/M. 2416 *Tetra Laval/Sidel* [2004] O.J. L 43/13; decision annulled under appeal in Case T–5/02 *Tetra Laval v Commission* [2002] ECR II–4381; as confirmed in Case C–12/03P *Commission v Tetra Laval*, not yet reported). The European Commission is contemplating issuing guidelines on how to deal with such transactions. By way of example, these issues are discussed in the case analyses of Case COMP/M.3083 *GE/Instrumentarium* [2004] O.J. L 109/1; and Case COMP/M.3333 *Sony/BMG* [2005] L 62/30 (see ss.9.3.3 and 9.3.4).

The test applied in European competition law to assess whether or not a concentration warrants regulatory intervention is contained in Article 2(3) of the Merger Regulation. This Article reads as follows:

"A concentration which would significantly impede effective competition in the common market or in a substantial part of it, in particular as a result of the creation or strengthening of a dominant position, shall be declared incompatible with the common market".

Clearly, the formulation is such that it requires detailed analysis as to how the anti-competitive effects and the pro-competitive effects of a concentration are assessed and balanced. This chapter will elaborate on both (a) the possible anti-competitive effects of concentrations (which result in an augmentation of market power and the related deadweight loss to society, i.e. allocative inefficiency), and (b) the potential benefits to society through a net welfare gain (which can materialise through the efficiencies a merger may generate, i.e. productive and dynamic efficiency).[6] More often than not, a particular concentration may combine anti-competitive and pro-competitive effects. This basic economic dilemma poses difficult problems for competition authorities.

This chapter is split into four sections. After this introduction, in the second section, the current legal framework for assessing horizontal concentrations is presented. The focus will be successively on market shares and concentration indices, the analysis of the anti-competitive effects and efficiency considerations. In addition, the second section will summarise the main insights from economic theory on horizontal concentrations. For an appropriate understanding of the anti-competitive effects of horizontal concentrations, a distinction must be made between single firm dominance and two types of oligopolistic behaviour: non-coordinated effects and coordinated effects. After a discussion of both types, this section will conclude with an analysis of efficiency gains that may be generated by concentrations. The third section of this chapter will then turn to the question of whether current European competition law in the field of merger control is consistent with economic principles. This will be done by discussing a number of recent cases.[7] Due to its forward-looking nature, merger control is characterised by a high level of complexity, as well as discretion. It will be shown that economic analysis and empirics may be instrumental in improving the quality of merger control. Contrary to the relatively short case discussions in previous chapters, which were contained in several boxes, the complexity of the merger cases warrants a more elaborate discussion in the main text of the book. In this way, topics such as the economic evaluation of the main rules of the substantive law on

---

[6] We do not deal with the procedural aspects of merger control here. For the general aspects, we refer to Ch.10 on enforcement. For a detailed legal analysis, we refer to N. Levy, *European Merger Control Law: A Guide to the Merger Regulation* (2005).

[7] To illustrate the type of antitrust issues that may be encountered when assessing horizontal concentrations, cases discussed in this chapter include: Case COMP/M.1672 *Volvo/Scania* [2001 O.J. L 143/74 (focus on non-coordinated effects); Case COMP/M.3083 *GE/Instrumentarium* [2004] O.J. L 109/1 (focus on unilateral/non-coordinated effects in oligopolistic markets); Case COMP/M.3216 *Oracle/PeopleSoft* [2005] O.J. L 218/6; and Case COMP/M.3333 *Sony/BMG* [2005] L 62/30 (focus on coordinated effects in oligopolistic markets).

mergers, various measurement techniques and a review of the more controversial aspects of competition law and economics already discussed in previous chapters (in particular, market definition) can be better covered. The fourth section contains the conclusions and an outlook.

9.2 General framework for assessing horizontal concentrations

The European Commission assesses the anti-competitive consequences of a concentration through a two-step process. As a first step in such assessment, market structure is analysed. However, as will be documented, market shares and concentration levels are seen only as useful first indicators for reviewing horizontal concentrations. If market structure is such that it seems to require an in-depth analysis, the Commission will move to the second step of the assessment and analyse the anti-competitive effects of the concentration. The structural changes caused by horizontal concentrations raise two potential competitive concerns. First, by eliminating the competition which exists between the parties prior to the concentration, the amalgamation may weaken to a significant degree the strength of the overall competitive constraint acting on one or more of the parties. Second, post-concentration the nature of competition may have changed in such a way that firms that were previously not coordinating their behaviour are—post-concentration—more likely to coordinate, or that firms which were already coordinating prior to a concentration find this easier and more stable. The first part of this section will present the relevant theoretical economic insights, which may help in assessing the (controversial) anti-competitive effects of horizontal concentrations. In the last part of this section, the relevance of efficiency considerations will be discussed. Efficiencies flowing from concentrations may counter or even outweigh potential anti-competitive effects. However, the standards for assessing efficiencies are probably even less settled than the standards for assessing the potential anti-competitive effects of a transaction. Where appropriate, a brief comparison with US antitrust law will be included to provide a broader framework of analysis and enable a balanced judgment of the strengths and weaknesses of European merger control.

9.2.1 Market shares and concentration levels: useful first indicators for reviewing horizontal concentrations

Horizontal concentrations have two effects on market structure. First, they reduce the number of competing firms. Second, they increase market concentration, as the post-concentration market share is larger than either of the parties' share prior to the concentration. It follows from the structure–

conduct–performance paradigm[8] that concentrated markets perform poorly and, hence, that structural remedies (prohibition of a concentration, divestitures) may improve market performance. In practice, the implementation of this basic (though controversial) insight is far from easy. Even if economists agree that there is a relationship between concentration and size of firms on the one hand, and the costs–price margins in a particular market on the other hand, they disagree about the relevant numbers. The first part of this section will elaborate on the use of market shares and concentration indices by both the European Commission and the US antitrust authorities in their assessment of horizontal concentrations.

Market shares and concentration levels are generally found to "provide useful first indications"[9]—no more, no less—of the market structure and of the competitive importance of both the parties to a concentration and their competitors. Market shares and concentration levels are derived from previously defined relevant markets. Market concentration is a function of the number of firms in a market and their respective market share. In order to measure concentration levels, antitrust authorities[10] often apply the so-called Herfindahl–Hirschman Index (or HHI)[11]:

- The HHI is calculated by summing the squares of the individual market shares of all the market participants. For example, a market containing five firms with respective market shares of 40, 20, 15, 15 and 10 per cent has an HHI of 2,550.

- The HHI ranges from close to zero (in an atomistic market) to 10,000 (in a monopoly).

The HHI has become the standard of choice only relatively recently, though. In the early days of US antitrust, use was made of the CR4 (see below).

9.2.1.1 Market shares in US antitrust law

Section 7 of the Clayton Act[12] stipulates that "no person ... shall acquire the whole or any part of the assets of another person ... where ... the effect of such acquisition may be to substantially lessen competition". In *du Pont*,[13] the Supreme Court decided that "Section 7 is designed to arrest in its incipiency

---

[8] See Ch.3, s.3.5.
[9] See EC Horizontal Merger Guidelines, para.14, and also US Horizontal Merger Guidelines, at 1.51.
[10] See, for example, EC Horizontal Merger Guidelines, paras 16 and 19–21; and also US Horizontal Merger Guidelines, at 1.5.
[11] Derived from A.O. Hirschman, "The Paternity of an Index" (1964) 54 Amer. Econ. Rev. 761; and A.O. Hirschman, *National Power and the Structure of Foreign Trade* (1945). The mathematical formulae utilised in the HHI may be obtained from the appendices to R.A. Miller, "The Herfindahl–Hirschman Index as a Market Structure Variable: An Exposition for Antitrust Practitioners" (1982) 27 Antitrust Bull. 593 at pp.615–618; and D.S. Weinstock, "Using the Herfindahl Index to Measure Concentration" (1982) 27 Antitrust Bull. 285 at pp.298–301.
[12] 15 U.S.C. 18 (1973 and Supp. 1995).
[13] *United States v E.I. du Pont de Nemours and Co*, 353 US 586 (1957), at 589.

... the substantial lessening of competition". To determine whether there is reasonable probability of a substantial lessening of competition, the courts have subsequently focused on whether such mergers will cause the merged entity to have enough market power so that it could profitably increase prices.[14] The decision to investigate and challenge a merger often lies with the federal agencies where the stated antitrust concern of the US regulators' 1992 Horizontal Merger Guidelines is market power, with market concentration being rated as a "useful indicator" of the likely competitive effects of a merger.[15] Therefore, careful attention is paid to the initial level of concentration and the predicted change in concentration due to the merger.[16] This reflects a view that anti-competitive harm is an increasing function of concentration. In principle, however, concentration has not served as a presumption of "guilt". Instead, it has served to determine which cases should be investigated, concentration being a necessary, but on its own an insufficient, condition for a merger challenge.[17]

The US approach has developed from the 1960s when the US Supreme Court formally condemned mergers between horizontal competitors with only minimal market shares,[18] referring to market share data as "one of the most important factors to be considered when determining the probable effects of the combination on effective competition in the relevant market".[19] Also, the idea was advanced that incipient market power should be blocked, even if the transaction was efficient.[20] The Supreme Court retreated from its extreme structuralist approach in 1974 when it held in the *General Dynamics* decision[21] that non-market share issues had to be examined as well.

9.2.1.2 Market shares in European competition law

The EC Merger Regulation itself does not establish a methodology for assessing whether a merger actually creates or strengthens a dominant position. It merely states that, when performing the appraisal of whether a concentration

---

[14] *United States v Mercy Health Services, Inc*, 902 F. Supp. 968 (N.D. Iowa 1995), at 975; vacated as moot, 107 F. 3d 632 (8th Cir. 1997); quoting *United States v Philadelphia National Bank*, 374 US 321 (1963), at 362.
[15] Section 1.51 of the US Horizontal Merger Guidelines.
[16] See Section 0.1 and 1.0 of the US Horizontal Merger Guidelines, stating that the creation, strengthening or exercise of market power is likely only if concentration is significantly increased, resulting in a concentrated market. See Section 1.51 of the US Horizontal Merger Guidelines for the general standards of concentration.
[17] M.B. Coate and F. McChesney, "Empirical Evidence on FTC Enforcement of the Merger Guidelines" (1992) 30 Econ. Inquiry 277 at pp.291–292.
[18] *United States v Philadelphia National Bank*, 374 US 321 (1963), at 364–365: the Court was "clear the 30% presents [a threat of undue concentration]", and that an increase in the market share from 44 to 59% "plainly ... must be regarded as significant".
[19] *Brown Shoe Co, Inc v United States*, 370 US 294 (1962), at 343.
[20] *ibid.*; *United States v Von's Grocery*, 384 US 270 (1966). As the dissenting opinion to the latter case shows, "the Court makes no effort to appraise the competitive effects of this acquisition". See *ibid.*, at 282 (Stewart, J., dissenting).
[21] *United States v General Dynamics Corp*, 415 US 486 (1974). See also M.B. Coate, "Economics, the Guidelines and the Evolution of Merger Policy" (1992) 37 Antitrust Bull. 997 at pp.1009–1010.

is compatible with the Common Market, the European Commission takes into account:

- First, "the need to maintain and develop effective competition within the Common Market, in view of, among other things, the structure of all markets concerned and the actual or potential competition from undertakings located either within or outside the Community" (Article 2(1)(a) Merger Regulation); and

- Second, "the market position of the undertakings concerned and their economic and financial power, the alternatives available to suppliers and users, their access to supplies or markets, any legal or other barriers to entry, supply and demand trends for the relevant goods and services, the interests of the intermediate and ultimate consumers, and the development of technical and economic progress provided it is to consumers' advantage, and does not form an obstacle to competition" (Article 2(1)(b) Merger Regulation).

All early European Commission merger decisions, in which the proposed concentration generated high market shares, have lead the Commission—as later confirmed by the Court of First Instance in *Gencor*[22]—to define what may be understood by a "dominant position" in the merger context[23]: "the ability to act to an appreciable extent independently of its competitors, customers, and, ultimately, its consumers".[24] This is not materially different from the definition of dominance as applied under Article 82 EC. In *Boeing/McDonnell Douglas*,[25] the European Commission refers quite explicitly to Article 82 EC, as:

> "The market power of Boeing allowing it to behave to an appreciable extent independently of its competitors, is an illustration of dominance as defined by the Court of Justice of the European Communities in its judgment in *Michelin*".[26]

Importantly, the connection between the substantive test contained in the Merger Regulation and economic analysis was already made in *Renault/Volvo*.[27] In this case, the European Commission indicates its belief that there exists a very close link between the ability to act independently and the ability to increase prices without losing market shares.[28] Market share figures as applied in defining dominance for purposes of Article 82 EC "make a good

---

[22] Case T–102/96 *Gencor v Commission* [1999] ECR II–753, para.200.
[23] See, e.g. Case IV/M.004 *Renault/Volvo* [1990] O.J. C 281/2, para.22; Case IV/M.053 *Aérospatiale-Alenia/de Havilland* [1991] O.J. L 334/42, para.56.
[24] This is confirmed in the Commission Notice on the definition of the relevant market for the purposes of Community competition law [1997] O.J. C 372/1, para.10, explicitly referring to the definition given in Case 85/76 *Hoffmann-La Roche v Commission (Vitamins)* [1979] ECR 461. Dominance is thus "less" than monopoly or quasi-monopoly; see P. Christensen, P. Owen and D. Sjöblom, "Mergers", in *The EC Law of Competition* (J. Faull and A. Nikpay ed., 1999) para.4.141.
[25] Case IV/M.877 *Boeing/McDonnell Douglas* [1997] O.J. L 336/16, para.37.
[26] At the same time, the CFI made it clear in *Tetra Laval/Sidel* that the assessment of potential abuse is the exclusive domain of Art. 82 EC and should not play a part in the merger review context.
[27] Case IV/M.004 *Renault/Volvo* [1990] O.J. C 281/2.
[28] *ibid.*, para.14.

starting point" for the analysis under the Merger Regulation, but should be used with caution. The assessment of market shares has consequently moved from an almost mechanical measurement towards taking into account the context of a market's characteristics and the nature of competition in it.[29]

In a mature market, a high market share is more likely to confer market power than it would in a dynamic market subject to innovation and rapid change.[30] It follows that market shares represent an important factor as evidence of a dominant position, provided that they not only reflect current conditions but are also a reliable indicator of future conditions. The dynamical aspects of a market as indicated by entry and exit, fluctuations of market share and the pace of technological change and innovation have clearly come to play a prominent part in the European Commission's approach, pointing towards the need to make some sort of prediction about future developments when assessing mergers. This is probably what the Commission implied when it stated[31] that the test of dominance is to be understood as an appreciable freedom of action unlimited by actual or potential competition. The European Court of Justice's *Kali and Salz* ruling may be quoted to confirm these earlier findings, obliging the European Commission to assess dominance using a "prospective analysis" of the reference market[32] and concluding that:

"A market share of approximately 60 percent ... cannot in itself point conclusively to the existence of a collective dominant position on the part of those undertakings".[33]

In *Gencor*, the Court of First Instance reconfirmed that market shares play a "highly important" role, immediately putting its findings into perspective, however, by corroborating this finding to be limited to a case-by-case approach, not binding the Commission in subsequent cases. At best:

"...the view may legitimately be taken that very large market shares are in and of themselves evidence of the existence of a dominant position, save in exceptional circumstances".[34]

It remains to be seen how the modified language of the substantial test in Article 2(3) Merger Regulation—now referring to "significantly impeding effective competition"—will ultimately affect the assessment of anti-competitive effects in this regard. Indeed, according to the EC Horizontal Merger Guidelines, "very large market shares" (this time defined as 50 per

---

[29] In Case IV/M.068 *Tetra Pak/Alfa-Laval* [1991] O.J. L 290/35, para.23, the European Commission said that a "market share as high as 90% is, in itself, a very strong indicator of the existence of a dominant position. However, in certain rare circumstances even such a high market share may not necessarily result in dominance. In particular, if sufficient active competitors are present on the market, the company with the large market share may be prevented from acting to an appreciable extent independently of the pressures typical of a competitive market".

[30] See, e.g. Case IV/M.206 *Rhône-Poulenc/SNIA* [1992] O.J. C 212/23.

[31] European Commission, *XXI Annual Report on Competition Policy 1991* (1992), p.362.

[32] Joined Cases C–68/94 and C–30/95 *French Republic and Société Commerciale des Potasses et de l'Azote (SCPA) and Entreprise Minière et Chimique (EMC) v Commission* [1998] ECR I–1375, para.221.

[33] *ibid.*, para.226.

[34] See Case T–102/96 *Gencor v Commission* [1999] ECR II–753, paras 199–216.

cent or more) may in themselves be evidence of the existence of a dominant market position.[35] It is noteworthy that the EC Horizontal Merger Guidelines also confirm (paras 17–18) that:

- the presumption of dominance based on such "very large market shares" may be rebutted (if, for example, smaller competitors have the ability to act as a sufficient constraint through their incentives to increase production);

- lower market shares may still raise competitive concerns in view of other factors (such as, for example, the strength and number of competitors, the presence of capacity constraints, or the level of substitution between the products of the parties to the concentration);

- where market shares remain below 25 per cent, however, it is presumed that the concentration will not bring about any anti-competitive effects (see also Recital 32 Merger Regulation).

9.2.1.3 Concentration levels in US antitrust law: from CR4 to HHI

Initially, the US Supreme Court found that high concentration established a rebuttable presumption of illegality,[36] stating that:

> "... a merger which produces a firm controlling an undue percentage share of the relevant market and results in a significant increase in concentration of firms in that market is inherently likely to lessen competition that it must be enjoined in the absence of evidence clearly showing that the merger is not likely to have such anti-competitive effects".[37]

This strict policy approach was formalised under the US Department of Justice's (DOJ's) (initial) 1968 Merger Guidelines, applying the so-called CR4 analysis for determining the degree of concentration in a market. CR4 is an abbreviation for concentration ratio for the top four firms. The CR4 approach has two significant drawbacks, as it does not take into account: (a) the relative sizes of the leading companies; and (b) the total number of firms in the market or the market shares of the companies below the four largest.[38]

The only indication of the conduct feared was a single sentence in the US (1968) Merger Guidelines stating that a concentrated market, where a few

---

[35] See Case T–102/96 *Gencor v Commission* [1999] ECR II–753, para.205.

[36] *United States v Philadelphia National Bank*, 374 US 321 (1963), at 363.

[37] The Court offered no indication, however, as to the basis for its view that concentration and competitive effects were so closely linked. Instead it referred to *inter alia* D.C. Bok, "Section 7 of the Clayton Act and the Merging of Law and Economics" (1960) 74 Harv. L. Rev. 226 at pp.308–316 and 328. In a subsequent case, the Court stated that "it would seem that the situation in the aluminum industry may be oligopolistic. As that condition develops, the greater is the likelihood that parallel policies of mutual advantage, not competition, will emerge", see *United States v Aluminum Co of America (Alcoa)*, 377 US 271 (1964), at 280.

[38] See Section 5 of the 1968 Guidelines; for example, a firm with a share of 15% in a highly concentrated market (four-firm concentration ratio over 75%) could not buy a rival with a share over 1%. No safe harbours existed. See D.S. Weinstock, "Using the Herfindahl Index to Measure Concentration" (1982) 27 Antitrust Bull. 285 at pp.285–286.

firms account for a large share of the sales, tends to discourage vigorous price competition by the firms in the market and to encourage other kinds of conduct such as use of inefficient methods of production or excessive promotional expenditures of an economically undesirable nature.[39]

Since the 1982 revision of its Merger Guidelines, the US DOJ tried to quantify some of the criteria that should be considered in interpreting the merger at hand. The US DOJ stated as its unifying theme that "mergers should not be permitted to create or enhance market power or to facilitate its exercise". The reason for this focus on market power was that the result of an exercise thereof is a transfer of wealth from buyers to sellers and a misallocation of resources.[40] Market power was defined as "the ability of one or more firms to maintain prices profitably above competitive levels for a significant period of time". Single firm conduct could be either that of a monopolist or of a firm well short of it, while as for multi-firm conduct the 1982 Guidelines made frequent reference to the prospects for post-merger collusion.[41] This collusion hypothesis suggests that while concentrations may be motivated by efficiency considerations, they may also be motivated by the prospect of escaping competition in favour of oligopolistic market structures. Concentration remained relevant, because it was found much easier to raise prices above a competitive level and keep them there in a highly concentrated market.[42] For the first time, the HHI was used as the way of measuring market concentration.[43] The 1984 revisions to the US DOJ's Merger Guidelines did not alter the treatment of competitive effects as touched upon in the 1968 Merger Guidelines, however.

While the joint 1992 Horizontal Merger Guidelines retained the focus and definition of market power of the earlier US Guidelines, the discussions of the potential adverse competitive effects of concern (the means by which market power may be exercised and the circumstances in which such conduct is likely to be successful) have been substantially revised. Coordinated interaction and unilateral conduct of the merged entity are placed on an equal footing. Market concentration, while still a significant component of the analysis, is less determinative of enforcement agency action than under previous Guidelines. The US (1992) Horizontal Merger Guidelines provide an analytical framework for evaluating concentration evidence in determining whether a merger is likely to have adverse competitive effects, consisting of five steps:[44]

(1) market definition, measurement, and concentration;

(2) competitive effects;

[39] Section 2 of the 1968 Guidelines.
[40] Section 1 of the 1982 Guidelines.
[41] Section 1 and 3 A II of the 1982 Guidelines. The concern for multi-firm exercise of market power is explained as that "where only a few firms account for most of the sales of a product, those firms can in some circumstances co-ordinate, explicitly or implicitly, their actions in order to approximate the performance of a monopolist."
[42] US Department of Justice, "Explanation and Summary of the Merger Guidelines", reprinted in: (1982) *Trade Reg. Rep. (CCH)*, No. 546, 58.
[43] Section 3 A of the 1982 guidelines.
[44] Section 0.2. of the US Horizontal Merger Guidelines.

(3) entry analysis;

(4) efficiencies; and

(5) failure or exiting assets.

The US (1992) Horizontal Merger Guidelines use the HHI as their primary market concentration guide, with concentration levels of 1,000 and 1,800 as the two key levels. The HHI embodies two aspects of the distribution of market shares in an industry: (a) the dispersion in shares, indicating whether they are spread out or relatively equal; and (b) the number of firms in the industry. The acceptance of the HHI was probably brought about by Stigler who suggested that the HHI is an appropriate measure of concentration "if we wish concentration to measure the likelihood of effective collusion".[45] As compared to the CR4, all firms are now included in the measurement with the shares of the larger firms given greater weight than those of the smaller companies, to offer a more complete picture of the whole market.[46] The obvious drawback is, of course, that information about the individual market shares for each of the firms in the market is required.

According to the US (1992) Horizontal Merger Guidelines, the following thresholds are relevant in deciding whether mergers will be challenged:

- any merger in a market with a post-merger HHI below 1,000 is considered unlikely to be challenged;

- a merger in a market with a post-merger HHI above 1,800 is likely to be challenged if the parties to the merger have market shares that cause the HHI to increase by more than 100, unless other mitigating factors exist such as ease of entry;

- mergers in the "in-between" markets with moderate post-merger concentration levels between 1,000 and 1,800 require further analysis before a decision is made whether or not to challenge.

This three-tier approach to industry concentration makes it possible to rule out regulatory challenges to certain mergers based on the HHI alone.[47] No sound economic reason exists, of course, for picking out particular levels of the HHI as danger points; they do, however, seem fairly consistent with the available evidence.[48] Setting the trigger levels of the HHI too high has the risk of letting too many anti-competitive mergers go by unchallenged; on the other hand the consequence of setting these levels too low would be a substantial number of

---

[45] G.J. Stigler, "Monopoly and Oligopoly by Merger" (1950) 40 Amer. Econ. Rev. 23 at p.55.
[46] This multifacet interpretation of the HHI is derived from M.A. Adelman, "Comment on the 'H' Concentration Measure as a Numbers-Equivalent" (1969) 51 Rev. Econ. Statist. 99 at pp.99–101.
[47] J. Greenfield, "Beyond Herfindahl: Non-structural Elements of Merger Analysis" (1984) 53 Antitrust L.J. 229 at p.232.
[48] R. Schmalensee, "Horizontal Merger Policy: Problems and Changes" (1987) 1 J.Econ. Perspect. 41 at p.49.

cases claiming offsetting efficiency effects with a fairly good chance of success.[49]

It is important to note that in the USA, the application of the set levels of HHI has not been overtly mechanical. First, as evidence from the case law shows, the courts have, as Coate puts it, "hardly validated the Guidelines' wording of challenge in all but extraordinary circumstances"[50] (which would imply that most mergers in highly concentrated markets are anti-competitive). Overall a lack of entry barriers makes it hard for the enforcement agencies to convince the courts of the dangers that collusion is immanent,[51] and even merger to near monopoly may be allowed if sufficient evidence exists to support the inference of no anti-competitive effect.[52] In fact, the HHI levels as identified in the 1992 Guidelines are well below actual enforcement trends. In a high profile speech, then-Deputy Assistant Attorney General Kolasky provided statistics showing that successful merger challenges were generally brought by the DOJ in cases where the post-merger HHI levels are in the 2,000–3,000 range (often on coordinated effects theories). For example, in 1990–91, the average post-merger HHI was 3,801, with an average HHI change of 1,798. Remarkably, in 2000–01, these numbers had risen to average post-merger HHI levels at 5,215, with average HHI changes of 1,729.[53]

Second, evidence reveals that the HHI is not a sufficient statistic for determining the effects of concentration on non-competitive behaviour. The HHI may only be used as the crudest of indicators as to a serious analysis of a given merger, and this must raise questions about the likelihood of tacit collusion. After all, the link between concentration and the exercise of market power is recognised to be weak; the only thing that can be stated with any confidence is that concentration is a necessary condition for the effective exercise of market power.[54] While the numbers of the HHI look pretty much the same in the US (1992) Horizontal Merger Guidelines as they did in the earlier versions, the role assigned to market concentration, however, has been altered substantially. No longer are the US enforcement agencies likely to make a challenge based on market concentration data alone. Instead, at the highest levels of concentration adverse effects are presumed, but this may be overcome by showing that the factors set forth in the remainder of the 1992 Guidelines make it unlikely that the merger will create or enhance market power or facilitate its exercise in the light of market concentration and market shares. By adopting such a presumptive approach, the 1992 Guidelines underscore the importance of other market factors, as well as market concentration, in the agencies'

---

[49] This setting becomes even more realistic if the relevant market is defined too narrowly, see F.M. Fisher, "Horizontal Mergers: Triage and Treatment" (1987) 1 J. Econ. Perspect. 23 at p.32.

[50] M.B. Coate, "Economics, the Guidelines and the Evolution of Merger Policy" (1992) 37 Antitrust Bull. 997 at p.1016.

[51] See, e.g. *FTC v Promodes*, 1989–2 Trade Cas. (CCH) para.68,688 (N.D. Ga. 1989); *Waste Management v United States*, 743 F.2d 976 (2d Cir. 1984).

[52] *United States v Syufy Enterprises*, 712 F.Supp. 1386, aff'd, 903 F.2d 659 (9th Cir. 1990).

[53] William J. Kolasky, "Coordinated Effects in Merger Review: From Dead Frenchmen to Beautiful Minds and Mavericks", Speech, Washington, DC, April 24, 2002.

[54] R. Schmalensee, "Horizontal Merger Policy: Problems and Changes" (1987) 1 J. Econ. Perspect. 41 at p.49.

assessments (or the likely competitive effect of mergers).[55] In sum, the US (1992) Horizontal Merger Guidelines have been applied in a largely pragmatic manner.

9.2.1.4 Concentration levels in European competition law

Also under European competition law, market shares are not to be detached from the effect the merger has on concentration.[56] Prior to the issuance of the EC Horizontal Merger Guidelines, only general inferences could be drawn from the precedent case law.[57] The Guidelines now offer a standardised approach similar to that of the USA. The European Commission clearly points out that "market shares and concentration levels provide useful first indications of the market structure" and that although current market shares are the norm, past or future market shares may be useful in dynamic industries.[58]

In terms of HHI, the relevant levels are the following:

- any merger in a market with a post-merger HHI below 1,000 is considered unlikely to be challenged;

- any merger in a market with a post-merger HHI between 1,000 and 2,000 is considered unlikely to be challenged, if the increase in HHI is below 250 (except in "special circumstances");

- any merger in a market with a post-merger HHI above 2,000 is considered unlikely to be challenged, if the increase in HHI is below 150 (except in "special circumstances");

- the "special circumstances" listed concern concentrations involving entrants, important innovators, cross-shareholdings, mavericks, evidence of past or ongoing coordination or facilitating practices and one party's pre-merger market shares in excess of 50 per cent.

These HHI levels are—again—an initial indicator of competition concerns. However, the European Commission stresses that they do not give rise to a presumption of either the existence or the absence of such concerns.[59] Although it is slightly early in the existence of the EC Horizontal Merger Guidelines to consistently review actual application levels, it may be noted that EC HHI levels are slightly higher than US levels (albeit distinctly below Kolasky's figures discussed in the previous subsection) and may hence reflect more realistically the European Commission's level of intervention (while still

---

[55] Thereby following the richer analysis of the Supreme Court's decision in *United States v General Dynamics Corp*, 415 US 486 (1974); instead of the rigid structuralist approach of *United States v Philadelphia National Bank*, 374 US 321 (1963); see P.T. Denis, "Advances of the 1992 Horizontal Merger Guidelines in the Analysis of Competitive Effects" (1993) 38 Antitrust L.J. 479 at p.507.
[56] See B.E. Hawk and H.L. Huser, *European Community Merger Control: A Practitioner's Guide* (1996), p.169, for a general discussion of the case law.
[57] For an overview, see P.D. Camesasca, *European Merger Control: Getting the Efficiencies Right* (2000), pp.95–108.
[58] EC Horizontal Merger Guidelines, paras 14–16.
[59] *ibid.*, paras 19–21.

providing sufficient discretion for the Commission to form its initial opinion of the likely effects of a proposed concentration).

9.2.2 Competitive assessment of horizontal concentrations

9.2.2.1 Current rules of EC merger control

According to the EC Horizontal Merger Guidelines:

> "A concentration may significantly impede effective competition in a market by removing important competitive constraints on one or more sellers, who consequently have increased market power. The most direct effect of the merger will be the loss of competition between the merging firms. ... Non-merging firms in the same market can also benefit from the reduction of competitive pressure that results from the merger, since the merging firms' price increase may switch some demand to the rival firms, which, in turn, may find it profitable to increase their prices".[60]

The EC Horizontal Merger Guidelines go on to explain that non-coordinated effects can emerge in settings of single firm dominance, as well as in oligopolistic markets. The Guidelines then discuss a number of factors which may influence whether or not non-coordinated effects are likely to result from a concentration: merging firms having large market shares, merging firms being large competitors, customers having limited possibilities of switching suppliers, competitors being unlikely to increase supply if prices increase, newly created entities being able to hinder expansion of competitors, and concentration eliminating an important competitive force.[61]

According to the Court of First Instance in *Gencor*:

> "A merger in a concentrated market may significantly impede effective competition, through the creation or strengthening of a collective dominant position, because it increases the likelihood that firms are able to coordinate their behaviour in this way and raise prices, even without entering into an agreement or resorting to a concerted practice within the meaning of Article 81".[62]

The EC Horizontal Merger Guidelines elaborate that a concentration may make coordination easier, more stable and more effective for firms that were already coordinating before the concentration. Such coordination may involve (a) keeping prices above competitive levels, (b) limiting production or the amount of new capacity brought into the market, (c) dividing up the market, or (d) allocating contracts in bidding markets.[63]

Coordination is more likely to emerge in markets where it is relatively simple to reach a common understanding on the terms of coordination. In

---

[60] EC Horizontal Merger Guidelines, para.24.
[61] *ibid.*, paras 24–38.
[62] Case T–102/96 *Gencor v Commission* [1999] ECR II–753, para.277.
[63] EC Horizontal Merger Guidelines, paras 24–38.

Airtours, the Court of First Instance added that three conditions are necessary for coordination to be sustainable:

● each member of the dominant oligopoly must have the ability to know how the other members are behaving in order to monitor whether or not they are adopting the common policy;

● there must be adequate deterrents to ensure that there is a long term incentive in not departing from the common policy; and

● the foreseeable reaction of outsiders, i.e. current and future competitors, as well as of consumers, must not jeopardise the results expected from the common policy.[64]

In the following, the distinction between non-coordinated effects and coordinated effects will be highlighted. The section will then go on discussing successively the theoretical underpinnings of non-coordinated effects and coordinated effects. The third section of this chapter will further explore the relevant issues in assessing the competitive effects of concentrations by discussing four cases: *Volvo/Scania* (focus on non-coordinated effects), *GE/Instrumentarium* (focus on unilateral/non-coordinated effects in oligopolistic markets) and *Oracle/PeopleSoft* and *Sony/BMG* (focus on coordinated effects in oligopolistic markets).

For a brief discussion of the procedural aspects of merger control in the EC, reference is made to Box 9.1. Jurisdictional aspects are contained in Chapter 10, section 10.3.2.1.

Box 9.1: Procedural aspects of merger control in the EC

The EC process for reviewing concentrations can be described as largely administrative. The same officials from the Competition Directorate General (DG Comp) will review the concentration, engage with the parties and draft a final decision to be taken by the college of European Commissioners. Only after the European Commission has taken its final decision can parties take recourse to judicial review before the Court of First Instance. In the following, the EC process is discussed; subsequently, the checks and balances of this process are presented.

The 2004 review to the Merger Regulation maintains the system of mandatory notifications for concentrations which reach the turnover thresholds contained in Article 1 Merger Regulation. Notification is made by completing a Form CO, a time-consuming and cumbersome exercise requiring detailed legal and economic analysis. The result of notification is that the timeline for review begins to run; in the meantime, the proposed concentration is suspended (implying no implementation before clearance by the European Commission and no preliminary contacts or exchange of information between the parties' businesses).

Prior to the notification, parties to a concentration often engage in

---

[64] Case T–342/99 *Airtours v Commission* [2002] ECR II–2585, para.62.

informal discussions with DG Comp to address jurisdictional issues (for example, referral) and legal issues (for example, market definition, remedies), as well as the scope and preparation of the notification (Form CO). After the notification, phase 1 of the review starts (see Article 6 Merger Regulation), in which the Commission (through its officials at DG Comp) undertakes a preliminary review of the concentration. The deadlines to undertake this preliminary review are fixed: 25 working days for a normal review, extended by 10 working days in case of remedy discussions (to alleviate competitive concerns) or a referral request pursuant to Article 9 Merger Regulation (see Box 10.1). At the end of phase 1, the Commission either decides that the concentration does not raise competitive concerns and is cleared to proceed (eventually subject to remedies) or that further investigation is necessary. If the outcome of a phase 1 review is that the Commission needs further information to take a final decision, an in-depth review is opened in phase 2 (see Article 8 Merger Regulation). The deadlines to undertake this in-depth review are 90 working days, which can be extended to 105 working days in case of remedies. For complex cases, the deadline for decision can be extended by an additional 20 working days (but only at the parties' request or with their consent), but after this, a final decision must be taken (resulting in clearance, possibly with remedies, or prohibition).

During the Commission's investigation, a number of meetings with both the notifying parties and third parties are envisaged under the Merger Regulation and its various implementation tools. Such meetings can be informal "ad hoc meetings", "state of play meetings" or "triangular meetings" (involving DG Comp, the notifying parties and third parties). In phase 2, the statement of objections, access to file provisions and the oral hearing (under the direction of a neutral hearing officer) formalise this exchange of views. Additional checks and balances of the Commission's internal process are contained in the "Best Practice Guidelines", available on the DG Comp website. They also include a peer review system (the so-called "devil's advocate panel"), in which the DG Comp officials leading the investigation present and defend their findings and preliminary conclusions to a number of (uninvolved) colleagues.

In terms of external checks and balances, as was noted in Chapter 1, the Court of First Instance has turned itself into a serious address for appeals against European Commission decisions, at least in the merger area. Without doubt, the Court of First Instance's judgments in *Airtours*, *Schneider/Legrand* and *Tetra Laval/Sidel* will go down in legal history as the demise of the DG Comp's specialised Merger Task Force. Prior to these three judgments, the Merger Task Force had near-mythical status inside DG Comp and the legal community; post-*Tetra Laval/Sidel*, it was quietly disbanded. Importantly, the Court of First Instance has implemented a fast track procedure to ensure appeals against merger decisions can be dealt with in a timely fashion, a crucial aspect in providing a viable appeals system in what is essentially a fast-moving process.

In sum, in the EC reviewing concentrations is basically a front-loaded administrative notification process. It may be noted that the EC process is thus different from the US process, which is in essence judicial. In the USA, initial contacts with the agencies (FTC or DOJ) are relatively informal. Only once competitive concerns surface does the review process kick in, but then, massive amounts of data need to be provided. Furthermore, each time the agency wishes to obtain further information, it needs to go to court and have a judge sanction its request and further action. Obviously, this provides for immediate checks and balances to the regulatory intervention. However, as a direct consequence the review process in the USA also becomes entirely open-ended, i.e. it is near impossible for the parties to a concentration to predict when final relief is in sight.

9.2.2.2 Distinguishing two types of oligopolistic behaviour

Other than by single dominant firms, competition may be threatened in two ways.[65] These two ways are conceptually distinct even if sometimes hard to distinguish in practice. The first threat to competition comes from so-called non-coordinated effects that arise where market concentration is high enough for non-competitive outcomes to result from the individual profit-maximising responses of firms to market conditions (without any of the firms involved being individually dominant, however). The second threat to competition comes from so-called tacit collusion or coordinated effects.

Before turning to the assessment of single firm dominance and the functioning of non-coordinated effects, it is important to identify the relation of the latter concept with coordinated effects. Both are instances of oligopolistic behaviour. Where they differ is in the way that the firms involved take into account their competitors' behaviour. Non-coordinated effects are a form of individual rivalry, implying that firms will take their competitors' behaviour as a given. Market power may nevertheless arise, if some or all of the firms are able to raise prices profitably above competitive levels (through, for example, technological advantages, product differentiation or entry). Coordinated effects have as a necessary condition that firms act with the intention of influencing the future actions of their competitors.

Even though non-coordinated effects thus imply that firms do not expect to influence their competitors, firms in such a setting will remain responsive to market conditions and take their decisions regarding prices and other competitive parameters in a way that corresponds therewith (i.e. to market conditions being the result of the decisions of other firms). Hence, another way of identifying the conceptual difference with tacit collusion lays in the "passive" nature in which firms subjected to non-coordinated effects will adapt to market conditions.

For the purposes of assessing the likelihood of anti-competitive effects that

---

[65] J.B. Baker, "Developments in Antitrust Economics" (1999) 13 J. Econ. Perspect. 181 at p.189. Compare for an overview R.B. Starek, III, and S. Stockum, "What Makes Mergers Anti-competitive?: 'Unilateral Effects' Analysis under the 1992 Merger Guidelines" (1995) 63 Antitrust L.J. 801.

could arise out of a proposed concentration, Ivaldi *et al.* suggest that, first, one needs to establish how a given concentration affects what would happen to prices, output and other features of a market if firms responded in an individually rivalrous way to market conditions (i.e. through single firm dominance or through non-coordinated effects), without increasing the likelihood of tacit collusion. The second task is then to assess what the impact of the concentration may be on the incentives for tacit collusion.[66]

9.2.2.3 Theory of single firm dominance and non-coordinated effects

When there is a limited number of firms remaining post-concentration, anti-competitive outcomes may arise particularly if products are imperfect substitutes (product differentiation), even while belonging to the same market. Expert studies recently commissioned by the European Commission helpfully set out the theoretical underpinnings of non-coordinated effects[67] and provide a detailed assessment of product differentiation and the impact this has on the review of concentrations.[68]

When assessing concentrations, the focus is regularly on (Bertrand) price competition or (Cournot) quantity/output competition as these are most likely to be affected within the timeframe of such review.[69] A substantial difference to market outcomes arises when firms react to each others' prices or quantities. When firms are principally reacting to each others' prices, it is the presence of some reasonably close substitute that is crucial for establishing competitive conditions (i.e. it matters most that there be some close competitor, not how many close competitors there are). When firms are mainly reacting to each others' quantities, the numbers of competitors will matter as well as the extent to which their products are substitutes (i.e. it matters not just that there be some competition but that there be enough of it).

Whether firms compete on prices or quantities, a concentration between competitors increases the remaining firms' market power (i.e. both the newly created entity and its competitors), thereby leading to higher prices and lower output (absent offsetting pro-competitive efficiency gains). The concentration will have an impact on both the newly created entity and the remaining competitors. The newly created entity will be able to coordinate the prices of its products perfectly. But, if the two products are to some extent substitutable, raising the price for one product implies some consumers will buy more of the other product (or, reducing the supply from one product increases the price of the other product). Prior to the concentration, each firm would have considered the potential losses of business to its rival "costs" of raising its own price. The concentration removes these costs and hence creates the incentive to

---

[66] M. Ivaldi, B. Jullien, P. Rey, P. Seabright and J. Tirole, *Economics of Unilateral Effects* (Final Report Prepared for DG Comp, 2003), p.7.
[67] *ibid.*
[68] R.J. Epstein and D.L. Rubinfeld, *Effects of Mergers Involving Differentiated Products* (Final Report Prepared for DG Comp, 2004).
[69] Depending on the nature of the industry, longer term decisions such as investment, product choices and R&D may also play a role.

raise price and/or reduce output. The extent of the price rise and/or output decrease depends on (a) the degree of substitutability between the respective products and the remaining ones, and (b) on the nature of competition (Bertrand or Cournot). A concentration between firms that produce close substitutes is more likely to raise prices than a concentration between firms producing imperfect substitutes (*viz.*, a newly created entity will raise prices to a lesser extent if other competitors produce close substitutes, the latter effect being more important in Bertrand price competition settings, since the elimination of competition between substitutes will matter more).

The impact on the remaining competitors depends considerably on the type of competition. A concentration in either a Bertrand or a Cournot setting limits the competitive pressure on the other firms (i.e. through an increase in the newly created firm's prices, *viz.* reduction in their output). However, the likely reaction differs.

Where firms compete on price, these prices are often strategic complements. An increase in the price by the newly created entity will typically lead competing firms to increase their own prices (although to a slightly lesser extent). Such a—from the newly created entity's perspective—positive reaction will encourage the concentration to further raise prices. Thus, because of strategic complementarity of prices, the price effect is exacerbated.

Where firms compete on quantities, these quantities are often strategic substitutes. A reduction of output by the newly created entity will typically lead competing firms to expand their own output (although not fully compensating the initial output reduction). Still, this often attenuates the incentives of the newly created entity to reduce its output.

The bottom line is that ignoring the incentives of competitors to react to a proposed concentration in a non-coordinated setting (but also in a single firm dominance setting) will tend to produce a biased assessment of the likely impact of the concentration. For an industry where price competition is important, this bias will underestimate price rises. Where quantity competition is important, the bias will lead to an overestimate of likely prices.

9.2.2.4 Theory of coordinated effects

For explicit coordination and the application of Article 81 EC, the reader is referred to the discussion in Chapter 5. An expert study recently commissioned by the European Commission sets out the theoretical underpinnings of tacit collusion.[70] Coordinated effects (tacit collusion) can arise when firms interact repeatedly. They may then be able to maintain higher prices by tacitly agreeing that any deviation from the collusive outcome would trigger some retaliation. To be sustainable, retaliation must be sufficiently likely and costly to outweigh the short term benefits from cheating on the collusion. These short term benefits, as well as the magnitude and likelihood of retaliation, depend, in turn, on the characteristics of the industry.

[70] M. Ivaldi, B. Jullien, P. Rey, P. Seabright and J. Tirole, *Economics of Tacit Collusion* (Final Report Prepared for DG Comp, 2003).

Ivaldi *et al.*[71] helpfully outline the factors which may be relevant in the assessment of coordinated effects that may arise from concentrations:

- Number of participants: a concentration that eliminates one of the significant competitors contributes to make collusion more sustainable.

- Entry barriers: collusion is more of a concern in markets with high entry barriers. This has two implications. First, a concentration that would raise entry barriers (e.g. by uniting two potentially competing technologies) would thus tend to facilitate collusion. Second, collusion should be a concern for merger control only in those markets where there are significant entry barriers in the post-concentration situation.

- Frequency of interaction: collusion is easier when firms interact more frequently. This factor is less likely than others to be directly affected by a concentration but is relevant to assess whether collusion is an important concern.

- Market transparency: collusion is easier when firms observe each other's prices and quantities. This factor thus contributes to determine whether collusion is an important concern; in addition, however, some concentrations may have a direct impact on market transparency. For example, a vertical merger between a manufacturer and a distributor may allow the manufacturer to have better access to its rivals' marketing strategies.

- Demand characteristics: collusion is easier in growing markets (taking as given the number of competitors, that is, ignoring the possible positive effect of demand growth on entry) than in declining markets and in stable markets than in fluctuating markets. These factors are useful to assess the seriousness of the collusion concern but unlikely to be directly affected by a concentration.

- Innovation: collusion is easier to sustain in mature markets where innovation plays little role compared to innovation-driven markets. This is an important factor for assessing whether collusion is a serious concern. In addition, a concentration that enhances the new entity's R&D potential may contribute to make collusion more difficult to sustain.

- Symmetry: it is easier to collude among equals, that is, among firms that have similar costs structures, similar production capacities, or offer similar ranges of products. This is a factor that is typically affected by a concentration. Concentrations that tend to restore symmetry can facilitate collusion, whereas those who create or exacerbate pre-existing asymmetry are more likely, all things equal, to hinder collusion.

- Product homogeneity: this factor has a more ambiguous impact on the likelihood of collusion, since it affects both the incentives to undercut the

[71] M. Ivaldi, B. Jullien, P. Rey, P. Seabright and J. Tirole, *Economics of Tacit Collusion* (Final Report Prepared for DG Comp, 2003), pp.11–67.

rivals and their ability to retaliate. Product differentiation can, however, have an impact when it contributes to introduce asymmetry between firms (e.g. when firms offer goods or services of different qualities); also, product homogeneity can make the market effectively more transparent. Overall, this factor, which is necessarily affected by concentrations, can be useful to assess the plausibility of collusion.

- Multi-market contact: collusion is easier to achieve when the same competitors are present in several markets. Multi-market contact is thus relevant to assess the plausibility of collusion; in addition, a concentration can increase significantly the number of markets on which the same firms are competing, in which case it may reinforce the possibility of collusion.

- Demand elasticity and buying power reduce the profitability of collusion; in addition, large buyers have more latitude to break collusion. This is mostly relevant to assess the potential relevance of collusion, although buyer concentration can also have a direct impact.

- Other factors are also relevant, such as the existence of structural links or of a "maverick" firm. Thus a concentration—or a concentration remedy— that would create such links or remove a maverick would be more likely to facilitate collusion. The particular organisation of the markets (e.g. auction design for bidding markets) can be relevant to assess the plausibility of collusion.

Clearly, the above listing allows for a number of general conclusions concerning the role of coordinated effects in concentration-type cases. First, some factors that may or may not be affected by the concentration at hand have a decisive impact on the firms' ability to sustain tacit collusion. These factors include entry barriers, the frequency of interaction and the role of innovation. There is little scope for collusion in the absence of entry barriers, or if firms interact very infrequently, or else in innovation-driven markets. Therefore, whenever an industry presents one of these features, collusion is unlikely to constitute a significant concern.

Second, some factors are both relevant and likely to be directly affected by concentrations. These factors include of course the number of market participants, but also the degree of symmetry among those participants. By eliminating a competitor, a concentration reduces the number of participants and thereby tends to facilitate collusion. This effect is likely to be the higher the smaller the number of participants left in the market. In contrast, a concentration that would create or reinforce asymmetry in costs, production capacities or product ranges would tend as such to make collusion more difficult. Of course, such a concentration would at the same time both reduce the number of participants (which is good for collusion) and introduce additional asymmetry (which is bad for collusion). However, as long as the number of key variables remains limited, it is possible to evaluate a trade-off between these two conflicting effects. Other factors in this second group would be the removal of a maverick firm, as well as the existence of structural links.

Third, there is a series of factors that can have an influence on the sustainability of collusion, possibly to a lesser extent, and that may or may not be directly affected by concentrations. Among these, the degree of market transparency appears to be a key factor. Other factors include product differentiation, the characteristics of demand (demand trend and fluctuations, as well as demand elasticity and buying power), multi-market contact, or the organisation of particular markets (such as bidding markets). These dimensions are relevant to assess the plausibility of collusion, particularly when the factors of the first two groups do not suffice to send a clear signal.

At the end of the day, however, the assessment of coordinated effects remains inherently complex. Some of the factors listed above may partially offset each other, in both theory and practice. Instead of advocating a checklist approach to identify potential cases for regulatory intervention (as was the widespread belief in the legal community before the Court of First Instance stepped in and overturned the original *Airtours* decision), it is crucial to understand why (or why not) each dimension is relevant in the particular concentration under review.

9.2.3 Efficiency considerations

Conceptually, as well as from a practical/empirical perspective, efficiency considerations pose a number of awkward questions to any competition authority that wishes to engage in a coherent review of concentrations. Such considerations, in a way, often boil down to a balancing act between anti-competitive effects (determined using a prospective analysis of the concentration) and—possibly even more ephemeral—pro-competitive effects (projecting potential future costs savings to a transaction not yet consummated).

There have been no clear-cut cases under European competition law that contain a worked-up discussion of efficiencies.[72] It may be noted that there have been two relatively recent cases in the USA and Canada. In the US case, *Heinz/Beech-Nut* (2000), efficiencies were fielded without changing the ultimately negative outcome,[73] while the Canadian precedent, *Superior Propane/ ICG* (2000), was successful.[74] A detailed discussion would go beyond the scope of the present work, however. In the following, both the conceptual and the practical/empirical issues surrounding efficiency considerations will be analysed. Thereafter, the solution opted for in the EC Horizontal Merger Guidelines will be described.

---

[72] The state of affairs prior to the issuance of the EC Horizontal Merger Guidelines is described in P.D. Camesasca, *European Merger Control: Getting the Efficiencies Right* (2000). There have been no clear-cut precedents since then.

[73] *FTC v Heinz Company, et al.* No.1:00 CV 01688 (DDC).

[74] *Canada (Commissioner of Competition) v Superior Propane Inc*, Competition Tribunal 1998–002, Reasons and Order dated August 30, 2000.

9.2.3.1 Private profitability versus social welfare

The conceptual perspective may be set out by contrasting how (a) a proposed concentration would affect the private profitability for the firms involved, and (b) how the concentration would affect social welfare.

Concentrations often have the potential to be privately profitable,[75] as they offer the opportunity to internalise (at least in part) the consequences of a price increase. A price increase affects aggregate industry output levels. Firms could choose to collude to lower output and raise profits; they could also merge and internalise this externality. One way or another, aggregate industry profits would increase. However, social welfare is not well served if output is lowered as a result of a concentration. How does this relate?

Salant, Switzer and Reynolds show that some exogenous concentrations would induce losses for the firms involved, even when the concentration creates such large efficiency gains through scale economies that it would be socially advantageous.[76] Confirming Stigler's earlier finding,[77] their model shows that the parties to a concentration do not capture all the profits resulting from the transaction; rather because of this externality, concentrations which increase total industry profits need not be privately profitable. Following on from Salant, Switzer and Reynolds, it may be noted that the welfare consequences of concentrations are not always well defined. In particular, combining the assets of the firms combined through a concentration increases the output the newly created entity can produce at given average costs, as it faces a different maximisation problem because of its altered costs function and new strategic considerations. Basically, the new firm emerging after the amalgamation is effectively larger than each one of the pre-concentration firms.

Subsequently, Davidson and Deneckere,[78] as well as Perry and Porter,[79] identify the principal behavioural as well as structural characteristics that will give rise to the necessary incentives to merge. Farrell and Shapiro[80] then provide a model broad enough to explain the adjustments of prices and quantities in response to a concentration in an oligopolistic Cournot-type

---

[75] See for a differing opinion, H. Schenk, "Fusies, Efficiëntie en Mededingingsbeleid", in *Economisch Beleid in een Ondernemende Samenleving* (B. Dankbaar and F. Becker ed., 1997), p.111; R.E. Caves, "Mergers, Takeovers and Economic Efficiency" (1989) 7 Int. J. Ind. Organ. 151.
[76] S.W. Salant, S. Switzer and R.J. Reynolds, "Losses from Horizontal Merger: The Effects of an Exogenous Change in Industry Structure on Cournot–Nash Equilibrium" (1983) 98 Quart. J. Econ. 185 at pp.185–186.
[77] G.J. Stigler, "Monopoly and Oligopoly by Merger" (1950) 40 Amer. Econ. Rev. 23 at pp.27–31.
[78] C. Davidson and R.J. Deneckere, "Horizontal Mergers and Collusive Behavior" (1984) 2 Int. J. Ind. Organ. 117, develop a model under product differentiation.
[79] M.K. Perry and R.H. Porter, "Oligopoly and the Incentive for Horizontal Merger" (1985) 75 Amer. Econ. Rev. 219, develop a model for homogeneous products.
[80] J. Farrell and C. Shapiro, "Horizontal Mergers: An Equilibrium Analysis" (1990) 80 Amer. Econ. Rev. 107 at pp.109–126.

industry.[81] Assuming a concentration to be privately profitable,[82] they show that concentrations raise prices if they do not generate synergies between the merging firms, with high market share firms needing to achieve "impressive synergies" if their merger is to reduce price.[83]

The crucial conceptual improvement of the Farrell and Shapiro analysis emerges from emphasising the *external* welfare effects of the concentration on consumers and non-participant firms, instead of trying to distinguish some hard-to-prove effects of the concentration that are internal to the firms involved. Positive external effects thus could imply an increase in social welfare. If non-participant firms reduce their output, the concentration may lower welfare even though it is profitable, and this will be more likely if collusion is facilitated, oligopolists compete in price among differentiated products, or if the combined market share of the firms involved is large, relative to the shares of the firms outside the concentration.[84] On the contrary, if the outsiders expand their output considerably in response to the concentration, a significant welfare gain can be provided.[85]

Few real-life industries, however, would be compatible with the Farrell and Shapiro assumptions.[86] Still, the following implications for European competition law can be drawn:

- From the efficiency perspective, a large increase in HHI levels should be viewed with suspicion; but, there is no reason to be more concerned about whether concentration levels as such are high or low.[87]

- Focusing on the external welfare effects of a concentration presupposes that the regulator dealing with this concentration is not making any evaluation of its desirability, bringing the theoretical inclusion of the efficiency defence in line with the European Community's goal of establishing an open market economy. Accordingly, approving a concentration on the basis that it has no adverse external effects on the interests of third

---

[81] Farrell and Shapiro's Cournot model may be extended to allow for tacit collusive behaviour, as is shown by F. Verboven, "Corporate Restructuring in a Collusive Oligopoly" (1995) 13 J. Ind. Organ. 335.

[82] J. Farrell and C. Shapiro, "Horizontal mergers: An Equilibrium Analysis" (1990) 80 Amer. Econ. Rev. 107 at pp.116–117. See also G.J. Werden, "Horizontal Mergers: Comment" (1991) 81 Amer. Econ. Rev. 1002; J. Farrell and C. Shapiro, "Horizontal Mergers: Reply" (1991) 81 Amer. Econ. Rev. 1007. The ideal solution to this assumption would be a workable theory of the firm.

[83] J. Farrell and C. Shapiro, "Horizontal Mergers: An Equilibrium Analysis" (1990) 80 Amer. Econ. Rev. 107 at pp.111–114.

[84] *ibid.*, at pp.114–120; A. Jacquemin, "Horizontal Concentration and European Merger Policy" (1990) 34 Eur. Econ. Rev. 539 at p.543.

[85] In Cournot theory, the presence of small firms with little market power is not desirable, as large mark-ups are associated with large market shares and large firms have lower marginal costs. This leads J. Farrell and C. Shapiro, "Horizontal Mergers: An Equilibrium Analysis" (1990) 80 Amer. Econ. Rev. 107 at p.119, to conclude that more concentration among the non-merging firms makes it more likely that the merger will be externally welfare-enhancing.

[86] P.D. Camesasca, *European Merger Control: Getting the Efficiencies Right* (2000), pp.68–70.

[87] R.D. Willig, "Merger Analysis, Industrial Theory, and Merger Guidelines", Brookings Pap. Econ. Act., Microeconomics 281, 286 (1991).

parties would leave private agents free to pursue their own advantage without regulatory intervention.[88]

9.2.3.2 Efficiency requirements under a consumer welfare standard

While Williamson's partial merger to monopoly model[89] required "relatively large price increases for the net allocative effects to be negative", contemporary developments have evolved now to demanding "impressive" synergies in order to allow efficiencies to make a positive impact on the assessment of concentrations. Even more far-reaching conclusions can be drawn when quantifying the efficiencies by confining them to those leading to *immediate* consumer benefits through lower prices; they would plainly require enormous costs savings to count as benefits at all. The latter has been demonstrated by two papers.

In the most recent paper, Froeb and Werden develop a test for welfare-enhancing concentrations among sellers of a homogeneous product.[90] Referring to a concentration's net effect on price, this paper derives a simple condition for implementing that standard as the touchstone for the concentration's legality when the industry equilibrium is static Nash in quantities. Under this strict Cournot setting, the authors provide a calculation determining the marginal costs reduction for the merging firms producing homogeneous goods which is necessary and sufficient to offset the incentive to restrict output and hence the marginal costs reduction necessary and sufficient to prevent a diminution in consumer welfare. Thereby they manage to quantify in part the general findings of the Farrell and Shapiro model. Without entry or efficiencies, an amalgamation causes the merged firm to reduce output as a result of which total industry output falls (causing prices to increase)—even though remaining competitors will respond by increasing their own output. If, however, the concentration also reduces the merging firms' marginal costs, as can be demonstrated, then the cost reduction tends to offset the anti-competitive effects of the concentration on prices. A sufficient reduction of the newly created firm's marginal costs would then result in an actual increase of total industry output and the related decrease in industry price. Froeb and Werden provide a table enumerating the sufficient reduction condition for plausible elasticities of demand under various changes in concentration, finding (a) the necessary marginal costs reductions to be quite sensitive to the elasticity of demand; (b) modest marginal costs reductions (e.g. 5 per cent) preventing price increases following concentrations of modest size; and (c) "implausible" large costs reductions (e.g. 20 per cent) to be necessary to prevent very large mergers from raising prices.

---

[88] P. Seabright, "Regulatory Capture, Subsidiarity and European Merger Policy" (1994) 57 *European Economy* 81 at p.93.
[89] See Ch.2, s.2.3.2.
[90] L.M. Froeb and G.J. Werden, "A Robust Test for Consumer Welfare-Enhancing Mergers among Sellers of a Homogeneous Product" (1998) 58 Econ. Lit. 367.

Most real-world markets tend to cover differentiated goods, however, and this is where the second paper by Werden[91] comes in. Considering a differentiated goods industry under Bertrand price competition, Werden demonstrates that marginal costs reductions necessary to restore pre-concentration prices can be calculated without making any assumptions about demand. The paper provides a robust and practical method for determining whether a particular merger enhances consumer welfare. When demand is elastic and pre-merger competition lively, synergies of 25 to 60 per cent would be necessary to prevent prices from rising and antitrust from intervening under the consumer welfare standard.

The inclusion of the redistribution effect, including all or part of the wealth transfer, will greatly reduce, or even eliminate, the possibility of successfully conducting an efficiency defence.[92] It is thus of the utmost importance to have clear guidance on how much weight should be given to the requirement that efficiency gains should be passed on and under which timescale. Also, a confrontation with these more advanced ideas inevitably superimposes directional guidance on how analytical concepts and techniques should be used to evaluate business behaviour as they may provide valuable insights, but do not always fit easily with existing theory and policy.[93]

9.2.3.3 Efficiencies in the EC Horizontal Merger Guidelines

The solution opted for in the EC Horizontal Merger Guidelines—similarly as under Section 4 of the US Horizontal Merger Guidelines[94]—is to acknowledge efficiencies as a potential counterbalance as part of an "overall competitive appraisal" within the meaning of Article 2(2) and (3) Merger Regulation.[95] This will be the case if the European Commission is in a position to conclude "on the basis of the sufficient evidence" that the efficiencies generated by the concentration are "likely to enhance the ability and incentive of the newly created entity to act pro-competitively for the benefit of consumers, thereby counteracting the adverse effects on competition" which the transaction might otherwise have (para.77). Thereto, the efficiencies have to (a) benefit consumers, (b) be specific to the concentration, and (c) be verifiable.

For efficiencies to benefit consumers, they should be substantial and timely, and should, in principle, benefit consumers in those relevant markets where it is otherwise likely that competition concerns would occur (para.79). The EC Horizontal Merger Guidelines list the following examples (paras 80–82):

[91] G.J. Werden, "A Robust Test for Consumer Welfare Enhancing Mergers among Sellers of Differentiated Products" (1996) 44 J. Ind. Econ. 409. See also above, at s.9.3.1, on the measurability of efficiencies under the modern approach.

[92] Concurring: S.S. Crampton, "Alternative Approaches to Competition Law" (1994) 17 World Competition 55 at p.68.

[93] In general, compare W.E. Kovacic, "Administrative Adjudication and the Use of New Economic Approaches in Antitrust Analysis" (1997) 5 Geo. Mason L. Rev. 313.

[94] For a discussion, see P.D. Camesasca, European Merger Control: Getting the Efficiencies Right (2000), pp.276–292.

[95] EC Horizontal Merger Guidelines, para.76, referring also to Recitals 4 and 29 of the Merger Regulation, as well as Art. 2(1)(b) of the Merger Regulation.

- cost savings in production, leading to a reduction in variable or marginal costs; reductions in fixed costs are considered less likely to result in lower prices for consumers, while cost reductions resulting from anti-competitive reductions in output are excluded;

- R&D and innovation efficiency gains leading to new or improved products;

- in the context of coordinated effects, costs savings leading to increased production and reduced prices, thereby reducing the newly created entity's incentive to coordinate its market behaviour.

Timeliness and the incentive on the part of the newly created entity to pass efficiency gains on to consumers is often related to the existence of competitive pressure. The EC Horizontal Merger Guidelines therefore apply something like a sliding scale approach: the greater the possible anti-competitive effects, "the more the European Commission has to be sure that the claimed efficiencies are substantial, likely to be realised, and to be passed on, to a sufficient degree, to the consumer". It is, as such, "highly unlikely" that mergers to monopoly would be waved through on the basis of efficiency claims (para.84).

For efficiencies to be specific to the concentration, they need to be a "direct consequence" of the concentration, and impossible to achieve to a similar extent by less anti-competitive alternatives. The firms involved have the onus to demonstrate that there are no less anti-competitive, realistic and attainable alternatives (such as licensing arrangements, or a cooperative joint venture).[96]

For efficiencies to be verifiable, the European Commission must be "reasonably certain" that the efficiencies are likely to materialise and are substantial enough to counteract a concentration's potential harm to consumers. If quantification is impossible, "it must be possible to foresee a clearly identifiable positive impact on consumers" whereto "the longer the start of the efficiencies is projected into the future, the less probability is assigned to them".[97]

At the time of writing, the EC Horizontal Merger Guidelines have not yet been tested on the point of efficiencies. If the experience with their US counterpart is of any guidance, however, then it may be expected that the occurrence of a successful efficiency defence will be relatively rare (which is also in line with what economic theory and research currently tell us). What is clear, however, is that the guidance provided is relatively vague and that the European Commission will leave it to the parties to come up with a convincing rationale.[98]

---

[96] See EC Horizontal Merger Guidelines, para.85.
[97] ibid., paras 86 and 88, the latter listing the type of evidence that can be relied upon.
[98] Outside DG Comp, it is to be noted that the European Commission's DG Enterprise has recently come up with two expert studies on the topic of efficiencies. See M. de la Mano, *For the Customer's Sake: The Competitive Effects of Efficiencies in European Merger Control* (Final Report Prepared for DG Enterprise, 2002); and S. Bishop, A. Lofaro, F. Rosati and J. Young, *The Efficiency-Enhancing Effects of Non-Horizontal Mergers* (Final Report Prepared for DG Enterprise, 2005)

9.3 Case discussions

In the third section of this chapter, four recent merger cases will be discussed. The aim of this section is to illustrate the increasing economic sophistication in assessing concentrations. The case analyses will be preceded by an overview of the available empirical techniques for assessing the likely effects of concentrations.

9.3.1 Quantifying market power

In recent years—and to an important measure as a result of regulatory demand in both the USA and Europe—a significant effort has been made in industrial organisation economics to provide empirical support for the assessment of market power and the likely effect of concentrations. Improved computer technology has enabled the collection of wider data sets at lower handling costs. Also, econometric technique has leapfrogged since the 1980s, while game theory has progressed the study of imperfect competition. The main instance where quantitative analysis is applied is for defining relevant markets.[99] However, each of the available techniques can be applied for the more general purpose of measuring market power. Ivaldi et al.[1] distinguish two segments of quantitative techniques: (a) empirical reduced-form analysis, and (b) empirical structural-form analysis.

Empirical reduced-form analysis includes statistical techniques that can be used to provide empirical evidence on issues of proof raised in antitrust cases. Numerous examples exist, such as regressions, factor analysis, correlations, Granger causality and co-integration tests. Using these techniques, the relationship that can be established between the facts of a specific case and economic models is either indirect, incomplete or informal. More useful for benchmarking purposes is the so-called empirical structural-form analysis. Here, the quantitative analysis is driven by an economic model, serving as a tool to interpret the relations that exist among the data measuring the competitive effects at hand (i.e. a behavioural approach). Two points are to be kept in mind. First, the relevance for the case at hand is not always clear-cut. Second, the availability and quality requirements of the data are tough. In practice, the choice between a reduced-form and a structural-form analysis, or a combination of the two, is often a matter of data availability.

---

[99] See Ch.4, s.4.2.2.2.
[1] See Annex to M. Ivaldi, B. Jullien, P. Rey, P. Seabright and J. Tirole, *Economics of Unilateral Effects* (Final Report Prepared for DG Comp, 2003) (also contains an overview of the various techniques and their technical implications as applied to the assessment of concentrations).

9.3.1.1 Structural-form analysis

The setting of a structural-form analysis is generally a static oligopoly with differentiated products, as this case underlies most modern industrial organisation analyses. Structural-form analysis starts from the presumption that market power does not result from the small number of competitors only; it also depends on the degree of substitutability among products. This is shown graphically in Box 9.2.

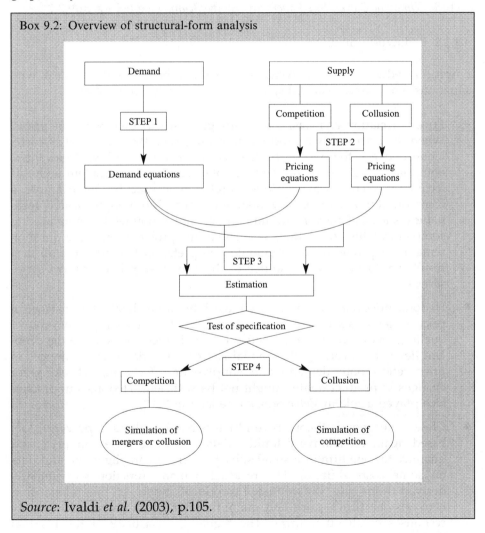

Box 9.2: Overview of structural-form analysis

Source: Ivaldi *et al.* (2003), p.105.

As shown in the figure, a first step normally is to define a demand model to approximate behaviour of consumers, then to specify supply (comprising a costs function and an objective function). The third step in a structural-form analysis uses statistical methods for fitting the economic model to the observed data, in order to obtain values for the demand and costs models, which, in turn, determine the equilibrium relationship between prices and market shares.

There are various techniques and applications including, among others, almost ideal demand system (AIDS) models, logit models, models testing for efficiency gains, market conduct tests using conjectural variations and dynamic models, and bidding market analyses. All require relatively detailed data sets and face a variety of theoretical and/or technical complications.[2] Frequently quoted examples where structural-form analysis was applied include *Kimberly-Clark/Scott Paper*[3] and *Volvo/Scania* (see below, at 9.3.2).

9.3.1.2 Reduced-form analysis

Empirical reduced-form analysis, on the other hand, exists to deal with situations where data availability is low. The main techniques[4] are:

- Price correlation analysis, using (straightforward) time series of prices. When the prices of two products move together, the coefficient of correlation between the two series of prices is positive and high (relevant to both market definition and evidence of collusion). The problem with this technique often lies in spurious correlations caused by, for example, a common component or raw material input.[5] More sophisticated techniques, such as Granger causality and co-integration tests, can be used to complement the correlations and solve this problem. Still, the question remains of providing an economic interpretation behind the statistical result (i.e. to identify the source of the relationship between two price series).

- Hedonic price analysis can be used to exhibit or invalidate the existence of price differentials (while monitoring for potential changes in product quality), based on price data and product characteristics. Here the problem lies with covering all potential sources of variability: as changes in price reflect both demand and supply-side effects, just checking for changes in product quality might not be sufficient. Hedonics in practice also played a role in *Volvo/Scania* (see later at 9.3.2).

- Closer to economic theory is residual demand analysis, a powerful tool based again on relatively limited data sets (time series on price and quantity for one firm or a small subset of firms in an oligopoly, and data on some costs shifters). The residual demand function subsequently derived from any differentiated products model is the relationship between one firm's price and quantity, taking into account the supply responses of all other firms. The higher the elasticity of the residual demand curve (i.e. the more competitive its market surrounding), the

---

[2] For detail, see M. Verbeek, *A Guide to Modern Econometrics* (2nd ed., 2004).
[3] Discussed earlier, in Ch.4, Box 4.3.
[4] For a technical overview, see S. Bishop and M. Walker, *The Economics of EC Competition Law* (2nd ed., 2002).
[5] See Ch.4, s.4.2.2.2.

lower the capacity of the firm to raise its prices. The problem lies in observing the costs of other firms, which more often than not will require the use of proxies that could introduce sources of measurement error. Conversely, with data available from all firms, this technique would equal performing a structural-form analysis.

- Price concentration studies evaluate the relationship between price and concentration in a given industry, based on the structure–conduct–performance paradigm. If one accepts that market structure measured by the level of concentration affects market performance measured by the level of price, then—where regressions show a strong positive correlation between price and concentration—a concentration which has a significant effect on concentration levels should raise anti-competitive concerns. When this technique is performed at firm level, it faces an endogeneity problem. The level of concentration measured by the firm's market share is usually not independent of the level of price itself. Even if feedback is accounted for, this technique does not account for efficiency gains and the existence of differentiated products, making its application questionable.[6]

By means of illustration of the various theoretical and empirical points discussed, sections 9.3.2 and 9.3.3 contain an analysis of two non-coordinated effects concentrations where sophisticated economics played a major role: *Volvo/Scania* and *GE/Instrumentarium*.

9.3.1.3 Coordinated effects

Compared to the difficulties related to proving non-coordinated effects, reviewing coordinated effects is made all the more difficult as there are no really good economic models available to incorporate the various factors listed above, let alone models that would subsequently yield clear-cut predictions in such an inherently forward looking exercise as is merger control.

While the evaluation of both non-coordinated effects and coordinated effects calls for a structural quantitative approach, establishing the link between structure and conduct requires much more prospective and qualitative analysis for tacit collusion-type transactions. Two recent examples from the precedent case law illustrate this point well: *Oracle/PeopleSoft* and *Sony/BMG*. They will be discussed in sections 9.3.4 and 9.3.5 below.

9.3.2 Case example: *Volvo/Scania*

One of the first examples of an in-depth review of non-coordinated effects is offered by the European Commission's prohibition of the proposed *Volvo/*

---

[6] For a detailed discussion of the structure–conduct–performance paradigm and the wider policy issues entailed, we refer to Ch.3, s.3.5.

Scania concentration.[7] The Commission found this deal would cause serious competition law concerns by creating or strengthening dominant positions in a number of national markets for heavy trucks (Finland, Ireland, Norway and Sweden), touring coaches (Finland and the UK), intercity buses (Denmark, Finland, Norway and Sweden) and city buses (Denmark, Finland, Ireland, Norway and Sweden).[8] The case provides a classic example of a horizontal merger creating single firm dominance in a number of differentiated product markets.

9.3.2.1 Competitive issues

In finding that the concentration would create single firm dominance, the European Commission gave strong weight to the merged company's high market share in the relevant markets (ranging from 50 to 90 per cent). Moreover, Volvo and Scania were each other's closest competitors with a long history of significant competition between them. Furthermore, the barriers to entry were high, requiring large investment over a significant period of time. In the light of industry critique of this decision (mainly arguing that the Commission failed to take sufficient account of the globalisation of the markets, the existence of potential competitors and the fact that European companies must grow in order to face competition from huge competitors outside Europe),[9] as well as the fact that the subsequently proposed *Volvo/Renault* concentration[10] was approved, this case illustrates well the advantages of an analysis supported by quantitative evidence over an analysis based purely on qualitative argumentation.

The core issue in this case boiled down to the definition of the relevant geographic market, which turned out to be national in scope. In its assessment the European Commission relied on sophisticated econometric simulation analysis,[11] most illustrative of which is the heavy trucks market (to which the remainder of the discussion will be limited).

---

[7] Case COMP/M.1672 *Volvo/Scania* [2001] O.J. L 143/74.
[8] *ibid.*, paras 213 and 331.
[9] Compare S.O. Spinks, "Recent Cases under the Merger Regulation", Speech, Brussels, October 10, 2000.
[10] Case COMP/M.1980 *Volvo/Renault V.I.* [2001] O.J. C 301/23. It should be noted that Volvo committed to several remaining links with Scania, which then established a strategic alliance with the Volkswagen group. Compare Vereinigte Wirtschaftsdienste, VW—Beabsichtigen nicht den Kauf des Volvo-Anteils an Scania, March 22, 2001; Reuters, VW-Aufsichtsrat billigt Erwerb von Scania-Anteilen, April 2, 2000.
[11] A public version is available as a CEPR working paper (No.2697): see M. Ivaldi and F. Verboven, *Quantifying the Effects from Horizontal Mergers in European Competition Policy* (2000). Compare also F. Verboven, "Het Gebruik van Simulatieanalyse in het Europese Fusiebeleid" (2001) 2 Markt en Mededinging 60; W. Bishop, "Economic Aspects of Recent Merger Cases", Speech, Brussels, April 27, 2001.

9.3.2.2 Market definition

In the published decision, the product market description is rather short and does not refer to the SSNIP test,[12] subdividing the truck market into three categories: light duty trucks (under 5 tons), medium duty trucks (5–16 tons) and heavy duty trucks (over 16 tons). In the heavy truck market (the only category where the parties' market shares were substantial) a further sub-segmentation was noted between rigid trucks (integrated vehicles from which no semi-trailer can be detached) and tractor trucks (vehicles from which the semi-trailer can be detached). Although full substitution between these two sub-segments is not possible, the European Commission found that switching production from the supply point of view does not involve substantial costs. "Heavy trucks" thus constituted the relevant product market.

The analysis of the geographic market was carried out in more detail, resulting in the conclusion that the markets are national in scope.[13] The evidence available to the Commission showed that Volvo and other suppliers of heavy trucks have applied significantly different prices and margins for comparable products in different Member States (see below). This, as well as non-price evidence (models and technical configurations differ considerably because of local consumer preferences and national technical requirements, the importance of profits from after-sales services may induce dealers to charge higher prices to foreign customers and there are large variations in market shares across countries), warrants the conclusion that conditions of competition in the heavy truck market differ from one Member State to another.

9.3.2.3 Simulation analysis, hedonics and regressions: will the concentration raise prices?

To get to this conclusion, the European Commission relied in part on the aforementioned simulation analysis describing the price setting in the market for heavy trucks. In short, this econometric method refines the outcome commonly obtained by using more indirect concentration indices (see below) by taking into account not only differences in average price between different markets (as in a classic price concentration study), but also differences in the quality of the product sold and differences in the pricing strategy of the different manufacturers. This type of analysis requires high quality data from both the parties to the merger, as well as from competitors, while also necessitating some restrictive assumptions to be made.[14]

The starting point is a so-called hedonic price analysis, which compares the price of products whose quality changes over a period of time or over product space, due either to technological or subjective factors, or other services and

---

[12] See Case COMP/M.1672 *Volvo/Scania* [2001] O.J. L 143/74, paras 13–30. On the SSNIP test, see Ch.4, s.4.2.2.

[13] *ibid.*, paras 31–75.

[14] Compare the aforementioned materials on the case, as well as Office of Fair Trading, *Quantitative Techniques in Competition Analysis* (1999), pp.49–52, discussing hedonic price analyses.

optional equipment. Clearly this is the case in differentiated product markets, such as trucks which come in many different configurations (different body types, engine sizes, axle configurations, cab sizes and different carrying capacities). Furthermore, customer requirements differ across Europe (e.g. Nordic customers are allowed a larger carrying capacity; customers located in hilly areas need larger engines). In such circumstances price analysis has to be adjusted to properly account for quality differences or quality changes, purging the appraisal that pure price differences between standardised products can be isolated.

Using regression techniques it is possible to estimate the price position of the different manufacturers in each country, while allowing for the variations in the configurations of the trucks sold. These purged prices can then be used to carry out other price tests on the basis of which the inter-substitutability of the different trucks can be estimated. The study thus finds that a hypothetical price increase of 5 per cent is profitable in almost all countries under scrutiny (except Austria, Germany, Italy and Luxembourg). A different picture emerges for a hypothetical price increase of 10 per cent. On the one hand, such a price increase is unprofitable for nine countries. On the other hand, for markets where the price increase is profitable, it is frequently more profitable than the 5 per cent increase. This is most notable in Sweden, Norway, Finland and Denmark. The following box may illustrate this.

Box 9.3: Case Volvo/Scania: potential market power for heavy trucks			
	Profit change of merging firms from alternative price increases		
Price increase	**5**	**10**	**25**
Austria	−0.70	−5.96	−35.09
Belgium	1.05	0.49	−8.63
Denmark	1.63	2.09	−2.25
Finland	251	2.98	−4.89
France	0.18	−1.40	−13.86
Germany	−0.23	−2.79	−19.70
Greece	1.39	−0.02	−14.49
Ireland	2.12	170	−10.02
Italy	−1.14	−7.63	−41.79
Luxembourg	−0.07	−1.51	−11.86
Netherlands	0.77	−2.47	−26.70
Norway	2.74	358	−2.37
Portugal	1.16	−0.12	−13.37
Spain	0.23	−2.05	−18.65
Sweden	2.95	491	567

United Kingdom	1.28	0.49	−11.04
European Union	1.00	49	−14.32

Source: M. Ivaldi and F. Verboven, *Quantifying the Effects from Horizontal Mergers in European Competition Policy* (2000).

The results contained in Box 9.3 may also be interpreted in terms of the market definition based on the SSNIP test. Following the rule that the relevant market is the minimum number of firms that can profitably raise prices by 5 per cent, heavy trucks manufactured by the merged entity by itself would constitute the relevant market in 12 out of 16 countries. Under a 10 per cent increase the merged entity constitutes the relevant market in 7 out of 16 countries.

Although these impressive numbers are still considered "conservative" by the authors of the study,[15] the European Commission, in the end, chose not to use it and based its decision on the more traditional evidence available (see above). The reason for this lies in data shortcomings. Due to the time constraints imposed by the Merger Regulation, the study relied on list prices for one type of truck in the various countries. These prices, however, are far from the economic reality and the true transaction prices actually paid (taking into account discounts, etc.). Moreover, transaction prices differ substantially across Europe (list prices only serve as the starting point for the bargaining ploy). Furthermore, the type of truck chosen was not sold in all countries. In sum, one might say that the result was that the study gave "information on products which no-one bought at prices that no-one paid".[16] But, nevertheless, this case shows that econometrics, if applied carefully, can play an important role in merger control proceedings.

9.3.3 Case example: *GE/Instrumentarium*

In early 2003 General Electric announced its US$2.3 billion purchase of the Finnish medical equipment maker Instrumentarium (operating under the brands Datex-Ohmeda, Spacelabs Medical, and Ziehm). The European Commission and the US DOJ conducted largely parallel investigations primarily focused on the potential unilateral effects of GE's acquisition, referring to the possibility that the proposed concentration would lead to a post-merger price increase due to the unilateral action of the merged parties. In contrast to another parallel merger review in 2001 involving GE, the controversial EC prohibition of GE's proposed acquisition of Honeywell, in this instance, both jurisdictions arrived at a similar decision, with the EC reaching its decision

[15] M. Ivaldi and F. Verboven, *Quantifying the Effects from Horizontal Mergers in European Competition Policy* (2000), p.19.
[16] W. Bishop, "Economic Aspects of Recent Merger Cases", Speech, Brussels, April 27, 2001.

during what has been termed an effective transatlantic coordination on an analysis of a common set of facts.[17]

9.3.3.1 Competitive issues

The European Commission opened a detailed second-phase investigation to assess the unilateral effects in terms of the competitive impact of the transaction particularly in the markets for patient monitors, C-arm mobile X-ray machines, and mammography equipment. The investigation also included clinical information systems and software purchased by hospitals, where the Commission had been concerned that the companies would hold too high a post-merger share. Moreover, the Commission was also interested in the possible vertical foreclosure effect of the strong position Instrumentarium had in a complementary market for the sale of anaesthesia delivery machines, which need to interconnect easily with patient monitors during surgical and other operating room procedures.

Despite high post-merger market shares in several product markets, the merger was ultimately cleared subject to a set of relatively novel structural and behavioural undertakings. In order to receive that regulatory approval, GE undertook the sale of Instrumentarium's Spacelabs patient monitor subsidiary and entered into a series of supply agreements with its purchaser to ensure that its divested anaesthesia equipment, patient monitors and clinical information systems will interoperate with independent third parties' devices.[18]

The merger review analysis in Europe was notable in that a number of empirical economic analyses were employed by the European Commission and the parties with a high level of transparency. The Commission's internal devil's advocate panel was used to scrutinise the arguments of the case team, leading to a significant change to the course of the investigation. Such a process paved the way for a model of merger reviews and reliance on econometric evidence to follow under the European Commission's Chief Economist.

9.3.3.2 Product market definition

The European Commission's overlap analysis between the merging parties initially identified five overlap product markets resulting from the proposed merger.

First, patient monitors are machines that monitor physiological reactions during medical treatment and recovery. These monitors are used in a range of medical care areas in a hospital or other clinical setting and can be manufactured and assembled to serve customised to that area's specific monitoring

---

[17] The level of cooperation included extensive discussions, covering timing of the reviews and key substantive questions, including the appropriate market definitions.

[18] The US DOJ concluded that the transaction would substantially lessen competition in the sale of monitors used for patients requiring critical care and mobile C-arms used for basic surgical and vascular procedures. The DOJ settlement reached with GE in February 2004, required the company to divest two Instrumentarium businesses—Spacelabs and the Ziehm C-arm X-ray machines for surgical and vascular procedures.

needs. This customisation results in a level of segmentation across patient monitors reflecting price variations and differences in purchasing routines/ processes in each care area:

- Perioperative (PO) monitors are specifically used in operating room and post-operative settings typically connected or networked to anaesthesia machines. Purchasing of such equipment is unique to the operating room care area and is orchestrated by the anaesthesiologists associated with that area.

- Critical care (CC) monitors differ in that they do not require the ability to be networked to anaesthesia machines and are generally used to monitor patient vital signs including blood pressure, body temperature, cardiac activity and other patient responses. Procurement of critical care monitors originates in a specific care area separate from anaesthesia and surgical specialists, typically with physician and other clinical specialists.

Because of the technical specification made at the time of purchase, substitution between PO and CC monitors is not practicable. Additionally, for large health care institutions, purchasing of such equipment is typically organised through a tender process designed to capture the specific needs of each clinical care area. Review of supply-side considerations found that interchangeability in production processes was relatively easy due to flexible production processes and that monitors are assembled components with easy access to components from outsourced third parties. In spite of this degree of production flexibility, the European Commission found that R&D activities tend to focus uniquely on either PO or CC monitor features contributing to greater difficulty for the R&D benefits to be applied across patient monitor segments. Moreover, software innovations raise technical barriers between the two monitor segments. PO monitor advances reflect improved abilities to measure neuro-muscular systems while advances in CC monitors reflect concern with the ability to non-invasively monitor blood pressure, temperature and cardiac activities. Recustomising CC monitors to serve PO applications is prohibitively difficult. The Commission found this separate product market segmentation is also reflected in the varying market shares both the merging parties and their competitors exhibit across these monitor segments.

Second, mobile C-arms are X-ray machines used in clinical situations to provide continuous viewing during diagnostic, surgical and interventional procedures. The European Commission's market investigation concluded that there existed three separate product markets for mobile C-arms customised to use in cardiac (or advanced vascular), vascular, and lower-end orthopaedic and other simpler surgical procedures.

Third, mammography devices are specific types of X-ray machines designed to produce views of internal breast tissue. A further distinction was made by the European Commission between the traditional analogue imaging and the recent (improved) digital imaging technique. The digital technique is likely to replace the analogue over time, but the Commission determined that they currently were in separate product markets.

Fourth, anaesthesia equipment used to deliver anaesthesia gases to surgical patients was determined to be a unique product market, due to the high degree of product differentiation and the unique specifications this equipment must meet. The Commission relied on a recent prior case to support this view.

Fifth, clinical information systems are used for automating patient records, medical readings and other clinical information. The Commission found these systems constitute a separate product market due to their distinct software enabling the exchange of electronic medical data in real time at the point of care.

9.3.3.3 Geographic market definition

The parties to the concentration proposed that the relevant geographic markets for this range of medical devices are EEA-wide based on a common legal framework set out by the 1993 Medical Devices Directive (93/42/EC). It was argued that this view was also based on supply-side substitution and centrally organised production, low transportation costs and low barriers to access to or establishment of a viable distribution network.

The European Commission's market investigation showed that the markets for patient monitors (PO and CC), C-arms and mammography devices, anaesthesia machines and CIS systems are actually national in scope. This definition was based on the observation of varying market positions across Member States among the product manufacturers. The Commission concluded that these different market structures suggest that competitive conditions vary across Member States leading to distinct geographic markets. The Commission found this consistent with its findings of the unique list prices and varying discount levels across Member States, reflecting different discounting schemes and different net transaction prices across Member States. The need for effective product distribution and reliable after-sales services including capacity for local training, installation and continuous maintenance also contributes smaller, national markets.

9.3.3.4 Theories of consumer harm and anti-competitive effects: bidding markets, differentiated markets

As in prior unilateral effects cases, the European Commission conducted typical market share and market structure analysis, as well as assessing qualitative information regarding the nature of the competition in the defined markets. What is notable is that in this review, a number of empirical (and econometric) analyses were undertaken by the parties and the Commission, particularly in analysing bidding data in evaluating whether the market shares of the merging parties overestimate or underestimate their market power. Specifically, the Commission examined the available bidding data and concluded that GE and Instrumentarium were close competitors. GE was the most frequent second bidder to Instrumentarium in customer bids for PO monitoring equipment.

The European Commission concluded that the market for PO monitors, in particular, is a mature, consolidating market made up of differentiated products offered by the range of suppliers. Hospital customers express their demand through calls for tenders with detailed technical specifications, limiting the set of suppliers able to submit credible bids. The Commission concluded that the market shares of the merging parties were large enough in some of the national markets where the post-merger shares were in the range of 50–60 per cent and higher, with several post-merger shares twice as large as the next closest competitor, to conclude the possible existence of a dominant position.

The merging parties argued that the bidding nature of the market reflected a situation where major rivals as well as small players could act as competitive constraints to any attempted price increase. Therefore, they concluded that market shares do not accurately reflect the actual competition in such a market. The European Commission took the view that, although the markets for monitors and other equipment were procured through a bidding or tender process, the actual value of such tenders is relatively low and the annual number of tenders relatively high to suggest that this market functions more like a standard differentiated product market with customer preferences captured by the technical specifications. Therefore, once customer preferences are expressed and the range of eligible bidders is determined, the tendering process reflects more a buyer-negotiation process where customers would switch to another eligible supplier in response to a material price increase. To the extent that this substitution between products was observed, the European Commission determined that market shares do contain important competitive information reflecting actual purchasing decisions.[19]

To assess this issue, the Commission undertook an in-depth analysis of the available bidding and win–loss data to assess the nature of competition and the actual closeness of substitution between the monitored products. In this effort the Commission accepted data and econometric studies from both the merger parties and third party competitors as well as gathered data from other parties during its investigation. These statistical analyses measured both the win–loss patterns as well as the level of discount offered as an indication of the closeness of substitution between competitors and their products. This allowed the Commission to assess the competitive constraints exerted by the merging parties on each other by revealing that for several Member States, Instrumentarium appeared to bid lower when GE was also present in the bidding and further noted that when GE and Instrumentarium were present, Philips tended to bid lower than when only one of the two merging parties was present. The European Commission concluded that, post-merger, Philips would likely offer smaller discounts and be less competitively constrained during the bidding process.

Given that the merging parties were each other's closest competitors at least in some Member States, the Commission's analysis of the available bidding data also was used to quantify the possible price effect of the proposed acquisition—demonstrating that GE's percentage price discounts to customers were higher when Instrumentarium was also participating in the bidding.

---

[19] See also Paul Klemperer, *Bidding Markets* (Report prepared for the UK Competition Commission, 2005) for a detailed discussion of the "fallacy" of the "bidding market" argument.

A notable milestone was reached during this merger review process when the European Commission gave the merging parties' economist confidential direct access to the data submitted, contributing to a new level of transparency and statistical robustness of the conclusions.

On the basis of the bidding data provided and collected, and the Commission's hospital survey data, an evaluation of the competitive role played by the smaller fringe suppliers showed that such fringe players could not currently be considered as credible rivals in the PO monitor market as they often lacked the perceived quality reputation and the established distribution network customers preferred. The ability to provide a high level of maintenance and other after-market service over the estimated seven to ten year product life cycle was critical, and something smaller firms were unable to effectively provide.

The extent to which the potential for competitive constraints to be provided by the powerful hospital and other health care institutional buyers was found by the European Commission to be limited because the customer base is highly fragmented and the value of each tender is relatively small in proportion to a supplier's sales. Also, the technical requirements for PO monitors limited the number of suppliers hospital customers face in any given tender, restricting the potential for countervailing buyer power.

Although capacity and productive barriers to entry appear to be low in the PO monitor market, the European Commission's market investigation showed that it can take between two and five years and significant regulatory approval to develop and introduce a new PO monitor. Under such conditions, smaller fringe competitors cannot be expected to represent significant entry/expansion following the transaction.

In light of the European Commission's investigation, it was determined that the merger would create a dominant position in the market for PO monitors in five national markets: Spain, the UK, Sweden, France and Germany.

Using the same set of statistical analyses performed in assessing the nature of PO monitors, the Commission concluded that in the market for CC monitors, a GE and Instrumentarium merger would not lead to the creation of a dominant position largely because GE and Instrumentarium were not each other's closest substitutes, as a greater number of firms are able to credibly supply hospital demand for CC monitors.

In the mobile C-arms markets, for both vascular and lower-end X-ray applications, similar analysis of the bidding data revealed Instrumentarium not to be GE's closest competitor, leading the Commission to conclude that the post-merger market share data may overstate the impact of the combined market power.[20]

The European Commission viewed the analogue mammography market to

---

[20] The US DOJ concluded that a significant number of customers view the GE and Instrumentarium orthopaedic-vascular C-arm products as close substitutes, and do not view the products of other vendors to be equally close. As is typical in US merger decisions, there is little publicly available description beyond the documents issued with formal Complaint that reflects the nature and methodological approach to the US review and decision. Although, the DOJ did retain outside "economic auction specialists", it is not widely known how the US DOJ used or interpreted any empirical bidding analyses in its review.

be different from the other medical equipment reviewed in this merger in that the purchase process is not conducted through tendering but sales are made more frequently to private entities through more typical price quote-negotiation processes provided by the local distributor. As stated above, the mammography market has become a mature market—in the sense "that this technology has reached its limits"[21] with demand-side sales declining as obsolete equipment is replaced by digital equipment over the next three years. Combined with the results of the statistical analysis of the available bidding data, Instrumentarium was not found to be GE's closest competitor at both the EEA and Member State level. Furthermore, the presence of Instrumentarium as an independent bidder in a tender was not found to systematically influence the size of the discount offered by GE.

Even though the merged entity would have significant post-merger market shares of analogue mammography equipment, the evolution of these shares had been declining in all the Member States where the horizontal overlap is significant, leading the European Commission to conclude that the merger would not lead to the creation of a dominant position in the market for mammography devices. As analogue mammography devices are soon to be replaced by digital devices, the Commission assessed the impact the merger would have on the emerging digital mammography market. Because Instrumentarium did not currently serve, nor did it have plans to introduce a digital mammography device, the Commission concluded that the merger would not reduce potential competition or limit innovation in the digital mammography field and that there exists a sufficient number of potential suppliers such that competition would not be affected by the transaction.

9.3.3.5 Vertical effects, foreclosure

In addition to the horizontal effects, the Commission concluded that there would be vertical effects relating to the market power stemming from Instrumentarium's well recognised brand and its position as one of the two market leaders in anaesthesia delivery machines. Relying to some extent on a previous merger decision in the same market, the Commission determined that there were high barriers to entry in that considerable sunk cost investment, including a high level of R&D, a well developed distribution and service network, and close commercial relationships with hospital and other health care institutions, is needed to successfully serve this segment.

The vertical issue is related to the fact that anaesthesia machines and PO monitors are complementary products used simultaneously during patient surgery, requiring not only a commercial marketing link but also an interoperability link. These links require cooperation between the anaesthesia device supplier and the PO monitor supplier to effectively integrate the devices. Independent PO suppliers will need access to detailed anaesthesia machine product specifications in order to effectively interconnect performance on this critical device. The need for this integration led the Commission

[21] Case COMP/M.3083 *GE/Instrumentarium* [2004] O.J. L 109/1, para.254.

to propose that post-merger the combined entity would be in the position to foreclose its rivals' access to its anaesthesia machines by withholding cooperation with independent PO suppliers in the timely sharing of changes or upgrades in system architecture or other cost-raising effects.

In light of the proposed transaction, the Commission was concerned that the combined GE/Instrumentarium entity would be in a position to exploit its anaesthesia machine market power to the benefit of increasing its own PO market power. The Commission presumably recognised that this incentive would have existed for Instrumentarium alone, before the merger, but that Instrumentarium's pre-merger product range was limited enough to force it to use an open architecture approach in order to maximise the level of interoperability between its anaesthesia machines and other PO monitor suppliers' products. This vertical foreclosure issue was acknowledged early on in the merger investigation process, prompting GE to offer a remedy to divest Instrumentarium's Spacelabs division while the in-depth investigation was still ongoing. In light of this offer, the Commission did not have to come to a conclusion of the potential vertical foreclosure effect, but instead used the remaining investigation to market test the proposed commitments.

9.3.3.6 Remedies

While divestiture commitments remain the European Commission's typical remedy in response to the horizontal competition concerns identified by the Commission, a far-reaching and novel remedies package was reached including both structural and behavioural commitments.

Instrumentarium's Spacelabs division, which manufactures the gas monitoring module and anaesthesia supply machines, was divested. In addition, GE agreed to divest all tangible assets and proprietary know-how related to the Spacelabs division of Instrumentarium. GE also offered three OEM supply agreements for purposes of supplying PO monitors to interconnect with anaesthesia machines manufactured by Instrumentarium's Datex-Ohmeda division, allowing this divested business to offer combined PO systems and thereby achieve a level of commercial viability. The goal is to ensure that the divestiture will enable the purchaser to be a "competitive force of size, presence and strength similar to GE's position" in the PO market prior to the merger.[22] This comprises a range of assets particularly specific to the patient PO monitoring platform. This will also include the transfer of key personnel enabling the creation of sales teams in every Member State and appropriate distribution staff with access to anaesthesiologists in charge of procurement.

In addition, the purchaser of the divested assets will have access for ten years to Instrumentarium's gas modules for PO monitor applications on favourable pricing terms. It is interesting to note that prior to the merger, GE did not have access to these gas modules, so this feature of the remedy package is likely to put the purchaser in a more advantageous position than GE held prior to the merger. Ultimately, with modifications, the Commission

[22] Case COMP/M.3083 *GE/Instrumentarium* [2004] O.J. L 109/1, para.338.

reached the Open Interface Commitment, specifically addressing the inter-operability between anaesthesia machines and third party PO and CC monitors. This behavioural remedy is designed to ensure access to technical assistance and consultation and to provide independent third parties with access to physical components and devices at reasonable non-discriminatory market prices.[23]

9.3.4 Case example: *Oracle/PeopleSoft*

In October 2004, the European Commission approved, without any conditions, Oracle Corporation's proposed US$7.7 billion hostile takeover of rival software company PeopleSoft.[24] This approval followed a US judge's ruling permitting the merger to proceed in September. The US Department of Justice (DOJ) had sought to block the transaction and embarked on a five-week trial in the northern district of California.

9.3.4.1 Competitive issues

The European Commission had been primarily concerned about the impact of Oracle's acquisition on the markets for business applications software (as opposed to consumer software) called enterprise application software (EAS), which is used by companies to coordinate and plan their financial and human resources activities. The relevant market was ultimately defined as high-function financial (FMS) and human resource (HR) management sold by Oracle, PeopleSoft and worldwide leader SAP.

The Oracle/PeopleSoft merger was jointly reviewed by the US and EC merger authorities and is notable in that it represents an interesting view into the nature and extent of convergence between the interpretation of economic evidence and its effect on the enforcement outcomes in these two key jurisdictions.[25] It stands as a good example of both the complexities and the investigational efficiencies that can result from such a joint review. In addition,

---

[23] This commitment went further to appoint an independent trustee assisted by an independent expert with knowledge of the relevant industry and with recourse to fast track arbitration dispute resolution procedure under the control of the Commission. OSI Systems, Inc of Hawthorne, California, agreed in January 2004 to purchase Spacelabs Medical, for approximately US$57 million.

[24] Case COMP/M.3216 *Oracle/PeopleSoft* [2005] O.J. L 218/6.

[25] US DOJ, FTC and EC Commission, *Best Practices on Cooperation in Merger Investigations* (2002). Where the US and EC are reviewing the same transaction, "both jurisdictions have an interest in reaching, insofar as possible, consistent, or at least non-conflicting, outcomes". This joint statement is designed to promote "fully-informed decision-making on the part of both sides' authorities, to minimise the risk of divergent outcomes on both sides of the Atlantic, to facilitate coherence and compatibility in remedies, to enhance the efficiency of their respective investigations, to reduce burdens on merging parties and third parties, and to increase the overall transparency of the merger review processes". Available on the DG Comp website. Although there have been many joint EC/US merger reviews since the Merger Regulation took effect in 1990, surprisingly only one case, Case COMP/M.2220 *GE/Honeywell* [2004] O.J. L 48/1, resulted in a significantly divergent enforcement outcome.

the European Commission's decision is notable because it marks the first time its five-month merger approval process has been stretched out to more than a year (such long reviews are more common in the USA). The deal was notified on October 10, 2003, suspended once and then reactivated, and then suspended a second time in April.

9.3.4.2 Product market definition

The European Commission reached a preliminary opinion that the transaction could lead to competitive concerns in the separate markets for HR and FMS high-function software solutions for large corporations served by Oracle, PeopleSoft and SAP.

To further improve its market definition process, the EC based its identification of high-function HR and FMS software demand using a three-pronged selection criteria identifying high-function software as bids as those (a) with a net licence value of greater than €1 million; (b) sold to corporations with €1 billion in annual revenues; (c) with at least 10,000 users/employees. The net licence value of an amount greater than €1 million was based on its market investigation and an analysis of the Oracle bid data. The great majority of respondents in the market investigation confirmed that 10,000 employees/users and €1 billion in company annual revenues would represent appropriate thresholds for large and complex firms requiring high-function HR and FMS software. These thresholds are also consistent with industry reports.

Both merger review authorities in the USA and in Europe excluded the competitive impact provided by outsourcers and best-of-breed[26] solution vendors, arguing that outsourcers overwhelmingly use Oracle, PeopleSoft or SAP as platforms in providing their outsource service, suggesting that those vendors will ultimately control its prices and availability in the outsource arena. Best-of-breed solution providers were also found to not be in the relevant market due to the high integration costs associated with the implementation of a number of small packages to provide a full range of core functionality.

9.3.4.3 Geographic market definition

The geographic dimension of the market was informed by average regional discount data presented by Oracle showing that average discounts between Europe and the USA were virtually identical (approximately 45 per cent), suggesting that European and US prices are likely constraints on each other. Based on this evidence, the European Commission concluded that the relevant geographic market was worldwide, as no specific barriers or other technical hurdles exist to limit suppliers from responding to large corporate bids

---

[26] "Best-of-breed" suppliers offer sophisticated solutions for a particular pillar of Enterprise Application Software, but do not offer a range of applications (suites). Best-of-breed software therefore has to be integrated in the existing applications environment that might require substantial integration costs.

worldwide, although it did allow that the relative strength or share of sales may vary by region.[27]

9.3.4.4 Theories of consumer harm and anti-competitive effects: initial simulations

The European Commission initially believed that the transaction could lead to both unilateral effects and coordinated effects, where the three-to-two resulting duopoly could successfully coordinate, with no viable outsiders able to destabilise such a duopoly.[28] On the basis of this early appraisal, the Commission issued a Statement of Objections in March 2003, and following the Oral Hearing, issued a request for further information. It is important to note that the early bidding data provided the basis for developing the theory of consumer harm. The information and economic evidence provided in response to the request for further information provided more extensive data. The economic analysis of these data contributed to the US trial court finding for Oracle, and the European Commission revising its preliminary opinions on the nature of the market and the impact on competition, finally granting unconditional clearance.

At the outset of the parallel merger reviews, both authorities were influenced by a (admittedly simple) regression analysis provided by PeopleSoft (it is important to note that PeopleSoft was a hostile acquisition target) demonstrating that, on average, the elimination of one bidder/competitor would reduce the average discount by 15 per cent. The numerous customer responses were also consistent with the notion that for some customers, the product differentiation was such that Oracle and PeopleSoft were the only two vendors capable of bidding on a given customer HR or FMS application. Using the same body of data and evidence, both authorities came to an early conclusion that Oracle was PeopleSoft's closest competitor, and that the elimination of such a key vendor would lock-in some customers, which would likely lead to increased prices and reduced product innovation.

The European Commission maintains that merger simulation is a useful tool in analysing the potential effects of a proposed merger. Merger simulations conducted by both authorities also played a role in the preliminary competitive assessments. The EC economists used an auction model to simulate the effect of the merger, which allowed for uncertainty about the buyers' valuation of the alternative solutions. The model predicted not only substantial price increases due to the reduction of bidders from three to two, but also tried to estimate the effect of the merger on consumer surplus. The European Commission submits that the use of simulation models depends critically on the ability of the model to adequately capture the fundamental mechanisms that

---

[27] The European Commission did note in its decision that Oracle had originally argued in an oral hearing that the geographic market was EEA-wide, whereas in the US trial it argued that the geographic market was global.

[28] The DOJ did not directly allege or present evidence at trial regarding coordinated effects, but did offer argument in a post-trial brief suggesting that it was plausible for a post-merger Oracle and SAP to tacitly collude to allocate markets along industry sectors.

drive the behaviour of the different market participants. However, it maintains that such necessary simplifying assumptions are not fatal as any economic model used in a prospective merger analysis is necessarily based on assumptions and that models can provide a high degree of transparency of the underlying assumptions and logical consistency in the model framework.

9.3.4.5 Theories of consumer harm and anti-competitive effects: in-depth assessment of sophisticated bidding data

On September 25, 2004 the US trial court rejected the DOJ's product market definition and found instead that Microsoft and Lawson participated in the market, as well as other (mid-market) vendors, best-of-breed solution and other companies providing outsourcing. The US trial court found that there was no reliable way to split the customers between high-function and the smaller mid-market segments and, therefore, combined the two segments. The US court also rejected the DOJ's geographic market definition, finding the market for business software was global. Consequently, the US court found that the DOJ had failed to establish that the merged firm could exercise market power and thus, that the merger would not substantially lessen competition.

When additional information and more extensive bidding data (Oracle submitted bid data for over 700 bids with detailed information about the list price, number and identity of bidders) were provided after the conclusion of the US trial, the European Commission also revised its opinion of the number of viable competitors serving its high-function HR and FMS markets. The benefit of these data and the trial court deliberations allowed the EC to conduct additional and more robust econometric analyses demonstrating that the number and identity of the bidders did not systematically affect the discounts offered by Oracle.

This finding opened the possibility of an evaluation of the extent to which other vendors could be considered viable competitors in the high-function HR and FMS markets. Although the data limitations did not permit detailed specification for econometric testing, the European Commission did accept that it provided anecdotal evidence that other suppliers besides SAP and PeopleSoft were able to win bids (or qualify as runner-up to other bids) for high-function HR and FMS applications with a net licence value of more than €1 million—including Lawson, Intentia, IFS, QAD and Microsoft. This new information also suggested that software product repositioning among these additional vendors was possible.

In its final evaluation of the bidding data, the European Commission determined that the absence of a significant, appreciable effect on the number and identity of the final round bidders in the bidding data regressions did not enable it to show anti-competitive effects from the merger. However, this result was not taken as proof that the merger would *not* have harmful effects on customers. In addition to these empirical results, the Commission based its decision on the broader set of competitor and customer questionnaire responses, and the large body of documentary and US trial court evidence. The interpretation of this broader information set allowed it to conclude that the software buyers were sophisticated enough to structure and control the bidding process such that maximum competitive pressure would be exerted on the bidders, sometimes re-inviting previously excluded bidders. Combined with the continued presence of SAP (always recognised to be a larger player in the EU), the European Commission finally concluded that Oracle would not be in a position to raise prices post-merger.

Furthermore, to the extent that coordination between market participants would be facilitated as a result of the merger, the Commission concluded that given that the market includes not only the three main players but at least four other smaller, but viable players, a theory of consumer harm based on coordinating competitive behaviour could not be plausible. The range and diversity of the full range of vendors made it very unlikely that the *Airtours* conditions could be met in a market which also includes Lawson, Intentia, IFS, QAD and Microsoft, as it would likely be difficult to reach common understanding, especially in such a differentiated product market where transparency is reduced and retaliation made more difficult.

9.3.5 Case example: *Sony/BMG*

In January 2004, Sony and Bertelsmann notified the competition authorities of their plan to create a full-function joint venture (SonyBMG) for their global recorded music business. This concentration was also investigated by the competition authorities in the USA and in Europe but resulted in much less transparency about the parallel processes.[29] The US FTC opened an investigation, but produced no published account of its reasoning or proceedings before closing its inquiry in July 2004 without taking any enforcement action, nine days after the European Commission decided to clear the joint venture. In a press release, the FTC stated that:

> "... throughout the course of their respective investigations, the FTC and the EC Competition Directorate's staff consulted and cooperated with each other under the terms of their 1991 cooperation agreement and 2002 Best Practices on Cooperation in Merger Investigations".[30]

9.3.5.1 Competitive issues

In its initial review, the European Commission solicited responses from customers and other competitors and provisionally concluded that the national markets for recorded music are dominated by five global record companies (the so-called majors) including Sony Music, BMG, Universal Music Group, Warner Music Group and EMI, which jointly have a market share of between 72 and 93 per cent in the EEA countries. Universal is the largest player and the

---

[29] Case COMP/M.3333 *Sony/BMG* [2005] L 62/30.
[30] See FTC press release of July 28, 2004 "FTC Closes Investigation of Joint Venture Between Bertelsmann AG and Sony Corporation of America." (*www.ftc.gov/opa/2004/07/sonybmg.htm*).

combined SonyBMG is of approximately equal size. Apart from the five majors, a fringe of many small independent record companies exists which together have a market share ranging between less than 5 per cent and almost 35 per cent in different countries. The market for recorded music has been characterised by a significant drop in demand (a decrease in sales of about 20 per cent between 1999 and 2003), which was accompanied by a slight decrease in real wholesale prices.

Based on its initial investigation, the European Commission issued a Statement of Objections and requested detailed transaction data from the five majors for several years from all EEA markets. The empirical analysis and interpretation of this economic evidence formed the basis of its ultimate decision to allow the joint venture to proceed. The focus of the EC's investigation was the effect of the joint venture on the market for recorded music, which constitutes the largest part of the decision, but the decision also dealt with effects on upstream and downstream markets (music publishing and online distribution), on which SonyBMG would not be active itself but which could be affected by the joint venture.

9.3.5.2 Market definition

In its review, the European Commission identified three distinct markets for (a) recorded music, (b) online distribution of music, and (c) music publishing.

The Commission chose a broad approach towards the product market definition and decided that the relevant market for recorded music in general was the appropriate market within which to evaluate this transaction, without seeing a need to define narrower markets based on genres or categories of recorded music (such as singles, albums or compilations). The Commission followed the parties' definition of the geographic scope of the markets for recorded music being national, mainly due to a national organisational structure of the record companies, differences in consumer preferences between countries and, finally, differences in prices.

The Commission did not follow the parties' arguments that the online distribution of music was part of the market for recorded music but instead found the markets for the distribution of physical media and the online distribution of music to be distinct markets. Among the reasons for this distinction was that online music sales were characterised by different demand, namely for individual tracks and not for entire albums, and differences in the control that suppliers have over the use of the product after it is purchased by the consumer (the so-called digital rights management for online music). On the supply side, online and physical distribution of music were found to be entirely different. The Commission furthermore defined two separate markets for the wholesale licensing to online music services and the retail distribution from online music services to final consumers. Due to the characteristics of the licensing structure, both markets were found to be national.

Finally, the European Commission defined the publishing of music (requiring mainly mechanical and performance rights for the distribution of music) as being an upstream market for the distribution of recorded and online music. Music publishing involves the authors and composers of music, whereas the recording business involves the singers and musicians. The Commission left open the question whether there could be separate markets for music publishing based on different types of rights and whether the geographic scope was national or wider.

9.3.5.3 Pricing parallelism, focal points and potential strengthening of collective dominance

In its focus on the market for recorded music, the European Commission's competitive impact analysis was based on a coordinated effects theory focused on the possible strengthening of a collective dominant position of the five major record companies maintained by tacit collusion. The Commission had requested large amounts of price and sales data for several years for all EEA markets from the five majors; its analysis was however focused on the five largest countries.

The Commission analysed whether the pricing data revealed a coordinated pricing policy among the majors. For that purpose, a subset of the data limited to the sales of the top 100 single album CDs (as opposed to single CDs, maxi CDs and albums with more than one CD) to the top 20 customers was used to compare average net wholesale prices between majors (the parties criticised the European Commission for using average prices, arguing that these could be affected by mere product mix changes). The Commission furthermore regarded the focus on the top 100 albums to be justified by the fact that these covered 70 to 80 per cent of the majors' total music sales and were thus considered representative.

The Commission took a three-step approach for the analysis: (a) to look for parallelism in average net prices; (b) to examine whether list prices (published prices to dealers or PPDs) could have been used as focal points to coordinate net prices; and (c) to investigate whether the majors' discounts to significant customers were aligned and sufficiently transparent to be monitored by each other.

In all of the five countries, the EC economists found that there was some degree of parallelism in the pattern of average net prices between the five majors, which was less pronounced in Germany. The price differences between the majors were generally found to be confined to a relatively narrow band. The list prices were found to be potential focal points, as the differences between the various PPDs of different majors were relatively close to one another and that even though each major had a high number of different list prices, a very small number of these accounted for the vast majority of sales. These prices were also found to be transparent as they can be gathered from the majors' catalogues.

The European Commission did not find significant differences on the overall discount levels between Sony and BMG. On the individual customer level, however, differences between the discounts granted by the two merging parties were found to be large enough to let the Commission conclude that there was no sufficient alignment in the discounts to establish existing coordinated behaviour, even though response to customer questionnaires suggested that the majors were aware of each others' discounts.

The Commission went on to analyse whether the markets were characterised by features that made them conducive to collusion. Although the physical characteristics of CD albums and the way they are marketed are relatively homogeneous, their content was found to be rather heterogeneous, which makes tacit collusion more difficult. The Commission acknowledged that the variety of list prices complicated monitoring, while at the same time finding that monitoring only a limited set of albums (the top 20 selling albums of each major) would allow the record companies to assess the pricing for about half of the total sales. The publication of weekly hit charts including sales of each album, the limited number of large customers and the frequent contacts between all majors' sales personnel and the wholesalers/retailers were found to be facilitating collusion. However, the difficulties to monitor certain types of discounts were found to be substantial and no evidence could be established that the record companies had solved this coordination problem.

Next, the Commission investigated whether retaliation against deviators was feasible and whether evidence of past retaliation could be found. Three potential mechanisms were identified: (a) a return to competitive behaviour; (b) the exclusion of a deviator from compilations; and (c) retaliation in different markets (publishing and online). However, no evidence could be established that any of these methods had been used in the past to punish a deviator or that explicit threats in that direction had been made.

Although the Commission contended that some degree of pricing parallelism had been found, no conclusive evidence could be established regarding the existence of a collective dominant position of the five majors in any of the EEA countries.

Besides reviewing recorded music in detail, the European Commission noted that the market for online distribution of music is relatively recent and still small. The Commission found that the majors had a similar or even stronger position in the market for wholesale licences for online music than in the market for recorded music. Prices charged for licences to online music providers were in a limited range but different usage rights made a comparison difficult. The Commission found that the prices charged to online music providers did not reflect the cost savings that could be achieved in comparison to the distribution of physical music recordings, but concluded that there was not sufficient evidence for a finding of existing collective dominance or that collective dominance was likely to be created by the joint venture.

9.3.5.4 Vertical issues and foreclosure

Based on concerns raised by third parties, the European Commission also examined whether the joint venture could lead to single dominance in some countries due to Bertelsmann's position in the TV and radio broadcasting sector. The theory was that SonyBMG could foreclose competitors if Bertelsmann refused to let them advertise and promote their artists on TV and radio.

The Commission, however, found that the joint venture did not reach the market share threshold of single dominance in any country and that Universal had comparable market shares in several countries. Nor did the EC find any evidence that the foreclosure of rival record companies would have been a profitable strategy for Bertelsmann.

For these reasons, the European Commission cleared the merger on July 19, 2004, without conditions or obligations. Impala, an organisation of several independent music companies, has recently challenged the clearance decision of the EC before the CFI.[31]

9.4 Conclusions and outlook

Until very recently, public policy toward horizontal mergers remained primarily structural[32] with traditional merger analysis on both sides of the Atlantic essentially following an indirect two-step procedure. The first step involves market definition for each product or service provided by the merging firms, whereas at the second stage of the assessment market shares are calculated in order to make predictive inferences on the likely economic effects of the merger. This structural focus may be welcomed because it allows relatively quick inferences to be made on whether a merger requires an in-depth analysis. If such in-depth analysis is indeed required, however, a thorough assessment of the nature of competition is needed. Apart from the (often used) presumptions on market shares, the analysis of concentrations thus necessitates a case-by-case assessment of the facts so as to determine the likely effects of the merger on prices, output, and other dimensions of competition and welfare.

Recently, the European Commission—prompted by the Court of First Instance—has begun the systematic use of quantitative methods to check real-world welfare effects in complex cases. New econometric tools enable the analysis of concentrations to move away from structural presumptions and take a more direct approach by looking at the price constraining effects of a concentration and analysing whether the removal of these constraints would lead to an increase in consumer prices. These advances in the development of quantitative methods may lead to an exponential growth in the use of empirical methods in antitrust cases.[33] Individual transactions may be broken down into finely-parsed product categories such as stock-keeping units for

---

[31] Case T–464/04 *Impala v Commission*.

[32] For an overview, on Europe, see e.g. A. Bertolini and F. Parisi, "The Rise of Structuralism in European Merger Control" (1996) 32 Stanford J. Int'l L. 13; and compare D. Neven, R. Nuttall and P. Seabright, *Merger in Daylight: The Economics and Politics of European Merger Control* (1993). On the USA, see G.J. Werden and L.M. Froeb, "Simulation as an Alternative to Structural Merger Policy in Differentiated Products Industries", in *The Economics of the Antitrust Process* (M.B. Coate and A.N. Kleit ed., 1996), pp.65, 70–78; and M.B. Coate, "Economics, the Guidelines and the Evolution of Merger Policy" (1992) 37 Antitrust Bull. 997.

[33] J.B Baker and D.L. Rubinfeld, "Empirical Methods Used in Antitrust Litigation: Review and a Critique" (1999) 1 Amer. Law Econ. Rev. 386.

products sold at retail.[34] If one can estimate individual and cross-price elasticities over a period of time, highly sophisticated economic models of competition may be developed. This may make the structural market share-based analysis partly redundant for certain differentiated product mergers,[35] even though this is still an open invitation for controversy in the antitrust world.

The implications for the control of concentrations and mergers are far-reaching.[36] A direct approach to assessing the competitive effects of a concentration yields additional information beyond the traditional standards. The reason is that changes in post-merger prices are captured, which may differ widely depending on particular economic conditions in a given industry. From a technical point of view, economic models can include expectations of reduced marginal costs so that the effects of merger efficiencies in the form of cost reductions may be incorporated into the analysis of a merger.

Still, differing meanings for even basic economic concepts (such as market power and dominance) leave substantial scope for subjective interpretation by the individuals and institutions involved in a merger control case, ranging from judges and competition authorities to lawyers and expert witnesses. This becomes all the more far-reaching as there are hardly any simple connections to be made between the merging firms' shares and the merger's effect on price and total welfare.[37] Naturally, if it is not even possible to link the market share presumptions to any explicit notion of price or total welfare effects without quantification of the anti-competitive effects, it is almost meaningless to trade-off explicitly any efficiency effects of mergers leading to a reduction of marginal or fixed costs for the merging firms.[38]

In sum, the main economic concern arising from concentrations is that

[34] See J.B. Baker, "Contemporary Empirical Merger Analysis" (1997) 5 Geo. Mason L. Rev. 347 at pp.348–351 for an introductory overview.
[35] See J.A. Hausman and G.K. Leonard, "Economic Analysis of Differentiated Products Mergers Using Real World Data" (1997) 5 Geo. Mason L. Rev. 321 at p.338; J.B. Baker, "Contemporary Empirical Merger Analysis" (1997) 5 Geo. Mason L. Rev. 347 at p.351; G.J. Werden, "Simulating the Effects of Differentiated Products Mergers: An Alternative to Structural Merger Policy" (1997) 5 Geo. Mason L. Rev. 363 at p.384. Undertaking a valiant stand to defend the Merger Guidelines, J.F. Rill, "Practising What One Preaches: One Lawyer's View of Econometric Models in Differentiated Products Mergers" (1997) 5 Geo. Mason L. Rev. 393 at pp.402–409, concludes that "such a shift in the analytical paradigm, though theoretically subtle, is practically dangerous, particularly when the reliability of the models is hampered by limiting assumptions and/or data availability", as it can lead to "unpredictable and unsound enforcement". Similarly aversion may be encountered in *Moore Corp Ltd v Wallace Computer Services, Inc*, 907 F. Supp. 1545 (D. Del. 1995). See C.K. Robinson, "Quantifying Unilateral Effects in Investigations and Cases" (1997) 5 Geo. Mason L. Rev. 387, on an integrated approach.
[36] See, for example, J. Hausman, G. Leonard, and J.D. Zona, "A Proposed Method for Analysing Competition among Differentiated Products" (1992) 60 Antitrust L.J. 889.
[37] The critique on structural merger analysis is not without precedent; see R.S. Markovits, "International Competition, Market Definition, and the Appropriate Way to Analyse the Legality of Horizontal Mergers under the Clayton Act" (1988) 64 Chi.-Kent L. Rev. 745; L. Kaplow, "The Accuracy of Traditional Market Power Analysis and a Direct Adjustment Alternative" (1982) 95 Harv. L. Rev. 1817 at pp.1826–1832; R. Schmalensee, "Another Look at Market Power" (1982) 95 Harv. L. Rev. 1780 at pp.1799–1800.
[38] Coming to a similar conclusion, see G.J. Werden, "Simulating the Effects of Differentiated Products Mergers: An Alternative to Structural Merger Policy" (1997) 5 Geo. Mason L. Rev. 363 at p.368 (efficiency effects cannot be considered systematically because anticompetitive effects are not quantified in any comparable way).

consumer prices may increase, while econometric tools available show that gains in efficiency may or may not outweigh increases in price.[39] This makes the economic argument in support of an enhanced consumer welfare standard as the relevant guide for antitrust ever stronger. In complex cases requiring a sophisticated assessment of the competitive effects of the concentration at hand, it also underscores the necessary preference for the more refined mode of analysis offered by contemporary economics as compared to the structural analysis commonly adopted in the not-so-very-distant past.

---

[39] J. Hausman, G. Leonard & J.D. Zona, "Competitive Analysis with Differentiated Products" (1994) 34 Ann. Econ. Statist. 159 at p.174.

Chapter 10

··

ALLOCATION OF COMPETENCES IN THE FIELD OF COMPETITION LAW: CENTRALISATION OR DECENTRALISATION?

10.1 Introduction

In recent years, an intensive discussion about coordination, convergence and harmonisation of competition laws as a response to market globalisation has arisen. This debate takes place both within the European Union and on a global level.[1] The economic analysis of regulatory competition (as opposed to harmonisation) is closely linked to the discussions about interjurisdictional competition, centralisation versus decentralisation, and competitive federalism. In the quasi-federal institutional framework of the European Union, the principle of subsidiarity is the crucial concept to decide the desirable degree of (de)centralisation. The most detailed statement of the principle can be found in Article 5(2) EC:

> "In areas which do not fall within its exclusive competence, the Community shall take action, in accordance with the principle of subsidiarity, only if and in so far as the objectives of the proposed action cannot be sufficiently achieved by the Member States and can therefore, by reason of the scale or effects of the proposed action, be better achieved by the Community".[2]

Powers should thus be granted to the institutions of the European Community only when it has been established that Member States cannot satisfactorily exercise them (except for matters falling within the exclusive competence[3] of the European Community institutions).

Competition policy is not an exclusive competence of the European Community. Member States have retained the power to enact their own competition laws. There are, however, a number of important qualifications to this rule. First, in the field of merger control, supervision by competition authorities of Member States is excluded for mergers having a Community dimension. Thresholds based on the worldwide and Community turnovers of companies involved in a merger are used to draw the borderlines of the Member States' and Community's jurisdiction. The powers of the Member States' competition authorities are limited to concentrations not reaching the relevant thresholds (one-stop-shop principle). Second, the EC rules governing cartel agreements and abuses of dominant position apply to activities which "affect trade between Member States". These terms are widely interpreted, so that in many cases European competition rules will take precedence over national competition laws because of the supremacy of Community law. Third, Regulation 1/2003 has strengthened the principle of supremacy of European competition law and thus has further restricted the scope for different rules of national competition law. When agreements may affect trade between Member States, national competition authorities and judges must also apply Article 81 EC. According to Article 3(2) of Regulation 1/2003, the application of national competition law may not lead to the prohibition of

---

[1] D. Neven and L.-H. Röller, "Institution Design: the Allocation of Jurisdiction in International Antitrust" (2000) 44 Eur. Econ. Rev. 845; A. Guzman, "Antitrust and International Regulatory Federalism" (2001) 76 N.Y.U.L. Rev. 1142; E. Graham, "Internationalizing Competition Policy: An Assessment of the Two Main Alternatives" (2003) 48 Antitrust Bull. 947.

[2] A slightly different formulation can be found in the (not yet ratified) Treaty establishing a Constitution for Europe. See Art. I–11(3).

[3] For a discussion of this concept, see: T.C. Hartley, *The Foundations of European Community Law* (1998), p.112. For the definition of exclusivity under the envisioned system post-modernisation, compare Art. 3 of the Proposal for a Council Regulation on the implementation of the rules on competition laid down in Arts 81 and 82 of the Treaty and amending Regulations (EEC) No.1017/68, (EEC) No.2988/74, (EEC) No.4056/86 and (EEC) No.3975/87, COM(2000)582.

agreements which do not restrict competition within the meaning of Article 81(1) EC or fulfil the conditions of Article 81(3) EC. The duty to simultaneously apply national competition law and European competition law (Article 82 EC) also applies in cases of abuses of a dominant position that have an impact on interstate trade. However, the national competition authorities and judges retain the possibility of applying stricter national rules to unilateral conduct. As specified in the recitals of Regulation 1/2003, these stricter national laws may include provisions which prohibit or impose sanctions on abusive behaviour towards economically dependent undertakings.[4] Fourth, even though Regulation 1/2003 leaves scope for the Member States to apply national rules to agreements not affecting interstate trade, the wish to guarantee the uniformity of national competition laws may prevent Member States from continuing their own diverging competition policy. As a consequence, at present there are great similarities between the European competition rules and the competition laws of many Member States. In the 1990s, Member States that previously had no competition laws (or did not actively enforce them) introduced new rules which are almost an exact copy of the relevant substantive provisions of the EC Treaty and the European Merger Regulation.[5] Also, Member States who had their own tradition in the field of competition policy have aligned their rules closely with those of European competition law.[6]

Apart from the substantive law, attention must be paid to the allocation of tasks in the field of enforcement. Even if cases are governed by European rules, decentralisation remains possible in the field of enforcement. There has always been a remarkable combination of centralised rule making and decentralised enforcement. The so-called modernisation of European competition law has consolidated this system of centralised substantive rules and decentralised enforcement with respect to Articles 81 and 82 EC. Since the European Commission has lost its enforcement monopoly, different national competition authorities and judges will compete with each other in enforcing the cartel prohibition and the assessment of abuse of a dominant position.

The modernisation project, as contained in Regulation 1/2003, is an example of how decentralisation may create scope for competition between jurisdictions. Four types of (more or less intensive) regulatory competition can be distinguished, according to the extent of mobility factors between different jurisdictions.[7] If information flows exist between jurisdictions (which remain

---

[4] Regulation 1/2003, [2003] O.J. L 1/1, para.8 *in fine*. Several Member States (Germany, France, Italy) have enacted laws protecting economically dependent firms from abuses by firms enjoying market power in relation with specific customers (in German: "relative Marktmacht"). Regulation 1/2003 reconfirms that also European competition law does not only pursue efficiency objectives but also aims at protecting freedom of business decisions and individual economic independence (recall the discussion in Ch.2, section 2.4.5).

[5] Clear examples include the Italian, the Dutch and the Belgian competition laws.

[6] This is the case in the United Kingdom after the passing of the Competition Act of 1998, which came into effect in March 2000, and in Germany after the seventh amendment of the *Gesetz gegen Wettbewerbsbeschränkungen* (GWB), which entered into force in July 2005. For an economic analysis of British competition law, see M.A. Utton, *Market Dominance and Antitrust Policy* (2nd ed., 2003).

[7] These distinctions are borrowed from: W. Kerber and O. Budzinski, "Towards a Differentiated Analysis of Competition of Competition Laws" (2003) 1 *ZWeR—Journal of Competition Law* 411.

isolated from each other as far as mobility of goods is concerned) they can learn from the experiences of competition policies in other countries and imitate superior competition rules (type I regulatory competition through mutual learning). If there is also mobility of goods and services (but immobility of factors of production), competition laws can have an impact on the international competitiveness of domestic firms. This can lead to incentives to adopt superior competition policies of other countries, in order to increase successes in international trade (type II regulatory competition through international trade). If, additionally, individuals, firms and factors of production (particularly capital) are mobile, competition laws can be chosen by moving between jurisdictions (type III regulatory competition through interjurisdictional competition). Finally, an additional type of competition can be distinguished if individuals and firms enjoy free choice of law, so that they can choose between different competition laws (and/or enforcement regimes) independent from their location or the market in which they do business (type IV regulatory competition through free choice of law).

The structure of this chapter is as follows. In the next section, an overview will be given of the economic criteria to decide in favour of or against decentralisation and competition between competition laws. The benefits and costs of both options will be discussed. On the one hand, decentralisation and competition between competition laws may allow the satisfaction of a greater number of preferences and enable learning processes. In addition, competition authorities of the Member States may be better able to gather the information which is needed for the enforcement of the rules in their respective jurisdiction. On the other hand, decentralisation and competition between competition laws may cause negative externalities in other jurisdictions, so that choices made by national authorities have a negative impact on the overall welfare of the Community. There is also the risk of a "race to the bottom", that is a competitive process leading to "bad" law benefiting companies and harming consumers. Scale economies may also be lost in the case of multiple legal rules. Finally, there is a danger of "regulatory capture": regulators who are too close to the firms to be regulated may lose their independence.

In the following section, the criteria for an economic assessment will be contrasted with the actual scope of (de)centralisation and competition between competition laws in the European Union. The central question is whether the current division of competences between national authorities and the European Commission can be supported by economic arguments. Particular attention will be devoted to the question whether the existing European institutional framework allows an optimal degree of (de)centralisation and regulatory competition (both with respect to the substantive rules and enforcement), so that the advantages of such processes are maximised while at the same time the disadvantages are minimised.

10.2 Lessons from economic theory

In a perfectly competitive market the free choices of buyers and sellers produce an efficient outcome.[8] The achievement of allocative efficiency in perfectly competitive markets for goods and services suggests that the same benefits may be reaped in a multi-government system that imitates the structure of the market. Hence, the starting point in an economic analysis of diffusion of competences in a federal state or a quasi-federal structure, such as the European Community, is that two (and preferably more) legislators are better than one. However, this argument in favour of competition between legislators, and thus decentralisation allowing for such competition, suffers from all the drawbacks of the static model of perfect competition and will only be briefly presented. Apart from the static analysis, arguments in favour of decentralisation follow from a dynamic view. Competition between legal orders makes it possible to gather knowledge about costs and benefits of alternative legal rules. Finally, the need to cope with informational asymmetries between regulatory authorities and regulated firms is a third argument in favour of decentralisation.

Economic analysis also suggests a number of reasons in favour of centralisation and harmonisation of competition laws. Markets for legislation may fail in the same way as ordinary markets for goods or services do not generate efficient outcomes because of market imperfections. Consequently, the need to cope with externalities between jurisdictions is a major argument in favour of centralised decision making. The danger of destructive competition between jurisdictions, also known as the risk of a "race to the bottom", is a second argument which may justify centralisation and harmonisation of competition laws. It must be added that competition between competition laws may also generate a "race to the top" that may be equally sub-optimal. Finally, centralisation may be warranted when extending the size of the jurisdiction allows the achievement of scale economies and transaction costs savings. All these arguments are particularly relevant in the European context, as will be illustrated in the third section of this chapter.

10.2.1 Benefits of decentralisation and competition between jurisdictions

10.2.1.1 The Tiebout model

Theory tells us that if competition between sellers of products may lead to allocative efficiency, the same beneficial results may be reached when legislators compete. This argument is based on Tiebout's theory[9] on the optimal

---

[8] See Ch.2, s.2.2.
[9] C.M. Tiebout, "A Pure Theory of Local Expenditure" (1956) 64 J. Pol. Econ. 416.

provision of local public goods.[10] In a world of purely private goods, individuals can buy different bundles of goods adapted to their tastes and consume them separately. In contrast, congestible public goods that are consumed and financed in common do not allow people with a variety of tastes to live side by side without difficulty. In the latter case, people may be better off if they can cluster together in communities with others who have similar tastes. For example, people who like to swim can decide to live in a community with a public swimming pool; others who prefer to read books may move to a community offering the library facilities necessary thereto. The idea behind an optimal decentralised offer of public goods is that people with the same preferences live together in small communities. If there is a sufficiently large number of communities which offer diverging packages of local public goods and people can freely move—or "vote with their feet"—an optimal organisation of public services will follow.

Tiebout's theory is only valid if the following assumptions are satisfied:

- there must be a sufficiently large number of providers of public goods (local communities);

- there must be no restraints inhibiting perfect mobility between communities;

- there must be no information deficiencies;

- there must be no externalities;[11]

- municipalities must be able to exclude "free riders" from the services offered; and

- there must be no scale economies which necessitate cooperation between communities to profit from efficiency savings.

Enterprises and citizens may have heterogeneous preferences not only with respect to public goods, such as local infrastructure for playing sports and libraries, but also as to their preferred set of laws. Tiebout's model can be extended to legal rules and institutions. Indeed, laws also have public goods' characteristics. A legal rule is indivisible: one person's enjoyment of a particular kind of legal protection does not preclude others from that enjoyment. A

[10] A public good is a commodity, the benefit from which is shared by the public as a whole, or by some group within it. The text book example is national defence. Public goods combine two characteristics. First, consumption is non-rivalrous: consumption by one person does not leave less for others to consume. Second, public goods are non-excludable: it is impossible or too costly for the supplier to exclude those persons who do not pay for the benefit. In contrast, private goods are rivalrous and excludable. Examples include apples and shoes. The characteristics of public goods explain why the free market will not offer an optimal quantity of public goods. However, if remedies to the problem of excludability can be found, as is the case with "club goods", private market solutions remain possible. Club goods are non-rivalrous but excludable: a person who is not a member of the (e.g. tennis) club will not be able to profit from the services provided.

[11] An externality exists when a person (in Tiebout's scenario, a community) does not enjoy all the benefits or incur the costs that result from the actions undertaken (i.e. the provision of the public good).

legal rule is also non-excludable: legal subjects not paying taxes cannot be denied legal protection. Jurisdictions may offer individuals and firms a varying set of legal rules and institutions: the more legislators and enforcement agencies compete, the more preferences may be satisfied. Firms and individuals may also "vote with their feet" and choose the jurisdiction which in their view offers the best set of laws or system of enforcement. The government closest to the people will best be able to tailor solutions that adequately address the people's problems. Decentralisation and competition between competition laws enables legislators to choose those rules which best serve the goals preferred by the local population.

In the case of competition between legislators also, a competitive equilibrium will ensue, but this outcome is again dependent on the restrictive assumptions mentioned above. In reality, the conditions for Tiebout competition may not be met. First, the number of jurisdictions to choose between may not be sufficiently large to allow individuals and firms the choice of their preferred set of competition rules and system of enforcement. Second, there may be restraints on mobility between jurisdictions. It is well known that capital is more mobile than individuals (labour forces), who may be hesitant to move to another country for personal or family reasons. In this respect, it must be added that Tiebout's theory remains valid in the absence of physical mobility (migration), provided that individuals and firms are free to select the jurisdiction whose principles are to apply to their transactions.[12] If there is free choice of law (type IV regulatory competition), an important advantage in comparison with type III regulatory competition through interjurisdictional competition is that legal rules can be chosen without having to accept the whole bundle of public goods, taxes and regulations of the respective jurisdiction. This may lead to very intense regulatory competition.[13] Finally, market imperfections on the markets for legislation (in particular externalities and information problems) may necessitate centralisation to improve upon efficiency. This last point will be further elaborated upon below (see section 10.2.2).

10.2.1.2 Competition as a learning process

Apart from their ability to satisfy more preferences, decentralisation and competition between competition laws bring other advantages. Competition between jurisdictions may generate all the benefits of a learning process. Differences in rules allow for different experiences and may improve an understanding of the effects of alternative legal solutions to similar problems. This advantage relates both to the formulation of the substantive rules and their enforcement.

The theoretical background of this argument can be traced back to the reasoning of Nobel Prize laureate Friedrich von Hayek about the fundamental

---

[12] R.J. Van den Bergh, "Towards an Institutional Legal Framework for Regulatory Competition in Europe" (2000) 53 *Kyklos* 442.
[13] W. Kerber and O. Budzinski, "Towards a Differentiated Analysis of Competition of Competition Laws" (2003) 1 *ZWeR—Journal of Competition Law* 411.

limitations of human knowledge.[14] It cannot be assumed that law makers know the best legal rules in advance. The quality of the performance of legal rules and systems of enforcement in a given jurisdiction is revealed by comparing it with the performance of different legal rules and systems of enforcement in other jurisdictions. The Hayekian concept of "competition as a discovery procedure" entails parallel experimentation with new problem solutions and the imitation of the successful solutions by others through learning. This Hayekian concept is closely linked to the idea of "yardstick competition", implying that information about the quality of the performance of governments and enforcement agencies is revealed by comparing it with the performance of others. Hayek's ideas are also close to the Schumpeterian concept of competition as a process of "creative destruction", implying continuous innovation and imitation.[15]

Mutual learning processes may alleviate the convergence of legal rules and amount to an *ex post* or market-based harmonisation of laws and systems of enforcement. Hence, competition between jurisdictions in the European Union does not necessarily imply that rules will greatly differ (as is often feared by lawyers who care mainly about legal certainty). Member States may decide to amend their laws in response to superior legal solutions adopted in another Member State. Competition between legislators and legal uniformity is thus not mutually exclusive. Whereas unification and harmonisation by means of central rules (EC Regulations and Directives) imply forced coordination of legislative provisions in the Member States, dynamic competitive processes may produce voluntary harmonisation. The result of the process of innovation and subsequent amendment may be a substantial uniformity across the Member States.[16] However, it should be added that, from a Hayekian evolutionary point of view, the notion of *ex post* harmonisation is misleading. The fundamental knowledge problem is never finally solved and, therefore, a certain degree of diversity should be kept in order to guarantee the flexibility and learning propensity of the legal system.

Processes of experimentation and mutual learning are effective under all types of regulatory competition. Under type I regulatory competition, states that do not amend their laws in response to another state's innovation run the risk that voters will negatively assess the performance of their government by comparing it with the performance in other countries.[17] Under type II regulatory competition, international trade between jurisdictions (decreasing exports and increasing imports) offers an additional transmission mechanism

[14] F.A. von Hayek, "Competition as a Discovery Procedure", in *Studies in Philosophy, Politics and Economics* (F.A. von Hayek, 1978), p.66.
[15] See Ch.3, s.3.7.1.
[16] The scope of such a voluntary harmonisation may be larger than the degree of uniformity brought about by centralisation. Directives, for example, often contain escape clauses or grant the Member States a number of options to choose between, that may endanger the goal of full harmonisation.
[17] If voters have insufficient incentives to become familiar with foreign competition policies and their performance in other countries, there may be other agents who can influence innovation and imitation. Experience shows that economists and legal scholars, who have a strong stake in innovative policy making, not only influence the academic discussion but may also effectively contribute to policy changes.

through which competition between competition laws can become effective. In jurisdictions with lenient competition policies, export-oriented firms suffer from low international competitiveness and the import-substituting industries are strongly challenged by foreign competitors. Moreover, the consumers in particular jurisdictions, in which there are only few producers, finance foreign monopoly rents by paying higher prices. These effects may provide incentives for politicians to adjust their regulatory regime towards more effective competition. Under type III regulatory competition, firms may wish to locate in highly competitive national markets to improve their competitiveness. Politicians may have incentives to adjust the competition laws in order to increase the inflow of capital and labour, which contributes to increasing domestic welfare and to avoiding that mobile production factors are driven away. Finally, under type IV regulatory competition, law subjects may fully profit from trial and error processes and will simply choose the laws that are best adapted to their preferences.

10.2.1.3 Informational asymmetries

A preference for decentralisation also follows from the need to cope with informational asymmetries between regulatory agencies and regulated firms. Decentralisation is the more efficient, the more valuable local information is for appropriate rule making and enforcement. The asymmetry of information between regulatory authorities and regulated firms may be analysed as a principal–agent problem. Regulatory authorities (both national and supranational) have an information disadvantage *vis-à-vis* the firms they have to control; the former may be seen as the principals and the latter as the agents. Out of self-interest the agents may be unwilling to reveal all the information needed by the principals. A related danger is the communication of false information. It may be argued that it is more difficult for firms to hide or misrepresent information to decentralised agencies than to a more remote agency. This is certainly true in the field of competition law. Information provided by firms may be cross-checked against information from competitors, consumer organisations and official sources. If such cross-checking is difficult, local agencies will still have a better view of the market than a supranational agency.

Decentralisation may thus be advocated because it reduces the agency problem. There are also, naturally, intermediate solutions between full decentralisation and full centralisation.[18] First, decentralised information gathering can help to remove much of the information asymmetry faced by central regulatory agencies. A second alternative to the choice between centralisation and decentralisation is the coexistence of national and supranational procedures. In the third section of this chapter, it will be shown that the European system of enforcement has moved from the former to the latter

---

[18] Compare D. Neven, R. Nuttall and P. Seabright, *Merger in Daylight: The Economics and Politics of European Merger Control* (1993), p.198; K. Gatsios and P. Seabright, "Regulation in the European Community" (1989) 5 Oxf. Rev. Econ. Pol. 37.

alternative and now consists of parallel competences combined with a division of work that leaves the most important cases to be decided by the European Commission.

10.2.2 Disadvantages of decentralisation and competition between jurisdictions

The obvious counterargument to the benefits of regulatory competition is that competition in the market for legal rules and systems of enforcement, as in any other market, may not function properly because of market imperfections. In this respect, attention must be paid to the problem of externalities and the risk of a "race to the bottom". In addition, centralisation and harmonisation of laws may be justified when it generates important scale economies and/or transaction costs savings.

10.2.2.1 Externalities

Externalities between jurisdictions are a powerful argument in favour of centralised rule making. If EC Member States enact legal rules that are likely to cause negative externalities for other Community members, centralisation may be needed to guarantee that the externalities are internalised. The externality problem arises in many fields: air pollution is an obvious example.[19] The problem is more pervasive, however. If allocative efficiency is to be reached in a federal state, preferences for inefficient rules in any field of law may be satisfied only to the extent that costs are borne by the population preferring such rules.

In diverging policy fields, including competition policy, jurisdictions may cause adverse externalities for other countries. This is the case with both the formulation of divergent substantive rules and the decentralised enforcement of common prohibitions. Also parallel enforcement of common prohibitions may generate interstate externalities. National competition authorities may not take into account the effects of their decisions on other national authorities. Because of the resulting regulatory externalities, splitting competences between competition authorities may lead to inefficiencies compared to action by a single (central) competition authority. Positive externalities occur when action of all competent competition authorities is necessary to give full effect to the activity of a single competition authority. Positive externalities will be underprovided because competition authorities producing the externalities only account for the effect of their action on themselves. Negative externalities occur when the action of one competition authority reduces the value and exploitable rents of another authority. Negative externalities will be

---

[19] See R.J. Van den Bergh, M. Faure and J. Lefevere, "The Subsidiarity Principle in European Environmental Law: An Economic Analysis", in *Law and Economics of the Environment* (E. Eide and R.J. van den Bergh ed., 1996), p.121.

overprovided because individual competition authorities do not account for the negative effects of their decisions on other authorities.[20]

When substantial externalities between jurisdictions occur, centralisation and (some degree of) harmonisation may be necessary. However, before jumping to such a conclusion, it should be investigated whether bilateral agreements between the jurisdictions involved are not better than centralised solutions, such as full harmonisation. The reason may be the availability of information and the negotiation and enforcement costs at different regulatory levels. In the Law and Economics literature this alternative to centralised decision making is known as Coasian bargaining.[21] The Coase theorem tells us that if there are well specified property rights, full information, and low transaction costs, the efficient solution will result through bargaining between the jurisdictions without any need for intervention by a central authority. Hence, an important task for the European Union is to provide an institutional framework in which Coasian bargaining is possible. However, if the number of jurisdictions affected by the externalities is too large or reaching agreements is impeded by opportunistic behaviour, centralisation, eventually including (some degree of) harmonisation of laws, may be needed.

10.2.2.2 The risk of a "race to the bottom"

Competition between jurisdictions is often criticised because it would cause a "race to the bottom".[22] States may wish to outbid each other in designing lenient competition laws in order to attract business to locate in their jurisdiction. Firms may have incentives to locate in "cartel paradises", either because they think that market power in domestic markets will improve their competitiveness on international markets or because they want to reap profits from domestic markets.

The theoretical basis for this fear is the existence of prisoners' dilemmas[23] between jurisdictions. When the European Commission proposes harmonisation of laws, it usually refers to the need to prevent inequality of competitive

---

[20] B. De Poorter and F. Parisi, *Modernization of European Antitrust Enforcement: The Economics of Regulatory Competition* (George Mason University School of Law, Working paper series 24) (2005) (available at: *http://law.bepress.com/gmulwps/gmule/art24*).

[21] Named after Nobel Prize Winner Professor R.H. Coase, who is generally considered a founding father of New Law and Economics in which economic insights are used outside the field of antitrust, such as private law. The Coase theorem was developed in: R.H. Coase, "The Problem of Social Cost" (1960) 3 J. Law Econ. 1.

[22] Fear that destructive competition between states might produce undesirable results in the form of "bad law" has often served as an argument for centralising certain areas of law. The race to the bottom argument has been advanced by US scholars in the contexts of corporate law and environmental law. However, with respect to corporate law, the view that states would engage in a race for the bottom in which they would attempt to outdo each other for the favour of corporate managers to the ultimate detriment of shareholders has been sharply criticised; see R. Romano, "Law as a Product: Some Pieces of the Incorporation Puzzle" (1985) 1. J. Law Econ. Org. 225; R. Romano, *The Genius of American Corporate Law* (1993). Similarly, with respect to environmental law it has been shown that the fear of a race to the bottom is both theoretically unsound and without empirical proof; see R.L. Revesz, "Federalism and Environmental Regulation: An Overview", in *Environmental Law, the Economy, and Sustainable Development* (R.L. Revesz, Ph. Sands and R.B. Stewart ed., 2000), p.37

[23] For a discussion of this concept, see Ch.5, s.5.2.2.

conditions across the Member States. This fear may be rephrased in economic terms as the danger of prisoners' dilemmas. States may operate, not in a market-like setting, but in a prisoners' dilemma game. When legislators can be analogised to firms selling in a competitive market, decentralised rules may be preferable. In contrast, when states compete under prisoners' dilemma conditions, national rules will produce a result that is worse than a federal rule.[24] A state will only gain in the struggle to attract business by choosing in favour of laxness when other states do not act in the same way. However, if all other states follow, only the businesses will gain. Regulatory laxness may occur when substantive rules have to be enacted, and this may also happen at the enforcement stage. Although all jurisdictions could be better off with appropriate competition laws that are effectively enforced, a sub-optimal equilibrium with an insufficient level of protection of competition may ensue. If jurisdictions compete with each other under the conditions of a prisoners' dilemma, there will be a "race to the bottom" and centralisation will then be required to generate efficient outcomes.

Prisoners' dilemmas can appear under each type of regulatory competition, with the exception of yardstick competition (type I regulatory competition, where there are only information flows between jurisdictions). Under type II regulatory competition through international trade, a deterioration of the quality of competition law may occur as follows. Strategic competition policies, which deliberately protect market power in domestic markets, may attract foreign investments. Such competition policies can take three forms. First, jurisdictions can allow their enterprises to obtain market power in domestic markets, if this will allow them to achieve efficiency gains in related international markets. Second, market power in domestic markets can be tolerated to support the attainment of market power in international markets. Examples of such competition policy strategies include the exemption of export cartels and the strategic use of merger control to support the creation of national champions. Third, competition policies may allow firms to reap profits from domestic market power in order to use them to cross-subsidise losses from predatory campaigns on foreign markets.[25]

Under type III regulatory competition, the prospect of attaining market power in domestic markets without effects on international trade can make it attractive for firms to move into another jurisdiction. The strategic competition policies just described may also provide incentives for firms to locate within jurisdictions adopting such policies, if they value the freedom to form cartels and reap monopoly profits higher than the protection against those types of conduct if performed by their competitors. Hence, production factors may flow to jurisdictions that do not enact appropriate competition laws.

Finally, a prisoners' dilemma emerges when firms are left free to decide under which competition rules they want to do business in a particular market (type IV regulatory competition). Although firms might be interested in being

---

[24] S. Rose-Ackermann, *Rethinking the Progressive Agenda: The Reform of the American Regulatory State* (1992), p.167.
[25] W. Kerber and O. Budzinski, "Towards a Differentiated Analysis of Competition of Competition Laws" (2003) 1 *ZWeR—Journal of Competition Law* 411.

protected from anti-competitive behaviour by others, firms trapped in a prisoners' dilemma will choose lenient competition laws that do not restrict their business decisions on the market.

With the exception of type IV regulatory competition (forum shopping), it seems that the argument about destructive competition on the market for competition laws is mainly theoretical and lacks sufficient empirical proof. Member States may be of the opinion that advantages in international trade are to be gained by exposing domestic firms to competitive forces in their home markets rather than protecting them from the effects of competition. Additionally, firms may decide to relocate their businesses not because of the prospect of a lax antitrust jurisdiction but primarily for different reasons, such as the level of taxes, the degree of unionisation of the labour force, and the quality of the infrastructure. Nevertheless, it cannot totally be excluded that considerations relating to the stringency of competition laws matter at the margin.

There is also the counterargument that competition between jurisdictions may cause a "race to the top" rather than one to the bottom. Generally speaking, antitrust laws do not seem to hinder worldwide competitiveness in light of the fact that business people in other countries are bound by no such laws. Successes in international trade are achieved through technological leadership, which is not necessarily due to monopoly power but may be the consequence of strong competitive pressures on the home market. Hence, competition policy may improve international competitiveness, contrary to the arguments in favour of an industrial policy favouring big enterprises through lax merger control or allowing anti-competitive practices. In this context, it must however be added that a "race to the top" does not necessarily lead to efficient outcomes. A rush towards overzealous competition authorities may result in too high a number of unnecessary prohibitions (type II errors). In discussing whether competition between jurisdictions causes either a "race to the bottom" or a "race to the top", one should always bear in mind that the optimal level of antitrust enforcement is not necessarily the "top" reached by unlimited regulatory competition.

10.2.2.3 Scale economies and transaction costs savings

From an efficiency viewpoint, centralisation may also be defended because of scale economies and transaction costs savings. If scale economies are important, central rule making may be required. National defence is an obvious example; local communities could not efficiently provide this public good. Scale economies may also be important in the production of the information needed to formulate and/or enforce legal rules. Some information relevant to the entire European Community can be most efficiently provided by Community institutions. Uniform legal rules also maintain economies of scale in production and distribution arrangements. If diversity in rules prohibits firms from using the same production and marketing techniques in larger areas, scale economies may be lost. The 1992 Internal Market Programme aimed at the removal of technical barriers caused by divergence in national regulations.

The savings resulting from this removal were estimated to be substantial, although different in magnitude across industries.[26] Also in the field of competition policy, firms will save on transaction costs if they do not need to have their business practices and contemplated mergers checked by several competition authorities acting in parallel.

10.2.3 A Public Choice perspective

The economic analysis above has made clear that arguments may be advanced in favour of both decentralisation and centralisation. So far the discussion has proceeded on the assumption that regulatory powers are allocated in such a way as to maximise social welfare. However, private politics rather than global welfare may be the driving force behind (de)centralisation. It is well known that private interests may have an important impact on the contents of legal rules. The same is true with respect to decisions about whether to regulate at Community or national level(s). Interest groups will have a preference for rules being formulated at the level at which their strength is greatest relative to that of other groups with divergent interests in the same area.[27] Hence, the question arises which interest groups may succeed in "rent seeking" at the expense of the public at large. The role of pressure groups, bureaucracies and utility-maximising judges will be analysed in turn.

Interest groups may be strong enough to pervert regulatory agencies. When not all interests are equally well represented, regulatory capture becomes possible. A general lesson from Public Choice is that industry groups will be more powerful lobbies than consumer groups. To be a powerful lobby the interests represented must be homogeneous and benefits from lobbying should not flow to outsiders who do not pay for the benefits generated (free riders). Consumer groups are large and have heterogeneous interests; excluding free riding is equally very difficult or impossible. By contrast, some industry interests are represented by well organised pressure groups that are able to cope with the free riding problem easily through compulsory membership. This argument is used to support the claim that the professions (medical doctors, lawyers) have been successful in generating rents for existing practitioners.[28] Large firms will also be powerful lobbyists: they may gather information about the substantive and procedural issues concerned at low costs (as a by-product of their other activities); they may also have more at stake and may therefore be better able to spread the fixed costs of information acquisition.[29]

---

[26] European Commission, *The Single Market Review: Impact on Competition and Scale Effects* (1997).
[27] E. Noam, "The Choice of Governmental Level in Regulation" (1982) 35 *Kyklos* 278.
[28] R.J. Van den Bergh, "Self-regulation of the Medical and Legal Professions: Remaining Barriers to Competition and EC Law", in *Organised Interests and Self-Regulation* (B. Bortolotti and G. Fiorentini ED., 1999), p.89.
[29] D. Neven, R. Nuttall and P. Seabright, *Merger in Daylight: The Economics and Politics of European Merger Control* (1993), p.175.

Centralisation may weaken the power of some interest groups (e.g. middle-class retailers), but other groups may gain when competition policy is centralised (e.g. farmers). Some interest groups (e.g. insurance companies) appear to be equally powerful both at the supranational and at the national levels, although there may be some differences across Member States. The group exemption for cartels on insurance markets illustrates how centralisation may even cause costs of market power in Member States where competitive markets existed before.[30]

The possibilities of regulatory capture have their limitations in the design of regulatory institutions. Although appropriate institutional design will not prevent regulatory capture altogether, it may nevertheless limit its scope. With respect to competition policy in general and merger control in particular, Neven, Nuttall and Seabright[31] indicate three different responses to the problem of regulatory capture: accountability, independence and transparency. Mobility is one of the best guarantors of accountability: firms and individuals who are unhappy with substantive rules of law and/or their enforcement simply move to another jurisdiction. When mobility is limited other devices are necessary to guarantee that regulatory agencies are held to account, through the political process, to the general public. The argument for political independence rests on the fact that compared to the voting public at large, special interest groups can more easily influence politicians. Finally, transparency may reduce the informational asymmetries, aid regulatory agencies to commit themselves to a given regulatory policy, and cope with unequal costs of gathering information.

Attention must also be drawn to the bureaucrats' self-interest in power and prestige and to the behaviour of utility-maximising judges. According to classic Public Choice analysis, the behaviour of bureaucrats may be explained by assuming that they pursue their self-interest, which includes salary, reputation and power. Contrary to managers of private firms in competitive markets, bureaucrats must not assess the marginal costs and benefits of their actions. As a consequence, the budget of the bureau will be maximised regardless of the quality of bureaucrats' performance and productive inefficiency will ensue.[32] However, the extent of the welfare losses may be reduced by competition between different departments that have to compete for budget allocation[33] (as is the case with the different Directorate Generals within the European Commission). In addition, the bureaucrats' self-interest in power and prestige may be secured better by high status and agreeable work tasks, rather than budget maximisation.[34]

Insights from Public Choice are equally relevant in explaining the behaviour of courts. Following the assumption that judges behave rationally, it may be

[30] See M. Faure and R.J. Van den Bergh, "Restrictions of Competition on Insurance Markets and the Applicability of EC Antitrust Law" (1995) 48 *Kyklos* 65.
[31] D. Neven, R. Nuttall and P. Seabright, *Merger in Daylight: The Economics and Politics of European Merger Control* (1993), pp.164–165.
[32] W. Niskanen, *Bureaucracy and Representative Government* (1971).
[33] A.I. Ogus, *Regulation Legal Form and Economic Theory* (1994), p.69, with further references.
[34] P. Dunleavy, *Bureaucracy and Public Choice: Economic Explanations in Political Science* (1991), Chs 7 & 8.

expected that they will try to maximise their utility by gaining prestige with their audience (lawyers and process parties) or by lowering the pressure of work.[35] From this perspective the scope and contents of judicial decisions may be explained. An example is the *Keck and Mithouard* judgment of the European Court of Justice in which an excessive workload was explicitly mentioned as a reason for reconsidering the existing case law on free movement of goods.[36] To judge the conformity of national regulations that indistinctly apply to both domestic products and imported goods with the fundamental EC principle of free movement of goods, the Court introduced a distinction between product-related rules (for example, composition of foodstuffs) and selling arrangements (for example, prohibition of sales at loss prices or with low profit margins), suggesting that the latter may escape from the ban of measures having equivalent effects as import restrictions, contained in Article 28 EC. Obviously, this distinction is not in harmony with economic insights since the efficiency losses caused by rules restricting sales methods may be substantial. In a later judgment, the Court clarified that selling arrangements nevertheless may infringe Article 28 EC if they prevent access to the market by products from another Member State or impede access any more than they impede the access of domestic products (for example, an outright advertising ban).[37] The dichotomy between product-related rules and selling arrangements was kept intact, however.

10.3 The allocation of competences in European competition law

In this section the insights from the economic analysis will be contrasted with the current division of competences between national authorities and the European Community in the field of competition law. The central question is whether the existing institutional framework allows an optimal degree of decentralisation and regulatory competition, so that the net benefits of such processes are maximised.

---

[35] R.D. Cooter, "The Objectives of Private and Public Judges" (1983) 41 *Public Choice* 107 at p.129; P.H. Rubin, "The Objectives of Private and Public Judges: A Comment" (1983) 41 *Public Choice* 133 at p.134.
[36] Joined Cases C–267/91 and C–268/91 *Criminal proceedings against Bernard Keck and Daniel Mithouard* [1993] ECR, I–6097, para.14.
[37] Case C–405/98 *Konsumentenombudsmannen (KO) v Gourmet International Products AB (GIP)* [2001] ECR I–1795. See the annotation by G. Straetmans in (2002) 39 C.M.L. Rev. 1407.

10.3.1 Advantages of decentralisation and competition between competition laws

10.3.1.1 Satisfying more preferences: a comparative perspective on the goals of competition law

Building upon Tiebout's classic article, a case can be made for divergent competition laws because preferences may differ with respect to the goals to be achieved. In the first and second chapters of this book it was stressed that allocative efficiency is not generally accepted as the sole goal of competition law. Competition policy may embrace a multitude of goals. In contrast with the USA, pluralist views have continued to predominate in Europe, even though the European Commission has limited the goals of competition law to allocative efficiency and consumer welfare in its most recent policy documents.[38]

The multiple values underlying competition policy and law become even clearer at the Member States' level. This is true both with respect to the assessment of anti-competitive agreements and practices as well as merger control. For example, in France and Belgium the principles of competition law do not apply fully to restraints arising from the application of statutory or regulatory law.[39] The inclusion of such a provision allows for various exceptions based on a wide range of public interest considerations. In apparent contrast with the competition laws of the Member States, the Norwegian Competition Act explicitly embraces "efficient utilisation of society's resources" as its purpose.[40] Oslo thus seems closer to Chicago than any other European city. In the following, the recent changes of German competition law will be presented to illustrate how harmonisation may put the achievement of policy goals, which are not shared by the European Commission, at risk.

Rather than emphasising efficiency goals, German competition law (*Gesetz gegen Wettbewerbsbeschränkungen*, hereafter abbreviated GWB) traditionally protects freedom of competition as such.[41] This approach opens the door for rules aiming at protecting small and medium-sized businesses and other policy considerations that are not in harmony with an efficiency (and consumer welfare) approach. The old German system was based on the prohibition principle, but various modifications were made by distinguishing between different types of cartel agreements. Some cartel agreements became valid after simple notification (*Anmeldekartelle*); others became valid unless the competition authority opposed such validity within three months (*Widerspruchskartelle*) and a third category comprised agreements which needed explicit permission (*Erlaubniskartelle*). Consequently, in the old version of the GWB, the basic prohibition of cartels was tempered by a long list of exceptions

---

[38] Guidelines on the application of Art. 81(3) of the EC Treaty [2004] O.J. C 101/97.
[39] Art. 10 Ordonnance 86–1243, JORF, December 3, 1986 (France); Art. 47 Wet Economische Mededinging (Belgium); Art. 16 Mededingingswet, March 22, 1997 (The Netherlands).
[40] Art. 1 Act No.65 of June 11, 1993 relating to competition in commercial activity.
[41] See also the discussion of the ordoliberal views (Freiburg School) in Ch.3, s.3.4 and Ch.7.

allowing, *inter alia*, agreements to improve the competitive position of small and medium-sized firms (Section 4 old GWB on *Mittelstandskartelle*), administrative exemptions allowing structural crisis cartels for socio-political reasons (Section 6 old GWB), and other exemptions based on a general provision enabling the Federal Minister for Economic Affairs to permit cartels in exceptional cases in which the restraint of competition is necessary because of overriding concerns for public welfare and the economy as a whole (Section 8 old GWB). In addition, the prohibition of minimum resale price maintenance did not cover books, and this was justified by so-called cultural reasons (Section 15 old GWB). The seventh amendment of the GWB, which entered into force in July 2005, aligned German competition law closely with European competition law. As a consequence, the list of specific exemptions was deleted—with the exception of the provision on *Mittelstandskartelle*—and replaced by a general and directly applicable exception rule similar to Article 81(3) EC (*Legalausnahme*). To some extent, the seventh amendment of the GWB sacrificed German preferences regarding goals of competition law on the altar of the European internal market. The application of EC inspired rules, both with respect to agreements having an impact on interstate trade and domestic agreements, has been justified by the need to create a "level playing field" for companies active in EC Member States.[42] The price to be paid for the uniformity of German competition law and European competition law, however, was the exclusion of an exemption regime that reflected German preferences on the goals to be achieved by rules of competition law.[43] In contrast with the agreed upon harmonisation of the rules on cartel agreements, the German government insisted on maintaining a stricter control on unilateral anti-competitive conduct than provided for by the rules on abuse of a dominant position contained in Article 82 EC. Consequently, the German rules on protection of economically dependent small and medium-sized enterprises against discrimination and exclusionary practices (such as sales at loss prices) by economically more powerful competitors (Section 20 GWB) have been kept intact. This clearly reflects the differences between the German and the European Commission's views on the goals to be achieved by competition law. Whereas the latter view increasingly stresses economic efficiency and consumer welfare as the sole goal of competition policy, the latter still insists on protection of individual economic freedom and the related concern to protect small and medium-sized enterprises.

---

[42] Bundesministerium für Wirtschaft und Arbeit, Begründung zur siebten Novellierung des GWB, 4 (available at: *www.bmwi.de*).

[43] The scope for satisfying divergent preferences becomes clear when the wording of Art. 81(3) EC is compared with the relevant provisions of the old GWB. Three examples may suffice. First, s.6 old GWB allowed for the exemption of crisis cartels if these were necessary to reduce overcapacity, without requiring proof that the four cumulative conditions of the European rule were satisfied. Second, s.7 old GWB (inserted in the German competition law by the sixth amendment) contained a catch-all provision to grant exemptions, which was similar to Art. 81(3) EC but did not contain the criterion of "improvement of technical and economic progress", in order to exclude industrial policy considerations in the assessment (Begründung zur siebten Novellierung des GWB, 12). Third, the Minister of Economic Affairs could exempt cartel agreements when this was deemed necessary for reasons of public interest, thus allowing for a broader policy assessment than possible in the framework of Art. 81(3) EC.

Merger control is another policy field where preferences concerning the goals to be achieved may differ. In the vision of things of some Member States, any assessment of mergers involves politically conflicting goals and should, therefore, be decided by the competent Minister. In France, the Minister of Economic Affairs decides whether a concentration creating or strengthening a dominant position contributes in a sufficient way to economic and social progress to compensate this disadvantage.[44] In the United Kingdom, decisions are taken by the Secretary of State for Trade and Industry on the basis of an even broader criterion of "public interest". As a consequence, employment or regional policy considerations as well as efficiency considerations can be relevant in the overall assessment of mergers.[45]

Economic theory teaches that allocative efficiency is improved when a greater number of diverging preferences is satisfied. There is no economic reason why competition laws should not reflect different views in different countries as long as costs and benefits remain in the jurisdiction that enacted the rules. In the opposite case, the magnitude of the ensuing externalities may be an argument in favour of harmonisation of laws. However, to ensure efficient competition à la Tiebout, a large number of competitors is required. In theory, in the enlarged European Community a choice among 25 different competition laws is possible. In practice, the choice is more limited because of the one-stop-shop principle in merger control and the broad interpretation of the requirement that interstate trade must be affected (Articles 81 and 82 EC). It should also be obvious that the recent transplantation of many EC rules into the national legal orders of some Member States has restricted the choice between competition laws. Instead of creating the conditions for Tiebout competition, the current trend is thus rather moving away from the conditions to maximise economic welfare in the European Union.

10.3.1.2 Enabling learning processes

The importance of learning processes with regard to the protection of competition should be obvious. Competition law is plagued by great uncertainties in designing the most appropriate substantive rules and methods of enforcement. Each competition law regime tries to cope with complex problems by using a complex set of rules. Many rules of competition law contain vague concepts that may be illuminated by different economic theories on, for example, entry barriers and predatory pricing. Given its crucial importance for the decision of real-life cases, the most pressing example to illustrate the need of experimentation and mutual learning is the definition of the relevant market.[46]

Both the substantive legal rules and the methods of enforcement may differ substantially. As to the former, by way of example, reference can be made to the discussion on the appropriate standard of merger control (dominance test

---

[44] Art. 42 Ordonnance 86–1243, JORF, December 3, 1986.
[45] See also W. Möschel, "The Goals of Antitrust Revisited" (1991) 147 J. Inst. Theoretical Econ. 9.
[46] See the discussion in Ch.4.

in old European competition law, the SLC test (substantially lessening competition) in the USA and the criterion of significant impediment to effective competition in the new EC Merger Regulation). As to the latter, the discussion of the type of sanctions, the range of antitrust offenders who can be sanctioned and the magnitude of the sanctions in US antitrust law and European competition law (fines on companies only or also fines on individuals and imprisonment) may be recalled.[47] In recent years, some Member States (United Kingdom, Ireland) have criminalised the most serious infringements of the competition laws (see Box 8.1), whereas other Member States still rely exclusively on administrative and civil sanctions. Consequently, Europe has become a laboratory in which the effects of differences in systems of enforcement can be tested. This will allow for learning processes that may be very valuable for designing the optimal system of enforcement. This state of things also shows that learning processes never end and that, as it was argued by Hayek, the notion of *ex post* harmonisation is misleading.

The current "spontaneous harmonisation" inhibits trial-and-error processes in the area of competition law where learning-by-doing is very important. A comparison with US antitrust law or with competition laws of the Member States may reveal that the wording of the European competition rules is either over- or under-inclusive. Also, the current European rules are not entirely consistent with lessons from economics and may lead to effects which are exactly the opposite of the goals for which they were enacted.[48] Under such circumstances there should be scope for competing rules; harmonisation is unwarranted since it entails the import into the Member States of all inefficiencies inherent in European competition law. Crucial learning processes are excluded if competition rules are made uniform throughout the entire common market. Here, one example may be recalled to demonstrate that national competition laws may do a better job and that the effects of harmonisation (either forced or spontaneous) may be perverse. As explained in Chapter 6, the old German approach to vertical restraints, in particular the treatment of vertical price fixing (see Box 6.2) avoided some of the inefficiencies of European competition law. Unfortunately, the impact of this German rule has been negligible because of the broad interpretation of the requirement of impact on interstate trade. In contrast with Article 81 EC, the old German GWB clearly distinguished between horizontal and vertical agreements.[49] At the outset it seems rather odd to qualify vertical restraints contained in contracts between manufacturers and distributors as agreements restricting competition because manufacturers and dealers are not competitors. Only when markets are concentrated and significant entry barriers exist will vertical restraints endanger competition. The anti-competitive effects of horizontal agreements are much more worrisome than the limited foreclosure effects of vertical restrictions.

---

[47] See Ch.8, s.8.2.
[48] Examples are discussed in Ch.6, s.6.4.5. (adverse effects on market integration flowing from European competition rules on vertical restraints) and Ch.7, s.7.2.2.1, Box 7.2 and s.7.5.2.2 (counterproductive effects on market integration flowing from the prohibitions of price discrimination and predatory pricing as abuses of dominant position).
[49] See Ch.6, Box 6.2.

Therefore, a control of vertical restraints *ex post* by means of an abuse principle as it existed under German law seems preferable to submitting vertical restraints to a prohibition principle, as is the case under current European competition law.[50] After the coming into force of Regulation 1/2003, which requires the simultaneous application of national competition rules and European competition law with the latter taking precedence over the former, the German legislator decided to give up the economics-based definition of cartels (which excluded agreements between non-competing firms) to enable a uniform application of the GWB to both interstate and domestic agreements.[51] The treatment of vertical restraints under European competition law is also at the same time inconsistent and ineffective: fully integrated firms are allowed to implement almost any contract internally, whereas the legality of vertical agreements between independent firms is subject to restrictive conditions.

10.3.1.3 Decentralised enforcement as a remedy for information problems

Compared to the European Commission, the competition authorities of the Member States may have an information advantage *vis-à-vis* the firms to be controlled. National competition authorities are generally better placed to assess matters that are concentrated in their particular state. On the other hand, the risk of regulatory capture at lower levels of government may be higher. National authorities may be inclined to favour national interests. Officials of a central antitrust authority are more remote from the firms they have to control and may thus act in a more independent way, making them less vulnerable to regulatory capture. As a consequence, an optimal mix of competences will be required to reach efficient outcomes. The problems posed by regulatory capture are discussed below (see 10.3.3). Hereafter, the current enforcement system of Regulation 1/2003 is described and its ability to reduce information asymmetries is assessed.

A first step towards overcoming information asymmetries is cooperation between competition authorities. Before the modernisation project contained in Regulation 1/2003 came into effect, Member States already had an obligation to cooperate with the investigation procedures of the European Commission. The Commission was empowered to obtain all necessary information

---

[50] The prohibition principle flatly outlaws particular business practices in a statute unless a statutory exemption or individual dispensation again makes them lawful. The abuse principle does not ban particular business practices unless, and until, the competition authorities use their review powers to intervene against such practices. It must be added that after the entry into force of the new-style block exemption on vertical restraints (Regulation 2790/99), the practical difference of both approaches became less significant. Indeed, a safe harbour was created for non-blacklisted clauses used by suppliers having a market share not exceeding 30%. For a more detailed discussion, see Ch.6, s.6.3.2.

[51] The following quotation is highly illuminating: "Die bisherige deutsche Systematik ist zwar wettbewerbspolitisch sachgerecht und führt auch zu praktisch befriedigenden Ergebnissen. Angesichts des erweiterten Vorrangs des europäischen Rechts wird jedoch zukünftig im Grundsatz das europäische Modell fur vertikale Wettbewerbsbeschränkungen übernommen, um die Einheit des Wettbewerbsrechts zu bewahren." (Begründung zur siebten Novellierung des GWB, 2).

from both governments and competition authorities of Member States, as well as from undertakings and associations within those Member States (Article 11(1) of Regulation 17). Moreover, the competent authorities of the Member States could be asked to carry out on the spot investigations on the Commission's behalf (Article 13(1) of Regulation 17). When the Commission carried out its own investigations, it could require the assistance of national authorities (Article 14 of Regulation 17).

If the information asymmetries are very serious, a further step towards decentralisation may be necessary. Regulation 1/2003 has given full powers to all national competition authorities and judges to apply Articles 81 and 82 EC. Compared to the enforcement monopoly of the European Commission, the application of Article 81(3) EC by many national competition authorities and courts allows better access to the relevant information. National competition authorities and judges can more easily take a closer look at the markets and firms to be controlled. Their information advantage will be the greatest when the anti-competitive effects of agreements manifest themselves mainly within the territory of a single Member State. National competition authorities are generally better placed to assess effects that are concentrated on their particular state and can thus be better placed to control these transactions.

The European Commission's Notice on cooperation within the Network of Competition Authorities states that a competition authority can be considered to be well placed to deal with a case if three cumulative conditions are met: first, the agreement or practice has substantial direct actual or foreseeable effects on competition within its territory, is implemented within or originates from its territory; second, the authority is able to effectively bring an end to the entire infringement; and third, the authority can gather the evidence required to prove the infringement.[52] The first and third conditions reflect the information advantages of national competition authorities; in this respect the Notice gains support from the economic criteria in favour of decentralisation. The harmony with the economic analysis is not complete, however. If agreements or practices have effects on competition in more than three Member States, the European Commission is seen as particularly well placed to deal with the case. This rule cannot be unreservedly supported by information advantages on the side of the European Commission. For example, a supranational competition authority may face greater information problems than the national competition authorities to establish dominance in four different national markets. Centralised enforcement will only save on costs if the information gathered for one market is also relevant for the other markets. Coexistence of supranational and national enforcement procedures, allowing several national competition authorities and the European Commission to act in parallel, seems better suited to benefit from information advantages where they exist. The exclusion of parallel action (in the case where effects on competition arise in more than three Member States) seems to be inspired by other reasons, such as the wish to avoid inconsistent decisions and to increase the

---

[52] Commission Notice on cooperation within the Network of Competition Authorities, [2004] O.J. C 101/43, para.8.

legal certainty for firms. However, if the savings brought about by greater legal certainty for firms are outweighed by the increase in information costs concerning the existence and effects of anti-competitive practices, the centralised enforcement may be inefficient.

10.3.2 Disadvantages of decentralisation and competition between competition laws

10.3.2.1 Interjurisdictional externalities

Competition between jurisdictions will only lead to allocative efficiency if the costs and benefits of law making are borne entirely within the jurisdiction where the legal rules are enacted and enforced. Externalities also occur in the field of competition law and thus raise the question whether they warrant centralisation. Below it is investigated to what extent the current division of competences between national competition authorities and the European Commission is able to cope with the problems posed by interstate externalities. It will be shown that the interpretation of the criterion of impact on interstate trade causes interventions by the Commission that cannot be supported by economic criteria. Whereas European competition law thus seems to be over-inclusive in the interpretation of the substantive cartel prohibition, there is a risk that the current decentralised system of enforcement may be under-inclusive. The new system may be biased towards granting too high a number of exemptions (type I errors), and this may ultimately lead to a deterioration of the quality of competition law enforcement. Finally, the criteria for delineating jurisdiction in the Merger Regulation are not fully appropriate for guaranteeing that interstate externalities are internalised. Each of these points is discussed in turn.

Cartels: the requirement of impact on interstate trade   For cartel agreements to be screened by the European Commission, the relevant criterion is whether they affect interstate trade. This requirement is broadly interpreted, however. Also purely national agreements may have effects on interstate trade in the sense of Article 81(1) EC. The European Court has decided that, in assessing whether an individual agreement is in breach of Article 81(1) EC, not simply the individual agreement but the entire economic and legal context must be investigated.[53] This reasoning has brought many agreements of an apparently domestic nature within the reach of the European prohibition. It has enabled the European Commission to exercise jurisdiction in a number of areas where the degree of effect on trade between Member States appears to be minor. A few examples may illustrate this point. According to the case law of the European Court of Justice, the Commission has jurisdiction over nationwide

[53] Case 23/67 *Brasserie de Haecht v Wilkin* [1967] ECR 407; Case C–234/89 *S. Delimitis v Henniger Bräu* [1991] ECR I–935.

distribution systems reducing the attractiveness of market entry for impor-ters,[54] aggregate rebate systems discouraging the imports of foreign products,[55] and refusals to supply local retailers without objective justification.[56] The latter case is the most dramatic example of the use of European competition rules to combat restrictive practices without any international spillovers. The market affected was clearly national (even local) with, at most, minor effects on imports or exports. Also with respect to the other cases the argument may be advanced that the costs of market power were borne by the consumers of the country to which exports were discouraged. Therefore, it seems more natural to have the foreclosure effects controlled by the competition authority of the import country.

Cartels: decentralised enforcement of Article 81 EC The information advantages at lower levels of government and the potentially beneficial effects of learning processes are powerful arguments in favour of decentralised enforcement of European competition law. However, decentralisation of enforcement efforts also comes at a cost. Parallel enforcement of competition law may generate interstate externalities. National competition authorities may not take into account the effects of their decisions on other national authorities. Because of the resulting regulatory externalities, splitting compe-tences between competition authorities may lead to inefficiencies compared to action by a single competition authority (European Commission).

Positive externalities occur when action of all competent competition authorities is necessary to give full effect to the activity of a single competition authority. Suppose that a restrictive agreement causes harm in three Member States and that one of the competent competition authorities establishes an infringement of Article 81 EC. If this decision is not sufficient to bring the entire infringement to an end or sanction it adequately, the decision of the acting authority will cause a positive externality by increasing the value and exploitable rents to the other two competition authorities. Positive externalities will be underprovided because competition authorities which produce the externalities only account for the effect of their action on themselves.

Negative externalities occur when the action of one competition authority reduces the value and exploitable rents of another authority. For example, an exemption by one competition authority dissipates the value of a second exemption by a competition authority in another Member State. Similarly, a leniency fine reduction from one national competition authority dissipates the value of a subsequent fine reduction by another national competition authority. Negative externalities will be overprovided because individual competition authorities do not account for the negative effects of their deci-sions on other authorities. Drawing upon these theoretical insights, one may

---

[54] Case IV/147 *Centraal Bureau voor de Rijwielhandel (Dutch bicycles)* [1978] O.J. L 20/18.
[55] As in the case of the Belgian wallpaper manufacturers, see Case 73/74 *Groupement des fabricants de papiers peints de Belgique v Commission* [1975] ECR 1491.
[56] Case 126/80 *Salonia v Poidomani and Baglieri* [1981] ECR 1563. This case concerned a complaint by a retailer in Ragusa who was not supplied with newspapers and periodicals by a wholesaler whose warehouse was also in Ragusa.

expect that the direct applicability of the exemption provision will increase the overall amount of exemptions.[57]

The adequate answer to the positive and negative regulatory externalities described above is centralised enforcement. The EC system of parallel enforcement provides only partial solutions to the externalities problem. If the costs of either non-enforcement or too lenient an enforcement of competition law in one of the Member States are borne by businesses and consumers in other Member States, centralised enforcement may be needed to ensure that these interstate externalities are internalised. The European Commission retains exclusive jurisdiction if a restrictive agreement or practice affects competition in cross-border markets covering more than three Member States. In this way, the under-provision of positive externalities by competing national competition authorities is overcome. If the agreement or practice has substantial effects on competition in two or three domestic markets, the European Commission's Notice provides for parallel action by the national competition authorities involved.[58] Also in the latter case, centralised enforcement may be favoured to avoid opportunistic behaviour of one or two of the competent authorities. The exclusive jurisdiction of the Commission in cases where competition is affected in more than three Member States is also a way to avoid the negative externalities of the system of parallel enforcement. If the targeted agreement or practice affects competition in two or three Member States, only coordination of regulatory action may minimise the distortions described above. In this respect, it may be deplored that the Guidelines on cooperation within the Network of Competition Authorities are not legally binding. National competition authorities may suspend a proceeding when another national competition authority is dealing with a case, but they have no obligation to do so.[59] Consequently, there remains scope for negative externalities across jurisdictions.

Mergers If a proposed merger is only evaluated in the Member State where the merging firms have their main centre of operations, a bias in favour of national interests cannot be excluded. Significant cross-border effects will not be adequately internalised by national agencies: "typically the costs of market power to foreign customers will be given less weight than the rents of market power to domestic interests".[60] An excessively national focus in the control of such mergers may thus lead to distorted judgments. Hence, an argument can be made in favour of multiple controls. Contrary to competing national environmental regulations, decentralised competition laws may be able to cope with negative external effects. A downstream Member State cannot use a veto right to ban emissions from an upstream Member State. In

---

[57] B. De Poorter and F. Parisi, *Modernization of European Antitrust Enforcement: The Economics of Regulatory Competition* (George Mason University School of Law, Working paper series 24) (2005) (available at: *http://law.bepress.com/gmulwps/gmule/art24*).
[58] Commission Notice on cooperation within the Network of Competition Authorities, para.12.
[59] *ibid.*, paras 20–22.
[60] D. Neven, R. Nuttall and P. Seabright, *Merger in Daylight: The Economics and Politics of European Merger Control* (1993), p.196.

contrast, mergers that would allow firms to extract consumer surplus abroad will not pass without the consent of the competition authority of the harmed countries. Under competing national competition laws, mergers having extra-territorial effects will be controlled by the competition authorities of all Member States involved. The combined application of several national control procedures may, however, cause problems of coordination and increase legal uncertainty.

The latter concerns are a major reason for the division of work in the field of merger control as adopted by European competition law. When mergers have to be supervised several times legal uncertainty will increase, especially when the appraisal criteria differ across countries. When the Merger Regulation was introduced in 1989, the basic idea was a one-stop-shop review system, i.e. the concentration would be notified to either the European Commission or one or more Member States, but no parallel jurisdictional wrangling would take place. For the purposes of the present discussion, the Merger Regulation thus contained an explicit choice between centralised and decentralised review of concentrations. Centralised review was reserved for concentrations with a Community dimension, providing exclusive competence to the European Commission if the Merger Regulation applied. The jurisdictional thresholds for determining whether or not the centralised authority—the Commission—would review a concentration having such Community dimension were contained in Article 1 of the Merger Regulation, which introduced a number of turnover thresholds.

After the 2004 review of the Merger Regulation, the current thresholds are as follows. A merger has a Community dimension if two positively formulated conditions and one negatively worded requirement are met. Positively, (a) the combined aggregate worldwide turnover of all the undertakings concerned must exceed €5,000 million; and (b) the aggregate Community-wide turnover of each of at least two of the undertakings concerned must be more than €250 million. Negatively, (c) even if these thresholds are reached, the merger will not be supervised by the European Commission if each of the undertakings concerned achieves more than two thirds of its aggregate Community-wide turnover within one and the same Member State (Article 1(2) of the Merger Regulation).[61] Since the 1997 amendments to the Merger Regulation, the European Commission must be notified of concentrations satisfying all the following thresholds: the (a) combined aggregate worldwide turnover of all the undertakings concerned exceeds €2,500 million; and (b) in each of at least three Member States the combined aggregate turnover of all the undertakings concerned is more than €100 million; and (c) in each of the same three Member States identified for the purpose of (b) above, the aggregate turnover of each of at least two of the undertakings concerned exceeds €25 million; and

---

[61] Exceptions to these rules are contained in the so-called German clause (Art. 9 of the Merger Regulation) and Dutch clause (Art. 22(3) of the Merger Regulation): the first clause allows for national merger control even if the thresholds are reached, whereas the second clause provides for the possibility of European merger control below the thresholds mentioned in Regulation 4064/89.

(d) the aggregate Community-wide turnover of each of at least two of the undertakings concerned is more than €100 million.[62]

With the 2004 review in sight, the European Commission decided to amend the original system by introducing a fine-tuned referral system to supplement the basic turnover-based thresholds. The exclusive competence for the Commission was maintained if concentrations were found to have a Community dimension (still through only slightly amended turnover thresholds), but the basic system was changed to allow better allocation of cases between the Commission and the Member States as application in practice had shown national filings with multiple Member State authorities to have become a regular occurrence (often, the relatively high turnover thresholds in the Merger Regulation were not met, while the much lower national thresholds were quite easily breached). The referral system—which though originally contained in the Merger Regulation, was burdensome—was seen as a means to improve the allocation of cases between the centralised and the decentralised authorities (the main concern being one of administrative efficiency). The referral system is summarised in Box 10.1.

Box 10.1: Referral system of the Merger Regulation

The key elements of the revised referral system are (a) simplified criteria for referral, to be applied for by using the new Form R/S, (b) application also at pre-notification stage (at the parties' request only—post-notification, referral can be at request of the parties, the European Commission or the Member States), with (c) legally binding deadlines, clearly expressed in working days. New, for pre-notification, Article 4(4) of the Merger Regulation contains the process of referral from the European Commission to the Member States, and Article 4(5) of the Merger Regulation the process from the Member States to the European Commission. Revised, for post-notification, Article 9 of the Merger Regulation contains the process of referral from the European Commission to the Member States, and Article 22 of the Merger Regulation the process from the Member States to the European Commission.

In detail, this amounts to the following:

Pre-Notification Referral: from the European Commission to the Member States:

- transaction with a Community dimension but parties believe it "may significantly affect competition" within a "distinct" national market;

- parties make request to the Commission for early referral;

- the Commission transmits request to a "network" comprising of the Commission and all Member State authorities;

---

[62] Compare C. Ahlborn and V. Turner, "Expanding Success? Reform of the EC Merger Regulation" (1999) 19 E.C.L.R. 249.

- competent Member States must express agreement within 15 working days;

- if agreement from the Member States is forthcoming, the Commission must decide within additional 10 working days;

- if full referral, then there is no need for a Community notification;

- parties proceed with national notification.

Pre-Notification Referral: from the Member States to the European Commission:

- no "Community dimension", but case reviewable in three or more Member States;

- parties make request to the Commission for early referral;

- the Commission transmits request to the network;

- the Member States decide within 15 working days;

- no national notifications before referral decision;

- if all competent Member States agree: exclusive jurisdiction by the Commission, and no national notifications;

- if one competent Member State disagrees: no referral, and national notifications.

Post-Notification Referral: from the European Commission to the Member States:

- "Community dimension" case notified to the Commission;

- a Member State makes a request within 15 working days from receipt of Form CO;

- test: the concentration threatens to significantly affect competition within a distinct market; or the concentration affects competition in a distinct market which is not a substantial part of the common market;

- the Commission decides, applying the "distinct market" test, under full administrative discretion;

- deadline: 35 working days (or 65 working days if phase 2 is already initiated);

- partial or full referrals possible;

- Article 9(6) of the Merger Regulation: Member State must inform parties of preliminary results within 45 working days after referral.

Post-Notification Referral: from the Member States to the European Commission:

- concentration falls within national jurisdiction;

- a Member State makes a request within 15 working days from national notification or knowledge of transaction;

- test: the concentration threatens to significantly affect competition within a national market and affects interstate trade;

- the Commission informs all Member States of such request;

- Member States decide whether to join request within 15 working days;

- suspension of national time limits pending decision on referral;

- the Commission decides within additional 10 working days whether to examine case on behalf of the requesting Member State(s);

- if the Commission examines the case, no application of national law in referring Member State(s).

How can the current EC competition rules delineating jurisdiction between national and European competition authorities be assessed? Starting from the insight that externalities are a powerful argument in favour of centralisation, the case for control under European competition law will be stronger the more significant the externalities problem. Under the Merger Regulation the scale of the parties to the transaction is crucial for determining whether the merger will be supervised by the European Commission. Neven, Nuttall and Seabright have argued that it would be more natural to let the absolute size of the spillovers determine whether the Merger Regulation should apply. Small transactions may have substantial spillovers which will not always be considered appropriately by national antitrust authorities. To avoid this kind of distortion they suggest a threshold requiring that of the worldwide annual turnover half of the turnover within the EC must take place outside the Member State with the largest share of the combined turnover.[63] Such a rule would better enable the EC to investigate transactions that give rise to significant international spillovers. In sum, the thresholds of the Merger Regulation may be seen as an attempt to limit intervention by the central authority to cases that may not be appropriately dealt with by national agencies. Unfortunately, the Merger Regulation does not adequately reach the goal of internalising interstate externalities because the scale of the transactions is not the best way of determining the magnitude of the spillovers.

The referral system has a number of pros and cons. On the upside, if the system works well, the most appropriately placed authority (centralised/

---

[63] D. Neven, R. Nuttall and P. Seabright, *Merger in Daylight: The Economics and Politics of European Merger Control* (1993), p.198.

decentralised) deals with the case, the number of multiple filings is reduced, deadlines are strict and legally binding, and the pre-notification system allows for early decisions to be taken at the request of the parties to a concentration. On the downside, referral may significantly delay the review of concentrations, the Form R/S is a cumbersome tool (closely resembling the Form CO in terms of information required from the parties to a concentration), and some issues may remain unresolved (for example, referral from the Member States to the European Commission is foreseen for such cases that require filing in three or more Member States—but one single Member State can block the referral; also, conflicting referrals cannot be excluded pre- and post-notification). Although a number of high-profile referrals have already taken place at the time of writing (perhaps unsurprisingly, mainly the large Member States with a sophisticated antitrust background—Germany, UK—have been actively involved), it is too early to comment whether or not the fine-tuned referral system optimises the allocation of cases between the centralised and decentralised authorities. Still, the modifications to the referral system at least provide for a viable corrector to the turnover-based thresholds for determining jurisdiction in cases where turnover does not clearly identify cross-border effects.

10.3.2.2 The race to the bottom

The view that divergent (applications of) competition laws may lead to "bad" rules did not have a prominent place in the recent debate on the modernisation of the system of enforcement.

However, the text of Regulation 1/2003 shows that the European Commission is concerned about divergent competition laws for another related reason, namely that such differences create unequal conditions of competition for firms active in the internal market and are at odds with the goal to create a "level playing field". Simultaneous application of national competition laws and European competition law has been criticised since it may subject companies active in Member States having enacted strict rules to prohibitions that do not apply in Member States, where national competition laws are more lenient. In order to "create a level playing field for restrictive agreements" Regulation 1/2003 has excluded such divergences when national competition laws are applied to agreements which may affect trade between Member States. In the latter case, national competition authorities and judges must also apply Article 81 EC. According to Article 3(2) of Regulation 1/2003, the application of national competition law may not lead to the prohibition of agreements, which do not restrict competition within the meaning of Article 81(1) EC or fulfil the conditions of Article 81(3) EC. The duty to simultaneously apply national competition law and European competition law (Article 82 EC) also applies in cases of abuses of a dominant position that have an impact on interstate trade. However, the national competition authorities and judges retain the possibility of applying stricter national rules to unilateral conduct. As specified in the recitals of Regulation 1/2003, these stricter national laws may include provisions which prohibit or impose sanctions on abusive behaviour towards economically dependent undertakings.[64] On top of the convergence rule, national competition authorities cannot—when ruling on agreements and practices under Articles 81 and 82 EC which are already the subject of a Commission decision—take decisions, which would run counter to the decisions adopted by the European Commission (Article 16(2) of Regulation 1/2003).

The "level playing field" argument will not be further commented upon. From an economic perspective, it is not the right approach to decide in favour or against (de)centralisation and harmonisation of laws.[65] Instead, the analysis below will focus on the crucial question whether European law is able to avoid a "race to the bottom" if the result of such regulatory competition would be a sub-optimal competition law (both in terms of substantive rules and their enforcement). As indicated above, a race to the bottom is most realistic under type IV regulatory competition. If firms can choose which competition rules apply to their transactions, irrespective of the place where their business is located or where their practices generate anti-competitive effects, an overall deterioration of the quality of competition law is to be expected. Hence, there is a need for an appropriate legal institutional framework that prevents the negative effects of such "forum shopping". Below it will be investigated whether European law is sufficiently able to minimise the risk of inadequate competition on the market for competition laws. In this discussion, attention will also be paid to the opposite view that competition between legal orders creates a "race to the top". Also in the latter case, the enforcement level may be sub-optimal.

General assessment of European competition law   In an early publication on antitrust law and federalism, Easterbrook has described how a "race to the bottom" on the market for competition laws would look.[66] He suggested the following wish list for firms in search of monopoly profits. First on the list would be a monopoly protected by the state but not regulated in any other way. Second on the list would be a cartel enforced by the state. Third on the list would be a law lifting the antitrust laws.

European law limits the scope for Member States to grant firms any of these wishes. Existing state protected monopolies have been deregulated, even in

---

[64] Regulation 1/2003, para 8 *in fine*. Several Member States (Germany, France, Italy) have enacted laws protecting economically dependent firms from abuses by firms enjoying market power in relation with specific customers (in German: "relative Marktmacht"). Regulation 1/2003 thus reconfirms that also European competition law does not only pursue efficiency objectives but also aims at protecting freedom of business decisions and individual economic independence (recall the discussion in Ch.2, s.2.4.5).

[65] In fact, a "level playing field" cannot be achieved by harmonising parts of the legal system, since competition may then shift to the non-harmonised parts. The ultimate answer to this problem is an outright full harmonisation of the entire legal system, which cannot be reconciled with the subsidiarity principle. Moreover, harmonisation of laws does not affect non-legal factors which have a direct impact on equality of competitive conditions, such as access to raw materials and climate conditions. The "level playing field" argument seems to be a popular argument with European bureaucrats willing to justify interventions in national legal systems, but owes its strength mainly to the fact that it is constantly repeated rather than to economic analysis.

[66] F. Easterbrook, "Antitrust and the Economics of Federalism" (1983) 26 J. Law Econ. 23.

markets which were long considered natural monopolies.[67] Cartels protected and enforced by state regulation may be prohibited on the basis of a combined use of the Articles 3(g), 10 and 81 EC.[68] Member States may not adopt or maintain in force any measure which could deprive the competition rules of their effectiveness. Following this principle, the European Court of Justice struck down several national regulations restricting competition, such as the Belgian rule requiring travel agents to observe the prices fixed by tour operators and prohibiting the grant of rebates to consumers.[69] Price restrictions may also be considered as measures having the equivalent effect of import restrictions in violation of Articles 28 and 29 EC.[70] Finally, a complete lifting of national antitrust laws seems unrealistic. In the past, there existed different statutory traditions in Europe. Countries adopting the "abuse principle" rather than the "prohibition principle" were qualified as "cartel paradises". Under the former regime, restrictive agreements are valid until the competition authority is able to prove that any particular agreement constitutes an abuse, and then with prospective effect only. Under the latter regime, agreements are prohibited and exemptions possible only after notification. In addition, even private parties may sue in court. These divergent systems reflect differences in the support for the competition principle. The "abuse principle" has meanwhile been abandoned.

Because of the very wide interpretation of the phrase "trade between Member States", there are not many agreements of commercial significance which remain outside the range of Community law. In general, agreements must satisfy both Article 81 EC and national law. If the agreement is forbidden by Article 81(1) EC, the rule of supremacy of European law makes national exemptions impossible. In such a case, Member States can not undersell each other (race for the bottom) in allowing anti-competitive practices. In the converse case, where the cartel is outside the scope of the European prohibition, national authorities are still free to intervene so that competition between competition laws remains possible. This competition may be for the top, instead of being a race for the bottom.

Scope for forum shopping: merger control   Some rules increase the scope for prisoners' dilemmas rather than reducing it. Although the diffusion of powers between competition authorities has been fixed by the Merger Regulation and the free choice of the controlling agency (type IV regulatory competition through free choice of law) has consequently been limited, in practice firms

---

[67] The deregulation of the telecommunications sector may serve as an example.
[68] Case C–13/77 *GB-Inno-BM v ATAB* [1977] ECR 2115.
[69] Case 311/85 *Vereniging van Vlaamse Reisbureaus ASBL v Sociale Dienst van de Plaatselijke en Gewestelijke Overheidsdiensten* [1987] ECR 3801.
[70] Case 229/83 *Association des Centres distributeurs Edouard Leclerc and others v Sarl "Au Blé Vert" and others (French Books I)* [1985] ECR 1. In this case resale price maintenance for imported books was held to violate the free movement of goods; the only exception to that would be if it were established that the original exports of the books had been for the sole purpose of circumventing the French legislation by subsequent re-importation.

may seek to change the content or the form of the contemplated transactions in order to have them controlled by a preferred competition authority.[71] Although the prospect of alternative jurisdictions will presumably be a relatively minor consideration in the majority of deals where the commercial rationale dominates, these considerations may matter at the margin. At this point, it should be noted that also the Community antitrust authorities take part in the competition on the market for competition laws. In the field of merger control, where some scope exists for tailoring deals in such a way that they fall under a preferred jurisdiction, the European Commission has responded by introducing flexible procedures, allowing for decisions to be taken at relatively short notice. The competition between competition laws may thus be won by central rules. If control of a merger by the European Commission is preferred to control by national antitrust authorities, a (presumably large) minority partner may be added to increase the turnover of the undertakings concerned and make the merger a matter for the Commission. Aside from its competitive advantage resulting from issuing decisions in a short timeframe, the Commission may be the preferred agency for another reason. When national competition authorities treat potentially anti-competitive mergers more strictly, firms may wish to change the contemplated merger in order to have it controlled in Brussels. It is, for instance, remarkable that German firms seem to have preferred the EC system to that of the Bundeskartellamt.[72]

Scope for forum shopping: joint ventures Changing the form of the contemplated transaction may also create scope for forum shopping. For example, with respect to joint ventures there is some evidence that firms have changed the form of the joint venture because they wanted it to count as concentrative and thus be subject to the Merger Regulation.[73] Early on the European Commission issued a Notice to inform parties about the characteristics qualifying a concentration to be either concentrative or cooperative under Article 3 of the Merger Regulation.[74] While the former qualification resulted in the joint venture falling under the assessment procedures and timetable established under the Merger Regulation, the latter brought the transaction within the scope of Article 81 EC. Procedures under Article 81 EC are more cumbersome,

---

[71] The arguments are derived from D. Neven, R. Nuttall and P. Seabright, *Merger in Daylight: The Economics and Politics of European Merger Control* (1993), pp.79–80.

[72] The German antitrust authorities have expressed concern from the outset that the Merger Regulation may be too lax. Officials from the Bundeskartellamt indicated that their assessment would probably have been different in cases, such as Case IV/M.12 *Varta/Bosch*: see D. Neven, R. Nuttall and P. Seabright, *Merger in Daylight: The Economics and Politics of European Merger Control* (1993), p.81.

[73] D. Neven, R. Nuttall and P. Seabright, *Merger in Daylight: The Economics and Politics of European Merger Control* (1993), p.195.

[74] Commission Notice on the concept of full-function joint ventures under Council Regulation (EEC) No.4064/89 on the control of concentrations between undertakings [1998] O.J. C 66/1. A joint venture was to be characterised as concentrative if it performs on a lasting basis all the functions of an autonomous economic entity (positive condition) and if it does not have as its object or effect the coordination of the competitive behaviour of undertakings that remain independent of each other (negative condition).

however. They are open-ended and tend to be lengthy; their implementation is perceived to be rather more inflexible and decisions have limited duration, whereas there is no such time limit under the Merger Regulation. Although this explains the incentives for parties to a joint venture to change the form of their transaction to ensure that it falls under the Merger Regulation, this may have added to the indirect costs of merger control. As it stood, the Commission's policy induced firms to engage in concentrations which tend to be durable, rather than in cartel agreements which are unstable by their very nature.

Since the one-stop-shop principle excludes control of mergers by Member States above the Community thresholds, this development may have indirectly favoured substantial increases of the concentration ratios in many European industries. Hence, after much discussion, the 1997 amendments to the Merger Regulation introduced a new provision, the current Article 2(4) of the Merger Regulation, incorporating the Article 81 EC analysis into the assessment of compatibility under the Merger Regulation in the case of structural joint ventures having coordination effects. This change is to be welcomed as it avoids the difficulty of determining coordination effects at the jurisdiction stage, while subjecting all structural joint ventures to the same stage one and stage two timetables applicable to concentrations. Firms' incentives to engage in more durable concentration-style transactions for purely procedural reasons have thus been diminished, although it must be pointed out that applying Article 81 EC to joint ventures governed by the Merger Regulation ensures continued legal complexities.[75]

Scope for forum shopping: decentralised enforcement of the cartel prohibition Under the old regime of centralised enforcement there was no scope for forum shopping. If the agreement had been exempted under Article 81(3) EC, either because the European Commission had given an individual exemption or when a Regulation containing a group exemption applied, the national courts and competition authorities could not disregard the terms of the exemption. Hence, there was no scope for the application of a different and stricter national solution and competition on the market for competition laws was excluded.

The latter conclusion no longer holds under Regulation 1/2003. Scope for a "race to the bottom" has been created by offering many national courts the power to grant exemptions from the cartel prohibition. Member States willing to attract businesses could try to abuse the directly applicable exception system to create new cartel paradises. However, the scope for laxness is limited since many anti-competitive practices will be outlawed by blacklists contained in block exemptions. The new enforcement regime may also cause a "race to the top", however. A lack of uniform application of Article 81 EC across national competition authorities and national courts may create incentives for

---

[75] For further discussion, compare C.J. Cook and C.S. Kerse, *EC Merger Control* (4th ed., 2005), pp.61–62; G.A. Zonnekeyn, "The Treatment of Joint Ventures under the Amended Merger Regulation" (1999) 19 E.C.L.R. 414.

plaintiffs to bring cases in jurisdictions that have a reputation as strict enforcers. Decentralisation will cause inefficiencies if the ensuing enforcement level is not optimal. Forum shopping may cause a race for the top, in the sense that there might be an overall stricter level of competition enforcement. This effect is amplified by the freedom of Member States to impose stricter national rules, including criminal sanctions.[76] From an efficiency perspective, selective litigation of competition cases may create enforcement costs that outweigh the benefits of the preserved competitive processes. In addition, the system of parallel competences may lead to high error costs, in particular type II errors (false negatives) caused by excessively zealous law enforcers. These inefficiencies could be avoided by a centralised system of enforcement. Under Regulation 1/2003, the discrepancies caused by forum shopping should be corrected by coordination within the Network of Competition Authorities. However, the case allocation provisions of the Guidelines are not binding and Member States have been left free to impose stricter competition rules and sanctions.

10.3.2.3 Scale economies and transaction costs savings

A large number of legislators may also hinder the achievement of scale economies. If such economies are important in the process of law making decentralisation will be too costly. If the data needed to formulate and/or enforce legal rules are relevant for the entire European Community, centralisation may save on information costs. Uniform legal rules also maintain economies of scale in production and distribution arrangements. Enterprises that are active in many Member States profit from unification and harmonisation since uniform rules reduce the costs of doing business.

The argument about legal certainty, which is emphasised in the legal literature, points in the direction of transaction costs savings. The relevant question is then whether transaction costs of diversity in rules outweigh the benefits of competing rules. The great majority of lawyers and business people welcomed the new national competition laws, which are almost identical to the European competition rules. The reasoning goes that if competition laws varied across Member States, more uncertainty as to the precise contents of competition rules would result. Different rules or interpretations make the outcome of antitrust proceedings less predictable. If European competition law was the only yardstick, legal certainty would follow from the Community antitrust practice. Under uniform competition rules firms and consumers must not spend on search costs. They do not have to inform themselves about differences in the substantive laws of the Member States and the way in which these rules are enforced. These transaction costs savings may be very

---

[76] This was discussed in Ch.8, Box 8.1. Specific problems may arise where individual executives are assisting their company's effort to cooperate with the European Commission, but could find themselves subjected to criminal charges in a Member State. See: J. M. Joshua and P.D. Camesasca, "Where Angels Fear to Tread: The Commission's 'New' Leniency Policy Revisited" (2005) *The European Antitrust Review* 10

important for firms that are active in interstate commerce. Uniformity also tends to produce a more stable and predictable case law.[77]

Although legal certainty may be rephrased in economic terms as a factor that reduces information costs, there are serious problems with the argument. A wholesale adoption of the European competition rules necessarily entails the importation of the inefficiencies that are inherent in them. To put it simply: lawyers might feel happy with certainty about the contents of economically inefficient rules. The reduction of information costs is only one part of the economic analysis; another part is the assessment of incentive costs due to legal rules that may induce inefficient behaviour or simply ban efficient conduct. These inefficiencies may outweigh any savings on information costs. An analysis that only considers information costs and neglects incentive costs is necessarily incomplete. Moreover, economic analysis has shown that inefficient rules will be challenged in the courts.[78] In the EC context, inefficiencies may induce lobbying with the regulator to change the rules to the benefit of interest groups only. The history of the group exemptions in European competition law illustrates that some interest groups were able to obtain approval of their distribution agreements by the European Commission.[79] This led to an inconsistent treatment of qualitative selective distribution and franchising agreements, on the one hand, and quantitative selective distribution and exclusive distribution, on the other. All these restrictions on competition may be defensible because of free riding concerns, and the differences in legal treatment are thus not justifiable.[80] In the past, the possibility of obtaining block exemptions restricted to specific sectors of the industry invited additional rent seeking. Given the degree of discretion enjoyed by decision makers and the risks of regulatory capture, the costs of inefficient rules may not be underestimated. In short, before concluding in favour of centralisation the costs of uniformity must be taken into account. These costs are not negligible since, in spite of the recent reforms, European competition law still contains a number of rules that may reduce economic welfare.

10.3.3 A Public Choice perspective

10.3.3.1 The formulation of substantive rules and legal certainty

Welfare considerations alone cannot explain the current allocation of regulatory powers in the field of competition law. Political factors have to be taken into account when a full explanation for the current substantive rules

---

[77] S. Rose-Ackermann, *Rethinking the Progressive Agenda: The Reform of the American Regulatory State* (1992), p.172.
[78] See P.H. Rubin, "The Objectives of Private and Public Judges: A Comment" (1983) 41 *Public Choice* 133.
[79] Regulation 123/85 on Block Exemption of Motor Vehicle Distribution and Servicing Agreements, [1985] O.J. L 15/16.
[80] See R.J. Van den Bergh, "Modern Industrial Organisation versus Old-fashioned European Competition Law" (1996) 17 E.C.L.R. 75.

and their enforcement is sought. First, the importance of some economic arguments supporting (de)centralisation is often strengthened by their attractiveness from a political point of view, rather than by their intrinsic value. As indicated above, harmonisation of laws may be defended on grounds of scale economies and transaction cost savings. Lawyers often tend to overemphasise the savings generated by what they call legal certainty. Even though uncertainty about the precise meaning of a legal rule and the way in which it is enforced causes costs, one should not forget that there may be offsetting benefits in terms of creativity and innovation as well as the possibility of satisfying a greater number of preferences concerning the contents of legal rules on competition. When political reasoning takes precedence over economic reasoning, the qualifications to the underlying economic argument may be lost from sight.

Legal certainty is a very important issue for a number of pressure groups: large industries and specialised competition lawyers both benefit from the adoption of familiar rules. First, large business firms wish to be informed as soon as possible about the legal validity of cartel agreements or the compatibility of a proposed merger with the applicable competition rules. The legislative records of national competition laws enacted in the 1990s make clear that transplantation of the EC rules into national competition laws was defended by large firms. In Sweden it was argued that uniformity between EC law and national law is an advantage for export businesses since the same rules will operate in the common market and at home.[81] Dutch large firms considered certainty as to the law of the utmost importance in the competitive struggle on the European markets because US firms may be tempted to use the possibility of initiating legal proceedings with the European Commission or national judges as a competitive weapon.[82] A preference for EC rules is also to be found in the advice of the Economic and Social Committee on merger control. In this document, one can read that European industry favours a lowering of the thresholds because controls by different national competition authorities would increase legal uncertainty. Moreover, the EC Merger Task Force is applauded for its flexibility and ability to reach decisions with only short delays. More scope for national merger controls is rejected because an extension of national competence would only result from "wrong ideas concerning subsidiarity".[83] Second, established competition lawyers prefer imitation of EC rules to the adoption of more innovative solutions. The transplantation of European competition rules into national legal systems increases the predictability of the decisions by national competition authorities. This may explain why a full acceptance of economic analysis into European competition law was delayed up until the 1990s. Specialists in

---

[81] See the Swedish Promemoria (Ny konkurrenslag—en promemoria från Näringsdepartementet 1992), 32–33; and the Swedish proposition (Regeringens proposition 1992/93: 56 Ny konkurrenslag-stiftning), 18–20.
[82] See the arguments advanced by Philips in the *Staatscourant*, March 10, 1995, p.5.
[83] Additional Opinion of the Economic and Social Committee on the Report from the Commission to the Council on the implementation of the Merger Regulation [1994] O.J. C 388/41.

competition law may wish to protect their human capital and prefer a quiet life to a hard time of study.

It is important to realise that the universal application of EC-like rules advocated by large firms may harm smaller firms. The savings in information costs (thanks to legal certainty) accrue to export industry but are achieved at the expense of industries competing only in the home markets.[84] The adoption of the European competition rules also entails the acceptance of the inefficiencies inherent in them. It has been shown in Chapter 6 that the European Commission is unwilling to take full account of the free riding argument with respect to the legality of vertical restrictions in distribution agreements between manufacturers and small retailers.[85] In short, pleas for legal certainty may be the flag under which powerful interest groups (large firms, antitrust lawyers) achieve benefits at the expense of interests that are not well organised (small firms, consumers).

10.3.3.2 The enforcement of the European competition rules

An economic analysis of the new regime of decentralised enforcement is also incomplete without a Public Choice perspective. Centralised enforcement may be preferred if the risk of regulatory capture at lower levels of government is higher. National competition authorities may be inclined to favour national interests. Officials of a central antitrust authority are more remote from the firms they have to control and may thus act in a more independent way, making them less vulnerable to regulatory capture. However, the achievement of these advantages at the central level requires that several conditions are satisfied. Competition authorities should be responsible for the consequences of their decisions; they should be independent from the interest groups they are supposed to control and decision processes should be transparent to outside observers. Accountability implies that competition authorities must be politically responsible for their decisions. If accountability is limited, devices to guarantee independence and transparency become of crucial importance.

European Commissioners are politicians. Although they are required to forswear national allegiances on joining the European Commission, it would be naive to think that there is no risk of national capture. This risk has even been institutionalised in the enforcement procedures. Before taking formal decisions under Articles 81 and 82 EC, the Commission is required to consult the Advisory Committee on Restrictive Practices and Dominant positions. This Committee is composed of representatives of the Member States' competition authorities. The meetings of the Committee are not open to the public. The Committee's opinion is attached to the draft decision when it is sent up to the Commissioners for approval, and may, at the recommendation of the Committee, be published.[86] Although the Committee's opinion is not binding, it is

---

[84] See with respect to the Swedish law: A.C. Stray Rysdall, "Towards a Nordic Competition Law" (1996) 109 *Tidsskrift for Rettsvitenskap* 332.
[85] See Ch.6, s.6.4.
[86] L. Ritter, W.D. Braun and F. Rawlinson, *European Competition Law: A Practitioner's Guide* (3rd ed., 2004), p.1104.

clear that the decision procedure with respect to Articles 81 and 82 EC has many features which allow for capture by national interests. The same is true for the procedure of merger control. The Advisory Commission on Concentrations, consisting of representatives of the Member States, meets with the Commission's staff during the investigation and before the results of the investigation will be published.[87] It is significant to add that there are also Advisory Committees for specific sectors of the economy.

Moreover, in the European Union a single body (the European Commission) is responsible for antitrust enforcement. The Commission is both prosecutor and judge.[88] All stages of the procedures (notification, investigation, negotiation, decision and political review) are assigned to the Commission, subject to the qualifications on internal and external (Court of First Instance) checks and balances, discussed elsewhere in this book.[89] The unification of roles in the EC may improve the efficiency of the procedure and its clarity and predictability to the parties concerned, but it reduces transparency from the point of view of the general public.[90]

Profiting from Public Choice insights, the European system of enforcement may be criticised in several respects. The main weakness of the EC procedures is that political arguments will be considered even though they are supposed not to be referred to. It would be naive to think that political arguments will not be contemplated if they are not explicitly mentioned in the relevant competition law provisions. A competition authority can only be truly independent if it is not forced to take account of political arguments in the assessment of anti-competitive practices. Real independence requires that political modifications of decisions are taken by a separate agency. A division between the decision stage and the stage of political review may contribute to the independence of the competition authority. Such a functional division of powers may also contribute to transparency. The advantage of a division of functions is that political modifications can only be made after the decision by the competition authority. If this decision is previously published, the political arguments for changing the decision will have to be spelled out clearly. This transparency may reduce the informational asymmetries and aid a competition authority to commit itself to a given policy. In some Member States the scope for regulatory capture is limited in three ways: (a) rules improving political accountability, (b) a division between the decision stage

---

[87] D. Neven, R. Nuttall and P. Seabright, *Merger in Daylight: The Economics and Politics of European Merger Control* (1993), p.218.

[88] In US antitrust terms "the Commission combines the functions of prosecutor, judge and jury" (I. Van Bael, "The Antitrust Settlement Practice of the EC Commission" (1986) 23 C.M.L. Rev. 61). In reaction to complaints about this improper combination of functions a Hearing Officer has been appointed within DG COMP.

[89] See Ch.8, s.8.3.2.

[90] D. Neven, R. Nuttall and P. Seabright, *Merger in Daylight: The Economics and Politics of European Merger Control* (1993), p.215.

and the stage of political review, and (c) rules on incompatibilities. More information on the Member States' competition laws can be found in Box 10.2.

Box 10.2: How Member States' competition laws try to cope with regulatory capture
A comparison between the antitrust procedures of the European Community and those of the Member States reveals how far accountability, independence and transparency are currently achieved under either centralised or decentralised competition laws. If such a comparison shows that decentralised competition authorities are politically accountable, enjoy a greater degree of independence and that the decision making at national levels is more transparent than at the level of the Community, the argument in favour of decentralisation will be strengthened.

Some national competition laws contain rules which try to improve political accountability. For example, the Belgian antitrust authority must submit a report to the parliament which informs all interested parties about the enforcement of the competition rules.[91] The German Monopolies Commission (*Monopolkommission*) publishes a report every two years concerning the evolution of concentration in Germany. These reports are submitted to the government which must then clarify its position *vis-à-vis* the legislator.[92] This broadens and deepens public debate of competition policy issues. So far there is no European Monopolies Commission with similar tasks.[93]

In the EC a single body (the European Commission) is responsible for antitrust enforcement. By contrast, in some Member States a functional division of powers between different bodies has been preferred. For instance, in Belgium restrictive practices and mergers have to be notified to the *Dienst voor de Mededinging* (Competition Agency) which will also carry out the investigation, but decisions will be taken by the *Raad voor de Mededinging* (Competition Council). The Agency is composed of civil servants whereas the Council has 12 members, half of whom are administrative law judges, the other half being experts in competition matters. The Council is presided over by a judge.[94] The separation of powers is even clearer in the United Kingdom. The body responsible for investigation of a proposed merger (the Monopolies and Mergers Commission) is neither the party to whom mergers must be notified (being the Director General of Fair

---

[91] Art. 41 Wet Economische Mededinging.
[92] s.44 (3) GWB. The Monopolkommission may also draft reports concerning competition issues on its own initiative.
[93] The establishment of a European Monopolies Commission is defended by C.D. Ehlermann, "Reflections on an European Cartel Office" (1995) 32 C.M.L. Rev. 471.
[94] See, for further discussion, K. Platteau, "Competition Law in Belgium", in *Competition Law in the EU, its Member States and Switzerland* (F.O.W. Vogelaar, J. Stuyck and B.L.P. van Reeken ed., 2000), pp.497–556.

Trading), nor the party taking the decision, who is the Secretary of State for Trade and Industry.

The head of the Community competition authority (Commissioner for Competition) is a politician, whereas the competition authorities of the Member States are usually headed by civil servants or administrative law judges.[95] Political independence is further guaranteed by rules imposing incompatibilities between membership of the antitrust authorities and leading functions in firms or professional associations.[96] By contrast, the European Commission is a collegiate, political body.[97]

Transparency is improved if the influence of considerations other than competition aspects is made visible. The risk that political negotiations distort the character of the investigations and influence the final decision without clearly being visible appears to be less serious in the Member States. German competition law aims at protecting the *Bundeskartellamt* from political influence. According to Section 42 GWB mergers may get the approval of the Minister of Economic Affairs if the restrictions of competition are compensated by general economic advantages or predominant motives of public interest ("aus überwiegenden Gründen der Gesamtwirtschaft und des Gemeinwohls"). Experience with this rule has made it clear that the political pressure exerted upon the Minister of Economic Affairs was greater than expected. To cope with this problem the law was changed. An approval now requires a report by the *Monopolkommission* prior to the decision by the Minister. The new procedure does not succeed in banishing entirely the influence of political pressures, but it makes those pressures clearly visible. The German system clearly contrasts with European merger control, where economic and political influences may distort the actual analysis of the competition aspects of cases.

The discussion of regulatory capture has recalled that private interests, rather than social welfare, may be the driving force behind regulatory reform. The changes introduced by the modern system of enforcement of Articles 81 and 82 EC may equally be explained from a Public Choice perspective. For a good understanding of the division of work between the European Commission and national courts and competition authorities, economic theory on bureaucracies is highly illuminating. Obviously, the growth of centralisation increases the workload of the central authorities. Bureaucrats motivated by self interest may want to maximise the budget of the bureau[98] or try to achieve higher status, while at the same time making work more agreeable.[99] The latter

---

[95] The only countries in which decisions are taken in ministries are the United Kingdom and the Netherlands. In the latter country the creation of an independent competition authority is envisaged, see C.D. Ehlermann, "Reflections on an European Cartel Office" (1995) 32 C.M.L. Rev. 471.
[96] See s.51(5) GWB (Bundeskartellamt) and s.45(3) GWB (Monopolkommission).
[97] In the past, there were proposals to establish an independent European Cartel Office. See, for a critical analysis of these proposals, C.D. Ehlermann, "Reflections on an European Cartel Office" (1995) 32 C.M.L. Rev. 471.
[98] W. Niskanen, *Bureaucracy and Representative Government* (1971).

option, reducing the workload while at the same time gaining more prestige, is not inconsistent with the different phases in the system reform. In a first phase, a reduction of the workload was achieved by leaving the treatment of the "simple" cases and the purely technical legal questions to national judges. As soon as matters became more complicated and especially when economic and political arguments could influence the ultimate decision, the European Commission kept the last word. With the exception of the granting of exemptions, the Commission's advice on legal issues was not binding. However, given their unfamiliarity with competition law, many national judges followed the Commission's advice in most cases.[1] Consequently, the Commission's ability and willingness to help poorly qualified national judges added to its prestige. Regulation 1/2003 has institutionalised the prestige of the European Commission as the most important enforcement agency. The Commission leads the enforcement efforts by concentrating on the most severe infringements, deciding landmark cases and punishing infringements that affect more than three Member States.[2] The supervisory role of the Commission is guaranteed by the duty imposed on national competition authorities to inform the Commission prior to or immediately after the first formal act of investigation.[3] The most delicate cases may be withdrawn from the national authorities. The Commission has also kept a guiding role: it may give advice on difficult cases and intervene before national courts. In sum, the workload of the Commission is reduced, it has kept the highest profile in the enforcement efforts and it has preserved enduring control on national authorities and judges. Utility-maximising bureaucrats could not dream of a better outcome of the system reform.

10.4 Conclusions

The central question of this chapter was whether rules of competition law should be enacted and implemented at the central European level or left to be decided and enforced by the Member States. In the policy discussion, a major argument to justify decentralisation is that it may allow a division of labour, which permits the central authority to chase the most serious infringements. The question of whether decentralisation is desirable requires a much more refined analysis, however. According to the subsidiarity principle contained in Article 5(2) EC, matters that can be better taken care of by the Member States should not be entrusted to institutions of the European Union. Subsidiarity in the area of competition law has two aspects: both the formulation of the substantive rules and their enforcement may take place at the national, rather

---

[1] P. Dunleavy, *Bureaucracy and Public Choice: Economic Explanations in Political Science* (1991).
[1] "What would be the point of such opinion if the Commission does not expect that they will be followed by national courts?", citing J. Bourgeois, "EC Competition Law and the Member State Courts", in: Fordham Corp. L. Inst. 1993, 493 (B. Hawk ed., 1994).
[2] Notice on Cooperation within the Network of Competition Authorities, paras 14–15.
[3] *ibid.*, para.44.

than the European, level. There is no (or very little) competition as far as the formulations of the substantive rules are concerned. At present, Member States' competition laws are aligned closely with European competition rules. The picture is different with respect to the enforcement of the competition rules. Whereas there has always been some degree of decentralisation (enforcement of Article 81(1) EC by national courts, cooperation between the European Commission and judges), the new enforcement regime takes subsidiarity a decisive step further. In interpreting and enforcing the rules, the European Commission has now shared competences with the competition authorities and judges of the Member States. Consequently, different national authorities and judges compete with each other in enforcing the cartel prohibition and the assessment of abuse of a dominant position.

Decentralisation may allow competition between legal orders, which in turn may achieve important efficiency benefits. If Member States are left free to decide on the content of their competition laws, a greater number of diverging preferences concerning the goals to be achieved may be satisfied. In addition, competition between competition laws enables learning processes. Creativity and innovation are very important in a complex field such as competition law, which is plagued by many uncertainties and inconsistencies. Finally, decentralisation makes it possible to profit from information advantages at lower levels of government. The latter arguments are relevant both for the formulation of the (substantive) competition rules and their enforcement.

The counterarguments, which highlight the disadvantages of decentralisation, follow from the important insight that competition on the market for competition laws, as in any other market, may not function properly because of market imperfections. The relevant market failures include the problem of interstate externalities and the risk of sub-optimal races to either the "bottom" or the "top". National competition policies may cause negative externalities in other jurisdictions: for example, merger control may emphasise efficiency savings on domestic markets and neglect the anti-competitive effects on foreign markets. Also decentralised enforcement of common prohibitions causes externalities. Positive externalities occur when action of all competent competition authorities is necessary to give full effect to the activity of a single competition authority. Negative externalities arise when the action of one competition authority reduces the value of the intervention by another authority. A race to the bottom will result if firms decide to relocate their businesses in order to attain market power in a lax jurisdiction or are left free to decide that their behaviour will be governed by the most lenient competition rules. Conversely, a race to the top may materialise if there is a rush towards overzealous competition authorities, resulting in a large number of type II errors (false negatives).

An economic analysis of decentralised enforcement is incomplete if insights from Public Choice are neglected. Private interests of industry groups and bureaucrats, rather than the public interest, may be the driving force behind decentralisation.

The major challenge for the design of an optimal competition regime for the European Union is to make sure that the benefits of decentralisation can be reaped and to prevent, at the same time, the potential inefficiencies of competition between competition laws. In this chapter, it was shown that the current legal framework is deficient from the perspective of optimising the net benefits of competition between Member States' competition laws. The trend of spontaneous harmonisation, which provides Member States with incentives to align their competition laws closely to the European rules, decreases the possibility of satisfying divergent preferences concerning the goals of competition policy and inhibits learning processes. The latter negative effect is mitigated by the new system of decentralised enforcement (Regulation 1/2003), which enables national agencies to improve the quality of the decision making by using economics-based interpretations of vague concepts and stimulating the use of quantitative techniques to prove violations of the competition laws.

The current legal framework does not guarantee that interstate externalities are internalised. Centralised supervision of cartel agreements, abusive practices by dominant firms and mergers may mitigate judgments biased in favour of national interests and overcome difficulties of monitoring cooperation between competing antitrust authorities. Unfortunately, from the perspective of internalising interstate externalities, European competition law is both over- and under-inclusive. With respect to the control of anti-competitive agreements and practices, the boundary between community competition law and that of the Member States is the requirement that the agreements or practices "may affect trade between Member States". In practice, this requirement is no effective limitation of the European Commission's powers because of an excessively broad legal interpretation. As far as the substantive rules on restrictive agreements and practices are concerned, European competition law thus is over-inclusive. In contrast, the Merger Regulation does not adequately reach the goal of internalising interstate externalities since the scale of the transactions (turnover thresholds) is not the best way of determining the magnitude of the spillovers across Member States. Also the new European rules on decentralised enforcement of Article 81 EC (Regulation 1/2003) are under-inclusive, since they fall short of guaranteeing that national competition authorities fully internalise the costs and benefits of their decisions for the competent agencies in other Member States. Since positive externalities tend to be underprovided and negative externalities are apt to be overprovided, the new enforcement system may be biased towards granting a too high number of exemptions. Only coordination of the enforcement initiatives at both the central and decentralised levels may minimise the distortions described above. Unfortunately, the Guidelines on cooperation within the Network of Competition Authorities are not legally binding.

Similar conclusions have been reached with respect to the ability of European law to prevent inefficient races either to the bottom or the top. On the one hand, the risk of a race to the bottom is reduced by rules of European law limiting the freedom of Member States to enact laws only benefiting firms and harming society at large. On the other hand, there remains scope for "forum shopping". In the field of merger control, changes to the form of the contemplated transaction may allow companies to choose their preferred supervising agency as well as the control procedure. Firms may thus opt for European merger control instead of (more stringent) supervision by the competition authorities of the Member States. After the entry into force of Regulation 1/2003 the scope for forum shopping has been further increased. The system of parallel competences may lead to high error costs (type II) if there is a race to the most zealous competition law enforcers. This effect is exacerbated by the competence of Member States to impose stricter rules, including stiffer (criminal) sanctions. These inefficiencies could be avoided by a centralised system of enforcement.

Finally, a Public Choice analysis has shown that centralisation is not the perfect institutional design that will exclude the scope for regulatory capture. Information asymmetries between competition authorities and firms may argue in favour of a decentralised competition policy. These benefits in terms of reduction of information costs may, however, be outweighed by the increased danger of regulatory capture. In general, the competition authorities in the Member States are independent of the government, whereas the European Commission is a collegiate, political body. The current European procedures obscure which kinds of political pressure were actually most influential in determining the outcome of cases. Decentralisation does a better job in mitigating the risk of regulatory capture than is often assumed. Of course, the relative strength of the interest groups will differ across countries and industries. If agencies are captured by national interests, supranational bodies will be able to reach more objective decisions. If lobbies represent sector rather than national interests, centralisation alone will not cure the problem.

INDEX